*Edited by Dean G. Peerman
and Martin E. Marty*

Ⓛ

Lutterworth Press
Cambridge

Lutterworth Press
P.O. Box 60
Cambridge   CB1   2NT

British Library Cataloguing in Publication Data
A handbook of Christian theologians.
1. Christian doctrine. Writers, ca 1800–1964
I. Peerman, Dean G. (Dean Gordon)   II. Marty, Martin E. (Martin Emil),
1928–
230' .092'2

ISBN 0-7188-2793-7

A HANDBOOK OF CHRISTIAN THEOLOGIANS
Enlarged Edition

Copyright © 1965 assigned to Abingdon
Additions copyright © 1984 by Abingdon Press

Additions include Introduction to the Enlarged Edition, the chapters in Part IV,
and the revised Notes on Contributors.

Scripture quotations are from the Revised Standard Version of the Bible,
copyrighted 1946, 1952, © 1971, 1973 by the Division of Christian Education of
the National Council of the Churches of Christ in the U.S.A., and are used by
permission.

MANUFACTURED BY THE PARTHENON PRESS AT
NASHVILLE, TENNESSEE, UNITED STATES OF AMERICA

CONTENTS

IV. Recent Theological Work

INTRODUCTION

A Handbook of Christian Theologians is a companion volume to *A Handbook of Christian Theology.* The earlier handbook, published in 1958, provided readers with 101 brief definitions of theological terms as used in present-day religious writing. *Theology* is a term which refers to words and ideas about God and the world. These words and ideas do not make their way in disincarnate fashion but are developed and discussed by individuals called theologians. In each generation those who form words and ideas about God and the world give a distinctive shape and pattern to these words and ideas. No one can profess to have a rounded view of theology without looking squarely at theologians. Twenty-six authors propose to do just that in the present book.

As inheritors of a pattern and a procedure, we are grateful for the achievement of the earlier handbook. At the same time, we confess to a certain uneasiness as we apply the term "Christian" to a group of men who happen to belong to the non-Roman-Catholic half of the Christian world. With the exception of the Russian Orthodox thinker Nicolai Berdyaev, all the theologians discussed herein could be classified as Protestant. The absence of Roman Catholic thinkers is not the only limitation imposed by the brevity of this work. We have concentrated first on the giants who gave a new language to theology in the nineteenth century. The second part of the book deals with a number of thinkers who refined that tradition. In the third section we turn to the main line of theological thought of the past three decades.

Such an outline finds us neglecting much liberal theology of the second through the fourth decades of our century. In particular we have had to slight philosophical theology. Readers who are familiar with this form of inquiry will note the absence of chapters on William Ernest Hocking, Edgar S. Brightman, William R. Inge, Henry Nelson Wieman, and numbers of others whose stature is comparable to that of many of the twenty-six who are included. We apologize for not being able to include in one volume all those we would have liked to include (particularly do we regret the omission, owing to an unfortunate concatenation of circumstances, of a scheduled essay on the great nineteenth-century theologian Ernst Troeltsch); nevertheless we justify this handbook on the grounds that the twenty-six theologians dealt with represent types of theologizing which have evoked much curiosity throughout the Christian world. Perhaps in a future volume it will be possible to enlarge the number of prominent thinkers to be given handbook-sized attention.

The earlier handbook listed its 101 theological concepts in alphabetical order. Such an arrangement is not feasible here. The present volume has a plot—one which tries to do some justice to three general ways of talking about God and the world. While no convenient labels adequately describe these three ways, we shall try to characterize them.

Each of the three sections begins with one or two theologians who have employed the category "religion." That is, they began their enterprise by giving due notice to human experience of the spiritual or the divine. Any history of theology in the past two centuries must begin with Friedrich Schleiermacher. He came upon the scene at the end of the Enlightenment, after men had long been speaking about laws of nature and nature's God. Suddenly, with Schleiermacher, all the categories of Christian thought were reinvested with meaning. In the United States, Horace Bushnell, working independently, came to beknown as "the American Schleiermacher"; he shared Schleiermacher's interests and his somewhat romantic view of human response.

In the early twentieth century Rudolf Otto, a devotee of Schleiermacher, traded upon the newer interests in world religions and concentrated on "the holy" as a basis for theology.

More recently, the Swedish theologian Anders Nygren has made a motif-study of religion the basis of his work.

The second cluster of thinkers in each of the three sections come at the data of theology from a different viewpoint. They breathe the historicizing spirit of the past century and a half. The giant who stands at the head of this line is Albrecht Ritschl. In the Ritschlian lineage historians such as Adolf von Harnack stressed the empirical side of the record of faith. The Ritschlians were also well known for their accent on the ethics of Jesus and on the concept of the Kingdom of God. Albert Schweitzer used the tools of history against historicism, but he too accented the ethic of the Kingdom. A half-century earlier, in England, F. D. Maurice worked out a Kingdom-concept which shared many of the Ritschlian ethical interests. William Temple is a twentieth-century representative of this line. In America, Social Gospel advocate Walter Rauschenbusch blended historical and ethical interests. Canadian-born D. C. Macintosh was noted for his attempt to locate theology in empirics, psychology, and history.

In the twentieth century, pure-form Ritschlianism has been out of fashion. The painstaking methods of biblical and historical inquiry have lived on, however, in men like Gustaf Aulén, who insists that his systematic theology is not normative but descriptive. They are also recognizable in the notable tradition of biblical theology, upheld herein by the British New Testament scholar C. H. Dodd and the Continental exegete Oscar Cullmann.

The third line begins with Søren Kierkegaard, who is often regarded as the father of modern existentialism. He and those who share his attitude are less interested in propositions about faith than in the study of existence and of the encounter between God and man. The remarkable British Congregationalist P. T. Forsyth introduced the concern for this encounter into Anglo-American theology. The highly individualistic Russian exile Nicolai Berdyaev refined this way of doing theology. On the Continent, Karl Heim employed existentialist methods to relate Christian faith to the scientific order.

The last eight thinkers dealt with in this volume have all been influenced by existentialist thought, though they are at variance with each other in many ways. The brothers Niebuhr, for example, share much of the Ritschlian interest in ethics and history. Karl Barth, Emil Brunner, Friedrich Gogarten, Rudolf Bultmann, and Dietrich Bonhoeffer are among the theological giants of the past four decades in Germany and Switzerland. In a variety of disciplines they have tried to relate the Word as witnessed in the early Christian documents to man as he is today. Paul Tillich began with many of these Continental interests, but in recent decades in America he has come to be known chiefly for his concern with correlating theology and philosophy.

If these men could be easily labeled or classified, there would be need not for a handbook of theologians but only for a guidebook to theological types. But however individual and personal the approaches of the twenty-six theologians may be, the broad classifications centering on the motifs of "experience," "empirics," and "existence" should help guide the reader.

We are deeply indebted to Marvin Halverson and Arthur A. Cohen, the editors of the earlier handbook, who began the work on this one. To them goes the credit for the original conception, the selection of most of the subjects and authors, and editorial supervision and correspondence over a period of years. They and we have in each case sought to select an author whose name has been associated with the subject. Some of the authors have studied under the theologians whose lives and works they discuss; others have written extensively about them elsewhere. While the writers are generally sympathetic with the work of these masters, they are noted theologians in their own right; we have encouraged them to be critical.

The transition in editorship unavoidably occasioned some delay in the publication of this book. Whoever has pursued two dozen theologians around the world through their academic schedules, their researches, their sabbaticals, will understand that a work of this kind cannot be produced overnight. We mention this in order to explain that some of the essays were prepared earlier than others; hence not all the authors were able to refer to materials produced during the past year or so. Many of the authors provided extensive bibliographies. Recognizing the limitations of space in a handbook, we have had to do away with these. Instead we have selected one work by and one work about each theologian, with the hope that readers who are making a first acquaintance with the subjects of these chapters will find their appetites whetted for further association with them (extensive bibliographies are easily available elsewhere on almost all twenty-six). The authors of the chapters should not be defaulted for the absence of comprehensive reading lists; the brief suggestion comes from the editors.

We thank Messrs. Halverson and Cohen, the twenty-six authors, and Cecelia Gaul and Joanne Younggren for their assistance in bringing this manuscript to fruition.

Dean G. Peerman
Martin E. Marty

INTRODUCTION TO THE ENLARGED EDITION

Exactly a generation has passed since *A Handbook of Christian Theologians* appeared. That volume went to press during the Second Vatican Council. In the introduction we apologized for the absence of Roman Catholics in a book with the word *Christian* in the title. This enlarged edition makes up for that deficiency. Five of the new subjects and six of the authors are of that Catholic tradition. It would have been useful, had not the constraints of space prevented us from doing so, to have retrieved some Catholic giants who made their mark earlier in the century: Jacques Maritain, Karl Adam, Yves Congar, and others. Yet we must leave such retrieval to other editors with other concepts. Only Pierre Teilhard de Chardin in this collection belongs to that earlier generation, and he left his public mark largely toward the last third of this century.

The deaths of most of the twelve giants who appeared in the last third of the first edition have occurred since its publication. They were part of a theological impulse which began in Europe after World War I. They gave shape to mainstream Protestant theology until the middle of the 1960's. Their passing, like the falling of great oaks, left a void on the landscape and exposed a great deal of empty sky. For a time people feared that only scrub oak and weak underbrush could struggle to grow in their shade. Not many of the newer theologians are household names the way Karl Barth's or Paul Tillich's were, but we were impressed to see that there were plenty of "schoolhold" names. That is, they belong to people who were well known in academic theology and who were giving shape to inquiry in the present generation. Some figures like Teilhard and Hans Küng did become widely known and their books were best-sellers. Yet even the slightly less well-known ones here included merit attention. Writers in a few secular and religious journals, for example, attributed to Karl Rahner the qualities of mind not seen since Thomas Aquinas on Catholic soil. His very extensive writings exercised great behind-the-scenes influence on Catholic and Protestant alike.

This time, even more than before, the editors' chief problem turned out to be the issue of exclusion. There were far more deserving candidates than we could include. Had we felt free to change the concept of the book, there would have been many more chapters. The original concept seemed to offer the only way to give coherence to this book, even as it must await successors. This is not, then, an "equal-time" book, one which keeps in mind all elements in the Christian tradition. Had it done so, Alexander Schmemann might well have represented Orthodoxy, Gustavo Gutiérrez would have been a strong candidate for Latin American representation, and Rosemary Ruether or one or more of her colleagues could have represented feminist theological endeavors. Within a generation they and their counterparts in the orbit of "black theology," African theology, or any of a number of other rooted theologies which have not derived from the sources that produced the first group of *Handbook* people would have won a place.

It happens, however, that whenever we took surveys or soundings to determine candidacies for inclusion, advice usually came that we should restrict this book to that Euro-American academic tradition which had been predominant in libraries, bibliographies, councils of churches, and classrooms from the mid-sixties to the mid-eighties. Numbers of our subjects' peers are not here, and their exclusion was sometimes a bit arbitrary. However, readers of this volume, we believe, are getting their time's and money's worth; this book bursts at its seams, its bulk gives its publisher a case of nerves and its editors a sense that they sneaked in all that could be crammed and fit between the covers.

Pierre Teilhard de Chardin, as Christopher F. Mooney notes, is a senior figure who was free to have influence only after his death. While his stock may not be as high as it once was, Teilhard left a legacy of evolutionarily synthetic and Christianly spiritual thought that inspired a subsequent generation of thinkers. Karl Rahner, who observed his eightieth birthday and who died in the season of our editing, had unmatched influence in and beyond Catholicism.

The next three thinkers have slightly specialized followings. Helmut Thielicke, who is not always seen as a seminal thinker, gained importance as a bridger of continents and between mainstream and evangelical worlds. At the same time, he also bridged between the academy and the church and gained a great reputation as a preacher. Jacques Ellul, a French lawyer and social critic who is one of the few lay people in this collection, is hard to classify. His following has included many of the socially intense evangelicals who have felt less congeniality with many of the liberal theologians of the century. The same is true for Carl F. H. Henry, the most notable of the theologians who are formally self-classified as "neo-evangelical" or, more recently, simply as "evangelical." While Henry and his constituencies have sometimes complained of isolation among the theologians whom they might not call evangelical, there are reasons, implies Gabriel Fackre, for the old lines between camps to erode. Henry is by far the most plausible choice of figures for an appraisal of this prospect of erosion.

Paul Ricoeur and Edward Schillebeeckx are both senior figures at the time we write; yet their influence came later than that of the first five figures, at least so far as North American theology is concerned. Ricoeur spent the 1970's on a major project in hermeneutics, and Schillebeeckx published enormous works on *Jesus* and *Christ* in the same period.

The other five of the new subjects have the aura of "mid-career" about them. Wolfhart Pannenberg's thought took interesting turns in the decade before this edition, while Jürgen Moltmann continued on a course of work that inspired much of the liberation theology in Latin America and political theology elsewhere. David Tracy has come to the fore in the newest generation of American Catholics, and he is the kind of thinker whose "foundational" work helps shape the thought of others who may build on different foundations, or build different ways on foundations like his own. John B. Cobb, Jr., is in the front rank of "process theologians." He opens a line of inquiry that is not developed in the other thinkers who appear here. Hans Küng needs little introduction; he symbolized the new generation that emerged during Vatican II, and he may be the best-known theologian in the world.

Those who may feel that it is a bit "clubby" to stay in continuity with the concept of the *Handbook* of 1965 will find that the subject matter and style of the thinkers and the approaches of this quite diverse set of authors will engage them in an astonishing number of ways. If a future *Handbook,* whether from this publisher and these editors or from others, changes the concept, becomes "representational," and illustrates the vitalities of Christian thought all over the world, in and beyond the academy, we are confident that such thought will be grounded in no small measure on people who laid the foundations here described. If these figures and their kind have to yield space to such new generations, that would be no surprise to any of them. They all have recognized the fact that Christian thought has developed and how it has done so. They ought to: they have been among the prime developers and initiators of change in our half-century.

Dean G. Peerman
Martin E. Marty

I
The Nineteenth—century Traditions

FRIEDRICH SCHLEIERMACHER

Richard R. Niebuhr

Religiously speaking, we must concede the nineteenth century to Schleiermacher. No other judgment is possible when one takes account of the development of Protestant thought in the extraordinary epoch that embraces the French Revolution and Immanuel Kant at its beginning and the First World War and Ernst Troeltsch and Adolf von Harnack at its conclusion. The great human struggle of these times in the West took on, for Protestantism, the form of an effort to establish once again the Reformation's steady and clear sense for the true roots of personal faith and religious community, in the aftermath of the critical destruction of rationalistic orthodoxy and the cooling of the tepid ardor of deism. But the endeavor's success depended upon the ability of its leaders not only to recognize the symptoms of atrophy in their inherited systems but to use creatively the most profound ideas that had taken possession of the Enlightenment and that were pulsing in the social, political, and intellectual ferment of Europe and America.

Among the most important of these: the idea of history as a story of events with a content whose human meaning could be divined through critical and imaginative reconstruction and so appropriated as an enrichment of the present; the idea of reaon as an operation or deed of the human spirit, capable of disciplined employment as the instrument of liberation from man's "self-incurred tutelage" but also freighted with the pathos and finitude of that spirit; the idea of the individual endowed with inalienable rights and a self-consciousness competent to range through all of human experience and reduce it to the order of the moral and aesthetic judgments of the mind; the idea of science as the pursuit of universal truth through which universal community arises; and the idea of religion as an inborn personal sense for the true and the eternal, drawing its vitality from a source much earlier in human nature than the speculations of metaphysical philosophers and officially sanctioned systems of theology. Schleiermacher by no means carried all or even one of these ideas to the highest stage that the century was to achieve, but he lived more actively among them than any other man of his profession and gave them the added impetus of his own genius through his books, teaching, and personal engagement in the history of Germany, so that the theologians of the 1960's have still to reckon with him above all others as the progenitor of the spirit of modern religious understanding. Kierkegaard is the only other who can approach him on this score, but due to his wider interests, deeper sympathy for the church catholic, and superior systematic powers—along with the fact that Kierkegaard became an influence only after 1918—Schleiermacher for better or worse continues to bear this responsibility.

Schleiermacher's popular reputation as philosopher of religion and theologian lives chiefly in and through two books: *On Religion, Speeches to Its Cultured Despisers*, a product of his youth; and *The Christian Faith*, the dogmatic theology that is his magnum opus. However, both of these works emerged so naturally out of his personal history and the intellectual modes and problems of the times that the outlines of Schleiermacher's biography belong indispensably to any introduction to his intellectual achievements. The chronological beginning of such an introduction is 1768, when Friedrich Daniel Ernst Schleiermacher was born into the family of a Prussian army chaplain stationed in Breslau. Although the father was a Reformed clergyman, he wished for his children a Moravian nurture, and so it was that Friedrich was imbued from his earliest years with the one form of eighteenth-century Protestantism that preserved and cultivated the religion of the heart, namely, pietism. Schleiermacher liked to think that he always remained a Moravian in sentiment, and later on his letters to his sister, who had entered one of the community's "sister homes," show his continued affection and respect for the way of the Herrnhutters. But he himself was forced to break both from them and temporarily from his family when he found that his teachers carefully screened from their charges every breath of the new intellectual life of Europe. He departed for the university at Halle with the despairing consent of his father and very little money. There he lived with his uncle, read Kant, listened to lectures on theology in the Protestant orthodox tradition and took his examinations for ordination without particular enthusiasm. Schleiermacher's real entrance into consciousness of self and world appears to have begun after his university days, when he took the position of tutor in the family of Count Dohna and on its East Prussian estate encountered for the first time the mixture of intimate family relationships with lively and intelligent sociality for which his nature had a hitherto unrealized affinity.

Beginning in 1796, Schleiermacher came fully into his youthful powers in response to the stimulus of Berlin's philosophical and literary romanticism, fused with a fashionable social life that centered for him and his friends in the home of Henrietta Herz, wife of a wealthy Jewish physician. In addition to discharging his duties as preacher to the Charité hospital, he worked intensively in his own philosophical studies and rapidly emerged as a leading personality in the aforementioned salons and as a man with a great capacity for friendship. Friedrich Schlegel, with whom he shared his rooms, acted as his tutor in the Romantic spirit and taunted him for his literary unproductivity until, having reached the age of twenty-nine with nothing to show for his promise of originality, Schleiermacher pledged to do something and wrote the *Speeches* on religion. He was the only clergyman among his circle, and it was thoroughly characteristic of him that he used this occasion to issue both a critique of his friends' world view and an apology for his own identity and vocation as a preacher by expounding the mood and themes of Romanticism—especially the idea of individuality—in such a way as to argue that the life uninformed by the cultivation of personal religion and religious community is artificially sterile and out of joint with universal being. The book's instant acclaim emboldened the author to publish in the following year (1800) *The Soliloquies,* a species of literary confession written in the ethical-heroic and often too sentiment-ful style of Fichte. Its theme was a continuation of that of the *Speeches,* the idea of the individual as an underivable and unrepeatable self, a unique microcosmic statement of the macrocosm and "compendium of humanity." True human freedom, he philosophized, is to recognize and develop one's identity in the only real world, the "eternal community of spirits."

The *Speeches* brought Schleiermacher to the threshold of his public career, but Schlegel was responsible for another stage in his growth that proved finally to be of still greater significance, when he proposed that they translate and edit the dialogues of Plato. Even though Schlegel soon lost interest in the project, Schleiermacher persevered in what was to him a labor of love. All the other minds that had worked upon his—Spinoza, Leibniz, Kant—now found their true interpreter and critic in the literary and philosophic master of dialogue. As Wilhelm Dilthey wrote of him, Schleiermacher was a "Plato-kindred spirit," and thereafter his reflection was stamped with two Platonic ideas: that of the highest good as the life-giving and organizing principle of human action, and that of reason as the unending historical dialogue of mind with mind.

The Berlin years dissolved in melancholy. Schleiermacher had fallen in love with Eleonore Grunow, the wife of another minister. With the Romantics, he advocated the moral justification of divorce, but Eleonore, although unhappily married, was prevented both by her conscience and her fear of wounding her family from taking such a step, and Schleiermacher had finally for her sake and on account of the uneasiness of his church superiors to resign his post and become a provincial pastor. To his sister, Charlotte, he had written in 1801 that he would gladly sacrifice his prospects of national renown for marriage. "Except in domestic life, all that we enjoy and all that we attempt, is but vain illusion." His despondency was correspondingly great in 1802 upon his leaving Berlin. However, the personal tragedy weakened his ties with Romanticism, while the isolation of his parish gave him time for writing a critical examination of ethical theory, published under the title *Kritik der bisherigen Sittenlehre,* as well as for the continuation of his translation of Plato. This period of two years was the beginning of his final maturation and of his career as systematic philosopher and theologian.

When he was called to the university at Halle in 1804, he resolved to give his life to the university and the church. He lectured on philosophical ethics, hermeneutics, or the discipline of interpretation, dogmatic theology, Paul's Letter to the Galatians, and began work on his book *Brief Outline of the Study of Theology,* a descriptive, critical account of the interrelations of the several theological sciences. The best insight that we have into the state of his religious and theological principles at this time comes from a small publication titled *Christmas Eve (Die Weihnachtsfeier),* which he cast in the form of a dialogue among a group of friends and family members gathered together to exchange gifts and converse about the meaning of the nativity. In some respects, and especially because of its highly stylized form, the book recalls the *Speeches* and the *Soliloquies;* it is also, like the other two, transparently autobiographical, reflecting the circumstances of the life of Schleiermacher and of several of his friends. But its content presages his later dogmatic theology, *The Christian Faith,* particularly in his effort to deal with the growing skepticism concerning the historicity of Jesus and with the characterization of Christian faith as rooted in a feeling or a mood that seizes the individual from without and transforms all the elements of his inner being and outer world into the component moments of "a universal pulsing of joy." Such a joy, the father of the family group declares, cannot originate in the divided consciousness of the fallen and corrupted individual; hence "we look for one point . . . from which this impartation went forth, although we know that it must go forth again from each individual as self-active. . . . That one, however, who is seen as the point of origin of the church . . . that one must already be born as man-in-himself, as the God-man."

At Halle, Schleiermacher had also been appointed preacher to the university, and as Napoleon invaded the German lands he started to develop a style of "political" preaching, illustrated in his second book of sermons (1808). In the second edition of the *Speeches,* prepared during this time, he warned that Napoleon meant to extinguish both Protestantism and the German spirit. In fact, the French army did capture the city, close the university, and occupy Schleiermacher's house. Without a salary, he and his sister held on as long as their means allowed, refusing another appointment, until there was no more hope for a reopening of classes. He then returned to Berlin and his friends. There King Friedrich Wilhelm III made him a preacher to Trinity Church in 1809, a pulpit that was occupied conjointly by a Reformed and a Lutheran minister. Schleiermacher regarded the terms of Prussia's peace with France as dishonorable, and he intensified his preaching against the background of the political disquiet and national confusion of those days. Dilthey attributes to him an effectiveness equal to Fichte's in arousing the spirit of freedom in the citizens of Berlin. Schleiermacher even joined the patriots who sought to promote war. He also supported from the pulpit and otherwise the liberal social and political reforms advocated by Baron von Stein—reforms which Prussia greatly needed, since it still existed on a feudal level far below England and France. Schleiermacher did not regard these activities as incidental or injurious to his vocation because of his conviction—set out most carefully in his ethics —that the individual must participate fully in the several spheres of public life in order that a healthy balance may be struck and preserved between them for the good of both the national entity and the individual citizen. After the retreat of Napoleon from Russia and the liberation of Prussia, along with many other liberal leaders Schleiermacher fell into official disfavor and was accused of antiroyal sentiments; but he continued to speak and act in accordance with his conscience on all issues that came within his competence. During the second decade of the century, church politics figured increasingly among these, and Schleiermacher's position propelled him into the debate and polemics attendant upon the efforts to reform the organization of the Protestant church and concomitantly to unify its Reformed and Lutheran branches. Here again he felt obliged to oppose the king when the latter tried to reform the liturgy without heeding the principle of church representation in the matter. The church union, however, was finally accomplished and Schleiermacher was able to preach the sermon at the celebration of the event on Palm Sunday, 1822.

In 1809 Schleiermacher at the age of forty married the young widow of a close friend. When two years later he was called to a chair of theology at the University of Berlin—he himself had been active in founding the university as a member of the state's department of education—the scope of his life and work was defined. His letters to his wife and children show him as a devoted and gentle patriarch. His labors in the academic arena speak for themselves. While continuing to hold his pulpit, he assumed an ever enlarging responsibility as professor, lecturing on each division of theological studies save the Old Testament, and on dialectics, history of philosophy, psychology, and political science, as well as hermeneutics and philosophical ethics. His colleague in the neighboring faculty of philosophy was Hegel, and there can be little doubt that the ethics upon which Schleiermacher worked intensely year after year constituted his own critique of this greatest of German idealists, although we find no mention of Hegel by name in the notes from these lectures. Of all these undertakings only the dogmatic theology issued in a book, whose full title is *The Christian Faith, Presented in Its Inner Connections according to the Fundamentals of the Evangelical Church.* It appeared in two parts, in 1821 and 1822, and again in revised form in 1830. He had hoped to prepare his dialectic (his critical analysis of human self-consciousness) for the press also, but only the introduction was completed before his death in 1834. Friends and pupils compiled his notes and literary remains, so that in addition to individual critical editions of his most important works we today have thirty-two volumes of his essays, addresses, sermons, articles and lecture notes, plus several collections of his letters, of which that edited by Dilthey and translated by Frederica Rowan is the most extensive. "The art of making time do," Schleiermacher once wrote to his friend Frau Herz, "is, after all, a great art; nay, I might almost say, the most important one in this world next after the art of loving, for upon this depend all others."

To his contemporaries, Schleiermacher's principal métier appeared to be society and friendship, earnest conversation, lecture and sermon. It was his habit to speak almost extemporaneously or from the briefest notes, and his congregation in Trinity Church was crowded with "Moravians, Jews, baptised and unbaptised, young philosophers and philologists, elegant ladies" and many others. But his *Brief Outline on the Study of Theology,* notes on dialectics and on ethics, and, above all, *The Christian Faith* exhibit systematic powers unequaled in the history of Protestant theology. In fact, Schleiermacher steadfastly took care to inform each side of his daily life with the corrective of his experience in the other. He could not countenance a sharp division between the personal and the scientific and had no use for the still-prevalent image of the scholar as a solitary archivist or seer. It is moral man who perceives, reasons, and strives to know; the real world is humanity, and into such a world it is that we are born and attain to consciousness. Self-consciousness arises in response to the words and gestures of others. Indeed, thinking is but inner speaking, as speech is the outerside of thought and the organ of the commonalty of reason.

Schleiermacher used the teaching-learning situation, that is, the dialogue, as the paradigm of man's rational activity, thereby emphasizing that insofar as all communication occurs within a particular historical language, be it classical or modern, all thinking and knowing has its genesis likewise in a given time and place as response to the uttered judgments and analyses of other historical selves. To the extent, then, that an individual's judgments are made possible by the public speech within which he thinks, each deed of reasoning reflects and is conditioned by the history of the language; to the extent that each such judgment represents a criticism and reformulation of the statements of the other, it constitutes a new moment both in the history of the self and of his culture. Our reasoning, therefore, even the highest and most abstract, takes its departure from no absolute beginnings or wholly self-evident first principles but from the history of other minds. Schleiermacher alluded to the experiential basis of this principle in the *Soliloquies*, where he wrote that he could not appropriate anything new, except in the company of friends and colleagues. The detailed import of the principle is spelled out in his philosophical ethics and in his dialectics, in which he presents a full-scale analysis of human consciousness and selfhood in the polarities of spirit and nature, mind and body, self and object, individual and community. Practically, these convictions led Schleiermacher to conceive of the university as a federation of faculties or sciences rooted in the history of a people and its language and to define its function as the critical preservation and extension of the knowledge contained potentially in that history. On his terms it is manifestly impossible to assign to any single discipline the position of queen of the sciences; rather, the natural and the human studies (*Geisteswissenschaften*) require each other collectively and severally as equally active partners in the unending dialectic of reason.

Over against his more thoroughly idealistic contemporaries, therefore, Schleiermacher had to reject the notion of an intuition of the absolute or of the appearance in human consciousness of pure, undifferentiated reason. Thinking is the deed of a naturally and historically individuated subject; the ground of all being cannot be an object. He was more than willing to ascribe to philosophy the title of the highest knowledge, for he regarded philosophizing as the natural and most original business of the human understanding, but the plurality of historical languages and the still incomplete state of the empirical sciences testify that it also is perpetually becoming itself and is never whole. Only when all historical information has been gathered in, when the natural basis of human consciousness is known in the totality of its relations to the cosmos, and when the inner individuality of all selves is fully revealed and understood, will the highest knowledge assume its true and final form and philosophy be perfected.

This doctrine of the sciences made it entirely natural for Schleiermacher to conceive of the university as the proper place for the study of theology. While he could not tolerate the pretensions of speculation to independence of or priority to historical life, neither could he have accepted the cogency of objections to the dialogue of philosophy and theology. In a most revealing letter to Friedrich Heinrich Jacobi, he made use of his favorite image of polarity to depict the relations of the heart and the head, of faith and reason: "Understanding and feeling [the organ of piety] in me . . . remain distinct, but they touch each other and form a galvanic pile. To me it seems that the innermost life of the spirit consists in the galvanic action thus produced in the feeling of the understanding and the understanding of the feeling, during which, however, the two poles always remain deflected from each other." Therefore, he wrote, his philosophy and dogmatics were "firmly determined not to contradict each other, but for this very reason, neither pretends to be complete; and as long as I have been able to think they have always been more or less attuning themselves to each other and drawing nearer to each other."

Despite the incredible busyness of his life, Schleiermacher was throughout really governed by that one galvanic principle to which he referred in his letter to Jacobi—the interaction of pulpit and contemporary intellectual culture, first in Berlin among the Romantics, then in Halle, and once more in the capital. The theological formulation of the problem with which he wrestled can be simply stated: what is the nature of the creature, man, whose existence is determined both by God and the world? Schleiermacher sought an answer that would do justice to his conviction that the two poles of religious self-consciousness and understanding energize the total field of man's life without destroying each other. The supposition that these two foci of human existence can be isolated from each other and considered apart was as little tenable to his disposition as the old Orthodox division of reality into a supernatural and a natural world, incorporating parallel structures of being that miraculously impinge only from time to time, according to the inscrutable will of their maker. So long as this kind of division lies as a presupposition of thought, the intellectual life of Christendom will find itself caught in the hopeless shuttlecocking of rationalism to biblicism and naturalism to supernaturalism and back.

> One age bears the penalty of the misdeeds of another, but seldom knows how to redeem itself, except by the perpetration of a new misdemeanour. By the utter subversion of the letter of the Scriptures all historical continuity was dissolved and it is as great madness to destroy such continuity in religious matters as in political matters. *That* had therefore, to be re-established; but as Tieck has admirably expressed it, in attempting to screw the thing back we shall only be destroying the historical continuity in the opposite direction.

Consequently, Schleiermacher addressed himself to the inquiry after that in human nature from which the sense of destiny, absolute dependence, and election arises—in a word, religious identity—and then to the exposition of the growth and conformation of this consciousness in the polarity of self and world. By abandoning the natural-supernatural dichotomy, he was returning to the prescholastic idea of man and the world that we find in the church fathers and the biblical milieu, in which the operations of nature and grace and the natural and theological virtues cannot be neatly segregated and labeled, and man is conceived to be not yet fully human and in possession of his "nature" until his genesis and destiny in the divine economy are fully understood and appropriated.

> . . . I have placed myself on the footing to demand of others that they shall prove to me where is the ultimate limit of nature. When, therefore, my Christian feeling is conscious of a divine spirit indwelling in me, which is distinct from my reason, I will never give up seeking for this spirit in the deepest depths of the soul's nature; and when my Christian feeling becomes conscious of a Son of God, who differs from us in another way than merely being better than the best of us, I will never cease to search for the genesis of this Son of God in the deepest depths of nature, and to say to myself, that I shall most likely learn to understand the second Adam just as soon as the first Adam or Adams, whose coming into existence I must also admit without being able to understand.

But Schleiermacher, of course, could not simply repristinate the earlier theology; he had to think this idea afresh in the language and concepts of the epoch.

This he set out to do for his *Speeches* on religion in order to show his Romantic friends the culture-affirming character of piety and the integral place of religious self-consciousness in the full development of the human spirit. Two of the points that he insisted on here and always thereafter are of the greatest moment for the whole of his religious and theological view. One of them is that the deeply personal locus and ramifying nature of piety make religion impossible except in community. Religiously we are no less dependent for the birth of self-consciousness upon the stimulus and response of personal encounter than we are intellectually, and, as Schleiermacher's life encompassed broader responsibilities for the church, he came to see that likewise the religious consciousness requires a tradition, a common and public medium, a cultus, that the individual may both teach and learn, just as the university or science needs a common vocabulary and knowledge of its history. While he was intensely and perennially involved in the analysis of the ethical meaning of personal individuality, he had no patience for the anti-institutional individualism that issued in superiority or indifference rather than reform. This grasp of the meaning of community for historical development, for the moral life of the individual, and of the meaning of the individual as the historical source of life, criticism, and progress for the community enabled Schleiermacher to hand on to Protestantism a renewed understanding of the church and a means of transcending the alternative of viewing faith as a purely private, personal affair or as adhesion to a time-sanctioned, unalterable institutional form. In effect, he recovered for Protestantism something of Augustine's vision of men living in commonweals according to the agreement of their loves for the good. But Schleiermacher accented the equality of all citizens of the city of God (he himself regarded the distinction between clergy and laity as functional only), and always insisted that the common life of the church must proceed afresh from each of its members. The Christian consciousness is not implanted in the community by any man or office but by the Spirit, and the task of the minister is to address and elicit that Spirit in each of its members.

Religion, then, is not the creation of ecclesiastical institutions and dogma; rather, it is their creator. It emerges out of a prior community and is rooted in a dimension of self-consciousness that cannot be expunged from the nature that is fully human. Here we have the second of the points that is first made in the *Speeches,* and it constitutes the best-known element in Schleiermacher's work. Religion or piety is an original form of self-consciousness that is not to be identified either with doing and morality or with knowing and science. In the *Speeches* Schleiermacher gives to it the name of feeling and again of intuition (*Anschauung*). Later, in the *Christmas Eve,* he speaks of the Christian feeling and mood, in his philosophical ethics of feeling as a subjective knowing; in the dialectics it is the representation of the transcendent ground of being, and in *The Christian Faith* he defines religion as an immediate self-consciousness and a feeling of absolute dependence.

Despite these changes and additions in Schleiermacher's terminology, the general intention of his language and ideas is relatively clear. First of all, he firmly disavowed the reduction of religion to moral sanctions or its identification with good works. Again, religion is not the fruit of assent to dogma, nor is it dependent for its actualization upon theological systems. Nor is its truth to be found in the purer concepts of speculative philosophy. To the Romantics he explained the content of feeling as harmony with the All; piety is "a sense and taste for the infinite," an awareness that the infinite is immediately present in the finite self and that the self is a unique statement of the universal concourse of being. The religious moment is not one of mystical absorption and loss of identity, but a moment in which identity is received and affirmed, while the kinship of self with all other being is intuited through an immediacy with the All that almost suspends the distance between subject and object. Consequently, religious experience is the sensitizing nerve of consciousness, the eye of the self upon the world of humanity. "What is finest and tenderest in history . . . can only be comprehended in the feeling of a religious disposition." Religious feeling is really the expression of that which is most original in the self, the welling up of being or life in the form of an historical existence that is at once related to all being and inwardly individuated. When this inner sense is raised to the level of thought and discourse it has already been partially dissipated, but its energy and quality pervade all that the pious individual is and does.

As he worked further into his philosophy, ethics, and systematic theology, Schleiermacher tried to introduce more precise distinctions among the grades of feeling and to give a fuller account of the way in which it becomes ingredient in the specifically Christian consciousness and of its theological significance. In his dialectics and ethics he makes clear that he means by feeling not a "faculty" but a quality of self-consciousness. Its content is the inner individuality of the self that cannot be derived from membership in a species, people, or community. As feeling selves we are enveloped in an awareness of the peculiar and inexplicable givenness of our existence in our world for which no object of perception and thought or of will and activity can furnish an explanation. It is the "original expression of an immediate existential relationship," the form of self-consciousness that is anterior to all subject-object relations and is in fact the source of the special affective content that distinguishes the doing and thinking of one self from another. No single moment of temporal activity or consciousness—including even the consciousness of the self as an object or a "me" over against the "I"—can adequately symbolize or exhaust the content of feeling, for the fundament of feeling is really the life-unity of the individual and the source of the imagination that synthesizes the elements of thought and volition into organic wholes.

Hence the difference between authentic and ephemeral art depends upon the degree to which the artistic representation embodies a will to create that has been thoroughly mediated by the permanent feeling of the artist. And insofar as all historical acts and thoughts are meditated or spontaneous expressions of such feeling (or mood), life itself is art and interpretation, the setting forth of self and the critical, intuitive reconstruction of the inner individuality of others. When considered at its utmost inner reach, such feeling bespeaks the radical unfreedom of the self, its "absolute dependence," and the "whence" of this immediate existential relationship and givenness of self-consciousness, Schleiermacher writes in the most famous paragraph of *The Christian Faith* (§4), is what we mean by "God."

God is therefore not an object of knowledge in the ordinary sense of the term, for an object in the knowing relationship is by definition a being that enters into consciousness and differentiates it, calling forth a particular response, and no response or series of responses of intellect and will can suffice to express the God-relationship. Consequently, Schleiermacher found no profit in the efforts to demonstrate the existence of God, for concepts—which are the only fruit of demonstration—are later products of the dialectical skill of the mind and at best symbolically evocative of that which is earliest in the self's history. Schleiermacher quite naturally hesitated to speak of a knowledge of God or of feeling as cognitive; God is "known" only in the sense that there is a certain analogy between knowing and feeling. That is to say, as in knowing, the subject is determined by the object, submits himself to the object, as it were, in an attempt to reconstitute the object ideally in himself, so through feeling the subject-self likewise is aware of being determined. But it is a determination or placing of the self as such, and, furthermore, of the self in the totality of its relations to and in the world. "What we call feeling here is the immediate presence of the whole, undivided personal existence, both sensible as well as spiritual, the unity of the person and its sensible and spiritual world." And such feeling arises, as we have already seen, not in the isolated man but in the participant of the world of humanity. It is called forth by the gestures and religious addresses of others, and, more generally, by the whole style of their personal bearing, and it takes on the historical character of the particular community in which the individual is nurtured. Thus the Christian faith can be simply defined as that feeling or consciousness whose entire content refers to Jesus Christ as its mediator. Schleiermacher's dogmatic theology is in· fact a description of the content of this consciousness, exemplifying his contention that theology is not a species of theoretical knowledge but the statement in the most precise, dialectical language available of the personal consciousness that the Christian community shares in.

There could be no question in Schleiermacher's mind about the propriety of calling Christianity a religion among other religions. By virtue of his analysis of the nature of human existence, he must necessarily have ranged Christianity alongside all the other manifestations of the human phenomenon and comprehended it under the general rubric of immediate self-consciousness and feeling. Nor could he have defended it, on his terms, as attesting to its own uniqueness through its infallible dogma and correct doctrine. Those who discover the distinctiveness or superiority of Christian faith here intellectualize and scholasticize its genius and so misplace it. All that really marks it off from other religions is to be found in the specific structure and quality of its consciousness, as it appears in the person of Jesus Christ, in his individuality and life and in the communication of the same to others.

Continuing in the tradition of the Reformation, Schleiermacher understands the church's origin and mission to be in preaching, the proclamation of the word. But the word proclaimed is not understood as doctrine to which the proper response is assent. The word is vessel of life. The church is the historical community deriving from Jesus' own self-impartation in parable, discourse, and deed, and the life of the church is the appropriation of that impartation and the re-enactment of its communication through the preaching and hearing, sacrament and communion, that form the Christian consciousness into the mind of Christ and the people into his body. The work of Christ is "person-forming," and the Christian church is the people who know themselves as persons through him. The essential type of Schleiermacher's theology is the ancient idea of the divine economy, in which the redeemer is presented as the last Adam, the Son of Man, the recapitulator and perfecter of the race. Christ appears in history with a sinless humanity, a humanity uninterruptedly and fully indwelt by God—by which Schleiermacher means that Christ's total consciousness of world and self was wholly dominated and regulated (not extinguished) by his God-consciousness. He was further marked by a fully developed consciousness of man, by a sympathy, that brings community into being about himself. In relation to him and in dependence upon him, the human consciousness belonging to historical, adamic manhood experiences the pain of its own dividedness and inconstancy, the guilt of its suppression of the feeling of absolute dependence, and the confusion in its resulting disorderly consciousness of self and world. But this awareness of sin is at the same time also an awareness of the potency of Christ's God-consciousness and of its already begun creative work in the self.

Thus the Christian is one whose consciousness is historically mediated by Jesus Christ and structured by the antithesis of sin and grace. He is caught up in a tide of pain and joy. Schleiermacher does not actually give much attention to these affective states in his dogmatics, although the whole conception of feeling and religious self-consciousness is rife with possibilities for an extensive phenomenology of the Christian "mood." The reader must turn back to the earlier *Christmas Eve* and to the occasional references in the letters for hints of his mind on this aspect of the subject. Quite characteristically, and in keeping with his view of sin as a state of inchoateness and imperfection of consciousness, he designates the pain of Christian faith as melancholy rather than remorse, "a holy sadness"; "I always picture to myself Christian piety . . . as excitatory of pain. But it is the sweet pain of melancholy so well calculated to soothe other pains. Surely, if there was any good in Saul's soul, it must have been an *adagio* that exorcized the evil." However, joy is the term he most frequently gives to the disposition created by faith, and it, in turn, is best interpreted by Schleiermacher's commitment to the belief in providence. This is the dominant theme in his treatment of the doctrine of God: the divine determination of all things, God's *eudokia,* "good pleasure." Much of the subsequent interpretation of Schleiermacher's theology has been so preoccupied with his startling use of human feeling that it has forgotten the consistency with which he defined it as a God-determined feeling that becomes actual "only as consciousness of His eternal power." Hence Christianly potentiated feeling leads away from all speculation about the separate operations of justice, mercy, and love in the Godhead, and their reconciliation. The divine love is simply the inclusive name that faith gives to the totality of the content of the God-consciousness as it arises through the work upon us of Christ's person, and so all the distinctions between real and possible, freedom and necessity, that are derived from historical judgments are inapplicable to the being of God, who is present in the consciousness imparted by the Redeemer in one way only, as choosing and ordaining what is and comes to be.

As a theologian Schleiermacher belongs unmistakably to the tradition of Augustine and Calvin, and if one judges him only from the dogmatic point of view, his handling of the divine government and of Jesus Christ as the mediator of the true consciousness of God is enough to establish him as the most powerful systematic mind in this line since the Reformation. He gave to the Augustinian-Reformed spirit a fresh embodiment that has enabled it to live on in modern times. Undoubtedly, however, his greatest achievement is his articulation of the self-consciousness and the God-consciousness that relate to feeling. In doing so, Schleiermacher sought and gained for faith and theology an independence of speculative philosophy and scholastically inclined theology and rationalism. With his idea of human nature and individuality, in effect he laid down a religious world view that culminates in Christian faith. Here again, by teaching that the consciousness of self and world remains confused and intermittent until it is clarified and ordered by the God-consciousness mediated through Christ's person, he points directly back to the ideal of Augustine, who pictured the remembering, thinking, willing soul as fully self-conscious only when it remembers, thinks, and wills its creator; and to that of John Calvin whose *Institutes of the Christian Religion* begins with the declaration that the sum of human wisdom consists of two parts—the knowledge of God and of man.

Theology since Schleiermacher, in turn, points back to him in its development of a number of themes. Among them is the search for the human ground of the experience of and knowledge of God, the religious a priori—not a term Schleiermacher used—as carried out by Ernst Troeltsch and Rudolf Otto, although 'the former is much more faithful to Schleiermacher's meaning than the latter. More generally, however, the whole quest of the nineteenth-century theologians for the moral, personal, or existential heart of the movement of faith, as exemplified in Coleridge, Albrecht Ritschl, and Wilhelm Herrmann, is to be identified with Schleiermacher's idea of theology and religion. Troeltsch's essays on the historical nature of the Christian faith and community, together with his effort to analyze their relations to culture, are also inspired significantly by the insight into the character of religion and Christianity that Schleiermacher emphasized from his *Speeches* and *Brief Outline of the Study of Theology* to *The Christian Faith*. The present-day concern for Christocentric theology has its origin in Schleiermacher also, though his Christocentrism is certainly not that of the objectivist species of neo-orthodoxy espoused by the school of Karl Barth. Nevertheless, *The Christian Faith* first demonstrated the need of recognizing that the mind of the church is wholly determined by the mediator of its faith; the person and work of Christ inform not just Christology but the whole scope of theology. And, finally, we have to thank Schleiermacher for establishing high on the list of virtues indispensable to honest theology the resolution to maintain Christian thought in the painful but necessary dialogue with the faculties of the university and their secular sciences—the most valuable trait of Protestant liberalism in the last century and this.

Bibliography

Friedrich Schleiermacher, *The Christian Faith*, H. R. Mackintosh and J. S. Stewart, eds., N. Y., Harper, 1963, 2 vols. (Harper Torchbooks).

Richard R. Niebuhr, *Schleiermacher on Christ and Religion*, N. Y. Scribner's, 1964.

HORACE BUSHNELL

Sydney E. Ahlstrom

Horace Bushnell (1802–76) was the most creative and interesting theologian to emerge from the New England Puritan
tradition during the nineteenth century. Like the great eighteenth-century claimant to that distinction, Jonathan Edwards,
he spent his entire active career in the local pastorate, devoting
much attention to the problems of conducting a viable parish
ministry. Like Edwards, too, he broadened his range of concern to include many of the oldest and deepest issues of Christian theology, but he did so by concentrating on certain of the
most critical problems rather than by a systematic discussion
of Christian dogmatics. Also like his great New England predecessor he took with great seriousness the apologetic task of
justifying God's ways to his fellow men and made his total *opus*
as classic a theological expression of romanticism as Edwards
had of the Enlightenment. He eminently deserves the titles
given him: the "American Schleiermacher" and "father of
American religious liberalism." Such designations, however, are
only a partial indication of his claim to remembrance and they
veil many factors which have sustained or actually widened interest in his thought for over a century.

Bushnell's insights into the nature of language, communication, symbolism, community, and nationhood have almost
limitless applicability. Christian thinkers of all persuasions have
continued to draw upon his views of the family, conversion,
congregational life, religious nurture, spiritual growth, and the
nature of dogma. Americans from North and South may in time
come to appreciate his profound understanding of the Civil
War, just as historians, literary critics, sociologists, and philosophers are becoming aware of his penetrating and fruitful analysis of the social dimensions of human thought and institutional
life. Man in community is the persistent theme of his most enduring thought; the contextuality and interpenetration of all

things, in history and nature, was a constant preoccupation. Out of these interests grew another lasting contribution: his lifelong and ever intensifying meditations on the meaning of love, forgiveness, sacrifice, and reconciliation. In the last analysis it may be that Bushnell's undoubted relation to the rise of liberal theology in the American churches is a relatively minor and transient aspect of his significance. Be that as it may, Bushnell is most certainly to be remembered for what he thought and wrote rather than for what he did in his fairly uneventful life as a pastor. "My figure in this world," he once wrote, "has not been great, but I have had a great experience." After a brief account of his career, therefore, we will here be concerned with the writings that grew out of that experience.

Horace Bushnell was born in the village of Bantam, two miles from Litchfield hill in Connecticut, the first child of Ensign Bushnell, a farmer and a Methodist, and Dotha (Bishop) Bushnell, a gentle and pious Episcopalian. "My mother's loving instinct was from God," he said in his characteristic way, "and God was in love to me first therefore; which love was deeper than hers, and more protracted." Three years later the family moved westward to a farm in New Preston, Connecticut. As he delightfully described it a half century later, it was an "Age of Homespun" wherein the internal economy of a household could be calculated by observing the sheep in the pasture, and when on winter mornings children went to school warmed by wool shorn from sheep individually remembered. In these isolated rural surroundings he experienced the meaning of a covenanted New England community under about as favorable circumstances as persisted anywhere in the early nineteenth century. Even the old Puritan Sabbath—beginning at sundown on Saturday—was observed in the more pious homes. In the local Congregational church he "owned the covenant" in 1821, and he recalled the sturdy piety of that congregation with gratitude. "If the minister speaks in his great-coat and mittens, if the howling blasts of winter blow in across the assembly fresh streams of ventilation that move the hair upon their heads, they are none the less content if only he gives them good strong exercise. Under their hard . . . stolid faces, great thoughts are brewing and these keep them warm." Not surprisingly young

Bushnell left for Yale College two years later with plans to enter the ministry.

During his college years his faith deteriorated and these plans changed. After being graduated in 1827, he taught school for a time, served as associate editor of the New York *Journal of Commerce,* then returned to Yale to study law, serving meanwhile as a tutor in the college. In 1831, however, just when almost ready for admission to the bar, his religious doubts were dissolved during a revival in the college; he experienced a deep renewal of Christian commitment. A friend remembered a confession that anticipates the theologian: "My heart wants the Father; my heart wants the Son; my heart wants the Holy Ghost." The student of law transferred thereafter to the university's theological department, which was then looked upon as being unusually progressive in tendency, with the eminent Nathaniel William Taylor as its head and dominant personality. Taylor was a metaphysician in the tradition of eighteenth-century Scottish common sense philosophy; and the "New Haven Theology" was under fire from the more conservative bastions of New England orthodoxy for its modifications of the old views of Jonathan Edwards on God's glory, original sin, and man's utter dependence on divine grace. Taylor made man's freedom a cornerstone of his rationale for revivalism in a democratic ethos.

Bushnell was actually to occupy much of the new ground Taylor had broken, but he did not admire the eighteenth-century rationalism that still prevailed at Yale. Insofar as the characteristic temper of his developing thought was owed to other thinkers (and he was not prodigal with admissions on such matters) it was rather to Samuel Taylor Coleridge, whose *Aids to Reflection* brought him to see "a whole other world . . . a range of realities in a higher tier. . . ." In due course, too, he, like so many dissatisfied American religious thinkers, would be stirred by Friedrich Schleiermacher's discussion of the Trinity which Professor Moses Stuart of Andover Seminary published in the *Bibliotheca Sacra* in 1835. Bushnell was to express nevertheless a kind of romanticism that was indigenous to America; and he naturally imbibed much during these and subsequent years from the Transcendentalist ferment beginning to be felt in Boston and soon to be dominated by the figure of Ralph Waldo Emerson. Even his undeniable romanticism, however, would largely be excogitated by himself in solitary meditation. As a biographer remarked, "He published first and read later."

In 1833, having been licensed to preach, he accepted a call from the North Church in Hartford, which in 1824 had been formed by seceders from the revivalistic First Church, with merchants and retailers the dominant element in the congregation. Bushnell was its third minister. (Later in the same year he married Mary Apthorp of New Haven.) At the time he admitted to certain doubts about the significance of infant baptism, but his congregation had confidence in his seriousness and dedication. During his long ministry he healed the contention within his parish between "New Haven" and "Old School" factions, and by a determined effort to comprehend opposing views won the loyalty and deep regard of his congregation. They remained steadfast even when he was being vigorously attacked for his alleged departures in doctrine. In 1852 when moves were being made to bring him to trial for his views, North Church withdrew from the local consociation so as to preclude an ecclesiastical process. The hostility of most of his fellow ministers in and around Hartford did not therewith abate, but with the passing years he played an active and farsighted role in many civic affairs, and his memory has been substantially honored by a grateful city.

Bushnell's first major publication and the one which has probably had the most sustained influence was on *Christian Nurture* (1847; revised edition, 1861). The original lectures as well as the book revealed his continuing concern with the meaning of baptism. They documented a fundamental shift in his own thinking, and in the longer perspective they mark a turning point in Congregational church history. *Christian Nurture* is a thoroughgoing, indeed a classic critique of views which were intrinsic to Puritanism and heavily accentuated by the Great Awakening. Bushnell returns to an older conception of baptism and nurture. He stressed the churchlike quality and genuinely redemptive role of the family and, inversely, another theme that would concern him increasingly, the familylike quality of the true Christian congregation. Attacking the notion of the Christian life oriented on brimstone, conversion, and revivals, he insisted that a child of Christian parents should never know himself as being otherwise than Christian. Though fairly conservative in doctrinal framework, though widely acclaimed in antirevivalistic circles, even by Professor Charles Hodge of Princeton Seminary, and though consonant with other critiques of latter-day Puritanism, the book ran counter to the mainstream of American evangelical Protestantism and marked its author for the time being as a dangerous innovator. In time, however, the negative animus of the work faded from view; it came to be appreciated as an important commentary on the practical and familial significance of infant baptism and a pathbreaking inquiry into the nature of character formation, subconscious influences, and the social dimensions of life and learning. As reinterpreted by persons of more naturalistic bent, his work became a pioneer expression of "progressive education" and a veritable bible of the Christian education movement. Bushnell's own interpretation was perhaps more "familial" than sacramental; and the book illustrates his persistent effort to make the church's message meaningful to people who were becoming increasingly removed from their traditional Christian moorings. He was determined to strike a respondent chord in the sentiments—and the sentimentality—of an urban middle class which was almost invulnerable to older revivalistic techniques. "If Bushnell could not appeal to his public as Christians," writes one biographer, "he knew they would listen as parents." In a striking way both Bushnell's circumstance and his response anticipated the impact of another century's social change on the Protestantism of America's urban middle classes.

God in Christ (1849) is Bushnell's central work. It consists of a Dissertation on Language and three discourses: on the Atonement, the Divinity of Christ, and the problems of "Dogma and Spirit" in the reviving of religion. These addresses were delivered in 1848 at the Harvard Divinity School, at Yale College as the *Concio ad Clerum* to the assembled ministers of Connecticut, and at Andover Seminary. They announced themes which were to remain at the foreground of his own thought, and brought Bushnell into the center of New England's theological discussion, provoking a storm of controversy. One old participant in those conflicts wrote in 1902 that "it is impossible for those who have come upon the stage of public life within the last thirty years to realize the intense excitement and tremulous apprehension caused by these charges of heresy against so prominent a character."

The lectures which precipitated Bushnell's temporary ostracism were preceded by deep spiritual crisis and a specific experience of widened mystical vision, to which the writings of Madame Guyon and Fénelon made a vital contribution. In his wife's words, the year 1848 became "the central point in [his] life. . . . He had reached one of those headlands where new discoveries open to sight." When criticism arose over these discoveries, he defended and amplified each of his positions in *Christ in Theology, Being the Answer of the Author, before the Hartford Central Association of Ministers* (1851). His treatises on *The Vicarious Sacrifice* (1866) and *Forgiveness and Law* (1874) provided still more complete statements of his view of Christ's atoning work, a profounder general understanding of reconciliation, and a deepening conception of God's sacrificial love. In this cluster of works one confronts the heart of Bushnell's theological message.

At the head of these productions stand the writings on language which had been maturing at least since a lecture on "Revelation" given at Andover in 1839. This theme was rightly judged by his daughter to be "the key to Horace Bushnell." He expounds the implications to be drawn from the organic character of the family, the state, and above all, the church. He delineates the social nature of language, and therefore its many-layered, metaphoric structure, its evocative function, its symbolic value. Poetry, to him, is the norm of language and "religion has a natural and profound alliance with poetry." Theological terms and doctrinal creeds, therefore, become lifeless and artificial counters or rationalistic prisons of the spirit if their form and history and atmosphere are not entered into and appropriated. Even when we proceed in this way of "participation," we cannot assume the adequacy or completeness of what we say. When we venture beyond the merely physical in our discourse, even the law of contradiction does not apply. "Accordingly we never come so near to a truly well rounded view of any truth, as when it is offered paradoxically; that is, under contradictions; that is, under two or more dictions, which, taken as dictions, are contrary to one another." How this could relate to a matter such as the atonement, he made clear: "It would not be as wild a breach of philosophy itself, to undertake a dogmatic statement of the contents of a tragedy, as to attempt giving in the same manner the equivalents of the life and death of Jesus Christ." Here is indicated the problem Bushnell created for his stricter, less imaginative brethren in the ministry: it was not so much that he was heterodox as that he made heresy a very elusive thing. As for creeds, "one seldom need have any difficulty in accepting as many as are offered him." Bushnell might even have seen *some* value in the diction of his archcritic, Bennet Tyler, who "writes about the human spirit as if it were a machine under the laws of mechanics."

Yet Bushnell was not an apostle of intellectual license; there was drive and purpose behind his own diction and intuitive methods. On the divinity of Christ, the trinity, revelation, conversion, the atonement, and on the comprehensive questions of nature and the supernatural (to be discussed below) Bushnell was moved by a single conviction: that the depths and riches of the Christian faith, so powerful and certain a reality in his own life, were being lost to his own generation and, *a fortiori,* to future generations because the entire world was entering "a new age of doubt." He saw it engulfing the churches at home and the mission fields abroad. Yet to him Christ was

> the Grand Chief Miracle of the world . . . a Saviour come to bring salvation. Mankind can rely on no stock powers in human nature; men are not going to mend themselves; neither history or evolution will avail. Nothing short of a salvation brought down from out of nature and above, in his divine person, can be any sufficient remedy. This most certainly is what is given us for gospel, and this we are firmly to hold and boldly publish.

Bushnell's Christology, accordingly, did not accent the human, historical Jesus, but dwelt upon the divine Christ with such insistence as to stir up legitimate cries of docetism and

Patripassianism. Neither did Bushnell "naturalize" the church. It was to him not simply a human historical organization but a new society "called the kingdom of heaven, . . . the Society of Life, the Embodied Word . . . the body of Christ, the fullness of him that filleth all in all." His instrumental view of the trinity likewise had man's experience of the Godhead as its point of departure. And in 1848 he professed an inability to speak of the divine nature, except that God is one and that he manifests himself to men as Father, Son, and Spirit. This was a modified Sabellianism. But his later thought moved toward the Athanasian position developed at the Council of Nicaea.

Bushnell had no desire to alter or blunt the offense of the kerygma; he did not seek to remove the scandal of the cross; he was willing "that we maintain our ground in what are called offenses against reason." But he did not want needless scandal or the wrong offense; he would not maintain offenses "against immutable morality." In a general way this brought him into conflict with the inelastic, propositional, "rationalistic" Calvinistic-Puritan dogmatic structures which to his mind had incarcerated the religious spirit in New England. He wished to make theology experientially relevant and morally powerful; and the atonement inexorably became the focus of his concern. Especially in need of revision, he thought, were those doctrines which explained the atoning work of Christ as a legal or penal "satisfaction" of God's wrath. This "theory" he could not countenance even if he had to assert that what "the Master's words have been plainly teaching for eighteen hundred years" was not discovered until the true insight came to him on a "particular day of accident" six months before the publication of his final treatise!

Bushnell's "moral theory" of the atonement took its rise from his persistent pondering of man's own experience of love, and a deep conviction, expressed in *Forgiveness and Law,* that "a grand analogy, or almost identity subsists between our moral nature and that of God." In his lecture of 1848 he had insisted that Christian preaching must include or comprehend both historic views of the atonement: (1) the *subjective* view that Christ's work was to change the lives of men, to "redeem us from all iniquity"—that "God was in Christ, reconciling the world unto himself"; and (2) the *objective* view that Christ "died for us" as a propitiatory sacrifice that we might be accounted righteous before God. His own emphasis, however, is "subjective," with the stress falling on the way Christ's work upheld the "sanctity of the Law" and on the danger of preaching forgiveness without demanding reformation of character. In *The Vicarious Sacrifice* he further expounds this conception of love as being "essentially vicarious in its own nature." Christ's sacrifice, therefore, is universally comprehensible, not a forensic mystery or a governmental transaction: it is God's healing work.

Finally, shortly before his death, Bushnell moves explicitly toward a traditional position by underlining the "Godward" element in the atonement, though he still employs his analogical moral argument. This last phase of Bushnell's thinking was preceded by a genuine reappropriation of Jonathan Edwards, perhaps especially a radical distinction between natural virtue and "true virtue" which he could not have accepted when he was writing *Christian Nurture*. There also came over Bushnell in these later years an awareness of tragedy that stood in sharp contrast to the evolutionary optimism of his age. "Christianity is a mighty salvation, because it is a tragic salvation . . . in an essentially tragic universe . . . with a fall and an overspreading curse at the beginning, and a cross in the middle, and a glory and shame at the end. . . ." True forgiveness, he now insists, is not a simple cleaning of the slate; it involves suffering for and with the offender quite regardless of his merit or comeliness. True forgiveness is impossible unless the wronged party take on himself the experiences of the malefactor. In like manner God himself, by his great sacrifice, is propitiated and inclined to mercy.

Nature and the Supernatural (1858) is the most comprehensive and wide-sweeping of Bushnell's major treatises; it deals with nothing less than the one "system of God." In this one system "nature" is seen as that realm of being which is governed or determined by law; the "supernatural" as that which is *not* in the train of cause and effect but which acts upon the chain from without and out of its own agency. These realms are seen as consubstantial or interpenetrated so that man and all living things, and how much more one knows not, partake of or participate in the supernatural and are in this way divine. The whole realm of spirit or freedom, in other words, was conceived of as supernatural, or transcendental in an Emersonian sense. On this foundation Bushnell then expounds his views of sin, miracle, incarnation, revelation, and Christ's divinity, all along vigorously defending these Christian views from skeptical attack. In this work as in no other the full scope, though by no means the full power, of his "romantic orthodoxy" is made manifest, as is the preponderant place that the apologetical task takes in his thinking.

As in all of his works one may note in this one an oscillation between liberal and conservative positions. A kind of incompleteness in the work also suggests that he had bitten off more than he could chew. Neither his historical nor philosophical preparations had been extensive enough to enable him to carry out a sufficiently penetrating work. His understanding of science and its method, moreover, was too limited to permit a fulfillment of his chosen apologetical task. The book's shortcomings explain why John Fiske, long before he became a famous evolutionary philosopher, saw in Bushnell what he took to be the hopelessly antiscientific bent of all Christian theology. Misunderstanding science and miscalculating the power and permanence of the rising philosophies of social and religious Darwinism, Bushnell probably overestimated the need for radical theological restatement. During most of his life his fears of popular skepticism overrode his own fundamental conservatism.

There were extremely liberal theological implications in much that Bushnell wrote, especially in his views on the essence and purpose of dogma and on nature and the supernatural. On public affairs, however, and in social philosophy he was a moderate conservative, suspicious of popular democracy and an admirer of the great Whig, Daniel Webster. Convinced that the wealth, health, and social excellencies of New England were the fruits of the Anglo-Saxon genius and Puritan piety, he was not sympathetic with the new, predominantly Irish and Roman Catholic immigrants who were moving into the New England cities and factory towns during his lifetime. He was very active during the 1840's in forming a Protestant League and Christian Alliance to combat the Roman Church, and the chief public result of his trip to Europe in 1845–46 was an outspoken open letter to the Pope, denouncing his despotism. His strategy in these efforts was to create a united Protestant front. He hoped that the various denominations would submerge their distinctive tenets and combine against the mutual enemy. His aims, thus, were practical rather than ecumenical in the modern sense. He believed that "most of what we call division in the Church of God is only distribution." The creed-based Evangelical Alliance did not interest him. It is a fact, moreover, that Bushnell's anti-doctrinal liberalism did provide a rationale for the emerging type of common-denominator Protestantism that replaced the Puritan tradition in New England during the later nineteenth century.

Given these fears and this orientation, it goes without saying that in the great agitation over the "church question," which during these same years preoccupied leading theologians on the Continent, in Great Britain, and in America, Bushnell felt none of the "catholic" tendencies of the Oxford or Mercersburg movements. Though deeply imbued with romanticism in the general sense of that many-sided term, Bushnell, like so many thinkers of Puritan background, including Emerson, was relatively untouched by the historical interest usually associated with the impulse. Neo-medievalism held no charms for him, nor did the contemporary renewal of interest in the Reformation and the early church. Anglicanism at times seemed almost as menacing as Rome.

In the great sectional controversy that was racking the country throughout his adult years Bushnell was, of course, morally opposed to slavery and he criticized both the compromises of 1820 and of 1850; but he was not an abolitionist. Though he attacked the Kansas-Nebraska Bill and applauded antislavery victories in Kansas as a turning point in American history, he discountenanced most forms of antislavery activity. He was convinced that northern population growth would combine with other natural pressures to extirpate slavery in God's good time. In 1860 he did not like the "provoking uppishness" of the Republican Party but was gratified to see an "honest man" replace an "inveterate huckster" at the helm. Lincoln, he said in February, 1861, "may turn out one of the best and even ablest Presidents we have had." News of the Emancipator's assassination left him grief-stricken.

The awesome experience of a nation in arms had meanwhile added depths to Bushnell's understanding of sacrifice and expiation, a fact one may observe in his wartime sermons and in his two last treatises on the atonement. He was also led by this total experience to a profound application of his organic view of the state as a holy commonwealth. The Civil War he saw as a veritable *Volkskrieg* in whose antecedent iniquities both North and South were implicated and by which both were chastised. From it emerged a *nation* where before there had been only a group of states "kenneled under the constitution." The country's great tragedy had at least opened the possibilities for national rebirth and rededication; it had been "good" in the way Good Friday was good.

In all that he thought and wrote Bushnell was to a degree victimized by the increasingly superficial nurture and tastes of his Victorian audience; like Mark Twain he had to yield to the sentimental preferences of a "fastidious people." Caught between the regnant tradition of Congregational revivalism and the social amenities of the Episcopal parishes, he was during most of his career a kind of anticipatory prototype of the twentieth-century minister to suburbia. Notwithstanding these shortcomings and obstacles, Bushnell singlemindedly devoted his mature life to the exposition and deepening of an experience, insight, and vision which had been given him. In his later years he transcended both his times and his milieu. He produced a well-nigh classic theological literature which is justifiably compared with that of Albrecht Ritschl and, even more, Frederick D. Maurice. Bushnell made an enduring contribution to American educational theory, intellectual history, and, above all, to American theology and church life.

Bibliography

Horace Bushnell, *Christian Nurture,* New Haven, Yale, 1948.

Barbara M. Cross, *Horace Bushnell, Minister to a Changing America,* Chicago, Univ. of Chicago, 1958.

ALBRECHT RITSCHL

A. Durwood Foster

Through the last quarter of the nineteenth century the most prominent figure in German and in all Protestant theology was Albrecht Ritschl of Göttingen. A generation later, as H. R. Mackintosh observed, he was "behind a passing cloud."[1] The cloud was less simple oblivion than misrepresentation and misguided secondhand opinion; whether it really is passing remains to be seen. But in any case, the thrust of Ritschl's work has so basically coincided with the modern theological task as to identify his importance with the possibility and destiny of modern Christianity in general. Not even Schleiermacher, whom Ritschl acknowledged as "theological lawgiver" especially in this respect,[2] can be said to have compassed with such self-conscious intensity *both* poles of the modern theological problem: on the one hand man's existence shaped by the conditions of modernity, and on the other, the biblically grounded Gospel. Ritschl drew angry fire from modernists who would relinquish the Bible as well as from biblicists who would reject modernity. His polemical sharpness also antagonized many whose intentions did not sharply differ from his own. But all who follow the path of mediating theology in the larger sense stand greatly in his debt. Through one of the most crucial periods in the intellectual history of Christendom he was the theologian's theologian, who worked more effectively than anyone else to save the openness, the honesty, and the relevance of Christian thought. Among those who seek a responsible theology today, his successors include the emphasizers of biblical church dogmatics as well as the emphasizers of correlation with contemporary existence. And while neither Barthians nor Tillichians have been duly mindful of his services, this very fact indicates that the present

[1] *Types of Modern Theology* (London, Nisbet, 1937), p. 141 n.
[2] *A Critical History of the Christian Doctrine of Justification and Reconciliation* (Edinburgh, Edmonston & Douglas, 1872), p. 442.

day has not settled its account with him. It suggests that when and if modern theology should take another look, it might still find in Ritschl essential aid.

I

The son of a distinguished Lutheran preacher and bishop, Ritschl was born in Berlin in 1822. He grew up in Stettin amid a dedicated engagement with the affairs of the church. In the home were established significant insights into the deeper meaning of Christian spirituality and the "Reformation life-ideal." Fellowship with God in spite of confessed sin, unshakable trust in the divine providence, humility, patience, and prayer within the supporting communion of the church, cheerful striving in one's moral vocation—these were the indelible features of a *way of life* which the theologian later confirmed through wide-ranging historical study and for which he sought systematic intellectual formulation. But Ritschl remembered that such formulation is preceded by the nurturing objectivity of the church, that feeling and will have place with knowledge, and that abstract and traditional conceptions must appeal to practical need and experience.

Already committed to theology, in 1839 Ritschl entered university life with a "speculative urgency to grasp the highest."[3] But though he dug deeply in historical, biblical, and systematic subjects, neither at Bonn, Halle, or Heidelberg was he able to gain a "right understanding" of what had become and was to remain central for him: the Christian idea of reconciliation. At Tübingen he found some temporary satisfaction in the Hegelian standpoint and published his first work (*Das Evangelium Marcions und das kanonische Evangelium des Lukas*, Tübingen, 1846) as a disciple of F. C. Baur. However, the agreement with Tübingen was revoked as Ritschl independently reworked the sources for his own lecturing in New Testament and historical theology, begun at Bonn in 1846. In an 1851 article on the state of Synoptic Gospel criticism, he reversed his earlier position on Luke and declared against Baur for the priority of

[3] O. Ritschl, article on Ritschl, in *Realencyklopädie für protestantische Theologie und Kirche*, 3d ed., Vol. 17, p. 22.

Mark.[4] The break became definite with the second edition, in 1856, of his important monograph on the rise of the old Catholic Church, where Ritschl argues that the history of the early church is not a logical synthesis of primitive Jewish and Gentile Christianity (*Die Entstehung der altkatholischen Kirche,* Bonn, 1st ed., 1850). On the contrary, the New Testament canon, for all its variety, is grounded in the unified apostolic witness to Jesus as the Christ; the Judaizers condition this mainly as a rejected countermovement, and the Hellenic world, in mediating the transition to ecclesiastical forms, dilutes and obscures the original substance, as is seen particularly by comparing Paul with the subapostolic writers.

Desirous of greater academic freedom, Ritschl decided to leave Bonn in 1864 for Göttingen. There he taught for his remaining twenty-five years, declining invitations to Strassburg and (four times!) to Berlin. While he continued to lecture in New Testament, attention was henceforth given largely to systematic theology. At the height of his powers everything converged upon his lifelong focal interest in the doctrine of justification and reconciliation, wherein he saw the pivotal Christian teaching for which everything else was either presupposition or consequence. Following some solid preliminary articles, he began in 1870 the publication of his magnum opus, *The Christian Doctrine of Justification and Reconciliation.* The first volume (translated by J. S. Black, Edinburgh, 1872) dealt with the history of the doctrine. The second volume, on "the biblical matter of the doctrine," regrettably never translated, was a pioneering effort at critical biblical theology, presented at a time when the field was divided between fundamentalist biblicism and the scholarly quest for "pure" history. The third volume, appearing concurrently in 1874, gave the "positive development of the doctrine." Its English translation, marred by some unfortunate renderings, was completed in 1900.

The climax of Ritschl's career was the publication of his great work. It was primarily through it that he began to exert a wide and radical influence. Though always deprecating party spirit, he now encouraged the alliance of motives which began

---

[4] "Ueber den gegenwärtigen Stand der Kritik der synoptischen Evangelien," reprinted in *Gesammelte Aufsätze* (Freiburg, 1893), pp. 1 ff.

to characterize a school. Included were such ascending figures as Wilhelm Herrmann, Julius Kaftan, Adolf Harnack, and many others. This development, and the extension of Ritschl's influence not only in Germany but throughout the Protestant world, was reciprocally conditioned by the rise of an organized and vociferous opposition. Resultant controversy affected revisions of the main work, as well as several of his later small pieces such as *Theologie und Metaphysik* (Bonn, 1881). However, the continued pursuit of historical interests bore further fruit in a massive account of Pietism, *Geschichte des Pietismus* (Bonn, 3 vols., 1880–86), and his concern for religious education showed itself in a Gymnasium text, *Instruction in the Christian Religion* (Bonn, 1875; translated by Alice Mead Swing, 1901). Although the latter proved too condensed for its original purpose, it is the only fully outlined systematic statement of Ritschl's thought ever provided.

Death came to Ritschl in 1889, after a lifetime of vigorous health had been interrupted by a heart attack in the preceding autumn. Suffering through the last months, Ritschl, according to his son and biographer, manifested the same patience and humble trust as when deprived of his beloved wife some twenty years earlier. Though he devoted his life to the vocation of academic theology, the root substance of that theology was a practical faith which the man sincerely believed and lived.

II

"In reference to method," wrote Ritschl with better insight than many of his interpreters, "[Schleiermacher] is my predecessor."[5] The agreement goes beyond formal procedure to theological motive and to the positive conception of the Christian faith, though in the latter there are also crucial differences. Like Schleiermacher, Ritschl accepts the theological task as that of reconceiving faith with the modern world responsibly in purview. The pledge of this reconceiving is taking with inward seriousness the questions arising in principle from the age, in particular from natural science, biblical research, comparative religion, and philosophy. In expounding the finality of the Christian revelation, Ritschl deals trenchantly with everything

[5] *Theologie und Metaphysik* (Bonn, Marcus, 1881), p. 54.

from Enlightenment ethical criticism to "Life of Jesus" historicism and the possibility of personal beings elsewhere in the
universe. Thus Otto Ritschl's remark that the apologetical tendency is "entirely foreign" to his father holds true only so far as
apologetics is limited to the explicit arrangements of conversing
with unbelief.[6] The remark is misleading if the best defense for
faith is at bottom its systematic correlation with modern intelligence.

Correlation implies independence and interdependence.
Christianity must be exhibited as discrete from scientific knowledge and the cultural functions, yet as humanly imperative.
Though heteronomy must be avoided, man's needs nevertheless
are shown to correspond with the Christian answer. The former
requirement—that man shall be free—is not for Ritschl a mere
concession to Kant and modernity; it is an innermost element of
the Gospel. Sincerity about this gives genuine integrity to his
synthesis, however anthropocentric some may hold it to be. In
creation, in redemption, and in the world's final goal, God intends man's spontaneity as a moral and spiritual person. Christianity, as indispensable means and form, accords with the end
and self-fulfillment of humanity itself. This is the basic intention of the Ritschlian "proof of the necessity" of Christianity.
Thus, while maintaining "as the foundation-principle of the
Evangelical Church that Christian doctrine is to be obtained
from the Bible alone,"[7] Ritschl can also censure J. C. K. von
Hofmann for knowing "nothing except Biblical theology" and
for refusing to seek a "necessary concatenation between revelation and the necessary idea of God, and the necessary view of
the world and human history."[8]

However, Ritschl is well aware that faith cannot be logically
coerced. Following Spener he appeals to the motto that "whoever
willeth to do the will of God will know the truth of Christ's doctrine."[9] He concedes that "the proof is nothing but a demonstra-

[6] *Albrecht Ritschls Leben*, 2 vols. (Freiburg, Mohr, 1892–96), Vol.
II, p. 167.

[7] "Instruction in the Christian Religion," in A. T. Swing, *The Theology of Albrecht Ritschl* (London, Longmans, Green, 1901), p. 172.

[8] *A Critical History*, p. 540.

[9] Cf. John vii: 17; *The Christian Doctrine of Justification and Reconciliation*, translation edited by H. R. Mackintosh and A. B. Macauley,
2d ed. (Edinburgh, Clark, 1902), pp. 8, 24–25.

tion of the harmony of the ideas which are bound up together in the Christian view of the world and the Christian view of the self. The man who altogether rejects this system of ideas will find their proof meaningless too."[10] The conditions of the proof include, then, both a deciding and a participating subjectivity reminiscent on the one hand of Kierkegaard and on the other of Schleiermacher. But for Ritschl the dialectic of individual subjectivity is assimilated into a kind of historicized Kantian practical reason. He reasons, that is, in terms of universal moral ends informed by the categorical imperative, yet he knows that such ends are historically conditioned and that their universality must be asserted teleologically rather than typically or statically. The moral and spiritual goal of all history appears concretely through a given historical community and can be fully known and validated only within the living faith of that community. But the fact that the Gospel can be confirmed only through commitment to it does not diminish the role of reason in the understanding, outworking, and communication of faith. In principle the Christian revelation pertains to every man's destiny, since it clarifies and fulfills that toward which moral and religious experience are universally reaching. Moreover, faith implies a world view alongside which no fully coherent or adequate alternative is possible. The disjunction of the practical and the pure reason is therefore only provisionally and not finally possible. For, as Ritschl points out with respect to the moral proof of God, either the account of things must stop short of the whole, which betrays the aim of philosophical theory, or it must embrace the subjective moral exigencies which are an ineradicable part of the whole.[11] Faith, its primacy presupposed, proves itself through meeting practical personal concern and therewith through its power to illuminate the whole.

It may seem surprising that faith's relevance for a view of the whole is maintained along with a severe restriction upon the use of metaphysics in theology. The contemporary neo-Kantian skepticism which, in von Hartmann's phrase, turned theory of knowledge into "theory of ignorance," does not lead Ritschl to dispense entirely with metaphysics. He insists that theological

[10] *The Christian Doctrine of Justification and Reconciliation*, p. 530.
[11] *Ibid.*, Chap. IV, especially pp. 223–25.

science is obligated to clarify metaphysically its epistemological assumptions, and he attempts this in his own case by affiliation with his Göttingen colleague Hermann Lotze.[12] Yet for two related reasons Ritschl speaks out against substantive intrusions of metaphysics. First, faith has its own source and security quite apart from metaphysical props. It is wrong, therefore, to articulate the faith as though it had to be prefaced and buttressed by "natural theology"—a procedure which the Reformers succeeded in interrupting only temporarily. Here as elsewhere Ritschl says that the Reformation must continue. In the second place, perhaps an even more decisive ground for the stricture against metaphysics is the specific character of the biblical God. Ritschl argues that metaphysics, in Aristotle and traditionally, investigates being merely as being. But the radically personal God of the Bible cannot be subordinated to a theory of being in general or being itself. Thus the *analogia entis* is repudiated, not in favor of sheer transcendence but for the sake of the decisive analogy of the Divine Fatherhood apprehended by faith through Christ.

While acknowledging the difficulties of defining religion as such, Ritschl makes use, as Schleiermacher had, of a regulative concept of religion. This serves to clarify the relation of faith to philosophy, science, and morals; it aids in the discrimination of what is essential within the heterogeneous totality of the received tradition; and it provides for a critical and consummating relation of Christianity to the other religions. Ritschl's concept diverges from that of his predecessor in centering upon the rectification and ultimate guarantee of personal worth. The content of religious concern is fully clarified in the Christian affirmation of the individual person as God's child and image, exceeding in value the whole world. This corresponds to Ritschl's personalistic theism, the lack of which he regards as Schleiermacher's crippling defect. Also involved is concern for personal eternal life, or the dominion of personal values in relation to God, as against any kind of mystical absorption. The Christian hope for what may lie beyond earthly death is not analyzed by Ritschl, though he clearly rejects the notion of the indefinite temporal survival of a detached soul. He continually attacks that relig-

[12] Cf. *ibid.*, pp. 19–20; *Theologie und Metaphysik, passim.*

iosity which would contract man's eternally significant being into an inward detachable substance. On the contrary, integral to every person is the context of responsibility and community. The essential self cannot be divorced from moral life in history, and here too eternal life must manifest its primary import.

The other main component of Ritschl's regulative concept of religion is the determination that all strictly religious knowledge is comprised of independent value-judgments. Unlike theoretical knowledge, the affirmations of faith root in immediate personal concern. They belong properly to the subjective and not to the objective consciousness, to the practical rather than to the pure reason. As one would say today, they are radically "existential," with no admixture of merely intellectual cognition or information. Thus Ritschl opposes the Reformation idea of faith as trust (*fiducia*) to the Thomist notion that an independently determinable intellectual content must be assented to as an integral part of faith in addition to trust. His assertion is not that faith is intellectually formless but that it is *"in intellectu tanquam in subjecto."*[13] That is, the intrinsic intellectual structure of faith is inseparable from the subjective movement of feeling and will which faith essentially is. The "faith which is believed" is indefeasibly conformable to the "faith which believes" as trusting response to the God revealed in Christ. Decision for Christ thereby stipulates no preamble of metaphysics, dogma, or historiography.

However, faith *is* conditioned by the human situation. It presupposes the ultimate practical concern which is independent of special theoretical acquirements and peculiar emotional temperament. It is not the needs merely of an elite which Christ answers, but the universal personal question of our final meaning and being. This question, in turn, is posed by the two intermingling factors of finitude and sin. Man experiences the limitations of natural and social life—smallness, weakness, death—as threats to the life of the spirit. But guilty alienation from God compounds and gives sting to these limitations by cutting off the hope of overcoming them. Thus the resolution of the human predicament must deal with the problem of guilt as well

---

[13] *The Christian Doctrine of Justification and Reconciliation*, p. 105.

as the problem of finitude. It must include justification as an integral element in the securing of one's ultimate personal meaning and worth.

In the order of being, though not in the order of knowing, this construction of the human situation implies more fundamental premises regarding God's nature and purpose as well as the nature and end of man. Partly these have to do with the personality of God, which Ritschl not only affirms on a biblical basis but also defends rationally. Strauss and others (including thinkers as far back as Plotinus) have objected that personality would mean inadmissible dividedness in the Absolute. But, says Ritschl, this is the case only if the Absolute be conceived as empty space. Now on the one hand the merely negative concept of undividedness does nothing to explain our world as a unified and yet developing manifold. On the other hand personality is the best analogy we have for representing dynamic diversity within unity, especially with respect to spiritual and moral purpose. Unless the Absolute is personal there is no hope for fulfillment of the religious concern for ultimate personal meaning; nor, certainly, is there any basis for responsibility, sin, and guilt. As for the dividedness and multiplicity of finite personalities, neither of course can be carried over to God. But why should either be? God's personal will is the ground and embracing unity of the creation, history and end of finite but genuinely free moral and spiritual persons. There is still a structural over-againstness of man and God, but this depends upon the creative act of God. It is God's eternal purpose that man's moral and spiritual history should occur and should be consummated in Christ. This is the goodness of creation.

Of equal moment with the rejection of an impersonal Absolute is Ritschl's critique of the ethical premises determining the traditional concept of God. He observes that in classical orthodoxy as well as in its Socinian antithesis the original relation of God to man has been controlled largely by notions of merely impartial justice or equity. On the one hand the assertion of the transcendent and arbitrary divine majesty has implied toward the created order an essential indifference, the logical consequences of which have been exposed by Duns Scotus. This implicit indifference entirely justifies the argument of Socinus that

God might as well forgive sins freely. On the other hand there has been juxtaposed with the idea of indifference that of the divine moral government of the world. But the understanding of this latter element has been shaped not so much by the Bible as by the model of the Greek city-state whose tyrant impartially guards the laws and administers punishments and rewards. Again with respect to this model, Socinus is right that the idea of forgiveness cannot be combined with that of justice. The trouble, Ritschl argues, is that orthodox theology has never given methodical centrality to the specifically Christian norm. From Augustine onwards, Christ and the Gospel have been subjoined to a frame of reference erected on other grounds. Schleiermacher, once again, has pointed out the right direction by defining Christianity as the religion in which everything is related to the redemption wrought by Jesus. But Schleiermacher has not heeded well enough his own insight, and in particular he has not been aware of the decisive importance of the Old Testament as the special context of Jesus' person and work. Thus while Schleiermacher has understood the necessity of construing creation and redemption in close interdependency, his *Glaubenslehre* does not, in Ritschl's judgment, represent either the one or the other with sufficient fidelity to the biblical revelation.

With the whole Bible as background, "the content of the Divine will is to be deduced from the revealed reciprocal relations between Christ and God, and from no other principle."[14] There results from this a view quite opposed to that of indifferent majesty or impartial justice, for God must now be understood radically as the Father. From the beginning—that is, essentially and from eternity—our world and history are grounded in the purposing righteous love whose reality Christ fully discloses. The divine aseity and justice do not stand over against this disclosure; they too are known through and determined by it. God in himself is God for man and with man in Jesus Christ. But for Ritschl the purpose which is revealed through the Bible and climactically in Christ is more than merely a soteriological one. As given in the notion of covenant

[14] *Ibid.*, p. 237.

and supremely in that of the kingdom of God, it aims at a universal community whose form is personal freedom and whose content is righteous love. Within the embracing goal of the kingdom everyone has an individual moral vocation which ideally includes the development of autonomous personality in dedicated service to the whole. Ritschl holds that only by being committed to the will of God in Christ—that is, to the good will for the whole—can true liberty be attained.

In the doctrine of providence faith affirms, without being able to demonstrate even for itself, that the entire world order subserves God's kingdom. How, then, is providence related to the history which has occurred before and apart from Christ, and how is it related to sin and evil? Ritschl wrestles with these problems but concedes the impossibility of fully solving them. He rejects twofold predestination and chides Augustine, Luther (in respect of *De servo arbitrio*), and Calvin for "unwarranted overstepping of theological competency."[15] Consciousness of election in Christ does not imply that some individuals were passed over and others picked out from an array of neutral prehistorical souls. The unevenness of personal destiny, rooting as it does in natural and historical contingency, may presumably have been presupposed by the end of an uncoerced moral and spiritual development of mankind. In any case, no life where love and moral value have been experienced is devoid of eternal significance. Yet Ritschl is far from claiming that any nice balance can be struck between a partly known divine plan and the actual course of history. At least non-Christian history does not stand under the condemnation of God. The heathen are not threatened with eternal punishment. It is as though Ritschl would have us think that sufficient unto them is the meaning they have.

Sin can be partly understood as conditioned by finitude, in particular by ignorance. But since it roots in moral freedom it cannot be wholly explained in any way. In this connection Ritschl regards the traditional doctrine of original sin as worse than useless. For by exaggerating the powers of Adam, it renders the first sin more inexplicable; and by referring subse-

[15] *Ibid.*, p. 126.

quent sins back to the first, it obscures present responsibility for them. Furthermore, the doctrine tends to swamp the field of necessary moral discriminations with a blanket description that cannot be taken seriously in practical life. The premises of education as well as normal moral intercourse refute it. The function of the doctrine has been to overthrow human merit and thus register the need for redemption. But its use for that purpose is "just as appropriate as it would be to use a boulder to kill a gnat."[16] Nevertheless, man's guilty alienation from God does pose a felt need that becomes the more drastic as the sinner compares himself with Christ. Also of fundamental importance are the socio-historical structures which Ritschl groups under the "kingdom of sin, . . . a substitute for the hypothesis of original sin which gives due prominence to everything that the notion of original sin was rightly enough meant to embrace."[17] All sin is forgivable so long as conditioned by ignorance, or, in other words, so long as it has not hardened into a final rejection of God. We can assert no actual instance of such hardening, identified as the sin against the Holy Spirit, though its real possibility must be maintained. God's love constrains, but Ritschl will not allow that it coerces the will of man.

Evil, in distinction from sin, "signifies the whole compass of possible restrictions of our purposive activity."[18] It cannot in general be regarded as punishment, which presupposes conscious guilt. On the other hand, the Christian may regard evils, retrospectively and presently, as disciplinary or as sent by God for a good end. But Ritschl takes even Schleiermacher to task for knowing too much about the matter. He cautions that we should not expect to find a reason for every misfortune. What we can hold to is trust in providence, confident that in everything God works for good with those who love him. The treatment of this subject supports Ritschl's claim that he never denied mystery, but only desisted from speaking whereof he knew not.

The source of confidence in God's providence is the historical Jesus Christ mediated through Scripture and church. In this

[16] *Ibid.*, p. 340.
[17] *Ibid.*, p. 344.
[18] *Ibid.*, p. 351.

matter Ritschl has been misrepresented through equal and opposite oversimplifications of his position. He has been denounced for trying to strip away faith from the "bare facts" of
the original Jesus and, at the same time, for dismissing objective historiography. Actually, he insists on maintaining both
history and faith. At the pole of the original datum both the
historical figure and the apostolic witness are integral. At the
pole of contemporary appropriation, the faith of the church is
primary, but historiography has place. Ritschl argues that the
facts about Jesus cannot be finally estimated on objective
grounds alone. On the other hand, he enjoins and strives for a
rigorous employment of scientific criticism and its results. Faith
genetically does not hang on these results, but Ritschl could
never with Kierkegaard have called them "rubbish." For they
do help to clarify faith and relieve it of corruptions. As a biblical scholar he is tendentious, and his work is now dated; but no
adequate assessment has yet been given of Ritschl's pioneering
effort to combine historical and theological exegesis.

It is not the witness of faith but the pre- and post-historical
transmutations of Jesus over against which Ritschl sets the historical figure. The normativeness of the latter stands against
Logos speculation and "spiritual-Christ" fanaticism. The idea
of pre-existence is not to be wholly cast out, since it expresses
the conviction that Jesus and the Kingdom are grounded teleologically in the divine eternity. But what is thus grounded is
the historical personal wholeness of Jesus, not an abstracted,
somehow previously subsistent element. In an analogous way
Ritschl interprets the continuous power of the exalted Lord, although here, there is the severe special problem of conceiving
the Easter event. On the resurrection Ritschl is diffident, not to
say cryptic, apparently having reached no precise conception.
Clear, however, is the principle that the living presence of
Christ to faith has for its *content* the biblically portrayed person. The spiritual is bound to the historical. Resurrection and
glory do not belong to an abstracted, now independent element,
but to the life that was lived and the cross that was borne.

To know Christ is to know his benefits, not to speculate
about the union of his natures. But while the person is measured
in the work, the work itself is inseparable from the definite fea-

tures of the historical life: the perfect sonship of trust and love, the dedication of everything independently human to the purpose shared with God, the tested but unbroken fidelity to vocation. These features permeate the life and cannot be isolated in one aspect or moment such as the teaching or the suffering on the cross. Faith, in apprehending this one life as the model and power of its own being, affirms that Jesus is the unique Son and final revealer of God. In the Nicene and Chalcedonian formulae Ritschl senses a detached scientific interest which should not be prescriptive for faith. But he can assert Christ's Godhead as "the worth to be put on those human achievements of his which suffice for our salvation."[19] Ritschl emphasizes Christ's humanity; yet in two ways he maintains the divinity: formally, in the unity of Christ's will and purpose with God's; and efficiently (so to speak), according to the paradox of grace stated by Paul in Phil. ii: 13. Thus, in Christ's human will and purpose God meets us; and we also give thanks to God for the mystery of this uniquely transparent humanity. Scientifically we cannot penetrate to the "special conditions of Christ's dependence upon God, however indefinite the formula in which we might express them."[20] But while Christ is a free and fully human personality, he is *as such* also the Divine Word, which "includes in itself the characteristic working of God, and is simply inconceivable without it. . . ."[21]

In the traditional scheme of the three offices, Jesus is prophet in revealing God's reconciling, Kingdom-forming will. He is priest in that, according to his unique vocation as God's intermediary, he lives and suffers for our sake in founding the community of forgiveness. His kingship, established through the first two offices, is especially manifest in patience and in humble, serving love. The three offices interpenetrate, but Ritschl occupies himself especially with the priestly function. Against orthodoxy the Socinian criticism is cogent, yet it is devoid of the religious and historical consciousness that Jesus is the redeemer and the founder of the community of redemption. The same lack is found in Kant and the ethical philosophy of the

[19] *Ibid.*, pp. 437–38.
[20] *Ibid.*, p. 439.
[21] *Ibid.*

Enlightenment. Jesus is reduced to a prophet who announces God's pardon as a timeless truth. But can we have more than this without recourse to the idea of substitutionary appeasement? Throughout his adult life Ritschl struggled earnestly with this problem, keeping it in continuous development through the various volumes and editions of his work. Consequently, at some points it is difficult if not impossible to compose his over-all or even his final view. For instance, the first volume of the major work, reviewing the history of doctrine, leads one to expect that a more strictly "objective" construction of the atonement will be forthcoming than is actually the case in the third volume. But even in the third volume, and in the last edition of it, there is still an unmistakable tension and oscillation. The evolution of Ritschl's thought, as he himself insisted, was strongly conditioned by the biblical investigations of his second volume—especially the inquiry into the concepts of sacrifice and the divine righteousness. Ritschl became convinced that the normative biblical meaning of sacrifice centers in the overcoming of alienation and the re-establishment of communion, not in any kind of payment to God. Divine righteousness he came to understand as the faithfulness with which God carries out his loving purpose to found the Kingdom, not as a separately constituted, fixed justice which requires satisfaction in itself. These insights weighed against any purely objective view of the atonement.

Nevertheless, Ritschl does in two ways assert an objectively grounded atonement. In the first place Jesus gives himself as sacrifice "for us" (in our behalf, not in our place) in living, suffering, and dying for the redeemed community. His deeds of active and passive obedience form the once-for-all established bridge for reconciliation with God. More than mere teaching, they are there for us in history, not as causing God's mind to change, but as providing the concrete means of change in us. In the second place, however, Ritschl wishes to recognize in Jesus' work a more purely objective representation. The Kingdom-forming personal life of Jesus is the end for which God creates and governs the world. In the actuality of this life, therefore, there is a reconciliation of the world to the divine purpose. Jesus sums up, as it were, and offers back to God the justification of the historical and human venture. In accepting this representation God accepts all those who participate in and are identified with it; He sees the world and more particularly the redeemed community through and in Christ.

Ritschl's principal motive in holding out for an objective dimension in the atonement is his commitment to Luther's "in spite of" as a fundamental characterization of the Christian life. The good news of Christ is that sinners are justified and accepted while still in their sins. Thus, as against Roman and Pietist tendencies, the Reformation insists upon the synthetic concept of "pronouncing righteous" (*Gerechtsprechung*) instead of the analytic "making righteous" (*Gerechtmachung*) in describing God's handling of the sinner in Christ. For this reason justification cannot in all respects be identified with reconciliation, although the two are inseparable. Justification is the beginning and the foundation of reconciliation; but it does not imply, in any other sense than the turning to Christ in trust, that reconciliation already is accomplished in the sinner. Justification and reconciliation are a single doctrine, yet a twofold one. Correspondingly, there is the tension between justification by faith and the necessity of good works which Ritschl saw to be determinative of the whole structure of Christian life. For while he gladly embraced the idea of *justus et peccator*, he reproved Luther for unfairness to the Epistle of James. The Christian man is also blessed in his deeds.

"Christianity," accordingly, "resembles not a circle described from a single center, but an ellipse which is determined by two *foci*."[22] Every moment in the circumference of Christian existence is a function both of the graceful indicative and of the moral imperative. Christ restores sinners to fellowship with God, but he also enlists their discipleship for the Kingdom. The imperative defines the sin which alienates us as well as the goal which engages our no longer alienated freedom. The indicative overcomes our alienation and bestows upon us the power freely to embrace the imperative as our own. But the two foci do not coalesce. For justification is in spite of unrighteousness, and the law of righteous love impinges in spite of justification. Yet there

[22] *Ibid.*, p. 11.

is an inner relation between faith and works in the freedom over the world and for God which Ritschl understands as the content of eternal life. For this freedom is concretely given and exercised, not outside the world—in the monastery or the life beyond—but in and for the world, after the model of Jesus himself.

Wherever the liberty of the Christian man is exercised, God's Kingdom is incipiently present. The model of its full realization is Christ, but it comes into being in the measure that Christ-likeness prevails among men: in the measure, that is, of reverent trust, humble patience, fidelity to vocation, and serving love. Though he would apply the goal of the Kingdom to the transformation of society, there is in Ritschl no simple progressivism or utopianism. The Kingdom is more within and above history than at the end of it. Nor is it possible to formulate for the Kingdom a rigid code of ethics. For love, the highest righteousness, cannot be translated into prescriptions. It is mediated in incalculable ways through the individual's disposition and is essentially qualified by the individual in his unique contexts.

The church, in Ritschl's view, is not the Kingdom either in fact or in principle. For if it were the Kingdom it would be subject to the perfectionism of the imperative, whereas actually it is grounded in the indicative of grace and is the mediation of the same through prayers and sacraments, proclamation and teaching. The Kingdom is manifested spontaneously from within the church, but it does not define the essential being of the church. Yet Ritschl stresses the church in some respects more than he does the Kingdom. The concrete life of the forgiven, worshiping, aspiring fellowship is actually the first principle of his theology. From within the church Ritschl takes his bearings with respect to Jesus Christ, its ground, as well as to the Kingdom, which is its goal. We do not first grasp the full compass of our sin, then settle accounts with God in Christ, and thereupon wind up in the church. On the contrary, through and within the church we come gradually to understand our sin, and likewise we grow in the knowledge and grace of our Lord Jesus Christ. It is consonant with this orientation that Ritschl appeals theologically to Christian experience and to hymnody, and that he evinces so much concern not only for the history of doctrine but also for Christian education, for the overcoming of the church's dividedness, and for a theology of the laity. The Roman ecclesiology errs not in emphasizing the importance of the church, but in identifying it with the priestly hierarchy. The church is the whole body of those who are indwelt by the Holy Spirit, the Spirit of Christ. This Spirit is nothing less, according to Ritschl, than the very knowledge which God has of himself in Christ. It is the power of the grace and truth which the church has beheld and which motivates its mission to mankind: the bread of its own life and the light of the world.

III

Ritschl's theology is certainly not able to save all the phenomena of the historic faith. The sense for mystery and for the awesome holiness of God registers too faintly. The cross and the resurrection do not as such retain their traditional centrality. The communion of the Christian with God is inadequately portrayed—Ritschl could not bring himself to appreciate even his friend Wilhelm Herrmann's attempt to supply the portrayal. In general the emotional and quasi-mystical phenomena of the Christian life are intolerantly handled. In this and other matters a combative will tends to shape exaggerated antitheses. Yet who would favor wholly suppressing this approach for the sake of irenic synthesizing? Moreover, it would be smug to assume that there is today a firm universal position from which can be read off pat judgments against Ritschl. Even his stricture against metaphysics remains problematic rather than simply wrong-headed, and the burden of proof must lie on those who would tell us that he was no more than a blunderer in philosophy.

Appreciation is confused by the unfinished or fluctuating aspect of some of his key ideas: the relations of eternity and time, of will and knowledge, of the kingdom and the church. At these points, of course, one wrestles with perennial difficulties of Christian understanding; and the same is true with respect to what surely is a fundamental problem in Ritschl's thought: Christ's role as the mediator of our salvation. In bringing God to the sinner, how shall it be that Christ does not stand between the sinner and God? On the one hand, as Ritschl sees it, Christ bestows upon us the fellowship with the Father which he himself enjoys; he is the model of our own redeemed God-relatedness. But on the other hand, it is only in or through Christ that God views and receives us, not in terms of our own individuality. In the one image, corresponding to reconciliation, we are in personal communion with our heavenly Father, whose solicitous love misses every lost sheep. In the other image, corresponding to justification, a Christo-monism displaces the concern for our personal response to God. Perhaps the images cannot finally merge. For, as Ritschl knows so well, the Gospel proclaims new being and yet acceptance in spite of our lack of new being, so long as we cling to Christ.

Aside from the great stimulus he gave to the development of critical-historical perspective, a comprehensive estimate of Ritschl's success will depend first and most generally upon how seriously one takes *both* poles of the mediating theological task: the biblical message *and* the human situation. Secondly it will depend, on the one side, upon how biblicistic one insists upon being about the Bible, and, on the other side, upon how practically or existentially (rather than theoretically or ontologically) one thinks the situational base line must be traced. In the third place and quite particularly, it will depend upon how radically one is willing to construe man's subjective autonomy. If one is instinctively hostile to "anthropocentrism," or if one regards Christianity as only a rescue operation, it will be difficult to see much good in Ritschl. But if one believes that creation and redemption themselves have basically to do with human freedom, then Ritschl's theology may well be one of the noblest efforts yet made to reconcile the graceful divine sovereignty with the dignity of truly responsible though sinning manhood.

Bibliography

No books by Albrecht Ritschl have been available for some years.

Hugh Ross Mackintosh, *Types of Modern Theology: Schleiermacher to Barth*, London, Nisbet, 1956, Part V.

FREDERICK DENISON MAURICE

William John Wolf

Frederick Denison Maurice, described by Masterman as "the greatest thinker of the English Church in the nineteenth century," was born at Normanstone in 1805. His father was a Unitarian minister who had once been a younger colleague of Joseph Priestley. Young Frederick with three older and four younger sisters knew an affectionate, tightly knit family until about the age of ten when some of his sisters and finally his mother left Unitarianism for the strict Calvinism of the Baptists. To prepare himself for the study of law Frederick lived for some time in London with a family closely allied to the Wilberforces and to evangelical circles in the Church of England. At Cambridge he took a first class in civil law but could not receive the degree because he would not subscribe to the Thirty-nine Articles. At college he was introduced to Plato and Coleridge. With his lifelong friend John Sterling he moved to London in 1827 to write for and finally to edit a literary journal.

His dissatisfaction with Unitarianism was resolved when he became a member of the Church of England and returned to university study to prepare for its ministry. At Oxford he finished his novel *Eustace Conway* and was ordained in 1834. *Subscription No Bondage,* his defense of the Articles as requirements in the universities, deserves study today apart from its dated controversy as a thoughtful analysis of the theological foundations of education and culture. In 1870 as he drew near the end of his career he indicated its importance in his own understanding of his work. "No book which I have written expresses more strongly what then were, and what still are my deepest convictions."[1]

He exercised a deep pastoral and preaching ministry as chap-

[1] *The Life of Frederick Denison Maurice, Chiefly Told in His Own Letters; Edited by His Son Frederick Maurice,* 2 vols., (N.Y., Scribner's, 1884), I, p. 174.

lain of Guy's Hospital in London. At first he welcomed the Anglo-Catholic revival of the Tractarians, but he was soon drawn into controversy over Pusey's beliefs on baptism.

Maurice married Annie Barton, sister of Sterling's wife. In 1845 she died, leaving him with two small boys. Later he married Georgiana Hare, half-sister of Julius Hare. Maurice was appointed professor of English literature and modern history at King's College, London. Afterwards he accepted the chair of divinity in its newly added theological college. He gave up Guy's Hospital to become chaplain of Lincoln's Inn, a center for students.

His theological masterpiece is *The Kingdom of Christ* (1838), which began as a series of letters to a Quaker "concerning the Principles, Constitution and Ordinances of the Catholic Church." His revision of 1842 was edited in 1958 with helpful notes by Alec Vidler. The first half consists of an analysis of Quakerism, pure Protestantism (Lutheranism, Calvinism, Zwinglianism, Arminianism), Unitarianism, contemporary religious, philosophical, and political movements, and Roman Catholicism. His basic conclusion is that nearly every one of these movements is right and truthful in its positive assertions but wrong in its negations, which are compounded into systems that further divide men and shatter the unity of Christ's church. Rarely has a man been able to live and think himself more imaginatively and appreciatively into the beliefs of others. Maurice is a Christian Socrates meeting other Christians on their own ground. The second half of the book describes the "hidden hunger" of the previous systems and interprets the Bible as the progressive manifestation of covenantal relations between God and man in terms of family, then nation, and finally church as the kingdom of Christ. The "signs of a spiritual society" are then analyzed in the order in which men are drawn into communion with Christ: baptism, the creeds, forms of worship, the eucharist, the ministry, and the Bible. Relations between church and nation are described, and the Church of England, particularly its party structure, is analyzed with respect to the previous problems and concerns. A common misunderstanding of Maurice is to regard this book simply as an apology for the Church of England.

I am not ignorant, also, that the hints which I have offered in opposition to systems may, themselves, be turned by myself or by others into a system. . . . On the other hand, if there be anything here which may help to raise men above their own narrow conceptions and mine, may lead them to believe that there is a way to that truth which is living and universal, and above us all, and that He who is Truth will guide them in that way—this which is from Him and not from me, I pray that He will bless.[2]

The Kingdom of Christ sets forth theological principles which have yet to come into their own in the ecumenical movement. As the Protestant churches see beyond pan-Protestantism to an ecumenism that is genuinely catholic and as the Roman Catholic Church comes out of its isolationism and loses what one of its theologians has called its "anti-Protestant face," Maurice's modestly offered "hints" will become increasingly central to ecumenical discussion and action. Already there are studies of the cosmic nature of the church by French Roman Catholic writers like de Lubac that resemble Maurice's positions. Father Bouyer comments that if anyone has seen the principle that is needed "to resolve the crisis endemic in Protestantism" it is Maurice.

Maurice is often described as the founder of Christian socialism. This description may actually be the source of more confusion than light. Maurice was not interested in a specific set of social goals for which legislation was to be sought. He was interested in a theological analysis of political and economic reform, in providing educational opportunities by founding colleges for working men and women, and in challenging his theological students to concern for the social imperatives of the Gospel. He helped set up a series of workers' cooperatives. "Competition is put forth as the law of the universe. That is a lie. The time is coming for us to declare that it is a lie. I see no way but by association for work instead of for striking. Hence my notion of a Tailors' Association." Maurice with Ludlow and Charles Kingsley was the senior statesman in a group loosely called Christian socialists, who met weekly after the

[2] *The Kingdom of Christ*, 2 vols., rev. ed. (London, Everyman's Library, 1842), II, p. 332.

events of 1848 and later published "Tracts on Christian Socialism." The name had been suggested by Maurice, but his own comment indicated his orientation. The title "would commit them at once to the conflict they must engage in sooner or later with the unsocial Christians and the un-Christian Socialists." He felt that the nation was related to the church much as the law is related to the Gospel. The church must educate "the conscience of the nation." "The time is come . . . when a nation must be felt to be *not* a formal corporation but a spiritual reality, a society of which we *can* predicate spiritual conditions and spiritual emotions, which can repent and be reformed as an individual can."[3] In an Advent sermon for the turbulent year of 1848 he asked: "Do you think that the invasion of Palestine by Sennacherib is a greater event than the overthrow of nearly all the greatest powers civil and ecclesiastical in Christendom?"

Attacked on all sides by the politically conservative papers of both low and high churchmanship, Maurice gave his enemies the opportunity they were seeking to impugn his orthodoxy when he published in 1853 his *Theological Essays,* his second best known work. He had criticized the popular view of the endless (i.e., eternal) nature of future punishment. His own understanding of the word "eternal" was drawn from such Johannine texts as "This is life eternal, that they might know thee the only true God, and Jesus Christ, whom thou hast sent." After much controversy he was dismissed by the Board of King's College for somewhat undefined opinions "of a dangerous tendency . . . calculated to unsettle the minds of the theological students."

In 1860 Maurice was appointed to St. Peter's, Vere Street, London. In 1866 he became Knightbridge Professor of Moral Theology and Moral Philosophy at Cambridge. The remainder of his life was spent in university surroundings where he also had cure of souls at St. Edward's. The substance of his Cambridge lectures is preserved in his immense two-volume work on the history of *Moral and Metaphysical Philosophy* and in his lectures on casuistry entitled *The Conscience.* He died on Easter Monday 1872 as he prepared to receive Holy Communion.

[3] *The Prophets and Kings of the Old Testament,* 2d ed. (Boston, Crosby, Nichols, 1853), pp. 403 ff.

Most of Maurice's writing was called forth by specific controversies. This occasional character of his thought with its demands on the modern reader for a detailed knowledge of Victorian England is doubtless one of the reasons why he has been so neglected until comparatively recent years. Any deep knowledge of him requires a complementary study of his life. Here there is an excellent resource at hand in the two volumes of his *Life* by his son Sir Frederick Maurice. This is largely a collection of his letters.

In 1842 he wrote *Three Letters to the Rev. W. Palmer*, defending the proposal of a Jerusalem bishopric with the German Lutherans. In *The Epistle to the Hebrews* (1846) he replied to Newman's *Theory of Development*. He delivered the Boyle Lectures on *The Religions of the World*, a work that both pioneered in the field and enjoyed immediate popularity. In 1859 he fiercely attacked Mansel's Bampton Lectures in *What Is Revelation?* Mansel was skeptical about our ability to know God, but argued that since the philosophical alternatives to Christian theism became entangled in unsolvable problems we might accept Bible and tradition. Maurice considered this the very worst of apologetical methods and held out for God's gracious self-disclosure as the Word that really enlightens every man.

Maurice's use of the Scriptures was precritical and constitutes a problem to the student today who works through his otherwise excellent commentaries or sermons on the Bible. Some of the more outstanding of these are: *The Prophets and Kings of the Old Testament, The Unity of the New Testament, The Doctrine of Sacrifice, The Patriarchs and Lawgivers of the Old Testament, The Gospel of St. John, The Epistles of St. John, The Gospel of the Kingdom of Heaven,* and *The Commandments Considered as Instruments of National Reformation.* The extent of his writing is amazing. One estimate runs to more than 16,300 octavo pages.

METHOD AND STYLE

The interpreter of Maurice's thought is considerably helped by its inner consistency from the time he sought ordination in the Church of England until his death. Very few changes are to be recorded. He remained loyal to the basic principle of Christ as king, which he had established very early. He found, however, ever more fascinating ways of illuminating man's cultural task in its light.

Many times Maurice made clear his opposition to system-building. While he modestly described his vocation as "metaphysical and theological grubbing," this phrase really expressed his deliberated choice of the method of laying bare the theological presuppositions of culture and of dogma. "Now to me these words [system and method] seem not only not synonymous, but the greatest contraries imaginable: the one indicating that which is most opposed to life, freedom, variety: and the other that without which they cannot exist."[4]

Behind this opposition to system is something of Kierkegaard's existentialist protest. The note of struggle in finding "the truth-for-him" is present in a letter: "I can say, I did not receive this of man, neither was I taught it. Every glimpse I have of it has come to me through great confusions and darkness."[5] His chief opposition to systems of doctrine, however, was founded on his respect for the facts of historical existence. In this Maurice expresses both the Englishman's empiricism against the conceptualism of Continental thinkers and the Anglican's respect for historical institutions as points of departure for theological analysis.

> When once a man begins to build a system the very gifts and qualities which might serve in the investigation of truth, become the greatest hindrances to it. He must make the different parts of the scheme fit into each other; his dexterity is shown, not in detecting facts, but in cutting them square.[6]

One of his letters provides insight into his understanding of the theologian's task.

> . . . theology is not (as the schoolmen have represented it) the climax of all studies, the Corinthian capital of a magnificent edifice, composed of physics, politics, economics, and connecting

[4] *Kingdom of Christ,* I, p. 238.
[5] *Life,* II, p. 16.
[6] *Ecclesiastical History,* p. 222.

them as parts of a great system with each other—but is the foundation upon which they all stand. And even that language would have left my meaning open to a very great, almost an entire, misunderstanding, unless I could exchange the name theology for the name *God*, and say that He Himself is the root from which all human life, and human society, and ultimately, through man, nature itself, are derived.[7]

An unfortunate hurdle for the reader of Maurice is his style, which can be and often is opaque and confused. Every reader finds himself at times trying to translate his author. This problem is partly the result of Maurice's extensive use of the Socratic method of inquiry, in which it is not always clear whether the evaluation and exposition is to be regarded as Maurice's or that of his imaginary interlocutors. Sometimes it reads like dictation that has suffered from interruptions. In spite of all this, however, there are passages of great emotional intensity and conviction. Every now and then he has the gift for epigrammatic utterance that makes it worth searching for nuggets amid the slag.

THE BASIC CHRISTOLOGICAL PRINCIPLE

No theologian of Christendom has ever expressed with more passionate conviction and sustained throughout a lifetime with more fidelity and richness in his theological analysis of culture the biblical witness to the cosmic setting of Christ's person and work. Christ, the Eternal Son of God, is "the Head and the King of our entire race." That is the heart of the Gospel as Maurice understood it.

In a letter to his son he wrote: "I was sent into the world that I might persuade men to recognize Christ as the center of their fellowship with each other, that so they might be united in their families, their countries, and as men . . ."[8]

The basic principle of all of Maurice's theology is that God has created and redeemed all men in Christ. This he believed to be the basic witness of the creeds and behind them of the en-

[7] *Life*, II, p. 136.
[8] *Ibid.*, I, p. 240.

tire biblical revelation. Incarnation-atonement in a trinitarian setting is the key feature for understanding every other Christian doctrine as well as the human situation.

> My desire is to ground all theology upon the name of God the Father, the Son, and the Holy Ghost; not to begin from ourselves and our sins; not to measure the straight line by the crooked one. This is the method which I have learned from the Bible. There everything proceeds from God; He is revealing Himself. He is acting, speaking, ruling.[9]

Maurice felt that contemporary theology, whether Roman Catholic or Protestant, whether Anglo-Catholic or Anglican Evangelical, had wrongly oriented itself around the sinfulness of man as the actual (even if not explicit) starting point. He proposed instead the divinity of the early creeds, which do not mention the fall of man. It should be noted here that Maurice held to a literalistic view of Genesis and thus believed in the fall as historical fact. Yet Maurice had understood that we know Adam and man through Christ and not *vice versa*.

> Protestants and Romanists, even while they denounce and excommunicate each other, yet appear to recognize the fact of depravity, of Evil, as the fundamental fact of divinity. The fall of Adam—not the union of the Father and the Son, not the creation of the world in Christ—is set before men in both divisions of Christendom as practically the ground of their creed.[10]

The theocratic principle in Maurice's thought that Christ is the head of all mankind is never left in isolation. It is always immediately correlated with the nature of the church and her function in the world. To Miss Williams Wynn he wrote in 1858:

> I do therefore anticipate a very deep and searching reformation, one which cannot be attended with less trials, one which I trust is to issue in greater blessings than the Reformation of the sixteenth century. . . . I feel very strongly that the ascension of our Lord into the heavens, and the glorification of our nature in

9 *The Doctrine of Sacrifice* (London, Macmillan, 1893), p. xii.
10 *Conflict of Good and Evil*, p. 170.

Him with the corresponding truth that the Church exists to witness of Him, not only as her Head, but as the Head of every man will be the battle-cry that will rally Protestants and Romanists, hungry seekers after wisdom, lonely tatterdemalions without bread, about the one standard . . .[11]

Maurice held his understanding of *Christus Consummator* in close association with what might be called *Ecclesia Consummatrix*. It remains to underline the significance of this fundamental Christological principle for such other doctrines as revelation, man and sin, the church and the sacraments.

REVELATION AND SCRIPTURE

In spite of his precritical attitude toward biblical study, Maurice anticipated many of today's theological commonplaces about revelation and its modes. He distrusted the scholastic distinction between natural and revealed theology on at least two grounds. He could not accept the notion that there were two pathways to the knowledge of God, especially that there could be one initiated from the side of man by something called "unaided reason." In today's terminology we would say that he believed in general revelation. "I hold that *all* our knowledge may be traced ultimately to Revelation from God."[12] He repudiated "the contemporary rage for apologetical literature." In the second place, he refused to class the Gospel as a religion among the religions of the world. The Bible is not about religion, but about the acts of the living God. ". . . we have been dosing our people with religion when what they want is not this but the living God."[13]

Maurice's use of the Bible has sometimes been criticized as "Platonizing eisegesis." There is no question about the impact of Plato on his thought. Yet even there the influence is more in terms of a method of inquiry than of substantive propositions. *The Kingdom of Christ* reminds one at once of Socrates seeking the definition of justice by questioning conflicting schools of

[11] *Life*, II, pp. 316–17.
[12] *Sequel to the Inquiry, What Is Revelation?* (Cambridge, Macmillan, 1860), p. 97.
[13] *Life*, I, p. 369.

opinion. Maurice, of course, is leading his respondents on to the admission that there actually is a Catholic Church in their midst to which each bears a partial witness. Probably the criticism of Platonism is rooted in the recognition that for Maurice the Johannine writings are very much the clue to his understanding of the Bible as a whole. It might even be permissible further to limit the field by saying that within the Fourth Gospel it is the prologue which is the key.

The Bible is the witness to the kingdom of Christ, and that kingdom is the real theme of the Old Testament and the source of half-truths in other religions and philosophies. Actually Maurice in interpreting any passage tried to understand its simplest context as well as its historical context. Then he tried to show how the historical facts therein narrated also were pointers to God's universal kingdom and in particular to the constitution of all men in Christ. He believed that the Holy Spirit would reveal the relevance between these insights and the situation of the preacher or reader of the Bible. He believed deeply in the self-authenticating character of revelation.

> I use them [the Scriptures] because I conceive they set forth Christ as the Son of God and the Lord of every man. I do not use them because I think they set forth some standard which is good for a set of men called Christians, who are different from other men, and who have not the same God with other men. I use the Scriptures to show us what I believe is the law and the life for all of us, that law and life of which men in the old world had only a partial glimpse. I should not use them if I thought them less universal and more partial than the books of heathens or of later moralists.[14]

For Maurice the Bible is not a solitary fact. He seeks to lay bare the organic connection that actually exists between church, creeds, and Bible. His Anglican heritage with its respect for Bible, tradition, and reason received a creative reinterpretation in depth.

> He who dwells with us and governs us, the Ever-blessed Word, has formed us to be one in Him; He seeks to make us one by

---

[14] *Epistles of St. John* (London, Macmillan, 1867), p. 14.

bringing us to a knowledge of Himself: for this end He has revealed Himself to us, and has preserved the revelation in a book; this revelation He has entrusted to His Church, that she may impart it to men, and train men to apprehend its contents; the Church, in the exercise of her functions, has from Scripture formed a creed which is the first step in her scheme of education; when men were awakened by this creed, it became her duty to use the Bible, that they might know the certainty of those things wherein they have been catechised; with this Bible, she is able to cultivate the reason, which is the organ wherewith we apprehend spiritual matters; the Church tried what she could do without the Bible, and she became weak; the Bible has been set up against the Church, and has been dishonored; the Reason has been set up against both Church and Bible, and has become partial, inconsistent, self-contradictory. Finally, bitter experience must lead us at last to a conviction, that God's ways are higher than our ways; that a universal Church, constituted in His Son, and endowed with His Spirit, is the proper instrument for using His universal book; and this book the instrument for educating the universal reason.[15]

MAN AND SIN

It is evident from the previous statement of Maurice's Christological principle what his method will be in evaluating the human situation. Christ precedes Adam in the order of being. When it is written in Genesis that man has been created in the image of God, Maurice at once understands that man has been created by the Eternal Son and that this image can therefore not be destroyed by sin. We are "not to think that the world was created in Adam, or stood in his obedience; for the Scriptures of the New Testament, illustrating those of the Old, teach us that it stood and stands in the obedience of God's well-beloved Son; the real image of the Father, the real bond of human society and of the whole universe who was to be manifested in the fulness of time, as that which He had always been."[16]

This means that when Christ comes he comes not as an alien

[15] *Kingdom of Christ* (1838), II, pp. 87 ff.
[16] *The Patriarchs and Lawgivers of the Old Testament,* 5th ed. (London, Macmillan, 1878), p. 66.

intruder into the world and to men, but as the redeemer of his own creation. While Christ brings us the utterly new gift of redemption, he does not extricate us from the race but restores us to our true life as men created in his image.

It is clear that such a presentation will entail a different understanding of sin than the traditional one which speaks either of a total loss of the image of God or of certain aspects of the image. For Maurice, sin is to be understood not so much prospectively as in conventional treatments which develop sin as the prelude to redemption, as retrospectively in the sense that we are members of a race that has been redeemed by the incarnation of the Word, by his bearing the sins of the whole world and by his resurrection from the dead on the plane of our history.

There is no minimizing of the Atonement in Maurice's work. Indeed, the opposite is the case, for his firm convictions about the work of Christ in overcoming sin led him to demote the doctrine of sin from its too dominant place in popular theologies. Maurice's view of the Atonement in *Theological Essays* has been characterized as close to the moral theory. This is only a partial description, although perhaps justified because of the obscurity of expression in that work. His own view of the Atonement is best set forth in *The Doctrine of Sacrifice,* one of the clearest of his writings. Tracing the sacrifices of the Old Testament in a way that would need much correction today from newer historical perspectives, Maurice holds that the New Testament asserts sacrifice as the great principle of the divine obedience of the Son before the world existed. What is new here is the careful linking of the Trinity and the idea of creation with the concept of Atonement.

> . . . we see beneath all evil, beneath the universe itself, that eternal and original union of the Father and the Son . . . which was never fully manifested till the Only Begotten by the eternal Spirit offered Himself to God. The revelation of that primal unity is the revelation of the ground on which all things stand, both things in heaven and things in earth. It is the revelation of an order which sustains all the intercourse and society of men. It is the revelation of that which sin has ever been seeking to destroy, and which at last has overcome sin. It is the revelation of

that perfect harmony to which we look forward when all things are gathered up in Christ . . . when the law of sacrifice shall be the acknowledged law of all creation.[17]

Maurice views sin from the angle of Christ's accomplished work; from this angle he cannot, I feel—contrary to his critics —be accused of underestimating the power of sin. Sin, for him, is to be defined as self-willed isolation from the true constitution of man as created and redeemed by Christ. Sin is man's refusal to acknowledge his true center in Christ, and his desperate effort to establish a false independence. Since Maurice took the fall as a historical event, his interpretation that it must not be the base for theology is all the more remarkable to us who usually describe it as a myth that lays bare deep insights into the human situation. Maurice also believed in the devil, but refused to grant that the world was properly his possession.

Maurice's criticism of Calvinism was that it misinterpreted God's election and predestination in a narrowly individualistic and exclusivistic way that made a travesty of the biblical witness that Christ was himself the elect and predestinated One and that the whole race, not just a favored few, was included in him. This perspective is quite close to Barth's criticism of Calvin. Maurice claimed that the constitution of the race in Christ is the proper background for appreciating the power of Luther's concern for justification by faith and of keeping that cardinal insight uncorrupted. But Protestantism found it almost impossible to submit its doctrine of justification by faith to the *experience* of justification by faith. As a result ". . . when assent to the doctrine of justification was substituted for belief in the Justifier, Protestantism went into the lean, sickly and yet contentious stage of its existence, only to emerge from that into indifference —a mere denial of Romanism."[18]

THE CHURCH AND ITS SIX SIGNS

For Maurice the church was organic to the Gospel. It is the body of Christ, given life by its head, that exists to show the world its true center and by articulating the law of mutual sacri-

[17] *Doctrine of Sacrifice*, p. 194.
[18] *Life*, II, p. 615.

fice to support the unity of both nations and families. Maurice held that the church was really the world when the Christological principle was rightly understood.

> The world contains the elements of which the Church is composed. In the Church, these elements are penetrated by a uniting, reconciling power. The Church is, therefore, human society in its normal state; the world, that same society irregular and abnormal. The world is the Church without God: the Church is the world restored to its relation with God, taken back by Him into the state for which He created it.[19]

It was not customary in Maurice's time to develop the idea of the church as the Israel of God. With a thoroughly scriptural analysis he traced a series of covenants between God and Abraham and the Israelite nation to show that family and nation are preliminary manifestations of church structure. *The Church a Family,* one of his most helpful books, carried on this theme. The ultimate pattern of unity is God Himself who as the Blessed Trinity expresses the ground of the family principle. He described the fundamental position of the *Kingdom of Christ* as follows: ". . . there rose up before me the idea of a *Church Universal,* not built upon human inventions or human faith, but upon the very nature of God himself, and upon the union which He has formed with His creatures."[20]

Just as the church had a history in Israel and in the New Testament period, so it has today. It is to be recognized by concrete facts of historical existence, not just in theological ideas. The theologian does well to accept the historical givenness of the signs of the church. These as facts are more impressive in their witness to the "Universal Society" than in the views men have entertained about these facts.

The fundamental sign of church life is baptism, whereby men are forgiven their sins and are incorporated into Christ and realize their status as sons of God because of the objective and racial atonement effected by Christ. Maurice liked to call baptism "the sacrament of constant union." He stressed the importance of sacraments as demonstrations of the free grace of God

[19] *Theological Essays* (Cambridge, 1853), p. 403.
[20] *Kingdom of Christ,* I, p. 14.

in Christ and as salutary checks to any excessive preoccupation of man with his own feelings or faith.

> Outward signs and tokens have a great worth. They attest the reality and the universality of God's gifts, as in the case of the water in baptism and the bread and wine in the Lord's Supper. They prevent men from fancying that their thoughts, and impressions, and beliefs, create the blessings which are bestowed upon us by God's free grace.[21]

Baptism interprets to man the human situation. Maurice has a way of bringing all his previous insights together when he seeks the depth of his next point. Notice the themes hitherto separately developed now focused on baptism:

> I have maintained that Christ, by whom, and for whom all things were created, and in whom all things consist, has made reconciliation for mankind; that on the ground of this atonement for mankind, God has built His church, declaring men one family in Christ. . . . And [we believing] that the mark of that universal body or fellowship, appointed by God Himself is Baptism, do, without fear or scruple, asseverate of ourselves, and of all others who will come to this holy Baptism, of all who bear the marks and impress of that nature which Christ took, in His birth, of the blessed Virgin; that they are admitted into these high and glorious privileges; that they are brought into a state of salvation; that they are made sons of God and heirs of everlasting life. . . . And in saying this, we contend that we give faith . . . a ground upon which to stand, and which otherwise it cannot have.[22]

The second sign of the kingdom of Christ is the fact of the two creeds which confess the triform name into which we are baptized. The creeds are not digests of doctrines; they are our protection against theological systems. To say the creed is to confess the name, to make an act of allegiance to a person. Baptism is the sign that we are saved by grace; the creed that we are saved by faith.

[21] *Acts of the Apostles*, p. 188.
[22] *Kingdom of Christ* (1838), I, pp. 88 ff.

The third sign of the church is the existence of set forms of worship such as are collected in the Book of Common Prayer. Maurice is one of the deepest interpreters of liturgics. He rejoiced that the ordinary Englishman expressed his worship in forms derived from the Hebrews, the Greeks, and the Latins. It was evidence to him that the church transcended space and time. Like most engaged today in the liturgical movement he held that "the prayers written in the first ages of Christianity are in general more free, more reverent, more universal, than those which have been poured forth since."[23]

The eucharist is the fourth sign. It testifies that because of Christ's sacrifice once and for all perfected on Calvary a "living and perpetual communion" has been established between God and man. It expresses Christ's "continual presence with His universal family." More significant than the debates over the manner of Christ's presence, Maurice maintained, was the reality of that presence as sheer fact. There was social meaning to the eucharist and an eschatological anticipation of the new age. Here his biblical orientation saved him from any Platonism, although even so he cannot be said to have given to eschatology that weight which it has held recently in biblical studies and theology. He was too Johannine for that. Maurice felt personally that the eucharist expressed a depth and a practicality that man could not find elsewhere, not even in the Bible. "Ask yourself then solemnly and seriously: 'Can I find Christianity—the Christianity I want—a Christianity of acts, not words, a Christianity of power and life, a divine, human, Catholic Christianity for men of all countries and periods, all tastes and endowments, all temperaments and necessities so exhibited as I find it in this Sacrament?' "[24]

The ordained ministry is the fifth sign of the church. It testifies that there is a permanent structure in the life of the church, a representative office of sacrificial service that unless it is kept faithfully may congeal into a hierarchy, making the church only another expression of the world. Maurice wrote that the four Gospels might be described as "The Institution of a Christian Ministry." The historic episcopate, he believed, expressed the

[23] *Ibid.*, II, p. 30.
[24] *Ibid.* (1838), I, p. 287.

reality of universal communion in the church and was the order that stood in essential succession to the apostolate.

> I believe that He meant His Church to stand in certain permanent and universal institutions . . . in a permanent ministry through which He should declare His will, and dispense His blessings to the whole body, and the main office in which should be that apostolic office which belongs characteristically to the new dispensation, seeing that it expresses the general oversight of Him, who no longer confines Himself to any particular nation, but has ascended upon high that He might fill all things.[25]

Although he considered the episcopate necessary, he did not, like the Tractarians, unchurch those who had lost it. The bond of communion might be broken and yet many ties with the universal church might still stand. Unlike the Tractarians he refused to define the limits of the church. "I cannot answer the question; I believe only One can answer it; I am content to leave it with Him."[26] Nothing would more falsify the picture than to describe Maurice as expounding Anglicanism as a system superior to other systems. He who was *persona non grata* to all the parties within the Church of England in his day and who warned against parties and systems, even to the extent of calling those who said they had no party the expression of the worst partisanship, was not likely to suggest that Anglicanism as such was what creation had been awaiting. The power of Maurice as a reconciler is illustrated in a letter to Erskine of Linlathen:

> The English *Church* I look upon as merely one branch of the true Church; and every *system*, whether called Evangelical, Liberal, Catholic, or purely Anglican, which has been invented by the members of that Church in former times and in our own day to express their notion of the Church, I look upon as "of the earth earthy," and as much carrying in it the seeds of destruction as the systems of the different sects which have revolted from her. The Church—it seems to me—is a part, the highest part, of that spiritual constitution of which the nation and the family are lower and subordinate parts; implied in the acts we do and the

---

[25] *Three Letters to the Rev. W. Palmer,* p. 8.
[26] *Epistle to the Hebrews,* p. cxxiv.

words we speak, established before all worlds, manifested as the true and everlasting kingdom when the Son of God died, rose, and ascended on high . . . testified as the common property and inheritance of men by certain forms and ordinances which convert it from an idea for the mind into an actual reality for all who will enter into it and enjoy it, and which prove God to be true though all men be liars.[27]

Since the sixth sign of the universal church, the Bible, has already been treated in the section on revelation, it remains to make a brief summary and evaluation. In *Christ and Culture* Richard Niebuhr cites Maurice as more clearly expressing the position that Christ is the transformer and converter of culture than "any other modern Christian thinker and leader." In spite of its being largely precritical, his sustained exposition of the Bible anticipates the christological interpretation of history held by many contemporary biblical theologians. Social prophet, yet deficient in eschatological perspective, he may be called "a thoroughgoing Johanninist" in his Christian humanism. His ecumenical theology is just beginning to come into its own with its reconciliation in depth between Catholicism and Protestantism. Maurice many times described his whole ministry and authorship as a search for unity.

The idea of the unity of the Father and the Son in the Holy Spirit, as the basis of all unity amongst men, as the groundwork of all human society and of all thought, as belonging to little children, and as the highest fruition of the saints in glory, has been haunting me for a longer time than I can easily look back to.[28]

[27] *Life,* I, pp. 306 ff.
[28] *Ibid.,* p. 414.

Bibliography

Frederick Denison Maurice, *The Kingdom of Christ,* new ed. based on 2d ed. of 1842, Alec R. Vidler, ed., London, SCM Press, 1958.

Alec R. Vidler, *Witness to the Light: F. D. Maurice's Message for To-day,* N. Y., Scribner's, 1948.

ADOLF VON HARNACK

Wilhelm Pauck

I

Harnack was born on May 7, 1851, in the Baltic city of Dorpat in Livonia, which was then and is now again a Russian province. His forebears had come there from Germany. His paternal grandfather, a tailor, hailed from East Prussia, and his maternal grandfather, a professor in the University of Dorpat and for many years its rector, was a native Westphalian. His father, Theodosius Harnack, a strict Lutheran with pietistic leanings, was a professor of practical and systematic theology, first in Dorpat, then for thirteen years (1853–66) in Erlangen, Germany, and then again, for the rest of his life, in Dorpat (he died in 1889).

Adolf Harnack and his three brothers (they were all unusually gifted) received their education in Erlangen and Dorpat. In October 1872 he left home in order to complete his studies in the University of Leipzig.[1]

In 1873 he wrote and published his doctor's dissertation on an early Gnostic text. Shortly thereafter (1874) he began his academic career as a church historian, first as a *Privatdozent* (1874) and then as a professor-extraordinary (1876), in Leipzig. In 1879 he was appointed to a professorship in Giessen. From there he moved to Marburg (1886). Two years later he was called to the University of Berlin. By then he had already acquired fame as a teacher, researcher, author, and critic and

---

[1] Hans Lietzmann writes in a commemorative article (*Theologische Literaturzeitung* 76, 1951): "When as a young student I became acquainted with Harnack in Venice, he told me one evening during an unforgettable conversation about his upbringing. As if he were telling a fairytale he said: 'We were four brothers, and when we left home, our father gave each of us one thousand dollars and told us that we should make good. All four of us did make good—and I still have the thousand dollars.'"

as an organizer of scientific projects.[2] This call was opposed by
the Supreme Council of the Evangelical Church. Being the
highest office of the Prussian state church, the council was entitled to exercise a veto right of sorts on appointments to the
theological chairs in the universities. However, both the faculty
and the Ministry of Education strongly desired Harnack's appointment. On their recommendation and on that of Chancellor
Bismarck and his cabinet, Emperor William II, then at the very
beginning of his reign, overruled the church office and affixed
his signature to the document of Harnack's appointment (September 17, 1888).[3]

The objections of the churchmen were based chiefly on Harnack's *History of Dogma* (3 vols. 1886–89; 4th ed., 1909).
They consisted mainly of the following charges: (1) that he
doubted the traditional views concerning the authorship of the
Fourth Gospel, of the Letter to the Ephesians, and of the First
Epistle of Peter; (2) that he was critical of miracles and, specifically, that he did not accept the conventional interpretation
of Christ's virgin birth, resurrection, and ascension; and (3)
that he denied the institution of the sacrament of baptism by
Jesus. No attempt was made to refute these views on the basis
of historical scholarship from which they were derived; only
the irreconcilability of Harnack's views with the doctrinal authority of the church was stated.

All this cast a dark shadow upon Harnack's academic position. Indeed, it lay upon his entire career. Even at this time, to
be sure, Harnack was of the conviction that the gospel of Jesus
Christ had nothing in common with the doctrinal authority exercised by an ecclesiastical hierarchy or by a bureau of church
officials. But the church to which he belonged felt it necessary
to maintain this very authority. He could therefore hardly avoid

[2] In 1876 he founded (with his friend Emil Schürer) the *Theologische
Literaturzeitung,* which is still one of the foremost critical reviews of
theological scholarship. (Harnack was its sole editor beginning in 1881
and held this post for many years.) In 1881–82 he began (in cooperation
with his friend O. von Gebhardt) the publication of the series *Texte
und Untersuchungen* which, in the course of time, became a mine of
information on the history of the ancient church.

[3] Cf. Walter Wendland, "Die Berufung A. Harnack's nach Berlin,"
Jahrbuch für brandenburgische Kirchengeschichte 29 (1934), pp. 103 ff.

some kind of conflict with it. Nevertheless, it was a source of deep sorrow for him that, throughout his life, he was denied all official recognition by the church. He was not even given the right to examine his own pupils as they entered into the service of the church. Yet for many years he was the most influential theological teacher in the land. Hundreds, nay, thousands of students who later became ministers gave him an enthusiastic hearing, and scores of them were inspired by him to prepare themselves for theological professorships, which then became centers from which his views were spread to ever widening circles. As a member of the theological faculty of Germany's most distinguished university, which was maintained and supported by the state and protected by it as to its academic freedom, he made an incisive contribution to the training of the leaders of the Protestant Church. This church was united with the same state, yet it never invited him to take a seat at its councils, synods, or boards, and it never gave him any assurance that as a theological teacher he was one of its spokesmen. Thus Harnack could not but be deeply disappointed in his strong desire to serve the church.[4]

In a wider sense he served it, of course, through his prolific authorship. Most of his more than sixteen hundred large and small writings were devoted to the study of the history of the church.[5] The New Testament, the Church Fathers, but also the Reformation and Protestantism furnished him the main themes.

Certain of his works have already become classics. His *History of Dogma,* for example, will have a permanent place among the masterpieces of theological literature. Though it will be superseded in specific parts here and there, it will always be recognized as a most suggestive work of historical interpretation, grandly conceived and executed with superior skill as to both

[4] The only opportunity he had to satisfy this wish was given him through his membership in the Evangelical-Social Congress (one of the voluntary associations so distinctive of modern Protestantism), whose purpose it was, outside the official church but through a membership that was recruited from the ranks of church members, to give concrete expression to the Christian responsibility for the social-political order. Harnack was its president (1903–12).

[5] Cf. Friedrich Smend, *A. von Harnack: Verzeichnis seiner Schriften* (Leipzig, 1931), which lists 1611 titles.

style and content.[6] The work on *The Mission and Expansion of Christianity during the First Three Centuries* (2 vols., 1902; 4th ed. 1924) is almost of the same quality. His *History of Ancient Christian Literature* (3 vols., 1893–1904) laid the foundation for all further critical studies in patristics.

Few works of modern theological literature have created as much excitement and stirred up as much furor as Harnack's *Wesen des Christentums* (*What Is Christianity?*, 1900; 15th ed., 1950). It is the transcript of a student's stenograph of a course of lectures delivered to students of all faculties in the winter semester 1899–1900. Troeltsch[7] thought it was representative of all theological work based on historical thinking. It certainly has become generally regarded as the one book which more directly than any other represents so-called liberal Protestant theology.

Harnack continued to publish scholarly and popular writings throughout his life. His authorship extended over fifty-seven years, from 1873, when he published his dissertation on Gnosticism, to 1930, when his publications ended with an article on the name of Novatian. His first important scholarly work had been a prize essay on Marcion (unpublished) for which the University of Dorpat had given him a gold medal; his last significant book was devoted to an interpretation of the same heretical figure,[8] and it stirred up considerable excitement.

In his capacity as a historian, Harnack was elected in 1890 to the Prussian Academy of Sciences in Berlin. Theodore Mommsen, one of its most distinguished members, gave him an enthusiastic welcome. Here he soon became organizer and

[6] One of Harnack's admirers, the French Jesuit scholar J. de Ghellinck, wrote about it (*En marge de l'oeuvre de Harnack. Gregorianum* 11 [1930], pp. 513f.): "Everyone knows the three volumes of his *Dogmengeschichte*, though it is perhaps correct to say that more people talk about them than read them." (*Chacun le s connait bien qu'il soit peut-être exact de dire que les trois volumes de sa Dogmengeschichte ont trouvé moins d'hommes pour les lire que pour en parler.*)

[7] Cf. Ernst Troeltsch, *Was heisst "Wesen des Christentums"?* (*Gesammelte Schriften* II [1913], p. 387): *Harnack's Schrift is gewissermassen das symbolische Buch für die historisierende Richtung der Theologie.*

[8] *Marcion: Das Evangelium vom fremden Gott* (Berlin, 1921; 2nd ed., 1924).

chairman of the editorial council of the *Critical Edition of the Greek Christian Authors of the First Three Centuries*. Furthermore, he learned to relate theological scholarship to that of other disciplines. It was a signal honor that he, the theologian, was invited by the Academy to prepare its history which was planned to be published in connection with the celebration of its two-hundredth anniversary, in 1900. Harnack punctually fulfilled the assignment. In three volumes, he offered not only an interpretation of the activities of the Academy but, in connection with it, also a history of modern scholarship.

At the dawn of the new century, he was at the height of his career. When the anniversary of the Berlin Academy was celebrated in a glittering ceremony, he was the official orator. It so happened that, just then, he occupied also the post of rector of the University of Berlin. Moreover, at this time his fame was spreading throughout the world in connection with the publication of the book *What Is Christianity?* He wielded great influence on educational affairs through the office of the Ministry of Education, who frequently sought his counsel.[9] Ever increasingly he became a representative personage. The public saw in him scholarship personified. William II, the German Emperor, gave him special recognition, first by inviting him into his company and then by bestowing special honors upon him.[10]

All this had an effect upon his academic career. To be sure, church-historical teaching and research continued to be his primary love and labor. But in the course of time he came to assume two further professional responsibilities. Indeed, he said of himself that he was active in three different careers. In 1906 he accepted the appointment to the post of Director General of the Royal Library[11] in Berlin, the largest and most important library in Germany. Some of his friends were disturbed; they feared that he might gradually abandon his theological career. But Harnack wrote to his friend Professor Martin Rade in Marburg:

[9] At one time the rumor was abroad that he would be appointed Minister of Education.

[10] He raised him to the dignity of hereditary nobility. Harnack was the last scholar so honored in royal Prussia.

[11] After World War I it was called the Prussian State Library.

You come to know the world only in so far as you influence it. My new position will not make me a librarian so much as an organizer. I hope that my friends will find that theology is not made the loser thereby but that all branches of learning, including theology, will make a gain. I have *done* little in my life, and I should like, in a modest way, to supplement my work of lecturing and writing by a "doing" from which the whole community can profit. The church has not offered me an opportunity of this kind, and if such work were offered to me now, it would come too late for me.[12]

He proved to be an excellent organizer and a brilliant administrator. Hence nobody was much surprised when, in 1911, he accepted also the post of President of the Kaiser Wilhelm Gesellschaft.[13] This was a foundation organized (in connection with the celebration of the centennial of the University of Berlin and sponsored by the German Emperor) for the purpose of launching scientific research institutes in which scholars would pursue pure and applied research of a kind which the universities could not afford to become engaged in, on account of their primary responsibility for teaching and professional training. Under Harnack's leadership and with the support of government and industry, the foundation rapidly established several research institutes. Almost immediately they won worldwide recognition and influence.

Harnack continued to be president of the Kaiser Wilhelm Gesellschaft until the end of his life. He led its affairs when it assumed broader and poignantly practical responsibilities during World War I, and he saw it through the turmoil caused by Germany's military defeat and through the ensuing period of monetary inflation and economic depression. In the spring of 1930 these duties led him to Heidelberg, where a new institute of medical research was to be opened. There he died, after a brief illness, on June 10, 1930.

In 1921 he had become a professor emeritus. He then gave up all administrative duties connected with his professorship and he also retired from the library, but he continued to teach

[12] Agnes von Zahn-Harnack, *Adolf von Harnack,* 2nd ed. (Berlin, 1951), p. 325.
[13] Now called Max Planck Gesellschaft.

(on a reduced schedule, of course) for several years.[14] In the spring of 1929 he delivered his last lecture in the University of Berlin and at the same time closed his seminar on ancient church history, over which he had presided continuously for 108 academic semesters. It always had been the center of his work and the headquarters of his professional labors. For in connection with the broad influence he exercised and throughout the deep impact that went forth from him to all fields of cultural endeavor, he always remained first of all a church historian and a theologian. Indeed, he embodied in his person a kind of cultural Protestantism, which was deeply anchored in his personal faith and reached out broadly upon the wide field of human civilization.[15]

II

Whatever may have been the secret of Harnack's power and whatever was the source of his accomplishment as a scholar, administrator, public figure, and representative man, one can say that he was what he was and that he produced his great

[14] In the fall of 1921 the German Government offered him the post of ambassador to Washington, D.C., but he regretfully declined the honor.

[15] Harnack was a person of great charm. This is the impression one obtains from reading the biography which his daughter Agnes wrote with a rare and congenial understanding of her father (cf. footnote 12). It is also the testimony of all who knew him well. At the memorial service held at the University of Berlin, Professor Erich Seeberg spoke of "his dutiful discipline in so ordering his daily life and dividing his time that he was able to accomplish so much—coupled as this discipline was with a chivalrous and objective formality in his dealings with men and in the management of his relations with them." (Erich Seeberg, *Adolf von Harnack,* Tübingen, 1930, p. 25.) At the same occasion the rector of the university, Professor Erhard Schmidt, a mathematician, characterized him as follows (*ibid.,* p. 6): "Harnack was of a noble, aristocratic character; his outward distinction was softened by a generous, considerate, and kind disposition. In conversation, he never let one feel his superiority; on the contrary, he enhanced the self-confidence of the one who was speaking with him by rearranging in a most agreeable way whatever was being said to him and putting it in such a form that the other took great delight in the thought he had expressed." There is a fine characterization of Harnack in Erich Fascher's *Adolf von Harnack—Grösse und Grenze* (Berlin, 1962).

works in the way he did because he was an unusually gifted teacher.

One who was one of his students in Leipzig, at the very beginning of Harnack's career (in 1877–78), wrote, almost fifty years later, in the following enthusiastic way of the impression Harnack (who was then still in his twenties) made upon him and his fellow students:

> We had the feeling that a new world was dawning upon us. We had been trained by capable teachers and we were taking courses from eminent professors and well-known scholars. But here we were touched by the aura of genius. Harnack combined in himself in a unique way the qualities required of a scholar with the gifts of a born teacher: concentrated inquisitiveness; tireless industry; the ability of ordering and forming his materials; a comprehensive memory;[16] critical astuteness; a clear and considered judgment, and, together with all this, a wonderful gift of intuition and combination and, at the same time, a marvellously simple, lucid, and appealing manner of presentation. And, to top it all, he also had not infrequently the good fortune of finding and discovering something new. To every subject and field of study he gave light and warmth, life and significance. In both theory and practice he was a master of the teaching method.
>
> He came to his classes only after thorough preparation. He was never without notes, but he spoke extempore . . . without affectation or pathos and never seeking cheap effects. He talked eloquently and from an even inner participation in what he was dealing with, without trying to excite or overwhelm his hearers. Yet he was fascinating and convincing. He was illuminating through the gentle compulsion of complete objectivity. He was conscientious and accurate but not pedantic, nor did he get lost in details. Without minimizing or concealing difficulties, he explained the problems at hand with vividness as to their logical form and material content. He made the past live through the present and let the present explain the past.[17]

---

[16] Harnack's brother-in-law, H. Rassow, writes (*Christliche Welt* 44, 1930), p. 728: "I asked him once: 'How much time would you need in order to memorize one page of Greek that you had never seen before?' He replied: 'If I read the page slowly, I would know it by heart.'"

[17] *Christliche Welt* 35 (1921), p. 315. The writer was Prof. W. Bornemann.

Many other testimonies prove that these striking words express the experience and judgment of the large circle of Harnack's students and pupils. Among these none is perhaps as telling as that of Dietrich Bonhoeffer, who was a member of Harnack's last seminar and who spoke in the name of his fellow students at the memorial service on June 15, 1930, in Berlin.[18] He said, among other things:

> He got hold of us in the way a real teacher gets hold of his pupils. He shared our questions, even though he confronted us with his superior judgment. We assembled in his home for a serious piece of work on the history of the ancient church, and there we came to know him and his unerring striving for truth and clarity. All mere talk was foreign to the spirit of his seminar. He demanded absolute clarity. This did not exclude the possibility that very personal and inmost questions were raised. He was always willing to listen to questions and to answer them. All that mattered to him was the honesty of the answer. Thus we learned from him that truth is born only from freedom.[19]

We should note that as a teacher Harnack was a historian and that as a historian he was a teacher. The role of the teacher is almost identical with that of the historian. In a certain sense every true teacher is a historian, and nobody can be a true historian unless he is willing to be also a teacher. For, in every present, men find that they must come to terms with the cultural legacy which they have inherited from their fathers. They must take possession of it and incorporate it into their own lives. They must fit it to the requirements of their own situation and thus transform it and then transmit it to their children and children's children.

Civilization is a product of education and a learning process at the same time. Men are engaged in it in order to relate the values produced by past generations to the needs of the present; at the same time, they endeavor to hand them on to future generations. Whoever, therefore, furthers human culture is in a real sense a teacher as well as a historian, for as he hands down

[18] Bonhoeffer was executed because he opposed the Nazi dictatorship. Harnack's eldest son, Ernst, experienced the same fate.

[19] "Adolf von Harnack," *Ausgewählte Reden und Aufsätze*. Berlin, 1951, p. 210.

the cultural traditions of the past to those around him, he acts as a historically responsible educator.

In this sense, Harnack was a supreme teacher-historian.[20] His writings as well as his activities clearly prove that he believed it to be the highest task of the historian to prepare his fellow men for right action in the present.[21] "Only that history which is not yet past but which is and remains a living part of our present deserves to be known by all," he wrote.[22] Hence he regarded all history as mute if it is nothing but a display of an antiquarian interest or if it is dealt with only in terms of archaeology, i.e., understood to be the mere record of past human life.[23]

The following statement sums up Harnack's fundamental conception:

> We study history in order to intervene in the course of history, and it is our right and duty that we do this, for if we lack historical insight we either permit ourselves to be mere objects put in the historical process or we shall have the tendency to lead people down the wrong way. To intervene in history— this means that we must reject the past when it reaches into the present only in order to block us. It means also that we must do the right thing in the present, i.e., anticipate the future and be prepared for it in a circumspect manner. There is no doubt that, with respect to the past, the historian assumes the royal function of a judge, for in order to decide what of the past shall continue to be in effect and what must be done away with or transformed, the historian must judge like a king. Everything must be designed to furnish a preparation for the future, for only that discipline of learning has a right to exist which lays the foundation for what is to be.[24]

[20] Cf. W. Pauck, "Harnack's Interpretation of Church History" in *The Cultural Heritage of the Reformation*, 2nd ed., Chicago, 1961, pp. 337ff.

[21] Cf. Hans Lietzmann, *Gedächtnisrede auf Harnack. Sitzungsberichte der Akademie der Wissenscheften in Berlin*, 1931, p. LVIII.

[22] In "Sokrates und die Alte Kirche,"*Gesammelte Reden und Aufsätze*, 1951, p. 25.

[23] Cf. *Wesen des Christentums*, p. XVII, and *Reden und Aufsätze*, Vol. IV, p. 5.

[24] *Über die Sicherheit und Grenzen geschichtlicher Erkenntnis. Reden und Aufsätze*, Vol. IV, p. 7.

We would misunderstand the import of these words if we took them to imply that Harnack was not concerned about the objectivity of historical research. He was wont to say that he was doing his work as a historian on three levels, namely, source criticism, representation, and reflection, and that he felt most at home on the third level.[25] And it is a fact that he devoted rigorous and time-consuming effort to the establishment of the accuracy and reliability of his sources, and that he took great care to represent and interpret these sources as diligently and objectively as possible. But he was also painfully aware of the limits that are set to the historian as he attempts to reconstruct, to relate, and to interpret past actions and events. He shared to some extent the skeptical judgment of Goethe[26] who is reported to have said in a conversation with the historian Heinrich Luden: "Not all that is presented to us as history has really happened; and what really happened did not actually happen the way it is presented to us; moreover, what really happened is only a small part of all that happened. Everything in history remains uncertain, the largest event as well as the smallest occurrence."

As a historian, he therefore did not try to tell *wie es eigentlich gewesen* (what really happened), and, indeed, he avoided all biographical history because he suspected that it represented, especially in regard to motivations, a necessarily unsuccessful engagement with insoluble puzzles and inscrutable enigmas. Instead, he chose to study the development of institutions, i.e., states, societies, groups, and corporations and their established practices, customs, laws, codes, and authoritative rules. He interpreted institutional history as a history of ideas, for he felt that one cannot understand the development and the power of institutions unless one knows the direction along which they are moved by the ideas that govern and maintain them. For example, he believed it to be the historian's task to show to what extent an institution has succeeded in incorporating the idea or purpose for the concrete expression of which it was founded, or

---

[25] The remark is reported by Walter Koehler. Cf. *Theologische Blätter* 7 (1930), p. 168.

[26] Cf. his lecture "Die Religion Goethes in der Epoche seiner Vollendung," *Reden und Aufsätze*, Vol. IV, p. 157.

in what way an institution has striven to maintain itself even after losing the right to exist because the purpose which called it into being became invalid or lost its directive power. He even dared define the norm by reference to which the historian can judge what institutions or institutional functions deserve to be maintained—that within them which preserves life. And he was persuaded that "only that line of action and that power preserve life which liberate men from the 'service to that which passes away,' from enslavement to mere nature, and from servitude to one's own empirical self."[27]

III

Among Harnack's books the *History of Dogma* is the clearest expression of this basic conception of the historian's task. It shows concretely how and to what extent he tried to carry out his historical principles in his own field of study. He himself describes the importance of his interpretation of the history of dogma in the following way:

> By delineating the process of the origin and development of the dogma, the "history of dogma" furnishes the most suitable means for the liberation of the church from dogmatic Christianity and for the speeding up of the irresistible process of the emancipation which began with Augustine. But it also witnesses to the unity of the Christian faith in the course of history by furnishing proof that the actual significance of the person of Jesus Christ and the principles of the gospel were never lost sight of.[28]

In writing the history of dogma, i.e., the history of that authoritative ecclesiastical doctrine concerning the person and work of Christ, God incarnate, which every Christian had to accept on peril of being excluded from the communion of salvation, Harnack desired to show, in the first place, how it happened that the gospel of Jesus Christ, which in its nature has nothing in common with ecclesiasticism and with authoritarian

[27] Cf. his lecture "Was hat die Historie an fester Erkenntnis zur Deutung des Weltgeschehens zu bieten?" in *Ausgewählte Reden und Aufsätze*, 1951, p. 192.

[28] Cf. *Grundriss der Dogmengeschichte.* 9th ed., Berlin 1921, p. 5.

statutes and doctrines, became embodied in the cultic-hierarchical practices and, especially, the doctrinal institutions of the church. But, in the second place, he wanted to offer proof, by historical analysis, for the thesis that if the gospel is to retain its living power today, it must be freed from identification with dogma. Indeed, it was his major point that the dogma originated in the effort of the ancient Christians to render the gospel comprehensible in the concepts of the Hellenistic world view and that they therefore expressed it in the thought forms of Greek philosophy and science. Then he drew the conclusion that, after having been maintained for centuries through the doctrinal authoritarianism of the church, the dogma has been coming to an end in the way the various Christian churches and groups have come to deal with it: In Eastern Orthodoxy it has become an uncomprehended relic kept alive only in the cultus and the liturgy; in Roman Catholicism it has become submerged in the hierarchical-sacramental order of the church, culminating in the absolute authority of the Pope; the Reformation invalidated it in principle by the rediscovery of the gospel and by the assertion of its primacy in all Christian thought and life. However, the Reformers failed to recognize the full revolutionary significance of this rediscovery: instead of making room in all Christian thought for the gospel alone, as they said it was their purpose, they coupled the reformation of the church on the basis of the gospel with the conservation of the dogma, in the interest, so they believed, of catholicity. Thus it came about that the churches of the Reformation faiths—Lutheranism, Calvinism, and Anglicanism—exhibit in their orders and practices the religion of the personal faith in Christ's gospel of forgiveness in the context of authoritarian churchmanship. They have always required of the faithful obedient submission to the authority of ministers and ecclesiastical officials who are duty-bound to maintain conformity with the dogma.

It was Harnack's conviction that the Reformation must go on. Inasmuch as "every really important reformation in the history of religion was primarily a critical reduction,"[29] Luther's rediscovery of the gospel must be completed by the emancipa-

---

[29] *Wesen des Christentums,* p. 160.

tion of Christianity from doctrinal authoritarianism. He believed that the Hellenization of the gospel which began with the formulation of the Logos-Christology and culminated in the promulgation of the Nicene dogma of the Trinity and of the Chalcedonian dogma of Christ, very God and very man, was a historical decision through which the Christian church succeeded in maintaining its identity in its confrontation with Hellenistic civilization and the Roman Empire, but he was also convinced that this Hellenization does not need to be continued forever, especially if this perpetuation can be accomplished only through an authoritarianism and an intellectual servitude which are irreconcilable with the gospel and its spirit. Having in mind Luther and the Reformation, he summed up his basic view in the following words:

> Christianity is something else than the sum of doctrines handed down from generation to generation. Christianity is not identical with biblical theology nor with the doctrine of the church councils, but it is that disposition which the Father of Jesus Christ awakens in men's hearts through the gospel. All authorities on which the dogma is based are torn down—how then can the dogma possibly be maintained as an infallible teaching! Christian doctrine is relevant only to faith; what part can philosophy then have in it? But what are dogma and dogmatic Christianity without philosophy?[30]

He concluded by asking: "How can there possibly be a history of dogma in Protestantism in view of Luther's 'Prefaces to the New Testament' and in view of his writings on the principles of the Reformation?"[31]

And with respect to the various historical forms which Christianity assumed in the course of time, beginning with the so-called Jewish Christianity of the Apostolic Age, he wrote:

> Either Christianity is . . . identical with its first form (in this case, one is forced to conclude that it came and went at a certain time) or it contains something which remains valid in historically changing forms. Starting with the beginnings, church

[30] *Dogmengeschichte,* 4th ed., Vol. III, pp. 896f.
[31] *Ibid.,* p. 898.

history shows that it was necessary for 'early Christianity' to perish in order that 'Christianity' might remain. So too there followed, later on, one metamorphosis upon another.[32]

We must acknowledge that this interpretation is thoroughly historical. By combining historical exposition with historical criticism, Harnack drew the full consequences from the application of the historical method to the Christian religion. In fact, he replaced the dogmatic method, which had been employed for so long a time in Christian thought, by the historical method. In doing so he brought to a culmination the approach which had first been introduced into Christian theology by the historical theologians of the Enlightenment, especially Johann Salomo Semler (d. 1791), and which then resulted in the interpretation of Christianity as a "development" at the hands of Ferdinand Christian Baur (d. 1860) and Albrecht Ritschl (d. 1889), whom Harnack regarded as his immediate predecessors. He relied on the work of these historical theologians and brought it to a climax insofar as, in following out the implications of the historical method, he substituted for the traditional dogmatic norm of Christian theological truth the historical concept of the nature of Christianity (*Wesen des Christentums*). Thus he hoped to replace theological dogmatism by historical understanding.

In the introduction to a new edition of his lectures on the nature of Christianity, he wrote: "Historical understanding is achieved only as one makes the effort to separate the distinctive essence of an important phenomenon from the temporary historical forms in which it is clothed."[33] In these lectures which constitute a summary and a popularization of the results of his scholarly investigations, he tried to achieve this understanding

---

[32] *Wesen des Christentums*, p. xix. Cf. *Dogmengeschichte*, 4th ed., p. 85: "The church historian is duty-bound not to be satisfied with the establishment of the fact that the Christian religion underwent changes but to examine to what extent new forms of it were able to protect, to implant, and to instill the gospel. In all probability the gospel would have perished if the form of 'early Christianity' had been preserved in the church; but, as a matter of fact, early Christianity perished in order that the gospel might prevail."

[33] *Wesen des Christentums*, p. xix.

by identifying the nature of Christianity with the gospel and its influences. He therefore dealt first with the gospel of Jesus Christ, then with the impact which Jesus himself and his gospel made upon the first generation of his disciples, and finally with the main types of the Christian religion as they developed from the changes which it underwent in its encounter with different human conditions. He proposed to discover the common features shared by these movements by testing them at the gospel. Furthermore, he believed that he would be able to define the principles (*Grundzüge*), i.e., the main characteristics of the gospel by verifying them through a study of the various ways by which the gospel was understood in the course of church history.

It is often said that Harnack identified the nature of Christianity with the teachings of Jesus. But this is an undiscriminating simplification of his view. He did not think it possible, it is true, to define the Christian religion apart from the gospel of Jesus Christ, but he did not isolate this gospel from its historical impact, nor did he absolutize it on the basis of the New Testament, where it is recorded in its earliest form. No historical form of Christianity, he believed, should be absolutized or regarded as normative.[34] "One may say," he wrote, "that Paul or Augustine or Luther were right [in their conception of the Christian gospel], yet one must never go so far as to regard their Christianity as Christianity itself."[35] He was persuaded that wherever the gospel of Jesus Christ is actually believed, i.e., where it is really apprehended by way of a commitment to God derived from faith in this gospel (i.e., so that this commitment is a certain trustful disposition of the heart), there Christianity is realized: the impulse which motivates such an actualization and the fountain which feeds it is the gospel—the gospel which Jesus proclaimed and of which he was the concretion in his historical humanity.

Harnack never stated in so many words what he conceived

[34] *Ibid.*, p. 113: "The gospel did not enter the world as a statutory religion and it can therefore have no classical and permanent manifestation in any form of intellectual or social expression, not even in the first one."

[35] *Ibid.*, p. xviii.

the nature of Christianity to be (and we should realize that no historian would attempt to offer a final definition!), but he undertook again and again to define the gospel. We must take care not to isolate certain ones of these definitions from the rest lest we illegitimately distort his thought.

He loved to quote Luther's saying, supposedly under the assumption that it summarized the gospel: "In forgiveness of sins there is life and bliss." Or he said: "The religion of the gospel rests upon . . . faith in Jesus Christ, i.e., because of him, this particular historical person, the believer is certain that God rules heaven and earth and that God the Judge is also the Father and Redeemer."[36] In the *History of Dogma* he asserted that the gospel as the New Testament presents it is something twofold: (1) the preaching of Jesus, and (2) the proclamation of Jesus as the Christ who died and rose again for the sake of sin and who gives the assurance of forgiveness and eternal life.[37]

Many, therefore, misunderstand Harnack when they hold that he thought that the gospel consists ultimately only of the teaching of Jesus. There is, of course, no denying that he put great stress on the teaching of Jesus. Indeed he has become famous for the definition he offers in *What Is Christianity?:* in the teaching of Jesus there are three circles of thought, each of which contains the whole proclamation: (1) the Kingdom of God and its coming; (2) God the Father and the infinite value of the human soul; (3) the better righteousness and the commandment of love.[38] He was concerned to emphasize that this teaching must be received with full seriousness. For he was persuaded that it was not something merely provisional which must be differently understood in the light of Jesus' death and resurrection, as if only a certain conception of the person of Christ (for example, that he was the "Son of God," etc.) could ensure the proper comprehension of the gospel.[39]

"Not the Son but alone the Father belongs in the gospel as Jesus proclaimed it."[40] By saying this, Harnack in no way in-

[36] *Dogmengeschichte*, 4th ed., p. 70.
[37] *Ibid.*, pp. 65f.
[38] *Wesen des Christentums*, p. 31.
[39] *Ibid.*, p. 86.
[40] *Ibid.*, p. 86.

tended to minimize the significance of Jesus. He wanted only to make sure that the gospel was understood as a religious-moral proclamation addressed to man's conscience which requires from him a decision for or against it and will then bring about a transformation of his inner disposition. He desired thus to avoid the impression that the gospel must be taken to be a revelation of an extraordinary sort which can be maintained only on the basis of certain metaphysical views about God, Christ, man, and the world.[41] He felt it necessary to insist on saying that "Jesus does not belong to the gospel as one of its elements,"[42] for, in fact, he thought of him as highly as possible.

> He was the personal concretion and power of the gospel and we still perceive him as such. For none has ever known the Father in the way he knew him, and he gives this knowledge to others, thereby rendering "the many" an incomparable service. He leads them to God, not only by his word but still more by what he is and does and, finally, by his suffering. It is in this sense that he said not only this: "Come unto me all ye that labor and are heavy laden and I will give you rest," but also this: "The Son of Man is not come to be ministered unto but to minister and give his life as a ransom for many."[43]

Throughout his life Harnack was certain that because of this gospel Christianity was *the* true religion. "It is *the* religion," he wrote, "because Jesus Christ is not one among other masters but *the* master and because his gospel corresponds to the innate capacity of man as history discloses it."[44]

In order to do full justice to Harnack's basic conception, we must note also that he frequently pointed out what the gospel

[41] Cf. *ibid.*, p. 122: "For most of us this identification [of the Messiah with the Logos] is unacceptable because our thinking about the world and about ethics does not lead us to conclude upon a Logos as being [*einen wesenhafter Logos*]. To be sure, the affirmation 'The Logos has appeared among us' had an exciting effect, but the enthusiasm and the rapture of soul which it evoked did not lead with certainty to the God whom Jesus proclaimed."

[42] *Ibid.*, p. 87.

[43] *Ibid.*

[44] *Die Aufgabe der theol. Fakultäten und die allgemeine Religionsgeschichte. Reden und Aufsätze*, Vol. II, pp. 172f.

and the Christian religion are not. "The Christian religion is something lofty and simple and is concerned only about one point: eternal life in the midst of time through God's power and in his presence. It is not an ethical or social arcanum for the purpose of preserving all sorts of things or of improving them. Even the mere question of what it has contributed to the cultural progress of mankind does harm to its spirit."[45] It is an error, therefore, to apply the gospel directly to secular affairs and to deduce detailed prescriptions and statutes for their regulation from it.[46] It is something religious; indeed, it is religion itself and as such a disposition of mind marked by worship in spirit and in truth. Hence it cannot and must not be expressed in laws and regulations or in a worship through signs, liturgical rituals, and idols.[47] Its true nature is threatened if it is linked with or confined to authoritative forms of faith and order, dogma and liturgy, law and hierarchy. Ecclesiasticism, so Harnack affirmed, frequently imposed a terrible burden upon the gospel, but it never succeeded in suppressing its power.[48] However, the most momentous conformity which, he thought, ecclesiastical authority has been wont to require and still requires of Christians is the doctrinal one. This is detrimental to the gospel not because of doctrine as such (though the gospel is not a doctrine!), but because of the fact that, from the beginning, Christian dogmatic thought was combined with Greek philosophy of religion and with the intellectualism characteristic of this philosophy. The result was not only that the Christian faith came to be dependent upon metaphysics but also—and this was an observation which Harnack thought was amazing and shocking—that a "fancied Christ was put in the place of the real one." [49]

IV

These several points are an indication of the program which Harnack advocated (explicitly and implicitly) for Christianity

---

[45] *Wesen des Christentums*, p. 5.
[46] *Ibid.*, pp. 38, 71.
[47] *Ibid.*, p. 141.
[48] *Ibid*, p. 158; *Dogmengeschichte*, 4th ed. p. 82.
[49] *Wesen des Christentums*, p. 140.

in the modern world. In conclusion, we now direct our attention to his major programmatic convictions and recommendations.

We must give priority to a concern which runs through his entire theological work, namely that Christians should be freed from the requirement of holding certain rigidly defined doctrines and of maintaining other traditions only because they are regarded as authoritative in connection with a dogma whose absolute validity is simply taken for granted or affirmed without question. During the negotiations about his call to the University of Berlin he addressed a memorandum to the Ministry of Education in which he made the following declaration:

> Neither exegesis nor dogmatics but the results of church-historical research will break the power of the traditions which are now burdening the consciences of men. Cardinal Manning once made the following frivolous statement: "One must overcome history by dogma"; we say just the opposite: Dogma must be purified by history. As Protestants we are confident that by doing this we do not break down but build up.[50]

Harnack's whole theological work can be regarded as a commentary on this statement. He wanted to see authoritarian dogmatic thinking replaced by historical thinking. He knew how difficult it would be to achieve this goal. For he was aware of the fact that "there is nothing more conservative and unyielding than ordered religion."[51] Indeed, he had the greatest respect for the Roman Catholic Church because it had succeeded in maintaining itself throughout many ages by means of this conservatism. "The Roman Church," he said, "is the most comprehensive and powerful, the most complex and yet most uniform structure which known history has produced."[52]

In order to liberate the gospel from the connection with this powerful institution, Harnack believed that the Reformers had had to renounce in some way the Roman Catholic ideal of building a visible Kingdom of God on earth and of penetrating the realm of nature with the power of grace and holiness; but

[50] November 27, 1888. Agnes von Zahn-Harnack, *op. cit.*, pp. 130f.
[51] *Wesen des Christentums*, p. 104.
[52] *Ibid.*, p. 166.

in order to return the Christian religion to its spiritual core, they had no choice but to effect a tremendous reduction.[53] The result was that the gospel was once more clearly seen in distinction from Roman ecclesiasticism. However, the Reformers did not go far enough. They abolished Roman ecclesiasticism in the name of the Word of God and they assailed its foundations, but they left the dogma intact. Luther had a certain historical sense, and to some extent he was able to apply historical criticism to purely dogmatic authority. For example, he rejected the notion of the infallible authority of the papacy by pointing out that it was the product of changing history. But his thinking was not really determined by historical sense.[54] Hence he was unable to recognize the Scripture as a historical product. For the same reason, he argued that the dogma promulgated by the ancient councils of the church was valid inasmuch as it agreed with the Word of God. The other Reformers, with the exception of a few humanistic representatives of the Reformation's left wing, followed in Luther's train. Hence, so Harnack concluded,

> Protestantism was unable, from the beginning, to develop fully, consistently, and strongly. It continued to be heavily burdened with Catholic remnants. When the Enlightenment finally came to its assistance, it brought with it a certain unproductive self-sufficiency which spoiled everything. Because of this, it failed to recognize the historical element through which faith in God the Father is linked with Jesus Christ.[55]

Modern historical theology must, Harnack contended, complete what the Reformation began. The application of historical thinking to all parts and phases of the Christian religion would make it possible, he believed, for the gospel of Jesus Christ to run a free, unhindered course in the world. "It must become possible," he wrote, "that one may openly say that such and such teachings and affirmations of the creeds are incorrect and

[53] *Reden und Aufsätze,* Vol. IV, p. 338 (in an address in commemoration of Albrecht Ritschl).
[54] *Dogmengeschichte,* Vol. III, 4th ed., p. 867.
[55] *Ibid.,* p. 906.

that nobody is forced to confess in the Divine Service what outside it he does not need to confess."[56]

He hoped that the time would come when traditional dogmatic Christianity would be replaced by an undogmatic Christianity.[57] At the end of his life he stated that he felt a certain kinship with the Congregationalists and the Quakers.[58] There can be no doubt that his whole theological outlook was similar to that of the "theologians" of the American denominations which represent the so-called free-church tradition.

There are three great themes to which he returned again and again in connection with his advocacy of the undogmatic, historical thinking in religion and theology: (1) the canonical authority of the Old Testament; (2) the doctrine of Christ; (3) the unity of Christendom.

(1) In order to release Protestantism from the shackles of literalistic biblicism and the dogmatics connected therewith, and in order to be consistent with the historical interpretation of the Bible—indeed, in order just to "honor the truth"— Har-

[56] Agnes von Zahn-Harnack, op. cit., p. 315.

[57] In this connection, it is interesting to note that throughout his career, Harnack found himself unable to regard systematic or dogmatic theology with the same seriousness which the "dogmatists" were accustomed to demand for it from themselves and others. For example, Theophil Wurm, later Bishop of Württemberg and widely known as a prominent opponent of Hitler, reports that Harnack said in the course of a seminar which Wurm, then a student, attended in 1894 (cf. Theol. Blätter 9 [1930], p. 273) that he would propose the following outline to anyone wishing to write a dogmatic theology: "Part I: The teachings of Jesus and the apostolic interpretation of them. Part II: Mysteries; in this part, he added, one could proceed to speculate as much as one liked." And Karl Barth writes (Kirchliche Dogmatik I; II [1938], pp. 403f.) that in the last conversation they had together, Harnack told him that if he had to write a "dogmatics," he would entitle it: "The Life of God's Children." Barth goes on to explain that Harnack intended by this suggestion to propose the substitution of the traditional kind of dogmatic theology by the personal confession of a Christian who had achieved maturity by letting his thinking be centrally determined by the history of Christianity. See also the remarkable book by Walter von Loewenich, Luther und der Neuprotestantismus. Witten, 1963, esp. pp. 118–29.

[58] Cf. his correspondence with Prof. Erik Peterson, reprinted in the latter's Theologische Traktate, München, 1951, p. 258.

nack felt that the Protestant churches should break with the tradition of treating the Old Testament as a book of canonical authority. In his work on Marcion he wrote (and he was then at the end of his career):

> In the second century, the rejection of the Old Testament would have been a mistake and the Great Church rightly refused to make this mistake; its retention in the sixteenth century was due to the power of a fateful heritage from which the Reformers were not yet able to withdraw; but its conservation as a canonical book in modern Protestantism is the result of a paralysis of religion and the church.[59]

Harnack did not mean, of course, to suggest that Christians, and particularly the historians and theologians among them, should no longer study the Old Testament. On the contrary, he thought that from the historical point of view it would always not only be good and useful but also necessary to read it in relation to the New Testament. But he was convinced that only the New Testament was the basic Christian book and that it alone, therefore, should be held as Holy Scripture.

This view called forth a storm of protest and it still does. Harnack's critics felt that he was assailing the very foundation of Christianity. Karl Barth, for example, responded to Harnack's insistence that Protestantism should "clearly decide" against the canonicity of the Old Testament, by saying: "In respect of this we merely remark that if the Evangelical Church were to do this, it would lose its identity with the Church of the first seventeen centuries."[60] It is difficult to imagine that this point would have greatly impressed Harnack, for his whole proposal was inspired by the realization that, in terms of historical reality, modern Protestantism is not and cannot be "identical" with the church of former ages.[61]

[59] *Marcion: Das Evangelium vom fremden Gott*, 2nd ed., Leipsig, 1924, p. 217.

[60] *Kirchliche Dogmatik* I; II, p. 82.

[61] Agnes von Zahn-Harnack cites (*op. cit.*, pp. 244f.) a letter which her father wrote to Karl Holl with reference to the discussion which his book on Marcion had elicited: "Is it not so that the Ancient Church was not aware of the fact that truth too develops? . . . I did not find it

(2) Of much greater importance to Harnack was his hope that modern Christians would free themselves from the burden of the dogma about the person of Jesus. Even as late as 1925, he said: "By combining all the various affirmations about Christ in the one confession and witness that he is the mirror of God's paternal heart,[62] one can get free from the entire ancient dogma and, at the same time, hold fast to the root of faith."[63] He was sure that it is not possible for any man on the basis of faith or knowledge to make any valid statements about Christ's nature and particularly his "divine nature." Christians must be content with the New Testament and leave room for the same diversity of thought and speech which the early Christians displayed in relation to their understanding of the lordship of Christ.

Harnack looked forward with keen anticipation to the Lausanne Conference on Faith and Order in 1927. He hoped that there the churches would achieve some clarity about Christology. In a memorandum he expressed the opinion that the deliberations of the conference were "a fateful hour of decision for the Christian church" insofar as they would either make a contribution to clarification and unification of a sort the churches had not experienced for centuries or increase the division of Christendom. Then he went on to say:

> There is a significant consensus in Christology. No one denies either the uniqueness or the unity of the person of the Redeemer; nor does anyone deny that the Christian faith is faith in the Father, the Son, and the Holy Spirit and that its universal confession is that in Jesus Christ the Word became flesh. . . . Should we not be satisfied with this consensus as it is expressed in the confessional affirmations that Christ is the "Son of God," the "God-Man," the "Image of God," "Our Lord"? In my judgment,

---

difficult to cause my children to accept the teaching that the Old Testament is now antiquated and only in certain parts still appealing and valuable. It is the law and history of the Jews; *our* book is the New Testament."

[62] This was a phrase of Luther's making (cf. his Larger Catechism). Harnack was very fond of it and used it frequently.

[63] Agnes von Zahn-Harnack, *op. cit.*, p. 161, in an address to the Evangelical-Social Congress.

this should be sufficient, and the churches would leave it to every Christian how he might further conceive the person of Christ. But, as a matter of fact, this consensus is not sufficient in our day; we need a formal decision, for, at the great ancient councils, the churches ordained that one must believe in the *two natures* of Christ and that any statement about him in which this speculation about his two natures is rejected must be considered heretical . . . But, in the course of the last two centuries, numerous Christians have found it impossible to express the faith in Christ through the speculation about the two natures, etc. . . . The Conference on Faith and Order will have to decide whether it shall demand that the dogmatic affirmation [that] Christ had two natures shall continue to be an affirmation of faith or whether it is prepared to reaffirm the faith in the Father, the Son, and the Holy Spirit and, therefore, also in the God-man Christ, but, as far as the churches are concerned, to make no binding rules about any further speculation.[64]

This expectation of Harnack was not fulfilled and has not been fulfilled to this day. No church body has ever officially renounced or given up or modified any dogmatic decision made by the official bodies of the ancient church.

(3) Harnack ardently believed in Christian unity. He was convinced that the Christian religion was the greatest force for the reconciliation of men with one another. He experienced with gratification the awakening of the ecumenical movement and entertained great hopes for it. But he felt strongly that such unity could be brought about only if all intolerance based on dogmatism and doctrinal authoritarianism would be banished from the life of the churches.

v

After the First World War the fashion of theological thinking changed radically. The leadership of Harnack, the historian, was replaced by that of Karl Barth, the dogmatist. The difference between them as to theological method was so great that Harnack, who was one of Barth's teachers, found himself utterly unable to follow Barth. "He was ready to acknowledge

[64] *Ibid.*, pp. 420ff.

Barth's deep seriousness, but his theology made him shudder."[65]

Barth has explained the difference between his own outlook and that of Harnack by pointing to the fact that, following Schleiermacher, all "modern" Protestant theologians pursued their work by proceeding *von unten nach oben* (from man to God) whereas he advocates a method which goes *von oben nach unten* (from God to man). There is much truth in this distinction. But saying this does not necessarily mean that truth is on Barth's side. He begins his theological interpretation with revelation, and God's revelation remains his theme throughout. But the question is, by what right he can begin and proceed in this way. For he is a man and as such he is bound to history and he should therefore be ready (but he is not!) to admit that like all other knowledge also the knowledge of God can be available to him only historically.

Harnack, by contrast, started with the assumption that, together with everything else that belongs to man's realm, the Christian religion also is something historical, a heritage with which every generation has to deal with respect to the past as well as to the future. Is then truth not on his side insofar as he insisted that the only adequate method of dealing with Christianity is the historical one? The discussion of this question will occupy theology for many years to come, and in this discussion Harnack's views will continue to be important.

[65] *Ibid.,* p. 415.

Bibliography

Adolf von Harnack, *What is Christianity?*, N.Y., Harper, 1957. (Harper Torchbooks).

Garland Wayne Glick, *The Reality of Christianity: A Study of Adolf von Harnack as Historian and Theologian*, N.Y., Harper & Row, 1967.

ALBERT SCHWEITZER

Fritz Buri

Albert Schweitzer belongs to humanity. His name and his work are known throughout the world. But even so, and despite the fact that, as it turns out, he has spent most of his life in Africa, he is still an Alsatian and Günsbach is still his home. In Günsbach he grew up, and in Günsbach his house stands—the house, built years ago with his Goethe-prize money, to which he always returned during the years when he still visited Europe, and which even today remains a meeting place for his worldwide circle of friends.

Up the Rhine, a two hours' journey by train, lies Basel. This town, already famous in the Middle Ages, has in recent years become known in all the world as the center where the theologian Karl Barth and the philosopher Karl Jaspers carry on their work. Karl Barth returned to this his home town at the beginning of the Nazi regime in Germany, and Karl Jaspers, having withstood the terrors of that regime, settled down there. In recent years students and scholars from all the world have come to this city on the great northward bend of the Rhine to listen to these two men.

Opposite Alsace, on the right bank of the Rhine, stretches the Black Forest. From this region comes Martin Heidegger, the fourth great philosopher of our era. (Ever since his years at Marburg, Heidegger has been a close friend of Rudolf Bultmann, Barth's opposite number, theologically speaking. It was from Heidegger that Bultmann took over the concept of existential interpretation.) Heidegger's name is bound up with that of Freiburg, the intellectual capital of the little land of Baden. As is well known, he was rector of the Freiburg university during the Nazi years, and since then has lectured there. He still lives in the Black Forest—whence the title of his collected essays, *Holzwege* (Woodland Paths).

Geographically, Günsbach, Freiburg, and Basel form a small

triangle. But in this little space a significant part of the most recent history of theology and philosophy has unfolded. For the names of the four thinkers who are associated with these three places must figure prominently in any account of the newest developments in theology and philosophy. The four men are indeed determinative for these developments, and even to-day are a center of world interest. One could most readily say of Schweitzer that this is not the case; he is the oldest of the four, and his great intellectual accomplishments belong to the first quarter of our century. So far as the theological and philo-sophical world is concerned, he seems to have vanished in the primeval forest. But from there the image of this *homo uni-versale* and friend of humanity shines forth, casting a radiance stronger than that emanating from any of his three younger contemporaries. At the beginning of the century he spoke the word about the eschatological character of the New Testament —the word that Barth (to be sure, in altogether different form: as theology of crisis) took as the point of departure for his own great achievement. On his part, Bultmann accepts as self-evident Schweitzer's argument concerning the primitive Chris-tian hope of the imminent coming of the end and its disappointment through history; and a great deal of Bultmann's opposition to Karl Barth goes back to this circumstance. Schweitzer's philosophical work, which remains incomplete, cannot stand comparison with that of Heidegger or Jaspers. But on the other hand, Schweitzer succeeded in formulating an ethical principle of elemental force and a view of the "decay and rebuilding of culture" with a clarity and a power of convic-tion that are matched neither in Jaspers' thought, which brings everything into a state of suspension, nor in Heidegger's ex-istential analysis of existence (*Dasein*) and philosophy of being.

Thus it appears that these four great thinkers of our time form a group whose interrelations are internal as well as ex-ternal. And this suggests that it would be in order to take a closer look at the significance of Albert Schweitzer in the frame of this "foursome" (to use an expression of Heidegger's). We shall first try to get a clear understanding of Schweitzer's basic concerns, which anticipated those of the three younger men in important respects. Then we shall analyze the relevant positions of the three others in order to show how, precisely against this background, Schweitzer's concerns can be newly appreciated today. In a critical analysis of this kind—an analysis such as Schweitzer himself did not carry out—the significance of his thought for our day can be truly assessed.

I

Schweitzer's theological and philosophical thought moves around two centers: the question of the historical Jesus and the problem of an ethic capable of undergirding culture.

For Schweitzer, the historical Jesus is the eschatological Jesus; that is, the Jesus who proclaims the immediately imminent breaking-in of the Reign of God in the sense of late Jewish apocalyptic. Anticipating the Last Judgment, Jesus preaches repentance, that is, a life lived in expectation of the New Eon. He is convinced that he is destined by God to be the future Messiah, and out of this messianic consciousness of himself he goes to his death, in order to bring in the New Eon and to suffer the tribulations of the End Time vicariously for the elect. Schweitzer arrives at this view of "consequent eschatology," on the one hand, through his research into the history of the attempts to capture the historical Jesus; on the other hand, this seems to him the best-supported hypothesis to clarify the oldest traditions by the methods of modern historical science. The outcome of Schweitzer's research, as stated in his *The Quest of the Historical Jesus,* is the thesis that since the *parousia* failed to eventuate, a de-eschatologizing of the Christian message necessarily set in. This thesis he pursues further in *The Mysticism of the Apostle Paul,* where he shows how Paul can hold on to the eschatological, saving significance of Jesus' death in spite of the contrary course of history: Paul interprets the proclaimed resurrection of Jesus as an emergent breaking-in of the New Eon into the Old, which still persists for a short time. The New Eon thus initiated is continued in the existence (*Dasein*) of the faithful, who think of themselves as those who died with Christ and are awakened to a new life in the Spirit. This is an ethically significant internalization of the Synoptic message of the Reign of God, and one that is in harmony with Jesus' call for repentance. But in John's Gospel it is externalized and made ethically questionable; for in that Gospel the primitive Christian eschatology and the Pauline Christ-mysticism are converted into the sacramental mysticism of the Hellenistic mystery cults—a change that became of decisive importance for the development of the church's Christ dogma.

Using the same methods as in his study of the problem of Jesus, Schweitzer deals with the problem of a worthy culture-ethic. In the two volumes of his *Kulturethik* that are devoted to this theme, and also in his volume on the "world view of Hindu thinkers," he examines the ethical content of various philosophical systems and ascribes positive value to this content in so far as it manifests a will to a culture-informing ethic and seems adequate to that end. Schweitzer shows that this will to culture is weakened, or falls victim to illusions, if it seeks a foundation in events in the world. But neither can it develop a world-forming ethic if, for the sake of its otherness from the world, it retreats from the world. From this problematic, Schweitzer draws the conclusion that ethics, if it is to fulfill its function, cannot take a world view as basis but can issue only out of a thinking will to life. To describe the posture of this will to life, raised to the level of thought and active in all life, he coined the formula "reverence for life." And in our time of decay he sees in that "reverence for life" the foundation for a possible rebuilding of culture.

All sorts of objections could be raised against these theological and philosophical ideas of Schweitzer's; and indeed, though they have been widely accepted and influential, there has been no lack of dissenting criticism of them. But before going on to consider positions held by others—positions from which Schweitzer's points of view might seem outdated and no longer tenable—we must emphasize two aspects of his thought that even today strike us as very modern, because they find parallels in the "foursome" mentioned above.

In his theological research Schweitzer stresses the absolute necessity of a strictly objective historico-critical scientific methodology. And he claims objective validity for his picture of Jesus. But we cannot fail to note that at the end of his *Quest* he speaks of another approach to Jesus. This special approach can be opened up through a single word, a word that, as the expression of Jesus' will, appeals to our will and prompts us not only to translate his message into our own way of looking at things but to obey the call we have thus heard. But, Schweitzer declares, this Jesus—the Jesus whose authority is experienced "from will to will," and in obedience to whom Schweitzer himself undertook his work at Lambaréné—meets us as "an unknown and nameless one"; that is, as one who will not fit into our conceptual schemes. Only as we obey him is the mystery of his personality revealed to us.

In regard to both the understanding of history and the problems of world view and culture, Schweitzer is well aware of the limits of objective, scientific thought and of the necessity and possibility of a direct connection between thought and being. As he sees it, this most intimate connection, which cannot be captured in a system, becomes evident to us as we pursue a way of thought and action determined by "reverence for life": "I am life, that wills to live, in the midst of life, that wills life." The open-endedness of an ethical world view that issues from a thinking experience of the will to life Schweitzer compares on one occasion to a cathedral, incomplete and forever incompletable, in whose choir the spirit ceaselessly worships.

That the formulations of these last two aspects of Schweitzer's thought are questionable cannot be denied. Their character as theology of experience and philosophy of life has been obvious from the beginning. Yet it is plain that they are nevertheless a direct bridge to the theology and philosophy of those three other thinkers—outwardly near to Schweitzer but inwardly very different from him—who have had an important part in helping to stamp the thought of our time through their emphasis on the limitations of science and their insistence on taking the impact of the existential moment into consideration as the basis of every metaphysic and ethic. That indeed is why we see Schweitzer with them as a foursome in the spiritual situation of our time.

II

In its day Schweitzer's "consequent eschatological" view of Jesus and of primitive Christianity had on the whole only a negative reception. It was Karl Barth who more than forty years ago set in motion what might be called a groundswell of eschatologism. This demolished some things that were obviously built on sand, but it has been ebbing for quite a long time now and has become a sort of Black Sea. True, the bibliography of the first edition of Barth's *Letter to the Romans*—which marks the breaking-in of eschatological Barthianism—cites Schweitzer's *Quest of the Historical Jesus.* But the eschatology of dialectical theology has nothing to do with the eschatological Jesus and his message of the emergent Reign of God as Schweitzer worked these out by the methods of scientific history. Even at the time Barth's *Romans* was published, leading New Testament scholars and historians averred that rather than interpret the Roman letter of the apostle Paul, he had put into it the sense of the crisis and impending fall of Western culture that beset him and many of his contemporaries in that first post-World-War period. (Since then, indeed, Barth himself has partly admitted as much.) Barth defended his unhistorical procedure by saying that he recognized historical science and its results as phenomena of this world, which, like everything in this world, stand under the weight of God's word, which breaks in vertically from above. As to the "talk about the nonappearance of the *parousia*," Barth asked: "How could that fail to appear which by its very nature can never come to pass?"—and thereby asked the same question in regard to every theory of salvation history. Every moment stands under the weight of eternity. The essence of the Christian's eschatological situation consists in his becoming aware that all worldly and human things are in a state of crisis. And this is to pronounce judgment on all human cultural activity. According to the theology of crisis, every cultural activity is a new attempt to build Babylonian towers. In this stage of his theology, then, Barth sees only disintegration; he does not admit the possibility of a rebuilding of culture. To be sure, this eschatological nihilism did not remain the final stage of his theology. In one of the later volumes of his *Dogmatik* there is even a section entitled "Reverence for Life." Here the "no" to a world spoiled by sin is canceled by a "yes" to God's good creation, and sin is declared to be nonexistent. But for all its beauty, the old Barth's praise of creation makes us think of a sinking sun that, after the struggle of the day, once more veils everything in a golden glow before it finally goes down and gives way to the night—after which, according to his present concept of eschatology as history of salvation, the true day will break in. Plainly, out of this hopeful but still rather weary evening mood there can develop no ethic that would match the message of him who said: "I came to cast fire upon the earth; and would that it were already kindled!"

III

The case is basically the same with Martin Heidegger. Granted, where Schweitzer took his Jesus-mysticism and his reverence for life as the point of departure for his thought, Heidegger took as his point of departure human existence, which cannot be grasped by the methods of science, and whose statements cannot be confirmed by any world view but stand contrary to all ways of looking at the world. On the one hand, however, in accord with the mood of that time—in which Kierkegaard (against whom Schweitzer had always warned as a sickly thinker) first found real acceptance—Heidegger chose as basis of his existential analysis the desperate situation of man, who sees himself delivered up to nothingness. This stance, of course, makes Heidegger sympathetic to the theology of crisis. On the other hand, Heidegger's existential ontology represents a substitute for the discarded, allegedly scientific world-view systematic; only that Heidegger's system is drafted with other means: so-called existentials of understanding in place of the categories of reason. In the measure that the analysis of this existential self-evidentness is rounded into a basic existential ontology, existence as the starting point is virtually betrayed in favor of a new system, under which the element of risk inherent in existence is surrendered in favor of an absolute standing beyond the subject-object antithesis. That Heidegger has surrendered the concept of existence as something that cannot be objectified but can only be experienced in specific historical materializations, is quite clear now that he has substituted being for nothingness and looks for salvation to a new advent of being—an advent in which being, in defiance of all human attempts to grasp it, will manifest itself in its truth. But this being-event of Heidegger's falls under the same objection that Schweitzer (in *Culture and Ethic*) raised against Hegel's metaphysic of being. Not irrelevant here is the fact that, as Hegel once saw absolute spirit in world history and the Prussian police state, so Heidegger saw the "saving event" in the Hitler regime.

IV

Heidegger's thought became influential in theology chiefly through Rudolf Bultmann. This was, however, his thought in its earliest form, before his "turning"—a way of thinking that, moreover, is probably still misunderstood. Bultmann, to be sure, comes from elsewhere altogether: from that field of theology which deals with historical criticism and history of religion, a field of which Albert Schweitzer was one of the last great consistent representatives. Bultmann never belies his origin. It accounts for his speaking in so matter-of-course a fashion of the nonfulfillment of the primitive Christian expectation of the end and of the obsoleteness of the mythological world-picture connected with it—as if he were totally unaware that, for Heidegger, this kind of scientific understanding of history represents an attempt to usurp being and is therefore a deficient mode of thought.

But as is well known, Bultmann aims not only to demythologize the New Testament proclamation but to understand it existentially—that is, as it bears on (and declares) the self-evidentness of human existence. In this positive part of his basic thesis he purposes to vindicate Heidegger's view of the historicity of existence (*Dasein*): as inner history, in contrast to external history. We are onlookers at external history—as though there were an absolute standpoint outside its relativity; we experience inner history when, waiving such questionable objectivity, we become aware that our life is caught up in it in some indescribable way, that we participate in it. Unlike the categories of external history, the existentials are affirmations of the historicity of our existence (*Dasein*). The eschatological event announced in the New Testament does not take place as an occurrence in the outer and inner world of space and time, an occurrence that can be described in terms of history of psychology; no, that eschatological event takes place where this message is proclaimed and the hearer unconditionally decides for it in his existence. Salvation becomes reality in a faith that newly understands itself.

From the point of view of this existential interpretation of the New Testament kerygma it is clear that Bultmann cannot simply acknowledge the nonfulfillment of the primitive Christian *parousia*-expectation and let the matter rest there; but that, on the basis of form-criticism, he can surrender the last remnants of a life of Jesus in favor of a kerygma of a salvation-event in Christ. (Here he goes beyond Schweitzer, and beyond consequent eschatology, which clung to some shreds of a life of Jesus.) We cannot go back of that salvation-event, because its historical origin—in the Jesus of Nazareth who still belongs to Judaism—is certainly not part of the kerygma's content. The primitive Christian kerygma proclaims not the historical Jesus but the risen Christ—even though in its proclamation of the Easter-event and the results thereof it speaks of none other than this same Jesus of Nazareth.

Today, to be sure, some of Bultmann's pupils are no longer content to accept this *skandalon* as the distinguishing mark of true kerygmatic theology; for in that paradoxical relation between an existentially understood Christ and the historical Jesus they can see no guarantee that this Christ of the kerygma is not after all a myth, no guarantee that the biblical kerygma will not be replaced by an existential anthropology. They fear that the Pauline and Johannine understanding of the kerygma will prove an obstacle to any concern to understand the historical Jesus. So the Bultmannians are setting out again, as Karl Barth mockingly said, to recapture the historical Jesus "with swords and sticks."

Undoubtedly it is possible to set up a picture of the "historical Jesus" on the basis of the Synoptic accounts. But, as is admitted, neither formally (i.e., in regard to the way in which it is arrived at) nor as concerns content (i.e., in regard to what it says) can this picture of the historical Jesus be distinguished from the existentially understood kerygma of the New Testament; rather, it represents only a particular part of this kerygma —that part which comes to expression in the Synoptic witness to Jesus. This method cannot take us back of the kerygma; that is, to the historical personality of the Jesus who speaks in the kerygma; or else we have tacitly discarded the existential interpretation and exchanged it once more for scientific historical criticism. For if we start out from the existential we cannot refer back to the categories of external history for our conclusions. A "historical Jesus" thus arrived at would only be a new edition of the Jesus whom the Ritschlians, in their day, thought they could lay hold of through the experience of faith. Even at that time Schweitzer most decisively rejected the Ritschlian Jesus in favor of a clear distinction between apprehension from history and apprehension "from will to will." Schweitzer's strictures on psychological historicism apply equally to today's existential historicism.

V

That Schweitzer's thought is still relevant today is plain when we compare his positions with those of Barth and Heidegger (and Bultmann and his school). It becomes even plainer when we bring his imitation of Christ through the ethic of reverence for life into juxtaposition with the philosophy of Karl Jaspers. Like Bultmann, Jaspers accepts Schweitzer's insight—which today is largely the common property of Protestant theology—into the significance for dogmatic history of the fact of the nonappearance of the parousia. Though he evinces considerable reserve toward the conclusions which, each in his way, Schweitzer and Bultmann have drawn from this historico-critical point of departure, Jaspers nevertheless counts these two as among today's most important representatives of scientific research into the history of primitive Christianity. True, he emphatically disclaims both Schweitzer's culture-ethic, which he regards as a demythologized form of Christianity, and Bultmann's existential interpretation of the New Testament, which he regards as a consequence of this demythologization. But this disclaimer arises from his basic philosophical position, which is of a different kind and is opposed both to Schweitzer's life-philosophy and to Bultmann's existentialism, as well as to their conception of science.

Schweitzer and Bultmann recognize only two (or three) ways

of understanding: historical science and understanding from will to will (Schweitzer), and faith in response to the kerygma in existential decision (Bultmann). Jaspers recognizes more ways than these. For him, the Schweitzer-Bultmann ways merely represent forms of an Encompassing. This Encompassing, however, takes forms in addition to "presentness" (*Dasein*) with its will to life, consciousness in general, in whose frame all our statements stand; and in addition to existence, which makes an unconditional decision in response to the call of transcendence. But it is not only the more comprehensive nature of Jaspers' periechontology[1] that is important in the context of this essay. What is of the highest importance is that, in consequence of this periechontology, the Encompassing does not in any of its forms reveal itself in an absolute and unequivocal fashion. Whether as presentness (*Dasein*), consciousness in general, or existence (to mention only these three possibilities), in each case it reveals itself as something altogether different from any or all of these, something we cannot grasp from any other point of view either, and dare not absolutize under its special aspect.

This is not the place to consider what this periechontological viewpoint means in regard to the existential ontology of Heidegger and Bultmann. Obviously, Jaspers can judge ontology only as a pseudo science which denies the existential—a pseudo science which in Heidegger's case leads to a romantic-poetic mythology of being, and in Bultmann's (in spite of his intention to demythologize) to a churchly-orthodox kerygma mythology. Where Bultmann does away with mythology, and Schweitzer translates mythology into ethics, Jaspers holds on to the declarative strength of the myth for existence. A science that thinks it can overcome the mythological way of expression not only misunderstands the nature of myth but itself becomes a sort of pseudo myth. And in this Jaspers sees the harmfulness of so-called demythologization.

Viewed in the light of Jaspers' conception of science, even

---

[1] "Periechontology" is an untranslatable coinage, combining the Greek word *periechō*, which means "to encompass, enclose, embrace, contain," and the word "ontology." Dr. Buri relates this term to Jaspers' concept of *das Umgreifende*, which we are here rendering as "the Encompassing."

Schweitzer's concern to translate his consequent-eschatological primitive Christianity into a universally provable ethic of reverence for life represents a sort of pseudoscientific remythologization. The questionable conception of the "thinking will to life" does justice to its real intent only when it is grasped in the sense of Jaspers' conception of existential thinking, i.e., the kind of thinking that is carried on in objective categories—but in that very process revolves around the nonobjectifiableness of the essence of existence, which essence cannot be universally proved but can only be appealed to. Moreover, from the point of view of Jaspers' schema of the Encompassing, reverence for life cannot be developed into a metaphysic of a universal will to life which is in conflict with itself but can be reconciled with itself through human action in love. Only beyond all rationalism and irrationalism can this speculation of Schweitzer's be positively valued as an expression of our understanding of existence. But probably that is what Schweitzer means when he builds a bridge from this crowning conclusion of his ethical thought to the Pauline Christ-mysticism, for in Christ he sees God's love becoming active as a transformation of man into a new creature.

Strangely enough, Jaspers has no sympathy for this eschatological Christ-concept. He sees in it only a God-man mythology which endangers the actualization of existence—a mythology that is evident in the Reformers' doctrine of justification, which was distilled from the original eschatological context of meaning. Because of this ominous misunderstanding of the Pauline Christology—a misunderstanding against which Schweitzer warns emphatically—Jaspers thinks that it is only to the so-called historical Jesus that a positive significance in the history of the human spirit can be attributed. But in this "so-called historical Jesus" Jaspers sees a towering embodiment of the ruin which inevitably befalls the human being (that is, man as an existence) as regards both his understanding of himself and his attempts to realize himself. For Jaspers this inescapable ruin in the border situations of life represents the place whence all patterns of thought are brought into flux and whence man, soaring up to the transcendence that forever eludes him, can experience himself as a present, a gift to himself.

This idea of existence as a present to itself, which man ex-

periences in the flight to the transcendent, is lucidly developed
again and again in Jaspers' philosophy. And indeed this philosophical ground-operation is indispensable for all thinking that
goes to the ultimate limits if it is to be saved from betraying existence to some massivity or other. Yet in comparison with the
vitality and nearness to reality of Schweitzer's thought and
work, Jaspers' thinking strikes us as carried on in exceedingly
thin air and as comprehensible only in a very abstract fashion.
Even so, today Jaspers' philosophy is indispensable for the interpretation and further development of Schweitzer's thought
and work. A Schweitzer understood from the viewpoint of that
philosophy will not have vanished in Africa's primeval forest so
far as we are concerned. Through the medium of Jaspers'
thought we are able to understand the forest physician's message as the direct, prophetic message it is, but also to appreciate
the continuing importance of his thought and research in the
frame of the "foursome" that distinguishes our place in history.

Bibliography

Albert Schweitzer, *The Quest of the Historical Jesus*, N. Y., Macmillan, 1960.

George Seaver, *Albert Schweitzer: The Man and His Mind*, rev. ed.,
N. Y., Harper, 1956.

SØREN KIERKEGAARD

Martin J. Heinecken

Søren Aabye Kierkegaard was born in Copenhagen, Denmark, on May 5, 1813, the seventh and last child of Michael Kierkegaard, a hosier, and Ane Sørendatter Lund. A distant kinswoman, Ane was Michael's second wife and the mother of all his children. She had been a servant in the house and Michael married her shortly after the death of his first wife. The first child was born four months later. This moral lapse, together with the fact that he had once cursed God because of his cruel lot on the barren Jutland heath, plagued the father all his life. When he came to Copenhagen and by a succession of strokes of fortune became a wealthy man able to retire at the age of forty, live in a great house on the square, and spend his time in security and comfort, he could not rid himself of the thought that he had committed the sin against the Holy Ghost and that God was mocking him. The discovery of the father's lapse played a decisive role in the life of the son, turning him for a while away from Christianity but eventually helping him to see that for a stricken conscience, the cross of Christ is the only answer. In fact, one of the decisive elements in Kierkegaard's development was his relationship with his father. He was the child of his father's old age and himself never knew any youth. He grew up in the strange house in the company of an old man who stimulated him with the power of his imagination and with his dialectical skill in debate with some of the more learned men of the town. But the strain of deep melancholy that plagued him all his life and never allowed the unspeakable joy of Christianity to take full possession thus had its natural roots in his heredity and home environment.

Søren was a precocious boy who made up for his lack of physical prowess by his sharp wit. He had a crooked back and walked with a limp, due probably to a fall in his childhood. He had the usual classical education and matriculated at the uni-

125

versity with the intention of studying theology, but the general liberal arts curriculum (languages, philosophy, physics, mathematics) and aesthetic studies (Faust, Don Juan, the Wandering Jew, fairy tales, Socrates, Mozart) engrossed his attention. He was earnestly in search of a cause to which he could give himself with unstinted devotion. The discovery of his father's guilt, followed by a period of dissipation and estrangement from his father, brought him finally, by what he himself ascribed to divine providence, to a decisive Christian experience. After the death of his father, who outlived all but two of his children and feared that he would outlive them all, Søren finished his master's thesis, "The Concept of Irony with Constant Reference to Socrates," and also passed with honors his examination in theology, which qualified him for a call to a parish.

There were two other events by which he felt that God was guiding him to his life's task. The one was his broken engagement with Regine Olsen and the other was the affair with the *Corsair*. There is no doubt about the genuineness of the love Søren and Regine had for each other, but the day after the engagement Kierkegaard declared he knew he had made a mistake. His diary and long sections of his pseudonymous writings betray the intense struggle he underwent. Finally he broke the engagement in what we can only, by Kierkegaard's own standard, regard as a "teleological suspension of the ethical." There are many surmises as to the reason, but Kierkegaard said he would carry the secret with him to the grave. "But there was a divine protest, that is how I understand it."[1] In *Fear and Trembling* he takes as his point of departure the story of Abraham and Isaac to show how unquestioning obedience to the divine command may involve a man in a "teleological suspension of the ethical" and so isolate him from the universal that it is impossible for him to communicate himself. The knight of faith who, like Abraham, receives back from God that which he gave up to him in trust, is to be distinguished both from the "knight of infinite resignation" who merely resigns himself to his loss and the "tragic hero" who, like Agamemnon with Iphigenia, makes his sacrifice for the sake of a greater gain. Kierkegaard realized

[1] *The Journals of Søren Kierkegaard* (London, Oxford Univ. Press, 1938), p. 93.

that he himself was not the knight of faith, but he did recognize what it meant to be one.

It was his refusal to marry that let loose the floodgates of his literary activity. Henceforth he devoted all his time to writing and in a few short years produced a body of literature which for its rich diversity in the realm of the aesthetic, of philosophy, of ethics, of psychology, of theology, of devotional writing, knows no equal. He praised his mother tongue as the finest and most flexible of instruments with which to give expression to the most profound as well as to the lightest thoughts. His writings abound in wit and humor, they are rich with imagery, they discuss with precision and the utmost dialectical skill the most difficult subjects, they probe to the depths of the human soul. The movement of "existentialism" derives its name from his emphasis upon the unfathomable mystery, the wonder, the terror, the joy and the burden of human existence. Like Socrates, whom he "approached with a palpitating enthusiasm that yielded to none" other than the God-man Himself, he had no interest in the study of the stones and the stars; his interest was in man himself. All his literature was devoted to but one thing. He had found the cause to which he could give himself with unstinted devotion, and that was to make clear in the midst of Christendom what it means to become and to be a Christian.

It was Kierkegaard's conviction that the Christianity of the New Testament was unknown in his day. The theologians and the preachers, led by Martensen, an outspoken Hegelian, were confusing the specifically Christian or biblical categories with those derived simply from the reason of the "natural" or unconverted man. Hegelian philosophy, as was the case with Aristotelian philosophy for Luther, was the object of his ceaseless, scathing attack. It confused God and man, put an end to ethics, destroyed the individual, and for existence as the time of decision it substituted the world historical process in which everything flowed together in a sea of mystification. If the Hegelian interpretation of Christianity were true, then all anyone had to do to become a Christian would be to think straight. Preachers would not be witnesses but professors, and pulpits nothing but lecture platforms. Difficult as some of Kierkegaard's polemic with Hegel is—because it is couched in the same terms—it clearly differentiates individual existence before the living God in the time of decision as man is confronted by the absolute paradox of the God-man, from the sort of monistic pantheism and worship of the state which has culminated in our day in totalitarianism and communism. All these developments Kierkegaard foresaw with amazing clarity. He was the Jeremiah, the weeping prophet of his day, whose clear warnings went unheeded.

The result of the church's proclamation in Kierkegaard's Denmark was that being a Dane and being a Christian were simply equated. Being a Christian meant being a respectable, prosperous, and satisfied citizen, content like a goose being overfed for Michaelmas and with no desire to use its wings and to fly.[2] People lived at the level of either the aesthetic or the ethical and at the level of universally human religiosity, but never became decisively transformed into being Christian.

The second crucial event that finally prevented Kierkegaard from accepting a call to a parish was the attack upon him by a rather dubious scandal sheet, the *Corsair*. Kierkegaard had attacked it in the hope that others would rally to his support. Instead, however, he was left in the lurch when the *Corsair* turned upon him and with a series of articles and cartoons made him the laughingstock of all the north country. It may appear as though Kierkegaard made far too much of this affair, but to one as sensitive as he this was a great blow. It isolated him more than ever and set him with resolution to his single task. Whereas before he had displayed joviality and wit, beneath which was hidden the most frightful melancholy, this was now scarcely possible any longer. He considered this a suffering which providence too had thrust upon him and not a self-chosen martyrdom.

The remainder of Kierkegaard's life was uneventful and was spent almost entirely in writing, until a year before his untimely death he made his uncompromising attack on the church of his day. Fortunately his patrimony was enough to keep him in comfortable circumstances. By the time it had given out, his life, too, was spent—and this, too, he attributed to providence.

[2] *Ibid.*, p. 54.

Except for two brief visits to Berlin and an occasional visit into the north country he never left the city of his birth. But what he lacked in breadth of actual experience in the world he made up for by the prodigious powers of his imagination. One hour on the Jutland heath, he said, was enough to educate a man in the school of possibility, for existence was for him the sphere of possibility where anything could happen and not at all the rationally determined world process necessarily bound to end in the *Kulturstaat*. Necessity, he said, belongs entirely to the sphere of logic, of static relationships, where nothing can happen. But life is not a logical system and history is the sphere of contingency. That is why man, who is free but not absolutely free, can find no security in existence short of coming to rest in the living God.

In order to make clear what it means to become and to be a Christian, Kierkegaard used a method of "indirect communication," sending out most of his books under a series of pseudonyms. This reflects his view that no matter what a man's profession may be, he actually "exists" in a way which may deny his profession. The professor who builds a beautiful castle of thought in which everything follows reason nevertheless lives in the hovel of actual existence by its side. There are thus mutually exclusive levels or stages or spheres of existence. A man will live either at the level of the aesthetic or at the level of the ethical in which the aesthetic is subsumed. Or he will live at the level of the specifically Christian and thus also give the aesthetic and the ethical their place. This is why Kierkegaard was nicknamed by his contemporaries "Either/Or." Either the aesthetic is dominant in a man's life, or he has made the transition by a "leap" to the sphere of the ethical. This "leap" from one existence to another Kierkegaard opposed to the Hegelian principle of mediation. In his view life is not a series of inevitable transitions but of discrete leaps of decision.

The aesthetic life, says Kierkegaard, is the uncommitted life, the life of the moment, the life that recognizes no binding universals but seizes what pleasure and significance it can from day to day. It is typified by the characters in the first volume of *Either/Or* and by some of the characters in *The Stages of Life*, particularly by John, the Seducer. This life, as is evident from the so-called diapsalmata at the beginning of *Either/Or*, is at bottom a life of despair. Instead of presenting such a life in the form of a lecture, Kierkegaard's method of indirect communication lets one see this man in action from the inside and experience with him what it actually means to exist in that sphere. So the reader cannot as a mere spectator know what is meant, but only by inner participation.

The sphere of the ethical is exemplified by Judge Wilhelm in the second half of *Either/Or*. This is the level of the universally human, where a man is guided by the recognition of universally binding ethical norms. It is here that the seriousness of life begins and all of life from the cradle to the grave is a time of trial in which a man must choose either to conform to the universally binding ethical norm or to depart from it. This is the task of life and no one can come to the teacher before life itself is ended and claim that he has finished his lesson and wants something else to do. Present-day interpretations of Kierkegaard which make him responsible for the complete subjectivism and moral relativism of the atheistic existentialists, for whom existence precedes essence and who contend that every individual makes his own values, are seriously mistaken. The ethical existence sphere is for Kierkegaard the sphere in which a man lives actually bound by absolute ethical norms. The ethical man is the one who is related absolutely to the absolute and relatively to the relative, and what makes this life at bottom a life of despair is the recognition that this is for the existing individual an impossibility. But there is a stage beyond the ethical—the specifically Christian—where the categories of sin and faith and love replace those of the universally human ethical norms.

The sphere of the ethical is at the same time the sphere of the universally human religiosity of which all men are capable by virtue of being human without entering into the decisive relation with Jesus Christ. Here lies the crucial difference between a "religion of immanence," in which a man is able to find God (the eternal Truth) within the depths of his own consciousness at any place and at any time because of his basic integrity, and Christianity, the sphere of the paradoxical in which man is forsaken by the hidden immanence of the eternal (the state of sin) and therefore can enter into the right God-relation only by having the Gospel preached to him at a specific time and place. In other words, a man's eternal blessedness depends upon his relation to a contingent historical event: the birth, life, death, and resurrection of the man Jesus. Any man of any generation can become contemporary with this contingent historical event, but only in faith. That is to say, there is no recognition of the revelation of God in Christ and the saving significance of his life and death for the sins of the world unless there is a transformation of existence. Of this transformation of existence any man in any generation is capable in the power of the Holy Spirit. Wherever the Gospel is proclaimed a claim is put upon man's existence; therefore the Gospel is apprehended only in "faith" or in "offense." He who makes the Christian profession cannot do so as a mere spectator, but only by living what he professes and by having passed by means of the leap of "faith" from the universally human religiosity A to the sphere of the specifically Christian religiosity B.

It is these distinctions between the existence spheres which Kierkegaard tried to make clear through his pseudonymous literature. *Either/Or* and *The Stages of Life* depict the first two alternatives. *Fear and Trembling* and *Repetition* point beyond the ethical to the specifically Christian. The *Philosophical Fragments* is his most significant and influential work in terms of establishing, merely as an experiment in thought, the difference between the religion of immanence and the religion of the Christian revelation. This work and its sequel, *The Concluding Unscientific Postscript*, in which the question discussed in the *Fragments*—"Can a man's eternal happiness be decided by his relation to a contingent historical event?"—is given its historical dress in Christianity, have been most important for the break with idealism and the return to the biblical categories which began in Germany with the bombshell of Karl Barth's *Letter to the Romans* (1919). *Fragments* and *Postscript*, written under the pseudonym Johannes Climacus, develop consistently the whole of Kierkegaard's thought. The first book is a model of precision and clarity in writing, coupled with beauty of expression (Swenson's is an excellent translation). There is in the world's literature no apology for the Incarnation that parallels the story of the king who loved the humble maiden and abandoned his throne in order to establish the absolute equality of love. In the second Kierkegaard pulls out all the stops of his genius and uses all the weapons at his disposal—dialectical acumen, sarcasm, irony, ridicule, humor, logic, pathos—in order to demolish Hegelianism and the pseudo-Christianity of his day and make clear the meaning of existence before the living God and the suffering involved in being a Christian who cannot give full outward expression to his absolute surrender to God. Without a grasp of these two books it is impossible to understand Kierkegaard and his influence on both theology and the development of so-called existentialism.

In *The Concept of Dread* and *The Sickness unto Death* Kierkegaard shows his genius as a psychologist of the human spirit, a quite different psychology from that which depends on objective experimentation. Here everything depends on the most astute kind of introspection and nothing is understood about human nature except that which is understood within. In fact all understanding of life itself is seen to be nothing but a form of self-understanding, for man will interpret all of history and its significance always in terms of the way in which he understands himself. True self-understanding, however, is possible only when one is first made known of God. The Socratic maxim "Self-knowledge is God-knowledge" must be reversed.

In *The Concept of Dread* he pseudonymously investigates the psychological state which precedes sin and out of which sin emerges with a leap. This state is that of dread or anxiety, to be distinguished from fear of a definite object and from the various forms of neurotic anxiety as the constant concomitant of man's freedom, which is not absolute. It is this basic undertone of anxiety which is the characteristic quality of man's existence in finitude as a center of responsibility before the living God. Man does not have an essence which is stable and which can maintain itself by itself. The human self is the self in relation to itself and other selves; it cannot maintain itself in equilibrium unless it is properly related to the being that posited it. Thus every man is in his existence confronted with the possibility either of coming to rest in the being upon whom he absolutely depends or of divorcing himself from that being in rebellious self-assertion. It is the latter possibility which every man finds realized in his life of conscious decision. This is the state of original sin in which every man finds himself, having leaped from the state of innocence prior to any decision whatsoever, in which the possibility of being able creates the dread before nothingness, into that of rebellious self-assertion. Adam's story is the common human story. Adam represents himself and the whole human race. At the beginning of human history sin enters by a leap out of the state of dread in which man exists in his finite freedom. Sin is not to be equated with finitude. Sin cannot be explained, but it is to be recognized and repented of. The delineation of the state of sin belongs to the sphere of dogmatics. Psychology can investigate only the psychological state preceding sin, which is the state of dread. The only real escape from the basic anxiety of existence is in the atonement.

In *The Sickness unto Death,* which should be read in close connection with *The Concept of Dread,* under another pseudonym Kierkegaard develops the meaning of selfhood and of the universal sickness of mankind which is despair or, in Christian terms, sin. Every man, whether he knows it or not, is in despair, and this is the only sickness which is unto death, for by it the self is destroyed. The ability to despair is man's superiority over the beast; to be keenly aware of this sickness is the Christian's superiority over the natural man, and to be cured of it is the Christian's joy. With the utmost precision Kierkegaard delineates all the subtle forms which despair takes in the human spirit. Basically all the forms of despair may be reduced to one—the unwillingness to be the dependent self, which in order to realize itself must be grounded transparently in the being that posited it. But this basic form of despair may manifest itself in one's failure to realize that he is a self, so that he merely vegetates instead of existing before the living God; or else in the despair of weakness, which simply succumbs to the fact of its dependency and does not take refuge in the possibility of God; or else the despair of defiance, which asserts itself boldly, making claim to autonomy where this claim is a usurpation. This state of despair is from the Christian point of view sin. It is not ignorance (the Socratic presupposition) but a position willfully maintained. Its only cure is in entering into the right God-relation through the miracle of faith.

While thus developing the meaning of the specifically Christian via his pseudonyms (and it is important for the reader always to keep in mind which pseudonym is speaking), Kierkegaard at the same time from the very beginning published a series of edifying discourses under his own name. These are not sermons, nor are they specifically Christian; though in the sphere of the universally human religiosity, they are for edification and deal with life's crucial situations. Often it is difficult for the reader to see why they are not specifically Christian, but a comparison with the later *Christian Discourses* and *The Works of Love* will show the difference. The difference lies in the mention of the paradoxical faith-relation to the God-Man, Jesus Christ.

When it became clear to Kierkegaard that those to whom he looked for support were not responding to his method of "indirect communication" he moved gradually to more direct address. In *Training in Christianity* and *For Self-Examination* the author calls for a return to New Testament Christianity. He clearly sets forth the nature of the "offense" presented by Jesus who in his lowliness nevertheless called all men unto himself. The Christianity of the New Testament therefore demands surrender to Jesus in his lowliness. There is no entrance to Christianity except through the gate of repentance, the recognition of sin, the surrender of faith, and the willingness to follow in the absolute surrender of obedience. Only then can the Christian life become all joy as it was meant to be. The comfortable life of respectable decency which knows nothing of sin or the offense or of suffering is castigated in no uncertain terms.

When even this more direct speaking failed to produce any response from the responsible authorities Kierkegaard ceased writing and waited. He waited for the death of Bishop Mynster, the respected friend and counselor of his father, whose services he regularly attended and whose sermons he read with the recognition that they were for edification. As long as Mynster was alive he could not bring himself to an open attack on the church. But after Mynster's death, when Martensen at the funeral declared Mynster to have been one of the true witnesses of the faith, the hour for direct action had struck. Even so Kierkegaard waited until Martensen had succeeded to the coveted office of bishop, but then he spared no one. The articles that appeared under Kierkegaard's own name and the series of pamphlets which Kierkegaard himself published under the title of *The Instant* are published together in English as *The Attack upon Christendom.* The uncompromising nature of this attack has been seriously questioned. If everything that Kierkegaard said is taken at face value then there was no shred of decency left anywhere in the church of Denmark either among the clergy, those "shopkeepers souls in velvet," or among the people to whom their Christian confession meant less than nothing except when it became necessary because of the state regulations pertaining to weddings, baptism of children, and funeral rites. According to Kierkegaard, all the priests were cannibals living off the blood of the martyrs, and he advised the people to stay away from the services. He himself refused on his deathbed to receive Holy Communion from a priest, although he would have received it from a layman—a fact which ought to silence those who claim that if Kierkegaard had lived longer he would have returned to Holy Mother Church. Kierkegaard understood the doctrine of the priesthood of all believers and part of his insistence was that only through an actual transformation of life could one come into possession of this priesthood, although the efficacy of one's witnesses did not depend upon this transformation but solely upon the power of the Word of God, which effects the transformation.

Many remonstrated with Kierkegaard for the severity of his attack, but he persisted in the conviction that only if he was uncompromising could he stir the church out of her complacency. As he said again and again, all he wanted was simple honesty, the admission that what was being preached and lived in Denmark was not New Testament Christianity. He knew, as no one else knew, the meaning of grace, and he wanted only that men should recognize their sinfulness and enter into the kingdom of God through the narrow gate of repentance and then live their lives accordingly: "Infinite humiliation and grace and then a striving grounded in gratitude, this is Christianity." Nor is it true that he advocated a mournful Christianity, celibacy, and the monastery. In the *Unscientific Postscript* he contrasts the Trip to the Monastery and the Trip to the Deer Park. His contention is that Christianity is suffering and that this suffering consists in the fact that it is impossible for a man to give unequivocal outward expression to his inward, singleminded devotion, as he is related "absolutely to the absolute and relatively to the relative." Therefore the medieval trip to the monastery deserves credit only for the seriousness of its intention and not because it succeeds in its purpose. The only alternative is fidelity to whatever calling a man feels himself called to by the exigencies of the moment. For Kierkegaard himself this meant the refusal to marry and his becoming the "corrective," the "pinch of spice" called for by the tasteless concoction being dished up as the "bread of life" in his day.

So Kierkegaard persisted in his merciless attack until one day he fell unconscious in the street. He spent several weeks in the hospital during which time he retracted nothing but, like Socrates, remained true in the hour of death to the manner of life he had lived in the market place. According to eyewitnesses he grew more ethereal as the end approached, and he died in the conviction that the joy which in this life had been denied him would be his in the eternal mansions through the merits of Jesus Christ his Lord. So his life was spent together with his patrimony in the pursuit of one objective: to make clear in Christendom what it means to become and to be a Christian.

KIERKEGAARD'S IMPORTANCE

The immediate effects of Kierkegaard's call to repentance in Denmark were negligible. A few of the clergy took it seriously and effected genuine reform. Some, like Ibsen's Brand, misunderstood and in their fanatic devotion only succeeded in wrecking the lives God alone could heal. Kierkegaard had to wait a hundred years for his day to come. Not only Karl Barth and his followers and in this country the so-called neo-orthodox school but all of Lutheranism, both in Germany and the Scandinavian countries and elsewhere, and particularly the free churches in England, in fact all of Protestantism as well as Roman Catholicism, have felt his influence. The theology of the future must inevitably come to terms with the issues he raised and the answers he gave.

Not only theology but also philosophy and psychology and the whole field of literature and the arts owe their debt to Kierkegaard in the development of that vast proliferation known as existentialism and covering everything from the preoccupation with the sordid side of life to the loftiest humanism in a world where God is dead and man as the only spearhead of freedom must in the full anguish of sole responsibility create his own values. In the vast Kierkegaardian literature there is enough for the greatest extremes to find something on which to capitalize and to outdo the master in following the whims of lonely subjectivity, but Kierkegaard must be allowed to speak for himself and he has made abundantly clear where he stood. In several treatises ("The Point of View," "The Present Age") he clearly elucidates the whole plan of his authorship and prophetically anticipates the course of human events in the development of the mass man and the loss of the individual in the monster of totalitarianism.

In addition to his view of the stages of life and of what constitutes authentic human existence, the following are distinctive elements in Kierkegaard's thought.

Christianity is absolute paradox. A paradox confronts one with a fact that is contrary to appearance, contrary to the general opinion, and also with propositions which are contradictory when used in attempted description of the fact. It is Kierkegaard's contention that while many paradoxes which confront us in life may be resolvable, either by clearer vision or greater knowledge, Christianity presents us with the absolutely paradoxical, i.e., with paradoxes which no existing individual, precisely because he exists in time and space and is not pure spirit, can resolve. For God there is no contradiction, but for the existing individual the contradiction remains. This is true, first of all, of the central fact of Christianity, the appearance of God in the flesh. No docetism, no Jesus of history, no rational Chalcedonian Christology nor any of the other attempts to resolve this paradox have been able to do justice to the full mystery of the incarnation in its once and for all uniqueness. That God was in Christ reconciling the world unto himself is true, contrary to appearance, for God does not appear visible to the senses in the carpenter of Nazareth and the man on the cross. It is true, contrary to the general opinion, for it is not the general opinion of men that the death of one can atone for the sins of all or even that there is need of such atonement. It is true, but not because man's reason gives him indubitable certainty that it could not be otherwise, or because by the accumulation of evidence a high degree of probability can be established for it. He who recognizes it to be so must first become transformed in his existence. He needs to recognize his predicament in sin and his need of a Saviour. Therefore the absolute paradox is that which blocks the way to a mere intellectual acceptance of certain propositions about God and confronts man with the living God Himself, to whom a man must surrender in "faith"—which is itself a paradox, inasmuch as it is at the same time the work of God in man that it is a human decision. The only alternative, therefore, to this God-wrought faith in which a man is absolutely humbled before God is an equally God-wrought "offense" in which the cross of Christ remains a stumbling block to the various forms of man's pride. And what is true of the central fact of the Christian faith, the Incarnation, is true also of all the specific Christian categories. They are all paradoxical and as such irresolvable by the existing individual. This is true of the mystery of the *creatio ex nihilo,* the fact that man remains lifelong a sinner and at the same time righteous, the fact, above all, of the resurrection from the dead. In fact, except in terms of the absolutely paradoxical it is impossible to make clear what is meant by the absolute miracle of grace in man's creation, redemption, and sanctification without reducing it to the merely astonishing. Here Kierkegaard was adamant. The only thing that he understood about the absolute miracle of God's love was that he did not understand it.

There is an absolute qualitative difference between God and man. This is the corollary to the recognition of the absolutely paradoxical, for it is precisely because the difference between sinful man and the holy God is not one of degree only but of kind that there is no resolution of the absolutely paradoxical until the end of the time of decision and the turning of faith to sight in the resurrection of the dead. It is a misunderstanding to suppose that this means a denial of the creation of man in the image of God or that it makes impossible any communication whatsoever with an absolute transcendent God, cut off by an unbridgeable chasm from his creation. The point is simply that it is not possible to get by degrees from the category "created and sinful man" over into the category "God." God and the world are in no sense necessary corollaries and between them there is no simple continuity. God's creation of the world and of man is a contingent and not a necessary event. It is also possible that if God so chose, God and the world should not be. The fact that God is the creator and man the creature establishes an absolutely irreversible relation and hence an absolute qualitative difference. Unless one begins with this premise there is no avoiding some subtle form of pantheism. The absolute qualitative difference therefore finds paradoxical expression in the fact that God is both absolutely transcendent and absolutely immanent, without any confusion of creator and creature. Moreover when Kierkegaard speaks of the absolute difference between God and man he is thinking not only of man as creature but of man as sinner. If God were perfection and man's predicament lay in his imperfection, then the degree of difference could readily be established and perfection quantitatively attained. But when God is holy and man is guilty before him, the sinner can only be redeemed and so spend eternity singing his redeemer's praise.

Truth is subjectivity. This does not mean for Kierkegaard that there are no truths that are independent of the knower. The truths of mathematics are what they are and are discovered by man with the powers of his reason. All the facts of life and history exist in time and space independently of being known by any particular individual. Above all, God is what he is, and he did what he did for man's redemption whether anyone believes it or not. In the moral realm it does not mean that each individual man is the measure of all things (Protagoras) and that all beauty is only in the eye of the beholder; there are ethical universals binding on all men. What Kierkegaard is insisting, however, is that God, the eternal truth, is not apprehended except in inwardness. There is no such thing as an "objective revelation" if by this is meant a direct visibility of God. It is paganism that believes the gods are directly discernible. God, when he is present in his creation, is discernible only in inwardness, with the eyes of faith. When God does appear he, the absolutely other, appears in the absolute likeness of man. Thus revelation and faith (or offense) are always corollary, and although God is "objectively" present whether discerned or not, there is, by definition, no revelation except where God is actually discerned. This discernment, however, always takes place in inwardness and can never be established in any other way. This inwardness is that of either "faith" or "offense" because revelation always puts its claim upon a person. This is the recognition that the Bible is testimony literature, witnessing to acts of God which do not appear as acts of God except to those who have been apprehended by them or to whom their claim is an offense. Jesus was the promised Messiah only to those who surrendered to his claim. To the others his claim was an offense. So there is no way to "prove," either from the fulfillment of prophecy or the "signs" he performed, that he was the one to come, since both signs and prophecies are susceptible of a different interpretation. Revelation is thus discerned in the inwardness of individual transformation. The Christian is reduced to being a witness to the mighty act of God in Christ. His method is that of "indirect communication." When he witnesses in both word and deed, nothing is communicated directly from speaker to hearer or from actor to observer; but when man witnesses, God communicates himself. This is the work of the Holy Spirit.

Hence Kierkegaard by no means destroys the so-called objectivity of revelation, reducing everything to a form of self-understanding, but he does insist on taking revelation seriously as revelation, and he takes seriously the Holy Spirit.

This also explains Kierkegaard's emphasis upon the individual. Each individual, in the strict isolation of his inwardness before God, must hear God put his claim upon him. Men enter one by one into the kingdom of God through the narrow gate of repentance as the sheep enter one by one into the sheepfold, each one known by his own name. As each one dies his death alone, so each one comes to faith alone in strict inwardness. This, however, is no denial of the fellowship of believers, apart from which no one can be a Christian.

It is in his analysis of existence that Kierkegaard has been most influential in the area of philosophy and psychology. Kierkegaard opposed the Hegelian notion of a world process unfolding with some kind of rational necessity and therefore bound to culminate in a certain way. There was no one quite as repugnant to him as the don who had read off the whole course of history in this fashion. History was for Kierkegaard the sphere of contingency, not of necessity. History, that of the individual as well as that of the world as a whole, is shaped by contingent acts of decision on the part of both God and man. Necessity is a logical category which belongs to the sphere of static relationships in which nothing can happen, as in mathematics and formal logic. Life, however, is not a logical system. This is Kierkegaard's so-called irrationalism—that reason is not the final arbiter, but existence itself in all its arbitrariness. God himself is love and not reason. The Logos that became flesh is not the world reason but the creative Word that brings into being that which it speaks.

For Kierkegaard, therefore, existence means man's peculiar predicament as the creature of God, dependent absolutely for his being upon that God's creative fiat. Yet man is a self, a center of self-awareness and of decision, who shapes himself by his decisions. This is precisely the precariousness of man's existence—that he is free to shape himself. There is no pattern to which he must necessarily conform. This enables an atheistic existentialist like Sartre to declare that in the absence of any God "existence precedes essence" and man therefore is precariously free to make himself into whatsoever he chooses within the limits of the particular givenness of his time and place. Man *is* this freedom, responsible to no one but himself and therefore beset with all the anguish and forlornness each decision entails, inasmuch as there is no God to forgive and no second chance and no way of altering a decision once made and acted upon. Kierkegaard, however, differs from this view, because for him man's existence is always responsible existence before the living God and because man was made in the image of God to reflect what God is, namely, love. All of life is the time and sphere of decision, in which man is on trial for eternity. The basic insecurity of life itself and man's involvement in sin can be escaped only in the "moment" of encounter with God in

Christ. Security is possible only in faith, peace of conscience is possible only in the forgiveness of sins, there is no "beyond" the tragedy of life except in the resurrection of the dead. Man does not escape life's involvements by escape into another realm of the eternal and unchanging, nor can he in this life progressively overcome the limitations of his finitude. He can only move forward into the new possibility that God alone creates in the "moment" of renewal. History remains the stage on which men are on trial for eternity.

Kierkegaard's importance for philosophy lies in the fact that he has turned the attention of the philosophers to an analysis of existence itself, a so-called phenomenological description of the human situation. This is what both Heidegger and Sartre attempt to give, operating, however, on the premise that there is no God and that if there is no God then man has no right either to assume a heaven of ideas to which his life is to conform. Atheistic existentialism takes seriously the alternative to faith in the living God and is thus a sort of vindication of Kierkegaard's *Either/Or*. "Rational metaphysics" is no substitute for faith in the living God. The alternatives are faith in the living God, a resolute nihilism, or a humanism that asks for no help from the skies.

Here lies Kierkegaard's importance in the field of Christian apologetics. There is no cogent rational defense of the Christian faith from outside the circle of revelation itself. Any defense of the faith is shameful and insidious betrayal. Christianity can only be proclaimed, so that it will put men before the clear choice of either "faith" or "offense." Christianity, therefore, must be distinguished not only from all the other religions of the world but also from all reasoned world views. The questions of ultimate concern are not answered by man in the predicament of his sinful existence, but must be answered by God Himself. Jesus is not the founder of a religion, but in him God speaks and acts in the fullness of time. This is where the so-called crisis theology got its impetus. The meeting with Jesus Christ is possible in any generation in the "contemporaneity of faith" (or offense). This meeting (*Begegnung*) is God-encounter and not a reasoning toward God. It creates a real crisis, a turning point, in which "eternity enters time" and creates the new. That is why also all "natural theology" with its reasoning toward God succeeds in producing only idols. God must be met face to face with his unequivocal claim and not arrived at as the end of an argument. There are some philosophers who recognize this and who have therefore given up the building of systems and the attempt to get a view of the whole while still enmeshed in existence. They consider their task to be the much more humble one of analysis, the Socratic task of the clarification of thought and of being the gadfly to all who are trying to understand. To this movement Kierkegaard may be said to have given impetus by his own attempt to make clear distinctions.

Kierkegaard hated what he called the "paragraph vulture," the person who gulps down a man's contribution to thought in neatly packaged form. What he dreaded most of all was to be appreciatively mentioned in the textbooks of the enlightened future and assigned his place in history by some pretentious don. Anyone, therefore, who writes about Kierkegaard must cry for absolution. Kierkegaard should be read himself or he should be left alone. He must be read in the way he intended to be read and in the context for which he wrote. Then the Either/Or with which he confronts the reader will be clear enough, as well as the sense in which he is and remains the "corrective" for every compromising theology and wishy-washy Christianity. Christianity is a radical cure and not a mild, sugar-coated sedative. To read Kierkegaard is to know what he has to say particularly to our age when the individual is lost in the mass and when general religiosity is confused with the specifically Christian and all awe and fear and trembling have disappeared from the God-relation.

Bibliography

Søren Kierkegaard, *A Kierkegaard Anthology*, Robert Bretall, ed., N. Y., Modern Library, 1959.

Walter Lowrie, *Kierkegaard*, N. Y., Harper, 1962, 2 vols. (Harper Torchbooks).

P. T. FORSYTH

Robert McAfee Brown

I ask'd the Lord that I might grow
    In faith and love, and every grace;
Might more of His salvation know,
    And seek more earnestly His face.

Instead of this, He made me feel
    The hidden evils of my heart,
And let the angry powers of hell
    Assault my soul in every part.

Lord, why is this? I trembling cried,
    Wilt Thou pursue Thy worm to death?
" 'Tis in this way," the Lord replied,
    "I answer prayer for grace and faith.

These inward trials I employ
    From self and pride to set thee free;
And break thy schemes of earthly joy
    That thou may'st seek thy all in Me."

(Olney Hymns, 1799, Book III, 36)

These words by John Newton (1725–1807), a twice-born slave-trader turned preacher, may not qualify as great poetry, but they describe an experience that rings a responsive note in the hearts of other "twice-born" Christians. And they furnish perhaps the most important clue to an understanding of the development and mature thought of Peter Taylor Forsyth, who on one occasion referred to them as "one of the greatest and most realistic utterances of Christian experience,"[1] and on another occasion, describing the course of his own spiritual pilgrimage, said that to him the words were "almost holy writ."[2]

[1] Forsyth, *Positive Preaching and the Modern Mind* (London, Independent Press, 1949), p. 106.
[2] *Ibid.,* p. 195. This section of his Beecher Lectures is the only place where Forsyth deals in any detail with his own theological pilgrimage.

144

The title of Newton's hymn is "Prayer Answered by Crosses," and if it is true that in his lifetime Forsyth experienced more than his share of personal crosses, it is even truer that the power to endure them came from his conviction that Christ had endured his cross in such a way that no other cross could finally threaten any of Christ's disciples.

Forsyth can be described in many ways, but perhaps the truest way would be to describe him as a theologian of the cross, provided we immediately add that his concentration on the cross did not mean a minimizing of the rest of the Christian message, but rather that the rest of the Christian message received its most concentrated expression in the cross. The holiness of God, the primacy of grace, the centrality of Christ, the significance of history, the basis of conduct—everything that is the proper concern of Christian theology and living was examined by Forsyth and illumined for him within the shadow of the cross of Christ, a cross that casts a shadow only because behind it is the bright light of the gracious God who has visited and redeemed his people.

BEYOND ORTHODOXY AND LIBERALISM

Forsyth did not come to this faith easily. It was a "hardly won" faith, possible because of a divine gift rather than a human achievement, based, as he once said, on atonement rather than attainment. It was a faith constantly under attack by Forsyth's contemporaries. The orthodox wrote him off because of his espousal of such things as biblical criticism, while the liberals (perhaps smarting under his strong attacks on them) looked on him as hopelessly out of date. The fact that he fits no theological pigeonhole is one sign of his enduring greatness. The gospel, he always urged, cannot be scaled down to any human system of thought. He has been called a forerunner of neo-orthodoxy, a "Barthian before Barth," a liberal evangelical (which is not the same thing as an evangelical liberal). But no tag quite fits, and he remains simply a man immersed in the good news of the Bible, particularly as seen through the eyes of the Reformers and Paul.

Forsyth was born in Aberdeen in 1848 in what were, even by

standards of a century ago, "humble surroundings."[3] He graduated brilliantly from Aberdeen University, spent a semester in Germany studying under Ritschl, and was ordained to the Congregational ministry in 1876. After serving in several important English parishes, he became principal of Hackney College, London, in 1901, a position he held until his death twenty years later. Beneath this apparently uneventful series of happenings an entire theological revolution took place. Reacting against a sterile orthodoxy that was crumbling under the impact of biblical criticism, Forsyth was at first a left-wing "liberal"—unashamedly so, as some of his earliest writings make clear. But in his pastoral contacts and, just as important, in his own life, he found that the liberalism of his time had no power. Its recasting of the Christian faith had a hollow sound. Forsyth gradually worked his way back from liberalism to the Bible, and through the Bible to the "Word behind the words," the gospel of the grace of God in Jesus Christ, a gospel contained in the Bible but not identical with the words of the Bible. "I was turned," he writes in a key sentence, "from a Christian to a believer, *from a lover of love to an object of grace*."[4] By about 1893 the new position had been secured, and a collection of Forsyth's sermons[5] preached before the turn of the century shows evidence of most of the themes that he was to pursue in his later and larger writings.

Forsyth was genuinely convinced, for reasons we shall presently examine, that the liberalism represented by R. J. Campbell's "new theology" represented the most serious threat to the Christian gospel since second-century gnosticism.[6] But he did not merely indict; he elaborated an alternative to what he rejected. One of his most frequent words in this endeavor was "positive"—he advocated positive preaching, a positive gospel, positive belief. But it must be clear that he did not advocate

[3] A full account of Forsyth's life is given in W. L. Bradley, *P. T. Forsyth, The Man and His Work* (London, Independent Press, 1952), and more briefly in my *P. T. Forsyth: Prophet for Today* (Philadelphia, Westminster, 1952).

[4] *Positive Preaching and the Modern Mind*, p. 193 (italics added).

[5] *God the Holy Father* (London, Independent Press, 1957).

[6] The terms of Forsyth's indictment can be found *inter alia* in *Positive Preaching and the Modern Mind*, Ch. VI.

what now goes by the name of positive thinking—a self-help religion astonishingly similar to the type of liberalism on which Forsyth turned his sharpest polemical weapons. But this word must stand as a reminder that for Forsyth the theologian's task had not been completed when the inadequacy of the alternatives had been exposed. At that point the task had merely started.

Honors came to Forsyth during his lifetime. He was elected chairman of the Congregational Union of England and Wales in 1904, gave the Beecher Lectures at Yale University in 1907, received a D.D. degree from Aberdeen University, and was recognized as one of the outstanding theological thinkers of his generation. But we have already indicated that during his lifetime he swam against the current theological currents. His return to the Reformers, to Athanasius, to Paul, set him against what he called the "sunny liberalism" in early twentieth-century Britain. Fifty years ago he was quoting Kierkegaard approvingly, but when he quoted Harnack it was in an effort to refute him. Men professed to find Forsyth's style too difficult—one critic compared his writing to "fireworks in a fog"—although the complaint may have arisen from his use of such difficult notions as regeneration, atonement, and reconciliation. But Forsyth recognized that a popular following was not the index of the truth of the free grace of God; he often quoted Melanchthon —"Our greatest enemies are the accommodating theologians" —and equally often stated that the proper theological stance in a day like his own must be modeled on Athanasius *contra mundum*.

So he was out of step with his own theological generation. He appears to be rather more in step with the current one, if it is too much to claim that the current generation is finally in step with him. The impact of two world wars has removed the heady optimism that seemed in Forsyth's lifetime to make his "positive gospel" redundant to forward-looking Christians. The external crisis of the 1950's and 1960's only serves to illumine the inner crisis that men always face, the permanent *krisis* of which Forsyth wrote so brilliantly. As a result, there has been in recent years a kind of "Forsyth renaissance" among younger churchmen in the Anglo-Saxon (and, interestingly enough, in the Japanese) Christian world. His major works have all been reprinted, thanks to the imaginative foresight of Independent Press and the indefatigable industry of Forsyth's daughter, Mrs. Jessie Forsyth Andrews, who has edited each volume for republication. Contemporary theologians of all stripes are finding that Forsyth speaks a word to them, and through them he is speaking a word to a wider audience than he ever had in his own lifetime.[7]

The Word and the World

What is his message?

Forsyth wrote so widely, in the course of twenty-five books and hundreds of articles, that a capsule version of his theology would be impossible. The books alone deal with the following range of subjects: art, the church, the holiness of God, Roman Catholicism, death, grace, homiletics, socialism, missions, prayer, marriage, authority, church and state, theodicy, war, the cross, the person of Christ, the work of Christ, the sacraments, and eternal life. And yet they have a unity. With a consistency almost unbelievable, Forsyth takes every topic with which he deals and examines it in the light of what it means in a world where there has been an empty cross and an empty tomb.

His method of doing this is one of his most important contributions, and this method we can only describe as christological. (Here is where Forsyth clearly foreshadows the emphases of the later Barth.) He insists that Christ is not only the Omega, to whom our thought must finally come and in bondage to whom it must finally be made captive if it is to be truly free, but Christ is also the Alpha, the beginning; and if we do not truly start with him, there is little chance that we will truly end with him. Long before the Continental theologians had made the antithesis popular, Forsyth was writing about "The Word and the World" and urging that the greatest decision the church continually has to make is whether to begin its life and thought with the former or with the latter. Forsyth was convinced that theology starts down a dead-end street when it starts with the

[7] It is a matter of continuing surprise that only one of his volumes—and one of the less significant—has been reprinted in the United States.

world, with man's "natural" experiences and reactions, his philosophies and schemes, and assumes that there is an easy transition from these to the heart of the gospel. In an atmosphere where this is the prevailing current of opinion, the first word of the gospel must be a judging and condemning word, pointing out that such an elevation of man's schemes is no more than an elevation of man himself, and that it quickly becomes the primal sin. It is not "natural" to kneel at the cross or see in it the only adequate revelation of the grace of God. There must be a radical break from "the speculative reason or the instincts of the heart" if the gospel of God's grace is to make its way into man's life.

This is not anti-intellectualism. If we are brought to the place where we see that our human schemes do not lead us to God but actually lead us further and further away from him, we may be brought to a radical change of footing in which we *start* with God's grace revealed in Jesus Christ and from that vantage point alone discover that we can proceed in faith and confidence. This is Forsyth's way of affirming that the Christian pilgrimage is a matter of "faith seeking understanding," and of affirming that understanding does indeed increase where faith is strong. "To begin with the world is to become dubious about the Word; whereas to begin with the Word is to become sure about the world. A philosophy can bring us to no security of a revelation; but a revelation develops a philosophy or a view of the world."[8]

"The Word," of course, is Jesus Christ, the Word made flesh. It is not the words of the Bible—here is where Forsyth breaks with views of plenary inspiration so popular in his day—but the One to whom the words of the Bible point. Since we could not know the Word apart from the Bible, any theology worthy of the name must be a biblical theology. But if we stare too intently at the words themselves we can miss the living Word behind them. Thus biblical criticism is not an end in itself; it exists, and it exists in honor, as a servant of the Word, as a means through which the Word can shine forth more brightly than before. There is a kind of criticism that is destructive of

[8] *Positive Preaching and the Modern Mind*, p. 170.

the gospel; Forsyth felt that Harnack's efforts at reconstruction had been particularly devastating. But rather than letting the radical wing of German critics sweep the field, he met them on their own battleground and used their methods for creative rather than destructive ends.

PROPER THEOLOGICAL METHOD

It was partly in terms of this intramural struggle for a proper understanding of the Bible, as well as in terms of the extramural struggle with contemporary culture, that Forsyth stressed the right of theology to employ methods proper to the nature of its subject matter. He insisted that it was improper and "unscientific" to take methods appropriate to the natural sciences for the investigation of *impersonal* data and insist that they be used to investigate the very *personal* claim about a Saviour of mankind from its sin and guilt. To Forsyth this demand, which is always being pressed upon the church, was a "dogmatism" far outweighing the supposed dogmatism of the dogmatic theologians. To proponents of such a claim Forsyth wrote, "You are doing to religion what you fiercely resent that religion should do to art or science. You are limiting its freedom by a foreign dogma."[9] Christian theology, concerned with One who saves from guilt, has every right to employ categories appropriate to the content of such a claim, and the categories will be categories of will and personality rather than slide rule and test tube.

But we must be aware that this concern was focused not only by the church's extramural battles, but was and is *the* issue within the church as well. It is the perennial temptation of the church to scale down its proclamation to terms that make it compatible with "the modern mind." When this happens, the norm becomes the modern mind, to which Christ must be accommodated, rather than a Christ with whom the modern mind must come to terms. If this is true, then Forsyth's insistence on the priority of the Word, and the legitimacy of the character of the Word dictating the categories of appropriate investigation, is a message the church needs to hear at every stage in its history, even though the precise terms of the basic conflict may differ in different ages.

[9] In *The British Weekly*, February 17, 1910, p. 557.

It must not be assumed that such a conclusion leads to cultural or intellectual obscurantism. There is the patent fact that it did not lead Forsyth to any such obscurantism, but rather intensified his concern in cultural areas, as the mere review of some of his book titles will indicate: *Religion in Recent Art; Socialism, the Church and the Poor; Christ on Parnassus, Lectures on Art, Ethic, and Theology; Marriage, Its Ethic and Religion; The Christian Ethic of War.* But more important is Forsyth's contention that a proper priority of the Word makes possible a proper understanding of the world, so long as the world is seen in the light of the Word. The gospel, Forsyth feels, must take seriously those insights about the human situation that come from the social sciences (e.g., the right of the individual to freedom from external authority) and from the physical sciences (e.g., the indubitable truth contained in the doctrine of evolution). Christians have much to learn about the human situation from non-Christians, and Forsyth wrote long articles about Hardy, Ibsen, and others to prove the point. He recognized that Aeschylus had much to tell the Christian theologian, and that Shakespeare could challenge a weak theology. But culture's gift to man is not so much a providing of answers as it is a showing forth of the depth of the human problem. In doing this it can point man beyond inadequate answers toward the one sure answer to human sin and human guilt (about which Ibsen and Aeschylus know so much)—the answer that is found in Jesus Christ and his cross. There are many schoolmasters besides the Law.

But it is not an easy step from culture to Christ; it is a gap. The gap is finally bridged by the movement from Christ to culture rather than vice versa, and only in the perspective of that movement can the continuities and the discontinuities be properly assessed.

"A Gracious Experience Which We Must Declare"

Theology, then, must be the servant of the Word who is Jesus Christ and grant him the priority that is rightfully his. This means neither believing doctrines about him (which was the error of the old orthodoxy) nor reducing his significance to that of an inspired teacher (which was the error of the new liberalism). It means recognizing that in Christ we have to do with "a gracious God" who transforms us through his relationship to us.

> The first feature of a positive gospel is that it is a gospel of pure, free grace to human sin. . . . The initiative rests entirely with God, and with a holy and injured God. On this article of grace the whole of Christianity turns.[10]
>
> To that gospel of grace, as we are continually sent forth from it, so we must continually return, to adjust our compass and take our course. . . . It is more than our base, it is our source. . . . Our theology is not a fixed system we must accept but a gracious experience which we must declare.[11]

"A gracious experience which we must declare." This raises a point of importance not only for the understanding of Forsyth but for the Protestant venture as a whole. Protestantism is often interpreted experientially; Catholicism is represented as having "fixed dogmas" while Protestantism is represented as a religion of experience. There is a certain truth here, but it is no more than a half-truth. No one inveighed with more fervor against equating Protestantism with "the right of private judgment" than did Forsyth. And yet no polemic against the autonomy of personal experience must be allowed to slip over into a polemic against the fact that faith must be experienced. For if the latter polemic is permitted, acceptance of the gospel becomes no more than acceptance of a number of intellectual propositions about the gospel. Forsyth often tried to indicate the fine line here by pointing out that *what* is experienced is more important than what is *experienced*. If the stress is simply on content, the result is creedalism or orthodoxy of a sterile kind. But if the stress is simply on experience, the result is subjectivism with no strings attached, in which the only norm of truth is vividness.

Faith, then, has a content, and its content is the Word of God incarnate in Jesus Christ who suffered on a cross for the sins of the world and was raised from the dead. But faith must also be an experience of this content, so that the "sins of the world" include "my" sins. In another of Forsyth's distinctions,

[10] *Positive Preaching and the Modern Mind,* p. 144.

[11] *Faith, Freedom and the Future* (London, Independent Press, 1955), pp. 119-20.

faith descends *to* experience but does not ascend *from* experience. Faith originates elsewhere than in ourselves; it originates in the decisive act of God in Jesus Christ, and that act has objective reality whether we acknowledge its reality or not. But that act exists in order to be acknowledged by us, and when it is, the life of the believer is changed. The gospel is not dependent on our experience for its validity. But its validity is confirmed in our experience.[12]

It is "a gracious experience," an experience of grace, "which we must declare."

REVELATION AS REDEMPTION

What must we declare? We must declare Jesus Christ. What must we declare about him? To this question the bulk of Forsyth's writings are addressed. There is no one book in which he has said it all systematically, although he comes closer to being a "systematic theologian" in *The Person and Place of Jesus Christ* than elsewhere. But so overpowering was the person and work of Jesus Christ to Forsyth that, as we have already intimated, his understanding of Christology shapes everything he wrote.[13]

Since Forsyth looks upon revelation primarily as deed rather than word, as act rather than declaration, a full understanding of who Christ is will be found not in what he said but in what he did. This does not mean that Jesus' teachings lack importance but that by themselves they are not a sufficient index of his importance. For this reason, among others, we must read the synoptics in the light of the epistles, realizing that it is from within the atmosphere of the epistles that the synoptics were actually written. Furthermore, we must not expect that Jesus will *say* everything that is to be said about who he is and what he does; instead he will *do* it, and the saying of it, the description of it, will be the task bequeathed to his followers.

[12] Forsyth develops these themes with great persuasiveness and in great detail in *The Principle of Authority*, 2d ed. (London, Independent Press, 1952).

[13] In what follows, I am drawing in part on the structure of my chapter on "The Cruciality of Christ" in *P. T. Forsyth: Prophet for Today*.

Christ came not to *say* something, but to *do* something. His revelation was action more than instruction. He revealed by redeeming. The thing he did was not simply to make us aware of God's disposition in an impressive way. It was not to *declare* forgiveness. It was certainly not to *explain* forgiveness. And it was not even to *bestow* forgiveness. It was to *effect* forgiveness and to set up the relation of forgiveness both in God and man.[14]

If Christ did not come to "preach the gospel," he did become a gospel to preach. He did what needed to be done and left to his followers the task of proclaiming what he had done, so that subsequent generations might enter into the orbit of the saving power of his deed.

This has important consequences for an understanding of revelation. It means, as Forsyth put it, that "revelation is redemption." God's revelation is not a report by someone (a prophet, an inspired teacher, or even a Son of God) that God is holy and gracious love; revelation is an act by which, at infinite cost to himself, the God of holy and gracious love restores us to fellowship with himself. It is not merely making plain that there is a chasm between holy God and sinful man; it is itself the bridging of that chasm. It is "creation instead of exhibition," "renovation instead of innovation," "resurrection instead of communication."[15] Revelation effects what it exhibits. A full understanding of revelation, therefore, comes only to those who have in fact been redeemed by it. It is not something that can be examined in an abstract, uninvolved way. The one who knows what revelation is, is the one whose life has been redeemed from sin and guilt and who has become a "new man" in Christ Jesus. "The article of Christ's deity," Forsyth writes, "is the theological expression of the evangelical experience of his salvation."[16]

THE WORK OF CHRIST

What does all of this mean for theology? It means something crucially important. It means that we are first confronted by

[14] *God the Holy Father*, p. 19.

[15] See Forsyth's contribution to *The Atonement and Modern Thought*, p. 80.

[16] *The Person and Place of Jesus Christ* (London, Independent Press, 1948), p. 74.

what Christ *does,* and that only thereafter can we begin to understand who Christ *is.* Put differently, it means that we can understand the *person* of Christ only when we have understood the *work* of Christ. Put still differently, it means that we can understand the meaning of the incarnation only when we have understood the meaning of the atonement. To know Christ is to know his benefits.

Now regardless of how Melanchthon came to feel about the latter statement (which he excised from later editions of the *Loci Communes*), it was a principle of utmost importance to Forsyth. The early Christians, he argued, were first confronted by the fact that in the cross of Christ a new relationship between God and themselves had been established. It was out of their indubitable experience of this new relationship that they went on to ask, "What must we affirm of one who could do this for us?" The work of Christ was and is the key to an understanding of his person. Forsyth felt (and he may have pressed this point too far) that theories about the person of Christ, as embodied in the later creeds and particularly that of Chalcedon, tended to become more and more speculative, and that they stood at a considerable remove from the heart of the gospel. A theory about Christ's person, he reasoned, was a secondary matter when compared to the reality of Christ's work. We must of course, he continued to reason, work out theories about Christ's person once we have been caught up in the reality of his work. Forsyth's most creative single book, *The Person and Place of Jesus Christ,* is an attempt to do just that. But this kind of analysis can proceed only if it is recognized that the redemptive deed has been done and that everything has been changed by it.

Everything. The redemptive act of God in Christ was cosmic in its dimensions. A "subjective" atonement was too weak to bear the burden of the full New Testament, Forsyth felt. An objective deed has been done. The relationship between God and the world has been changed. Men live in this new world, whether they are aware of it or not. This view (which can be compared to the "classic" view of the atonement presented in Aulén's *Christus Victor*) has significance not only for individual men but for the whole race, not only for a personal relationship to God but for an understanding of the meaning and sweep of human history.[17] We live in a redeemed world. Evil is still rampant—obviously. But its power is limited, for the real battle between God and the power of evil has already taken place. It took place on the cross. The last judgment is past. It took place there. Its effects are simply being worked out. This means that the Christian, while he must be concerned about evil in the world and is called upon to do battle against it, need never be overwhelmed by it. He may be perplexed, but not unto despair. Indeed he can be of good cheer, for he knows that Christ has overcome the world.

> The evil world will not win at last, because it failed to win at the only time it ever could. It is a vanquished world where men play their deviltries. Christ has overcome it. It can make tribulation, but desolation it can never make.[18]

Against this vast backdrop, in which Christ is seen as "the center of . . . history,"[19] we must underline certain further things Forsyth says about the cross. Not surprisingly, Forsyth looked upon the cross as something done primarily for the race rather than for the individual. Christ offers a complete and perfect obedience on behalf of all men, and his obedience is more important than his suffering. Part of Forsyth's stress on man's solidarity in guilt, and the need for a solidary deliverance, may have come as a reaction against the overemphasis in his day on religious individualism, but basically Forsyth stressed the point because it was what he found throughout the Bible, where God deals with his *people,* his chosen people, and with individuals as they are a part of that people.

> The first bearing of Christ's work was upon the race as a totality. The first thing reconciliation does is to change man's corporate relation to God. Then when it is taken home individu-

---

[17] Forsyth develops the implications of this in *The Justification of God* (London, Independent Press, 1948), a book on theodicy published in 1916, in the midst of World War I.

[18] *Ibid.*, p. 223.

[19] Forsyth anticipated Tillich's phrase in a series of Lectures given in 1909 and published in *The Work of Christ* (London, Independent Press, 1948), p. 107.

ally it changes our present attitude. . . . We must, therefore, avoid every idea of atonement which seems to reduce it to God's dealing with a mass of individuals, instead of with the race as a whole—instead of a racial, a social, a collective salvation, in which alone each individual has his place and part.[20]

To say that in his atoning act Christ is effecting (and not merely suggesting) a new relationship between God and man is to say that it is at the cross that we come to know the real meaning of grace. Forsyth was chary of using the word "love" to describe God, since the word had become sentimentalized in his day; when he did talk about God's love, he almost always made plain that he meant *holy* love. Holy love is a love that both judges and redeems. And we shall presently see that for Forsyth the cross is both the judging and redemptive act of God. But it is grace rather than love that most characterizes Forsyth's understanding of the cross. An atonement is not needed to make God's grace a reality; on the contrary, it is because God's grace is a reality that there is an atonement. Grace is not something Christ earns for us; grace is God giving himself to us in Christ. Quoting an author whom he does not identify, Forsyth writes, "Do not say: 'God is love. Why atone?' The New Testament says, 'God has atoned. What love!' "[21] Thus God and man are not "reconciled" by a third party, i.e. Christ, but God in Christ does the reconciling. Later on, to be sure, Forsyth speaks of the atonement as representing a "change" in God, but this has a special meaning for him:

> The distinction I ask you to observe is between a change of feeling and a change of treatment, between affection and discipline, between friendly feeling and friendly relations. God's feeling toward us never needed to be changed. But God's treatment of us, God's practical relation to us—that had to change.[22]

As Forsyth spells this out, using the story of the Prodigal Son as a human analogy, it is clear that what he means is that "The father's heart is the same, but his treatment must be different."[23]

[20] *The Work of Christ*, pp. 87, 96.
[21] *God the Holy Father*, p. 4.
[22] *The Work of Christ*, p. 105.
[23] *Ibid.*, p. 109.

So God needed no placation, but He could not exercise His kindness to the prodigal world, He certainly could not restore communion with its individuals, without doing some act which permanently altered the relation. And this is what set up that world's reconciliation with Him.[24]

The cross, then, does not exhibit God's changing mind; it is a revelation of God's unchanging mind and of the way in which, out of his grace, he deals with men in such a way that their guilt can be met and overcome.

To effect this new situation, the cross must represent both judgment and reconciliation. Sin must be judged, and it is judged there. But it is the judge himself who takes upon himself the burden of the penalty and curse. "There is a penalty and a curse for sin; and Christ consented to enter that region."[25] Forsyth frequently refers to the fact that Christ was "made sin" for us. So there is a judgment upon sin, but the very nature of this judgment means that it is also a reconciliation.

By reconciliation, Paul meant the total result of Christ's life-work in the fundamental, permanent, final changing of the relation between man and God, altering it from a relation of hostility to one of confidence and peace.[26]

The reconciliation does certain important things:

(1) It reveals and puts into historic action the changeless grace of God. (2) It reveals and establishes His holiness, and therein also the sinfulness of sin. And (3) it exhibits a Humanity in perfect tune with the will of God. And it does more than exhibit these things—*it sets them up*.[27]

THE PERSON OF CHRIST

So much, then, in briefest compass, for Forsyth's description of the work of Christ. The question with which we are now con-

[24] *Ibid.*, p. 109.
[25] *Ibid.*, p. 147.
[26] *Ibid.*, p. 54.
[27] *Ibid.*, pp. 180–81.

fronted is: What must be affirmed of one who could do this? Our treatment of this question can be briefer, for it is a question Forsyth has explored in one piece of sustained writing.[28]

What has just been affirmed about the work of Christ leads Forsyth to three inescapable conclusions about the person of Christ:

1. *His pre-existence.* If a modern man recoils from this conclusion, he must at least try to see the reason why Forsyth was led to make it. The reason is essentially a very simple one: "The soul's saviour could be no less a power than the soul's creator."[29] More fully:

> It was an inevitable rebound of spiritual logic under [Paul's] obsession by the Christ in glory. Such glory, such Godhead, could not be acquired by any moral victory of a created being within the limits of a life so brief as that of Jesus. In a similar application he worked back from the faith that all things were made *for* Christ to the conviction that, as the end was in the beginning, all things were made *by* Christ; and by a Christ as personal as the Christ who was their goal. And so, from the exalted glory of Christ, Paul's thought was cast back, by the very working of that Christ in him and in the whole consciousness of the Church's faith, to the same Christ from all eternity by the Father's side.[30]

2. *His kenosis, or self-limitation.* Once we accept the notion of pre-existence, we are forced to some kind of view of the self-emptying of Christ, if he is to lay aside his glory and become man in the full sense of the word. The problem for Forsyth is not whether there has in fact been such a kenosis but rather how we are to conceive of it. He suggests four human analogies, one of which may be cited here: A student with philosophic gifts has to lay aside his scholarly future because of the death of his father and devote himself to the family business. He gradually forgets most of what he once knew, and the joys of

[28] See Lectures 10–12 in *The Person and Place of Jesus Christ,* and also the earlier treatment, "The Divine Self-Emptying" in *God the Holy Father,* pp. 29–44.

[29] *The Person and Place of Jesus Christ,* p. 277.

[30] *Ibid.,* pp. 268–69.

philosophic thought are relegated to the past. Forsyth comments:

> Is this not a case where a moral and sympathetic volition leads to a certain contraction of the consciousness; not indeed by a single violent and direct act of the will, but by a decision whose effect is the same when it is spread over a life? . . . In applying the illustration to the theology of a kenosis in eternity, where a thousand years are but as one day, the element of time between choice and result in the earthly case is negligible.[31]

We can at least imagine, on these terms, how the eternal Son of God could engage in a similar voluntary contraction of consciousness and enter into the status of a real humanity.

A real humanity—even though he could not sin. Here a limit is reached, but it is not a limit that forces a docetic conclusion, for Forsyth suggests, "What if his kenosis went so far that though the impossibility [of sinning] was there he did not know of it?"[32] If this supposition is correct, it means that Christ's moral struggles and temptations were real and that consequently his is a real incarnation and not simply a theophany. In fact, from this perspective, "self-emptying" is not the best way to describe Forsyth's kenotic view. For he does not suggest that the divine attributes in Christ were discarded, but that they were retracted or condensed. Instead of being actual, they became for a time only potential. The "self-reduction" of God better describes the situation than the self-emptying. Omnipotence, for example, is not surrendered in this view; kenosis in fact provides a superior way of understanding what omnipotence really is.

> There was more omnipotence (if we can so speak) concentrated in the person of Christ than was spread in all creation. To appear and act as Redeemer, to be born, suffer, and die, was a mightier act of Godhead than lay in all the creation, preservation, and blessing of the world. It was only in the exercise of a perfect divine fullness (and therefore power) that Christ could empty and humble himself to the servant he became.[33]

[31] *Ibid.*, pp. 298–99.
[32] *Ibid.*, p. 301.
[33] *Ibid.*, p. 315.

3. *His plerosis, or self-fulfillment.* Many christological interpretations stop with kenosis. For Forsyth this is not enough. The self-humbling of Christ must be matched by an increasing fullness and glorifying of Christ. Through his entire lifetime, Forsyth asserts, Christ is growing into what he actually is. If in his kenosis Christ represents God's movement toward man, in his plerosis he represents man's movement toward God. In the latter he comes to fuller and fuller communion with his Father. His life is not static but dynamic, and the reality of his growth is assured because of his kenotic ignorance of his inability to sin. In this single personality, then, we have the movement manward and Godward that sums up the meaning of who God is and who man is and how they are related to one another.

What is the point of all this speculation? We may let Forsyth answer the question:

> What we have to ask about Christ, then, is this, what account of him is demanded by that work, that new creation of us, that real bringing of us to God, not simply in nearness but in likeness? We are to think about Christ whatever is required to explain the most certain thing in the soul's experience—namely, that he has given it the new life of God and mercy, and saved it from the old life of guilt, self, and the world.[34]

One may disagree with the specifics by which Forsyth carried out this program, but one cannot deny the validity of the concern to which he here gives such concrete expression. One who is dissatisfied with what Forsyth has done is under the necessity of providing a more satisfactory answer to Forsyth's inescapable question.

THE FACT OF THE CHURCH

But none of this can be left in an individualistic setting. Forsyth is not only a Christian but a churchman, and a high-churchman at that. He would, in fact, deny that one can be a Christian without being a churchman. Rather, he insists (and the italics are his): *"The same act which sets us in Christ sets us also in the society of Christ. It does so ipso facto, and not by a mere*

[34] *Ibid.,* pp. 346–47.

consequence or sequel, more or less optional. To be in Christ is in the same act to be in the Church."[35]

The church is not a human club established by like-minded individuals who want to get together occasionally; the church is the instrument established by God through which the fullness of the gospel is manifested. It is not a second chapter in the story of the Christian life, it is part of the initial chapter: "To be in Christ is *in the same act* to be in the church."

And since to be "in Christ" is possible only by the grace of God made known in Christ, so too the note of grace will be the note by which the life and message of the church are known. Speaking to his fellow "free churchmen" in Britain, Forsyth could write as early as 1896:

> The Church's changeless note is grace. The charter of the Free Churches is free grace. And the Free Churches are the inevitable response to that freedom of grace which is the one article of the gospel and the one source of the Church's being and well-being alike. If that ceases to be our note, we must cease to be at all.[36]

The place to see most clearly the nature of Forsyth's churchmanship is in his treatment of the sacraments. There is much in the first half of *The Church and the Sacraments* that is now dated, but there are few things in the whole Forsyth corpus more exciting or relevant today than Part Two, which deals with the sacraments.

Since the sacraments are means of grace, they must point unfailingly to the supreme embodiment of grace, the Word made flesh, and make that Word a living Word for us. "The sacrament of the Word is what gives value to all other sacraments. They are not ends, but they are means to that grace."[37] The sacrament of the Word can be communicated to believers by baptism or the Lord's Supper or preaching or Scripture or other means as well. All these can be sacraments of the Word as they

[35] *The Church and the Sacraments* (London, Independent Press, 1947), p. 61–62.
[36] *The Charter of the Church*, p. 6.
[37] *The Church and the Sacraments*, p. 141.

"convey" (a favorite word) the gospel to the believer and "bring home" (another favorite) to the believer the reality of the grace of our Lord Jesus Christ.

> The Word and the sacraments are the two great expressions of the gospel in worship. The sacraments are the acted Word— variants of the preached Word. They are signs, but they are more than signs. They are the Word, the gospel itself, visible, as in preaching the Word is audible. But in either case, it is an act. It is Christ in a real presence giving us anew his redemption.[38]

As this quotation clearly shows, Forsyth will not settle for a notion of sacraments as "memorials" or reminders. They may be that, but they are more than that. They are *acts*. They *do* something. In them the Word comes alive with re-creative power. Following Augustine, Forsyth can refer to sacraments as the Word made "visible." Nor is he afraid of terms like "real presence." For the sacraments convey grace and do not merely exhibit it.

His treatment of the baptism of infants is a case in point. At a time when this "ceremony" was being looked upon as a "dedication" of the parents, fittingly observed in a private home, Forsyth insisted that baptism—and particularly the baptism of infants—was an act *of* the church and *for* the church and that it "made visible" the true nature of the gospel of prevenient grace. Where does the church more vividly set forth the true nature of the gospel entrusted to it? The child does not know God, yet God claims him. The child does not choose God, yet in the act of baptism is made visible the fact that God has chosen him. Later on the child will have to do something about what God has already done. But the latter step, taken by the child at confirmation, will be no more than an acknowledgment of the reality of the former step, taken by God at baptism. When faith comes, it will be acknowledged as a gift, a gift made possible because grace has already been bestowed. "Infant baptism is a means of exhibiting to the whole Church and world this right relation of grace and faith, that grace precedes and is

[38] *Ibid.,* p. 176.

the condition of faith, that it is not its reward, and that the element of time between grace and faith does not wither nor change the grace and its power."[39] The act is not so much, at the moment, for the child as for the church. It is still proclamation *by* the church, but it is also *for* the church, since it conveys to those present the true reality of grace, the reality that as it is with this little child, so also is it with all those present whom God has chosen: "You have not chosen me but I have chosen you."

And all of this—church, Word, sacrament, congregation—not for the sake of an institution, but for the sake of a gospel that cannot be separated from earthen vessels like institutions any more than it can be equated with them. So there must always be prayer for the church, as Forsyth well recognized:

> We beseech thee, O Lord, for thy Church throughout the world. May it grow in the faith of the cross and the power of the resurrection. Keep it in thy eternal unity, in great humility, in godly fear, and in thine own pure and peaceable wisdom so easy to be entreated. Make it swift and mighty in the cause of the Kingdom of Heaven. Cover, stablish, and enlighten it, that it may see through all that darkens the time, and move in the shadow of thy wing, with faith, obedience, and sober power.[40]

CONCLUSION

A friend of mine, defending Forsyth's style against an over-rationalistic seminarian, once described it as a typical expression of "celebration theology," meaning by the term that every word Forsyth ever put on paper was an occasion to celebrate the reality of the good news, and call attention to the fact that something had really happened, and that therefore nothing could ever be the same again. This is one reason Forsyth is an exciting theologian; he is so obviously caught up in what he is writing about and so aware that the issues he is discussing are momentous. Many men disagree with Forsyth. Some of them

[39] *Ibid.*, pp. 220–21.
[40] *Intercessory Services for Aid in Public Worship*, p. 8.

accuse him of being hard to follow. A few have even accused him of being dull. But no one could ever accuse him of being trivial. It is the large issues he deals with, and he deals with them in such a way that lesser versions of the Christian faith are made uncomfortable in his presence.

When we are tempted to an individualistic Christianity, he reminds us of the inescapability of the church; when we tire of theology, he reminds us that an undogmatic Christianity is a contradiction in terms; when we want a "simple Jesus," he points out that our reconstructions are at the farthest possible remove from the New Testament; when we reduce the love of God to a magnified version of human emotion, he thunders to us of holiness and judgment and grace; when we scale our gospel down to what is palatable to our hearers, he challenges us with the stark alternatives of the Word or the world, and will brook no middle ground no matter how clever we are in answering him; when our preaching settles into mild exhortation, he confronts us with the necessity of preaching that is vigorous proclamation.

And yet, fortunately, such is the nature of his message that he cannot produce "followers." To be a "Forsythian" would be the greatest betrayal of all. Forsyth was first and last concerned to produce disciples. But not disciples of himself.

Bibliography

P. T. Forsyth, *The Person and Place of Jesus Christ,* Grand Rapids, Eerdmans, 1964.

Robert McAfee Brown, *P. T. Forsyth: Prophet for Today,* Philadelphia, Westminster, 1952.

II
Between the Times

RUDOLF OTTO

Bernard E. Meland

Rudolf Otto was the most memorable figure of my student days at Marburg University in 1928. I shall not easily forget my first glimpse of him. On my first Sunday afternoon in Marburg, having arrived from America only a few days before, I called at his home on Rotenburg Strasse. The maid, having managed to make out my garbled request, said one word, *"Augenblick,"* and hurried away to bring Professor Otto to me. I never actually heard Otto come. He just seemed to arrive, an invasion of hushed austerity. Professor Otto said two words: *"Bitte herein."* His towering, erect figure and kingly head, crowned with white hair that bristled upward, caused one to draw back a bit. Here was a presence! *"Der Heilige,"* as he was called by the students, was all you had expected him to be.

My year at Marburg was the last year Professor Otto lectured in the university. He retired at the close of that school term, having completed thirty years of teaching and research. Despite the fact that a persisting illness plagued him throughout that final year of teaching, I remember his lectures as being crisp and orderly, delivered with a directness that commanded attention. Otto spoke as one having authority. And authority is precisely what he had in the field of his special concern.

Rudolf Otto was born on September 25, 1869, in a town called Peine, twenty miles southeast of Hanover. He was educated at Erlangen and Göttingen, receiving his licentiate in theology in 1898 at Göttingen. In the same year he became a *Privatdozent* at Göttingen and remained on its faculty until 1914. During that time he was a colleague of the philosopher Edmund Husserl (1859–1938) and of the Friesian scholar Leonard Nelson. These two influences were to manifest themselves in Otto's own methodology. He left Göttingen in 1914 to join the theological faculty at Breslau, where he remained only three years before going to the University of Marburg. Here he was to rise to eminence as one of the major theological voices of postwar Europe.[1] And he continued to live in Marburg until his death in 1937.

Otto began as a Ritschlian theologian. Ritschl had been a member of the Göttingen faculty for a quarter of a century (1864–89) and his influence was still being felt in that place and elsewhere when Otto came to Göttingen as a theological student toward the close of the century. Harnack at Berlin and Herrmann at Marburg were at the height of their influence as exponents of the Ritschlian school. Students from America and Britain, who were to become eminent theologians in their respective countries, were finding their way to these centers for graduate theological study. Rudolf Otto belonged to the younger generation of Ritschlian theologians who had begun to turn back upon some of the emphases which had marked Ritschlianism in its earlier years. In this he was joined by his contemporary Ernst Troeltsch (1865–1923), who, like Otto, was concerned about the specific nature of religion but resisted the Ritschlian tendency to identify religion and Christianity. Otto went further in his deviation from the mainline of Ritschlianism by renewing a concern with philosophical inquiry preparatory to his effort to establish the religious a priori, and by acknowledging the mystical tradition as a fruitful source of data bearing upon numinous experience.

If one were to designate the central vein of Otto's scholarly concern, to which he directed inquiry along various lines throughout his theological career, it would be the teleology of the holy as disclosed in numinous experience. For it was in this dimension of man's experience, Otto believed, that the markings of religious specificity lay. The source of this notion is many-sided. Otto attributes the notion in its modern form to Schleiermacher who, he claimed, "rediscovered the *sensus numinous*."[2] Yet his own concern with it, he tells us, was prompted

---

[1] Cf. C. H. Herford, *The Post-war Mind of Germany and Other European Studies* (Oxford, Clarendon, 1927), p. 49.

[2] *Aufsätze das Numinose betreffend* (Gotha, 1923). Translated by Brian Lunn as *Religious Essays* (London, Oxford Univ. Press, 1931), pp. 68–77.

by his study of Luther early in his theological career.[8] Otto's
earliest published work, *Die Anschauung vom heiligen Geiste
bei Luther* (Göttingen, 1898), analyzes this problem historically. In later writings he continually refers back to Luther as
one who exemplified this quality of apprehension which conveyed the distinctively religious mode of truth, "the truth of
feeling." Yet it was Schleiermacher who provided Otto with the
initial theological stance by which this mode of truth and this
distinctive form of apprehension could be inquired into. Otto
cites *The Speeches* as being the primary source in this regard.
It is to be preferred, he said, to the later dogmatic work of
Schleiermacher, *The Christian Faith,* which he felt to be more
speculative. If one will simulate the imagery of Schleiermacher's
early work in which the sense of dependence becomes the point
or boundary at which the feeling of Infinite Unity is inferred,
one will have some notion of the starting point in Otto's own
reflections. This is not religious experience in the ordinary
sense of the term but an ontological moment or event, as it
were, in which human perception and the Wholly Other are in
juxtaposition. Otto insisted that Schleiermacher must not be
read simply as one appealing to the normativeness of religious
experience; nevertheless he was aware that the emphasis which
Schleiermacher placed upon God-consciousness in his more
mature theological work seemed to open him to this interpretation. Otto's concern was to center upon this ontological moment, this point of juxtaposition, and to find a way of attending
to the objectively numinous dimension of that experience. For
in this moment, he argued, is to be found the specifically religious occurrence.

Otto was helped in this effort by the philosophy of Jacob
Friedrich Fries (1773–1843), whose thought was being urged
upon the faculty and students of Göttingen at this time by Otto's
colleague Leonard Nelson, an ardent disciple of Fries. Before
examining this resource of Otto's constructive effort, however,
we need to consider his polemic against Darwinism and the naturalism it implied; for it was in this critique that he forged some

[8] Cf. *The Idea of the Holy* (London, Oxford Univ. Press, 1923),
Chap. XII.

essential tools of thought with which to build his case for specificity in religion.

Darwin's *Origin of the Species,* published in 1859, had become a thorn in the flesh of all idealists in the nineteenth century, including the Ritschlians. But the Ritschlians had found a way to circumvent direct argument with Darwinism by designating religion as man's act of defining himself over against nature. In this way the issue between science and religion did not arise in theology. Otto, however, saw this procedure as being too cavalier a way of avoiding the issue. His sympathies were with the Ritschlian solution. In fact one might say that his tendency to define man's spiritual nature over against his physical nature is one aspect of the Ritschlian legacy that persisted in Otto's theology. Nevertheless, his own association with scientists and philosophers led him to feel responsible as a theologian for arguing out the issues, which he did in great detail in his first major work, *Naturalistische und religiöse Weltansicht* (Tübingen, 1904; translated into English in 1907 as *Naturalism and Religion*). Otto's grasp of scientific details bearing upon Darwin's theory of evolution and the various vitalistic alternatives cannot fail to impress any reader. The position he took in discussing this problem is one which had become fairly well accepted among critical thinkers in religion. This was to the effect that evolution is to be acknowledged as an established fact.[4] And the significance of the mechanisms of nature for present forms of personality was in no sense to be denied. What Otto objected to in the Darwinian theory, however, was the claim that the evolution of man as a person is to be accounted for by natural selection, thus ascribing to chance occurrences of adjustment the full credit for man's advance as a human being. In this account of causality, teleology, the phenomenological tract of the Infinite Unity in nature and in human events, went by the board. "Darwin's danger," wrote Otto, "is in its radical opposition to teleology."[5] This is a revealing statement. It not only

[4] This notion was a familiar one in theological literature prior to 1859. Lotze's *Microcosmus* antedates the publication of Darwin's *Origin of the Species,* but it is commonly acknowledged that Lotze anticipated the evolutionary theory, as did others.

[5] *Naturalism and Religion* (London, Williams and Norgate, 1907), p. 89.

expresses succinctly the basis of Otto's aversion to naturalism, but it points to the mode of apprehension which he was to emphasize as being appropriate to religion as a numinous event. It implies seeing phenomena not only in relation to the Infinite Unity, but in terms of what that Unity intends, or toward what it tends. Kant's teleological judgment lay back of this way of thinking, and with it, Schleiermacher's view of Christianity as being a teleological religion.

One might assume that, in these remarks and others, Otto was anticipating emergent evolution. It is true that he was aware of the work of Lloyd Morgan, whom he cited as a representative of "the new vitalism." Otto approved of the direction of his thought in so far as it countered the mechanical theory and moved "towards a deeper conception and interpretation of reality in general, and towards a religious conception in particular."[6] The most important contribution which he saw coming from this new vitalism was "the fresh revelation of the depth of things and of appearance, the increased recognition that our knowledge is only leading us towards mystery."[7] A point that Otto was insistent upon, however, was that "the psychical is not derivable from the physical, does not arise out of it, is not secondary to it, but pre-eminent over it, is not passive, but creative."[8] Here he was asserting his transcendental idealism, which was to say that the source of personality and of man's spiritual dimension is the numinous realm. In mysticism and in the phenomenon of moral consciousness and moral freedom, he wrote, "there is implied something that is inaccessible to a purely rational consideration, and is directly related to mystery and divination."[9] In any effort to understand personality, then, Otto argued, "intuition and feeling must always play the largest role."[10]

Otto's concern to pursue the specifically religious dimension of man's experience thus led him to probe intuition and feeling as being the form in which apprehension of the numinous could be anticipated. In this effort he found the philosopher Jacob

[6] *Ibid.*, p. 275.
[7] *Ibid.*, p. 275.
[8] *Ibid.*, p. 306.
[9] *Ibid.*, p. 325.
[10] *Ibid.*, p. 325.

Fries more helpful than Schleiermacher. In his earlier writings Otto had favored Schleiermacher because of a wider scope in his ideas when discussing intuition and feeling; but in writing his philosophy of religion (*Kantisch-Fries'sche Religionsphilosophie,* 1909, translated as *The Philosophy of Religion Based on Kant and Fries,* 1931) Otto found it necessary to say in a footnote "I am now compelled to withdraw my remarks as to Schleiermacher's superiority to Fries." He had now become of the opinion that "in the philosophy of religion, the points of contact between Fries and Schleiermacher are less important than their points of differences; and where their views agree, Fries is quite original, and closer study proves him to be superior in comprehensiveness, thoroughness, and solidity."[11]

Otto, in discussing Fries's contribution to the understanding of intuition and feeling as modes of apprehending the numinous, points out an interesting linkage between Enlightenment thinking and that of Fries, and thus indirectly with his own in this regard, saying that a characteristic of the theological work of the *Aufklärung* is:

> the conviction that religion must have its own sources and a separate life of its own, not dependent on ingenious scholasticism, on reasoning and logic, on speculation, on learned research, on academic controversy and apologetics, on theological schools, on the grace of philosophers, on toilsome proofs. . . . It has its root in the general emergence of "lay Christianity" at the close of the Middle Ages, which carried the Reformation along with it, was continued in the Independents' Movement in England, and thence progressed towards Deism and "Aufklärung."[12]

In this respect Otto finds the *Aufklärung* to be a continuation "of Luther's way and Luther's mind." "Moreover," he continues,

> Kant's attempts at a philosophy of religion, artificial though they may be, are everywhere a plea for the very simplest lay religion and its assurance. The object of Kant's whole attempt is to make

[11] *The Philosophy of Religion* (London, Williams & Norgate, 1931), p. 15.
[12] *Ibid.,* pp. 34–35.

religious conviction safe from the artfulness of speculative thought and the roundabout methods of scholarship. Here as much as Locke, he appears for the "average man."[13]

It is at this point, Otto observes, and with affinity for this effort, that the work of Fries begins, which "in total contrast to the theosophical systems of his contemporaries" (Otto seems to have Schelling in mind here) "professes to do no more than this: to find a basis for the conviction already given 'by the first simple religious emotion.' "[14]

Fries, building upon Kant's theory of the antinomies, opposed the world of knowledge to the world of faith, demonstrating that "Faith is a form of higher knowledge, with a firm base in the reasoning intellect."[15] This line of reasoning led to his "doctrine of *Ahnung*," expressing "man's deepest need and longing" through feeling—a feeling best expressed as an aesthetic response as in the response to beauty and to sublimity. On the surface this appears to be subsuming religion under aesthetics; but Otto defends Fries against this implication, saying that it is rather a matter of availing oneself of the help which aesthetic judgment affords as a mode of apprehension. In aesthetic judgment we apprehend the unity of things under concepts and ideas in a way that differs from that of logic.

That is to say, in an undefined, obscure manner, by the way of "Ahnung" I gain real knowledge of the universe in a quite particular way, following the supreme laws of its unity and necessity, which are clearly presented in conceptual form in the Categories as a whole, and especially in the completed categories of eternity, spirit, freedom, and deity. In the obscure aesthetic knowledge I recognize, dimly and inexpressibly, ideal existence in the world of phenomena as perceived by the senses, ideal existence in general, without any determination of its particular and individual side. But this is not all. For it is precisely this world, actually known to us under categories and ideas, which is the spiritual world in reality, the world subject to the laws of Good and the Supreme Good, the "best work," the world of the

13 *Ibid.*, pp. 34–35.
14 *Ibid.*, pp. 36–37.
15 *Ibid.*, p. 43.

objective Final Purpose. And thus it becomes clear why the aesthetic comprehension, deep but obscure, is not merely of a "speculative" character; why it presents to the feeling something beyond bloodless forms of unity; why it gives these forms the potent emotional content that goes with them. In aesthetic ideas I gain an obscure comprehension of the unity and connection of true reality in the world of appearance, of this reality in its essential nature; and in so doing I also reach an obscure comprehension of its teleology.[16]

In passing from beauty to the sublime, such comprehension presents itself "with still greater force."[17] This aesthetic comprehension of objective teleology in nature and in individual phenomena, Otto continues, would correspond "to a divination of the world as governed by God in history and in the life of the individual."[18]

Otto is suggesting here that feeling, understood in this ontological context, is a mode of perception which apprehends not simply qualities that are subjective and transitory, but structural meanings, purposes, and tendencies bent on attaining such ends. And in this respect it enables us to see, as through a glass darkly, what is ultimate in the complex of experiences about us. In this sense it provides us with *a feeling of truth,* "the obscure knowledge of the Eternal in general and of the eternal determination of Existence."[19]

Otto's patient delineation of Fries's doctrine of *Ahnung* (a yearning which yields the feeling of truth) can be taken as a preliminary working out of his own understanding of intuition and feeling and of their role in pursuing the specific nature of the religious response. John Moore is correct, I think, when he says: "It is a complete mistake to treat *The Idea of the Holy* as if it were a complete account of Otto's theory of religion, for in it he emphasizes the non-rational aspect of experience in a way which is easily misunderstood unless seen against the background of his other works."[20] It is equally a mistake, I would

[16] *Ibid.,* p. 141.
[17] *Ibid.,* p. 142.
[18] *Ibid.,* p. 144.
[19] *Ibid.,* p. 229.
[20] John M. Moore, *Theories of Religious Experience* (N.Y., Round Table Press, 1938), p. 79.

add, to assume that one may move directly from Otto's earlier to his more mature efforts as if his method of "divination" rested back upon philosophical premises developed under the influences of Kant and Fries. To a considerable degree these influences persist and show through; but Otto was continuously restive under the recognition that both Fries and Kant veered off toward Enlightenment tendencies which elevated the rational and formal aspect of religion, tending to make of it one universal phenomenon. Thus he wrote,

> In Fries, as in the Deists, something which is, after all, wholly "Positive," something which is equivalent to Christian belief with its precise historical stamp rubbed away as far as possible, is taken as the religion, which is then placed in opposition to the "Positive religions."[21]

But the thrust of Otto's thinking was more concrete than this Friesian tendency implied. He was already participating in a mood of inquiry that sought to take particular instances of the numinous seriously even as he undertook to identify the nature of the religious a priori implicit in all of them. This was by way of attending to historical religions concretely and thus to see them in terms of their own specific offerings, while being attentive also to the comparative aspects of these several historical forms of faith.

Eight years after his work on the philosophy of religion had appeared, Otto published the book that was to bring him worldwide recognition, the title of which was *Das Heilige* (1917), translated into English in 1923 as *The Idea of the Holy*.[22] What was significantly new and fresh in this work was Otto's recognition of the fact that the "holy" as a category embraces di-

[21] *Philosophy of Religion*, pp. 146–47.

[22] The position developed in *The Idea of the Holy* has sometimes been represented as being in the nature of a theological retort to the interpretation of religion simply as social phenomena, to which the psychologist Wilhelm Wundt had given expression in his *Völkerpsychologie (Folk Psychology)*, which first appeared in 1910. Otto had written a significant review of Wundt's book, which evoked considerable interest. The essence of this critique, under the title "Myth and Religion in Wundt's *Völkerpsychologie*," appeared in the appendix of the German edition of *Das Heilige*, but unfortunately it was omitted in the English edition.

mensions of reality that go beyond the notion of goodness in the moral and ethical sense. This was one of the early thrusts of theological inquiry breaking through the stereotypes of moralism to which much of liberal theology had become addicted. It had the effect of seeing religious phenomena in a new and strange light, opening up vistas and depths of religious meaning which had long been obscured, and compelling a reassessment of religions, both historically and those near at hand, the dimensions of which had been radically curtailed by an arbitrary imposition of the moralistic measure.

Otto was not dissociating religion from its ethical aspect, any more than he was uprooting it from its rational side. His preliminary effort had been directed toward understanding religion in relation to ethical and rational cateogries. Now he was calling attention to its nonrational and nonmoral aspects. This was tantamount to announcing that religion as a numinous event eludes our human measure even as it participates in human forms. To those for whom all things must be made manageable within human bounds, Otto's thesis implied sheer irrationalism; but Otto was insistent that to speak of the nonrational aspect of the numinous was not the same as declaring religion irrational. It was rather to call attention to the fact that rational and moral descriptions of events are limited ways of speaking about them, viewing them under analogies drawn from human nature and experience and in relation to our human structure of realities. This restrictive way of speaking, he argued, is always distorting to a degree; but the degree of distortion is radically accentuated when we apply our mode of analogical or logical thinking to God and to the holy. In confronting instances which awaken us to these numinous realities, or in simply contemplating them, we encounter "a clear overplus of meaning." It was this "overplus of meaning" in the experiences of the holy which Otto sought to isolate in *The Idea of the Holy*.

We suggested earlier that one will be able to identify oneself with the imagery of Otto's thinking if one assumes the orientation implied in Schleiermacher's *feeling of dependence* in which the noumenal and the human consciousness are in juxtaposition. But this is only a starting point. The direction of Otto's thought is intimated in the correction of Schleiermacher which he. undertakes at this point. For in suggesting the term "dependence," Schleiermacher was employing "what is no more than a very close analogy." Schleiermacher distinguishes the feeling of religious dependence from other forms of dependence in the human situation, but "his mistake is in making the distinction merely that between 'absolute' and 'relative' dependence, and therefore a difference of degree and not of intrinsic quality."[23] The distinction, in Otto's view, is more radical than Schleiermacher implied, for the feeling of dependence in this numinous experience is "qualitatively different from such analogous states of mind."[24]

In this observation one will detect in Otto something of the postliberal emphasis which was to become increasingly more prominent in neo-Protestant thinking. Otto substituted for Schleiermacher's feeling of dependence the term "creature-feeling," which, in his judgment, was more expressive of the objective aspect of the numinous presence and more attentive to the reality outside the self. Furthermore, in applying to the object of this experience of creature-feeling the qualifying adjective *mysterium tremendum,* Otto meant to designate it "a unique 'Wholly Other' reality and quality, something of whose special character we can feel without being able to give it clear conceptual expression."[25]

Having designated the form and quality of the nonrational elements in numinous experience, Otto was at pains to make clear that in all religious discourse the rational and the non-rational traffic together. And all explication of numinous experience in religions takes the form of conveying the simultaneity of these two aspects.

The consciousness of a "wholly other" evades precise formulation in words, and we have to employ symbolic phrases which seem sometimes sheer paradox, that is, *ir*rational not merely non-rational in import. So with religious awe and reverence. In ordinary fear and in moral reverence I can indicate in conceptual terms what it is that I fear or revere; injury, e.g. or ruin in the

[23] *The Idea of the Holy,* p. 9.
[24] *Ibid.*
[25] *Ibid.,* p. 30.

one case, heroism or strength of character in the other. But the object of *religious* awe or reverence—the *tremendum* and *augustum*, cannot be fully determined conceptually: it is non-rational, as is the beauty of a musical composition; which no less eludes complete conceptual analysis.

Confronted by the fact of the non-rational thus interpreted we cannot be satisfied with a mere bare statement, which would open the door to all the vague and arbitrary phraseology of an emotionalist irrationalism. We are bound to try, by means of the most precise and unambiguous symbolic and figurative terms that we can find, to discriminate the different elements of the experience so far as we can in a way that can claim general validity.[26]

Theology, when it is true to its function, is thus "an attempted statement, in conceptual terms and by analogy, of something that at bottom is incapable of explication by concepts."[27]

But along with this sense of the uncanny and the mysterious in religious moments, said Otto, there is the experience of being drawn to this numinous event "as being uniquely attractive and fascinating." This, said Otto, conveys the "qualitative content of the numinous experience," as the *mysterium tremendum* conveys its form. The simultaneity of these two seemingly contradictory effects in the numinous experience, "the daunting and the fascinating," awe and attraction, is what lends depth and power to the religious moment. Man is simultaneously judged and made to stand back before the overwhelming impact of the Wholly Other, yet curiously and irresistibly drawn into its presence as being a visitation of grace. Otto saw in this latter aspect a transition into mysticism. At least mysticism seemed to him to present the most complete instance of "fascination." All religious moments, however, Otto suggested, in which "religious beatitude" or an experience of grace are experienced partake of this dimension of the numinous.

It is instructive to see how Otto dealt with such terms as "sin" and "forgiveness" in this context. These words had all but lost their distinctively religious meaning in the moral and ethical discourse then prevailing. Religion, however much it might em-

---

[26] *Ibid.,* p. 94.
[27] *Ibid.,* p. 53.

brace moral and rational restraints (and this was an important aspect of it for Otto), was seen to him to be first and foremost a thing of mystery emanating from a numinous realm. And when we speak of religious realities such as God, sin, forgiveness, redemption, we are using terms which connote an order, realm, or level other than that conveyed by rational or moral categories. Whenever we press these terms into rational or moral categories, he suggested, we are guilty of reductionism; we ignore the dimension of otherness which they in fact convey and thus profane their meaning. Rather than rationalizing or moralizing these terms, as he found liberals inclined to do, Otto insisted that we are to seek out helpful analogies that will continue to point our thought to what transcends human thinking, that is, to the realm of the numinous; to do so is to recognize the nonrational as being a qualification upon all rational and ethical categories. Accordingly, the righteousness of God, the work of grace, the fact of sin, the act of forgiveness, form a discourse appropriate to the numinous dimension that supervenes experience. Thus whereas Ritschl had defined forgiveness as an attribute of the Christian community founded by Christ, enabling the Christian to remain identified with the Kingdom of God as an ultimate end even as he participated in the Kingdom of sin, Otto sought to wrest this term from the human community as such. Forgiveness, he said, is a numinous act of the spirit transcending moral and rational good and investing them with a higher goodness through the judgment and grace of the holy.

Similarly, sin, in Otto's analysis, took on import beyond that of moral wrong. Sin, he wrote, is

not simply, and probably at first not at all, *moral* depreciations, but belongs to a quite special category of valuation and appraisement. The feeling is beyond question not that of the transgression of the moral law, however evident it may be that such a transgression, where it has occurred, will involve it as a consequence; it is the feeling of absolute "profaneness." But what is this? Again something which the "natural" man cannot, as such, know or even imagine. He, only, who is "in the Spirit" knows and feels what this "profaneness" is; but to such an one it comes with piercing acuteness, and is accompanied by the most uncompromising judgment of self-depreciation, a judgment passed, not upon his character, because of individual "profane" actions of his, but upon his own very existence as creature before that which is supreme above all creatures.[27]

Then Otto adds,

> And at the same moment he passes upon the numen a judgment of *appreciation* of a unique kind by the category diametrically contrary to "the profane," the category of "holy," which is proper to the numen alone, but to it in an absolute degree. . . . It is the positive *numinous* value or worth, and to it corresponds on the side of the creature a numinous *disvalue* or "unworth."[28]

Thus Otto opened up the line that he was to follow in pointing to the source of forgiveness, "the means of grace" which "springs directly from the idea of numinous value or worth," the awe of standing in a *mysterium tremendum* of good in contrast to one's unworthiness.

One will see here some survival of Kant's use of "the idea of value," "the idea of good," etc.; yet it is surcharged with the concrete, magnetic, and operational working of "the thing-in-itself." Husserl regarded Otto's *The Idea of the Holy* as an application of his phenomenological method to the study of religious phenomena. And, with qualifications derived from Otto's own history and creative effort, this in fact is what it was.

Otto was led in his study of the numinous to conclude that there is such a faculty as "divination," that is, a capacity "of genuinely cognizing and recognizing the holy in its appearances." He believed that both Schleiermacher and Fries had in their way rediscovered this faculty and described it in their explication of "contemplation" and "Ahnung," respectively. Both Schleiermacher and Fries, Otto pointed out, had represented this capacity of "divination" to be a universal one. Otto, on the other hand, was willing to speak of this capacity as being "a universal potentiality of man," but what appears as such, he argued, "is by no means to be found in *actuality* the universal possession of every, single man; very frequently it is only disclosed as a special endowment and equipment of particular gifted individuals."[29]

[28] *Ibid.*
[29] *Ibid.*, p. 149.

In view of his having come to this conclusion, it is not surprising that Otto was to give so much attention to the study of mystics, both Western and Eastern,[30] and to look upon mysticism itself as a resource of special significance in the study of religions. In these studies his pre-eminent figures were Eckhart and Sankara. Here, as in everything else Otto touched, the juxtaposition of the rational and the nonrational, the ethical and the holy, was in evidence. Thus he sharply distinguished these mystics of his choice from "the illuminists" with their "fantastic visions, occultism, or miracle-hunting" and found in their mysticism an ethical content along with the experience of grace.

Otto's concern with mysticism as a phenomenological study was genuine; and his own temperament, not to speak of his theological orientation, inclined him quite naturally to the pursuit of this study. Yet it would be a mistake so to emphasize Otto's interest in mystics as to obscure the very genuine concern he had in extending and nurturing a more general sensitivity and response to the numinous in all aspects of Christian life, especially in Christian worship. During the year I was in Marburg, Professor Otto was engaged in a remarkable experiment in liturgical reform, seeking to create within the forms of the evangelical Protestant tradition a service of worship in which numinous experience would be made central and commanding. I have described this experiment in worship in my book *Modern Man's Worship*.[31] The distinctive feature of Otto's order of service was the Sacrament of Silence, which came at the close of the service. The idea of a sacrament of silence, he says, was suggested to him while attending a Quaker meeting in Boston during one of his visits to the United States. It was to be the supreme mo-

---

[30] Cf. his *Mysticism East and West* (N.Y., Macmillan, 1932). (First published as *West-östliche Mystik*, Gotha, Klôtz, 1926.)

[31] (N.Y., Harper, 1934.) See also Otto's *Zur Erneuerung und Ausgestaltung des Gottesdienstes* (Giessen, 1925); *Chorgebete für Kirche, Schule und Hausandacht* (Giessen, 1925); *Liturgische Blätter für Prediger und Helfer* (Gotha, 1926–30); *Das Jahr der Kirche in Lesungen und Gebeten* (Munich, 1927); *Eingangspsalmen für die Sonntage des Kirchenjahres* (Munich, 1927). Otto has discussed "The Lord's Supper as a Numinous Fact" and "The Form of Divine Service" in his *Religious Essays*, Chs. VI and VII. See also his essay "Silent Worship" at the close of *The Idea of the Holy*, pp. 216f.

ment in the service when, as it were, the Wholly Other invaded the presence of the worshipers, confronting them with the magnitude of mystery and beatitude. The service as a whole was conceived within the pattern of a numinous event in which Scripture reading, music, and prayers as well as the sermon were viewed as being preparatory for the period of silence. Thus the Sacrament of Silence, coming at the close of the service, was the climactic experience toward which everything else in the hour of worship moved.[32]

Otto's concern with liturgical reform extended to other aspects of worship such as the writing of new hymns and a new prayer literature. His emphasis was upon creating a sense of urgency and expectancy in worship, consonant not only with his emphasis upon the numinous presence but with what he believed to be the insistent message of the Christian witness, namely, that a new age of salvation had come in Jesus Christ and is an ever-present reality in the Christian community, giving intimation of the coming Kingdom of God. In this, said Otto, is the church's charisma. Around this theme, he believed, a new church calendar should be written, every service addressing itself anew to this expectation.

Otto's concern with numinous experience as a phenomenology of the holy took him also into the field of the history of religions, where his reading and observations were vast. He had learned Sanskrit and thus had access to basic materials in the study of Hinduism and the religions of India, and through his travels in India he was able to observe and study religions close at hand. His translations of Hindu writings from the Sanskrit for the study of Hinduism as well as his studies of Hindu writings form a substantial portion of his published works. In addition to his study of Sankara reported in *Mysticism East and West*, Otto made a study of the eleventh-century Hindu theist Ramanuja, the theologian of the bhakti school. He translated the basic chapters of Ramanuja's system, which he published in 1923 under the title *Siddhanta des Ramanuja*. His book *Indian Religion of Grace and Christianity*, published in 1930, presents a study of Ramanuja's theology together with a com-

[32] I have reproduced one of Otto's Orders of Service in my *Modern Man's Worship*, showing his use of the Sacrament of Silence.

parison of the bhakti religion with Christianity. Otto also translated a number of Hindu texts into the German for the study of Hinduism, including *Dipika des Nivasa* (1916), dealing with the Hindu doctrine of salvation; *Vischnu-Narayana* (1923), one of the basic works in Hindu mysticism; and a philosophic treatise of Brahmanism, *Die Katha-Upanishad* (1936). In addition, Otto published several studies on the *Bhagavad-Gita;*[33] these appear in English in a translation from the German texts under the title *The Original Gita: The Song of the Supreme Exalted One* (1939).

Otto's last major work was his impressive *Reich Gottes und Menschensohn* (Munich, 1934), translated into English in 1938 under the title *The Kingdom of God and the Son of Man*. While this was a further inquiry into the numinous dimension of experience as a study in the history of religions, it can be said to be a kind of summation of his lifelong study applied to the Christian religion, and specifically to the person of Jesus Christ. As the late Joachim Wach pointed out in his moving essay on Rudolf Otto, this study of early Christian reports of Jesus and his teaching throws new light on this material from a source hitherto unnoted. Whereas scholars previously had discussed the relation of Christianity to Jewish, Hellenistic, Egyptian, Mesopotamian, and Syrian religions, Wach observes, Otto brought fresh understanding of "the influence of Iranian notions upon the concept which played so central a role in the Kerygma of Jesus, the idea of the Kingdom of God."[34] In this work Otto revived the theme of eschatology in the New Testament to which Albert Schweitzer had addressed himself a generation earlier. With his notion of the numinous Otto was able to lift up the meaning of the eschatological dimension as the mysterious presence of the end or of ultimate reality operating in the immediate moment of time. Or, as Otto himself put it, "The Kingdom, future and yet already dawning, is in truth a mystery. To grasp this mystery one needs the ability and the desire to

[33] Cf. *Die Urgestalt der Bhagavad-Gita* (Tübingen, 1934); *Die Lehrtraktate der Bhagavad-Gita* (Tübingen, 1935); *Der Sang des Hehr Erhabenen. Die Bhagavad-Gita* (Stuttgart, 1935).

[34] Joachim Wach, *Types of Religious Experience* (Chicago, Univ. of Chicago, 1951), p. 224.

see and hear rightly."[35] Or again, "It was the salvation of the new age which was visible to him who could see the mystery of the Kingdom as already present."[36]

I agree with Wach when he says that "this book actually represents one of the major contributions of the last decade to the understanding of New Testament theology and especially to Christological thought."[37] I would place it alongside Schweitzer's *The Quest of the Historical Jesus* (1910; German edition, 1906) and Bultmann's *The Theology of the New Testament* (German edition, 1948) as being one of three successive landmarks in the study of the problem of eschatology in recent biblical theological thought.

In this work more than in any other, Otto appears to be addressing himself to the specifically constructive theological problem of the New Testament. He does so, however, as a historian of religion, thus allowing his constructive concern to show through only incidentally. What is made clear is that Otto sees "the mystery of the Kingdom" as a persistent and significant dimension of the gospel teaching and thus takes his stand on the side of eschatology—yet in a way that enables him to integrate it with the ethical emphasis. Logically he could see that ethics and eschatology are contradictory notions. Nevertheless, he argued, they go together religiously, and these apparently contradictory dimensions of existence are not to be dissociated. They must be kept together as presenting on the one hand a life of obligation in the present world of existence, and, on the other hand, as holding before us an impending mystery that lends depth and expectancy to our immediate life. This mystery is not just an appeal to the future, but a new reality that in some respects has already come.

Otto followed the route of mysticism in specifying the numinous event, in which the mystery of the kingdom is made known, as the charismatic person of Jesus.

His charismatic gift was not an "accidens" in him, but was of the essence of his person, and helps to reveal its significance.

[35] *The Kingdom of God and the Son of Man*, new and rev. ed. (London, Lutterworth, 1951), p. 138.
[36] *Ibid.*, p. 146.
[37] Joachim Wach, *op cit.*, p. 224.

And only when we understand his person and its meaning is the meaning of his message of the kingdom disclosed. The kingdom for him was the inbreaking power of God into salvation, and he was not a rabbi but an eschatological redeemer, who was an integral part of the eschatalogical order itself. "Charisma" and kingdom of God belong together by their very nature and they illuminate one another.[38]

This much one must say, declared Otto, as a historian of religion; to speak otherwise would be to make a false reconstruction of events. Otto acknowledged that much that the historian of religion concerns himself with in explicating the psychic datum that is presented here will not concern the theologian; however, "the 'charisma', together with the *pneuma,* as an anticipation of the eschatological order is an essential element of a community which is intended to be a church of the Nazarene."[39] For Otto, then, the eschatalogical congregation or community is made the norm of the living church. And he closed with this telling conclusion: "That the church has lost its 'charisma,' that men look back to it as to a thing of past times, that men make it and the inbreaking kingdom belonging to it trivial by allegories, does not show this church is now on a higher level, but is a sign of its decay."[40]

The work of Rudolf Otto has been widely admired wherever an interest in the phenomena of religion has been in evidence and wherever a sensitive concern with the problem of religious faith has been acute. The scope of his influence was worldwide, and the effects of his scholarship, one may venture to say, are to be found among students of religions in all contemporary faiths of the world. Certainly his influence among historians of religion has been deeply felt. And within the period immediately following the publication of his *The Idea of the Holy* the effect of his work upon theology and religious thought, especially in Europe and America, was considerable. It is possible that Otto's chief significance in those years lay in his role as a transitional theologian. The insight which his method disclosed,

[38] *The Kingdom of God and the Son of Man,* p. 375.
[39] *Ibid.,* p. 375–76.
[40] *Ibid.,* p. 376.

making the apprehension of the holy analogous to, yet not coterminous with, numinous moments in experience, represented a revolutionary break through the monolithic world view of liberal theology and philosophy of religion. Otto's achievement here placed him at the forefront of that minority company of sensitive theologians who saw the limitations of the liberal theologians' methodology prior to the 1920's. In fact, among critical scholars Otto's work was the baseline from which other ventures in transcendent thinking were made. It succeeded in restoring to liberal theology a nonrational dimension sufficient to give it overtone and depth. The readiness with which this led to a liturgical renaissance in Protestantism is itself evidence of its re-creative force. For many liberal Protestants of that earlier period Otto pointed the way out of the rational-ethical wasteland into which they had come; yet he did so without denying the claims of either ethical or rational concerns. He restored to Protestant thinking enough apprehension of the holy, as distinct from rational and ethical categories, to enable liberal minds to grasp in contemporary terms the significance of such historic notions as *sacred, tabu, mysterium, demonic*. From this they were moved to recognize the reality of sin as a distinctly religious category to which words like "judgment," "grace," and "redemption" were immediately relevant. The strain, so evident in much of liberal Christianity of the period, to retain these classical words within its rational-ethical vocabulary was thereby relieved if not dispelled. The imagery of Reformation thinking, with much of its feeling tone, was again in force, yet in a way that did not rudely disavow the critical judgment of disciplined, historical thinking.

I think it has not always been recognized how responsive Rudolf Otto was to the stimulus of Luther. His idea of the holy, based upon what he called the numinous experience, was put forth within the context of the ethical problem as a repossession of Luther's sense of sin before the judging grace of a righteous God. His basic intention was to set the ethical category, which in Kantian thought had been made the equivalent of the holy, in a dimension of Otherness, bringing man's own formulations of the good under judgment and rendering it responsive to the higher goodness discerned in the grace of a righteous God.

As a statement of the phenomenology of spirit within that framework of thought it is difficult to see how Otto's formulation of the idea of the holy could be improved upon. For all of Otto's concern with the idea of the holy, however, his thought remains essentially under the dominance of rational-ethical categories. The holy appears as an overtone or supplement to it, but with no radically transforming consequences at the level of rational and ethical activity. Thus the effect upon thought and action appear to be more aesthetic than redemptive. This may not be altogether fair to Otto. Certainly his intentions were otherwise. Yet the ethicism of Kant, however deepened and heightened with a more vivid sense of the Wholly Other, persists. In this respect the dialectical theologians are partially justified in considering Otto to be within the liberal tradition, although some of their statements misinterpret and thereby misjudge Otto's efforts.[41] To identify Otto wholly with liberalism, however, in the static way in which they tend to do, is to overlook the important contribution which his thought made at a critical juncture of theological development. As we have indicated, his thought provided at least an imagery by which the beginnings of a more critical liberalism could be undertaken.

Yet it may not be assumed, I think, that Otto's contribution has been only transitional, his influence limited to the closing decades of the liberal era. What his role in the recent turn of theological affairs has been or now is, may not be readily recognized; nor has it, for that matter, been assessed. There are certain aspects of his thought which appear to participate in the current mood of theological inquiry. This perhaps may best be seen by comparing his thought with that of a theologian whose theology is clearly relevant to the immediate theological scene. The contemporary theologian nearest to Otto in feeling tone and in the formulation of his theology is Paul Tillich. Tillich has acknowledged his affinity with Otto's approach to theology. Speaking of the effects of his own early experience growing up in a Lutheran parish, Tillich writes:

[41] Cf. Emil Brunner, *The Philosophy of Religion* (N.Y., Scribner's, 1937), p. 104; and Karl Barth, *Church Dogmatics* I, (N.Y., Scribner's, 1936), Part I, p. 153.

It is the experience of the "holy" which was given to me at that time as an indestructible good and as the foundation of all my religious and theological work. When I first read Rudolf Otto's *Idea of the Holy,* I understood it immediately in the light of these early experiences, and took it into my thinking as a constitutive element. It determined my method in the philosophy of religion, wherein I started with the experiences of the holy and advanced to the idea of God, and not the reverse way. Equally important existentially, as well as theologically, were the mystical, sacramental, and aesthetic implications of the idea of the holy, whereby the ethical and logical elements of religion were derived from the experience of the presence of the divine, and not conversely. This made Schleiermacher congenial to me, as he was to Otto, and induced both Otto and me to participate in movements for liturgical renewal and a revaluation of Christian and non-Christian mysticism.[42]

One sees many parallels between Tillich and Otto stemming from this common orientation in method. In fact, Tillich's description of himself as being "on the boundary" aptly describes Otto's situation in many respects. This theological stance they both inherited from Schleiermacher, who saw the role of the Christian theologian of the modern period precisely in these terms. And this image of the theological task gives rise to other similarities. For example, Tillich's correlation of *kairos* and *logos* recalls Otto's attempt to hold the nonrational and the rational in juxtaposition. And Tillich's "ecstatic reason" has affinities with Otto's way of speaking about the cognitive element in the act of divination. Despite the fact that Otto resolves the eschatological problem within the mystical pattern, ascribing charismatic powers to Jesus, through whom *an inbreaking of the new order* is made manifest, one may say that at least the semblance of a dimensional theology (to use Tillich's phrase) is indicated here within the compass of historical experience. Tillich expresses this same note of innovation ontologically in his concept of the "New Being." Furthermore, one cannot fail to see that both men, in making the holy their starting point in method, have been driven to a symbolic discourse by way of

[42] Charles W. Kegley and Robert W. Bretall, eds., *The Theology of Paul Tillich* (N.Y., Macmillan, 1952), p. 6.

explicating "something that at bottom is incapable of explication by concepts" (Otto). Both men were indebted to the phenomenology of Husserl, and both men trace their early stimulus back to Schleiermacher, Kant, and Luther. Their distinctions arose chiefly from the fact that Otto followed Jacob Fries in formulating his philosophical method, while Tillich drew upon the ontological system of Schelling.

In so far as a dimensional theology finds it necessary to draw upon the notion of the numinous for its imagery of depth and upon a reconception of the doctrine of eschatology in which the numinous informs the meaning of intimations of depth and newness in existence, Rudolf Otto's contribution to theological thinking will continue to have force and influence.

Bibliography

Rudolf Otto, *The Idea of the Holy*, 2d ed., N.Y., Oxford Univ. Press, 1950.

Robert F. Davidson, *Rudolf Otto's Interpretation of Religion*, Princeton, Princeton Univ., 1947.

WALTER RAUSCHENBUSCH

Robert T. Handy

Walter Rauschenbusch (1861–1918) was a Baptist minister, church historian, and the leading exponent and theologian of the social gospel in America. He came into sudden prominence in 1907, and from then to his death he poured out the stream of lectures and writings on which his reputation rests. Three major and four smaller books from his pen appeared in that period of about ten years during which he was American Protestantism's best-known social prophet. At once deeply religious in personal life and vigorously progressive in social attitudes, Rauschenbusch's central effort was to bring into one the two dominating visions of his life, the religious and the social.

I

Rauschenbusch was born in Rochester, New York, on October 4, 1861, son of Karl August and Caroline (Rhomp) Rauschenbusch, who had migrated to the United States from Germany fifteen years earlier. His pietistic father had come as a Lutheran missionary, but was later converted to Baptist views. Beginning in 1858, he taught for thirty-two years in the German department of the Rochester Theological Seminary, devoting much of his scholarly attention to Anabaptist history.[1] Walter was brought up in the conservative German Baptist tradition. His formal education actually was begun in Germany, where he lived from 1865 to 1869. The following ten years were spent again in Rochester, where he attended a private school and a free academy. Summers were passed working on a farm in Pennsylvania. In 1879 the young man had a conversion experience which led to his baptism on confession of faith. Though later his theo-

[1] Carl E. Schneider, "Americanization of Karl August Rauschenbusch, 1816–1899," *Church History*, XXIV (1955), 3–14; Walter Rauschenbusch, *Leben und Wirken von August Rauschenbusch* (Cleveland, Ritter, 1901).

logical understanding of this event changed markedly, he always acknowledged that this "tender, mysterious experience" had great value for him. The deeply religious tone of his personal life remained undiminished, though his intellectual apprehension of the nature of Christian faith was to undergo a sharp reorientation.

Later in 1879 Rauschenbusch again went to Germany for a period of four years, studying at the Gymnasium at Gütersloh in Westphalia, from which he graduated in 1883 with first honors in classical studies. He mastered Latin, Greek, French, Hebrew, and German in those years, showed great interest in art and literature, enjoyed opportunities for travel on the Continent, and studied briefly at the University of Berlin. Resolving to enter the ministry, he returned to Rochester in 1883. His splendid educational preparation allowed him to complete his senior year at the University of Rochester at the same time that he commenced study at the Rochester Theological Seminary. A summer pastorate at Louisville, Kentucky, in 1884 convinced him that he had truly found his calling. He wrote: "It is now no longer my fond hope to be a learned theologian and write big books; I want to be a pastor, powerful with men, preaching to them Christ as the man in whom their affections and energies can find the satisfaction for which mankind is groaning."[2] He graduated from the German department of the seminary in 1885, and from the regular course the following year. Quite in keeping with the warmly evangelical emphases in which he had been schooled, he volunteered for foreign missions. But he was also acquainted with the critical scholarship of his time to the degree that the soundness of his views on the Old Testament were questioned by conservatives in his denomination, and he was refused.

He went instead to the pastorate of the Second German Baptist Church in New York City. Located on West 45 Street, the church was near the depressed area styled "Hell's Kitchen." The cornerstone of a new building was laid in 1889, but it was only two blocks away. Here he was confronted by the social problem in a most challenging way. Here he saw some of the

[2] Dores R. Sharpe, *Walter Rauschenbusch* (N.Y., Macmillan, 1942), p.54.

terrible human effects of poverty, unemployment, insecurity, malnutrition, disease, and crime. It was consistent both with the individualistic, warm-hearted piety in which he had been reared and also with his own understanding of Christian discipleship to reach out in love to help the victims of social misfortune and injustice. But it was difficult for him to find theological undergirding for the social concerns which he found he could not evade. His awareness of the social situation was sharpened in his very first year in New York by the work of Henry George, author of *Progress and Poverty* (1879) and advocate of the single tax. Rauschenbusch later declared that "I owe my first awakening to the world of social problems to the agitation of Henry George in 1886, and wish here to record my lifelong debt to this single-minded apostle of a great truth."[3] Thus awakened, he read widely in the social and socialistic literature of his day. He edited a short-lived paper for working people, *For the Right*. He played a role in some of the movements for social betterment.

Rauschenbusch was very much aware that his social views did not come from the church but from the outside, from personal contact with poverty and unemployment, from his own association with social reform literature and movements. To the earlier religious passion which had called him to the ministry was now added a social passion that engaged him in reformist writing and action. But how were these two passions of his life to be related? The individualistic, evangelistic interpretation of Christian faith which he had inherited and largely accepted scarcely provided resources for confronting the social problem; indeed, many denied that there could be any connection between the two. The effort to bring them together into a satisfying whole launched Rauschenbusch on the main work of his life, and led him to revise much of his understanding of Christian faith. As he later explained: "All this time my friends were urging me to give up this social work and devote myself to 'Christian work.' Some of them felt grieved for me, but I knew the work was Christ's work and I went ahead, although I had to set myself against all that I had previously been taught. I had

[3] *Christianizing the Social Order* (N.Y., Macmillan, 1912), p. 394.

to go back to the Bible to find out whether I or my friends were right. I had to revise my whole study of the Bible. . . . All my scientific study of the Bible was undertaken to find a basis for the Christian teaching of a social gospel."[4] That basis he finally did find in his discovery of the importance of the doctrine of the Kingdom of God, which for him bridged the gap between the religious and the social.

The misfortune of deafness, which befell him in 1888 when he arose too soon from a sick bed to minister to others, in a way contributed to his intellectual achievements, for it partially isolated him and provided more time than he might otherwise have had for concentrated study. But his thirst for a resolution of the tension between the religious and the social concerns of his life led him to take a leave from his parish in 1891. He surveyed conditions of life and labor in England, becoming acquainted with Fabian socialism and other social movements, and then went on to engage in New Testament study in Germany. His theological pilgrimage led him in a distinctly liberal direction. He accepted the critical approach to the Bible and the historical understanding of Christianity. He identified himself with the theological streams associated with the names of Schleiermacher, Bushnell, Ritschl, Wellhausen, and Harnack. During this year there came to him as a unifying concept the ideal of the Kingdom of God on earth. He described this turning point in these words:

So Christ's conception of the Kingdom of God came to me as a new revelation. Here was the idea and purpose that had dominated the mind of the Master himself. All his teachings center about it. His life was given to it. His death was suffered for it. When a man has once seen that in the Gospels, he can never unsee it again.

When the Kingdom of God dominated our landscape, the perspective of life shifted into a new alignment. I felt a new security in my social impulses. The spiritual authority of Jesus Christ would have been sufficient to offset the weight of all the doctors, and I now knew that I had history on my side. But in addition I found that this new conception of the purpose of

[4] *Rochester Theological Seminary Bulletin, The Record* (November 1918), pp. 54 f.

Christianity was strangely satisfying. It responded to all the old and all the new elements of my religious life. The saving of the lost, the teaching of the young, the pastoral care of the poor and frail, the quickening of starved intellects, the study of the Bible, church union, political reform, the reorganization of the industrial system, international peace,—it was all covered by the one aim of the Reign of God on earth.[5]

As a theological liberal he frequently criticized the individualistic and pietistic conservatism with which he had once been associated, though the deeply religious orientation of his life was not shaken but deepened. He remained always an "evangelical liberal," deeply influenced by liberal scholarship but grasped by a personally profound Christianity.

Inspired by his new vision and assured of his direction, Rauschenbusch returned to New York to throw himself into his religious and social tasks with a new enthusiasm. He spoke and wrote on the burning public questions of the day. To the Baptist Congress, of which he was secretary, he presented papers on ethical and economic issues. With like-minded brethren who were passing through crises similar to his, he participated in the organization of the Brotherhood of the Kingdom, a group of "thrice-born men" who met annually to stimulate each other's thinking and to advance the cause of social Christianity. At this same time he took a wife, the former Miss Pauline E. Rother, a Milwaukee schoolteacher. Mrs. Rauschenbusch made it much easier for her deafened husband to be at ease in public gatherings. Five children were born of the union.

In 1897 the pastor was called back to his native Rochester to teach New Testament interpretation in the German department of the seminary; at the collegiate level he also taught courses in natural science and civil government. Five years later he was made Professor of Church History on the regular faculty of the Rochester Theological Seminary. Though he wrote little as a church historian, he was a respected and popular teacher in the field. He utilized the concept of the Kingdom of God in organizing his courses. He gave special attention to the early centuries, to the history of baptism, to the Anabaptists, and to American church history.

The pursuits of scholarship and teaching did not at all blunt

[5] *Christianizing the Social Order*, p. 93.

his interest in the social question. He could not forget the sufferings of those among whom he had labored as pastor for eleven years. To discharge a debt to them he resumed work on a manuscript which he had started years before, a book "on social questions for the Lord Christ and the people." He knew the theme was an unpopular one; he was prepared for a storm of attack and perhaps even for dismissal. Just as the book was coming from the presses in the spring of 1907, he left the country on sabbatical. To his surprise, he returned to find himself famous. *Christianity and the Social Crisis* ran through six editions in two years; finally there were to be seventeen editions. The mature effort of a competent man and a brilliant writer, the book appeared at a time when the Progressive movement was rising in popularity and was affecting national legislation. It came at a moment when the muckrakers and reformers had convinced many Americans that social changes were desperately needed, and when liberal theology was winning a substantial following in many churches. Its patent sincerity and thoughtful merging of Christian and social motifs caught the imagination of many. Its careful elaboration of the ideal of the Kingdom of God on earth opened attractive vistas to a generation struggling with the perplexing social question. So the professor of church history from the moment of his return found himself in great demand to speak and write on social questions from the viewpoint of Christian faith. Sensing himself to be in the vanguard of a social and religious awakening, he responded as best he could to the many calls coming to him.

His second major work, *Christianizing the Social Order,* was published in 1912. The bulk of this large work, developed from his Earl Lectures at Pacific Theological Seminary and from his Merrick Lectures at Ohio Wesleyan, was devoted specifically to social issues, but characteristically the author insisted that "this is a religious book from beginning to end. Its sole concern is for the Kingdom of God and the salvation of men. But the Kingdom of God includes the economic life; for it means the progressive transformation of all human affairs by the thought and spirit of Christ."[6] In pointing the way to such a progressive transformation, Rauschenbusch drew heavily on the progressive social thought of his time.

[6] *Ibid.,* p. 458.

Rauschenbusch's message was also presented through a number of articles, pamphlets, and smaller books. In 1910 appeared *For God and the People: Prayers of the Social Awakening,* a little book which distinctively revealed the depth of his own devotional life. Two years later was published *Unto Me,* a small work addressed to social workers. In 1914 was issued another brief writing, *Dare We Be Christians?* In this commentary on I Corinthians 13 he developed his understanding of the meaning of Christian love. In another two years was produced his most widely circulated writing, a study book entitled *The Social Principles of Jesus.*

The climax of his productive decade came in 1917. In the spring of that year he delivered the Taylor Lectures at Yale; they were then published as *A Theology for the Social Gospel.* In this significant work the prophet of social Christianity took this as his main proposition: "We have a social gospel. We need a systematic theology large enough to match it and vital enough to back it."[7] Though he insisted that he was not a doctrinal theologian either by professional training or by personal habits of mind, he continued in what proved to be his last book to relate Christian faith to social concerns precisely by undertaking with considerable imagination to suggest what an adequate theology for social Christianity would be like. In this effort he drew freely on the liberal tradition in theology, and brought to clear delineation the vision of the Kingdom of God that had inspired him a quarter of a century before.

The outbreak of World War I in 1914 had brought deep anguish of spirit to him. He was almost as much at home in Germany as in America. He hated militarism, was inclined toward pacifism, and hoped that America could remain neutral. In the popular wave of revulsion against things German, some began to question his loyalty, though without foundation. His immense popularity declined somewhat. He was a saddened man; war for him seemed to be the negation both of Christianity and of social progress, the twin passions of his life. While the war was still raging, Walter Rauschenbusch, on July 25, 1918, died of cancer in his beloved Rochester.

---

[7] *A Theology for the Social Gospel* (N.Y., Macmillan, 1917), p. 1.

II

Rauschenbusch's public work was dominated by an effort to bring together things which had been separated to such an extent that many saw them as antithetical. Throughout his writings appear references to realities which many had difficulty in relating to each other: science and faith, culture and church, democracy and Christianity, ethics and theology, dogmatics and the social gospel. All these he sought to bring into a coherent whole; for him the Kingdom of God was the way to such unity. A strong sense of continuity between God and man and between God and the world informed his work. An important part of the reason for the appeal of his writings was that they were informed by a vision of a regenerated world; there was in them an arresting comprehensiveness of conception and understanding. However idealistic and perhaps even utopian they may seem to a later generation, they have a breadth and a boldness that is striking. Rauschenbusch sought to give as full and adequate a philosophy for personal and social life as he could. Thus, though he was not a theologian in the formal sense, and in no sense a theological system builder, his work was done in an effort to supply a whole view of the world and of human life.

In methodology Rauschenbusch was decisively influenced by a modern historical approach. His understanding of the Bible, the Kingdom of God, the Christian faith, the Christian Church, and the social situation was cast in terms of historical development. He was conversant with the critical historical treatments of the Bible and of the institutions of Christianity which stemmed from German scholarship; he was well acquainted with the work of the leading "scientific" church historian of the day, Adolf Harnack. His understanding of history was cast in the light of the theory of evolution; the developmental view was worked into the warp and woof of his thought. It was the historical approach which helped him to understand how the church and the movements for social justice had become separated. As he saw both in historical perspective, he could explain why the church had lost the initial social vision which had been hers, and why, in the absence of proper Christian influences, certain serious social conditions and movements for their amelioration had arisen. His dominating ideal of the Kingdom, which would bring the two together again, was shaped in the light of his historicism and developmentalism. He wrote: "Translate the evolutionary theories into religious faith, and you have the doctrine of the Kingdom of God. This combination with scientific evolutionary thought has freed the Kingdom ideal of its catastrophic setting and its background of demonism, and so adapted it to the climate of the modern world."[8] He further declared that the social gospel is always historically minded, always endeavoring "to see the progress of the Kingdom of God in the flow of history; not only in the doings of the Church, but in the clash of economic forces and social classes, in the rise and fall of despotisms and forms of enslavement, in the rise of new value-judgments and fresh canons of moral taste and sentiment, or the elevation or decline of moral standards."[9] The entire first half of the book which won national prominence for him was a sweeping historical interpretation. He traced the historical roots of Christianity to the Hebrew prophets, analyzed the social aims of Jesus in the light of the liberal historical criticism of his period, surveyed the social impetus of primitive Christianity and accounted for its loss in later centuries. Even in the latter half of the book, in which the modern social crises, the stake of the Church in the social movement, and suitable courses of action were discussed, there were many historical references. The strong stamp of the historical method and the developmental viewpoint can be plainly seen both in his most "social" book, *Christianizing the Social Order,* and in his most "theological" work, *A Theology for the Social Gospel.* Inasmuch as it was the historical approach that was setting the pace and posing the main questions in the American theological world in the early years of the twentieth century, it is understandable why a historian might make the leading theological contribution of the period.

The sources of Walter Rauschenbusch's social-ethical thought have been analyzed in a doctoral dissertation by Donovan E. Smucker, who finds four main influences operating upon him: pietism, sectarianism, liberalism, and transformationism. His

8 *Christianizing the Social Order,* p. 90.
9 *A Theology for the Social Gospel,* p. 146.

understanding of Christian faith was initially cast in a pietist framework through the influences of family and church; though he later moved out of this frame of reference, a deep personal piety and interest in evangelism remained. The sectarian influences came through the interests both his father and he himself had in Anabaptist thought; his Baptist understanding of the church and the Christian life have sectarian traces. The liberal thought provided the primary content of his position; the most influential theologian for him was Albrecht Ritschl.[10] Rauschenbusch's mature thought was also tempered by the transformationist outlook as presented by such Christian socialists as Frederick Denison Maurice and Charles Kingsley in England and Hermann Kutter and Leonhard Ragaz in Switzerland. Rauschenbusch drew on these influences in a free and often original way in framing the social gospel. Though he wrote from a liberal frame of reference, he never slavishly followed any one pattern, and he felt free to criticize the weaknesses of all. He could say, for example, "To concentrate our efforts on personal salvation, as orthodoxy has done, or on soul culture, as liberalism has done, comes close to refined selfishness."[11]

Rauschenbusch's theology for the social gospel was not a systematic one; indeed, he showed not a little of the distrust of metaphysical speculation and dogmatic thought that was common in his time. His was a theology of mediation, accommodation, and adjustment. For he could say,

> When the progress of humanity creates new tasks, such as worldwide missions, or new problems, such as the social problem, theology must connect these with the old fundamentals of our faith and make them Christian tasks and problems.
> The adjustment of the Christian message to the regeneration of the social order is plainly one of the most difficult tasks ever laid on the intellect of religious leaders.[12]

[10] Donovan E. Smucker, "The Origins of Walter Rauschenbusch's Social Ethics" (typed Ph.D. thesis, Univ. of Chicago, June 1957), p. 212; cf. his summary article, "Multiple Motifs in the Thought of Rauschenbusch: A Study in the Origins of the Social Gospel," *Encounter*, XIX (1958), 14–20.

[11] *Christianizing the Social Order*, pp. 464 f.

[12] *A Theology for the Social Gospel*, p. 7.

Though the statement came from his last work, it aptly summarizes the main thrust of his religious and theological effort.

The informing center of his work, ever since his vision of it in 1891, was the doctrine of the Kingdom of God. Not only was it the most important doctrine for him, but he insisted that it should bring about the revision of "all other doctrines so that they will articulate organically with it."[13] With great emphasis he could say:

> The Kingdom of God is the first and the most essential dogma of the Christian faith. It is also the lost social ideal of Christendom. No man is a Christian in the full sense of the original discipleship until he has made the Kingdom of God the controlling purpose of his life, and no man is intellectually prepared to understand Jesus Christ until he has understood the meaning of the Kingdom of God.

Rauschenbusch believed that the Kingdom was to come on earth in history; he explained that Jesus "never transferred the Kingdom hope from earth to heaven. The Kingdom is so much of this earth that Jesus expected to return to earth from heaven in order to set it up."[14] He believed that the Kingdom of God is divine in its origin, progress, and consummation, miraculous all the way, the continuous revelation of the power, the righteousness, and the love of God. It is the supreme purpose of God, to be realized not only by the redemption of man through the overcoming of evil but also by the education of mankind and the revelation of God's life within it. The Kingdom of God is always present and future, always coming, always pressing in on the present and inviting immediate action. Every human life can share with God in the creation of the Kingdom. The Kingdom is humanity organized according to the will of God, it is a nobler social order. It implies the progressive reign of love in human affairs, it advances wherever the free will of love supersedes the use of force and legal coercion as a regulative of the social order. The reign of love tends toward the progressive unity of mankind. The Kingdom must be the purpose for which the church exists, and gives the church the power to save.

Rauschenbusch did not neglect the doctrine of the church in

---

[13] *Ibid.*, p. 131.
[14] *Christianizing the Social Order*, pp. 49, 66.

his theology. He called the church "the social factor in salvation," and indicated the necessity of its being and function. His own church idea was much shaped by his Baptist background and commitments. He favored congregationally ordered, non-creedal, nonhierarchical, fully democratic churches.[15] For him church was always subordinate to Kingdom; the church was a perpetuation of the past while the Kingdom is the power of the coming age.

The Kingdom of God, Rauschenbusch taught, embraces all of life and realizes itself through the family, the economic organizations, and the state as well as through the church. The Kingdom of God is a historical force that can be progressively realized; humanity is on the march to the Kingdom of God. The Kingdom of God is not utopia; there is no perfection but only growth toward perfection. There can only be the approximation of a perfect social order. Yet Rauschenbusch dared to hope that a vastly better, if not entirely perfect, social order was at hand, a social order that would far more fully realize the Kingdom of God than anything the world had known. "The swiftness of evolution in our own country," he said at the end of his first book, "proves the immense latent perfectibility in human nature."[16] Interpreting the eschatological teachings of the gospels in the light of the evolutionary optimism of his time, he explained that Jesus took "his illustrations from organic life to express the idea of the gradual growth of the Kingdom. He was shaking off catastrophic ideas and substituting developmental ideas." Actually, Rauschenbusch was basing his interpretation of the eschatology of Jesus on a view that had already been sharply challenged by certain biblical scholars of the time. Though aware of their work, Rauschenbusch argued that "the professional theologians of Europe, who all belong by kinship and sympathy to the bourgeois class and are constitutionally incapacitated for understanding any revolutionary ideas, past or

[15] Cf. his articles, "Why I Am a Baptist," originally published in *The Rochester Baptist Monthly*, XX (1905–1906), 2–3, 85–8, 106–8, 134–6, 156–9; reprinted in *The Colgate-Rochester Divinity School Bulletin*, XI (December 1938).

[16] *Christianity and the Social Crisis* (N.Y., Macmillan, 1907), p. 422. For the full development of his teaching on the Kingdom see *A Theology for the Social Gospel*, pp. 139–45, 165 f., 227.

present, have overemphasized the ascetic and eschatological elements in the teachings of Jesus."[17] Hence he continued to understand Jesus' Kingdom teachings as anticipations of the fraternal ethics of democracy and prophecies of social common sense that were soon to be fulfilled.

The Kingdom is of God, but the theologian of the social gospel did not often touch directly on the doctrine of God. He put the doctrine of the Kingdom of God before the doctrine of God, insisting that the Kingdom is the necessary background for the Christian idea of God. Without denying God's transcendence, Rauschenbusch emphasized his immanence: "God is not only the spiritual representative of humanity; he is identified with it. In him we live and move and have our being. In us he lives and moves, though his being transcends ours." He indicated that the conception of God held by a social group is a social product and that such conceptions can change and grow. The concept of God which is dominant among a given people is influenced by the social relations under which they live; under tyrannous conditions the idea of God was tainted with the cruel hardness of society. But when Jesus took God by the hand and called him "our Father," he "democratized" the concept of God. "He disconnected the idea from the coercive and predatory State, and transferred it to the realm of family life, the chief social embodiment of solidarity and love. He not only saved humanity, he saved God."[18] The social gospel is to continue to free men from wrong conceptions of God, it is to continue what the Reformation began. The religious belief that he is immanent in humanity is the natural basis for democratic ideas about him. Rauschenbusch declared that the idea of solidarity, properly understood, acts as a theodicy; the consciousness of solidarity is the essence of religion. God is the ground of the social unity of all mankind.

Though Rauschenbusch rarely touched on the doctrine of God formally, everything he wrote referred, explicitly or implicitly, to Jesus Christ. The very soul of his own deep religiousness was his loyalty and devotion to Jesus. The following passage from a letter written in 1912 is very revealing:

[17] *A Theology for the Social Gospel*, p. 158.
[18] *Ibid.*, pp. 49, 174 f.

God and Christ may differ for my analytic intellect, but for my religious life they are convertible terms. The God of the stellar universe is a God in whom I drown. Christ with the face of Jesus I can comprehend, and love and assimilate. So I stick to him, and call him by that name. Let others do differently if they are differently made. I prefer to superimpose the two concepts on each other and get more out of each.[19]

His was a quest for the historical Jesus; from the scientific New Testament study of his time he found the Master coming out of the past with greater clarity. He saw the Jesus of history as a teacher of morality and the master of "the greatest and deepest and rarest secret of all—how to live a religious life." Jesus knew the Father; his religion flowed out naturally into all the relations of his life, reconstructing everything it touched. Jesus was the perfect religious personality; he rose above the temptations of mysticism, pessimism, and asceticism. Jesus incarnated a new type of human life; he was the first real man, the inaugurator of a new humanity. The social redemption of the entire life of the human race on earth was always the purpose of all that Jesus said and did and hoped to do. He put the Kingdom of God at the center of all his teaching. Rauschenbusch firmly believed that his own views about the Kingdom were solidly based on what Jesus had taught about it. For Rauschenbusch the social gospel must always be concerned about the progressive social incarnation of God. The Christology of the social gospel therefore focuses on how the divine life of Christ can get control of human society. Its emphasis is not on the speculative questions of the two natures in Christ, but on a real personality who could set the great historical process of redemption in motion. In Jesus the Kingdom of God got its first foothold in humanity; by virtue of his personality he became the initiator of the Kingdom.[20]

Throughout Rauschenbusch's work is to be found a con-

19 Quoted in Sharpe, *Rauschenbusch*, p. 322.
20 Cf. Chap. II, "The Social Aims of Jesus," *Christianity and the Social Crisis*, pp. 44–92; Part II, Chap. II, "The Social Christianity of Jesus," *Christianizing the Social Order*, pp. 48–68; *The Social Principles of Jesus* (N.Y., Association Press, 1916); Chap. XIV, "The Initiator of the Kingdom of God," *A Theology of the Social Gospel*, pp. 146–66.

tinuing discussion of the doctrines of sin and salvation, "the starting-point and goal of Christian theology," with special attention to their social dimensions. The climax of this discussion comes in *A Theology for the Social Gospel,* in which he declared that "my main purpose in this book has been to show that the social gospel is a vital part of the Christian conception of sin and salvation, and that any teaching on the sinful condition of the race and on its redemption from evil which fails to do justice to the social factors and processes in sin and redemption, must be incomplete, unreal and misleading."[21] In that book he caught up much that he had said before about the nature of social sin and salvation. For him sin was essentially selfishness, a definition which "furnishes an excellent theological basis for a social conception of sin and salvation." He believed that man rarely sins against God alone. A vision of the Kingdom of God makes clear the social dimensions of sin, for we see the Kingdom of God locked in struggle against the superpersonal forces of evil which together comprise a Kingdom of Evil. As men are turned from self to God and to humanity, they find salvation. A solidaristic religious experience is more Christian, Rauschenbusch believed, than an individualistic one.

Rauschenbusch based his social ethics on the teachings of Jesus concerning love. Hence he "made one of the outstanding attempts in modern Christian history to construct an ethic of love."[22] "The fundamental virtue in the ethics of Jesus was love, because love is the society-making quality," he once wrote, adding:

> Human life originates in love. It is love that holds together the basal human organization, the family. The physical expression of all love and friendship is the desire to get together and be together. Love creates fellowship. In the measure in which love increases in any social organism, it will hold together without coercion.[23]

The fullest development of his philosophy of love is in *Dare We Be Christians?*, which closes with the words: "Those who

[21] P. 167.
[22] Smucker, "The Origins of Walter Rauschenbusch's Social Ethics," p. 220.
[23] *Christianity and the Social Crisis,* p. 67.

take up the propaganda of love and substitute freedom and fraternity for coercion and class differences in social life are the pioneers of the Kingdom of God; for the reign of the God of love will be fulfilled in a life of humanity organized on the basis of solidarity and love." The Christianization of the social order will be accomplished by bringing it into harmony with the ethical convictions which we identify with Christ.

When he turned to the task of spelling out the specific details of the social ethic of love, Rauschenbusch drew heavily on the progressive, mildly radical, socialistic thought of his time. Private gain must give way to public good. Competition must give place to cooperation. Special privilege must yield to the principle of equal rights. To his joy, when he surveyed the American social scene in 1912 he could report that "four great sections of our social order—the family, the organized religious life, the institutions of education, and the political organization of our nation—have passed through constitutional changes which have made them to some degree part of the organism through which the spirit of Christ can do its work in humanity."[24] The next thing, he affirmed, was business, "the unregenerate section of our social order." Drawing his arrows from the quivers of the muckrakers, reformers, progressives, and socialists, he analyzed capitalism critically. He wrote of its competitiveness, autocracy, and commercialism. He criticized its tendency to grab for profits to the detriment of human values, its neglect of aesthetic interests, its crippling of the institutions of love. He summed up "the Christian indictment of capitalism" as follows: "Capitalism has generated a spirit of its own which is antagonistic to the spirit of Christianity; a spirit of hardness and cruelty that neutralizes the Christian spirit of love; a spirit that sets material goods above spiritual possessions. To set Things above Men is the really dangerous practical materialism." Against this, Rauschenbusch called for "a collective action of the community to change the present organization of the economic life into a new order that would rest on the Christian principles of equal rights, democratic distribution of economic power, the supremacy of the common good, the law of mutual dependence and service, and the uninterrupted flow of good will

[24] *Christianizing the Social Order,* p. 154.

throughout the human family."[25] These goals could be achieved, he thought, through the strengthening of the working class, the development of social insurance, the assurance of the right to employment, and the increasing of economic democracy by trade-unionism, cooperatives, and socialism. Rauschenbusch called himself a Christian socialist, but his was an evolutionary, nondoctrinaire, really nonpolitical form of socialism. He noted the dilemma with which organized socialism confronted Christians: "It is far and away the most powerful force for justice, democracy, and organized fraternity in the modern world. On the other hand, these moral elements are fused with an alloy that is repellent to their Christian instincts."[26] Hence he did not himself become a member of the Socialist Party; he could not identify the Kingdom of God with the socialist state, as some Christian socialists were doing. He recognized the "menace" of socialism, but insisted that the task of Christians was to make its menace small and its blessing great.

Not by revolution or swift overturn but by gradualism did he believe that the Kingdom would come. By shortening hours of work and raising wages, by providing adequate housing, by returning something of the "social dividend" to those who have helped make it, by putting "natural monopolies" under public ownership, could the coming of the Kingdom be speeded. Always he maintained that the social task was religious, and that the religious task was social:

It is not this thing or that thing our nation needs, but a new mind and heart, a new conception of the way we all ought to live together, a new conviction about the worth of a human life and the use God wants us to make of our own lives. We want a revolution both inside and outside. We want a moral renovation of public opinion and a revival of religion. . . . A righteous public opinion may bring the proudest sinner low. But the most pervasive scrutiny, a control which follows our actions to their fountain-head where the desires and motives of the soul are born, is exerted only by personal religion.[27]

[25] *Ibid.*, pp. 315, 323.
[26] *Ibid.*, p. 397.
[27] *Ibid.*, p. 459.

So Rauschenbusch hoped to link the evangelical gospel with the social gospel, to add the latter to the former, and thus to create a public opinion that would bring about renewal of both church and society.

III

Rauschenbusch was the best-known and most perceptive advocate of the liberal social gospel. Not only did he enjoy great prominence in the English-speaking world, but beyond, for writings of his were translated into German, French, Norwegian, Swedish, Finnish, Russian, Chinese, and Japanese. His counsel was sought by many, including such public figures as Theodore Roosevelt, Woodrow Wilson, and David Lloyd George. About two decades after his death Henry P. Van Dusen declared, "It is clear, it seems to me, that the greatest single personal influence on the life and thought of the American church in the last fifty years was exerted by Walter Rauschenbusch. Probably the three most influential men in American church history upon the thought of the church have been Jonathan Edwards, Horace Bushnell, and Walter Rauschenbusch."[28] And more than four decades after his passing, Donald B. Meyer called Rauschenbusch the "greatest spokesman" of the social gospel, the man who preached it "more glowingly and with more reasoned faith than any other of his generation of Protestant leaders." Comparing him with other figures of the time, Meyer concludes: "But it was Rauschenbusch who stood foremost, and although Rauschenbusch was hailed for many things, what stamps him most sharply in retrospect is his estimate of tactics, the first clear, concrete estimate in the annals of the social passion."[29]

After Rauschenbusch's death the social gospel and the liberal theology on which it was based developed in several different and not wholly consistent directions, none of which would probably have had his full approval. The basic synthesis for which he labored did not prove to be lasting. Some representatives of the social gospel tended toward a humanistic orientation and in

[28] Quoted in Sharpe, *Rauschenbusch*, p. 410.
[29] Donald B. Meyer, *The Protestant Search for Political Realism, 1919–1941* (Berkeley and Los Angeles, Univ. of California, 1960), pp. 15, 88.

their attention to the social minimized the religious; others focused their attention on one or two major social problems and neglected the larger scene. In the 1930's positions for which Rauschenbusch had stood tended to disintegrate under the attacks of dialectical and realistic theologians and social ethicists. In delineating what Jesus' concept of the Kingdom of God was, no doubt Rauschenbusch did read in too much of his own progressive and evolutionary views; he minimized the eschatological aspects of the Kingdom. In stressing the centrality of the Kingdom, he was inclined to slight the role and place of the Church in history. In proclaiming the immanence of God, he neglected biblical and theological themes concerning the transcendence, majesty, and sovereignty of God. In defining sin as essentially selfishness, he did not deal adequately with the classic Christian understanding of sin as pride and rebellion against God. In seeking to awake public opinion to the need for greater social righteousness, he relied too heavily on the power of press and platform and did not realistically enough count political costs of change. In estimating the degree to which the nation and its institutions had become Christianized, he was far too optimistic and scarcely read aright deeper undercurrents of criticism and confusion. Yet he avoided many of the pitfalls into which the later social gospel slipped. He understood the tragic character of life and warned that men and nations might take the wrong road. He never neglected personal religion; he never confused social reconstruction, important as he believed that was, with the Christian experience of salvation. Hence, though his formulation of the social gospel had its day and passed, it has made lasting contributions to theological and ethical thought. The man who led the attack on the liberal theology and its social gospel, Reinhold Niebuhr, expressed the hope that his own 1934 Rauschenbusch Lectures would be "an extension and an application to our own day of both the social realism and the loyalty to Christian faith which characterized the thought and life of one who was not only the real founder of social Christianity in this country but also its most brilliant and generally satisfying exponent to the present day."[30] What-

[30] Reinhold Niebuhr, *An Interpretation of Christian Ethics* (N.Y., Harper, 1935), Preface.

ever its limitations, the social gospel made a permanent contribution to Christian life and thought in America by effectively calling attention to the social dimension in all religious thought and by emphasizing in a way appropriate to an industrial society the importance of the quest for social justice. This was more the work of Walter Rauschenbusch than of any other one man.

Bibliography

Walter Rauschenbusch, *A Theology for the Social Gospel,* Nashville, Abingdon, 1961. (Apex Books).

Dores R. Sharpe, *Walter Rauschenbusch,* N.Y., Macmillan, 1942.

D. C. MACINTOSH

Herbert R. Reinelt

Douglas Clyde Macintosh was born in 1877 in Breadalbane, Ontario. After doing graduate work in theology and philosophy at the University of Chicago, he went to Yale Divinity School in 1909 to teach theology. On his way to Yale from Canada he was almost denied entrance when a border guard informed him that to enter for purposes of employment was in violation of the Alien Labor law. When he happened to mention that he was to teach theology at Yale, the guard said, "I thought you said you were going to work!" and promptly let him enter. Macintosh was also the center of a celebrated legal case in which he was denied U.S. citizenship by a five-to-four decision of the Supreme Court because of his refusal to agree to bear arms in time of war. He remained at Yale until his retirement in 1942. He died in 1948.

Macintosh's thought focuses on the problem of knowledge, particularly the problem of religious knowledge. His first major work, *The Problem of Knowledge,* is a critical examination of the fundamental alternatives in the theory of knowledge. His most important theological works include *Theology as an Empirical Science, The Reasonableness of Christianity, The Pilgrimage of Faith,* and *The Problem of Religious Knowledge.* He also is the author of numerous other books and articles in the field of philosophy and religion.

Theologically, Macintosh sought to come to grips with the problems that were presented to religion by the significant movements of thought in the nineteenth century. He was clearly disturbed by the extreme rationalism, disconnected from empirical data, which he felt to be a fundamental characteristic of much orthodox theology. He was equally disturbed by the retreat of faith before the advance of scientific knowledge. He felt that the major theological developments of the nineteenth century were inadequate because they failed to provide an adequate ground for knowledge of God and, consequently, for the clear understanding and pursuit of a meaningful religious life.

In responding to this situation, he was deeply impressed by the significance of scientific method for the discovery of knowledge. In this he reflects the general character of his time. He was influenced by the attempt of William James to study the varieties of religious experience and to base theological theory on the data studied. However, whereas James's work is disconnected from any specific religious tradition, Macintosh was striving to apply the empirical method to the defense of Christian faith. He was also a participant in the attempt to develop a critical realism in regard to the problem of knowledge, and his resulting theological theory reflects his concern that adequate foundation be given for genuine knowledge of God. In this respect some interpreters see him influenced by the Scottish Common Sense School of philosophy.[1]

PHILOSOPHICAL FOUNDATIONS

For Macintosh there can be no essential separation between theology and philosophy. Philosophical issues are of fundamental importance in the solution of theological problems. No theology is adequately critical which does not face the philosophical implications of theological affirmations. Every theology, for example, makes assumptions concerning the possibility and nature of knowledge, including religious knowledge. The problem of knowledge is crucial for the critical justification of theological thought. This outlook involved Macintosh in consideration of general problems in the theory of knowledge as well as in the development of a specifically religious epistemology.

The whole history of modern philosophy, culminating in the critical philosophy of Kant, had set the stage for consideration of the relationship of things as they appear to us to things as they are in themselves. Do we know reality itself in knowing the objects given in experience, or do we know only the appearances while reality itself remains unknown? For Macintosh

[1] Cf. Eugene Garrett Bewkes, "Common Sense Realism," in *The Nature of Religious Experience* (N.Y., Harper, 1937), pp. 1–25.

these are the two fundamental alternatives. The second alternative, that the object which is given in perceptual experience is totally different from the ultimate reality, he calls *dualism*. The logical consequence of this view, according to Macintosh, is agnosticism with respect to the independently real object. Nothing can be known about it. We cannot even know that it is.[2] The fundamental error of the dualist is to overlook the continuity of existence. If the appearance is that of a reality, then it is somehow continuous with it. If it is not in any sense continuous with it, we have no basis from which to call it an appearance of a reality.

The first alternative, says Macintosh, must be the correct one. The view that we know reality itself in knowing the objects given in experience is called *monism*. In monism there is at least partial identity between the object which is known and the independent reality. But within monism there are two alternatives. The *idealist* alternative is that there is complete identity between the object we know and the independent reality. The idealist says that there is complete identity because he holds that reality is idea, and since we directly experience ideas, we therefore directly experience reality. Since nothing in our idea is in principle unknown to us, we can know reality completely. The interpretation of the character of ideas may vary among idealists, but they uniformly hold that there is nothing which exists beyond ideas. Macintosh contends that the idealist's theory is clearly at odds with common sense experience and that for this reason the burden of proof for the theory rests on the idealist. He distinguishes many different types of idealism and examines the arguments for idealism with great care; he concludes that the arguments are inadequate to establish the truth of the theory. The argument is too detailed to be included here.[3]

The other alternative within monism is *realism*. The realist is defined negatively as one who holds that reality is not idea in

[2] Cf. *The Problem of Knowledge* (N.Y., Macmillan, 1915), Chaps. II–III, hereafter cited as PK; *The Reasonableness of Christianity* (N.Y., Scribner's, 1925), pp. 193 ff., hereafter cited as RC; "Experimental Realism in Religion," in *Religious Realism*, D. C. Macintosh, ed. (N.Y., Macmillan, 1931), pp. 349–52, hereafter cited as "ERR."

[3] Cf. PK, Chaps. V–IX; RC, pp. 168–186; "ERR," pp. 341–349.

any common meaning of that term. Since idealism—the attempt to identify appearance and reality by reducing reality to the appearances—has been rejected, some form of realism must be true, that is, there must be a reality which exists independent of experience and which can be at least partially known. *Naive realism* reduces the appearances to the reality—the conclusion opposite to that of the idealist. The naive realist holds that we directly experience realities without any intermediate appearances; thus there is no appearance distinct from reality. The problem with this view is that it is committed to the rationally unacceptable notion that if a person has contradictory experiences of the same object, the object must have contradictory characteristics.

An adequate theory of knowledge, then, must be a *critical realism* which recognizes a partial identity between ultimate reality and the way in which this reality appears to us—a theory that can account not only for the fact that we can know what is external to ourselves and independent of our knowledge of it, but also for the fact that the conditions of knowledge influence the character of the object known. The sensible qualities of objects are not independently real; therefore the perceived object and the independently real object are qualitatively distinguishable. However,

> there may still be such an existential unity or identity between them as to enable one to say with truth that an object which is real independently of our conscious experience has been presented in experience and directly known, even though not all the qualities of the independent reality have been directly presented, and even though not all of the qualities of the object as presented need be thought of as belonging to it in its independent existence.[4]

We know the reality through the appearance; it has at least an existential and numerical identity. We have here what Macintosh calls "perception in a complex"—the perception of a reality in and through the presented content of experience. Instances of such perception in a complex are involved in our

[4] RC, p. 198.

knowledge of physical movement, animal life, consciousness, the self, other selves, and, most importantly for the problem of religious knowledge, God.

Development of Theology as an Empirical Science

The consideration of the logical alternatives in the theory of knowledge lays the groundwork for the development of theology. A dualistic theory with respect to knowledge of God leads to agnosticism or to an uncritical dogmatism—uncritical because it is never possible to test the dogmatic claim with the religious reality. It is precisely at this point that Macintosh is extremely critical of many contemporary theologians—Tillich, Barth, and Brunner, among others—who represent this type of inadequate epistemological position.[5] On the other hand, idealism in religion reduces the religious reality, God, to some form of idea. The consequence of this type of theory is that God does not represent an independently existing reality. It is fatal to religion if true, for once God is understood not to exist the meaning of the religious life would be lost; the religious life has as its very essence the relating of man to God, who is understood to be a reality. Feuerbach epitomizes religious idealism, but Freud, Durkheim, and others are to be included among its adherents.[6] Idealism in religion is subject to the general criticisms of epistemological idealism and to other special objections as well.

If we are to deny neither the possibility of testing the truth of religion nor the possibility that religion is meaningful, we are driven toward some type of realism with respect to religious knowledge. Corresponding to naive realism is mysticism. As the naive realist who holds that we know reality as it is could not square his theory with the diverse experiences we have of reality, so the mystic tends to assert that we have direct knowledge of God and to deny the reality of ordinary experiences of other objects. But in denying ordinary experience mysticism is dogmatic and uncritical. In theology as in other fields of knowl-

[5] Cf. *The Problem of Religious Knowledge* (N.Y., Harper, 1940), Chaps. XIII–XIX, hereafter cited as PRK.
[6] Cf. PRK, Chaps. IV–X and RC, pp. 219–224.

edge the only justifiable theory is a critical realism which acknowledges a real apprehension of God through a complex of experience, which builds theology upon the data of religious experience and from which adequately tested truth may be derived. It is in order to meet this need that Macintosh develops his theology as an empirical science.

Scientific theology makes the same basic assumptions that ordinary science makes. It assumes the laws of thought, the methods and principles common to all scientific procedures, the results of other sciences.[7] One presupposition, already substantiated by the criticism of alternative epistemological theories, is the critically realistic view that knowledge of reality in general is possible. Scientific theology also assumes the principle of induction, that is, that the future will be like the past or, to state it otherwise, that nature is uniform. If the scientist is to generalize from his data he must make this assumption.

But there is one presupposition which is unique to theology: that of the reality of its subject matter. Theology of a scientific sort has the right to assume the existence of God. In defending this assertion Macintosh points out that scientific theology is only making the same sort of assumption that every scientific investigation makes. Every scientific discipline at least tentatively assumes the existence of its object from the outset. Without this assumption there could be no such discipline. The initial assumption is based on practical experience of the object in question prior to scientific investigation. Practical experience of religious reality is to be found in the religious life of mankind. In fact, the history of religion might be considered the history of empirical investigation of the divine. Those who would deny the right of theology to make this assumption do so on highly dogmatic grounds. The agnostic generalizes from the basis of his own ignorance of God that there is no such reality, but this sort of dogmatism is not in accord with scientific procedure.[8]

When critics accused Macintosh of dogmatically presupposing the existence of God, he defended the *logical* right of the

[7] *Theology as an Empirical Science* (N.Y., Macmillan, 1919), p. 28, hereafter cited as TES.

[8] TES, pp. 29–31.

theologian to make this presupposition on the basis of pre-scientific experience, just as the physicist presupposes electricity in order to investigate it. Macintosh of course granted that the preliminary presupposition of God is tentative and that any preliminary definition of the nature of God is necessarily minimal and subject to revision in the light of further investigation. However, he also suggested the alternative approach of introducing the consideration of the existence of God as a question to be settled by the empirical data of theology and not as a presupposition of theology. In this case a tentative definition of God would be hypothesized and then tested by reference to the data of the religious life.[9] Even the latter approach must make the assumption that there is meaningful theological or religious material which can be investigated and which will enable one to test theological hypotheses. Again, theology is no different from the other sciences in making this assumption.

The principle of induction or of the dependability of nature is also specified in Macintosh's scientific theology. If God is presupposed, this principle becomes the principle of the dependableness of God. Scientific theology could not proceed without the assumption that God will act in the future in ways consistent with those with which he has acted in the past. No generalization from given data would be possible without such dependableness. As the most fundamental assumption of theological science, this principle is the last to be verified; but no science is possible without it.[10] If God is not presupposed, then it must be assumed that whatever reality is the source of the religious life is consistent in its activity.

These presuppositions of religious inquiry having been acknowledged, the next step is to specify what experiences are religious as distinct from other types of experiences. Some criteria must be used in order to distinguish the data of theology from other data. The establishment of such norms presupposes that we have sufficient discrimination to be able to identify the essence of religion or the divine element in experience. Analysis of religion discloses that there are two fundamental elements in religion: first, our consciousness of ultimate reality as expressed

[9] Cf. PRK, p. 193.
[10] TES, p. 35.

in our feelings of absolute dependence, wonder, and awe, and, second, our sense of absolute values which are universally and finally valid.[11] Religion as a function in human life thus has its own unique concern. "The distinctively religious interest is an interest in the relation of reality to values."[12]

The criterion of the divine, therefore, is the unity of power and of value. Reality is felt as divine when it is felt to act in support of the highest values. Nothing less than a being which is ultimate in power and in concern for value could possibly be the object of religious worship, adoration, praise, confidence, and trust. Underlying Macintosh's theology is the conviction that men can know, at least in a general way, absolute values. Macintosh identifies these values with all those factors which contribute toward spiritual development, including rationality and knowledge of truth, righteousness and good will, true friendship and unselfish love; in short, with those values which contribute to intellectual, aesthetic, social, and moral development.[13] Macintosh, an ethical intuitionist, maintains that these values are "intuitively appreciable as intrinsic, ultimate, and universally valid, whether universally appreciated or not."[14] If a critical philosophy of values discloses absolute values to us and if reality steadfastly supports the achievement of such values, then we have evidence that the religious object exists.

Macintosh has been criticized at this point for subjecting God to human criteria. Does not such a theory define and analyze the nature and function of God in terms of a human value system?[15] Can God be God and be subjected to external criteria more ultimate than himself? Macintosh is quite clear that there can be no separation of the divine from value. Apart from the concern for value, there would be no ground for absolute reverence and devotion. Furthermore, are the criteria really external to the divine? We find not only that ultimate reality supports ultimate values, but also that it forces us in the direc-

[11] "ERR," pp. 307 ff.; cf. PRK, pp. 163–4.
[12] "ERR," p. 312.
[13] "ERR," p. 310.
[14] PRK, p. 374.
[15] H. Richard Niebuhr, "Value Theory and Theology," in *The Nature of Religious Experience*, pp. 93–116.

tion of such values, that is, it lays a claim upon us to realize these values. To seek other ends is to be disappointed and, finally, to be driven toward absolute values.

With these criteria we are able to give a preliminary definition of God. God is "the value-producing factor and behavior in the universe, driving toward right adjustment on man's part . . . ,"[16] "a dependable Factor, favorable to spiritual values, and responding to the right religious adjustment,"[17] "the ultimate Object of religious dependence, or the Source of religious deliverance."[18]

Given this preliminary understanding of God, the next step is to confront those experiences in which such divine ideals are being realized. In entering into such experiences we are in the presence of the divine, "an immanence of the divine within nature or humanity or both."[19] Such experiences are instances of religious perception, that is, experiences in which men feel the presence of the divine agency influencing their lives. This agency cannot be identified with human forces, whether the self or society as a whole, for it is responsible for the emergence of man in the first place and thus is prior to all human activities. The experience of this agency is an "experience of spiritual uplift through religious dependence," an "awareness of the presence and activity, within experience, of a Power that makes for a certain type of result in response to the right religious adjustment."[20] In this way what the divinely functioning reality does is revealed, discovered, and known.

Carefully criticized religious experience is thus the source of our knowledge of God. It is important to note that through religious experience we gain knowledge that God is and, in addition, we are able to gain knowledge concerning what God does. It is only at a later stage that we will construct a theological theory on the basis of experience concerning what God is. The next step, according to Macintosh, is to formulate carefully investigated experience into theological laws, that is, to generalize on the basis of experience.

[16] "ERR," p. 395.
[17] PRK, p. 197.
[18] TES, p. 27.
[19] PRK, p. 164.
[20] TES, pp. 31–32.

What we discover is that the reaction of God to man is conditioned by the adjustment of man to God. This adjustment can be positive or negative, responsive or destructive, depending on whether the motive in the action is directed toward proper ends and utilizes the proper means for seeking religious experience.[21] Positive response by God is contingent upon the right religious adjustment. Macintosh is critical of those theologians who claim that man has no part in the working of revelation. God does not act in such a way that man is a mere pawn in the process. Macintosh finds the analogy of sense perception useful. In sense perception we become aware of reality external to ourselves when we are willing to look, hear, taste, etc. When we allow our senses to work we become aware of the influence of reality upon us. The process of sense perception is the product of the use of human capacities and the action of external realities. The same thing is true in religious revelation or religious perception. Revelation or awareness of divine reality occurs only when men make use of their capacity to apprehend it and divinely functioning reality acts to reveal itself.

Making use of our capacity to apprehend the divine means making the right religious adjustment. The right religious adjustment includes (1) concentration of attention on spiritual and moral ends and upon God as the source of these ends and their realization; (2) absolute self-surrender to God and trust that God is a source of help for the attainment of spiritual development; (3) responsiveness to the guidance of God; (4) steady persistence in this attitude of responsive trust and confidence. If these conditions for religious knowledge are met, one will experience in one's life the effects of the activity of God and will know the reality of the working of God in human experience.[22] The right religious adjustment is essentially the same as the life of true prayer.[23]

What theological laws or laws of the religious life are discovered as a result of this experimental faith? They are in the first instance laws which deal with changes in the personal and volitional life of the individual. Macintosh formulates these in a general way: "On condition of the right religious adjustment

[21] PRK, p. 170.
[22] Cf. TES, p. 144; PRK, pp. 170–71.
[23] TES, p. 147; *Personal Religion* (N.Y., Scribner's, 1942), Chap. III.

with reference to desired truly moral states of the will (such as repentance, moral aspiration, and the moral elements in self-control, courage, victory over temptation, faithful service and patient endurance) God the Holy Spirit produces the specific moral results desired."[24] This is the theological law dealing with the elemental experiences of religious life. Macintosh also formulates a similar law dealing with composite experiences which involve such traditional ideas as regeneration, perseverance, and sanctification; salvation is the general term which encompasses all experience of this type. There are also secondary theological laws which deal with the emotional, intellectual, bodily, and social consequences of right religious adjustment.[25]

Macintosh's formulation of these laws in terms of the actions of God and the Holy Spirit has been criticized as assuming the spiritual or essentially personal nature of the divinely functioning reality. In *The Problem of Religious Knowledge* (Ch. XII) he meets the problem by reformulating the laws. For example, he states the elemental law of empirical theology or the law of the answer to prayer (the basic theological law) as follows: "A divinely functioning reality, on condition of the right religious adjustment for a specific volitional effect (the promotion of the good will) tends to produce a desirable change in that direction in the will and character of the individual concerned, and this may be regarded as the basic, dependable 'answer to prayer.' "[26] Laws are stated for conversion, regeneration, perseverance, spiritual health, sanctification, repentance, religious peace, joy, love; religious assurance, guidance, health; the salvation of social groups and society at large.

These laws are not exact in a quantitative sense; rather they are laws of direction and tendency. But for all that, Macintosh holds them to be truly scientific laws. They state constant relationships discoverable within the religious life. As in all science, there are constants and variables. Macintosh sought to delineate the constant relationships in the midst of experienced variation. The constants include nature with its laws, some aspects of human nature and of the social environment, and the being and

[24] TES, p. 148.
[25] TES, Part II, Chap. V.
[26] PRK, p. 203.

character of God, which is the most important constant for empirical theological laws. Among the variables are such factors as individual training and social environment. Most important, however, is the quality and degree of responsiveness of the individual and his particular religious adjustment.[27]

How does Macintosh avoid the criticism that these laws he has formulated do not refer to any external reality but are simply descriptions of the religious psychology of the individual? His answer is that it is not an either/or question. All of the theological laws are also descriptions of the psychology of the individual and can be formulated as psychological laws simply by dropping the reference to God or to divinely functioning reality. However, he contends that they are also evidences for the existence of God. Through these experiences we discover that reality is the cause of dependable results, and this is a disclosure of the dependable character of religious reality, whatever that reality may be. As already indicated, Macintosh holds that this reality is more than man since it antedates and is the cause of human existence.[28]

Theological laws formulate the character of the processes of our religious experience. But science is concerned with more than this. Scientific theory seeks an adequate understanding of the nature of the reality with which experience acquaints us. We acquire scientific understanding of the objects of the experience through our understanding of how the object acts. The same holds for theology as an empirical science. Once theological theory is formulated, it is then capable of further verification by repeated experimentation. It can be gradually substantiated by further positive results or it can be refuted by the discovery of falsifying facts.

On the basis of empirical investigation and the formulation of laws which generalize the results of that investigation, we can, in Macintosh's view, formulate a theological theory concerning the existence and nature of God. We can say that God is known to exist through the experience which we have of him. In addition we can say that he responds to the right re-

[27] TES, pp. 141–2.
[28] PRK, pp. 198 ff.

ligious adjustment; that he regenerates, maintains and promotes the moral and spiritual life; that he convicts of sin, gives peace, joy, and power to love; that he works not only in the life of the individual but in the life of church and of society. In other words, what is discovered in the theological laws can in theological theory be understood as the character of divinely functioning reality.[29]

We have now seen the general way in which Macintosh develops his scientific theology. But theology for Macintosh is more than an empirical science, as we shall see presently. Something must first be said of the limitations of scientific theology. It is limited to consideration of the uniformities discoverable in the data of religious experience and the understanding of the divine through this data. Though much can be known about the character of the divine processes and therefore something about the activities of the divine, we know little in this way concerning what the divine is. For example, we do not know whether divinely functioning reality is one or many. There may be one divine being which is the cause of these results; there may be more than one such being. Again, we do not know whether this being is personal or impersonal. We do not know whether God is more than the universe and its processes, that is, whether God is a being who in some way transcends the universe even though in his activities he is also immanent within the universe. Scientific theology cannot answer these questions. It formulates what can be scientifically known about divine reality, and it provides the indispensable basis upon which all further theological thought must be based and to which it must conform. But it is not adequate in itself to answer all the important questions with which the theologian is concerned.

Scientific empirical theology is not the whole of theology. Within theology proper we can distinguish scientific theology from normative theology and from metaphysical theology. Scientific theology alone gives us knowledge. In both normative theology and metaphysical theology we are dealing with reasoned belief or faith. Within theology one must distinguish that

[29] PRK, p. 209.

material which is fully verified from that which is practically imperative but only partially verified and that which is apparently valuable and not discredited.[30]

NORMATIVE THEOLOGY

Normative theology goes beyond science. As science has its data given to it through perceptual intuition in which reality is disclosed, so normative theology has its basis in what Macintosh terms religious or imaginal intuition. Such intuition is subjective; it is a strong feeling of the reality of an unperceived presence. It is a conviction concerning the nature of transcendent reality. Critical realism with respect to knowledge has disclosed that the reality we know is known only in part. Through our perceptual experiences we become aware of the existence of reality, and we are able to know something of what that reality does. Aside from this, reality transcends perceptual knowledge. But we do have convictions concerning the nature of transcendent reality. These convictions are largely subjective, based on our imaginal intuitions. An example of such an intuition would be the feeling that many men have that the God who exists is the God who is needed for the satisfactory pursuit of the religious life.[31] Such a belief is not known through experience to be true; nonetheless it is a conviction which is subjectively felt to be true.

Can such subjective beliefs form a part of theology? While they do not form a part of scientific theology, they can form a part of normative theology, provided they are critically evaluated and thus become justified as reasonable beliefs. Such evaluation demands that they be in accord with the criteria which govern scientific theology and that they be conformable to or coherent with what is discovered scientifically. In addition Macintosh introduces a pragmatic criterion to which beliefs must be subjected if they are to be regarded as reasonable. He formulates the principle of religious pragmatism thus: "We have the right to believe that those theological doctrines are true which are necessary for the maintenance of the morality which is necessary for the maintenance of the highest well-being of human-

[30] PRK, p. 201.
[31] PRK, p. 368.

ity."[32] Man must act. In practical life a belief is reasonable if it accords with our active tendencies. An idea is theoretically permissible as an object of reasoned belief if it is a necessary presupposition of actions directed toward realization of our fundamental human purposes. This criterion does not permit any belief which may be supported by false rationalization. Again, it must be remembered that it is one criterion along with those criteria which govern scientific theology and is subject to those criteria as well as to the previously formulated results of scientific theology. The pragmatic principle therefore does not stand by itself;[33] it is, however, a necessary further criterion of rational faith.

Given these criteria for testing our religious intuitions, what intuitions are acceptable in the light of critical evaluation? Meaningful religious life involves the commitment of man in trust and confidence that if his will is right he need have no fear of anything the universe can do to him. This moral optimism is practically necessary in that the commitment of one's whole life makes sense only when one feels that the best aims of man and the purposes of God coincide. Furthermore, such optimism is so inspiring that one may say that it is a condition for the realization of the highest ends.[34] Put another way, there emerges within the life of the religious man the imaginal intuition that God is supremely trustworthy and worshipful, fully adequate for all our religious needs.[35]

We are further justified, says Macintosh, in asserting the oneness, the integrated unity and consistency of God. The divinely functioning reality must be at least one, and the burden of showing that it is more than one is on him who would deny the unity of God. This is also justified by the principle of parsimony (not multiplying entities beyond necessity). The reasonable belief that God is one also includes the unity of the immanent and the transcendent aspects of God. Religious intuition also affirms the personal and conscious nature of God. Personality is the highest type of being that we know, and God,

[32] TES, p. 22.
[33] Cf. RC, pp. 17–25.
[34] RC, pp. 46–49.
[35] PRK, p. 361.

in dependably seeking the realization of the highest ideals, is disclosed to us as purposeful, conscious, and personal reality. He is sufficient in power for man's religious needs; this is the practical meaning of omnipotence. And he can be depended on in whatever place and under whatever circumstances we may find ourselves. We therefore can reasonably believe that he is omnipresent. Since he is able to do for us all that needs to be done in order to meet our practical religious needs, we can say that he is wise and, for every practical purpose, omniscient. God is holy love, that is, so far as his character is concerned the God needed for religious life can be reasonably believed to exist. At this point we are also justified in interpreting the effects formulated in the laws of scientific theology as the work of God, the Holy Spirit, rather than the work of a nonpersonal divinely functioning reality.

In the light of what we can reasonably believe about God we are able to say what we can reasonably believe about many other theological topics. A rational belief in immortality is a consequence of our trust in God. The ultimate conservation of all spiritual values, among which must be included the value of individual moral personality, is involved in the belief that God is great enough and good enough to overcome every ultimate threat or disaster. Man is of potentially infinite value as a means to the creation of spiritual values, and one of our basic intuitions is that he is intrinsically valuable in his own right. The values of character and friendship are inseparably bound up with the existence of the individual. Unless these values are to be lost, there must of necessity be continued existence of intelligence, memory, moral activity, and social relations.

In saying that God can be counted on to do all that needs to be done by him for the attainment of the highest spiritual value, we are dealing with the doctrine of divine providence. General providence has to do with the universal actions of God upon all human beings, bringing dissatisfaction and discomfort to those whose lives are morally evil and gradual growth in human fulfillment to those whose lives are directed toward the morally good. There is also special providence for individuals who make the right religious adjustment to God. The laws of scientific theology state what a providential God does for individuals who make the effort to fulfill the special conditions of the religious life.

Human freedom is implied in the foregoing and may, Macintosh declares, be reasonably believed to be true. If man ought to realize the values of moral and spiritual personality, then he must be able to do so. If this is true, then character and all of the other forces which play upon the life of the individual cannot be such that they determine without remainder the choices that man will make. The question of freedom turns on the question whether, in any given situation, the subject might have given more or less attention to an idea or stimulus than in fact he did. That is, though we act within a situation, our reaction to that stimulation, our evaluation of it, is a matter of self-determination within limits. If this is so, then it is at least theoretically possible that some of man's voluntary acts may transcend his already acquired character; rather than already achieved character simply continuing, a change of character may occur in the process of volition or action. Science cannot deny this possibility, and we are justified rationally in believing it as a requirement of moral faith.[36]

In the light of man's moral freedom, any divine predestination to moral evil or purely arbitrary election or rejection must, says Macintosh, be ruled out. A morally perfect God would not be willing for any man ultimately to perish. We cannot say that such a God would work an arbitrary miracle to help one individual and decline to do the same for another. Nor can we say that the disasters suffered by humanity through the orderly processes of nature are to be interpreted as the will of God. They occur within a context of order in which such events can happen as the result of natural processes, but they are not specifically a consequence of the will of God. The natural processes themselves are good, since they are conditions for consistent and integrated beings. Without stable processes within the universe, we could not plan for the future in any rational way, nor would the moral life itself be possible, for it presumes a world stable enough for us to carry out moral aims.[37]

We now come to the critical question concerning the rela-

[36] TES, pp. 68–71; RC, Chap IV.
[37] TES, Part III, Chap. V; RC, Chap. VII.

tionship of Christian faith to Macintosh's theology. Nothing that has been said so far depends uniquely upon the person and work of Christ. What has been said is, however, consistent with the Christian faith and in fact serves to explicate much that is contained within the Christian faith. To that extent, Christian beliefs have been shown to be scientifically verifiable and/or rationally justifiable. The whole of scientific and normative theology to this point can be seen as an apology for the truth of Christian faith insofar as Christian faith affirms these truths of scientific and normative theology.

The person and work of Christ has, however, a place within normative theology. For the Christian community and the Christian man, the life and death of the historical Jesus is apprehended in religious intuition as having normative value as a clue to the character, will, and attitude of the transcendent God. "To employ this idea of the Christ-like as a norm for the criticism of all intuitive faith in God is to make use of what is known as the Christocentric principle."[38] Jesus Christ becomes a principle by which the adequacy or inadequacy of our religious intuitions is judged. This does not mean that the attention of theology centers in concern with doctrines about Christ. The center of theological concern is God. What it means is that God is understood in his inmost nature to be like Christ.

But Jesus Christ is not *the* norm of theology for Macintosh. As we have seen, prior to any norms or criteria which we may use for judging what may be reasonably believed, are the criteria of theology as such. The christocentric principle within normative theology is acceptable because Jesus is found to be the primary example within human history of the right religious adjustment to God. When we study the attempts of man to relate himself in an adequate way to divine reality, we find that the highest fulfillment of this human potential is in Jesus; therefore the fullest revelation of God's will toward man is disclosed in Jesus' life.

Jesus Christ is the true moral example in that his love of man, his recognition of the true worth of men, and his regard for every human life exemplified the highest moral values and

38 PRK, p. 367.

made morality essentially social. He was also the true religious example in that he exemplified in his life the true way of man to God. Through a moral attitude toward a moral God, Jesus sought a relationship to God as the foundation for his relationship to men as well as for its own sake. His moral and religious life constituted a unity in which his life reflected its basis in the will of God. Moreover, he is the true revelation of God. He reveals God through his commitment to the divine in all that he does. His self-surrender to God and the divine quality in his life which came from this self-surrender means that what he does reveals God's will for man. God works in his life, therefore, so that he exercises the divine function of saving man from his sin. For the Christian community he is historically and psychologically the source of salvation. He is the Divine Man because of this divine immanence in him. In affirming the immanence of the divine in Christ, Macintosh does not mean to deny the immanence of the divine elsewhere. Jesus was united with God in the same way in which every human being ought to be united with God. Conversely, it is possible for others to be united to God in the same way in which Jesus was united to God. But the revelation of God in Christ remains normative for the Christian faith.[39]

Macintosh views the virgin birth story as legend, the messianic notions of the second coming and consequent judgment and election as fundamentally mythological. The doctrine of the Trinity, he holds, can be formulated in the light of this view of Christ. The transcendent God, the Father, is immanent in the universe as the Holy Spirit and in the person and work of Jesus as the Son. The transcendent God disclosed to normative theological faith is not different from the immanent God disclosed to empirical theology, and this one God is revealed in Jesus.

Thus in normative theology the revelation of God in Christ can legitimately become the standard by which other revelations are judged. It is consistent with the best that can be discovered through empirical investigation of religious experience, and it is confirmed practically in the life of the committed Christian. The essence of Christian faith can be subjected to

[39] Cf. RC, pp. 149–53; *Personal Religion*, pp. 112–19.

the most rigorous examination and can be shown to involve a reasonable belief.

METAPHYSICAL THEOLOGY

The final test of theology, according to Macintosh, is the submission of theology to the critical examination of metaphysics. Such final criticism by metaphysics is not unique to theology. Every discipline must finally find its ultimate justification through metaphysical analysis. It is the function of metaphysics to combine the more general results of the various sciences in a comprehensive and self-consistent world view. In the course of developing such a world view each of the various sciences will be subjected to critical examination of its assumptions.[40] Metaphysics will be changed by the inclusion of theological results among the data of metaphysics, and theology will be changed by the confrontation of theology with the other data of metaphysics.

An empirical theology will have both problems to suggest to metaphysics and solutions of problems for metaphysical consideration. Clearly, no final solution to the metaphysical problem of the relation of nature and the supernatural is possible which does not take into account the data of theology. Macintosh tentatively suggests that the answer to this problem may be to understand the physical universe as the body of God. We have already seen something of the consequences of theological thought for the problem of determinism and freedom. In addition to these problems, Macintosh sees the problems of substance and activity, mind and matter, body and mind, creation and evolution, mechanism and teleology, law and chance, the one and the many, the absolute and the relative, the finite and the infinite, and good and evil as fundamental metaphysical questions. In all of these questions theological considerations are relevant and no final answer is possible which does not take into account the results of theology. The problem with metaphysics has been that the natural sciences have developed more rapidly than the social and theological sciences, with the consequence that metaphysical solutions have tended to be

[40] PRK, pp. 374–5.

heavily materialistic. Careful and critical investigation can redress this balance.

Theology must, argues Macintosh, submit itself to metaphysical examination. If it refuses this final theoretical test, it would to that extent undermine if not lose the certitude of faith. Scientific theology has a firm basis in empirical knowledge. Combined with normative theology, it has become subjectively certain and reasonable faith. But this subjective certitude must become tentative for the purpose of metaphysical examination in order that it may pass from subjective certitude to objective certainty. Contrary to what Kierkegaard and Barth suggest, theology need not remain in the permanent tension of certainty and doubt. When every test has been supplied the resulting synthesis will be more and more objectively certain. Macintosh is convinced that the final solution of the problems of metaphysics will leave room for the truth of religious faith.[41]

The theological position which Macintosh developed sought to meet the need of religious man in the twentieth century by being adequately critical while at the same time grounding itself on the foundation of religious experience. He sought to provide justification for theological truths through critical philosophical analysis. He was also aware of the historical and psychological dimension of religion and sought to give a sufficient place to historically conditioned and psychologically important normative religious intuitions. Careful analysis of religious affirmations shows that there are levels of meaning and of truth. The aim of theology is to transform beliefs which rest on subjective certitude, so far as possible, to truths which are objectively certain. His final conclusion is that within the limits of what is logically and psychologically possible, "we have the moral right to believe as we must, if we are to live as we ought."[42]

[41] Cf. TES, pp. 249–62; RC, pp. 251–81.
[42] PRK, p. 382.

Bibliography

D. C. Macintosh, *The Problem of Religious Knowledge*, N.Y., Harper, 1940.

No detailed studies about Macintosh are available.

WILLIAM TEMPLE

Joseph Fletcher

Dorothy Sayers in an essay called "The Greatest Drama Ever Staged" says that official Christianity "of late years, has been having what is known as a bad press. We are constantly assured that the churches are empty because preachers insist too much upon doctrine—'dull dogma,' as people call it. The fact is the precise opposite. It is the neglect of dogma that makes for dullness. The Christian faith is the most exciting drama that ever staggered the imagination of man—and the dogma is the drama."

More than any other Anglican theologian in modern times, William Temple has recalled to modern Christians what strong meat the classical faith of the church can be. The Epistle to the Hebrews tells us that "everyone that uses milk is unskillful in the word of *righteousness,* for he is a babe." Archbishop Temple never failed to remark that in the Greek text the word used here is *dikaiosunee,* or "justice"—troublesome, radical, critical, prophetic judgment, not personal, mystical, private rectitude. "But strong meat belongs to them that are of full age, even those who by reason of use have their senses exercised to discern both good and evil" (5:14).

Possibly the most important lesson we have to learn from Temple's life and thought is that the dogma is the drama. The three areas of Christian leadership in which he was especially active were expository and apologetic theology, radical social analysis, and ecumenical thought and effort. In all these enterprises his contributions were solidly grounded in classical Christianity and in a consistently theological frame of reference. After a brief account of his life we will look at what he did and said in each of these three areas. It will be abundantly plain that he was first and foremost a theologian. Temple treated theology as it should be treated—as a method of faith interpretation applicable to every aspect of human life.

"Theological ideas," it has been said, "are created on the Continent, corrected in England, and corrupted in America." If

this tart saying has any basis in fact, William Temple played
no conscious part in the theological process it describes. Like
F. D. Maurice nearly a century before him, he neither cited nor
drew upon any Continental theological sources, and only a very
few Continental philosophers had any impact on him. He alone
among English-speaking theologians of the twentieth century
wrote with virtually no reference to such recent architects of
Protestant Christianity as Schleiermacher, Kierkegaard, Ritschl,
Troeltsch, Schweitzer, nor to those of our own time—Barth,
Brunner, and Bultmann.

It is not that Temple was a provincial or a chauvinist. He was
never "a little Englishman" or a Colonel Blimp in outlook and
feeling. As a young Oxford don he took a leave to sit at the
feet of Harnack and Simmel, and another to study with Eucken
and Wendt in Jena. He watched the contributions of Continen-
tals cross the Channel through the journals. He used Greek and
Latin freely and had a prodigious memory. No doubt his lack
of concern with Continental theology was in some measure due
to the Catholic and classical orientation of his theology. At the
same time his lifelong role in the ecumenical movement is evidence enough that he was not indifferent or antagonistic to
Reformation perspectives. Actually his writing was just as sparing of reference to Roman Catholics and the Orthodox as to
Continental Protestants.

Temple once told his wife that his highest wish was to "master
the great stream of classical theology," but not the Reformers
or the disputes of the Counter Reformation. The plain truth is
that Temple was every inch an Anglican, standing between
Romanism and Protestantism in the *via media* or bridge-church
position, at what the French scholar Father George Tavard has
called "the crossroads."[1]

PERSONAL HISTORY

William Temple, Archbishop of Canterbury, was the son of an
Archbishop of Canterbury. He was "born to the purple" on
October 15, 1881, the second son of Frederick Temple, at that
time Bishop of Exeter; he died on October 26, 1944. This was

[1] *Protestantism* (N.Y., Hawthorn, 1959), pp. 91–106.

the only father-to-son line ever to sit in St. Augustine's Chair. After becoming a "scholar" at Rugby he went on to Balliol College, Oxford, where as an "exhibitioner" he won honors in classics in the intermediate "moderation" (1902) and in his final examination or "greats" (1904). At Balliol the idealist Edward Caird—and especially his dialectical synthesis of supposedly conflicting views—was a significant influence on Temple. Of the three major concerns in Temple's life, two were already manifest in his undergraduate days—social redemption and the apologetic exposition of the Christian faith. The third, the ecumenical movement, came almost as early: while a young philosophy don at Queen's he began to take an active part in the Student Christian Movement. In 1910 he went as an S.C.M. steward to the Edinburgh meeting of the International Missionary Conference, and following that made a tour as an S.C.M. lecturer in Australia.

During his Balliol days he was elected president of the Oxford Union, a top university distinction. His involvement in social service through the university settlements in London's Bermondsey and Bethnal Green matured quickly into a conviction that the poor had to produce their own leaders and that education was a vital part of the strategy. For this reason he entered the Workers' Education Association with his school friend R. H. Tawney in 1905 and stayed on faithfully as its president from 1908 to 1924. At the same time he began to fly the flag of the Labour Party, keeping on as its consistent but not uncritical supporter all his life. He formally joined the party in 1918, remaining a "card carrier" until 1925, when he took his seat in the House of Lords. Then he quietly dropped his membership to avoid the side issues inevitably associated with adherence— or seeming adherence—to a doctrinaire position. At a Pan-Anglican Congress in 1908 and in *The Economic Review* he said, in language he later modified, that the alternatives were "socialism or heresy."[2]

Upon receiving his degree Temple was offered some thirty posts. He chose a teaching fellowship at Queen's College, and his remarkable gift for analysis and exposition of both abstract

[2] M. B. Reckitt, *Maurice to Temple* (London, Faber and Faber, 1947), p. 412.

and concrete questions soon marked him as a man to watch. Since early boyhood Temple had meant to be ordained, but in 1906 Francis Paget, the Bishop of Oxford, refused to order him deacon because he was only "very tentatively" inclined to accept the Virgin Birth and the bodily resurrection. Randall Davidson, successor to Temple's father at Canterbury, was less cautious and ordained him in 1908. In 1910 he accepted the headmastership of Repton, an old public school in the Midlands. However, he soon learned that he was out of his proper element, and when in 1914 Lord Chancellor Haldane offered him the benefice of St. James' Church in London's Piccadilly, he accepted it gladly.

In London, Temple's preaching and writing caught on with a socially varied public. In 1915 he was made honorary chaplain to the king, and crossed the war-hazardous Atlantic to deliver the Paddock Lectures (on Church and Nation) at General Theological Seminary in New York. In 1916 he married Frances Anson, secretary of the Christian Social Union, of which he was chairman. (No children were born of their lifelong marriage.)

The First World War and the turbulent years just after pushed William Temple into national prominence. The Church of England as the "established" church was under fire, accused of having sold out to Toryism and imperialism. In response to popular disillusionment with the church, Temple led what was largely a young men's fight for a truer measure of Anglican self-government and self-respect. It began first with the National Mission of Repentance and Hope, of which he was secretary; but after the report of the Archbishops' Commission on Church and State (Temple was its youngest member) appeared, the young men converted the mission into a new and broader program called the Life and Liberty Movement (1917).

Temple was chosen to be the leader of the movement and editor of its magazine *Challenge*. The movement aimed both at widening the Church's role in social and industrial life and at setting up a Church Assembly, or national synod. He resigned the St. James pastorate, dropping his income from 2,000 to 700 pounds a year in order to give full time to stumping the country. He sought life and liberty for the church—if necessary, he said, "even at the cost of disestablishment." Evangelicals and high churchmen alike joined in the campaign. Temple, with his love of causes and his distaste for church party-liners, was in his element. Then, in 1919, the House of Commons passed an Enabling Act for the Assembly—a victory for Temple, though less than what he wanted. Later on he was deeply disappointed by Parliament's refusal to allow the 1928 revision of the Prayer Book (and at his request his own funeral service in Canterbury was conducted according to the Revised Book). But in 1919 the Enabling Act was a great step forward.

That same year Temple was given a canonry at Westminster Abbey. It was an almost certain way-station to a bishopric, and in only two years' time he was nominated by Lloyd George as Bishop of Manchester. By then he had already published ten volumes of apologetics and philosophical theology and had contributed to various symposia, such as *Foundations* (1912), a work by seven Oxford theologians on Christian belief for modern times, and *Competition* (1917), produced by an interdenominational "collegium" dealing with social issues.

During his Manchester episcopacy, Temple began chairing the Archbishops' Commission on Doctrine (1925–38), and in 1924 he headed the Interdenominational Conference on Politics, Economics and Citizenship, held in Birmingham. He tried unsuccessfully to mediate in the national coal strike in 1926. He published eight more books. At the 1927 Lausanne Conference on Faith and Order he continued his ecumenical labors, serving as chairman of its continuation committee at gatherings everywhere in Europe. He also took part in the 1928 Jerusalem meeting of the International Missionary Council. In 1928 Prime Minister Stanley Baldwin persuaded Temple to accept the Northern primacy of York. Temple's exposition of theology to students gave him considerable stature in university circles. Sympathizing with the students' doubts and difficulties, he suggested that the church inaugurate a new "associate membership" for those whose fellowship was a moral and spiritual reality but not yet a settled intellectual certainty.

As Archbishop of York (1922–42) Temple became even more of a world figure. He was sworn in on England's Privy Council; an ardent advocate of the League of Nations, he preached at the Disarmament Conference at Geneva in 1932;

and he took the chair on Christian Unity at his first Lambeth (worldwide) Conference of Anglican bishops (1930). He continued to preach university missions; he delivered the Gifford Lectures at Glasgow (November 1932–March 1934); on behalf of the International Convention of the Student Volunteer Movement he revisited the United States (1935–36), at which time he lectured at Harvard, the University of Chicago, and Washington's College of Preachers. At the same time his energies were equal to meeting the demands of his diocese and his obligations as Metropolitan of his province. And with all this he managed to produce in his York period another dozen volumes, in addition to journal and magazine articles and chapters in such important symposia as *Contemporary British Philosophy, Revelation, Men Without Work,* and *Doctrine in the Church of England.*

Ecumenics was much to the fore in Temple's thinking. He worked for Christian unity on all fronts—in evangelism and missions, life and work, faith and order. In 1937 he was active on two commissions of the Oxford Life and Work Conference on Church, Community and State and drafted its Message. Two weeks later he moved to the chair of the Faith and Order Conference in Edinburgh. His leadership naturally put him in the chair of the provisional committee of the World Council of Churches, which met at Utrecht in 1938. In spite of Anglo-Catholic resistance he succeeded in winning the English church's approval of the World Council. Moreover, he asked the Cardinal Secretary of the Vatican for exchange of information and unofficial consultation with Roman Catholic theologians; the Vatican "saw no obstacles in the way."[3]

Cut off from the Continental churches by the Second World War, Temple marshaled his forces at home for the foundation of the British Council of Churches, saying in his sermon at its inauguration that "the primary need is for more clear and united testimony to Christianity itself. The difference between Catholic and Protestant is very small as compared with the difference between Christian and non-Christian." He attended the Amsterdam World Christian Youth Conference just before war broke

[3] F. A. Iremonger, *William Temple* (London, Oxford Univ. Press, 1948), p. 412.

out in the summer of 1939. His chairmanship of the 1941 Malvern Conference—intended to shape Christian thought for "a new society" as part of the nation's war aims—made it quite plain that as he saw it the Anglican communion was not any longer "the conservative party at prayer."[4]

Temple was enthroned at Canterbury as primate of all England on April 23, 1942, following Lang's retirement. It was, said George Bernard Shaw, "a realized impossibility." In plain fact it was rare indeed for a man of letters and learning to be elevated to that seat—in this case one who was also a social liberal, an irenic Christian, and as much distrusted by the Federation of British Industries as he was trusted by the broad mass of Englishmen. His sobriquet was "the people's Archbishop." In that moment of national struggle Winston Churchill had no alternative but to accede to the appointment.

The demands of a wartime primacy, however, were taxing in the extreme for Temple. With the appearance of his *Christianity and Social Order* in 1942, which in its first edition alone ran to 129,000 copies, all major publication ended for him. He lived only two and a half years longer, moving up and down and back and forth across the land—attending "Religion and Life" and Industrial Christian Fellowship meetings, giving quiet days for clergy and laity, lecturing to philosophical societies and civic gatherings, working in the House of Lords for measures like the Butler Act (an education bill). Many of these addresses were gathered together and published posthumously in a volume titled *The Church Looks Forward* (1944). Ironically, he died of gout in spite of being a teetotaler. His death in October 1944 came peacefully a week before his sixty-third birthday.

Temple was much more caught up in church administration and public affairs than the other theologians dealt with in this volume. The preceding account of his life and enterprise is therefore necessary background to an understanding and assessment of his thought. The full flavor of Temple's contributions to what he called "theological philosophy"—to say nothing of the other phases of his thought—comes only when those con-

---

[4] Cf. *Malvern, 1941: The Life of the Church and the Order of Society* (London, Longmans, Green, 1942).

tributions are viewed within the context of his ceaseless activity as a man of affairs. He believed that our times need what Thomas Aquinas did for his, but he never for a moment supposed this to be his own role. He produced no *Summa;* his extensive treatises *Mens Creatrix, Christus Veritas, Nature, Man and God* were put together in spare moments between speeches in the House of Bishops or the House of Lords, ecumenical meetings, episcopal duties, university missions. Yet the "system" implicit in the scores of volumes and essays he wrote is in nearly every way the most comprehensive, versatile, and lucid achievement by an Anglican theologian of this age. Had he gone into a purely academic career his gifts would have guaranteed him a prominent place in British intellectual life, but very likely at the expense of the scope and concreteness which brought his thinking into such close alignment with both the reformer's vision and the apologist's urgency.

THEOLOGY: EXPOSITORY AND APOLOGETIC

Temple approached virtually everything theologically. For him theology was a method, not primarily a body of doctrines. He was convinced that all human problems and concerns must be theologized, i.e., set in a framework of Christian faith. To do this obviously calls for a vast amount of integrative thought, hence his ceaseless concern with the relations of faith and reason. The Christian starts with faith, he held, then his reason uses faith to illuminate every question. Though sympathetic to Anselm's *credo ut intelligam,* Temple insisted that once the leap of faith is made, reason must come into play as its skillful servant and friendly critic. "Faith is not a conclusion but a starting point; reason will enrich its content." Thus "God is for faith not an interference, but a datum," because "the man of faith does not reach his faith by scientific inference."[5] Faith propositions are decisions, not conclusions; thus the so-called logical proofs of the existence of God are only arguments. God is not to be found through a syllogism or a microscope or a telescope.

[5] *Thoughts on Some Problems of the Day* (London, Macmillan, 1931), pp. 6–7.

"The primary assurances of religion are the ultimate questions of philosophy."

Reason is, in Temple's view, the lantern with which faith's light is focused. It is also the link between the Christian's believing and his behaving. In this sense Temple was a rationalist. He would not flout or ignore reasonable tests of faith's internal and external consistency. In his method reason's service to faith is correlation, not verification. He had no sympathy with Luther's reference to "Dame Reason" as a whore. As to Barth's dictum that "God is not only unprovable and unsearchable, but also inconceivable," Temple agreed on the first two points but not on the third. He was confident that "by analogy we make progress" in our pursuit of theological questions, "even though we never reach their ultimate solution."[6] He declared firmly, "I see no alternative to the acceptance of the method of analogy."[7]

Like his Balliol teacher Edward Caird, Temple was a man of coherent convictions; to use a distinction come into use since his day, his aptitude was for coherent rather than analytical reason; he thought inclusively, not exclusively. His amazing ability to find middle terms and to mediate apparently divorced or contradictory views in an irenic and conciliatory reinterpretation—so invaluable to the World Council of Churches in its formative, pre-Amsterdam years—he referred to as his "parlour trick." Dean Matthews said that Temple's "comprehensive" method was "fired" by a "synthetic impulse." Temple himself said it was his "temperamental disposition, fortified by the fact that my master in logic was Edward Caird, to start from the assumption that every conviction strongly held is at least partly true, and that, as a rule, our wisdom is to find out, if we can, where this partial truth fits into the whole fabric."[8] In short, his theological method was a decidedly Anglican one.

Temple's third primary category along with faith and reason was revelation. In his view revelation has two dimensions—divine initiative or self-disclosure, and human response or be-

---

[6] *Nature, Man and God* (London, Macmillan, 1935), p. 441.

[7] *Religious Experience* (London, J. Clarke, 1958), p. 231.

[8] Intro., O. C. Quick, *Gospel and the New World* (London, 1944), p. xii.

lieving apprehension. God makes His mind and will manifest both in His creation (general revelation or "natural theology") and in decisive direct action, most crucially in the God-man event in Christ (special revelation or "revealed theology"). But the total process of revelation is "the coincidence of divinely controlled event and minds divinely illuminated to read it aright."[9] Even the Bible, the Word of God, is refracted or sifted first through the finite personalities of its writers, then through those of its readers. What it reveals depends partly on how it says what it says, partly on how it is "heard." While this is obviously a theory of revelation by inspiration, it is not a gnostic notion of secret saving knowledge given to some and withheld from others; on the contrary, Temple always held that the "believing interpretation" is not a special gift at all but the work of the Holy Spirit through reason, the fellowship of the church, the sacraments, and character-forming experience in human society and brotherhood.

Temple's starting point in his Gifford Lectures was that the difference between natural theology and revealed theology is one of method only, not of content. By the same token he set aside the division commonly made between "philosophy" and "theology," claiming that it is intellectually unrealistic to call the first an enterprise of reason, the second of faith. He held that since reason and faith cannot be artificially disconnected or pulled loose from each other, the true task of theology is to reason clearly and fully (i.e., philosophize) about faith.

In the last analysis, Temple was convinced, faith is a matter not of holding correct opinions but of having personal fellowship with the living Lord. What is offered to men in revelation is not a truth or truths about God but God Himself. Two cardinal principles in Temple's method of theologizing were: (1) man's finite intelligence can at best only apprehend God, not comprehend Him, and (2) faith is essentially not belief about God but a relationship of trust (*pistis*), that is, a moral rather than an intellectual matter. His last formal counsel to "the younger theologians" was to urge their more serious consideration of experiential rather than propositional theology.

[9] *Revelation*, John Baillie and Hugh Martin, eds. (London, Faber and Faber, 1937), p. 107.

On the doctrinal side Temple's theology was centered in the incarnation. Affirming Jesus' simple statement "He that hath seen Me hath seen the Father," he saw Christian theology as "God in the light of the Incarnation" and Christian anthropology as "man in the light of the Incarnation." God became man and preached and taught and died on a cross and rose again. Temple never hesitated to insist on the absurdity and scandal of it, as seen from the Greek perspective. The God who dared to become not only a man but a criminal in a divine act of shocking sacrificial love—this God was his starting point.

At the same time, like F. D. Maurice, Temple in Platonic fashion declared that "Christ is not only *a* man, He is Man."[10] The incarnation added not merely another individual to the human race; it was the confluence of deity and humanity, which "raised our humanity to an entirely higher level, to a level with His own." Temple espoused a strong christocentric doctrine of man in terms of "solidarism" (cf. Maurice's "He is the Head of the Body"). He was confident that what had been done for man metaphysically or essentially or latently in the saving effects of the incarnation—this at-one-ment in Christ—would become historical or existential or realized. The membership of men one with another would come to be known and acknowledged here or hereafter by all. As to the question of the mode by which the divine and human were to be united, Temple was agnostic. He rejoiced that Chalcedon (A.D. 451) only affirmed the fact without saying how. "It would be disastrous," he said, "if there were an official Church explanation of the Incarnation."[11]

In the doctrine of "the Word made flesh" he found a theological foundation for Christian materialism—a dialectical materialism, not unlike Marxism's, in which the incarnational interpenetration of the spiritual and material, as of the divine and human, is the first principle. It was Temple who made the first major break away from idealism in post-Reformation Anglican theology. God acts in history through and by means of material things. Therefore, he said, "Christianity is the most avowedly materialist of all the great religions."[12] The incarnation

[10] *Christus Veritas* (London, Macmillan, 1924), p. 153.
[11] *Ibid.*, p. 134.
[12] *Nature, Man and God*, p. 478.

is a cosmic dialectic, as every sacrament is a particular dialectic. And why does God so act, giving up His wholly otherness? Said Temple, "Although He had no need of us for the fulness of His being, He has need of us for the satisfaction of His love. . . . The World minus God equals zero: God minus the World equals God."[13] Yet because of His loving nature, God conceives and creates and relates; while He does not need objects, He necessitates them!

Temple adhered too firmly to the biblical ethos to conceive of God as anything so impersonal as Being-itself. Men are men only because they are personal beings, and they are personal only because God is personal; they share this capacity for self-identity precisely because they are made in His image. God is not impassive but loving. Therefore God suffered in true patripassian fashion. "Suffering," Temple said, "is not the ultimate evil. Hate is the ultimate evil." In spite of his almost lyric admiration for Greek literature and philosophy, Temple rejected the classicist orientation at any point where it was in opposition to the biblicist orientation. "Christ," he acknowledged, "does not reveal all that is meant by the word God. There ever remains the unsearchable abyss of Deity. But He reveals what it vitally concerns us to know; He reveals God the Father."[14]

For Temple the concepts of incarnation and atonement were inseparable, that is, he saw the Christ event and its consequences as a unity. Some not too careful students of Temple have held that he strongly emphasized the incarnation but neglected the atonement. On the contrary, toward the end of his life, in a time of wars and revolution, he maintained that the contemporary upheavals in human hearts and societies called more for a theology of redemption than one of explanation. He came to emphasize the saving effect of God's incarnation and only secondarily saw in it the key to meaning and existence, for he wanted to encourage contemporaneity in the younger theologians. At the same time he insisted that these two "theologies" —the incarnation-centered and the atonement-centered—are only emphases, are actually part and parcel of each other.

13 *Ibid.*, p. 435.
14 *Readings in St. John's Gospel*, 2 Vols. London, Macmillan, 1939–40), Vol. I, p. 18.

Thus, as Temple saw it, the atonement has both an objective and a subjective side. The objective side is what God had done for man, His taking up of man's being into His own in a new creation ("redemption") and his incarnational revelation of Himself by word and deed. Yet Temple did not believe that the incarnation (nativity, ministry, crucifixion, resurrection, ascension) restored men to a right relation with God as far as God was concerned. "Christ's death and Resurrection did not cause God to be after their occurrence what He was not before." Nevertheless, the revelation of His love was an objective event and a new fact without which men could not be "saved," i.e., enter into the knowledge, worship, and service of God. The subjective side of the atonement is of course man's response to God's offer of Himself, a response which is free and uncoerced. The completion of atonement "is accomplished through our realization of the love of God."

Temple viewed the so-called "moral influence" theories as part of the truth about the atonement. He insisted that even if he wishes to affirm more concerning the atonement, every Christian can agree with Abelard that "Christ by His manifestation of His love awakens love in us, and that is the Atonement."[15] The unconquerable and creative love of God is manifested in the objective fact of the incarnation. The freedom of man is respected in the subjective side—man's ability to say Yes or No, or to say nothing, to God's redeeming sacrifice. But whether or not men respond, the facts of the "new creation" and the "new life" remain.

In Temple's theology, as in the gospels, the Kingdom of God is the key concept. By "Kingdom" Temple meant not so much God's realm as His rule, though his concept encompassed both. Inaugurated by Christ, the Kingdom is eventually to reorder and rule all the structures of life—economic, political, familial, personal, etc. Temple was no pietist, restricting redemption to purely individual and "religious" affairs. The Kingdom is for this world, though not "of" it. He was a "conversionist" in H. Richard Niebuhr's sense: one who believes that ultimately and progressively God's grace will convert the whole world to

[15] *Faith and Modern Thought* (London, Macmillan, 1910), p. 133.

His will for it. Temple never, however, endorsed the nineteenth-century idea of automatic or inevitable progress, or the idea of automatic harmony to be found in laissez-faire social philosophy; this error of the American liberal Protestant "social gospel" made little or no headway in either Anglican or Continental social theology. Temple's theology was neither a "bootstrap" one, claiming that men could build the Kingdom by their own powers, nor a "stalemate" theology, holding that God's will cannot be realized within history even though He is Lord of it, that it is something for "beyond" history only. In short, his eschatology was prophetic rather than apocalyptic or gnostic or "pie in the sky."

The church, as Temple understood it, stands in relation to the Kingdom as a means to an end. "As Christ's purpose was to found a Kingdom, so we should think of the Church as the army of that Kingdom." Temple never swallowed the Catholic "heresy" which treats the Church as an end in itself, the highest good. He held that it is related to the Kingdom as batter is to cake—a chief means and ingredient in God's purpose. Still, Temple acknowledged the importance of the extra-ecclesiastical work of the Holy Spirit and of the power of uncovenanted grace The Swedish bishop Yngve Brilioth remarked after Temple's death that "the criticism against Anglo-Saxon theology as founded on a superficial conception of the Kingdom of God cannot be applied to him."[16]

As a consequence of his personalist theology, Temple's anthropology was personalist. He conceived of both human and divine personality as "purposive will organized for action." Will, he held with Plato and Aristotle, is not a faculty or function like emotion and intellect, but the purposiveness which is released when they are integrated. To ask if the will is free is tautologically to ask, "Has the power to choose the power to choose?" Though almost completely ignorant of modern psychology, Temple had a realistic if unsophisticated understanding of it. He declared that personality is the capacity to choose rather than be "hung up" by conflicting desires and reasoning, and that the power of choice, or freedom, is the key to personal status.

[16] Iremonger, *op. cit.*, p. 605.

The end and aim of God's creative purpose, Temple held, is the realization of the full personal potential of every human being. In his view personality is the highest and the only intrinsic value, the only value which is always good in itself. Furthermore, he held that there is no good (value) of any kind at all apart from persons. The goodness of a thing "depends for its actuality upon the appreciating mind."[17] And he was insistent that society or fellowship is the matrix of personality; a person is a socialized individual. As he put it (with no knowledge of Buber's "dialogic" thesis), "I am only I in my relationship with You, and You are only You, or capable of being called an *I*, in your relationship with Me."[18] Community, he was sure, progressively engulfs and repairs all fragmentations—of nations, races, classes, etc.

The logic of Temple's understanding of God as purposive will, of creation as a process, and of the Kingdom as *for* yet not of the world, led him to a developmental view of history and providence. All things exist in dynamic, ascending grades, developing upward from matter to life to mind to spirit. Each grade, he said, develops only as it is indwelt by what is above, though it also depends on what is below it. All of this is a process of value-achievement. His world view was akin to Whitehead's and L. S. Thornton's theistic process-doctrine, and was suggested to him by the creative or emergent evolution of Samuel Alexander and Lloyd Morgan.

Temple's view of history as God's creative process was not only purposive (teleological); it entailed moral as well as technical and cultural progress. This is what it means, he insisted, to speak prophetically of God as the Lord of history. Moreover, he not only rejected "automatic" progress in society and culture but also distinguished sharply between moral progress at the level of nature and at the level of grace. Therefore, while he saw in history evidence of human success in moving from stupid to enlightened self-interest, apart from Christ he saw no possibility of disinterested love.

Contrary to the neo-orthodox emphasis, Temple was certain

[17] *Nature, Man and God,* p. 211.
[18] *Christianity in Thought and Practice* (N.Y., Morehouse, 1936), p. 68.

that modern secularized men are not half so blind to the reality of sin as they are skeptical about the reality of grace. He treated sin (especially "original" sin) as selfishness—"self-centeredness and all the welter of evil flowing from it." Most men, he contended, know this experientially even if they do not conceptualize it theologically. What men do not believe is that there is a power greater than their own to help them. Grace, he pointed out, is God himself—not something God "gives" but something He is, just as love is not something God "has" but something He is. In our experience of grace God gives Himself, as in the sacrament of the altar. And only God can rescue us from our self-captivity. "Education may make my self-esteem less disastrous by widening my horizon of interest; so far it is like climbing a tower, which widens the horizon for physical vision while leaving me still the center and standard of reference."[19] The Pelagian notion that men can of themselves overcome their selfishness was in Temple's opinion the only intrinsically damnable heresy.

The new self that God's love (grace) has "saved" reaches out for wider fellowship. "The true aim of the soul is not its own salvation: to make that the chief aim is to ensure its perdition; for it is to fix the soul on itself as centre."[20] Fellowship is the consequence of grace, as it is the goal of the creative process. Creation's "one increasing purpose" through the ages is to bring about the practical, conscious solidarity of mankind. It has been so from the start of the world. Temple was always careful to describe the "fall" not as an event but as a myth; he discarded all prescientific notions of aboriginal virtue. Savage men in the "garden" were innocent and therefore without virtue morally; their "fall" was a fall upwards to the knowledge of sin and hence to ethical decision and personal responsibility. At the same time, Temple insisted that "none of these evolutionary theories touches the centre of the problem," for over and beyond our not always seeing the goals and demands of God's will (good will), we often do see them yet turn our backs.[21]

Even though he expressed hesitation about "universalism,"

[19] *Christianity and Social Order* (N.Y., Penguin, 1942), p. 50.
[20] *Nature, Man and God*, p. 390.
[21] *Citizen and Churchman* (London, Eyre & Spottiswoode, 1941), p. 64.

on balance Temple was confident that God's love would win all men to full fellowship (sonship) with Him by means of their new creation in Christ—if not in this world then in another. He saw through to the hidden salvation-by-works doctrine lurking in the post-Reformation distortion of salvation by faith, i.e., the notion that men are "saved" by their faith in God, when in fact they are saved by His unshakable faith (*pistis*) in them. "All that we can contribute of our own would be the resistance of our self-will. It is just this which love breaks down, and in so doing does not over-ride our freedom but rather calls it into exercise."[22]

THEOLOGY: SOCIAL AND PROPHETIC

Temple's basic ethical position was relativistic. In his view the good is whatever is right, the right whatever is good, in the circumstances. The ideal or standard in his ethics was love as manifested in Christ. Reason, serving love, must in every situation weigh the factors as wisely as possible. What is right in one set of conditions may be wrong in another: "an act cannot, strictly speaking, be wrong in itself."[23] "Universal obligation attaches not to particular judgments of conscience, but to conscientiousness. What acts are right may depend on circumstances . . . but there is an absolute obligation to will whatever may on each occasion be right."[24] For this reason he opposed absolutist pacifism, even though he defended and protected pacifists. As a matter of Christian ethics he identified justice as the social dimension of the love norm. "It is axiomatic that Love should be the predominant Christian impulse, and that the primary form of Love in social organization is Justice. . . . Love, in fact, finds its primary expression in Justice."[25] In short, Temple regarded justice as love (neighbor concern) facing the fact that we have many neighbors, that rarely if ever is it just one individual whose claims are binding on us.

[22] *Nature, Man and God*, p. 469.
[23] *Essays in Christian Politics* (London, Longmans, Green, 1927), p. 123.
[24] *Nature, Man and God*, p. 405.
[25] *Christianity and Social Order*, p. 75.

A second feature of Temple's ethics was his concept of "natural order," which he sometimes called natural law. Actually, however, his personalistic view of value (it has to be worth something to some person) and his extrinsic, relativistic view of obligation (acts are never right or wrong in themselves) were not consistent with classical natural law theory. He never spoke, as would a Roman Catholic moral theologian, of "natural" moral laws "discernible by human reason" and "given in the nature of things." He believed that this doctrine had lost out when it had sought to fix forever a "special relation to a feudal and peasant society."[26] What he meant by "natural order" was a given God-willed, functional means-end pattern of life. For example, he argued teleologically that in the natural order of economics goods are produced to satisfy human needs, and finance assists the exchange of goods and labor: finance exists for production's sake, production for consumption's sake. When bankers control and even restrain industrialists, and industrialists control and even restrain the supply of goods, ends are subordinated to means, and *inordinatio* (i.e., sin) results.

Temple followed Aquinas and Aristotle in the view that man is a *zoön politikon,* a social being. A person, he said, is an individual in community: a socialized individual. Society is an "order" of creation: it is real or natural in the sense of original or elemental. Hence the social order was of vital concern to his basic relationship theology. The state he insisted, is only an agency of society (although important as such); politically to identify state and society or to subordinate society "is the one great heresy."[27] Hence his theological emphasis on democracy.

To Temple the state was good though corruptible; he did not concur with the libertarian notion that the best government is the least government. In fact, in this regard he stood in the tradition of Plato, St. Paul, Augustine, Aquinas, Luther, Calvin, Hooker, and (interestingly) Marx, rather than with John Milton, Thomas Jefferson, Guizot, Cavour, and the liberal Protestant separationists. This partly explains his genuine preference (even in the Life and Liberty Movement) for a church-state coalition provided it could be maintained on terms suitable to the Gospel's

---

[26] *Ibid.,* p. 79.
[27] *Christianity and the State* (London, Macmillan, 1928), p. 45.

integrity. "We have a divine commission; we exist as a divine creation. If the earthly State likes to associate with us, let it."[28]

Temple was too Anglican and too irenic to embrace a doctrinaire social ideology. He called himself a Christian socialist, in the line of F. D. Maurice, Kingsley, Westcott, Gore, and others. As an Oxford don he was a convinced adherent of evolutionary socialism, and he never abandoned it. Yet in a lecture tour in Australia in 1910 he was already qualifying his socialism by acknowledging some good in private enterprise; he favored "free enterprise conducted in a spirit of public service."[29] By the thirties he was an advocate of economic pluralism or a "mixed" economy. "Our problem," he said, "is to get the best out of both" capitalism and socialism.[30] For obvious theological reasons he was never a Marxist. Yet as a sacramentalist he appreciated the Marxist concept of dialectical materialism and once thought of calling his Gifford Lectures "A Study in Dialectical Realism." "The Christian understanding of history," he said, "has much closer affinites with the Marxist view than with the interpretations of Christianity in terms of idealistic thought."[31] Nevertheless, he found Marx "not a profound or an accurate thinker."[32] And he had a radical distaste for communist dictatorship. As a socialist he recognized that technology and interdependence ("collectivism") constitute an irreversible trend and that planning is necessary; hence, he argued dialectically, we can preserve personal freedom only by planning for it.

Temple thought that the church's task is to teach principles, the individual Christian's to try to find their application; he allowed for disagreement on the latter but not on the former. As to the pietistic objection that the church should not interfere with political and economic policies, he countered that through its members it "is bound to 'interfere' because it is by vocation the agent of God's purpose, outside the scope of which no human interest or activity can fall."[33] Needless to say, he met

---

[28] *The Church Looks Forward* (N.Y., Macmillan, 1944), p. 130.
[29] *Essays in Christian Politics*, p. 44.
[30] *Christianity and Social Order*, p. 102.
[31] *Religious Experience*, p. 254.
[32] *Christianity and the State*, pp. 82–83.
[33] *Christianity and Social Order*, p. 21.

strong and sometimes quite vicious opposition in big business and Tory circles—which only added delight to the English masses' pride in his leadership. Some of his concrete proposals (to be found in the Appendix to his *Christianity and Social Order*)—among them elimination of outside investors in favor of ownership of enterprises by their managers and laborers, public control of production, socialization of credit and banking, a "mutual-export" plan for international trade (a plan foreseeing the European Common Market), public ownership of urban land and control of rural land—are worth attention even today.

THEOLOGY: ECUMENICAL AND MISSIONARY

Christian unity took as much of Temple's time and attention as social witness, but it was a concern that found expression primarily in sermons and addresses rather than in published material. He was fully committed to the Anglican Communion as being both Catholic and evangelical, i.e., encompassing both the genius for order and the genius for freedom and personal decision. In Catholicism he saw the dangers of rigidity, lack of sympathy, legalism and magic; in Protestantism the dangers of sectarian atomization, one-sidedness at the expense of the total Christian heritage, and Pelagianism or self-sufficiency. Anglicanism, he believed, best avoided this complex of faults; it was therefore for him a bridge church to help reunite not only fragmented Protestantism and Orthodoxy but Catholicism too. As between the "high" and "low" wings of Anglicanism, the pluralist Temple usually endorsed their affirmations and discounted their negations.

In accordance with the Lambeth Quadrilateral, Temple held to the necessity of episcopal ordination, but he was always quick to point out that while such ordination confers authority to administer the sacraments, their power or efficiency comes from Christ. He declared that the requirement of administration by a priest has all along meant only that it *should* be, not "can only be."[34] He thought it "a shocking presumption to question

[34] *York Diocesan Leaflet* (July 1931).

the reality of the Sacraments administered, for example, in the Presbyterian Church of Scotland or the Lutheran Church of Germany."[35] Ordination by bishops is, he held, *bene esse* only. And this principle he extended to lay ministrations too—in emergencies, even of the eucharist (as with baptism). And he looked forward to the eventual ordination of women.

Temple worked by discussion and debate for "a fuller and worthier conception of the Church than any of us hold today."[36] In the meantime he held to the Quadrilateral, even to the point of opposing open communion except at ecumenical gatherings. The Church of South India's agreement on limited intercommunion with the Church of England had his full support, as did the C.S.I. itself. Temple was always definite about distinguishing unity from uniformity, and sought, as a good pluralist and dialectician, to avoid the latter. He favored doctrinal and liturgical variety within dogmatic unity. Concerning the C.S.I. he said to his high-church critics that it limited ordination to bishops, which is what the Anglican churches do, and he urged his critics to make sure they do not impose on others more stringent terms of union than obtain among the Anglicans themselves (a simple piece of ecumenical ethics!).

Temple foresaw a united church which would include all three basic principles of polity—episcopal, presbyterial, congregational—as well as the distinctive genius of both Catholic and Protestant Christianity. And his deep involvement in Protestant and Orthodox ecumenics never closed his eyes to Rome and its people. At many church assemblies he spoke of his regret at their absence. (He would have rejoiced at the presence nowadays of Catholic observers at such gatherings. He used to say, "I think reunion with Rome is so far off that it need not trouble us just now; there are other things to do; but I would certainly refrain from anything which made ultimate reunion more difficult. And so I hold fast to my Catholic doctrines."[37] Just as he warned the "party" men in his own communion that their real enemies are "the world, the flesh, and the devil," so he insisted that "the difference between Catholic and Protestant is very

[35] *Thoughts on Some Problems of the Day*, p. 112.
[36] Iremonger, *op cit.*, p. 406.
[37] In Harold Begbie, *Painted Windows* (N.Y., Putnam's, 1922), p. 187.

small compared with the difference between Christian and non-Christian."[38] The communion prayer for "the whole state of Christ's Church" is offered alike for Rome, the Eastern bodies, the Reformation churches, and the "sectaries."

The archbishop was twenty-five years ahead of the new emphasis in mission theology—the emphasis that the churches do not *have* missions but are missions. Said Temple: "To be a Christian is to be a missionary," drawing men to or driving them from Christ.[39] As with his view of creation, atonement, the Kingdom and so on, he saw conversion as a process rather than an event, gradual instead of suddenly effected. "The beginning is to admit the Lord to our lives at all. But when that is done there are many doors still to be opened."[40] He listed some of these doors: true citizenship, decent housing, economic democracy, wider education—not the pious abstractions and intimate personal details in the ordinary "devotional" treatise!

There were two cardinal principles in Temple's view of Christian mission. One was that Christian witness must be expressed through socially redemptive action and socially relevant theology, for the setting of today's evangelism is a sick society in need of the Christian remedy. But the remedy has to be offered in relevant terms, else it will be pushed aside; communication of the Gospel calls for social theology. The other principle was "the ministry of the laity"—because the laity constitutes the church in the world, and "the actual leavening of the world's lump with the energies of the Kingdom of Heaven must be done by laymen."[41]

Temple's faith was that God's creation, that is, His spreading Kingdom, was moving toward one world as well as one church. As with the ecumenical effort, so he found ecumenical politics in the League of Nations (and would have found it in the United Nations). In his theistic belief that history's process moves from heterogeneity to homogeneity he went far enough to predict that the Christian-unity effort would some day be superseded by a

[38] *The Church Looks Forward*, p. 32.

[39] *Basic Convictions* (N.Y., Harper, 1936), p. 79.

[40] *Personal Religion and the Life of Fellowship* (London, Longmans, Green, 1926), p. 81.

[41] *Citizen and Churchman*, p. 61.

faith-unity development. It gave Arnold Toynbee great satisfaction to quote in his *Study of History* from Temple's *Readings in St. John's Gospel:* "All that is noble in the non-Christian systems of thought or conduct is the work of Christ upon them and in them. There is only one divine light; and each has only a few rays of that light, which needs all the wisdom of all the traditions to manifest the entire compass of the spectrum."[42] Yet Temple was no eclectic. His Lord was, as he put it in the titles of his major expositions, *Christus Veritas,* the source of whatever is valid anywhere, and the *Mens Creatrix,* the creative guiding intelligence of all the world.

[42] *Readings in St. John's Gospel,* Vol. I, p. 10.

Bibliography

William Temple, *Nature, Man and God,* N.Y., St. Martin's, 1960.

Joseph Fletcher, *William Temple, Twentieth-century Christian,* N.Y., Seabury, 1963.

NICOLAI BERDYAEV

Matthew Spinka

Nicolai Berdyaev (1874–1948) has been steadily gaining recognition among the cultured Western circles as the philosopher of the spirit, of freedom, and as a fighter against the contemporary dominant secularist tendencies which deny man his spiritual nature and thus reduce him to a mere psychosomatic being. Accordingly, he stressed man's spiritual nature as against the generally held materialistic conception. He once defined his philosophy as

> the science of the spirit. And the science of the spirit is above all the science of human existence. It is in the human existence that the meaning of being is revealed. . . . And the existential philosophy is precisely the knowledge of the meaning of being through the subject. The subject is existential. . . . In that sense philosophy is subjective and not objective. It is founded on spiritual experience.[1]

But before Berdyaev arrived at this mature Christian and existentialist view of man and reality he had to struggle with views that were quite foreign to it. He was born in Kiev of an ancient Russian noble family. His father, Alexander Mikhailovich, was a retired officer of the Cavalier Guard, who intended his son for the elite military service. His mother was half French and never learned correct Russian. Nicolai had a brother, Sergei, fifteen years his senior, an eccentric, whose son, Alexander, is the sole surviving member of the Berdyaev family, and still lives in the Soviet Union. From childhood Nicolai felt "alone and rootless in this world,"[2] the real world being the one of his imagination. He was naturally of the Platonic bent of mind, and

[1] "Ma Conception philosophique du Monde," in *Bulletin de l'Association Nicolas Berdyaeff*, Paris, April 1953.

[2] Donald A. Lowrie, *Rebellious Prophet: A Life of Nicolai Berdyaev* (N.Y., Harper, 1960), p. 21.

256

this characteristic remained his guiding principle throughout life. He read all sorts of books before he entered the Cadet Corpus school at the age of ten. Left to himself, he developed an exceedingly strong tendency toward self-direction, refusing to accept orders from anyone. He became both physically and intellectually fastidious. In his old age he recorded in his spiritual autobiography: "I often close my eyes, ears, and nose. The world is filled with odors for me."[3] In the school he could not endure the coarseness and ignorance of the other boys as well as the poor quality of the teaching offered him, both of which he regarded as stupid. His philosophical precociousness set him apart from his fellows—a solitary, serious youngster eager to find some sense to life. He confessed in his autobiography that during his school days he was "a regular monster." Nevertheless, he graduated from the school, and at the age of twenty he entered the University of Kiev, enrolling at first in the natural science department—which was then exceedingly popular as being in line with the prevailing materialism; but within a year he transferred to the faculty of law. He continued his private devotion to philosophical studies as before—he had already become well grounded in Kant, Schopenhauer, Hegel, and Nietzsche. His only friend was Leon Shestov, a Jew, who later became a notable philosopher in his own right.

Berdyaev underwent a spiritual crisis which at first turned him against the existing conditions in society, particularly his own aristocratic class, and which led him, in 1894, to accept the then fashionable Marxism. But it was impossible for his independent spirit ever to become a doctrinaire conformist. Because of his unusual philosophical proficiency, he was acknowledged within a few years as the principal ideologist of the Social Democratic party in Kiev and as such was associated with Lunacharsky (later the Soviet commissar of education), and in Zurich he met Plekhanov. He plunged into the revolutionary activity among the workers and his fellow students; but finally, in 1898, the police arrested him along with 150 other students. After two years of imprisonment he was sentenced to

[3] *Samopoznanie* (Paris, YMCA, 1949), p. 351. My translation. (An English ed. was published by Macmillan in 1951, under the title *Dream and Reality: An Essay in Autobiography.*)

three years of exile in the Vologda province (an "easy" exile center). Berdyaev lived there in the best room of the best hotel of the town, free to have contacts with other revolutionaries, to order all the books he wanted, and to write and publish almost as he pleased (subject to moderate censorship). He published during this time his first major work, *Subjectivism and Individualism in Social Philosophy.* The book already betrayed a clear "deviationism" from orthodox Marxism of such of his fellow exiles as Lunacharsky and Bogdanov.

During the third year of his exile he was permitted to remove to Zhitomir in Volhynia. After his return to Kiev, Berdyaev made the acquaintance of Sergius Bulgakov, then professor of economics at the Polytechnic Institute, who was already moving from Marxism to Christianity. The latter ultimately entered the Orthodox Church as priest and after his exile from the Soviet Union became the outstanding Russian Orthodox theologian and the dean of the Paris Orthodox Theological Academy. He helped Berdyaev to make the transition to the Christian faith, although Dostoevsky's religious views had been even more influential in aiding him to make the radical change. This is particularly true of the concept of Christianity expressed with overwhelming power in Dostoevsky's "Grand Inquisitor," which Berdyaev made practically his own. Bulgakov was also instrumental in directing two sisters, Eugenie and Lydia Trushev, daughters of a prominent Kiev lawyer, to Berdyaev, who was already regarded as a dominant intellectual leader. He later married Lydia.

In 1904 Berdyaev moved to St. Petersburg and joined there the brilliant literary circle consisting of such luminaries as Vyecheslav Ivanov, Vasily Rozanov, Dmitry Merezhkovsky and his wife, Zinaida Hippius, as well as the symbolist poets Alexander Blok and Andrey Byely. They met weekly in Ivanov's celebrated "Ivory Tower." Berdyaev's definite conversion to Christianity falls within this period (1907), as is witnessed by his chapter contributed to *The Milestones,* a kind of manifesto of the seven contributors who thereby signalized the radical change of their views. Included among the contributors were the two later leaders of the Russian religious movement, Bulgakov and Frank. Nevertheless, the Christianity which Berdyaev now embraced was not the "official" kind identified with the Holy Governing Synod—to which he remained opposed, at times even violently. In his autobiography he writes: "I never pretended that my religious thought had a churchly character. I sought the truth and experienced as truth that which was revealed to me."[4] Along with the other Russian religious thinkers from Alexey Khomyakov onward, Berdyaev distinguishes between the Church composed of all who are truly redeemed and dominated by the spirit of Christ—this being the essential meaning of the Russian concept of *sobornost,* approximating the Western concept of the Church invisible—and the mere external and formal membership in the outward institution of the Church. Only the former compose the real body of Christ. It is this distinction which the official Russian Church repudiates. Nevertheless, Berdyaev did not reject the sacraments of the historic Church and did not neglect communicating in them. "Philosophy is my calling," he writes, "but sacraments of the Church are the very essence of life."[5]

In 1912 Berdyaev went to Italy for a year. It was at Capri that he at last caught a glimpse of his own religious vision of life and embodied it in "one of the most important books of his life, *The Meaning of the Creative Act,*"[6] to the fuller explication of which he devoted his entire subsequent literary career. After his return to Russia in 1913 he plunged into a violent struggle with the Holy Governing Synod by publishing an article titled "Quenchers of the Spirit." He was arrested and charged with blasphemy—an offense then punishable by exile to Siberia for life. But the outbreak of the First World War delayed the trial, and the subsequent catastrophe of the revolution quashed it.

During the war Berdyaev found himself unable to join either the revolutionaries, from whom he had felt estranged ever since his conversion, or the Kerensky regime. After the October Revolution he bitterly denounced the Bolsheviks, writing of them: "The Russian revolution has turned out to be a consistent application to life of Russian nihilism, atheism, and ma-

[4] *Ibid.,* p. 199.
[5] Quoted in Lowrie, *op. cit.,* p. 221.
[6] *Ibid.,* p. 134.

terialism. . . . This . . . leads to destruction of all values."[7] He likewise wrote a fierce denunciation of the revolution in his *Philosophy of Inequality,* which, however, could not be published in Russia. Berdyaev likewise refused Lunacharsky's appeal to writers to serve the new regime. Thereupon he and his wife and sister-in-law were compelled to join a labor battalion detailed to clean the railroad tracks in winter, when the temperature often fell to twenty degrees below zero. Nevertheless, he was invited to lecture in a state institution and allowed a free hand in choosing his subjects. He even organized a Free Academy of Spiritual Culture, which was permitted to exist for three years. At one time he was called before the dreaded head of the Cheka, Felix Dzerzhinsky, and in a forty-five-minute speech he frankly expounded to him his religious, philosophical, and moral reasons for the faith that was in him. Dzerzhinsky not only heard him through without interruption but even set him free and sent an escort to accompany him home; Berdyaev could not, however, leave the city without permission. In 1920–21 he was elected by the university faculty to lecture there—a remarkable tribute to him, since he had not finished his university course and hence had no degree. During the four years following the revolution he wrote several books of outstanding merit, characterized by a remarkable freedom of expression: *Worthiness of Christianity and Unworthiness of Christians,* which he had delivered as lectures to large audiences of skeptics and unbelievers; *Meaning of History,* which is also of permanent value for the understanding of his thought; and *Dostoevsky,* still one of the best interpretations of the religious message of the great novelist.

But in 1922 conditions changed for the worse, the men in power no longer "knew Joseph" and consequently decided not to tolerate those former intellectual leaders who still refused to conform to the new order. Berdyaev was imprisoned and banished along with others from the Soviet Union, and forbidden ever again to return on pain of death. He was at first taken to Berlin, which was then the intellectual center for the one and a half million Russian émigrés. Berdyaev always insisted that he

[7] Quoted in *ibid.,* p. 146.

was not an émigré but an exile, and as such was not well received by those who had left Russia voluntarily. But with the collapse of the German currency he could not make his very slender means suffice and moved, along with others of the intellectual elite in similar dire circumstances, to Paris, where he lived for the rest of his life. An English lady, Mrs. Florence West, an admirer of his religious philosophy, left him a legacy with which he was able to buy a small house in Clamart, a suburb of Paris, which thus became his permanent home.

The Paris period was Berdyaev's most fruitful in literary production. He published here in Russian the large number of books which in French, English, German, and many other translations made him famous and established him in the West as one of the most notable of contemporary Christian thinkers. He also engaged in other activities: he became the editor of the Russian publications issued in an astonishingly large number by the Y.M.C.A. Press, and which made it possible for the exiled Russian intellectuals to engage in literary work. Nowhere else had a similar opportunity been offered them. He also edited a periodical, *Put'* (The Way), which contains many valuable articles both by him and others. Furthermore he lectured extensively, particularly among the Russian youth, and entertained discussion groups in his own house. He did not participate to any great degree in the political activity of his fellow countrymen, and in turn was severely criticized by them. He even refused to follow Metropolitan Eulogius of Paris, the ecclesiastical head of the Orthodox Russians in the West, when the latter cut himself off from the Moscow patriarchal jurisdiction and placed himself under the authority of the Patriarchate of Constantinople. Nevertheless, Berdyaev continued to hold the metropolitan in high personal esteem. Toward the end of his life he conceived a great admiration for Father Stefan (Svetozarov), despite the latter's return to the Soviet Union. Father Stefan wrote of Berdyaev after the latter's death: "I consider him a faithful member of the Orthodox faith."[8] This testimony contrasts favorably with the adverse judgment of some outstanding Russian churchmen who denounce him as heretical,

[8] Quoted in *ibid.*, p. 221.

or at least insufficiently Orthodox. It must be remembered that in the religious sphere Berdyaev was isolated even from his wife, Lydia, who had been converted to Roman Catholicism before leaving the Soviet Union. He died in 1948 at his writing desk as he was ready to engage in his customary daily task.

We may now turn to a succinct summary of his religious thought, chiefly on the basis of his works published after his removal to Paris. They represent his mature thought, for they were written after he reached his fiftieth year. He always insisted that he was a religious philosopher, not a theologian. As such it was paramount that he establish, first of all, firm philosophical foundations for his religious faith. Starting with Kant, whose critical distinction between the phenomenal (scientific) and noumenal (ethical) realms he accepted as the basis of his own existential philosophy, he blazed a path to an apprehension of the spiritual realm—a position not reached by Kant, although the latter prepared the way for it. Accordingly, Berdyaev regarded Kant as the philosopher of freedom. Berdyaev makes a fundamental distinction between the world of objects and the world of the spirit. The former is subject to natural laws and therefore determined by them: there is no freedom in it. It is only in the latter, the spiritual realm, that freedom exists. He writes: "The chief characteristic of my philosophical type consists above all in that, that I have placed as the basis of my philosophy not being, but freedom. Not a single other philosopher has done that in such a radical form."[9] Man is a unique being in so far as he is the meeting point of both the material and the spiritual realms: he is thus a microcosm. Nevertheless, in him as in all reality the spiritual is primary; the objective, the ontological, is secondary. Being is identified by him with matter, while existence is synonymous with the spiritual realm, which is freedom. "Existence is not essence, is not substance; it is a free act."[10] "Spirit is not being, but the existent, that which exists and possesses true existence, and is not subject to determination by any being at all. Spirit is not a principle, but personality, in other words the highest form of existence."

[9] *Samopoznanie*, pp. 58–59.
[10] *Truth and Revelation* (N.Y., Scribner's, 1953), p. 12.

"Freedom cannot have its source in being, nor be determined by being: it cannot enter into a system of ontological determinism."[11]

Accordingly, in Berdyaev's view to identify the objective with the real, as is often done in scientific systems and is always done in materialism, is a fundamental and pernicious error. Science properly delimited deals exclusively with objects, matter, things, and as such is justified in its methods; however, this is far from including all reality, the existence proper where alone meanings are found. There are no meanings as such in objects, in mechanical contrivances, no matter how ingenious they might be. Meanings are imparted to objects solely by persons who alone are capable of conceiving them, since they partake of the spiritual realm: hence meanings are subjective, not objective.

The common misunderstanding of the proper character and function of these two realms results in "objectifying" the spiritual into the material, converting a subject into an object, a thing. To Berdyaev this represents the origin of most if not all the evil in the world. This is in essence what materialism invariably and necessarily does. The commonest example of this universal practice is the treatment of human beings as if they were merely psychophysical organisms, a chemical laboratory walking on two legs and driven by a variety of impulses all of which are physical. This denies man's spiritual nature and results in his being looked upon as a commodity: "in short, whenever man is used as a means rather than an end, objectification takes place."[12] This is for Berdyaev the "fallen world." And the worst about it is that it is we who create it; God does not. He afflicts no man, for there is no evil in Him.

> Objectification of the world takes place through our agency and for our sakes, and this is the fall of the world, this is its loss of freedom, and the alienation of its parts. . . . Objectification is the ejection of man into the external, it is an exteriorization of him to the conditions of space, time, causality and rationaliza-

[11] *The Beginning and the End* (N.Y., Harper, 1952), pp. 103–4.
[12] Matthew Spinka, *Nicolas Berdyaev, Captive of Freedom* (Philadelphia, Westminster, 1950), p. 107.

tion. But in his existential depth man is in communion with the spiritual world and with the whole cosmos.[13]

Consequently man, by being denied his spiritual nature and treated only as a physical being, is degraded, dehumanized, and his personality destroyed. No genuine community is possible where spiritual communion, the I-Thou relationship, is absent. All intercourse is reduced to a lower, impersonal level and thus "objectified."

It is on the basis of these considerations that Berdyaev constructs his concept of God and man. As for God, or rather the Godhead, He is in Himself beyond all possibility of apprehension by the human mind: for as well could a child scoop up the ocean in his sand pail as man by his mind grasp God in His essence. Nevertheless, it has pleased God to reveal Himself in such a way that man can grasp something of the divine. But Berdyaev never tires of warning men—particularly theologians —against assuming that they can construct a neat logical system in which to enclose and delimit even the revealed God. This is the distinction he makes between the "apophatic" and the "kataphatic" ways of knowing God—God apprehended in a mystical experience of the human spirit meeting with the divine Spirit, and a logical construct of a purely intellectual or philosophical system. Thus God has revealed Himself to some degree in nature and history, but this revelation is so variously conceived by men as to be self-contradictory, a matter of opinion and therefore relative. It is only in His revelation by incarnation in Jesus Christ that we possess an authentic, supreme, and final self-revelation of God, even though this is likewise but inadequately apprehended by men. We are thus reduced to a personal encounter with the divine in the depths of our consciousness—to an intuitive apprehension of God. "Christian dogma is merely a symbolism of spiritual experience."[14] God cannot be known by reason alone, or by some scientific method of analysis, for He is not an object, a thing, but Spirit, a subject. "Our knowledge of God is, therefore, basically intuitive, subjective, experiential, or, if you will not blanch at the word, mys-

---

[13] *The Beginning and the End,* pp. 56, 60.
[14] *Spirit and Reality* (N.Y., Scribner's, 1939), p. 140.

tical. It is neither exclusively intellectual, emotional, volitional, nor intuitive, but rather integral, combining all these four to-gether with the additional element that results from this integral approach."[15]

But Berdyaev's rejection of the ontological interpretation of reality, his insistence on the primacy of existence as against being, leads him to reject the current doctrine of God as cre-ator. God is *not* Being or the Ground of being, for He is Spirit.

> God does not act everywhere in this objectified world. He was not the Creator of this fallen world. He does not act and he is not present in plague and cholera, in the hatred which torments the world, or in murder, war and violence, in the trampling down of freedom or in the darkness of the ignorant boor. Doc-trines of that sort have even led men to atheism. . . . God is present and God acts only in freedom. . . . God is to be found in Truth, in Goodness, Beauty and Love, but not in the world order. . . . God is Spirit and he can operate only in Spirit and through Spirit.[16]

But in that case, how was matter created and by whom? This stark, unexplained dualism, even though it asserts an undoubted truth when applied to the perverted thought of man and the many evils consequent upon it, fails to account for the cosmic objective reality, which certainly cannot be ascribed to man's "objectification"! For it surely cannot be asserted that it was the perverted thought of man that created the material world. Whence then evil? The only glimpse of relief of this dilemma is in defining as evil only that which is the direct result of man's evil will, while designating the natural evils as calamities in-separable from the very nature of matter.

Accordingly, Berdyaev rightfully rejects any causal connec-tion between evil and God. He traces it to the nature of freedom: "Evil and suffering exist because freedom exists; but freedom has no foundation in existence, it is a frontier. But be-cause freedom exists, God himself suffers and is crucified. The Divine love and sacrifice are an answer to the mystery of free-

[15] My article on Berdyaev's existentialism in Carl Michalson, ed. *Christianity and the Existentialists* (N.Y., Scribner's, 1956), p. 63.

[16] *The Beginning and the End*, pp. 151–52.

dom wherein evil and suffering have their origin."[17] We are here touching upon some of the most difficult and controversial aspects of Berdyaev's thought: since evil originates in freedom, is God not responsible for making evil possible by creating spirits with the fatal endowment of freedom? In order to parry this thrust commonly made against his thought, Berdyaev resorts to Jacob Boehme's cosmogonic speculations and asserts that freedom is *uncreated, not* created by God. But it seems that this is more of an evasion than a solution of the mystery; it would have been better had Berdyaev followed his own advice and treated the mystery in the apophatic, rather than the kataphatic, fashion. He himself admits that the idea of "uncreated freedom" has been generally unintelligible to his readers, although for him it "has become ever more clearly etched." Nevertheless, he confesses that "I remained altogether alone in my view."[18] Perhaps he best expressed the necessity of such a view when he wrote: "Freedom cannot be derived from being, for it would then be determined."[19] Moreover, without freedom, men would not be intelligent, morally responsible beings, but mere automata.

Turning now to his conception of man, he asserts, following Kant, that human personality is the greatest value in the world: "I became a Christian not because I ceased to believe in man, in his dignity and supreme destiny, in his creative freedom, but because I sought a much deeper and more actual basis for that faith."[20] But it is the human personality that he identifies with the supreme value, not the psychosomatic organism that he calls individuality. Only as man secures spiritual victory over his physical nature—what Apostle Paul calls the flesh—does he become a person. Accordingly, personality is an attainment, not an endowment, and presupposes a struggle. Many, perhaps most, individuals never become persons. Nevertheless, the three elements composing man—body, soul, and spirit—form a unity.

> The individual is born within the generic process and belongs to the natural world. Personality, on the other hand, is a spiritual

[17] *Spirit and Reality,* p. 115.
[18] *Samopoznanie,* p. 239.
[19] *Toward a New Epoch,* p. 98.
[20] *Samopoznanie,* p. 191.

and ethical category. It is not born of a father and mother, it is created spiritually and gives actual effect to the divine idea of man. Personality is not nature, it is freedom, and it is spirit.[21]

Man is a whole creature, an organism compounded of spirit, soul and body. . . . *Spirituality* is not opposed to *body* or *matter* but implies its transformation . . . personality. Its realization is achieved through the victory of spirit over the chaotic elements of soul and body. . . . The spirit is derived from the Logos, while the soul is cosmic.[22]

Berdyaev thus accepts the Christian dogma of the "fallen" state of man, although he places the "fall" in the spirit's pre-existence.[23] The spirit fell by a free choice, not by any divine fiat of predestination. In its earthly existence it likewise remains in the "fallen" state by its own act of self-assertion. Therein consists its individuality. But man may be saved by the grace of God, which is ever available, ever offered to him, were he willing to accept it. Thus man's salvation from the state of alienation consequent upon his self-assertion is likewise an act of his own will, or rather an act of cooperation with the proffered grace of God. For God ever yearns that man should not perish but have eternal life; and He has revealed His gracious purpose supremely in Jesus Christ. For Christ is not only the revelation of God as *agape*—the love that seeks those who are not worthy of that love and could never deserve it by their own efforts, no matter how heroic; he is also the divine revelation of what man may and ought to be. The incarnation of the divine Logos reveals the God-Man and makes possible the transformation of the merely human into the divine-human. This is the doctrine of Godmanhood, taught by Eastern theologians from Irenaeus onward, but particularly in the recent Russian religious renaissance by Feodor Dostoevsky, Vladimir Soloviev, Sergius Bulgakov, and Nicolai Berdyaev. To use the latter's philosophical term, this is the process whereby an individual attains the status of personality. In it the spirit dominates the flesh and thus attains to freedom—for the spiritual realm is one of freedom. In it all action is freely chosen, not

[21] *The Beginning and the End*, pp. 135–36.
[22] *Spirit and Reality*, p. 40.
[23] *The Destiny of Man* (N.Y., Scribner's, 1935), p. 328.

governed by necessity or determinism: man is free from all fetters—his own passions which enslave him as well as from the "objectification" which prevails in the unredeemed society.

> The mystery of Christianity is the mystery of Godmanhood, the mystery of the meeting of two natures, united but not co-mingled. Man does not cease [to exist], does not become divine, but retains his humanity in the eternal life. I think that this idea is wholly orthodox, even though it is inadequately revealed in Orthodoxy and is often obscured by a monophysite tendency.[24]
>
> Man ought to be free, he dares not be a slave, for he ought to be man. Such is the will of God.[25]

> This deification or theosis . . . is neither a monistic identity with God nor a humiliation of man and the created world. Theosis makes man Divine, while at the same time preserving his human nature. Thus, instead of the human personality being annihilated, it is made in the image of God and the Divine Trinity.[26]

It follows, therefore, that since the attainment of personality is equivalent to salvation, those who do not attain it are necessarily excluded from this state, even though it is not by some inscrutable decree of God, or His predestination, but by their own failure to act redemptively. "Man is immortal and eternal as a spiritual being belonging to the incorruptible world, but his spirituality is not a naturally given fact; man is a spiritual being in so far as he manifests himself as such, in so far as the spirit in him gains possession of the natural elements. . . . Immortality has to be won by the person and involves struggle for personality."[27] Nevertheless, Berdyaev does not accept the tenet that the failure to win salvation in this terrestrial life is final: he clings to the possibility of other opportunities in the life beyond the grave (although he does not accept Origen's notion of universal salvation; that to his mind constitutes a denial of human freedom). Moreover, he shares the Eastern Orthodox hope in

[24] *Samopoznanie*, p. 195.
[25] *Slavery and Freedom* (N.Y., Scribner's, 1939), p. 48.
[26] *Spirit and Reality*, p. 149.
[27] *The Destiny of Man*, p. 325.

the cosmic redemption that includes in its scope all creation. "My salvation," he writes, "is bound up with that not only of other men but also of animals, plants, minerals, and every blade of grass—all must be transfigured and brought into the Kingdom of God."[28]

The redeemed society, then, consists solely of transformed men and women and is impossible on any other basis. As long as men are dominated by selfish motives they cannot create a good world. Accordingly, mere external change—cultural, political, economic—is inadequate because it does not transform basic human motives. All social achievements in the present era are only relative: they may improve the prevailing conditions and lessen some evils, but they do not cure them. It is for this reason that Berdyaev rejects Marxism, which he regards as "a lie." "Marxism is a lie, because God exists; that is, there exists a supreme power and the source of all power; there exists a spiritual, and not only an economic power."[29] But the bourgeois ideal of capitalism is equally materialistic, extolling economic well-being as the highest good, and therefore equally unacceptable. "Bourgeois life is dominated by money and social position. Another of its characteristics is a complete disregard of the human personality."[30] Thus the Christian ethic of redemption, of the transformation of the mainsprings of human conduct, is incompatible with the prevailing sociological and political notions of the world order. A radical improvement of society cannot be attained without a spiritual transformation. And this is a process that cannot be forced or imposed on society from without: it must be voluntarily undertaken by each individual. As long as men insist on doing their own will, so long will social evils, injustice, war, and misery afflict humankind. The Marxist dream of a perfect society that does not involve such a radical change is utterly naive, lacking in the elementary perception of the necessary conditions of its realization.

But this does not imply a rejection of the cultural, political, and economic means as subsidiary to the transforming process,

---

[28] *Ibid.*, p. 367.
[29] *Khristianstvo i klassovaya borba* (Paris, YMCA, 1931), p. 17.
[30] *Spirit and Reality*, p. 120.

provided they are guided and dominated by the redemptive motivation. In fact, Berdyaev places an extraordinary emphasis on such creative action on the part of redeemed men: he calls them to creativity. If Christian men should fail in the task of redemptive creativity, then the forces of evil would surely take over. In fact, that is exactly what is happening in the contemporaneous world where arts, literature, and cultural life generally are largely subserving the demonic rather than the divine aims. Because Christians have failed to exercise creative activity in arts, sciences, politics, and economy to a sufficient degree, these fields have been pre-empted by the forces of evil. Berdyaev castigated this creative lag in his early work in which he developed the thesis of "the worthiness of Christianity and the unworthiness of Christians." He has never tired of insisting that Christianity is not a passive and static but a dynamic and creative religion.

> It would be wrong and impossible to abandon society to the free play of evil forces and passively to await a miraculous transformation of the world, a new heaven and a new earth. . . . Society must struggle against evil, but in doing so it must preserve the value of personality and spiritual freedom.[31]

The task of the Christian Church consists primarily of bringing men to God who alone can act on their wills in the gracious process of spiritual transformation. And since God compels no one but awaits his free acceptance of the proffered grace, salvation is a synergistic process.

Berdyaev is also deeply concerned with history as far as its spiritual meaning is concerned. History is a record of humankind's wrong choices. It is the tragic story of the misuse of human freedom, of the self-assertion of the proud, strong, ruthless, grasping, ambitious, and the power-mad over the weaker or less well endowed of their fellows. This applies both to individuals and nations, or rather to the rulers of nations. All the suffering, misery, cruelty, injustice, and inhumanity originate from this root cause. But despite this tragic character of the story of humankind, it is not devoid of meaning. God reveals

[31] *The Destiny of Man*, p. 284.

His purpose in it, especially in Jesus Christ, in whom the divine has broken through into the human sequence of historical events. The goal and aim of history—properly speaking, of the *Heilsgeschichte,* the history of redemption—is the transformation of the human into the divine-human, the theanthropy. History is meaningless unless one sees the world order in the light of God's purpose. There can be no "progress" unless there exists a goal toward which humankind is tending. And the goal cannot be set by mere mechanical evolutionary process, because natural forces are determined by the natural law of cause and effect and therefore cannot foresee the goal and thus direct themselves toward it. They lack purposiveness, teleology, and therefore are devoid of meaning. Only God can set a goal for His world and humankind and thus impart meaning to the historical process. Accordingly, only those who believe in God and in His providence can discern a purpose in an otherwise meaningless and purposeless universe. They alone can hold the notion of "progress" without being guilty of an absurdity.

Berdyaev concludes that the present humanist-secularist era has exhausted its original creative energies and has for the past century turned upon itself in repudiating man as the measure of all values. Secularism, by denying God, has also destroyed man as a spiritual being. He writes:

> Man faces the threat that nothing shall be left of himself, of his personal and intimate life, no freedom for his spiritual life or his creative thought. He is submerged in huge collectives, subject to non-human commandments. It is demanded of man that he give himself up without reserve, to society, the state, the race, the class, the nation.[32]

> I find myself in complete rupture with my epoch. I sing freedom, which my epoch hates; I do not love government and am of religio-anarchistic tendency, while the epoch deifies the government; I am an extreme personalist, while the epoch is collectivist and rejects the dignity and worth of personality; I do not love war and the military, while the epoch lives in the pathos of war; I love the philosophical mind, while the epoch is indifferent

[32] *The Fate of Man in the Modern World* (London, SCM Press, 1935), pp. 12–13.

to it; I value aristocratic culture, while the epoch degrades it; and finally I profess eschatological Christianity, while the epoch recognizes only traditional-contemporary Christianity.[33]

In other words, Berdyaev holds that only Christianity properly apprehended may entertain a valid hope of creating a good and just society, a society of spiritually transformed men and women, voluntarily accepting the rule of God in their hearts—a veritable Kingdom of God. That Kingdom is realized at present in the hearts of those who have submitted their lives to God, and it will so continue to come to the end of time. But since it cannot be reasonably expected that *all* humankind will accept God's rule at any time in the future any more than it had accepted it in the past, the Kingdom of God shall never be completely realized on earth within the scope of human history. "The Kingdom of God cannot be thought as existing in time, it is the end of time, the end of the world, a new heaven and a new earth."[34] Thus Berdyaev's grandiose concept spans time and eternity. Nevertheless, the man who is committed to this glorious vision of the ultimate goal of the divine purpose need not sit in passive, idle expectation of it as if he could do nothing to bring it about or to hasten its coming. In fact, the spiritual transformation which he undergoes is an essential part of the transformation of the world. Since this "fallen" world has ever been created by man's "objectification" of it, the end of history will be brought about by the cessation of this perversion of reality. As this process is of human contrivance, its end must likewise be effected by human cooperation. This is Berdyaev's vision of the transformed humanity, and along with it of redeemed cosmos, at last realizing the original intention and purpose of God.

[33] *Samopoznanie*, pp. 280–81.
[34] *The Destiny of Man*, p. 367.

Bibliography

Nicolai Berdyaev, *The Destiny of Man*, N.Y., Harper, 1959. Harper Torchbooks).

Donald A. Lowrie, *Rebellious Prophet: A Life of Nicolai Berdyaev*, N.Y., Harper, 1960.

KARL HEIM

Carl Michalson

The thought of Karl Heim, late professor of systematic theology at the University of Tübingen in southern Germany, exhibits an astonishing range and versatility. Over a period of more than fifty years he wrote on the history of religions, philosophy, and natural science with the same vigor and skill that characterized his theology and ethics. He also produced biblical expositions and historical studies, including a treatise on Alexander of Hales and another on the problem of certainty in Christian doctrine to the time of Schleiermacher. Scores of his sermons were published, several volumes of which are in English. They reveal a fascinating combination of tender piety and disciplined penetration into personal and cultural needs. No crisis in the life of the German people seemed to escape his theological scrutiny. A fat volume, *Faith and Life* (*Glaube und Leben,* 1926), which someone has called "a thesaurus," embraces these essays over a period of twenty-five years.

Heim saw the care of the soul portrayed in the ministry of Jesus. Contrary to the stereotype of the German theologian, he made such pastoral concern central to his own vocation. Ecumenical involvement begun in his youth as secretary of the German Student Christian Movement persisted throughout his most mature work. To the very end of his life he deliberately resisted what he felt to be the theologian's cardinal ambition— the writing of a *Dogmatik*. During an Oxford Group meeting in England that ambition was revealed to him as a sin of pride and he surrendered it. In 1931 he began his closest approximation to a *Dogmatik,* a six-volume work entitled *The Evangelical Faith and the Thought of the Present* (*Der evangelische Glaube und das Denken der Gegenwart*). The first volume, *Faith and Thought* (*Glaube und Denken*), is his most significant work. In his preface he announced that he was definitely not writing "in the form of a *Dogmatik*. . . . We have enough text-

273

books on dogmatics." At least one theologian in Europe found it impossible to take that announcement lightly, for Karl Barth just four years earlier had launched his own leviathan.

Probably best known to the English-speaking world of the pre-World War II period was Heim's Protestant manifesto, *Spirit and Truth* (*Das Wesen des Evangelischen Christentums,* 1925). This was written in open dialogue with his famous Catholic colleague at Tübingen, Karl Adam. Since World War II Heim has been known across the world for his writings on natural science. This is a calamity, for it by-passes his most distinctive contribution, which is the methodological structure underlying his entire literature and which, more than the concerns of piety, dictated the direction of his theological writing. Heim aimed his communication of the Christian faith at levels of the human spirit which are often left untouched by the theological traditions stemming from seventeenth-century Protestant orthodoxy and from nineteenth-century liberalism. It is not mysterious, therefore, that a majority of the pastors in Germany today regard him as their principal teacher.

Here the mystery begins, however. The Continental theologians who remember him have appended him to their courses in the history of doctrine. His phenomenal life-span has made that a possibility. He was over eighty years of age when he died. But what of the contemporary pertinence of his work? I believe there are mainly two reasons for the relative neglect of Heim's thought among his colleagues today. The more immediate reason seems to be that the Barth and Bultmann circles have almost completely absorbed current theological attention. The less evident but equally instructive reason is that the theologians have been too disconcerted by Heim's method to sustain their interest. My account of Heim's contribution will attempt to provide the key to both circumstances. It can be found in what Heim conceives to be the responsibility of Christian apologetics.[1]

---

[1] In December 1953 the *Scottish Journal of Theology* printed my article on Heim entitled "The Task of Apologetics in the Future." I am indebated to the editors for permitting me to draw heavily upon the substance and language of that article.

I

The theologians who have noticed Heim have exhausted themselves attempting to locate his position within some standard camp. One group has labeled him "a rationalist." Did he not develop a philosophical basis for the Christian view of life? Was he not concerned with the intellectual possibility of the certainty of faith? Did he not restlessly seek for a "category" by which to express the Christian faith in terms comprehensible to contemporary culture? Is not that device reminiscent of the Schleiermacher-Troeltsch-Otto succession, with its tactic of religious a priori?

The testimony of this group is very confident. "Anyone who accepts Heim's world view is not yet a religious man," says one interpreter. "Heim's whole effort is a blunder which can be traced to his preoccupation with artful abstraction," says another. "Insoluble logic is more important to him than personal relations. His God is an 'it' and not a 'Thou.'" "He employs the experience of despair as a device for securing the certainty of faith." "In his desire for a science of the ultimate he wishes to stand where only God can stand." "He does not speak from a place within the Church." He "fails to follow the proper task of theology, reflection on the testimony and message of the Bible."[2]

These charges would be serious were it not for the almost comical fact that another block of interpreters arrives at a completely opposite conclusion about him. His tendencies, they say, are those of "an irrationalist." Does he not elevate God beyond the reach of human reason? Does he not exemplify a simple trust in the biblical revelation with its miracles and unique revelation? One rejects him because he denies that man is able to

[2] Paul Kalweit, *Die Christliche Welt*, J. 21, p. 562; Th. Steinmann, *Zeitschrift für Theologie und Kirche*, n.f., XIII, p. 49; W. Thimme, *Theologische Studien und Kritiken*, J. 105, pp. 25, 35–36; Karl Barth, *Die Kirchliche Dogmatik*, II,1, p. 225; Dietrich Bonhoeffer, *Christentum und Wissenschaft*, H. 12, p. 435; Hermann Diem, *Die Christliche Welt*, J. 46, p. 546; H. Obendiek, *Scottish Journal of Theology*, Vol. 5, No. 3, p. 259.

have communion with God outside of Jesus Christ. Another says, "He imports a *deus ex machina* into a sceptical philosophy." Another, "He is a reactionary irrationalist." Still another, "He neglects the rational in order to found religion on an irrational source."[3]

By these contradictory testimonies the critics fall against each other and the Heim mystery deepens. The more patient and discerning critics see both rationalist and irrationalist tendencies in Heim's work, but they fail to see how he has resolved these tendencies. He presents the puzzling appearance of one who attempts contradictory aims. Therefore, these analysts ask, "How can one combine in a single viewpoint an emphasis both on what is beyond the reason and what is a necessity within the reason," as Heim seems to do? "How can an intellectual impossibility become the basis for the intellectual possibility of Christianity?" "How can one express Tertullian's fideism in the patterns of pure mathematics?" Has not Heim "vacillated indefinitely between an austere metaphysical theology and a theology of individual experience"?[4]

Those more cautious and well-balanced critiques are as misguided as all the others, however. All seem to miss a central key which unlocks the mystery of Heim's theological significance. One may state it briefly. Heim's theological method is instructed by a sensitivity to the polarity, the tension, in human existence which is ineradicable from within existence. How does he know about this tension? In not one but two ways. He both lives as a man and is the beneficiary of the revelation which names the truth "Jesus Christ." These two standpoints are nowhere held in separation in Heim's position. The human situation is seen to be riddled with the agonies one associates with doubt, social hostility, suffering, guilt, and death. These agonies are the more acute for the fact that there appears to be

[3] Fernand Ménégoz, *Le Problème de la Prière*, p. 203; Friedrich Traub, *Theologische Studien und Kritiken*, n. j., 1917, p. 191; D. C. Macintosh, *The Problem of Religious Knowledge*, p. 350; Rudolf Paulus, *Zeitschrift für Theologie und Kirche*, n. f., 1922, p. 201.

[4] Karl Beth, *Theologische Rundschau*, V. 20, p. 94; Otto Hoffmann, *Theologische Studien und Kritiken*, 1922, p. 267; Julius Kaftan, *Studien zur systematische Theologie T. von Haering*, pp. 37, 39; Erich Przywara, *Stimmen der Zeit*, 1926, p. 353.

no satisfactory relief from them within the human situation. How does Heim know that? Has he personally played all the registers of life? That is not required of a man who has heard from within his life as a man the message of justification by faith alone. It is precisely the priority of faith in his method which makes it possible for him to participate profoundly in the life of the world.

For instance, he wrote as a *phenomenologist;* indeed, his first book in 1902 was an analysis of Husserl's phenomenological method. That means he dealt with the problem of life *as it appears,* and not simply as a deduction from the Christian revelation. Yet it was his position from within the faith that gave him his warrant for proceeding as a phenomenologist does, in honest pursuit of the problem of life as it appears, for that process of fundamental questioning would surely culminate in thirst for a meaning which does not necessarily appear. He also wrote as an *existentialist.* Heim was one of the first theologians in Europe to introduce Kierkegaardian insights, as well as one of the first to take up the work of Heidegger into theological reasoning. Yet it was as a steward of the faith that he had the confidence that the pursuit of meaning involves *all* one's faculties and commits one to decisive action upon the results of his search. And he wrote as an *ontologist.* That means he was not simply a metaphysician seeking for the origin or causes of things, for first principles. In that regard he was instructed by Ritschlianism. To say he was an ontologist means he examined and illuminated the fundamental structure of being in such a way as to relate the whole of one's life to the ultimate meaning in the whole of life. Along with Tillich and others in the days between the wars he defended the role of ontology in theology. However, it was clearer to him than to some others that theology precedes ontology and makes it possible, as even Plato and Aristotle seem to have believed. Finally, he wrote with a *hermeneutical* accent. By that is meant that the fundamental realities with which a theologian has to deal are meanings. This accent ought not be confused with a variety of Gnosticism for which sheer theological information was held to be redemptive. The intellectual propositions of a hermeneutical theology are different from those which specify that life means this or that.

The meanings which resolve the manifest and hidden agonies of life will be breathed with intimacy through such confessional language as "You mean everything to me!" and by that communication change the structure of life.

II

The primacy of faith in Heim's system ought to safeguard his otherwise secular methods from being dismissed, as Barthian-influenced theologians tend to dismiss them. Karl Barth has said *"Nein!"* to almost every major theologian of this century, and he has done it, as he himself says, like a roaring lion. His main prey have been theologians with an *Anknüpfungspunkt* mentality, which is a species of natural theology, deriving theological insight from sources other than God's special revelation in Christ. Therefore, to join forces with Heim would seem like an invitation to annihilation at Barth's hands, considering Heim's apparent deafness to the Barthian warning. The following typical citations from Heim's works are impressive evidence of his apparent methodological flirtation with natural theology:

"All reality speaks a common language." "Morality and religion are one and the same movement of life under two different viewpoints." "Every fleeting wish is indeed already a religion in miniature." "The demand of human relations is for another who himself needs no other." "There are only two possible reactions for the man in battle—stupefaction or prayer." "There is no experience of despair that does not give light to the horizon." "The despair which the conscience experiences is the foothold in the visible for the leap into the invisible." "Every forcible suppression of doubt is a direct blow at conscience. It destroys our reverence for truth, the highest faculty within us, which must be kept alive if we wish to know God." "An atheistic ontology is only possible on the grounds of an abstraction which neglects the why and wherefore of the existence of the real man." "We must find an answer to the question about how we may find a way from creation to the creator." "The leading of God can come to one in an entirely reasonable and commonplace form in which, after a laborious rational process through which I examine a given situation according to my best knowledge and conscience and enumerate all the reasons *pro* and *con*, I become stamped with the seal of certainty: 'This way must in the name of God be taken.' "[5]

Barth's own critique of Heim was relatively benign until he read Heim's statement disavowing works on dogmatics as acts of pride. It can truthfully be said of Barth that he never fought an offensive war. In the case of Heim, the casual sentence in his Preface provoked Barth's counterattack. In an open letter to Heim appearing in the periodical *Between the Times*,[6] Barth asked Heim to explain what he meant by that statement. But he said more. The students who moved back and forth between the two universities where Heim and Barth were teaching had told Barth some of the things Heim was saying about him in his lectures. Apparently Heim said that Barth's *Dogmatik* is "the summit of the unpleasant pride of modern secularism." To that Barth replied that Heim's theology was "the most recent form of the equally unpleasant humility of modern pietism." While Heim's personal history is laden with pietism, as his recent autobiography quite explicitly reveals, Barth's charge was theological in intention. Heim's approach to the Christian faith, Barth said, is a form of "psychologism," the very kind of anthropological exaggeration which makes bedfellows of nineteenth-century liberalism, pietism, and scholasticism. Each is a trend toward "point of contact" thinking, or natural theology.[7]

Barth's criticism of Heim is wrong. Heim's theology has never

---

[5] *Das Weltbild der Zukunft*, p. iv; *Leitfaden der Dogmatik*, 2nd ed., Vol. 1, p. 64; *Das Weltbild*, p. 193; *Glaube und Leben*, pp. 518–19; *ibid.*, p. 623; *Glaubensgewissheit*, 1st ed., p. 39; *Glaube und Leben*, p. 650; *Spirit and Truth*, p. 113; *Zeitschrift für Theologie und Kirche*, n. f., Vol. 11, p. 330; *Die Wandlung im naturwissenschaftlichen Weltbild*, p. 18; *Glaube und Denken*, 2nd ed., pp. 335–36.

[6] *Zwischen den Zeiten*, J. 9, h. 5, pp. 451–53.

[7] *The Doctrine of the Word of God*, p. 21. In one of his last written statements Heim conceded that pietism dominated his thinking, but defined pietism as "the conviction that there is such a thing as Christianity only on the basis of a 'conversion,' which means a turning about through which I cease to lead myself and by complete surrender put my whole existence under the leadership of Jesus Christ. If a conversion is the only way a man can be certain of his eternal salvation, then a theology can only have meaning if it serves the end of leading man to this decision." *Ich gedenke der vorigen Zeiten*, 1957, pp. 315–16.

been anthropological, except in the sense that his Lutheran Christology is anthropological. To begin with God's word in Christ, however, does not prohibit taking one's humanity with theological seriousness. Since the Enlightenment, of course, any alliance between revelation and human discernment has been looked upon with suspicion by both theologians and philosophers, for at that time philosophy declared its independence from theology and theology felt obliged to return the compliment. Therefore, in modern life philosophies have tended to absorb the functions of faiths. Barthianism alone of all the theologies today has attempted, like medieval scholasticism, to absorb the functions of philosophy.[8]

Heim's understanding of the relation of theology to non-theological disciplines antedates this curtaining off of the human and the divine disciplines. It is probably best exemplified in the philosophical theology of Augustine. Karl Heim can really be understood only in this setting. For that reason, judgments aimed at him from within the philosophy-blind post-Enlightenment theology are apt to miss the mark. If theology is separable from other spheres, it is insulated against their judgment. At the same time, however, in such a relation the judgment of theology upon other spheres is blocked by its own defenses. If theology is in any way dependent upon other spheres, its autonomy is threatened, being subject to the judgment of these other spheres. One of the rewards of that risk, however, is that the methodological lines by which theological perspective is communicated to other spheres are at least kept open.

It would be better to find a new name for what theologians used to do than to allow the theological task to be pinched by restrictions forced upon it by either secular or sacred sciences. Heim believed this so firmly that he entertained the notion of a completely different name for theology, namely, the "Science of the Ultimate." Such a science is interested in but one question: "What are the ultimate presuppositions which support our life

[8] Kazuo Mutō, a Japanese Christian teaching philosophy at Kyoto University, has helped me understand this about Barth. See my *Japanese Contributions to Christian Theology* (Philadelphia: Westminster, 1960), p. 133.

and how is the certainty of this foundation established?"[9] Heim
would not concede that there is a distinction between theological
responsibility and the type of search for a basis in life which
goes on outside theology, such as in the novel and the drama,
or even in newspapers and in politics. All are concerned explicitly or implicitly with the ultimate in existence, be they inside
or outside the church.[10]

Heim believed he was able to achieve as a result of his
method at least the outlines of a Christian ontology. There does
seem to be a convincing overlap between the human situation
as lived through by the concerned man and the divine revelation as witnessed within the Christian church. One would expect, therefore, that the effect of Heim's method would be to
break down the wall, if not to construct a bridge, between the
church and the world, between theology and philosophy, between faith and culture. It should be carefully noted that Heim
proposed no theological bridge "between God and man." That
task is out of the theologian's hands and, where attempted, is
nothing but a *Schneebrücke*, a bridge of snow.

Two major data dominate Heim's ontology. One is the thoroughgoing relativism of human existence. The other is what he
calls God's "dimensional" transcendence. These data are complementary. If there is a God of the sort confessed by the
Hebrew-Christian faith, then man has a permanent basis for his
life. The basis, however, would be not in man's life but in God's.
Therefore Heim could press man relentlessly with the question
of ultimate meaning because he knew from the outset that a
life unrelated to God is relatively meaningless. "A man must
have something permanent," Heim believed.[11] Human experience needs it, not because it feels the need, but because the
need is revealed to be inherent in the very structure of life.

By relativism Heim meant that in existence, as one can know
it by himself, there is no absolute point of reference. The
ontology underlying this assertion is constructed out of a view
of time. Man is completely embedded in time, or better, time

[9] *Glaube und Denken*, p. 22.
[10] *Die Wandlung*, p. 13.
[11] *Leben aus dem Glauben*, pp. 3, 4.

is completely embedded in man. The very structure of existence is time, and, like time, existence is running out. Within existence there is no security for existence. Man's life is a continuous trek across a never-ending watershed. Behind him is the irrevocable and certain past, powerless to help him in the present. Ahead of him is the uncertain future. Without the help of any final knowledge, man must act decisively toward the future. In the nature of time, moving forward as it does irreversibly, suspension of decision would be itself a decision to let time decide. The mistake of man is either to accept something in time as if it were final, or to fail to despair of its lack of finality. Either state would be a condition of "radical godlessness," which Heim describes as the lack of an Archimedean point for the orientation of one's life.

How does the human reason function within this time reference? Reason leads man restlessly from island to island but never finds a continent on which to build firmly. Within the ever-receding infinity called existence, the reason comes upon nothing which is not staggered by the question, Why? But the conscientious reason, the moral reason, the reason which is concerned with the total destiny of the person on behalf of whom it functions, is not content with this situation and tantalizes itself in an endless and exhausting search for a clue to transcendence beyond the situation. Life under these conditions can result only in either the crushing spiritual poverty one has learned to call despair, or a leap into some sort of saving faith. No faith could be regarded as a saving faith which does not transcend the limitations of the "time-form" from which it professes to bring deliverance. In his autobiography *Ich gedenke der vorigen Zeiten* (*I Remember the Days of Old*), Heim recapitulates the sheer geographical and political relativity he experienced in a trip around the world just after the First World War. Add to this experience his knowledge of Einstein's theory and you have what he called "the fundamental negative idea at the base of my whole theological work."[12]

The Christian belief in the transcendence of God both explains the relativity of the time-form and brings deliverance

---

[12] *Ich gedenke der vorigen Zeiten*, p. 224.

from it. Where there is only one God, all else is related to him, that is, all else is relative. Where there is only one Absolute, all else presupposes this Absolute. The very effort to know the Absolute depends upon the prior existence of the Absolute. Is God so transcendent, then, that He is out of touch with human experience? On the contrary. God is transcendent because he is so near, not because He is so remote. He sustains man's whole life, and one cannot see the place on which one stands. Is man therefore destined to live in ignorance of the one reality the knowledge of which can bring authenticity to his life? Not at all. The experience of thoroughgoing relativism is the presupposition for the raising of the question about the ultimate. The question simply waits upon the answer which only the ultimate can give, and give in its own way. The Christ-revelation is taken to be the answer of God to the question implicit in the structure of man's life. As such, it is an answer which arises not from the relative situation but is transcendent of the situation.

Yet throughout Heim's work he makes the claim for the rational certainty of the Christian faith. What could that mean within this ontological scheme of human relativism and divine transcendence? The allusion to certainty is a residuum in Heim from another day. The meaning, however, does not hinge upon the language. Heim is convinced that it is rational to affirm what is needed to make experience possible. The Christian revelation, then, notwithstanding man's inability to come upon it by himself, is a "rational event"—as Barth himself once called it.[13] For Heim it is not revelation but only the need of revelation which is given in human experience. When Barth complains that one cannot end with faith-certainty unless one has begun with it, he requires exactly what Heim has proposed. His theology begins from within the human situation at the point where the Christ revelation brings the ultimacy of the transcendent God to the contingency of existence.

III

The general lines of Heim's ontology were present in his theology from his earliest work. Pertinent elements in the new physics

[13] *The Doctrine of the Word of God*, pp. 152–53.

and biology, in existential philosophy, and in the political fortunes of the world have been blended with Luther's doctrine of justification by faith. The result has been no flatulent philosophy in waiting for some doctoral candidate to place it in the history of thought. Heim's work has been a spur at the flank of Continental life for over half a century.

The mobility of Heim's intellectual forces during this time is most impressive. In each succeeding decade he has shifted his key concept, always improving without essentially changing his fundamental structure. To shift the figure, he has felt it important to erect a readily traversible bridge between the Christian message and the world. It must be remembered that the bridge connects the Church and the world, not God and man. To use an Augustinian figure, the bridge is traversible when illuminated, and one who believes in the Christian doctrine of justification by faith or—what is the same—the doctrine of the Holy Spirit, knows that this is a *lumen aeternae* for the coming of which one can only wait. This primacy of God's action, however, in no way obviates for Heim the importance of building bridges.

In *Psychologismus oder Antipsychologismus* (1902) Heim set the pattern for his entire theological literature. In this very difficult little study of Edmund Husserl's pioneering work in logic, he attempted to show how it is possible to do theology without either metaphysics on the one side or the logic of the natural sciences on the other. An epistemology is required which will allow that at the base of thought processes there are presuppositions which are themselves unknowable. In his recent memoirs he notes how Martin Heidegger's *Sein und Zeit,* which virtually attempted the same kind of analysis, has now made that early work of his superfluous. I cite this comment simply to observe that he makes no such statement with reference to his other works.

Das Weltbild der Zukunft (1904) established Heim as an author at a time when he would rather have become a professor. The book was a study of reality documented from the modern sciences and from philosophy. His thesis was that in reality as it appears one has to do only with relationships, never with ultimate data. This very relativity of phenomena forces men to make decisions, even though a secure basis for such decisions is not given in the phenomena. It does not seem unreasonable, therefore, that there would appear to man what man himself needs but cannot voluntarily conjure up—the revelation of an absolute basis for decision in God's own decision.

Heim does not hide his disappointment at not being called to a chair of systematic theology as a result of this work. Actually, it was not the kind of work expected of dogmaticians in Germany at that time. Just to show that he could do it, he subsequently turned to more traditional historical studies, one on Alexander of Hales and another on the problem of certainty. Karl Barth is said to have confessed a similar motive behind his own *Anselm* study. Not until 1914 was Heim finally called to a professorship at Münster. Because of the war he could not take up this call until 1918. Two years later he won the post at Tübingen, which he held until retirement. I say "won" because a contest actually ensued with Rudolf Otto for that position. In his early student movement days Heim felt shunned by circles in Germany which associated him with an American brand of practical Christianity and a Methodist brand of evangelical piety. On one occasion when he sought the advice of Reinhold Seeberg concerning his vocational possibilities as a professor of theology, he was shocked when this famous teacher told him he should seek a chair of practical theology.

In 1916 his original insights concerning the decisional character of reality were sharpened in the direction of more fundamental theological concerns in the volume called *Glaubensgewissheit* (*The Certainty of Faith*). In the second edition of this work, appearing in 1920, the first significant shift in his position occurred. The "decision" category was replaced by a "destiny" category. Man's windowless decisions do not simply presuppose some transcendent light. They suffer a light burning in upon them. This category, suggested by Oswald Spengler, offered Heim the occasion to introduce into his method the more aggressive connotations of revelation, theologically expressed in the doctrines of predestination, grace, and the witness of the Spirit.

Within three years a third edition of *Glaubensgewissheit* appeared, which further clarified the structure in the relation which

God's destinating decision sustains to man's relative decisions. God is "the nonobjective perspective," drawing all visible experience up into the unity of His being, but Himself remaining invisible. This perspectival unity is at the ground of all experience as the very possibility of experience. One cannot know the nonobjective perspective point of all objective perspectives, but one cannot know anything else without it. The dependence here upon motifs from Kant is avowed.[14]

This development of categories prepared the way for the emergence of the category on which Heim based his magnum opus, *The Evangelical Faith and the Thought of the Present*. I refer to his most famous category of "the dimension." Heim believed that one who understands the meaning of the "dimensions" has come upon the primary and most important basis for understanding the mystery of existence. The illustrations are patent. The two-dimensionally minded primitive man was unable to make sense of his universe until someone announced the existence of the third dimension. The third dimension was nothing he could see, for one's perception presupposes it. Width and height stretch out before us, but depth is a straight line. If we observe it we see only the end of it, a pinpoint on the two-dimensional width-height surface. If we observe on the basis of it, however, the surface becomes deep with perspective. To say it more technically, on the basis of two-dimensional experience it is contradictory to assume that more than two straight lines may meet at right angles. Analogically, the God-relation is the depth dimension which, when one hears of it, comprehends all other dimensions and clarifies existence, without itself being perceptible.

The God-dimension is hidden, and it is the presupposition of a meaningful existence. But it is not a silent relation. It is characterized by "the word," an encounter similar to the relation between persons. Hence the analogy from dimensions serves an additional function. Heim has used it to express in somewhat logical language the poetical insights of Martin Buber's *I and*

[14] In 1932 G. C. Berkouwer wrote discerningly of Heim's theology as "the theology of the nonobjectifiable." See his *Geloof en Openbaring in de Nieuwere Duitsche Theologie (Faith and Revelation in the New German Theology)*, pp. 84–103 and 182–92.

Thou. There are two kinds of spaces: I-spaces and it-spaces. It-spaces are filled with contents which are exclusive of all other spaces, like the spaces on a checkerboard. The conflict in personal relations is a result of attempting to make it-spaces out of I-spaces. Either we draw circles around ourselves in such a way as to exclude others, or we introject the others into the circle of our own existence in such a way as to rob these others of their independence. I-spaces, however, are not content-spaces. They are dimensional-spaces. Therefore there may be an infinite number of these spaces without their excluding one another. An infinite number of lines may converge perpendicularly at the same point if there is a third dimension beyond height and width. At the same time, these dimensional spaces can meet without losing their distinctive identity. Two infinite planes may intersect without jeopardizing either their infinity or their distinctness. It-spaces meet by contact. I-spaces meet by encounter. The God-relation is of the nature of I-spaces.

The analogy from space has not overlooked the time analogy in which Heim's ontological structure was conceived. It-spaces are past time and I-spaces are present time. God Himself is an I-space with the unique character of eternal presentness. God is the "dimension of dimensions" which comprehends all other dimensions. That dimension actively confers meaning on all reality when the word of God, which is the point at which the world of experience is related to God, is present.

With the rise of National Socialism in Germany, Heim's categorial bridge-building suffered a moment of uncertainty. Since 1902 his method had assumed the ontological impossibility of relativizing the absolute and absolutizing the relative. Obviously it was always considered *morally* possible to invert the structure of life, to exchange the truth about God for a lie and worship the creature rather than the Creator. National Socialism, however, seemed to illustrate the possibility of embracing relativities as absolute without undergoing existential despair. Hence in the third edition of *Glaube und Denken,* which was the first volume of his six-volume work, Heim stressed what had nonetheless always been implicit. This volume is translated into English as *God Transcendent.* In it Heim indicated that analogies from the world are too weak to turn man from preoccupation with the world to faith in God. Man cannot by any observation of his own attain to the Christian knowledge of God. "We are thrown back on God's own revelation."[15] As Heim had said in his *Glaubensgewissheit*, "The hammer with which the smith strikes the anvil cannot forge itself. . . . Nor can thought prove its own presuppositions."[16]

IV

The best clue for understanding Heim's theology is what he believes to be the responsibility of a Christian apologetic. At this point he is most clearly different from the two dominating figures in Continental theology, Barth and Bultmann. The questions that emerge from a comparison of these three theologians are now helping to form the theology of the future.

In Heim's method an apologetic has three obligations. The first is to unmask the idols which the world destructively reveres. This is the offensive phase of apologetic. As such, it is simply a propaedeutic to Christian preaching. The second obligation is to preach the positive Christian message. The third is to provide a Christian view of life, a Christian ontology, a science of the ultimate that would relate the Christianized world meaningfully to its total environment. This is the phase of consolidation, organic to apologetics in general.[17]

The old variety of defensive apologetic in which the theologian felt called upon to justify the Christian message before the so-called bar of reason is utterly foreign to Heim's method. As he said, "We need an attitude which we do not need to defend . . . indeed, which can change the strategy from defense to attack."[18] Equally foreign is the still older method of rational attack upon non-Christian systems, characterized by Franz Overbeck as the intellectual equivalent of the medieval crusades. Heim is rather in the tradition of Pascal and Kierkegaard,

[15] *God Transcendent* (N.Y., Scribner's, 1936), pp. 230–31.

[16] Second ed., pp. 129–30.

[17] The strategy was outlined by Heim in an article called "Der gegenwärtige Stand der Debatte zwischen Theologie und Naturwissenschaft," *Theologische Studien und Kritiken*, 1908, pp. 402–29.

[18] *Der christliche Gottesglaube und die Naturwissenschaft*, Erster Teilband, p. 33.

applying a relentless critique to the roots of man's existence, and always upon the presupposition that the God revealed in Christ can alone re-establish the uprooted man on the soil of His truth. Apologetic attack is analogous to the way a physician attacks an illness. He is not so intent on defending his professional reputation as he is in effecting a cure.

Apologetic can lead only to the threshold of a Christian solution. Even then the threshold is no closer to heaven than to hell. The method is informed by Socratic midwifery, the maieutic method which Kierkegaard introduced into theology through his concept of irony. But where Socrates used the process of fundamental questioning to deliver the mind of its own innate wisdom, the great Christian apologists have simply disabused the mind of its barriers against the coming of the revelation.[19] The revelation itself is *sui generis*.

Heim's apologetic can be clearly seen in his latest work, his three volumes on natural science and the Christian faith, which are volumes four to six of his *Evangelical Faith and the Thought of the Present*. Following a lead from German physicist Pascual Jordan—that the language of today is the language of the natural sciences—Heim has gone to the trouble to think through the faith as it relates to the latest sciences and to communicate the faith in juxtaposition to scientific questions. Motifs in contemporary thought, inspired by classical materialism and Newtonian mechanism, attributing absoluteness and causal necessity to the objective world, do not need to be attacked by theology. The newer science has already discredited them. Physics, it seems, has been forced to become more philosophical by its successive reduction of matter to an indeterminate element, of space and time to relativity, and of mechanical necessity to acausality. The theologian in this context does not ask science to listen to the dogmatic conclusions of faith but simply to the wistfulness of science itself. After science has been allowed to interrogate itself, the faith introduces the meanings

[19] Emil Brunner's works also illustrate this method. He has given it the name "eristic" or "Christian Socratism," and he refers to it as "theology's other task," which was his way of saying that the writing of a *Dogmatik* does not exhaust the theologian's responsibility. *Zwischen den Zeiten*, 1929, pp. 255–276.

which are essential but inaccessible to science. The universe is sustained by a living God who relates Himself to the ongoing process as He will. That, roughly, is the thesis of volume five, *The Transformation of the Scientific World-View*.

Volume six, *Weltschöpfung und Weltende* (*Creation and Eschatology*), takes up the problem of the origin and end of the world. Here again the new science has destroyed the Laplacian and Newtonian concepts of a universe that is closed and self-existent. The universe is open at both ends. It has its beginning in an indefinable fog and its ending in what the scientists themselves call a "natural science eschatology," such as the notion of the heat death of the universe. The interpretative value of natural science in these instances, however, is candidly negative. It clears the air for what we need desperately to know about our universe but cannot know even from science. God is at the beginning and at the ending of time. While this affirmation cannot be made on the basis of a scientific method, it shockingly corresponds to the deepest though unanswered questions of science.

There is a vast difference between apologetic in this sense and natural theology. Natural theology, as Karl Barth has rightly called it, is a species of intellectual works-righteousness where the mind arrives at the truth of God, not independently of God perhaps, but independently of God's revelation in Christ. It is, therefore, a kind of theological peeping-tom act which spies on God independently of the manner in which God wishes to reveal Himself. It may succeed in finding out God's hands and feet, but as Calvin has said, it will not find His heart. The heart is the sole master of its secrets.

Why, then, an apologetic? Why not simply a quiet, patient waiting for God to break into our perception when and where He will? Apologetic proceeds neither out of skepticism of God's ability to make Himself known independently of apologetic nor on the basis of a theory of natural revelation. Apologetics answers to the call of Christ to preach the Gospel to the world. It is not difficult to be a man of the world to the men of the world if one is a Christian, for a Christian is always at the same time a worldling. Apologetics simply calls upon a man to do earnestly what comes quite naturally—to talk to one's neighbor in the terms of one's neighbor about the matter of our life and death. A man in Christ knows much more about his neighbor than the neighbor knows about himself, not by virtue of his neighbor-relation but by virtue of the transcendent perspective of the Christ-relation.

A man is never asked, however, to step from his false though orderly world view into an esoteric faith-relation whose contacts with the rest of reality are allowed to remain amorphous and chaotic. The Christian man has the privilege of living within a church which is constantly developing "an honest theology of cultural high standing," to use Paul Tillich's phrase. This is no longer apologetics in the sense of establishing a bridgehead on enemy territory. It is the consolidation of gains. Nor is it simply dogmatics or systematic theology in the sense of the exposition of the faith of the church. It is avowedly secondary to dogmatics, but not thereby without importance. It is a frankly bifocal enterprise which, while informed by the substance of Christianity, is patterned by the dominant issues in the culture of the time.

Despite my valiant effort to keep Heim's most respectable side forward, I must confess that I find his more popular later writings theologically inferior to his earlier work. Some might explain this apparent decline by the fantastic manner in which Heim wrote these books. Confined to bed with a heart ailment, he was permitted to dress and sit at his desk for but one hour daily. Whatever the reason, this later work deviates from his self-announced apologetic method. Until this time he had created categories which had theological and existential durability. Except for the first of his six volumes, these works abandoned categorial and analogical reasoning for sheer homily and illustration. The second volume, *Jesus der Herr* (*Jesus the Lord,* 1935), adds little to the understanding of christology and soteriology except sermonic lessons drawn from the feeling of need for a strong leader which National Socialism inspired. *Jesus der Weltvollender* (*Jesus the Fulfiller of the World,* 1937) adds even less to eschatology and supports a rather traditional view.

Most vulnerable of all are the three volumes on natural science. Due to his serious illness during the time these volumes were composed, Heim's publisher kept negatively critical reviews from him. Thus the benefit which comes from vigorous challenge was lacking in this process of composition. The most manifest difficulty is that the latest insights of natural science are used by Heim to justify traditional views of creation, miracle, and eschatology, views which many exegetes and theologians are no longer able to purvey as either mandatory or meaningful. An apologetic method which began with the capacity to sting the life of man with the sense of his inadequacy and to illuminate his life with the realization of God's adequacy ended in defense of doctrinal forms which had already begun to lose their meaning.[20]

How, then, does Heim stand up alongside the giants of the contemporary theological scene? A detailed comparison of the apologetic emphases of Barth, Bultmann, and Heim would be highly instructive. Suffice it here to make several generalizations.

Barth dismisses Heim's apologetic as a scholastic residuum in Protestant theology. Heim, however, believed that Barth defaulted in his leadership in the church's conflict with the unbelieving world. There is no disputing the fact that Barth has warmed the heart of the believing community. For that Heim recurrently professed his personal debt to Barth. Whether Barth has chilled the life of modern man with a "sublime monotony," as Heim has claimed, is a serious charge whose validity the future must appraise. At the same time there is already impressive evidence that a strategy such as Heim's could lead the church "out of the stuffy air of a closed space in which it spoils miserably, into the full expanse of world events."[21]

In the last years of his life Heim felt he had to choose between two projects, his memoirs or a critique of Bultmann. He wrote his memoirs. Bultmann was an enigma to Heim. That fact may indicate that Heim never really learned his lessons well from Heidegger. For Bultmann, hermeneutics is the sum and substance of the theological task. In that single discipline are embraced all the tasks which other theologies splinter into exegesis, dogmatics, apologetics, and preaching. Bultmann would

[20] Cf. also my analysis of Heim in *The Hinge of History*, esp. pp. 70, 71.

[21] Kurt Leese, *Zeitschrift für Theologie und Kirche*, J. 24, p. 120.

not have criticized Heim, as Barth did, for flirting with natural theology; he would have recognized the thoroughgoing Christocentrism of Heim's position. Bultmann would have criticized Heim for developing Christian world views which had no necessary relation to man's self-understanding and which therefore amounted to nothing but cosmological speculation. Barth is just as disconcerted as Heim by Bultmann's disavowal of apologetics. In his little writing on Bultmann, Barth admits that every time you mention apologetics in Bultmann's presence Bultmann "hits the ceiling." Barth cannot understand this, and says that "in some one sense all theologians in all times have been and even must be apologists as well."[22] What Bultmann means, however, is that the method of theology is no different from the tactic of exegesis or of apologetic. It is simply in the light of the Scriptures to understand the meaning of human existence.

Barth, by his exclusive preoccupation with the Christian gospel in its own terms, has run the risk of moving parallel to modern culture, although he himself understands that the connection between God and the world is a circuit which God, not the theologian, completes. Bultmann, with his concern for the meaning of human existence, has run the risk of changing the traditional form of the gospel, although not the gospel itself. Heim has run no risk. He has attempted to reach the world without jeopardy to the traditional form of the Christian gospel. Not even the pietistic community of Württemberg questioned his orthodoxy. He moved with no noticeable sense of intellectual agony back and forth from the existential needs of the modern world to what he took to be the historical facts of the first-century gospel. Behind the appearance of dialogue with the world, he has come close to maintaining a parallelism as sharp as Barth's while at the same time pursuing the interpretive task less courageously than Bultmann.

The great merit of Barth is that he has developed in theology today a conscience about the unique source of the Christian faith in the reality of God and His revelation. The merit of Bultmann is that he has been willing to lose his faith in its

[22] "Rudolf Bultmann: Ein Versuch ihn zu verstehen," *Theologische Studien*, Heft 34, p. 43.

traditional form in order to find it as a meaningful reality. It may well be enough to say of Karl Heim that he stood at a point of transition between these polar passions.

Bibliography

Karl Heim, *Jesus the Lord,* Philadelphia, Fortress Press, 1961.

Ingmar Haolmstrand, *Karl Heim on Philosophy, Science, and the Transcendence of God,* Stockholm, Almquist & Wiksell International, 1980.

III
Mid-century Classics

ANDERS NYGREN

Warren A. Quanbeck

Anders Nygren (1890–1978) is the most influential representative of the Lundensian school of theology, so named because of its origin in the University of Lund in Sweden. Gustaf Aulén and Ragnar Bring are other well-known theologians of this school.

Nygren was ordained to the ministry in the Church of Sweden (Lutheran) in 1912 and served as a parish pastor until 1921, when he was appointed docent (instructor) in the faculty of theology at Lund. In 1924 he was appointed to the chair of Systematic Theology and Ethics. In 1948 he was elected bishop of the diocese of Lund, continuing in this position until his retirement in 1959. He has been active in the ecumenical movement since the Conference on Faith and Order at Lausanne in 1927. He played a leading part in the Edinburgh Conference in 1937 and served as chairman of the Faith and Order Commission on Christ and the Church for more than a decade. He was among the leaders in the formation of the Lutheran World Federation, and served as its first president.

Nygren's range of theological interests has been broad, including the philosophy of religion, historical theology, ethics, and biblical exegesis. Until quite recently English readers had access only to his writings in historical theology and exegesis, a situation which has prevented a proper understanding of the purpose and development of his thought. His earliest writings were in the field of philosophy of religion, and in these works Nygren lays down the program which is carried out in the later works.

The first years of Nygren's work at the university were devoted to study and writing in philosophy of religion. His first major work was *Religious Apriori; Its Philosophical Presuppositions and Theological Implications* (1921). Condensed and popularized versions of this work appeared in Swedish and German in 1922 and in English in 1960. During this period he also wrote *The Scientific Foundation of Dogmatics* (1922), *The Question of Objectivity in Theology* (1922), *Philosophical and Christian Ethics* (1923), *Basic Questions in Ethics* (1926) and *Religiosity and Christianity* (1926).

His work in the history of thought includes his *History of the Christian Idea of Love,* appearing in two parts (1930, 1936) and in English translation as *Agape and Eros* (1932, 1939). He also wrote essays on *Primitive Christianity and the Reformation* (1932) and *The Atonement as a Work of God* (1932).

Later Nygren turned to biblical theology, publishing his *Commentary on the Epistle to the Romans* in 1944 (English edition 1949) and a pastoral letter to the clergy of the diocese of Lund (1949), translated into English in 1951 with the title *The Gospel of God*. In 1956 followed the volume *Christ and His Church,* closely related to the work of the World Council of Churches' Commission on Faith and Order. He also made important contributions to two volumes of essays: *A Book about the Bible* and *A Book about the Church.*

During Nygren's days as a student of theology there was serious question about the method, scope, and even the possibility of theology. The historical study of the Bible had brought into question the traditional doctrine of biblical inspiration and authority. The theology based on the traditional use of Scripture was further undermined by the philosophical work of Kant and his successors. The scholastic method of using the theological propositions of the Bible to construct a well-integrated picture of the transcendent realm was discredited. Some theologians were persuaded that with the disappearance of the transcendent realm as an object of study, they could only duplicate the efforts of students of philosophy or psychology of religion, comparative religion or ethics. Nygren set himself the task of discovering whether there is a legitimate scientific task for the theologian and what methods should be used to establish valid knowledge in this realm.

Nygren accepts the judgment of historical studies and critical philosophy on the traditional theological method, agreeing with Kant that there can be no science of the transcendent. What lies beyond the limits of human experience cannot become the object of scientific thought. Science must be based on the realities of human experience. If theology is to claim to afford valid knowledge it must meet two requirements: (1) it must first have its own subject matter for investigation and not be parasitic on some other discipline; and (2) it must have a scientific method of study which is appropriate to its subject matter. These requirements provide the starting point for Nygren's early essays in philosophy of religion. He seeks first to answer the objections of those who claim that religion is illusion and that a scientific study of religion can only end by demonstrating this fact. He also grapples with the objections of those who claim that theology is only a masked version of some other discipline, such as ethics, philosophy, or psychology.

Beginning with an examination of philosophy itself, Nygren insists that the requirements of scientific method be applied here first of all. Inasmuch as philosophy lacks the data for a study of the transcendent realm, it must forego metaphysical speculation and assume the humbler but more useful task of a critical examination of language and presuppositions. Philosophy is not a quest for some ultimate reality beyond experience, but an examination of the validity which is to be found within experience itself. The examination of language is designed to assist clarity in communication by eliminating ambiguity and confusion as far as possible.

When the critical examination of language has been accomplished, Nygren holds, the philosopher can undertake a second task: the examination of presuppositions. These are the concepts that underlie all our thinking and speech, but of which we are most frequently unaware. They are the unspoken assumptions of a period or a culture, judgments of fact or value whose truth or validity is not questioned, simply because everyone in a society accepts them. Nygren argues that it is the task of philosophy to uncover these hidden presuppositions, examine them, and make plain what are the basic principles or fundamental categories with which a period or society carries on its task of reflection.

Through his use of critical philosophy Nygren observes that there are four main areas of meaning, each corresponding to one of the inescapable questions which are fundamental to the life of the spirit. The first is the theoretical question, the question of truth. It is easy to show that this question is fundamental and essential, for if there were no difference between truth and falsehood, research would be meaningless, the search for causes and relationships pointless, speech and reflection in vain. The question of truth points to the area of the scientific. The second question is that of right and wrong, and the closely related question of good and evil. This too is obviously fundamental, for apart from it social life would be impossible and even individual character would be without foundation. The third question is that of the beautiful. It is more difficult to establish its fundamental character and less easy to refute aesthetic skepticism, but it is nevertheless an all-embracing form of the spiritual life. The fourth question is that of the eternal, the religious question. Positivism challenges the validity of this question, interpreting religion as a relic of an earlier and outworn stage of human existence. Nygren replies that this is to confuse religion with a primitive world view, and insists that the question of the eternal can be shown to be fundamental to the life of spirit. Each of the questions claims to be valid, and not simply for a single time or place but for all time. But none of these spheres —theoretical, ethical or aesthetic—realizes this presupposition in itself. Only in religion is this presupposition of the life of the spirit realized. Each of the other realms therefore ultimately depends upon the realm of religion, the question of the eternal.

By this analysis Nygren has attempted to establish the existence of four distinct areas of meaning: science, ethics, art, and religion. Each has its own distinctive approach to the data of experience. Each has its own use of language, must be dealt with in its own terms, and resists reduction to one of the others. The areas may indeed overlap, in the sense that a person may be concerned with several of them at the same time. The physician may be concerned as scientist with the nature of the ailment afflicting his patient, as ethical thinker may be troubled about the problem of informing his patient of his condition, and as religious man be seeking divine guidance in his dilemma. But his scientific thinking will not solve his ethical problem, nor can his ethical or religious reflection solve the scientific question.

The purpose of this analysis is to show that religion is an independent form of experience with its own context of meaning. Those who regard religion as strange ritual practices or merely mythological notions fail to understand it in its fullness and reality. For religion is not something accidental imposed upon human life from outside; it is the spiritual life itself in the deepest meaning of the term. Nygren points out that the independent status of religion has frequently been overlooked—by Kant, for example, who treats it as identical with ethics, or by Hegel, who identifies it with philosophy. But to understand religion the scholar must study it as it grows on its own ground and in accordance with its own laws. It can be rightly understood and expounded only from an essentially religious point of view, and any attempt to construe the meaning of religion by the application of laws which govern other spheres of the spiritual life is bound to fail.

Nygren points out an important difference between the scientific area and the other contexts of meaning. The scientific realm is "theoretical"; the others are "atheoretical." A statement in a scientific context can be verified empirically, and its truth or falsity conclusively demonstrated. But this does not hold in ethics, aesthetics or religion. Statements in ethics and religion are true or false only in relation to ultimate standards, and these standards cannot be verified empirically. There are different ethical and religious ideals, and which of them is right and true is a matter not of empirical verification but of personal decision and commitment. This does not mean that statements in these realms are unimportant or meaningless, but that they must be judged by standards different from those which prevail in the scientific context of meaning.

For the study of religion this means that a religious assertion is not to be dealt with in abstraction or removed from its context. There are different religions and each of them forms a complete constellation of meaning. Each has its own conception of the eternal and from this develops its understanding of the religious relationship, man's communion with the eternal and its social and ethical implications. For example, both Christianity and neoplatonism speak of the love of God, but this does not point to agreement or identity. What the love of God means in each of them must be understood in the context of the total constellation of meaning. One then discovers important differences between the religiosity of late Hellenism and that of early Christianity.

But in order to understand what is essential in religion, it is not enough to undertake a logical analysis of the concept of the eternal. Because the realm of religion is autonomous, by being subjected to logical analysis it can only be falsified and confused. It is important rather to turn to an examination of historical religions, and from a study of their features learn what content is to be put into the question of the eternal. Nygren contends that examination of the religions which have existed during the course of history does not support an evolutionary scheme in which there is unbroken development from primitive religion to complete "ethical monotheism." But he perceives that the question of the eternal occurs everywhere in certain fairly constant forms, and he singles out four of them: (1) All religions claim to unveil the eternal. Some religions have no idea of God, but there is no religion which lacks the idea of revelation, the disclosure of the eternal in the world of time. The revelation takes varied forms, ranging from fetishism and animism to mysticism, but in all there is a concern to open up the experience of the eternal. (2) All religions express the disquiet or judgment of the eternal. The eternal is regarded as mysterious and powerful, and he who approaches it must do so with gravity and earnestness. (3) Religion seeks to overcome the tension between the awareness of the eternal and man's knowledge of his unworthiness. It seeks ways to bridge the chasm between man and the eternal, to remove the barriers that separate them, to seek atonement or ways of purification. (4) Religion claims to be genuine fellowship and union between the eternal and man. The two cannot stand opposed to one another, but must be brought into union. The ways of doing so are very diverse, from totemistic eating of the deity at one extreme to the most sublime mystical awareness of union with God. With this analysis Nygren believes that he has detected the essential structure of religious experience. The four aspects appear in varying degrees and emphases in concrete historical religions, but all are present. But like the concept of the eternal, they are abstract—

tools to be used in the analysis of actual religions to see what content they are given.

With the task of philosophical analysis accomplished, Nygren turns to the second main part of his theological work, the task of developing systematic theology as a scientific discipline. It is the task of science to examine and comprehend a given subject matter. The science of systematic theology, according to Nygren, is given the task of understanding and expounding the Christian faith as it has developed over the centuries. It must show the essential content and meaning of the faith, pointing out its specifically Christian features and showing what makes it different from other religions. It is *systematic* theology in that it expounds the fundamental character and unity of Christianity and shows the relationship, structure and coherence of all the parts to each other.

Nygren's proposals for a scientific systematic theology are simple and for this reason attractive. But formidable difficulties stand in the way of carrying out this program. The great number and variety of theological expressions of Christianity seem to doom any project for finding the essence of the Christian religion. Viewed in the perspective of the contemporary church one sees Roman, Orthodox, Anglican, Lutheran, Calvinist, free church, and sectarian versions of Christianity. Historical perspective shows us the versions of Irenaeus, Origen, Augustine, the scholastics, Luther, Calvin, Schleiermacher, Barth, and others. Even if one limits the quest to the New Testament there is a bewildering variety: Christianity according to Paul, James, Peter, Matthew, Luke, John. What is to insure that Nygren's version shall not be merely another addition to an already long list of interpreters of Christianity? Nygren's answer is to propose motif research as the tool of the systematic theologian.

Motif research is a technique for discovering the fundamental idea or category of a religion. It seeks to set aside what is unique to individual interpreters of a religion and fasten on the elements which are essential and formative. Its procedure is to examine the historical evidence at hand for the understanding of a religion, form a hypothesis as to the fundamental element amid all the diverse expositions, and then test the hypothesis by checking it against the evidence. If the facts are not accounted for adequately, the hypothesis must be refined or reformulated. If the hypothesis does stand up to the facts, the indications are that it expresses the fundamental character of the religion being studied, and not merely peripheral matters. Nygren maintains that this is the proper scientific approach to the study of religion, and that it is capable of yielding valid results.

In the volume *Agape and Eros* we can view the method at work. The work has two parts, one dealing with the New Testament and the apostolic age, the second examining the history of theology to the Reformation in the sixteenth century.

Nygren begins with the recognition that Christianity is a religion and is therefore concerned with the question of man's relationship to the eternal. He then asks how communion with the eternal is achieved in Christianity, in order to see what content is given to the fundamental category of all religion. His hypothesis is that the fundamental category of Christianity is *agape*, the unmotivated love of God. The communion of man with God is brought about by God's manifesting his *agape*, by the fact that he takes the initiative, offers man his love in Jesus Christ, and invites man to receive the life which is thus proffered to him. Nygren proposes to show that this is the fundamental category of Christianity by demonstrating that it is (1) the unifying principle of the diverse theologies of the New Testament, (2) the common center of all the theologies which have developed in the life of the church, and (3) the essential meaning of the great dogmas of the Christian tradition, such as creation, incarnation, and resurrection.

He begins with the materials witnessing to the ministry of Jesus and shows how agape appears as the distinctive thrust of Jesus' teaching and of his understanding of his own ministry. On the basis of this material he formulates four characteristics of agape: (1) It is spontaneous and unmotivated. Christ shows his love by establishing fellowship with social and religious outcasts. (2) It is indifferent to value. God's love is not an irrational craving for spoiled goods. His love is addressed to the proud and complacent as eagerly as to the tax collector. (3) It is creative. What has no value in itself becomes valuable because God's love is directed to it. Man is not in himself of infinite value, but is invested with value because God cares for him. (4) It initiates fellowship with God. The greatest marvel of the divine love is not that it annuls death penalties or accomplishes deliverance, but that God gives himself to his creatures.

Where the older liberal theology liked to point to the contrasts between Jesus and Paul, Nygren shows that Paul's development of the agape theme is in full harmony with that of Jesus. The vocabulary is different, but the same central theme comes to expression, as in Paul's vivid awareness that the love of God met him just as he was acting most rebelliously, on his way to persecute the Christians of Damascus. Paul's proclamation of the cross is nothing other than an exposition of God's agape. This is plain also in his use of the term agape to describe the Christian's relation to his neighbor, and in his contrast between the way of knowledge which puffs up and the way of love which builds up.

The third movement in the analysis of biblical materials is the examination of the Johannine literature. Nygren regards this as the climactic formulation of the agape motif in the New Testament, although he points out the duality of the presentation. The strong concentration on the Christian love of the brethren achieves a high level of intensity but runs the risk of narrowing its scope to members of the community.

The analysis of biblical materials is followed by a systematic exposition of the *eros* motif in Hellenistic civilization. Nygren examines the writings of Plato as an unfolding of the religious outlook of Hellenism, and then studies the development of the theme in Aristotle and in neoplatonism. The closing section of the work is a contrast between biblical and Hellenistic modes of thought, sharpening the differences in the different dimensions of God's love, love toward God, love of neighbor, and love of self.

The second volume traces the development of the idea of love in the history of the church. A new element, inexplicably absent from the first volume, appears here: the *nomos* motif, the fundamental concept of rabbinic Judaism. The nomos type is exemplified in the writings of the Apostolic Fathers and Tertullian, the eros type in Gnosticism and Alexandrian theology, and the agape type in Marcion and Irenaeus. The discussion here is a tacit correction of the first volume, where the discussion of the agape motif in Paul had little to say about conflict with the nomos concept, even though Paul's theology was formulated in a struggle with rabbinic viewpoints concerning the proper interpretation of the Old Testament.

The remainder of the volume unfolds the development of a new synthesis in the theology of Augustine, and the twofold challenge to this synthesis in the sixteenth century. Augustine is viewed as a pivotal theological figure who combines elements of biblical and neoplatonic religion in a new formulation, the Caritas synthesis, which then dominated the history of theology for the next millennium. The Renaissance offered an effective challenge to it, seeking to return to the religious ideals of Hellenism. A second challenge appears in the Reformation, which attempts to renew the biblical agape motif.

The *Commentary on the Epistle to the Romans* is an eloquent testimony to Nygren's many-sidedness and versatility as theologian. He is not only a philosopher and historical scholar of distinction, but shows remarkable gifts as an expositor. The *Commentary* does not enter upon questions of textual criticism or an examination of literary forms and traditions, but comes to grips effectively with the religious content of the epistle and expounds it with clarity and simplicity. His treatment of the development of the argument of the letter is persuasive, even in such difficult and debatable sections as chapter seven or chapters nine to eleven.

The volume *Christ and His Church* also shows Nygren as an able organizer and expositor of complex and difficult biblical materials, and it illustrates the wide influence he has exercised on the character of theological discussion within the ecumenical movement. When after forty years of discussion of comparative ecclesiology the Commission on Faith and Order turned to study of the centrality of Christ and his relation to the church, Bishop Nygren's voice was one of the most effective in urging the change.

The Gospel of God, first written as a pastoral letter to the clergy of the diocese of Lund, shows yet another aspect of Nygren's theological work—his pastoral orientation and concern.

However intense his preoccupation with the problems of scientific theology, he has never permitted himself to overlook the central concern of the church, the communication of the gospel. An earlier work, *The Church Conflict in Germany*, shows another aspect of this concern. Written after a visit to Germany in 1933, the year of Hitler's accession to power, it shows Nygren's early perception of the true character of the Nazi movement and his anxiety that the church not be trapped into compromise.

But while we are impressed by the versatility of Nygren as theologian, it is highly probable that his most enduring contribution is to the history of Christian thought. *Agape and Eros* promises to be a lasting source of illumination on the meaning of the Christian theological tradition. His contribution to philosophy of religion may well increase in popularity among the devotees of linguistic analysis, especially if a projected volume on theological method is published. Others will agree with the criticism that the task of philosophical criticism is not done stringently enough, and that the formal questions addressed to the Christian tradition are not sufficiently formal, but ascribe an alien content to the Scriptures and thus distort the biblical message. Support for this contention is to be found in Nygren's neglect of the Old Testament as the background of the Christian community and his overlooking of the tension between *nomos* and *agape* in the development of the biblical message. He has also been criticized for being insufficiently radical in his proclamation of the kerygma to his own age, being so occupied with research into Luther's theology as to permit the historical presentation of that theology to serve as proclamation to the twentieth century.

Bibliography

Anders Nygren, *Agape and Eros*, Philadelphia, Westminster, 1953.

Gustaf Wingren, *Theology in Conflict*, Philadelphia, Fortress, 1958.

GUSTAF AULÉN

Gustaf Wingren

Gustaf Aulén was born on May 15, 1879. After receiving his early education in Kalmar, on the east coast of Sweden, he matriculated at the University of Uppsala, where he became an assistant professor in 1907. For the subject of his doctoral thesis Aulén chose the life and history of Henrik Reuterdahl, professor of church history at the University of Lund in the nineteenth century. After serving as an assistant professor in Uppsala from 1907 to 1913, Aulén transferred to the University of Lund, where he was a professor of dogmatics from 1913 to 1933. While in Uppsala, Aulén had continued his interest in the theological tradition of Lund, and so in 1914, as a young professor, he was quite prepared to deliver an inaugural lecture on the theme "Den Dogmatiska Traditionen vid Lunds Universitet" (The Dogmatic Tradition at the University of Lund). During his twenty years as a professor in Lund Aulén himself left his mark on that university's tradition. His personality and his books helped immeasurably to define what is meant by the term "Lundensian theology."

In 1933 Aulén's university work was broken off by his appointment as bishop of the Strängnäs diocese, a position he held for almost twenty years (1933–52). But even during these two decades he continued to engage in theological research. In 1937, at Edinburgh, he officiated as a vice-president of the World Conference on Faith and Order. Liturgy and church music have always been of great interest to Aulén; while he was a bishop the Swedish Church acquired a new hymnbook, a service book, a gospel book, and a missal, and he played an active part in shaping all four.

After retiring from the bishopric, Aulén returned to Lund and immediately busied himself in writing. Several books have come from him during his emeritus years, and in spite of his advanced age all of them suggest a youthful spirit. Aulén is still a member of the editorial staff of *Svénsk Teologisk Kvartal-*

skrift (Swedish Theological Quarterly), a periodical he began in 1925. Although it continued to be printed in Lund, Aulén remained its chief editor during his first year as Bishop of Strängnäs. Now he is the only surviving founder of the journal. Some important articles by him are to be found among its early volumes.

Aulén's most important work before he became a professor was *Den Lutherska Kyrkoidén* (The Lutheran Concept of the Church), published in 1912. At that time, unlike today, it was not customary for a European theologian to deal with the doctrine of the church. But Aulén was interested in that doctrine from the very beginning, and for two reasons. In the first place, it had been a dominant concern of the old Lundensian tradition dating from the middle of the nineteenth century. Aulén was well acquainted with this tradition and its outstanding figure, Henrik Reuterdahl, the subject of his doctoral thesis. In the second place, in Uppsala Aulén had been a pupil of Nathan Söderblom and Einar Billing, theologians for whom the concept of the church was central. The influence of these two sources is still evident in Aulén's emeritus work *Hundra ars Svensk Kyrkodebatt* (One Hundred Years of Swedish Discussions on the Church), published in 1953.

In 1917 Aulén published his first major work as a Lund professor—a textbook titled *Dogmhistoria* (History of Dogma). Designed primarily to aid students of theology, only at a few points does the book present results of independent theological research. Relying on synopses by such German scholars as Harnack, Seeberg, and Loofs, it traces the development of Christian doctrine from the first till the twentieth century.

Aulén's next book, *Den allmänneliga kristna tron*, appeared in 1923. Although this was also intended as a textbook, in it Aulén builds on a basis distinctively his own. The book, which has had five Swedish editions (the latest in 1957), appeared in 1948 in a U.S. edition under the title *The Faith of the Christian Church*.[1] Its influence has been important within as well as outside Sweden. The major sections of the work are "The Liv-

---

[1] The first American edition (Philadelphia, Muhlenberg, 1948) was a translation from the fourth Swedish edition (1943); the second American edition (Philadelphia, Fortress, 1961) is a translation from the fifth Swedish edition (1957).

ing God," "The Act of God in Christ," and "The Church of God." It is evident from this work that Aulén has his roots in Einar Billing's theology; it has the same basic structure as Billing's *De etiska tankarna i urkristendomen* (Ethical Ideas in Original Christianity, 1907) and his *Försoningen* (Atonement, 1908)—neither of which, unfortunately, has been translated into English. History, declares Aulén, is the workshop of God. In history, God presents himself as the "living God," accomplishing his utmost in his act in Christ, and out of this act arises the church. The book's three parts, it may be noted, make for a marked trinitarian theology.

Aulén's next work in the area of the history of Christian thought, *Den kristna gudsbilden* (The Christian Conception of God), first appeared in 1927 and was published in German translation in 1930 as *Das christliche Gottesbild*. In it Aulén manifests for the first time his concern to divide the history of dogma into distinct periods and to place the first Christian centuries and the Reformation on the same level. Both these periods he views as valid expounders of the biblical message. For both, God is the subject—the "living God" and the God of action in Christ. At the same time Aulén is critical of medieval scholasticism and Lutheran orthodoxy, which he sees as relatively similar. Thus he does not draw a line from Luther to Lutheranism but instead is inclined to note points at which Lutheranism withdrew from Luther—for instance, its tendency toward a juridical, legalistic interpretation of the atonement. For Aulén, then, Luther is to be allied more with the Fathers of the early church than with Lutheranism. Indeed, in Aulén's view, Luther belongs to the universal church. It is no accident that Aulén's theology has had wide acceptance outside Lutheranism in spite of its being grounded in Luther. Aulén believes that in this work he further developed the view of Luther held by Einar Billing and Nathan Söderblom. Nonetheless in certain respects his interpretation is independent of theirs.

Aulén's next important work also was of a monographic character: a historical study titled *Den kristna försoningstanken* (The Christian Idea of the Atonement), based on a series of lectures delivered by Aulén at the University of Uppsala in 1930 and published the same year. It was published in English in 1931 under the title *Christus Victor*, and since then it has appeared in several editions in English and likewise in French, Dutch, and Chinese. Presumably it is Aulén's most famous book. It presents much the same view of the periods of Christian dogma as his "The Christian Conception of God." Irenaeus, bishop of Lyon during the second century, is here regarded as the great Father of the Fathers. Aulén contends that Irenaeus and Luther essentially share the same understanding of the atonement. Both conceive of it not primarily as a sacrifice offered to God, delivered by man to a receiving God. Rather, they conceive of it as an act performed by God himself, an act accomplished by God in Christ in struggle against the evil powers of sin and death which have enslaved man. Divine struggle and divine victory characterize the work of atonement. Luther modifies the idea of struggle by introducing divine "wrath" and "law," but he nonetheless adheres to the view Aulén calls the "classic" idea of the atonement, which emphasizes a "line leading downwards from God."

Contrasting to the classic idea of the atonement is what Aulén terms the "Latin" idea, which views the work of atonement as a line "from man upward," accomplished primarily by Christ in his human nature and offered to a receiving God. Again we are confronted by the relationship between medieval scholasticism (Anselm) and Lutheran orthodoxy. Both espouse variations of the Latin idea and hence are alien to the theology of the Fathers and the Reformation.

The chief criticism to be made of Aulén's interpretation of the classic idea of the atonement is that it tends to ignore the human nature of Christ. His exposition never clearly answers the question why Christ had to fight against and triumph over the evil powers of the world as a tempted *man*. The reason for this weakness in Aulén's analysis may be that he begins with the second article of the Creed rather than the first, that of Creation. Irenaeus rightly delineates the act of God in Christ as *recapitulatio*, as an act which involves a restoration of man, a return to the purity of the creation.

Of the books Aulén has published in Lund since his retirement we have already mentioned *Hundra års svensk kyrkodebatt* (1953), which is not likely to be translated since it deals with a Swedish subject. Two other books from his retirement years, however, have already been translated into English: a work on the Lord's Supper, *För eder utgiven*, published in 1956, and a work on the ecumenical problem, *Reformation och katolicitet*, published in 1959. The former appeared in English translation in 1958 as *Eucharist and Sacrifice*, the latter in 1961 as *Reformation and Catholicity*. These works from the past decade must be seen against the background of the situation in the Church of Sweden. A vocal high-church group within it, influenced by foreign liturgical movements, at times takes positions contrary to some of the central emphases of Luther and the Swedish Reformers. This high-church wing is especially influential in the middle-Swedish dioceses, which at one time were primarily low-church in orientation.

Not least among them, the diocese of Strängnäs, where Aulén served as bishop, has acquired a high-church clergy in parishes which have been virtually without traditions and which often have very few churchgoers. Aulén himself holds a rather ambivalent position in relation to this Swedish high-church movement. His theology is decidedly on the side of the Reformation and Luther. But owing to his work in connection with liturgy and church music he is at the same time in rapport with the high-church group. Thus it is not surprising that Aulén's writing during the 1950's has sought to achieve peace and to give guidance to church groups of differing opinions.

Eucharist and Sacrifice is concerned with the controversial idea of sacrifice in the Lord's Supper. *Reformation and Catholicity* analyzes the place of the tradition and deals at length with the creeds of the Patristic period and the Reformation. Though Luther figures centrally in the latter work, the Lutheran reformation is regarded—as always in Aulén's works—from an ecumenical and catholic viewpoint.

What is characteristic and distinctive about Aulén's thought? His mentors Söderblom and Billing concerned themselves with the Bible and with Luther. In their biblical research they benefited from findings in the field of history of religion, and they had a positive attitude toward historical-critical exegesis. At the same time they used the then new knowledge of the Near East religions in such a way as to focus on what was uniquely biblical.

In this respect Aulén is very much their pupil. Throughout his works he is concerned to delineate the characteristics of the genuinely Christian faith. But quite new is Aulén's interest in the history of dogma, an interest that he manifested from the very beginning of his professional career. His first work during this period was a survey of the history of dogma, of the development of church doctrine from the earliest days to our own time, and he has retained his historical perspective, his interest in "periods." He is concerned to delineate the characteristic features of the early church, the medieval period, the Reformation, and so on. The uniqueness of Christianity he sees as involved in constant struggle throughout the different periods—for example against juridical, legalistic attitudes or against idealistic, subjectivistic conceptions of life. Sometimes what is genuinely Christian appears purely and clearly, sometimes it is obscured. This desire to maintain a historical outlook was not to be found in Billing or Söderblom.

Consequently Luther also is seen in a new light by Aulén; he emerges as a renewer of the biblical inheritance, whereas the periods before and after him—the periods of medieval scholasticism and Lutheran orthodoxy—were, in Aulén's view, unable to keep this inheritance fresh and vital. Both Billing and Söderblom did work on Luther, but they never placed him in such a perspective. Particularly new is Aulén's interest in the Church Fathers, primarily in Irenaeus, who had been of little interest to Aulén's teachers in Uppsala.

Aulén's predilection for the historical outlook and the dividing of church history into periods is best understood in the light of the Swedish theological examination system. As a rule in European universities, the study of the history of dogma and of Christian thought constitutes a part of the discipline of church history; the church historian deals with both the happenings and the thought of past eras. Systematic theology—for instance in Germany and Switzerland—is a quite independent discipline. In Sweden, on the other hand, the history of dogma and the history of Christian thought are subsumed under the discipline of systematic theology. While studying past periods seminarians also study systematic theology. Thus historical study is given a systematic orientation. The problem with this approach is that it tends to regard the uniqueness of the faith as resting in history; it never finds its way to the present age. In Sweden there is no effort comparable to Bultmann's program which regards the interpretation of the kerygma as the main task of theology. A Swedish scholar in the field of systematics is likely to devote his best years to historical research—a feature of Swedish theology which has been emphasized by Aulén's successors. Aulén's work *The Faith of the Christian Church,* however, is systematic in character yet presents the Christian faith to the man of today.

The "Lundensian theology" which thus came into view utilized much more than the old theology of Uppsala, historical theories shaped through contact with church historians and historians of dogma on the Continent. Of special influence was Adolf von Harnack. Harnack regarded the early dogma of the church as a corruption of the simple doctrine of Jesus. Aulén, however, has given much attention to the christological conflicts of the first four centuries, and he is convinced that the resulting dogmatic system served to guard the Gospel of the Apostolic Age against Gnostic and Arian inroads. This kind of positive valuation of the earliest dogma of the church has long been typical of Anglican theology; it is therefore understandable why Aulén's works have been widely read and appreciated in England.

In regard to the historical view of the theology of Luther, Aulén made use of German research, especially that of Karl Holl and his pupils. But exegetics and the theology of the Bible have always formed the basic ground of Aulén's work. Increasingly Aulén has cooperated with the exponents of the so-called realistic exegesis, established in Uppsala in the 1930's by Anton Fridrichsen. The symposium *En bok om kyrken* (A Book on the Church) is a result of the cooperation between systematic theologians in Lund and exegetes in Uppsala. When this book appeared in 1942 Aulén was no longer a professor at the University of Lund. But most of its articles were originally delivered as discourses at a conference in Nyköping in February 1942—and Nyköping is situated in the diocese of Strängnäs where Aulén was a bishop. That this place was selected for the meeting was no accident.

A number of scholars have raised questions concerning this cooperative effort between systematics and exegesis. Over the years there has arisen a strange alliance between, on the one hand, exegetical scholarship executed by young New Testament scholars in Uppsala and, on the other, certain doctrines of the Anglican and Roman churches. These scholars tend to put aside Luther's exegesis with arguments derived from high-church views. Against this background it is easier to understand Aulén's writings of the 1950's, which have helped foster a split between Swedish exegesis and Swedish systematics and have underplayed the Reformation inheritance. How to remove this crisis in Swedish theology is a problem which cannot be treated here.

When Aulén appeared on the scene soon after the First World War the situation was altogether different. At that time a liberal and subjectivistic theology was posed against a conservative and confessional theology, and Aulén found his own way between them. At about the same time dialectical theology made its way on the Continent. Aulén's emergence is not so distant but what many of us can remember the atmosphere in which his theology appeared. Those who were rooted in the liberal tradition at first regarded Aulén's theology as but a new form of conservative confessionalism. Aulén made no attempt to discover the "historical Jesus" or to anchor faith in a "religious disposition" or in subjective experience. He did not see a demarcation between the Gospels and Paul; on the contrary, he held that the act of God in Christ, as related in the Gospels, was properly interpreted by Paul and by the early Church Fathers.

Those rooted in the conservative tradition, on the other hand, viewed Aulén's theology as a new form of liberalism. Aulén did not reject historical-critical research on the Bible; indeed, he sought to learn from the exegetes—even from some of the most radical ones. He was respectful of scholars in the field of comparative religion and sometimes used their work in support of his own theses. Conservative readers were again distressed when they learned what Aulén had to say about Luther and Lutheranism. Just as Holl had emphasized the difference between Luther and Melanchthon and thus driven a wedge between Luther and Lutheranism, so also did Aulén criticize Lutheran orthodoxy, especially in regard to the view of the atonement which by stressing juridical "satisfaction" theories obscured "the unabridged act of God in Christ."

One might expect that a theology which thus disappointed both liberals and confessionals would have difficulty gaining acceptance. But such was not the case with Aulén's. After the First World War disillusionment with both confessionalism and liberalism set in, and Aulén's unfamiliar theology came as something of a relief—a theology that upheld both the classical dogmatic system and the right of free research into biblical texts. Especially appealing was Aulén's unusual coordination of incarnation and atonement. The Fathers' christological formulas concerning divine and human nature were reintroduced as bearers of the Gospel, witnessing to the act of God in Christ, to an atonement performed by God himself and offered as a free gift to all men through the church.

But the difference between Aulén's theology and the dialectical or "crisis" theology of Germany and Switzerland is also apparent. In his 1927 work, *The Christian Conception of God,* Aulén himself indicates awareness of this difference—a difference which can be traced to divergent historical sources. In the theology of Karl Barth the influence of Calvin and of medieval scholasticism, particularly Anselm, is considerable, while Aulén has been influenced instead by the antignostic Fathers of the early church. This means that the creation holds a more central position for Aulén—and in connection with creation the law also emerges as an essential concept. In the 1930's both Aulén and Barth analyzed and criticized the political situation in Germany and were staunchly anti-Nazi during the Second World War. Of personal importance to Aulén in this connection were his relatives and friends in occupied Norway. But the theological basis for opposition to Nazism was different for the two men. Barth's criticism of Nazism proceeded from the Gospel and from the second article of the Creed. Aulén's criticism had a much wider basis and was grounded in the fundamental theological concept of *Skaparene lag* (The Law of the Creator).[2] The Law of the Creator, ac-

[2] The lectures delivered by Aulén in the United States in the spring of 1947 are characteristic of this phase of his work. The lectures are gathered in a book titled *Church, Law and Society,* published in the U.S. in 1948 (N.Y., Scribner's).

cording to Aulén, is a guardian of the interests of the neighbor but is also a law for society as a whole. Aulén sees this law as a basis for cooperation between Christians and non-Christians. Clearly this idea relies on Luther's "two-realm" theory—an approach explicitly rejected by Barth.

It is evident that Aulén has influenced the whole of Scandinavian theology; his work has modified theological work in both Scandinavia and Finland, and as a result a new way of posing questions has emerged. To this should be added Aulén's influence on Anglican theology, primarily through *Christus Victor*. It is yet too early to give an opinion of Aulén's influence on American theology; study of his work began later in the U.S., but it continues to grow there. Especially interesting is Aulén's role in the inner circle of his former colleagues at Lund. Anders Nygren, beginning as a philosopher in the 1920's, wrote little in the area of systematics. In the 1930's, however, beginning with *Den kristna kärlekstanken* (*Agape and Eros*), he turned to a form of systematic theology termed "motif research." Nygren sees three motifs—agape, eros, nomos—as fighting for domination through the centuries. Sometimes the early Christian agape motif emerges, sometimes it is obscured by hostile motifs. In Nygren's view, to write systematic theology is to write the history of the conflict of these basic motifs. The division of church history into periods becomes also for Nygren a chief concern. But most importantly, once again the early church and the Luther period emerge as similar. According to Nygren's 1936 study, Irenaeus and Luther are history's two best proponents of the agape motif. This conclusion of Nygren's strikingly accords with Aulén's conclusion in his 1930 work on the atonement. Nygren's dependence on the Lundensian tradition is to be noted in two books by myself written in the 1940's: one on Irenaeus (translated into English in 1959 as *Man and the Incarnation*) and one on Luther (translated in 1957 as *Luther on Vocation*).

It is rather difficult to state in what respects Aulén and Nygren have influenced each other. They belonged to the same faculty during the years 1924–33. Aulén was the first to use the "period" approach and no doubt influenced Nygren in this regard. Nygren's work in philosophy of religion, however, is of primary and pioneering importance. His motif method has been most exhaustively developed by Ragnar Bring, his successor as professor of dogmatics at Lund.

But it is also true that Aulén has remained somewhat aloof from the later Lundensian theology and uses the term "motif" quite differently than does Nygren. Aulén sometimes views the motifs as composing a unity; a universal conception of Christianity would, for example, bring together "motifs" which might otherwise move in different directions. Aulén seeks to hold together that which is inclined to separate. A typical expression of his is "tension-filled unity." A sound theology, he maintains, holds together the wrath of God and the love of God—unites God's almightiness and his love. But Aulén's effort to hold together opposing elements preserves rather than smooths over tensions; he would sacrifice no element to attain a deceptive harmony.

Aulén is the connecting link between the theological renaissance in Uppsala after 1900 and the theological renaissance in Lund after 1920. He not only stands between those two revival periods but also belongs to both; while he remains faithful to his inheritance from his student years in Uppsala, he also adds to it his wide historical outlook, his work with periods of church history, his study of the Fathers and of classical dogma. All this is characteristic of Lundensian theology and is to be found again in the writings of Anders Nygren, who in turn has added his own contributions to the inheritance, notably his wide philosophical framework and his "basic motif" approach. Aulén has not a little to learn from the younger man Nygren; nonetheless Aulén, though drawing on the tradition of Billing and Söderblom, has furthered that tradition in a quite original and creative manner.

It might seem as if Aulén—viewed in this way as coming between Billing and Nygren—were a figure bound in time, tied to the first half of this century. Strangely enough, in Sweden Aulén is viewed in almost opposite fashion; his contributions to the present theological discussion seem fresh and alive: his words fit the present situation, they break down false contrasts, they point forward. Why is Aulén so well received? For one thing, it is evident that what was a new theological stance at the beginning of this century—that represented by Einar Billing and

Nathan Söderblom—does not today seem antiquated; indeed this older theology has come to life again. The fact that it has returned to life seems to be a part of a general European phenomenon; one can observe in several European countries a considered examination of that theology which tried to take seriously the historical-critical method in exegesis, in the conviction that just in this way the evangelical faith can be more fully comprehended. Furthermore, Aulén in his books of the 1950's has directed his attention to actual problems in today's theological situation—problems of Christian ministry, of Scripture and tradition, of the sacrifice in the Lord's Supper, which in Sweden are at the center of theological controversy. Owing partly to high-church opinions, partly to trends in New Testament exegesis (particularly in Uppsala), the question of the relation between the Reformation and the early Church Fathers has become paramount. On the basis of his previous research Aulén is exceptionally well suited to deal with this problem, and his frank and straightforward way of doing so is evidence that he is well aware of his responsibility.

When Aulén thus directs his attention to the state of affairs in Sweden he is at the same time expressing interest in the theological situation internationally. In *Eucharist and Sacrifice* he deals with several Anglican theologians, and in *Reformation and Catholicity* he discusses Roman Catholic contributions to the ecumenical discussion. The current theological situation in Sweden is such that discussion of foreign contributions seems to be the only hope of untangling the skein of persistent problems. It is significant that Aulén's books are so promptly translated into English. This fact also is evidence of the strength and relevance of his theology.

Bibliography

Gustaf Aulén, *The Faith of the Christian Church*, rev. ed., Philadelphia, Fortress, 1961.

No full-scale study of Aulén is available in English.

C. H. DODD

George B. Caird

Charles Harold Dodd was born on April 7, 1884, at Wrexham in Denbighshire, North Wales. At the age of eighteen he won a classical scholarship to University College, Oxford, and four years later was awarded his B.A. with a first class both in Honours Classical Moderations and in the Final School of Literae Humaniores. From 1907 to 1911 he was engaged in research, first in Roman Imperial Numismatics at the University of Berlin, subsequently in Early Christian Epigraphy at Magdalen College, Oxford. Concurrently with these studies he took a course of theological training at Mansfield College, Oxford, which led to ordination in 1912. After three years as minister of the Congregational Church at Warwick he returned to Mansfield College as Yates Lecturer (afterwards Yates Professor) in New Testament Greek and Exegesis. In 1930 he was appointed Rylands Professor of Biblical Criticism and Exegesis in the University of Manchester, and in 1935, with his election as Norris-Hulse Professor of Divinity at Cambridge, he became the first non-Anglican to hold a chair of divinity at either of the ancient English universities. Besides these regular appointments he has held a number of special lectureships: he was Grinfield Lecturer in the Septuagint at Oxford (1927–31); Speaker's Lecturer in Biblical Studies at Oxford (1933–37); Shaffer Lecturer at Yale (1935); Ingersoll Lecturer at Harvard (1935); Hewett Lecturer at Episcopal Theological Seminary, Cambridge, Mass., Union Theological Seminary, New York, and Andover-Newton Seminary (1938); and Olaus Petri Lecturer at Uppsala (1949). He was elected Fellow of the British Academy in 1946. After his retirement in 1949 he was for a time Visiting Professor in Biblical Theology at Union Theological Seminary, New York, and during this stay in the United States he was also Bampton Lecturer in America, Stone Lecturer at Princeton Theological Seminary, and, for the second time, Ingersoll Lecturer at Harvard. He returned to England in 1950 to become general director of the New Translation of the Bible—"The New English Bible," as it was later to be called. Since then he has been Syr D. Owen Evans Lecturer at the University College of Wales, Aberystwyth (1954), and Sarum Lecturer at Oxford (1954–55), and has been the first non-Anglican to preach the University Sermon at Oxford since the days of the Protectorate. His distinguished contribution to biblical scholarship has been recognized by honorary degrees from Oxford, Cambridge, London, Manchester, Aberdeen, Glasgow, Wales, Harvard, Strasbourg, and Oslo, and by honorary fellowships at Jesus College, Cambridge, and University College, Oxford.

Dodd's publications include over twenty books and about seventy articles, essays, lectures, and reviews, which between them cover a very wide range of New Testament study. But within the whole series may be discerned a leitmotif or principle of unity: the conviction that God is Lord of history, and that the word of God spoken in Scripture is so inextricably interwoven into the fabric of historical events that it can be let loose into the modern world in the fullness of its relevance and power only through historical criticism exercised with the utmost integrity and thoroughness. The importance of this principle can be seen if we set Dodd's work over against each of the five great schools of New Testament thought which have held the hegemony during his lifetime: the radical criticism represented by Wellhausen and Wrede and more recently by Loisy and Goguel; the *Religionsgeschichtliche Schule* of Reitzenstein and Bousset and their modern disciple Bultmann; the thoroughgoing eschatology of Weiss and Schweitzer; the form criticism of Dibelius, Schmidt, and Bultmann; and the revival of biblical theology, heralded by Barth's commentary on Romans. Dodd belongs to all of these schools and to none of them. He has responded to the stimulus of each of them, yet always with originality. He has frequently spoken and written with warm appreciation of their leading exponents, maintaining at the same time his critical independence.

In its inception radical criticism was a movement of emancipation from the dogmatic tradition of centuries, which had almost totally overlaid the real humanity of Jesus, except as an article in the Creed. The critics believed that by employing the methods of the secular historian they could probe behind the Christ of faith to find the Jesus of history. What they in fact did was to produce so many conflicting portraits of the Jesus of history that the whole quest ended in historical skepticism. In the reaction that followed there were many who turned for security to the verbal inerrancy of the Scripture, to the fortress of creed and ecclesiastical council, or to a theology of transcendence unassailable by the doubts of the historian. Dodd has been one of those who unswervingly maintained that, for those who believe in an incarnation, there is no avoiding the historic quest, and that it was not the methods of the critics that were at fault but their presuppositions.

> If we are bound to criticize the great critics of the last century, we are also bound to confess that where we have gone beyond them it is by standing on their shoulders. It is a testimony to the scientific integrity of the critical school that by applying their own methods more strictly it was led to discard many of the presuppositions upon which it formerly relied, and to arrive at what I believe to be a juster estimate of the material with which it deals. Be suspicious of any suggestion that we can afford to by-pass criticism. The way of advance lies through and not round the critical problem.[1]

The history-of-religion school thought that they had found the way through the critical problem. Christianity, they pointed out, did not come into existence in an intellectual vacuum. It had its roots in Judaism and spread rapidly into the gentile world of cults and philosophies, a world where there were "gods many and lords many." They hoped that by stripping off all that Christianity had in common with contemporary religions they would arrive at its essential core. Under their hands the picture of the first century background of Christianity was filled in with an immense wealth of detail. Dodd has hailed their labors as "the most distinctive contribution of the first quarter of the twentieth century"[2] and has himself provided a most important

[1] *The Bible Today* (Cambridge, The Univ. Press, 1946), p. 27.
[2] *The Present Task in New Testament Studies* (Cambridge, The Univ. Press, 1936), p. 14.

addition to them with his own researches into the Septuagint and the Hermetic literature. Nevertheless he has also criticized these scholars because they too readily believed that parallels were evidence of dependence, and because they envisaged early Christianity as an amalgam of beliefs and practices drawn from contemporary Jewish and pagan religion, whereas if they had regarded it in its wholeness they would have been struck by its coherence and distinctiveness. "To establish the derivation of an idea is not to explain it as an element in a new complex."[3]

Schweitzer's rediscovery of biblical eschatology had a transforming influence on the whole of New Testament scholarship, for it opened up the possibility, ignored by previous generations of scholars, that the apostolic faith of the New Testament, in which eschatology figured so largely, might actually be an accurate reproduction of the mind of Jesus, formed as it was by the expectations of apocalyptic Judaism. But Schweitzer carried out his reconstruction of the Gospel with an uncritical reliance on the least trustworthy strands of Synoptic tradition, never stopped to consider whether the Jews, Jesus, or the early Christians took their eschatological language with pedantic literalness or with an understanding of its symbolic character, and completely overlooked the fact that whatever concepts Jesus inherited were transmuted in the crucible of his experience. It was Dodd's concept of realized eschatology, the product of accurate and imaginative scholarship, that rescued Schweitzer's work from futility, as we shall see more fully below.

Form criticism began as a protest against the skepticism of the radical critics and ended by surrendering to it. The form critics believed that the Gospels were compiled out of small units of tradition which, during the period of oral transmission, circulated independently in a limited number of stereotyped forms; and they hoped that by classifying these *pericopae* according to their formal characteristics they would obtain a reliable index of their historical validity. They started from the well-established principle that the contents of the Gospels were preserved out of a larger mass of available material by a process of natural selection, since the early Christians remembered and

[3] *Ibid.,* p. 15.

recorded those sayings and stories which were relevant to their current needs and interests. Every *pericope* therefore had an identifiable *Sitz im Leben* or setting in the life of the primitive church. The next step was to attribute larger and larger powers to the community, which was supposed not merely to have preserved and molded the units of tradition, but in many cases to have created them to meet its own needs. The end of the process was Bultmann's conclusion that very little can be confidently asserted about the historical Jesus. The form critics used criteria which were far too subjective, ignored the established results of literary criticism, overlooked the presence of eyewitnesses in the early church, attributed incredible powers of invention to the community, and unjustifiably depreciated the historical value of Mark's outline of the ministry of Jesus. The positive results of their work would be meager indeed had not Dodd shown how their methods could be turned to more constructive use. He has used the form-critical classification of *pericopae* to demonstrate that, at one point after another in the Gospel narrative, sayings and stories with a wide variety of forms present us with a convergent testimony, which encourages us to think that we are in touch with authentic history and not merely with church tradition.[4] He has shown that the parables, though they may have had a setting in the life of the church in which they were given a general, moral interpretation, had their original setting in the tumultuous ministry of Jesus, as interpretations of the crisis and opportunity which his coming had brought upon Israel. Above all he has acknowledged the great service done by the form critics in drawing our attention to the period of oral tradition between the life of Jesus and the writing of the earliest documents, and has devised a reliable technique for recovering the content of Christian preaching and teaching during that formative generation.

Barth's *Romans,* published in 1918, was a great blast of the prophetic trumpet, recalling New Testament scholars from their preoccupation with details of literary and historical criticism (what the Germans call *Historismus*) to their proper task of expounding the Scriptures as the Word of God. In the excite-

[4] *History and the Gospel* (London, Nisbet, 1938), pp. 91–103.

ment of new discovery it had been all too easy to forget that the Bible is above all else a book about God. "Paul knows of God what most of us do not know; and his epistles enable us to know what he knew."[5] There can be little doubt that we owe to Barth the healthy revival of theology which has characterized biblical scholarship during the past forty years. Yet there were dangers in his exegetical methods which have become more apparent in his later work. While Bultmann has been telling us that it is impossible to attain a reliable historical picture of Jesus, Barth has been assuring us that after all this does not matter, since the Jesus of history is irrelevant to faith in Christ the Lord. As a historical figure Jesus is even "a little commonplace" in comparison with the founders of other religions and some of his own followers.[6] The revolt against *Historismus* has become an indifference to history.

Dodd was one of the first to respond to Barth's challenge. Within two years of the appearance of Barth's *Romans* he had published his first major work, *The Meaning of Paul for Today*. Here already we can find the distinctive note which Dodd was to sound so clearly in his later writings. The Word of God in Scripture is not a series of eternally valid propositions which can be disengaged from their temporary setting. It comes to us in the writings of individual men about particular events and situations; and both the individuality of the writers and the particularity of the events are an essential part of the divine revelation. We cannot claim that the Bible is God's word, unless we are prepared to allow its authors to speak for themselves in their own native accents; and we shall find what they say relevant to ourselves only when we have taken the trouble to discover how it was relevant to the circumstances of their own day.

The emphasis on the unity of revelation is salutary. But the question of the historicity of the Gospel narrative is not so easily disposed of. For better or worse, Christianity grounds itself upon a

[5] Karl Barth, *Epistle to the Romans* (London, Oxford Univ. Press, 1933), p. 11.
[6] See Barth's *The Doctrine of the Word of God* (Edinburgh, T. & T. Clark, 1936), p. 188.

revelation *in history,* and history consists of events (including the meaning borne by events, but necessarily including what actually happened). It remains, therefore, a question of acute relevance, what actually happened.[7]

Dodd's own doctrine of history was adumbrated in 1927 in a paper communicated to a conference of English and German theologians and subsequently developed in a series of three books, published between 1935 and 1938. The major premise of the argument is that history consists not of bare facts but of facts plus meaning, facts selected by the historian as worthy of record, because they seem to him to be significant. Some events are more significant than others; and it is not incongruous with the nature of history that there should be a unique event, an event of such absolute and universal significance that it could give meaning and purpose to all history. The minor premise (minor logically, but theologically far-reaching) is that according to the teaching of Jesus the Kingdom of God had become through his ministry a present reality, confronting men with an offer of redemptive power and a demand for instant response and unconditional obedience. The Law and prophets had held sway till John the Baptist, but now the Kingdom was being proclaimed, men were seeing and hearing that which prophets and kings had desired to see, something greater than Jonah the prophet and Solomon the king; already the guests were being summoned to the messianic banquet, already the strong man was bound and his house plundered, already the harvest was ripe for the sickle; and the night of crisis was at hand when the servants must be awake and prepared for the coming of their Lord.

The Jews had always believed that God was Lord of history, but, recognizing that God's intentions were never fully disclosed, let alone attained, in the actual events of their national life, they looked for a Day when God's reign of justice and peace should be established; and in that Day they found the meaning and purpose of all history. But for them it remained an ideal, an unfulfilled aspiration, sometimes even a phantasy. Jesus, in a

[7] *The Study of Theology,* K. E. Kirk, ed. (N.Y., Harper, 1939), p. 241.

great variety of most vivid imagery, declared that this eschatological Day had arrived. Thus, taught by Jesus, the early Christians believed that they had been witnesses to an event which was nothing other than the visitation of God, an event which was capable of giving meaning to all other events. The story of Jesus was sacred history, which carried with it the possibility that all history might be taken up into the same transcendent order.

> Whenever the Gospel is proclaimed, it brings about a crisis, as in the experience of the individual, so also in the experience of whole communities and civilizations. Out of the crisis comes a new creation, by the power of God. Every such occasion is the "fullness of time" in which the Kingdom of God comes. Thus history reveals its meaning as an order of redemption and revelation.[8]

The concept of realized eschatology rests on such overwhelming evidence that it must be regarded as one of the permanent gains of modern scholarship; but it has corollaries which have provoked a storm of controversy. If in the coming of Jesus the meaning of history is fully revealed and its purpose fully achieved, what are we to say about subsequent history, and in particular about the expectation of the New Testament that the historical process would end in a Day of the Son of Man? The *eschaton* of the Jewish hope was final chronologically as well as teleologically, as Dodd himself has pointed out. "It is such that nothing more could happen in history, because the eternal meaning which gives reality to history is now exhausted. To conceive any further event on the plane of history would be like drawing a cheque on a closed account."[9] Except in a highly figurative sense we can hardly be asked to believe that the world ended in A.D. 30! Dodd's answer is that the language of eschatology is figurative, that the end of the world, like its beginning, is a myth used to convey that which is essentially beyond history. "Jesus declares that this ultimate, the Kingdom of God, has come into history, and He takes upon Himself the 'eschatologi-

[8] *History and the Gospel*, pp. 181 ff.
[9] *The Apostolic Preaching and Its Developments* (London, Hodder and Stoughton, 1936), p. 206.

cal' role of 'Son of Man.' The absolute, the 'wholly other,' has entered into time and space." In so far as the Gospel writers speak of a future crisis, their tenses are a mere accommodation of language. "There is no coming of the Son of Man 'after' His coming in Galilee and Jerusalem, whether soon or late, for there is no before and after in the eternal order. . . . So far as history can contain it, it is embodied in the historic crisis which the coming of Jesus brought about."[10] This elimination of futurist eschatology creates exegetical and theological difficulties. The early church did not merely believe in the life everlasting, they expected as a coming event the *Parousia* of the Lord; and other scholars have not found it easy to follow Dodd in attributing this expectation to a wholesale revision of the teaching of Christ. Again, if the purpose of God is fully achieved in Christ, what meaning can we attach to the continuance of the historical order? Dodd does indeed grant that the *eschaton* is a beginning as well as an end, but it is the beginning of an otherworldly order not to be confused with history; yet his own emphasis on tradition in the life of the church implies that historic continuity has a place in the divine scheme of things. He allows, as we have seen, that those who in any age accept the Gospel, and with it "the whole rich content of the historical process," are to be taken up into the eternal order; but does not this mean that God is still working his purpose out, until the day when he declares it complete?

For such reasons as these some scholars have suggested that for "realized" we should substitute "proleptic" or "inaugurated" eschatology. By these terms we should be depicting the ministry of Jesus either as an anticipation of that which in essence remains future or as the beginning of a process yet to be consummated. Dodd has given a qualified assent to these suggestions, and in one of his latest works has declared that the Johannine formula, "the hour comes and now is," "probably represents the authentic teaching of Jesus as veraciously as any formula could," though he insists that both in the Fourth Gospel and elsewhere in the New Testament the emphasis remains on the "now is."[11]

[10] *The Parables of the Kingdom* (London, Nisbet, 1935), pp. 107–8.
[11] *The Interpretation of the Fourth Gospel* (London, Cambridge Univ. Press, 1953), p. 447.

It is important, however, that minor adjustments of this kind should not cause us to lose sight of the excellent reasons Dodd had for his original statement of his thesis. He was clearly anxious to avoid the quite unbiblical notion that with the coming of Jesus something was injected into history which would thenceforth work itself out by an evolutionary process to the ultimate denouement. He wanted also to underline the mythical nature of all eschatological language; and much work is still to be done on the relation of the literal to the symbolic in the language of the Bible. He was undoubtedly correct in saying that the first Christians thought of the life, death, resurrection, exaltation, and second advent of Christ as a single divine event, God's day of salvation in the midst of which they were living; and that it was only with the passage of time that they learned to distinguish the part of this event which was past from that which was future, the fulfilled from the unfulfilled. Even then it continued to be a permanent element in New Testament teaching that Jesus had died and risen as the inclusive representative and head of mankind, so that in him all men had vicariously attained their divinely allotted destiny. The eschatological problem turns out, in fact, to be a christological one—the relation of humanity to him who so identified himself with them as to undergo their judgment and achieve their salvation. This central theme of our faith will continue to exercise the minds of exegetes and theologians; and those that are wise will start at the point to which Dodd has led us.

In his inaugural lecture at Cambridge Dodd laid down a program of the three most pressing tasks awaiting the attention of New Testament scholars: the closing of the "gap between the facts of the life of Jesus and their earliest literary record"; the solving of the Johannine problem, earlier criticism's "most signal failure"; and the balancing of the centrifugal movement of analytical study by a centripetal movement which would recover the original unity of New Testament thought. It is characteristic of the man that what he preached to others had already been adopted as the agenda of his own future research, and that from the start these three tasks were seen to be intimately related to one another and to the problem of history as the arena of revelation.

The Fourth Gospel may well prove to be the keystone of an arch which at present fails to hold together. If we can understand how it came to be and what it means, we shall know what early Christianity really was, and not until in some measure we comprehend the New Testament as a whole shall we be in a position to solve the Johannine problem.[12]

The bridge designed to close the gap between the life of Jesus and the earliest written records had three main supports, strongly interlocked: the *kerygma* or apostolic preaching of the early church; its *didache* or ethical instruction; and the principle of selection and interpretation which enabled the first Christians to use the Old Testament as Christian Scripture.

Dodd's reconstruction of the apostolic kerygma begins with the earliest available evidence, the Epistles of Paul. In dealing with the pastoral concerns of the churches Paul occasionally refers to his own preaching or to the traditions which he received from those who were Christians before him, and occasionally also uses formulae of an almost creedal nature, from which he argues as though they were necessarily familiar to his readers. He carefully distinguishes between the foundation and the theological superstructure which he and others have built upon it, and, in spite of his claim to independence of the other apostles, he is insistent that his Gospel does not substantially differ from theirs. A similar pattern of preaching is to be found in the early speeches in Acts, where the author, whatever editorial freedom he may have used elsewhere, was apparently relying on traditions drawn ultimately from the Aramaic-speaking church of Palestine. The evidence of these two primary witnesses is confirmed by parallels in other New Testament writings, since what is common to several of the New Testament writers is likely to have formed part of their common background. The conclusion to be drawn from this is that behind the books of the New Testament there lay a common preaching tradition, which proclaimed that in the life, death, and resurrection of Jesus God had fulfilled his ancient promises given through the prophets, that Jesus was now exalted at God's right hand as Messiah and Lord, in token of which he had sent upon

[12] *The Present Task in New Testament Studies*, p. 29.

his followers the gift of the Spirit, that he was destined to be Judge of all men, but that in his name salvation was now offered to those who would repent and accept the Gospel. The nucleus of this kerygma was a series of events which had happened *sub Pontio Pilato* before many witnesses. But, as Dodd has repeatedly reminded us, bare facts become history only through the significance which the historian discovers in them. The early Christian preachers found a key to the meaning of the events they had witnessed in the eschatological expectations of their native Judaism. The Day of the Lord had arrived; and they pointed to the resurrection of Jesus and the gift of the Spirit—both eschatological events—as evidence that they were living in the midst of the *eschaton*, the final crisis of history, which could be expected to draw swiftly to its close.

The eschatological character of the primitive kerygma has one implication of immense importance. The early church did not invent realized eschatology. They were hardly capable of the drastic remolding of accepted ideas which this concept involved. Moreover, the concept is present throughout the recorded teaching of Jesus, and especially in the parables of the Kingdom, from which not even the most radical criticism can now reasonably excise it. Realized eschatology is thus our strongest guarantee that the apostolic faith of the New Testament had its origin not merely in the common kerygma of the primitive church, but in the preaching of Jesus himself.

The oral traditions of the early church included not only kerygma but *didache,* the ethical instruction by which the life of the community was governed. On this subject Dodd has been chiefly concerned to emphasize two facts. Jesus was known to his disciples and to others as Rabbi, and regularly displayed those qualities which were normally associated with the prophets; and it was expected both of a rabbi and of a prophet that his teaching would be committed to memory by his followers. Not only in the Gospels but in the Epistles as well we find ample evidence for the existence of an authoritative historical tradition, to which appeal could be made to settle matters of dispute. But the ethical teaching of the Epistles is also thoroughly eschatological. It is regularly introduced by a "therefore," which makes it a consequence of God's definitive act of grace. Browning might mock at the grammarian who "properly based *Oun*" and then had no more that he could do; but Dodd has raised *Oun* to theological status. "In the word 'therefore' lies much virtue: it implies that the direction of Christian action, in the variety of situations to be reviewed, is always to be determined by reference to what God has done for us in Christ."[13] But this eschatological character was stamped upon Christian ethics by Jesus himself. His teaching expresses the absolute obligation laid upon men by the presence of the Kingdom of God.

One of the most fascinating and convincing pieces of recent scholarly detection is Dodd's work on the use of the Old Testament in the New. For forty years this area of study had been dominated by Rendel Harris's theory that one of the earliest literary products of the church was a book of testimonies or proof-texts collected at random from the Old Testament for the benefit of Christian preachers, catechists, and apologists; and that it was from this book rather than from the Scriptures themselves that the New Testament writers drew their citations. To test this hypothesis Dodd worked through the New Testament and wherever he came to an Old Testament citation or reference, he turned to the Old Testament passage and underlined it. If Harris's theory had been sound, the underlinings should have been evenly scattered throughout the Old Testament. What Dodd in fact found was a heavy concentration of underlinings in a comparatively small number of passages of varying length. This suggested that the early church considered these whole contexts to be peculiarly relevant to the interpretation of their Gospel. The passages proved to be of three types: (a) Apocalyptic-eschatological Scriptures—Joel 2-3, Zechariah 9-14, and parts of Daniel; (b) Scriptures of the New Israel—certain prophecies of Hosea, Isaiah, and Jeremiah; (c) Scriptures of the Servant of the Lord and the Righteous Sufferer—the latter part of the Book of Isaiah and a group of psalms. The first group describes the supreme crisis of history in which Israel is to be delivered from her humiliation at the hand of evil powers through the vindicating action of God. In the second group Israel is humiliated by God's judgment on her sins, but

---

[13] *The Bible Today*, p. 82.

is to be redeemed by his forgiving grace and restored to ultimate sanctity and glory. The third group portrays Israel as an innocent sufferer who, at least in the Isaianic prophecies, is called upon to endure vicariously the judgment of God on the sins of others. Thus all three groups have a common plot, which enabled the early church to find the fulfillment of all the Scriptures in the drama of the suffering and subsequent exaltation of Jesus. But such a use of Scripture was a complete departure from all Jewish methods of exegesis; and it involved the assumption that Jesus had somehow identified himself with Israel in such a way as to fulfill her divinely appointed destiny.

> Very diverse scriptures are brought together so that they interpret one another in hitherto unsuspected ways. To have brought together, for example, the Son of Man who is the people of the saints of the Most High, the Man of God's right hand, who is also the vine of Israel, the Son of Man who after humiliation is crowned with glory and honour, and the victorious priest-king at the right hand of God, is an achievement of interpretative imagination which results in the creation of an entirely new figure. . . . This is a piece of genuinely creative thinking. Who was responsible for it?[14]

It was not the creation of Paul; he does not argue for this type of exegesis, but argues from it, as something already familiar to his readers. Either there was in the pre-Pauline church an anonymous genius who laid down the substructure of Christian theology without leaving any clue to his identity, or else, as the Gospels repeatedly affirm, the great theologian was Jesus himself. "To account for the beginning of this most original and fruitful process of rethinking the Old Testament we found need to postulate a creative mind. The Gospels offer us one. Are we compelled to reject the offer?"[15]

Dodd's *The Interpretation of the Fourth Gospel* is divided into three parts. In Part I, assuming that this Gospel was directed primarily not to Christian readers but to the serious pagan who could read it intelligently without any previous knowledge

---

[14] *According to the Scriptures* (London, Nisbet, 1952), p. 109.
[15] *Ibid.*, p. 110.

of Christianity (though he would find vastly more in it if he read it a second time after associating himself with the fellowship, traditions, and sacraments of the church), Dodd takes a series of soundings in the religious literature of the period to see whether he can identify these hypothetical readers. He concludes that the Gospel has affinities with the higher religion of paganism, exemplified in the writings of the Corpus Hermeticum, and with the Hellenistic Judaism represented by Philo. He does not suggest that the evangelist has derived the content of his message from such sources, but that he has deliberately adopted a theological vocabulary and imagery likely to appeal to "a wide public consisting primarily of devout and thoughtful persons . . . in the varied and cosmopolitan society of a great Hellenistic city."[16] Only by allowing for these affinities is it possible to distinguish the specifically Christian elements in his thought.

In Part II Dodd takes up one by one the leading ideas of the Gospel, adduces Hermetic and Philonic parallels, and traces them to their source in the Old Testament. In one instance after another he is led to conclude that the Hellenistic reader would find beneath the superficially familiar language something provocatively new. "The current conceptions of the higher religion of Hellenism have been taken up but entirely transformed."[17] This is not simply because John's thought is fundamentally more Jewish than Greek (though this is true), for Jewish ideas undergo at his hands a similar transformation. The transforming power is the apostolic tradition of the historical Jesus. Other commentators on the Fourth Gospel have in the past claimed that John transformed the apostolic Gospel by expressing it in terms of Greek philosophy. Dodd is suggesting that this is the exact reverse of the truth. It was not the apostolic tradition but the Logos doctrine of Philo and Poimandres which was transformed by the proclamation that the Logos became flesh.

In Part III, in defiance of all theories of dislocation, interpolation, and redaction, Dodd seeks to show that the Gospel, in the form attested to by all manuscripts, has a coherent struc-

[16] P. 9.
[17] P. 212.

ture dictated partly by the apostolic tradition, partly by the intricate pattern of ideas woven by the author, and partly by the theological program laid down in the Prologue.

Finally, the book has an important Appendix on the historical aspect of the Gospel, which is a shadow of good things yet to come. Dodd rejects both apostolic authorship, whether direct or indirect, and the dependence of John on the Synoptists, and declares himself in favor of the hypothesis that John had inherited an independent Judaean tradition which contained some material that reached the Synoptists by different channels.

A generation ago it was almost axiomatic that similarities between books of the New Testament were due to literary dependence of one author on another. The author of I Peter copied from Paul, John from the Synoptists; there were many who doubted whether Luke could have written Acts because of his manifest independence of the Pauline Epistles; and it was even suggested that John the Divine compiled his letters to the seven churches in imitation of the newly published Pauline corpus. Today, thanks largely to Dodd and those who have followed his lead, we have a more adequate picture of early Christianity. Whatever elements the New Testament writers have in common, whether kerygma or *didache*, Old Testament exegesis or catechetical and liturgical forms, are to be attributed to their common background in the traditions, the life, and the worship of the Christian community. This does not mean that we are to find the unity of the New Testament in a highest common factor, ignoring the intensely individual character of the various authors. No one who has taken seriously what Dodd has to say about the particularity of historical revelation could be content with such a view. It means rather that at the heart of the Gospel is a life, and the writers of the New Testament bear their particular but consentient witness to the meaning of that life and its impact on those who were most directly affected by its creative impulse. Only by understanding what it meant to live in that creative moment of history, from which all other history draws its meaning, can we ourselves come into touch with him who was its origin.

The ultimate test of New Testament scholarship is the picture of Jesus which emerges at the end of the process. From Dodd's writings we gain a picture adequate to justify Christian faith and worship. Jesus is first of all a historical figure deeply immersed in the affairs of his own time. His parables reveal "an untrammelled interest in real life," so that "the literature of the Roman Empire contains no other such vivid picture of the life of common men under its rule."[18] "He lived intensely in a particular historical situation, and the relevance of His teaching to that situation is part of its eternal significance. He dealt not with general abstractions, but with issues which the time raised acutely for the people to whom He spoke."[19] At the same time he was conscious of a unique calling—to be the eschatological Son of Man through whom God was to confront Israel with the ultimate crisis of her destiny. He was a profound and original thinker, capable of reminting the currency of theological speech, of transforming the eschatological hope of his nation into a present experience, and of grasping the Old Testament Scriptures entire, so as to find in them a new conception of God's purpose for his people and his Messiah. He was a man of faith, prepared to translate his vision into practice even at the cost of tragedy, in the conviction that God would honor his promises and vindicate his Servant. He was a man of love, who so totally identified himself with his wayward people that his heart was broken by their disobedience at the very moment when in their name he was offering to God the obedience they had failed to pay. To be with him was to be in the presence of God, to hear his words of pardon was to experience the divine forgiveness, and to understand his love was to have a new conception of God.

The spirit which has inspired Dodd's erudite and humane scholarship is best expressed in his own words. "The ideal interpreter would be one who has entered into that strange first-century world, has felt its whole strangeness, has sojourned in it until he has lived himself into it, thinking and feeling as one of those to whom the Gospel first came; and who will then return into our world, and give to the truth he has discerned a body out of the stuff of our own thought."[20] It is appropriate

18 *The Authority of the Bible* (London, Nisbet, 1928), p. 148.
19 *Ibid.*, p. 234.
20 *The Present Task in New Testament Studies*, pp. 40 ff.

that one who has set himself this lifelong ideal should have devoted the first ten years of his retirement to the *New English Bible,* helping to translate into the language of today not only the words of Holy Scripture but the accumulated wealth of dedicated learning.

Bibliography

C. H. Dodd, *The Authority of the Bible,* N.Y., Harper, 1958. (Harper Torchbooks).

Frederick William Dillistone, *C. H. Dodd: Interpreter of the New Testament,* London, Hodder & Stoughton, 1977.

OSCAR CULLMANN

S. C. Guthrie, Jr.

Oscar Cullmann was born in Strasbourg, February 25, 1902. He was baptized in the Lutheran Church of Alsace, and is still a member of the Lutheran Church (he was never ordained). He was educated in his home city, receiving from the University of Strasbourg in 1920 a bachelor's degree in literature for his work in classical philology, in 1924 a bachelor's degree in theology, and in 1930 a doctorate in theology for his dissertation on the Pseudo-Clementine writings. After teaching Greek and German in a Parisian secondary school in 1925–26, he returned to Strasbourg to become instructor in Greek at the university. From 1930–38 he was professor of New Testament and ancient church history there. Since 1938 he has been professor of New Testament and ancient church history at the University of Basel. Besides his work in Basel, he also teaches regularly at the École des Hautes-Études, in the philosophical faculty of the Sorbonne, and at the Protestant theological seminary in Paris. In Paris, as well as in Rome, where for a number of years he has lectured periodically at the Waldensian seminary, Cullmann has had fruitful contact with Roman Catholic theologians which has contributed in his writings to a renewed Protestant-Catholic conversation. Cullmann, who is not married, directs with his sister a theological student house in Basel.

Cullmann is a so-called biblical theologian. That is, he is first of all a New Testament scholar whose works are all primarily exegetical studies of the New Testament writings. But he does not consider his task to be exhausted by an analytic investigation of the language and historical setting of the early Christian writings and the comparison of the "religion" they embody with other contemporary religions. He seeks beyond this to identify and describe the unique theological character and central message of these writings. In order to understand his work, therefore, one must understand both his exegetical method and the theology which results from it.

THE THEOLOGY OF HEILSGESCHICHTE

How does one discover the essence of the early Christian faith? Cullmann never tires of repeating that the task of the biblical interpreter is simply to listen to what the authors of the New Testament have to say to us. He must guard against reading into the New Testament writings, or judging them by, his own philosophical or theological opinions. However difficult this may be, he must try to set aside all his preconceptions and presuppositions (including those he believes to be "Christian") and even his concern about whether what he hears is possible or believable. He has to be willing first of all to take the trouble to understand and present what is in the texts, however strange or contradictory it may be to what he thinks he already knows or can accept as a modern man. For Cullmann, this means especially that one must avoid the false methodology and therefore also the false conclusions of nineteenth-century historicism and of Bultmann and his school.[1]

While he agrees with the great biblical scholars of the past century that the only legitimate method of exegesis is the philological-historical one, and while he seeks the same "objectivity" they were concerned to achieve, Cullmann accuses them of finding in the New Testament only the preconceptions they brought to it. They stripped off as dispensable "form" whatever did not agree with, and discovered as "kernel" whatever did agree with, their own ideas about which of the events and words of the New Testament were scientifically and historically demonstrable, rationally and morally acceptable. As a result the "historical Jesus" they were so concerned to discover turned out to be only a reflection of nineteenth-century idealism.

[1] For Cullmann's description of his own methodology, see especially the prefaces to his various works and the article "The Necessity and Function of Higher Criticism," in his *The Early Church* (Philadelphia, Westminster, 1956). See especially *Christ and Time* (Philadelphia, Westminster, 1950) and *The Christology of the New Testament* (Philadelphia, Westminster, 1959) for his running criticism of Bultmann.

Against this kind of exegesis Cullmann has welcomed form criticism. With other form critics, he recognizes that the New Testament does not offer us only "historical sources," a collection of "facts" to be proved or disproved. It is the confession of faith or preaching (kerygma) of the early church. By its very nature it is *theology,* a biased *interpretation* of Jesus and his message, which we can see only through the eyes of the faith of the early church. In order to get to the real center of the New Testament, Cullmann contends, we cannot distinguish between what is historically genuine and false, essential and nonessential, primitive shell and eternal truth. We must seek to understand the faith of the early Christian community, the forms in which it expressed its faith, and the development of these forms in its life and worship.

But Bultmann's existentialist method of interpretation Cullmann sees as an equally false approach to the New Testament writings, and equally inadequate to get to the real center of the New Testament theology. Despite the fact that Bultmann also rejects the historicism of the past century, Cullmann accuses him of being finally guilty of the same basic error. He also refuses to let the New Testament speak for itself. He also reads into it his own philosophical presuppositions. The only difference is that the presuppositions are now those of existentialist philosophy. Specifically, what Cullmann finds wrong with Bultmann is his reduction of the "objective" events of God's revelatory action in Christ to subjective descriptions of the "self-understanding" of the biblical writers. We must speak again of this criticism of Bultmann, because it plays an increasingly important part in Cullmann's writings; first, however, we must speak of Cullmann's own concept of the center or essence of the New Testament which appears with this general rejection of Bultmann's methodology.

When one is willing to set aside all preconceptions and let the Scripture speak for itself, he discovers that the distinctive content of its proclamation is the *historical* witness it bears. The message of the New Testament is not just a metaphysical speculation, or philosophy of one kind or another, or general theological "truth" which comes to us in the *form* of history. It *is* history. It is not just some abstract propositions about God and man and their relationship, or about "authentic existence," but it is the proclamation of concrete historical events which took place at a particular time in a particular place. Every misunderstanding of the New Testament (whether that of the nineteenth century or Bultmann or any other) is the result of an interpretation which either does not understand or is not willing to accept this historical character of the message of the early church. This is the reason that Cullmann sees docetism as *the* biblical-Christian heresy.

"History" here means of course a special history: "biblical" or "revelatory" or (most often in Cullmann's writings) "redemptive" history (*Heilsgeschichte*). It is the history of God's self-revealing, saving action in the events which lead up to and follow from *the* self-revealing, saving event of the life and death and resurrection of Jesus Christ. This particular history, though unique in general world history, is nevertheless of the same character. It is different from history in general in that the events which compose it are the direct intervention of God in the world, and can therefore be perceived only by faith. They cannot be disproved or confirmed by scientific investigation as can the "facts" of "secular" history (here Cullmann follows the form critics). Yet these events are real historical events in time. They have to do above all with a real "historical" Jesus, not just with a mythological process of salvation described in terms of a historical figure. While we cannot use the New Testament writings to construct a "biography" of Jesus, we can show that the early church did not simply "make up" the content of its faith; rather, its faith resulted from words which Jesus actually spoke and events which actually happened concerning him (here Cullmann qualifies his acceptance of form criticism). Moreover, so decisive is this revelatory history that *all* history both before and after must be understood and judged in the light of it, so that history in general is only the working out of the plan of salvation made known and realized in the particular history recorded in the New Testament.

The theology of the New Testament, therefore, is the theology of *Heilsgeschichte*. All Cullmann's writings are devoted to explaining what *Heilsgeschichte* means and to fitting all theological concepts into the temporal scheme defined by his view of it.

THE BIBLICAL VIEW OF TIME

If the content of the early church's faith and proclamation by its very nature is *Heilsgeschichte*, then one can understand the theology of the New Testament only when he understands the concept of time it presupposes. Cullmann devoted his first major work, *Christ and Time*, to this problem, and all his subsequent works only develop in detail the position formulated here. According to the biblical view, time is understood in analogy to a straight line. The line is formed on the one hand by linking the individual moments of time (*kairoi*) in which God chooses to reveal himself and realize his plan of salvation; and, on the other hand, by linking whole periods of time (*aion*) which these particular actions mark off. Even eternity, "God's time," is not to be distinguished qualitatively from the time which falls between the particular acts in which God creates and ends the world. It is only quantitatively different, to be distinguished from "historical" time only by the fact that it is unlimited, stretching in unending duration "before" and "after" the beginning and end of time as we know it. The time line of the Bible, then, may be divided into three sections: the period stretching endlessly (eternally) backward from creation, the "limited time" between creation and end of the world, and the period stretching endlessly (eternally) forward from the end. This concept of time means that for biblical thought, time has meaning. It is "going somewhere" (in contrast to the "circular" time of the Greeks, which is meaningless because it is only the constant repetition of events and periods without direction or goal). This also means that salvation is expected to occur in time, and that although it will be finally realized only after the "present age," even then it will have a temporal character (in contrast to the Greek idea that salvation comes only by escaping from the prison of time into a "timeless" eternity which is understood in spatial terms of "this world" and "beyond" rather than in temporal terms of "now" and "then").

Judaism and Christianity share the idea that time is the framework for the execution of God's plan of salvation in such a decisive way that all history is at its deepest level the history of salvation. They also share the threefold division of time. Further, both superimpose on this threefold division a twofold one between the "present" and the "coming" age. That is, on the three-part time line of redemption they both locate a "mid-point," which is *the* event of salvation, the one event which gives meaning to and marks the fulfillment of the whole process of salvation which God has been progressively working out not only in and since creation, but even before then in his eternal predestination. The difference between the Jewish and Christian concepts lies in the *placing* of this mid-point. For the Jews it lies in the *future* with the still expected coming of the Messiah, and it coincides with the end of history. For the early church, however, the mid-point is no longer future, nor does it coincide with the chronological end of history. It is identified with the appearance and especially with the death and resurrection of Jesus Christ. The decisive event of salvation which the Jews still look forward to only at the end of time is seen by the early church to have happened before the end. And this means that the coming of the "future age" in which God's plan of salvation is to be fulfilled can no longer simply coincide with the end of time, but has broken into the middle of the "present age." Present and future can no longer be simply distinguished in the Jewish way. Although with Judaism the church also looks forward to the end of time which has "not yet" come, it claims in opposition to Judaism that the decisive center of time, the "fulfillment" of time, has already happened. The end can only be its final completion or confirmation. Salvation or the Kingdom of God to come at the end will only be the final realization of the Kingdom or salvation which has already come.

Cullmann often uses the following analogy to illustrate this complex situation: the decisive battle of a war may be won before the enemy is willing to acknowledge or even knows about it. Fighting may therefore continue for a time, although the outcome of the war has already been determined. The final "cease fire" and declaration of victory are only the inevitable result of the decisive battle already fought. For the Jews the battle which means God's victory and man's salvation has not yet been waged. It will be fought only at the end of time. For the Christians, however, Christ's triumph over death and sin in his resurrection and ascension means that the deciding battle has already been won. Although resistance may continue for a while, the final vindication of God and his gracious will can only make clear to all the victory already achieved.

According to Cullmann, all the theology of the early church is determined by this tension between present and future, "already fulfilled" and "not yet consummated." All periods of the time line must now be understood in the light of the new interim period which began with the resurrection of Christ and which will be concluded with his second coming at the end. Whoever cannot or will not recognize and respect first the linear concept of time which the Jews and the early church have in common, and then the radical change the event of Christ makes in this time scheme, will not be able to understand or share in the uniqueness of the faith and thinking of the New Testament.

Cullmann emphasizes in this context that this "already but not yet" theology of *Heilsgeschichte* is not only the early church's evaluation of the importance of Jesus. A careful exegesis of the Gospels shows that this temporal tension between present and future existed also for Jesus himself. He himself saw the future as already fulfilled in his person: with his coming, the Kingdom of God had come and the victory of God over Satan's kingdom had been realized. And yet he also anticipated a lapse of time (though not a long one) between the fulfillment he accomplished with his earthly work and the end of time when this fulfillment would be finally consummated with his coming again. Therefore Schweitzer, though right in seeing that the whole message of the New Testament is a thoroughly eschatological one, is wrong in seeing Jesus' own eschatology as only futuristic, and in attributing the "already fulfilled" side of the dialectic in the New Testament to the church's invention resulting from the "embarrassment" caused by Jesus' failure to fulfill the Jewish messianic hope for the end of time. C. H. Dodd is equally wrong in resolving the dialectic in the other direction with his "realized eschatology" which leaves no room for a final consummation still to come in the future. Bultmann, while maintaining a tension between the "present" and the "coming" age, reduces (demythologizes) it from a genuinely temporal tension between the now past historical event of Jesus Christ and the future historical event of the end to the "existential" tension in the subjective experience of the man who must decide "now" for or against the Kingdom.

CHRISTOLOGY AND HEILSGESCHICHTE

The mid-point which Christ marks in the time line of redemptive history is so important that the whole line may be called the "Christ line." Every point and every period in it must be understood as Christ-history. All *Heilsgeschichte is* Christology. To move, therefore, from Cullmann's *Christ and Time* (1945) to his later and most important work to date, *The Christology of the New Testament* (1956), is not to change the subject of discussion but to get to the heart of the matter.

It would be quite incorrect for us to be influenced by the Christological controversies in the church after the New Testament period to think that the earliest Christians were interested in the problem of the "nature" of Christ. For the early Christians the question "Who is Christ?" meant not "What is his nature?" but "What does he *do?*" They were not interested in his person as such, but in his work—or rather only in his person to the extent that it is revealed in his work. The Christology of the New Testament is "functional" Christology. It has to do not with philosophical speculations but with historical events. In other words, if *Heilsgeschichte* means Christology, then it is also true that Christology means *Heilsgeschichte*.

The early church had at its disposal certain concepts already familiar in Judaism with which to interpret the meaning of the work of Jesus and the events of his death and resurrection. They were the various messianic titles—titles which dealt not so much with the "person" or "nature" as with the function of the one who should come bringing salvation. The early church worked out its Christology primarily in terms of these Jewish titles. It also used some concepts and titles which came not exclusively from Judaism but also from Hellenistic religion. Nonetheless it is very important to see, Cullmann insists (especially against

Bultmann), that nothing of the Christology of the early church *originated* with these concepts, which were primarily mythological and gnostic; and that when it did take up these concepts, the church poured a new meaning into them, above all by relating them to real historical events having to do with the flesh-and-blood Jesus of Nazareth. Moreover, even the Jewish concepts were not in themselves adequate to express the uniqueness of Jesus but had to be adapted to what actually happened in him. The Christology of the early church is not an attempt to fit Christ into *any* conceptual scheme, but to adjust all concepts, of whatever origin, to the events connected with him. Only when we recognize this can we see the radical newness of the theology of the New Testament and its radical difference from a timeless mythology or nonhistorical kerygma.

We cannot discuss here Cullmann's careful investigation of the various titles with which the New Testament writers worked out their Christology. We may, however, see the results of his work by summarizing his reconstruction of the development of the Christology of the early church. Again in this context Cullmann emphasizes that all New Testament Christology is founded upon and begins with the life of Jesus himself, not with a ready-made mythology or eschatology, and not even with the experience and theology of the early Christian community after Easter. Jesus himself was conscious that he had to carry out God's plan of salvation. He knew that he had to do this by accomplishing the forgiveness of sins "for many" through his obedient death in fulfillment of the role of the "Suffering Servant of Yahweh." He knew that he had to introduce the Kingdom of God in fulfillment of the eschatological role of the "Son of Man," who had existed with God from all eternity and who would appear "on the clouds of heaven" at the end of time to judge and renew the world. In fulfilling this double function of humiliation and exaltation, he was so aware of his complete and unique oneness with the will of God that he was conscious beyond all human possibilities of being the "Son of God."

Already among Jesus' disciples during his life there were flashes of insight into his real identity and mission. But despite Jesus' allusions to his self-consciousness, his disciples generally could think of him only in terms of the political-nationalistic concept of the "Messiah." It was really only in the light of the events of Good Friday and Easter that the disciples began to understand who Jesus was. They now began to understand the meaning of the earthly life of Jesus and his role as Servant, and they were all the more interested in the future now that the Jewish messianic concepts had to be qualified by the fact that the Coming One was the Jesus who *had* come. But it was finally not so much the past or future events of redemptive history as the *present* upon which the thinking of the church concentrated, the time *between* the "comings." The community worked out its interpretation of the role of Christ in the present, above all in terms of the concept "Lord." What is the risen and coming Christ doing *now?* He rules as living and present Lord over his church, the world, and the life of each individual. This understanding of Jesus as Lord is not to be traced to the use of this title in other contemporary religions; rather, it grew directly out of the worship of the earliest community in which the presence of the risen Lord was directly experienced.[2]

So profound was this cultic experience of the present Lord, Cullmann believes, that it really was from this center that the whole line of redemptive history was given its Christological interpretation. All other titles must be seen in the light of the fact that the Jesus who *was* crucified and who *will* come again *is* the living Lord over both Church and the whole world. Indeed, not only must the past and future periods of *Heilsgeschichte* be related to this realization, but also the periods before and after history. If Jesus is really Lord, this must point to his oneness with God himself in eternity—to his "deity." He can therefore be called the pre-existent "Logos" or "Son of God" or even "God." Wherever in all periods of *Heilsgeschichte* God is at work revealing himself, there Christ must be. He *is* God in his self-communication.

The development of the New Testament Christology, then, is the direct traceable path from the self-consciousness of Jesus and the occasional premonitions of his disciples, to the Easter experience of the disciples, to the community's experience of

[2] See *Early Christian Worship* (Naperville, Illinois, Allenson, 1953). Also *The Earliest Christian Confessions* (London, Lutterworth Press, 1949).

the Lord in worship, to a deep theological reflection (especially in the Gospel of John and Hebrews) upon the connection between Christ and *all Heilsgeschichte*.

CHURCH AND WORLD IN THE PRESENT PERIOD OF HEILSGESCHICHTE

We have seen that for Cullmann the biblical *Heilsgeschichte* includes and gives meaning to all periods of the time line. And we have seen how he relates the Christology of the New Testament to all these periods. Yet it would not be correct to think that all these periods and Christ's work in them receive equal emphasis in the New Testament. We have also seen that Cullmann believes that the early church was above all interested in the *present* period and in the function of Christ as Lord in this period. Indeed, all other periods of redemptive history and all other functions of Christ were first understood and interpreted on the basis of the early Christians' belief that they stood already in the future age although the end had not yet come, and of their experience of the risen Christ in their common worship. Cullmann's works on the theology of the New Testament bear a corresponding emphasis. If his two major works, *Christ and Time* and *The Christology of the New Testament,* discuss the whole stretch of *Heilsgeschichte* and the Christological significance of it, most of his other works are devoted to an interpretation of the New Testament understanding of this present period. Even in the two big works this problem occupies a disproportionate amount of Cullmann's time and effort. A glance at his view of the church and the world in this period will at least indicate the direction in which he points in this context.

The period of *Heilsgeschichte* between the resurrection of Christ and his return is the period of the church.[3] The church began with the appearance of the risen Lord to his first disciples and it will end with his return. The meaning of its existence, its faith and life, its task in the world, can be properly understood only in terms of this position in the history of salvation; that is,

[3] For detailed discussions of the church, see *Christ and Time,* pp. 144 ff; *The Christology of the New Testament,* pp. 203 ff. Also *Baptism in the New Testament* (Naperville, Illinois, Allenson, 1950).

only in terms of the church's consciousness of living "between the times," in the eschatological tension between the "already fulfilled" but "not yet consummated" reality of the new age. The presence of the Holy Spirit in the church is a sign of this tension. Because of the Spirit's presence, the new life of the Kingdom of God which will come finally at the end is already realized in the members of the community, and yet it is a new life only provisionally realized, which can only be believed in, because the church is made up of men who are still sinners. The Lord's Supper is another sign of this tension, for at this celebration the church prays for the coming of the Lord at the end and yet experiences his presence already now in the gathered community. Preaching, the one great task of the church, is still another sign of the "already–not yet" dialectic. It is the call for all men to accept the Good News of the decisive battle won on Good Friday and Easter and of Christ's already effective rule over sin and death; and it is a call of promise and warning about his final victory which is coming. So important is the preaching of the church that one can say that the "between times" exists for its sake. It *is* the time of God's gracious patience which grants men still time to hear, repent, believe. The church thus actually participates in and carries forward the divine redemptive activity in history. It is the earthly center from which the lordship of Christ becomes visible, the center from which Christ the Lord rules and does his work in the world. However insignificant it may seem in world affairs, the existence of the church is the clue to what is going on in the world and what God is doing not only in "church" history, but also in the secular history of our time.[4]

What *is* going on in the world? Cullmann is not so much interested in the relation of *Heilsgeschichte* and Christ's lordship to secular history or culture in general as in their relation to

[4] This high evaluation of the church does not mean that the church itself may be absolutized. The church has authority only as it submits itself and its traditions to the proclamation of the unrepeatable event of salvation and the apostolic tradition concerning it which lie not *in*, but in the past *before* the time of the church. See Cullmann's criticism of the Roman Church at this point in his *Peter* (Philadelphia, Westminster, 1953, rev. and expanded ed., 1962) and in "The Tradition," in *The Early Church.*

political history. The problem of *Heilsgeschichte* and world history thus becomes the problem of church and state.[5]

The New Testament understands also the existence and history of the state in the light of the dialectic between the decisive battle already won and the final victory yet to come at the end. The lordship of Christ between these events is not only his rule over the church, but also his rule over the world of political powers—and at a deeper level over the invisible demonic "powers" which the New Testament sees as standing behind the state. Christ's victory on Easter was also his victory over the "princes of the world" who were ultimately responsible for his death. Therefore they and their empirical organ, the state, are now subject to Christ and are his "ministers." The difference between church and state is not that the members of the former serve Christ while the members of the latter do not, but that the former know of his lordship and willingly serve him, while the latter do not know of it and serve him unconsciously or even against their will. Not only the church, then, but also the state is God's instrument in the working out of his plan of salvation. Although it may not even know it, the state exists for the sake of maintaining the order and peace in which the preaching of the church before the end may be carried on. Christians for this reason have greater respect than any other citizens for the state, and are more concerned than any others that it be obeyed. They know that the state is subject to Christ and exists to fulfill his will.

This does not mean, however, that the state is absolutized. While the decisive battle over the powers of the world has already been won, in the present period of *Heilsgeschichte* the final victory has not been achieved. The "powers" are only "subjected," not yet "destroyed." They can still do damage. They constantly threaten to attempt to free themselves from the authority of Christ, and sometimes for a time seem to do so. Then the state, instead of creating order and peace for the church's work, becomes totalitarian, becomes the "beast" of Revelation 13, persecuting the church, which refuses to give to

[5] See *The State in the New Testament* (London, SCM Press, 1957) and "The Kingship of Christ and the Church in the New Testament," in *The Early Church.*

Caesar the absolute obedience which belongs to Christ alone. When the state thus oversteps its legitimate limits the church can only disobey it to that extent. Thus while Christians have greater respect for the state than anyone else, they are also more watchful for signs of self-deification in the state, and are more opposed to it, for they know about the dangerous demonic forces threatening to break loose there, and they see this political totalitarianism for what it really is, rebellion against the lordship of Christ.

On the ground that the New Testament does not do so, Cullmann does not attempt to answer the question how we know just when the state does or does not remain within its proper limits. The only clear case we are given in the New Testament is the situation in which the state claims emperor worship. Moreover, while he suggests that resistance is allowed in the case of totalitarianism, he offers no help about what the church's attitude should be when a state is simply unjust. This way of dealing with the problem of church and state is a good example of the way in which Cullmann relates all theological problems to *Heilsgeschichte,* particularly the present phase of it; and his willingness to let difficult problems which are not solved in the New Testament itself simply stand.[6]

CONCLUSION

One of the greatest virtues of Cullmann's work is his ability to deal with difficult problems of exegesis and theological interpretation in such a simple, clear way that not only technically trained scholars but any beginning student in theology can understand him. But this virtue is also the ground of most of the criticisms of his work: is not his theology of *Heilsgeschichte* too simple and generalized, too neatly schematized, to do justice to the complexity of the New Testament writings and their theological content? The most general criticisms in this respect

[6] While Cullmann is not so much interested in the life of the individual Christian as in that of the Christian and civil communities, when he does deal with the individual, it is also in terms of the "already–not-yet" dialectic. See especially his treatment of death and the "afterlife" in *Immortality of the Soul or Resurrection of the Dead?* (N.Y., Macmillan, 1958).

probably relate to his concept of time and to his Christology—precisely to the central themes of all his work.

Can the biblical concept of time really be so nicely diagrammed as Cullmann's time line suggests? Above all, can eternity legitimately be said to be only quantitatively different from time? Is not eternity in the Bible something different from both Greek timelessness and Cullmann's endless time? If God's and man's *time* are only quantitatively distinguished, what does this do to the relationship between God and man? Granted that Cullmann successfully shows that it is improper to read the Greek cyclical (or any other philosophical) concept of time into the New Testament, is he himself free from preconceptions about time? Is his own concept of time in terms of chronological succession not a modern concept read into rather than a concept derived from the Bible? To put the question in an even more radical way: even properly understood, is the biblical concept of time really the central concept which determines the meaning and content of all other concepts? Is everything in the Bible not related rather to *God* and to his acts than to time as such?

The same basic charge of oversimplification lies behind most criticisms of Cullmann's understanding of New Testament Christology. Granted that the Church has often separated the person and work of Christ in such a way that Christology has wrongly become a matter of metaphysical speculation about "substance" and "nature," is it a valid alternative to think only of a "functional" Christology? If Christ *is* what he does, is it not necessary on the basis of the New Testament itself to attempt some "ontological" statements about him? Or again, is not Cullmann's construction of the development of the Christology of the New Testament too neat and easy? Can everything be so certainly traced back to Jesus himself? Does so much depend on our being able to demonstrate a direct continuity between the theology of the church and the "historical Jesus"? Is the "self-consciousness" of Jesus a sound beginning point for ascertaining the "real facts" about who he was and what he did? Is Cullmann convincing when he grounds his opposition to the theory of a Hellenistic influence regarding the Christological thinking of the church on the "cultic experience" of the earliest community?

Behind some of these objections to Cullmann's work lies the difficult problem of the relationship between "biblical" and "systematic" theology. When his understanding, for instance, of time and eternity, or functional Christology, or the church-state relationship is criticized as inadequate, Cullmann answers that a New Testament scholar must permit questions that are not solved in the New Testament itself to stand as questions. He fulfills his function just by refusing to answer them, and by handing them in their proper form over to the systematic theologian. Is he right in so limiting the task of the biblical theologian, or is this also an oversimplification of his task?

Despite all criticisms, Cullmann's work will undoubtedly stand as an important contribution to the biblical-theological thought of our time. His careful, disciplined work of philological-historical research in the texts of the New Testament places him in line with the great critical scholars of the past and present centuries. His theology of *Heilsgeschichte,* with its constant emphasis on the fact that for the New Testament revelation has to do with concrete time- and space-bound historical events, is a formidable obstacle to the gnostic-docetic heresy which also in our time is a threat to a genuinely Christian theology. His consistent demonstration that Christology lies at the heart of all New Testament thought and his refusal to think of the person of Christ apart from his work has contributed significantly to the new understanding in this century of what is unique and central in the New Testament. His treatment of New Testament eschatology in terms of the "already–not yet" paradox offers a constructive alternative to the one-sidedness of Schweitzer and Dodd, and at the very least a serious challenge to the existentialism of Bultmann. Perhaps his most helpful insight has been his understanding of the greatly neglected importance of the meaning of the resurrection of Christ and his function as "Lord" for the "present" period of *Heilsgeschichte.* At this point Cullmann's theology of *Heilsgeschichte* becomes immediately relevant to the situation in which *we* live. *Our* church as well as the New Testament community, *our* world as well as that dominated by the Roman Empire, *myself* as well as the first century Christian—*we* are touched by this lordship. Here Culmann's theology ceases to be merely academic research and becomes itself the proclamation of Good News. Finally, his active and sympathetic participation in the renewed discussion between Protestant and Roman Catholic theologians during the past few years will certainly earn for Cullmann an important place in a new chapter in the history of Protestant-Catholic relations.

Much of what Cullmann has said has also been said by others, perhaps occasionally in a better, more nearly complete way. But he has never been concerned to lead the pack in discovering and defending the newest and most radically different theories of New Testament interpretation. He has never attempted to be "original" or to draw a school around himself. He has been content simply to work at the New Testament itself and patiently to report his findings. New Testament scholarship in the years to come will not be able to ignore or bypass him.

Bibliography

Oscar Cullmann, *Christ and Time, rev. ed.*, Philadelphia, Westminster, 1964.

No detailed study of Cullmann is available in English.

REINHOLD NIEBUHR

Hans Hofmann

There are two interrelated aspects of the church's theological task: that of intellectual self-reflection, whereby the church seeks to give coherent, systematic expression to its faith, and that of articulating that faith, which it affirms has definite implications for man and his life in society. Dogmatics is the term used to refer to the former aspect of the church's theological task; ethics, moral theology, apologetics to the latter. And it is in this latter aspect of theology that Reinhold Niebuhr has made an impressive contribution to twentieth century Christianity. However, as significant and perceptive as his thought has been, it is his approach, his stance, which is unique. Though other Christian thinkers, notably Karl Barth and Paul Tillich, appear to have eclipsed Niebuhr in popularity, to ignore his thought is to miss something that is crucial if the church is to retain and deepen its vitality. This essay, while attempting to delineate the major themes of Niebuhr's theology, also seeks to bring into prominence that in his thought which, owing to the almost idolatrous hold which dogmatics has come to have on thinking Christians on both sides of the Atlantic, has not received its full measure of recognition.

Reinhold Niebuhr was born in Wright City, Missouri, on June 21, 1892. His ancestry reaches back into the solid German stock of creative thinkers who anticipated and welcomed rational liberalism. Their faith and insights merged into a vision of a democratic realization of the Kingdom of God, in which the creative grace of God would cooperate with the well-meaning efforts of man to bring about a free and constructive unfolding of human potentials. However, neither Germany nor the Europe of the time was ready for such a development as was evidenced by the reaction to the Revolution of 1848. Reacting against the forces of nationalistic imperialism and political conservatism, Niebuhr's forebears immigrated to the United

States. On arriving they settled in the Midwest among other recent arrivals to the New World. The piety and vigor of these people gave every promise that they would be successful in the kind of venture that had been rebuffed by the Old World.

Such was Niebuhr's background. After attending the college and seminary of his denomination, the Evangelical and Reformed Church, Niebuhr enrolled as a graduate student at the Divinity School of Yale University. However, the needs of his family and his boredom with academic studies led him to set aside his plans for a teaching career. Instead, he accepted an assignment as pastor of the Bethel Evangelical Church, a newly established mission in Detroit. At the time, Detroit was in the throes of industrialization and was rapidly becoming the "motor capital of the world." It was his thirteen years' experience as a minister to people caught up in the juggernaut of American industrialization that shaped Niebuhr's development as a critic of both the church and American society.

In 1928 Niebuhr accepted a call to be Professor of Applied Christianity at Union Theological Seminary in New York City. During the years since, his thought has developed and matured, but its focus has not shifted. Through his lecturing and preaching as well as through countless books and articles, Niebuhr has devoted himself to analysis of and prescription for the problem which so forcefully confronted him during his pastorate in Detroit.

People who today exclaim that the church does not come to grips with the actual problems of its people should be reminded that over a generation ago a young pastor turned "tamed cynic" lamented that what he had learned at seminary was of little use to him in his ministry and that what he now needed to know had not been taught him. Tamed was his youthful idealistic conviction that his task was simply to apply his recently acquired theories; cynical was the doubt that he and the church had any future in Detroit's rising industrialism. Yet Niebuhr set himself the task of exploring the meaning and significance of the Christian Gospel in the context of modern industrial society. His experience in Detroit forced him to grapple with the problem of religion and society. He had seen at first hand both the plight of men caught up in industrialization and the failure of the church to minister effectively to them. For him the most pressing task facing the church became that of investigating the various forces which come into play when the Gospel confronts the world. Hopefully, such an analysis might be of genuine assistance to those who were seeking to be faithful to the New Testament injunction "to be in, but not of, the world." For Niebuhr, a stance for such an analysis that would both recognize the complexity of the problem and be faithful to the Christian perspective would have to be taken precisely at the point at which the Gospel and the world confront each other. To a great degree, Niebuhr's importance as a thinker rests on his skill in identifying that point of contact and his consistency in viewing all things in terms of it.

For Niebuhr the precise point at which the Gospel and the world confront one another is in man. Thus the focal point of Niebuhr's interest is man. Though he does not ignore other facets of theological concern, from the start it was the doctrine of man, theological anthropology, that consumed his attention. The title of his chief work, *The Nature and Destiny of Man,* delivered as the Gifford Lectures when he was at the zenith of his influence, summarizes what was Niebuhr's central concern. But before turning to Niebuhr's mature treatment of human nature, it would be helpful to our understanding of his thought if we became acquainted with the approach and major themes set forth in his first two important publications: *Does Civilization Need Religion?* and *Moral Man and Immoral Society.*

In *Does Civilization Need Religion?,* written just before his resignation from the pastorate, Niebuhr focuses on the problem of the relation of the Gospel and the world by investigating the nature and purpose of religion in human life. At this point he is not concerned to distinguish religion and Christianity—a distinction which has recently become quite fashionable in theological circles—since he still regards the latter as but a specific expression of the former. It was only after he began wrestling with the problem of revelation that Niebuhr became more circumspect in his view of Christianity as a specific expression of the religious consciousness. Nevertheless, it could be argued that Niebuhr was aware of the distinction between religion and Christianity very early in his career. For from the start the word "religion" had a twofold, almost ambiguous, meaning for Niebuhr. On the one hand, he uses the term when referring to the source of man's religious consciousness, i.e., God and his will for man. On the other hand, he often uses "religion" to refer to that which man constructs in order to blunt, domesticate, and replace true religion. These two meanings of religion, which he later distinguishes as prophetic religion (Jesus is interpreted as standing within this tradition) and priestly religion, really are the nub of the current distinction between Christianity and religion. However, especially in the earlier works, Niebuhr does not make this distinction clear and the student of his thought must discern from the context the specific meaning he has in mind.

The first point that Niebuhr examines is the place of religion in modern life. Niebuhr's answer to the question, Does religion have much of a place? is in the negative. Pointing to the tremendous changes which have marked the growth of modern society, he declares that religion has shown itself to be almost helpless in the face of the impact the technological revolution has been having on man, both individually and corporately:

> There are indeed many forms of religion which are clearly vestigial remnants of another day with other interests. They have no vital influence upon the life of modern man, and their continued existence only proves that history, like nature, is slow to destroy what it has found useless, and even slower to inter what it has destroyed.[1]

Nevertheless, despite the dismal performance of contemporary religion, Niebuhr does not conclude that religion has outlived its function and is thus only of antiquarian interest. To the contrary, he asserts that, because of what has been happening to man and society as a consequence of the Industrial Revolution, man needs more than ever before the resources provided by religion.

Niebuhr's experience as pastor to Ford workers made him keenly aware that a by-product of industrialization is the cheapening of the value of personality. It is in the face of this

[1] *Does Civilization Need Religion?* (N.Y., Macmillan, 1928), p. 3.

trend toward the devaluation of personality that he sees religion as making a basic contribution. Far from being outmoded, religion plays a crucial role in life in modern industrial society. To put the matter succinctly, it is Niebuhr's view that if religion is taken away from man, the integrity of his personality is undercut. When that happens, society loses its cohesiveness and integrity. Thus, since society requires religion for its own survival, one would expect to find religion wherever one finds men living in community. Concludes Niebuhr:

> Whatever may be said of specific religions and religious forms, it is difficult to imagine man without religion; for religion is the champion of personality in a seemingly impersonal world.[2]

Having suggested that religion and society come into focus in terms of man, Niebuhr devotes considerable attention to spelling out how the two interact in and on man. On the one hand, religion provides human personality with the foundation that enables it to function in society. It does this by stressing that there is a God who is personal and that God, society, and man are related in organic, personal fashion. By emphasizing the personal nature of the cosmos, religion underwrites the value of human personality. However, in modern society it is just this emphasis which comes most into question. Not only does the philosophical presupposition of modern society—naturalism—run contrary to that of traditional religion by depersonalizing the universe and nature, but, as Niebuhr saw so clearly in Detroit, the forces of modern civilization themselves depersonalize society and the individual. Hence in order to defend the sanctity of personality, religion must carry out the battle on two fronts. As well as demonstrating on a metaphysical level that the notion of a personal God is intellectually defensible, religion must also bring its forces to bear on society itself, seeking to make the latter more humane. Religion must bring its ethical insights to bear on the problems of modern society. In this regard Niebuhr insists that the forces of religion must do more than simply concern themselves with the nurturing of the individual in isolation from his involvement in the social matrix. Important as the

[2] *Ibid.*, p. 4.

personal development of the individual may be—and Niebuhr never overlooks this concern—it is his view that the individual can never be understood or helped except from within the social context, since its forces exercise a decisive influence on the individual's development.

It is this view that lies behind Niebuhr's involvement in the burning social issues of the day. Because he believes that the church has erroneously thought it possible to minister to the individual in isolation from social forces, Niebuhr has sought to redress the balance by involving himself, theoretically and personally, in social questions. In this regard he has come to exercise a great influence on the social and political thinking of the day. It is important to note, however, that he has been no mere social activist. He is well aware that individual as well as social factors are involved in the development of human personality.

Niebuhr has described himself as not a theologian but one concerned with ethics and apologetics.[3] However, his concern for ethics and apologetics must be understood in terms of his conviction that in the battle against the forces depersonalizing man the church has been engaged almost wholly on the metaphysical level. It is because the ethical front, which he regards as just as important as the metaphysical, is being ignored that he plunges into the battle at that point:

> The fact is that more men in our modern era are irreligious because religion has failed to make civilization ethical than because it has failed to maintain its intellectual respectability. For every person who disavows religion because some ancient and unrevised dogma outrages his intelligence, several become irreligious because the social impotence of religion outrages their conscience.[4]

On the other hand, Niebuhr is too subtle a thinker to view the problem of man in modern society simply as a matter of religion's providing man with the resources that will enable

[3] Charles W. Kegley and Robert W. Bretall, eds., *Reinhold Niebuhr: His Religious, Social, and Political Thought* (N.Y., Macmillan, 1956), p. 3.
[4] *Does Civilization Need Religion?* p. 12.

him to achieve personal integrity and build a more humane society. If Niebuhr insists that the notion of God as person is necessary in order that there may be a community of persons, he also recognizes that one's ability to regard God as personal depends on one's living in a society in which "person" has some meaning. Religion is not the panacea which has only to be applied in order to effect a cure for the human condition. Such a view is far too naive. To work against those forces in modern society which prevent the individual from becoming a person is not to play the part simply of the prophet decrying the fact that society has turned away from its Lord and succumbed to evil ways. Rather, to involve oneself actively in working for a more just and humane society is to give credence to the view that God is personal. It is to maintain the concept as viable for modern man. If society ceases to be personal, then it becomes nonsensical to talk of God as personal.

Niebuhr's view that religion and society are interdependent categories which come into focus in man provides the starting point and impetus for the task that has come to occupy his attention during his mature years—the analysis and elucidation of man's nature and destiny. It is in man that the gospel and the world come into direct confrontation. Hence, if one would understand the gospel and its relevance for life in the world, one must understand man.

Before we turn to an exposition of Niebuhr's doctrine of man, the reader should be reminded of the way Niebuhr uses the term "society." His understanding of the term is to be contrasted with that which it bears in modern social theory. As opposed to the social scientist, Niebuhr does not view society as a self-governing entity which exercises autonomy and supremacy over the individual. Nor does he accept the view that man, the individual, and society are mutually exclusive entities. Rather, society for Niebuhr is no more and no less than a collectivity of individuals. It possesses no reality apart from its reference to people. Its characteristics are those of man-as-such. It possesses no special mystique. The significant difference between man and society is that in the latter are revealed more nakedly the qualities possessed by individual man. For example, whereas the individual possesses one set of ethical norms, as a member of a group and as a consequence of interacting within the group, he subscribes to a morality of a much lower level. This situation exists for a very simple reason:

> In every human group there is less reason to guide and check impulse, less capacity for self-transcendence, less ability to comprehend the needs of others and therefore more unrestrained egoism than the individuals, who compose the group, reveal in their personal relationships.[5]

Thus Niebuhr's interest in society is partly motivated by his conviction that one can arrive at a clearer, more realistic understanding of human nature by analyzing group behavior than by analyzing the individual in abstraction. At the same time, it is important to remember that for Niebuhr the individual does not exist apart from the group. Fulfillment of life requires association with others. Yet such association creates as many problems as it solves. This leads Niebuhr to say that "the society in which each man lives is at once the basis for, and the nemesis of, that fulness of life which each man seeks."[6]

Having made these points at the outset of *Moral Man and Immoral Society*, Niebuhr then describes man's nature and function as they are revealed in the various forms of group life that make up what we call "society." The gist of his argument is that man, as a reasoning creature, has a capacity not only for self-consciousness and thus for selfishness, but also comes to the awareness that he counts for nothing in the universe. The latter discovery motivates man to seek to increase his power over others in order to win an illusory victory over his own insignificance. His will-to-live becomes transmuted into a will-to-power. Within the human soul, in self-consciousness, lies that which is at the root of the inhumanity and corruption that is everywhere so evident in human society. And in his analysis of the demonic nature of the groups which compose society, Niebuhr does not exclude a consideration of the corporate forms of religion. They, too, can be used as vehicles of man's will-to-

---

[5] *Moral Man and Immoral Society* (N.Y., Scribner's, 1932), pp. xi–xii.

[6] *Ibid.*, p. 1.

power and its resultant vitiating of human life. As history has shown, man has been all too ready to make religion "his" religion and to use it for his own selfish purposes. The main burden of Niebuhr's study is to demonstrate that at the root of the malfunctioning and breakdowns so obvious in social life is a split within man himself. Only when man is himself healed, Niebuhr insists, can the structures of his societal life function in a healthy and constructive fashion.

Just as the close interrelation of religion, society, and man is to be seen from a realistic appraisal of what is going on in the world, so, for Niebuhr, is that interrelation to be demonstrated by the manner in which society's splits and fractures are overcome. Since man is the center of the disturbance in society, when he is healed he mediates that which in turn renews society. Man is the connecting point where all the conflicts of society arise and the disturbances in the social order converge, but he is also that which mediates the forces which redeem society. It goes without saying that the resources which man makes available for the renewal of society are those of society.

Yet Niebuhr does not simply assert that it is religion which, through man, provides the wherewithal for the renewal of society. He comes to this conclusion only after investigating the question whether man is able to redress the grievances of the social order on his own. Though it is Niebuhr's central position that man mediates that which renews society, he nevertheless contends that man must look beyond himself for the resources of renewal. Society must be integrated if it is to be renewed. But man himself is in need of integration. He lacks the objectivity of judgment that would form a basis for social integration. Though man is the center of renewal, he is also the center of the disturbance. He must receive something from beyond himself which he can in turn mediate to society. It is at this point that religion becomes significant. Its function is to provide the resources which integrate man and through him integrate society. Its function is thus twofold.

Niebuhr understands the primary resource which religion makes available to man as that of a self-transcending goal: that which lifts him out of his narrow, self-centered preoccupations. This self-transcending goal not only helps man to see how narrow and self-seeking he is—and so enables him to be more equitable in his dealings with others—but also enables him to evaluate more fairly what is good for society. Freed from his own prejudices, man will be enabled to mediate between the rival claims which lead to the conflicts on the corporate level. Indeed, given a new perspective which transcends both the self and society, man will see that it is precisely the tendency in society to split into warring camps that makes it impossible for society to rectify human problems. One of the main insights given by religion is the realization that in social conflict there is never simply a right and a wrong side. To make such a division is not only to oversimplify but to preclude at the outset the possibility of solving any problems. It is only when man realizes that society is one that there is any possibility for true social progress.

In being given a new vantage point from which to view both himself and society, man should, says Niebuhr, manifest a humility born out of repentance. Freed from an exclusive concern for self, realizing with pain what his egocentrism has done to himself and others, man is filled with an understanding of and a self-giving concern for the needs of others. More important, he is freed from captivity to the notion that the true and the good function exclusively through him. He is open and ready for change that comes from elsewhere. Further, his awareness concerning the pervasiveness of self-love and the subtlety of its expression makes him humble as to the achievements he believes are possible in society. While working actively for the betterment of the individual and society, he realizes that the Kingdom of God lies in the future and that it is built by God. His realism concerning that which motivates the individual, not to mention social groups, makes him wary of any attempt by men, even churchmen, to build the Kingdom themselves. But at the same time he understands the idea of the Kingdom in corporate terms. He knows that true religion is no private affair. He works to change society, knowing full well that he can build nothing durable and lasting. Acknowledging the fact that he lives in a world vitiated by pride and self-aggrandizement, he recognizes that true religion is one of the forces encouraging change.

From the above general outline of Niebuhr's understanding of the interaction of religion, society, and man, and his view that man is simultaneously at the center of the conflicts disrupting society and the channel through which they are healed, we can see the focus and direction which his thought is to take. The focus is to be on man—his nature, his destiny, how the resources of religion are made available to him, etc. But the interest of Niebuhr in man is in man-in-society. For Niebuhr, there is no other man. Thus throughout his discussion of man's nature and destiny, he does not lose sight of the social dimension. Indeed, one of Niebuhr's greatest accomplishments is the single-minded thoroughness with which he devotes himself to the task of spelling out his doctrine of man as mediator between God and society. We now turn to a more systematic discussion of his understanding of that doctrine.

The sources of Niebuhr's understanding of man are the biblical revelation and his realistic appraisal of the human situation. He accepts the notion of "general" as well as "special" revelation. The former is synonymous with individual, private revelation, while the latter refers to God's self-revelation to man in history. He regards both types of revelation as essential and as implying each other:

> Without the public and historical revelation the private experience of God would remain poorly defined and subject to caprice. Without the private revelation of God, the public and historical would not gain credence.[7]

Thus while Niebuhr is quick to acknowledge that the biblical revelation is determinative as regards man's understanding of God and his ways with men, he is in essential disagreement with the more orthodox tradition, which affirms that it is only within "the circle of faith" that man, or God, is understood. Niebuhr believes it is possible to arrive at valid insights concerning man's nature and destiny apart from the biblical revelation (though these can easily be misunderstood). Here we can see in the background Niebuhr's concern to keep God and society in re-

---

[7] *The Nature and Destiny of Man* (N.Y., Scribner's, 1953), Vol. I, p. 127.

lationship. Because he affirms this tension he is ready to learn about man from other sources besides Holy Scripture. Yet he does view the latter as determinative.

For Niebuhr the unique and crucial contribution of the biblical tradition to the understanding of man is its myth of creation. According to the Genesis account, man is created "in the image of God." Niebuhr understands this to mean that man is placed between the Creator God and the rest of the created order. Man shares with the former the creative spirit and with the latter inescapable participation in matter. Man's uniqueness lies in his partial self-transcendence. By means of his understanding, man can rise above his immediate involvement in his life-context, but he cannot completely disentangle himself from it. Contrary to the Greek understanding of man, correct understanding, from the biblical point of view, does not necessarily result in correct action. For between man's knowing what is objectively constructive and destructive and his acting accordingly comes the lustful desire of man to prove himself God-like; i.e., independent and all-powerful:

> Man is insecure and involved in natural contingency; he seeks to overcome his insecurity by a will-to-power which overreaches the limits of human creatureliness. Man is ignorant and involved in the limitations of a finite mind; but he pretends that he is not limited. He assumes that he can gradually transcend finite limitations until his mind becomes identical with universal mind. All of his intellectual and cultural pursuits, therefore, become infected with the sin of pride.[8]

This assertion of independence alienates man from God and makes him a slave to the potentials of creation, rather than their master, which was God's original intention in creation. Niebuhr sees the myth of the tower of Babel as illustrating the perennial temptation of man to be completely autonomous and the confusion that results therefrom. But what is there about man which forces him to yield to temptation?

In answering this question Niebuhr attempts to understand and interpret the fall of Adam in such a way that it will be

[8] *Ibid.*, pp. 178–79.

readily accepted by modern man, and to this end he makes use of concepts drawn from the behavioral sciences. Of course, he does not regard Adam's fall as an historical event, in the sense that a specific person disobeyed God's command and implicated the rest of mankind in the consequences of his action. Adam means simply "man" and connotes the normal human propensity for inordinate self-concern. In attempting to explain why man is so unduly concerned about himself Niebuhr is led into an analysis of the nature of sin. Like Kierkegaard, he does not believe that it is possible to set forth the etiology of sin. Sin posits itself. This being the case, one can only trace the phenomenology of sin in human behavior and point to its consequences. This Niebuhr does so extensively that some critics regard his doctrine of man as sinner as his central contribution to contemporary Christian thought.

Departing from the traditional understanding of Pauline theology—that "the wages of sin is death," i.e., that death is the consequence of sin—Niebuhr does not view sin and death as having any direct cause-effect relationship. Rather, he speculates that, had man not sinned, death would not be an insuperable problem for him. But, since man is already sinful, death comes to exercise a tyranny over him. Death represents the unpredictable termination of man's opportunity to fulfill his life's ambitions. It is this insoluble tension between "finis" and "telos" that fosters man's anxiety. The injustice and competitiveness that mark human interaction on all levels are the paramount fruits of this anxious self-seeking.

In holding that sin posits itself Niebuhr means that man carries within himself a dual awareness. While man knows of his insurmountable finitude, he is also conscious of the totality of which he is a part. The resulting tension creates an anxiety in man which is unbearable but inescapable. This anxiety in turn gives rise to an insatiable temptation to escape the predicament of being human. Niebuhr locates his understanding of man as sinner in this ambivalence:

> The fact is that man is never unconscious of his weakness, of the limited and dependent character of his existence and knowledge. The occasion for his temptation lies in the two facts, his

greatness and his weakness, his unlimited and his limited knowledge, taken together. . . . His sin is never the mere ignorance of
his ignorance. It is always partly an effort to obscure his blindness by overestimating the degree of his sight and to obscure his
insecurity by stretching his power beyond its limits.[9]

Many have stumbled over Niebuhr's ambiguous statement
that "man sins inevitably, but not necessarily." Since he has
insisted that sin posits itself, Niebuhr now has to avoid the logical conclusion that God is the author of evil and man a prede-
termined sinner. This he does by means of his concept of
temptation. Niebuhr views God as providing the setting, while
man inevitably responds. Temptation implies not a causal necessity but an empirical inevitability. In short, Niebuhr does not
explain the nature of sin, but describes its setting and ingredi-
ents. The basic manifestation of sin is pride, which tempts man
to abuse his freedom. Standing at the juncture of nature and
spirit, man recoils into a dehumanizing identification with nature when the strain of proud self-assertion becomes too great.
This, which represents an escape from freedom and responsibility, Niebuhr calls sensuality. The two basic forms of sin are
pride and sensuality, the latter a derivative of the former. They
constitute the two ways by which man attempts to deal with his
position between God and the world. Man is created to obey
God, but he attempts to "play God." Rather than using this
world as he was intended to, man loses himself to it.

According to Niebuhr, the final proof that God is not the
author of sin is man's feeling of guilt. On this point Niebuhr
makes a sharp distinction between the exterior and interior
points of view concerning sin. What to the external observer
may appear to be the necessary outcome of prior decisions is
in reality the result of conscious choice by the agent reflecting
upon himself:

The fact of responsibility is attested by the feeling of remorse or
repentance which follows the sinful action. From an exterior
view not only sin in general but any particular sin may seem to
be the necessary consequence of previous temptations. . . . But

[9] *Ibid.*, p. 181.

the interior view does not allow this interpretation. . . . It discovers that some degree of conscious dishonesty accompanied the act, which means that the self was not deterministically and blindly involved in it.[10]

Niebuhr sees no difficulty in both maintaining human responsibility for actions and asserting their inevitability. Thus he avoids the unending debate between the idealistic contenders for absolute human freedom and the pessimistic advocates of mechanistic determinism. Niebuhr holds that man is not free as such, though he is free in his awareness of his limitations. At the same time, man is not determined in his awareness of motivation and decision, although the external observer, by hindsight, is able to establish a causal nexus between the two. For Niebuhr, freedom is always personal, while determinism is a scientific abstraction. He concludes his discussion of human freedom by asserting: "We cannot, therefore, escape the ultimate paradox that the final exercise of freedom in the transcendent human spirit is its recognition of the false use of that freedom in action. Man is most free in the discovery that he is not free."[11] Implied here is the assumption that in his actions man is always bound by his past and influenced by his expectations. Man's freedom centers in his acknowledgment that he must live in full recognition of his condition.

Niebuhr's discussion of man's status as sinner will be misunderstood if we lose sight of his insistence that man is the point of contact of the natural, social, and religious orders. Niebuhr's interest in analyzing man's nature is motivated by his concern to bring the resources of religion into play in society. As noted earlier, Niebuhr views man as the unique agent who mediates between religion and society. However, though man in his original state is depicted as being able to do so, man-as-sinner is not only unwilling but also unable to carry out his God-given assignment. In addition to describing man's plight following the fall, the Genesis myths depict the natural and social decay which follow upon man's disobedience. Interpersonal innocence gives way to deceit. Peaceful cooperation turns into

[10] *Ibid.*, p. 255.
[11] *Ibid.*, p. 260

competitive annihilation. Social tolerance degenerates into national and international rivalry and turmoil. The story of the flood portrays the depths of man's corruptive influence on both himself and nature. Yet at the same time this myth prefigures the saving grace of God. Just as the natural and social orders are vitiated by sinful man, so the grace of God will be brought to bear on these orders by man. Niebuhr continually attacks any religious understanding, be it pietism or moralism, which is preoccupied with the individual to the detriment of the corporate dimension.

It goes without saying that Niebuhr is well aware that only he who already stands convicted by the loving judgment of God is able to appreciate the full dimensions of man's sinfulness and its reverberations throughout the created order. Even —and perhaps primarily—man's religious notions constantly lead him to justify himself on the basis of his corrupted values. Niebuhr is vehement in stressing that Jesus of Nazareth was persecuted and delivered to his execution by the religious people of his time. But only by hindsight, after one has experienced the redemptive love of God, does one recognize that he has not only fallen short of any standard of perfection, but that his best deeds themselves have added to the corruption. Repentance thus has for Niebuhr the New Testament meaning of a radical about-face in attitude. The grace of God and the faith of man can bring this about.

At this point it must be reiterated that Niebuhr is not particularly interested in a full doctrinal exposition of either Christology or grace. Although he is pre-eminently interested in the work of the Spirit through man, Niebuhr does not intend to minimize the significance of Christology. He acknowledges that the penal theory of salvation on the cross must be kept in careful balance with the view of grace as the inner work of the Spirit. However, more christocentrically oriented theologians have pointed out that Niebuhr has been less than successful in maintaining the proper balance.

With respect to Christology, Niebuhr's interest centers in its ethical significance for man. The revelation of God's love in Christ denies once and for all the human ambition to self-justification—even that of the most pious. Niebuhr views the

Sermon on the Mount as underlining the fact that man, even regenerate man, is unable to fulfill God's law of love. The difference between the sinner and the redeemed is that the latter no longer aims at self-justification. Justified by grace, the redeemed man concerns himself with the real ethical question —how the law of love can be realized in human living. He knows this to be an ongoing task. Regenerate man realizes, on the one hand, that one can never prejudge how the law of love will function in human living, nor, on the other hand, can he claim to have fulfilled its demand in any given instance. He knows that Jesus' ethic is an "impossible possibility"; i.e., one is unable to prejudge the form love will take and to fulfill it in the concrete instance. Yet it is always relevant:

> The ethical demands made by Jesus are incapable of fulfillment in the present existence of man. They proceed from a transcendent and divine unity of essential reality, and their final fulfillment is possible only when God transmutes the present chaos of this world into its final unity. . . . The Kingdom of God is always at hand in the sense that impossibilities are really possible, and lead to new actualities in given moments of history. Nevertheless every actuality of history reveals itself, after the event, as only an approximation of the ideal; and the Kingdom of God is therefore not here. It is in fact always coming but never here.[12]

Niebuhr's ethic is a creative relativism, demanding that the Christian always consider the significance of the love of God in terms of his specific circumstances. Because he no longer aims at self-justification, the Christian can be realistic in his analysis of the problems before him and can accept the necessity for compromise. In this regard, Niebuhr quite properly can be called the "father of contextual ethics." His understanding of ethics has become dominant in American Protestantism.

Niebuhr's emphasis on the context of ethical decision leads him to investigate the two main components of human existence: history and the life of institutions. For him, the former connotes the temporal setting in which man functions. The

[12] *An Interpretation of Christian Ethics* (N.Y., Meridian, 1956), pp. 59–60.

latter, in their rise and fall, are the forces with which man must contend. As man's temporal setting, history is constituted of God's providence and man's ambitions. God uses man's ambitions to achieve his penultimate ends. Man, however, identifies his ambitions with God's will. The result is confusion. Dimly aware that his aspirations outrun his individual potentialities, man creates institutions in a vain attempt to transcend his limitations. Very quickly, however, these institutions, intended to be man's means of realizing his Promethean dreams, develop a life of their own and enslave him to their whims. The result is that man no longer controls either his individual or his corporate life. Institutional life apes the life of the individual by pursuing its own goals of dominance and permanence. And it does so with terrifying intensity.

As the institution seeks dominance and the assurance of its own survival it becomes increasingly susceptible to corruption and tyranny. Inordinate force calls forth counter-force. Unfortunately, the latter, though having begun as a redeeming corrective of the existing institutional injustice, itself becomes caught up in the inevitable process of seeking to be permanent. There is thus a vicious circle of degeneration at the heart of institutional structure. Every institution, the religious included, contains within itself the seeds of its own destruction.

Although the process described above assures that no institution can forever outlive its usefulness, such a control mechanism is purchased at an immense price in human suffering and despair. Aware that nature does not destroy as quickly as it creates, man attempts to alleviate his condition by taking matters into his own hands and subverting the established order. War and revolution, which really offer man little recompense, are the logical outcome.

Having described human life in society in these terms, Niebuhr asks himself what are the implications for the Christian who would live in such a world realistically but not cynically. It is at this point that eschatology assumes a special significance for Niebuhr. Christian man lives with a dual awareness which is succinctly expressed in the Johannine notion of "being in, but not of, the world." Though God's judgment will be revealed in its fullness only beyond history, Niebuhr nevertheless maintains that it has real implications within history. For the Christian, the eschatological parables bear witness to the only valid criterion for responsible human conduct. He is aware that God uses the changes and catastrophes of history to exercise his Lordship. Change and misfortune are not simply the result of man's blindness or of chance. They reveal God's judgment on man's individual and corporate pride.

Because he is aware that his true citizenship is in a Kingdom that will be realized only at the end of history, the Christian is able to withstand the buffeting that is his lot in this life. His realization that the Kingdom is not built by men's hands frees him to be a realist. He is saved from cynicism, however, by the knowledge that he has a God-given vocation. Niebuhr never tires in his insistence that, while the Christian cannot build God's Kingdom in history, he cannot escape involvement in God's ongoing action in history. Niebuhr's emphatic declaration that the Christian cannot abdicate responsibility for critical social involvement arises in this context. To be a Christian means to be radically in the world.

The limited scope of this essay precludes any discussion of Niebuhr's extratheological political theories. It must be pointed out, however, that Niebuhr has devoted considerable attention to the problematics of politics, especially in recent years. His theologically grounded suspicion of all ideologies has allowed him to raise a prophetic voice whenever there is a widespread tendency to interpret complex social movements in simple black-and-white terms. His wise insistence that crusading fanaticism, be it Communist, capitalist, or nationalist, always represents a terrible oversimplification, has had considerable influence on political thinking, both here and abroad.

Since there already exists a considerable body of critical literature concerning Niebuhr's work, we can limit ourselves to a brief estimate of his significance. There is no question but that among contemporary Christian theologians, Reinhold Niebuhr is the only native American to have achieved world-renown. His ability to combine unswerving realism and keen analysis has enabled him to cut through speculative theological systems in order to focus on the essential problem—how man is to understand himself as a citizen of two worlds. While some of his insights concerning man's nature may be inadequate in view of more recent findings, he has made a major contribution to theology by his concentration upon man as the point of contact of the Gospel and the world. Today, when systematic theology is regarded by many as the whole of the theological enterprise, Niebuhr's approach stands as a necessary and important corrective. In addition to reminding the church that it must ceaselessly struggle to relate itself to what is going on in the world, Niebuhr challenges us to develop a more comprehensive and creative understanding of man. To view man simply as a "child of God" and a product of society is no longer sufficient. As Niebuhr himself would readily acknowledge, the task which he embarked upon is still for us unfinished business.

Bibliography

Reinhold Niebuhr, *The Nature and Destiny of Man: A Christian Interpretation*, N.Y., Scribner's, 1946.

Reinhold Niebuhr: His Religious, Social, and Political Thought, Charles W. Kegley and Robert W. Bretall, eds., N.Y., Macmillan, 1956.

H. RICHARD NIEBUHR

Clyde A. Holbrook

Helmut Richard Niebuhr[1] has been called "a theologian's theologian"—a cryptic title signifying that by high professional competence he commanded the respect of his peers. Yet the title may be misleading. It suggests a pretentiousness of manner which found no counterpart in the man himself; it implies that his thought could be grasped only by theological experts; and in the popular imagination it may even tend to anchor him too securely in the role of a technician in theology, whereas his intellectual concerns ranged into the territories of ethics, sociological analysis, history, theological education, and on occasion, metaphysics. However the title be understood, it is intended to affirm that Niebuhr stood in the forefront of contemporary American theologians, and some would say he was the most influential, if not the most widely recognized, among them.

MAJOR PUBLICATIONS

Niebuhr came to the attention of the theological world with the publication of his sociological study *The Social Sources of Denominationalism* (1929). This work ruthlessly exposed the secular factors which have fragmented and distorted the Christian movement in America. It showed incisively how national-

[1] Born, Wright City, Missouri, 1894; graduate of Elmhurst College (1912), Eden Theological Seminary (1915), Washington University (1917), Yale Divinity School (1923), Yale Graduate School (1924); D.D. degrees from Eden Theological Seminary, University of Chicago, Wesleyan University; Litt.D., Franklin and Marshall College; S.T.D., Oberlin College. Ordained minister Evangelical and Reformed Church (United Church of Christ), 1916; pastor, 1916–18; professor, Eden Theological Seminary (1919–22, 1927–31); president, Elmhurst College (1924–27); 1931 member of faculty, Yale Divinity School; died 1962 while Sterling Professor of Theology and Christian Ethics at Yale University.

istic, economic, racial, and regional influences had molded Christianity into their own images. The book was not a "best-seller." Its impact remained largely restricted to the seminaries. Even there the prevailing liberal mind-set of the period greeted it with mixed feelings. Its strong critical tone appealed to many, but its implications for theological and ethical reassessment had yet to win their way. Whatever else his first major publication accomplished, it undoubtedly helped to bring Niebuhr to Yale Divinity School, where he wielded a potent influence upon the development of theology and Christian ethics.

If his first book rehearsed excessively the theme of the church's bondage to social forces, the balance was rectified in his contribution to *The Church against the World* (with Wilhelm Pauck and F. P. Miller, 1935) and in his study *The Kingdom of God in America* (1937). In the latter work he analyzed the several motifs of religious revolution which have guided and energized the Christian movement in its unending dialogue with American culture. Whereas his first book, he observed, had helped to explain why the religious stream had taken certain denominational configurations, this book showed the initiating forces in the religious stream itself, the nature of its unity and its capacity to mold rather than be molded by culture. By the use of the themes of the "sovereignty of God," "the reign of Christ," and "the kingdom on earth," he interpreted the Christian movement as a dynamic process rather than "as an institution or series of institutions." And in this light he showed the shaping and meaning of American history itself. Here Niebuhr displayed his talent for moving penetratingly in the fields of cultural analysis and theological construction. He had marked out the area where culture and faith interplay as a domain peculiarly his own. Here also had begun the tutelage of American theological students in the lively art of dialectical thinking, which moves back and forth between the relativisms of man's cultural productivity and the convictional options of Christian faith.

The broad theme of culture and faith never lost its appeal for Niebuhr. In a book which might be called the most technically theological of his major publications, *The Meaning of Revelation* (1941), he set his conception of revelation against the background of cultural relativism. He found that the absoluteness of Christian revelation does not call for a repudiation of this relativism but for its intensification, because the absolute God who reveals himself in Jesus Christ and through the Christian community relativizes all finite entities, including even the theologian's statements about the absolute! Therefore no place remains for the exaltation of man's historic actions to the level of the absolute and universal. But neither was Niebuhr content to leave revelation itself as a purely private and subjective act. Since revelation takes place within the Christian community, the individual's views on the universal deity are subject to the cross checking and correction of the Christian community in its historic and contemporary forms. Thus the historical and societal factors continue to be influential preventives against sheer eccentricity and antinomianism on the part of individual Christians.

Niebuhr's emphasis on the communal setting of revelation did not lend itself to the idea that all Christians will interpret the interplay of revelation and cultural forces in the same manner. The question of how the Christian and the Christian community are related to culture at large is not settled by recourse to revelation. Rather the Christian finds himself moving between the demands of God derived from revelation, the structural necessities of the Christian church, and the calls of the culture in which he lives his life. To this triple problem Niebuhr turned his attention in what is probably his most widely read book, *Christ and Culture* (1951).

In this work he traced the types of relations which the church has historically adopted in relating its understanding of the mandate of its Lord to culture. He built upon the foundation laid by Ernst Troeltsch's typology of the relation of Christianity to culture, but amended and supplemented it. In place of Troeltsch's threefold pattern—the church, sect, and mystical types—Niebuhr's treatment yielded a fivefold pattern. The two extreme positions he identified as Christ against culture and Christ in agreement with culture. These two types enter into the remaining three, but are reduced in their radicalness by their mutual interaction. The possibility of Christ in agreement with culture is exploited in the synthetic pattern, but here Christ is also regarded as above culture, acting as the supernatural transformer and goal of human aspirations and values. The dualistic type leans more heavily upon the Christ-against-culture pattern, as the Christian is subject both to the authority of the institutions of society to which he properly owes allegiance and to the Christ who is the judge of that society. The fifth type, the conversionist position, also maintains the opposition between Christ and culture, but in spite of man's fallen nature, which appears in various cultural embodiments and is transmitted by them, it maintains that Christ can effectively enter into the transformation of culture. It refuses to lead either to the extremes of a Christian separation from the world or to the inexorable agony called for by the dualistic pattern. The conversionist position was obviously most congenial to Niebuhr himself, although his identification with the position is something less than explicit.

In *Radical Monotheism and Western Culture, with Supplementary Essays* Niebuhr once more attacked the problem of culture and faith. Here he set forth, more fully than he had in *The Meaning of Revelation,* his conception of radical theocentrism as a form of human faith.

> For radical monotheism the value-center is neither a closed society nor the principle of such a society, but the principle of being itself; its reference is to no one reality among the many, but one beyond all the many, whence all the many derive their being, and by participation in which they exist. As faith, it is reliance on the source of all being for the significance of the self and of all that exists. . . . It is the confidence that whatever is, is good, because it exists as one thing among the many, which all have their origin and their being, in the One—the principle of being which is also the principle of value.[2]

In these abstract terms one can detect the overtones of the Augustinian and Edwardian modes of thought which have suffused much of Niebuhr's theological work.

In his exploration of the relation of this radical faith to competing objects of loyalty found in the religious, political, and

[2] (N.Y., Harper, 1960), p. 32.

scientific worlds, he showed the crucial battle of faith which is to be waged between the polytheisms of culture and the high and austere faith called for by the One God. Man's natural religion, as he was fond of pointing out, is polytheism or henotheism, each of which builds about itself exclusive societies between which struggles for power and influence continue. The faith of radical monotheism challenges the exclusiveness of these societies by virtue of its lodgement in the One who is the undergirding source of all being and value.

The supplementary essays which conclude the book have for the most part been previously published. They include his contribution to the definition and role of theology, the nature of value, the approach to the problem of God's existence, and the moral element in contemporary science. Although these essays appear as an addendum to the volume, each serves as an expansion or commentary upon themes broached in the main segment of the book.

Niebuhr did not confine his attention to theology and Christian ethics. In 1953 he was appointed the director of a major study of theological education in this country and Canada. With Daniel D. Williams and James M. Gustafson he helped prepare and edit three volumes and several bulletins dealing with the nature of the Protestant ministry, its aims and methods, as well as the criticisms launched against seminary education and recommendations for improvement. These books, published in the years 1956–57, comprised a thorough and searching analysis of the needs of the churches and theological schools, and they pointed the direction for theological studies.[3]

BACKGROUNDS OF NIEBUHR'S THOUGHT

Only with great hesitation can an attempt be made to designate several of the factors which provide a context for Niebuhr's

[3] A full bibliography by Raymond Morris of Niebuhr's writings and reactions to them may be found in *Faith and Ethics,* edited by Paul Ramsey (N.Y., Harper, 1957). *Radical Monotheism and Western Culture* and *The Responsible Self* (the latter published posthumously, N.Y., Harper, 1963) appeared after the bibliography was prepared and therefore were not included.

thinking. His was an evangelical heritage whose roots run back through the classical affirmations of the Protestant Reformation to Augustine and Paul. As a matter of personal conviction and thought, the sovereignty of God stands to the foreground. The God who is unapproachable in his awesome power, authority, and justice approaches man in Jesus Christ with a mercy which is powerful and a love which is just. Nothing escapes this One's searching eye; nothing in all creation falls outside the bounds of his care. The church dedicated to his service and worship is itself ever under the divine judgment and hope. It is called to be an obedient community under its Lord, yet its ranks number sinners whose obedience and trust, weak and fragile as these may be, are accepted by the grace of its Lord. Although there has always been in this heritage a danger of an ingrown pietism, a preoccupation with the soul and its travail, there stands beside this tendency a robust intent to infuse and transform the structures of civilization with that sense of prophetic judgment and loving mercy which the Christian community experiences in its own life. From its Calvinist sources this tradition draws its social passion to make the kingdoms of this world the Kingdom of its Lord. Yet it knows that within the limits of historic time and the conditions of human sin, this consummation remains a hope which judges the inadequacy of human effort yet energizes men to fresh assaults upon moral evils. The ethical notes which resound throughout this movement are those of gratitude and responsibility: gratitude for divine acceptance, which frees from self-interest, and responsibility to the source of men's hope and for the neighbor.

At the end of the First World War a vigorous theological movement, associated with the names of Karl Barth and Emil Brunner, broke upon the Continental theological scene. With its return to the Reformation insights of the transcendent divine sovereignty, the Lordship of Christ, the sinfulness of man, the importance of revelation, the sense of the significance of the church, and the reawakened exploration of what Barth called the "strange new world of the Bible" where "the Word of God" is anchored, the prevailing theological liberalism received a serious setback. In this country, which had known the "empirical" theology of D. C. Macintosh and the religious naturalism of H. N. Wieman as well as less radical forms of liberalism, there were few who were ready to understand or appreciate what seemed to many a perverse attachment to doctrines supposedly long since sent to the limbo of dead theological contentions. "Postwar pessimism," "failure of nerve," "retreat from reason"—these were some of the expressions which quickly sprang to mind to explain this strange treason to the conceptions of a benevolent deity, a prophetic Jesus, and a rationally humane human nature.

Among those on this side of the Atlantic whose sensitive minds were ready to catch the deeper meaning of the "crisis theology" were the Niebuhr brothers. The reading of man's situation found in the new movement was not for them a nostalgic return to the Reformation, nor a "bloodless dance of categories" extracted from Scripture by pedantic, closeted exegetes. Nor was it merely a transitory phase induced by postwar discouragement, soon to be replaced by a renascent confidence in man's upward social and moral progress. Rather it was a realistic description of contemporary man's condition when the inherited values of the Renaissance and Enlightenment had proved incapable of preventing war's horror, economic depressions, and incipient political anarchy. The value center of Western civilization had given way; it was time once more to reassess man's image of himself, to seek out once more the points where modern man's ailments arose and to rediscover the grounds of hope resident in the commanding convictions of once-powerful religious traditions.

The evangelical tradition in which the Niebuhrs were reared was of course congenial to the offerings of the neo-Reformation theology. And from this common ground, they each in his own way broke down the American wall of theological isolationism. They provided an opening for a two-way intellectual commerce between Continental theology and American liberalism, without themselves becoming mediating theologians. They did not give up their liberal concern with society's problems or the need for study of social structures; they did not yield to the biblicism inherent in much of the Continental movement; their terminology, though redolent with traditional concepts, was also a translation of a foreign theological jargon into a language which could be understood by the educated American. Together with Paul Tillich, whom they were instrumental in introducing to this country, they brought about a virtual theological renaissance, whose impact has been felt not only in the churches of America but among the "cultured half-believers and active disbelievers."

The richly varied academic tradition of nineteenth-century Protestant theology has also provided substantial fare for Niebuhr's theological stance. One may detect in his writings the impact of Kant and the post-Kantians, who had raised in an especially provocative way questions about the nature of theological knowledge and evidence as well as that more general distinction between theoretical and practical knowledge with which Niebuhr dealt in *The Meaning of Revelation*. Schleiermacher also continued to hold interest for Niebuhr as the pivotal figure whose treatment of theological method and revelation provided the setting for the development of both liberal theology and the reaction against it as seen in the early Barth. With these problems Niebuhr continued to wrestle in the development of his own theological style and his views on revelation. In the development of the latter, Kierkegaard, the creative, nonacademic mind of the nineteenth century, wielded a major influence. In Kierkegaard's existential stance and sharply dialectical thought, Niebuhr found re-enforcement and stimulation for his own conceptions of decision, reduplication in life of thought and in thought of life, participative knowledge, and of the importance of understanding faith in ontological rather than simply noetic categories. But perhaps no figure of the recent past laid so lasting an impress upon Niebuhr as did Ernst Troeltsch. On the one hand, Troeltsch struggled with the problem of historical method and its assertions, and on the other, the claims for the truth and uniqueness of Christian insights as based on historical events. The issue of universal validity as it stands confronted by the intransigent relativism of all historical phenomena, including the observer and interpreter as posed by Troeltsch's efforts, marked out the area within which Niebuhr accomplished much of his work. The same problem also directed him toward the development of a dialectical way of thinking by which he wove patterns of comprehension from the interplay between rigorous attention to the concrete events of human history and the deliverances of revelation. Hans Frei interprets Niebuhr's encounter with both Barth and Troeltsch as resulting in an effort "to unite a doctrine of radical monotheism and Christocentric revelation with an understanding of our life as responsible persons in an endlessly varied cultural history."[4]

Only brief mention may be made of others who have discernibly influenced Niebuhr. Jonathan Edwards, to whom Niebuhr gave protracted attention, weighed heavily in the formation of his own theories on value as well as in his theological understanding of American culture. Josiah Royce, with his treatment of the themes of loyalty and community, and F. D. Maurice, in whom, said Niebuhr, "the conversionist idea is more clearly expressed than in any other modern Christian thinker and leader," have both dealt with themes near to Niebuhr's paramount concern with culture. Martin Buber's "I-Thou" played an extremely important role in Niebuhr's formulations of the personalistic character of revelation. Indeed, much of Buber's influence on American Protestant thought probably came through Niebuhr's teaching and writings. Although one would have difficulty in tracking down with precision the influence of A. N. Whitehead, it could be maintained with some success that Niebuhr's sensitive concern for nature in the divine economy, his portrayal of the dynamic interrelations of created beings and relativistic interpretation of value, and perhaps certain tendencies to metaphysical formulation owe something to Whitehead's process philosophy.

Yet having said as much as this concerning influences, one realizes that all talk of formative factors comes to an end in the frustration of mere conjecture. The inexplicit influences of home and family, friends, and conversations with colleagues and students—the value of which Niebuhr was ever ready to acknowledge—may weigh as heavily as the formal, academic factors.

MOTIFS IN NIEBUHR'S THEOLOGY

If any one theme can be considered pivotal in Niebuhr's theology, it is his theocentrism. In *Radical Monotheism and*

[4] *Faith and Ethics*, p. 64.

Western Culture we have noticed his treatment of the concept
in relatively abstract or ontological terms. And in more personalistic terms it forms the burden of the concluding chapter
of *The Meaning of Revelation.*

To affirm the pre-eminence of God over life is not to offer
for logical or empirical testing a hypothesis about the possible
existence or nature of deity. Nor is it to be taken first of all as
doctrine to be defended through thick and thin. Rather it is the
confession that when a person and a community have been met
by the Ultimate One, revealed through Jesus Christ, life moves
from a new source of strength and intelligibility for which no
other finite, created being can be substituted. The mystery which
enfolds the beginnings and endings of life is illuminated by the
awareness of One whose knowledge and love meet man's search-
ings; the chaotic and mutually conflicting ends feverishly sought
fall into intelligible focus, and the potential meaninglessness of
human existence is subverted by a developing trust in Him who
is trustworthy above all others.

There may be other ways in which the question of God's
nature and existence may arise, but for Niebuhr the problem
was first of all practical, "a problem of human existence and
destiny, of the meaning of inner life in general and of the life
of self and its community in particular." Therefore his approach
to the conception of deity was by way of "the universal experience of faith, of reliance or trust in something," by which men
seek to find meaning in life. A study of the manifold faiths to
which men pathetically cling shows that polytheism is the
common form religious faith takes—a polytheism centered upon
the competing gods of success, sex, national honor, class, family,
and even religion itself. Yet none of these stands the test of a
universal and absolute commitment; none of these objects of
adoration sustains the erosive work of time and the destructive
power of fierce conflict for supremacy. "The causes for which
we live all die." Yet there is that which in Whitehead's terminology meets man as the Void or the Enemy, that implacable
reality which is the enemy of all the gods, but which itself is the
power by which all things come to be. For the Christian, as
Niebuhr understood the matter, the turning point comes when
man's faith is attached to the Void or Enemy, who in that faith
is found also to be the trustworthy Friend and Sustainer.

In that transition and its continuing impact lies the basis of a life lived not in restful ease but in hope and confidence, ever sensitized by repentance, thereby constituting the permanently revolutionary character of Christian existence. Henceforth in referring to God, implicitly if not explicitly, one confesses that He is "Our Father or Lord," since whatever assertions are made about deity are uttered from the ground of the faith relation itself. Questions about the First Cause, the nature of substance, or the Final Purpose are not to be pursued as though in independence of that relation satisfactory answers to life's meaning could be found. When questions such as these are posed they presuppose doubt about the existence and goodness of deity, which is to say that the questioner, if in earnest, has simply moved to some other faith in which doubt of deity becomes the first principle of inquiry. Or, one is asking a metaphysical type of question to which the proper answer must be given in metaphysical or speculative terms rather than in existential or religious terms. In fact, in these inquiries the term "God" has itself shifted in meaning, from the living God of personal encounter and faith to God conceived as an impersonal explanatory principle behind phenomena. But for Niebuhr conceptions of the latter type were beside the mark. God is not known as He is in Himself (aseity). Rather, "What is known and knowable in theology is God in relation to self and to neighbor, and self and neighbor in relation to God."[5] From within this intense interrelatedness of God and man in which, to be sure, not man but God is always first in a logical and valuational sense, the Christian theologian does his work of clarifying the nature of the relation itself. He does not possess faith without reason, nor reason without faith; he operates, so far as human capacity allows, with faithful reasoning to carry out the explicative and normative task which his vocation as theologian lays upon him. Thus Niebuhr's theocentrism manifests itself at last in dictating the context and mode in which the theologian works.

By saying that God is first, one is also affirming that revelation is first. It is the beginning point of theological reflection. For Niebuhr the term "revelation" did not refer to a method of private access to divine truths. It was not tied to the defensive

[5] *The Purpose of the Church and Its Ministry* (N.Y., Harper, 1956), pp. 112 ff.

strategy of churches who wish to safeguard their authority and influence over society. Nor was it an attempt to stir up the fires of the fruitless ancient controversy of faith versus reason by reversion to the biblical literalism of yesteryear. Rather, in turning to revelation the Christian movement once more seeks to understand its sources of vitality, to chart and correct its course in an era where the presuppositions and points of view with which men evaluate life are of crucial importance in understanding what is valuable and true. The reinvestigation of revelation takes place in a context of thought where men's statements about the universal or absolute are themselves neither universally valid nor absolutely true. And the theologian's problem is set by this realization that the relativity which marks statements made in other areas of thought no less marks statements which he makes. He must work, conscious that theological formulations of the past as well as his own are relativized by the cultural forces in which they arise. He can speak from no pinnacle of observation which is exempt from the cultural stream in which others are also immersed.

However, recognition of this fact does not in Niebuhr's view necessarily lead to skepticism nor to an irrational loss of confidence in reason itself. In the case of theology an adequately critical approach to its task may, within the segment of history for which it assumes responsibility, seek the intelligible patterns of the religious life of the Christian community, without at the same time demanding that its findings be normative for all religious life. Historical reason will know the "length of its tether," but it will not yield to the false notion that a conditioned standpoint must deny the reality of that which is seen from that standpoint. "It is not apparent," as Niebuhr argued, "that one who knows that his concepts are not universal must also doubt that they are concepts of the universal, or that one who understands how all experience is historically mediated must believe that nothing is mediated through history."[6] To be sure, all acceptance of reality is accompanied by some form of faith, but faith also finds justification in ways appropriate to its nature and by its fruits.

[6] *The Meaning of Revelation* (N.Y., Macmillan, 1941), pp. 18–19.

Thus the theologian, although confined "to the knowledge of God which is possible to those who live in Christian history," can think with Christianity about God from the standpoint which that position affords, interpreting, clarifying, and correcting the insights found there. He has no choice but to begin his work from those standpoints which have developed from revelatory events in Christian history. He also has the exacting task of spelling out the contemporary nature and significance of that reality as it continues to disclose itself. "Such a theology of revelation is objectively relativistic, proceeding with confidence in the independent reality of what is seen, though recognizing that its assertions about that reality are meaningful only to those who look upon it from the same standpoint."[7] Its characteristic mode of expression must therefore be confessional and non-defensive.

Niebuhr had many ways of describing revelation. In a general statement he spoke of revelation as an event which occurs in Christian history conditioning all thinking: ". . . through this happening we are enabled to apprehend what we are, what we are suffering and doing and what the potentialities are. What is otherwise arbitrary and dumb fact becomes related, intelligible and eloquent fact through revelatory event."[8] When he interpreted revelation more fully, he referred to it as

the moment in our history through which we know ourselves to be known from beginning to end, in which we are apprehended by the knower; it means the self-disclosing of that eternal knower. . . . Revelation means that we find ourselves to be valued rather than valuing and that all our values are transvaluated by the activity of a universal valuer. . . . When we speak of revelation we mean that moment when we are given a new faith, to cleave to and to betray, and a new standard, to follow and deny.[9]

That event in the internal history of the Christian community which makes sense of human existence in its heights and depths, which itself is intelligible and which, by the decision it calls

[7] *Ibid.*, p. 22.
[8] *Ibid.*, p. 138.
[9] *Ibid.*, pp. 153-4.

forth, sets in motion the unending transformation of mind and life, is revelation.

Although Niebuhr saw the locus of revelation in Jesus Christ, he carefully distinguished the role of Christ from the ultimate object of revelation. Christ does not take God's place. It is one thing to seek the triumph of Christ's cause; it is another matter "to substitute the Lordship of Christ for the Lordship of God," as though Christ's devotion to the will of the Father were a matter of indifference to Christian faith.[10] Christ's fidelity to the Father and his status as Son of the Father indicate that there is One beyond him to whose service he summons men. Even as he lived to God and through him God lived with men, so his followers are called to the double movement in the religio-ethical life; from the world to God and from God back into the cares and concerns of the world.[11] In Christ men may find what Niebuhr called "three notes": "The note that the valuing, saving power in the world is the principle of being itself; that the ultimate principle of being gives and maintains and re-establishes worth; that they [men] have been called upon to make the cause of that God their cause."[12] Thus Jesus Christ is inseparable from revelation, but what is revealed by him is the Ultimate One whom men meet in the personal encounter of the I-Thou relation.

In the outworking of revelation Niebuhr discerned a process which converts men's natural appreciations and evaluations of moral law, attitudes toward nature and science, history and religious knowledge. The moral law is now known as the demand of one from whom there is no escape, "whose seriousness of purpose will not suffer that his work be destroyed by the evasions and transgressions of this pitiful, anarchical creature. . . ."[13] It has universal sway, including in its domain both rational and arational creatures, "good" and "bad" people—as the world judges them. And since men are dealing with a living God, there can be no absolutizing of commandments into specific rules of conduct. "What is commanded by God is commanded anew in

[10] *Radical Monotheism*, pp. 59–60.
[11] *Christ and Culture* (N.Y., Harper, 1956), p. 29.
[12] *Radical Monotheism*, p. 43.
[13] *The Meaning of Revelation*, p. 165.

every new moment for that moment" and calls in turn for a resiliency of spirit answerable to a living authority, as well as to the concrete deeds of the situation. Similarly the human provincialisms and pride which infect men's views of nature are brought under judgment by revelation. When one meets the Creator, "it is no longer necessary to defend man's place by a reading of history which establishes his superiority to all other creatures. To be a man does not now mean to be a lord of the beasts but a child of God." Science is free to go about its business without fear of a new theological bondage in the light of a faith "that nothing God has made is mean or unclean," or forbidden to its search.[14] Man's natural knowledge and expectations about God are likewise cast in a transforming light by revelation. In Christ, God meets men "not as the one beyond the many" gods but "as the one who acts in and through all things." His unity of will draws men's disunity into a new integrity of being. His power, displayed in the apparent weakness of the cross, turns out to be a conquering power which makes even death its instrument of hope and salvation. His goodness reverses human expectations for self-centered benefits, and men discover that they "sought a good to love and were found by a good that loved them."[15]

It would be easy to conclude that since revelation takes place in what Niebuhr called internal history, he had lost sight of its relation to external history. Yet the dialectical bent of his mind can be seen in the way in which throughout his analysis of revelation he has also retained a firm grasp upon the realities of external events. He has continued to move between the realm of participative, lived history and the realm of speculative, observed history. Or as he flatly put it, "Internal life does not exist without external embodiment." Therefore the Bible, the traditions, rites, and story of the churches' behavior in history, as well as the events in human culture generally, have their part to play in the way in which the Christian lives his life. The life under revelation does not take place in a vacuum. Revelation cannot be reduced to publicly observed events, but the perspectives and attitudes it creates find expression in the public domain.

[14] *Ibid.*, p. 173.
[15] *Ibid.*, p. 189.

Though we cannot point to what we mean by revelation by directing attention to the historic facts as embodied and as regarded
from without, we can have no continuing inner history through
which to point without embodiment. . . . External history is the
medium in which internal history exists and comes to life.[16]

MOTIFS IN NIEBUHR'S ETHICS

Niebuhr left behind him no final, systematic treatise on Christian ethics. His posthumous volume *The Responsible Self* might
have been the prologue to such a work, but it must now remain
a broken fragment barely pointing directions which he might
have taken had time served him better. For the most part the
book does not introduce unfamiliar motifs of his thought, but
it does indicate his persevering interest in seeking out highly
illuminative symbols and figures in which to express the moral
life and the relevance of Christ to ethics. Here he offered a
phenomenology of the moral life cast in the model of man the
answerer or responder who seeks a fitting response to a situation.
In this analysis he construed the moral situation as such without
particular reference to Christian elements, but in the Appendix
of the volume he turned to the subject of adequate metaphors
and symbols in which to cast the role of Christ in respect to the
moral life. The conception of man the answerer Niebuhr saw
as the image in which ethical decisions in fact take place in any
community, but in the Christian community where his own
thought came to lodge he saw man as the being who is responsible to the dynamic, single God revealed in Jesus Christ. Thus
in this book as in his earlier works his radical monotheism
comes to the foreground as one of the central motifs of his
constructive endeavors.

From his radical monotheism was drawn his insistence upon
the relativity of all created beings, events, and principles. This
meant that one does not expect from Niebuhr the detailed laying
out of certain virtues, rules, or principles which popularly are
thought to constitute Christian ethics. Principles, values, virtues
may have their place within ethical reflection and action, but
Niebuhr would not hear of the absolutizing of any of them, not

[16] *Ibid.*, pp. 89–90.

even that of love. God is the only absolute and universal being; all else has a temporary validity. From the principle of radical monotheism also comes the freedom for the moral agent to take account of the many factors relevant to moral decision in concrete situations. He does not begin with some abstract norm which then is applied to specific cases; he begins rather with the concrete situation as interpreted in the light of what God has done and is doing—sustaining, judging, and redeeming. It is the obligation of the moral agent to reflect into that situation, with all the resources of knowledge and insight at his command, his understanding of the divine will. In general—and therefore in somewhat misleading terms—the Christian's task is to bring to bear, so far as possible, that sensitively unifying relation among beings which he finds disclosed by God in Jesus Christ.

No man's moral actions fulfill perfectly the imperatives of faith, but he stands justified by grace in his shortcomings. He cannot callously hold himself guiltless before men and God; repentant action is still called for. But grace operates redemptively by enabling him to accept himself with his failures and to get on with the job of responsible moral action without the self-concerned introspective scrutiny of motive which halts action. And the Lord of history takes even the misshapen products of human decision and action within the orbit of his grace and power, turning them into the service of his own glory. Man's job is to be a faithful, hopeful, and conscientious respondent to God's claim; it is not that of assuming proprietary obligations and rights over the universe.

Responsible moral action was in Niebuhr's view no simple matter. Faith calls men to know the technical dimensions of the situations wherein they are called to act. The secular world is laid under tribute with its knowledge of psychology, philosophy, sociology, economics, and government, for one does not become a Christian moralist or actor by closeting himself with books on "Christian ethics." As James Gustafson sees it, "Significant meaning and interpretation of life can be derived from disciplines which are not concerned with the ultimate meaning of life, or which even have a clearly inadequate view of life's meaning."[17] The structures of power and authority within which

[17] *Faith and Ethics,* p. 121.

life is lived, as well as the nature of the deeply personal and interpersonal relations by which values come into being, must be understood. If the Christian is to be relevant to his time and place, he must do vastly more than concentrate upon his motivations. Love, justice, and sincerity are no substitutes for knowledge. Neither are abstract speculations about value or ontology replacements for informed policy decisions.

Thus there seem to be several foci to Niebuhr's view of Christian ethics. The first is the revelational foundation which is spelled out in the theological and ethical implications of the permanently revolutionary character of the Christian life. The second is the intensely existential, participative character of ethical reflection, decision, and action. The third is the concern for social relevance and realism. And the fourth is the sense of the dynamic interrelatedness of personal, religious, and social factors in human history within which moral action takes place. The critical understanding of these foci as they continuously interplay within the Christian community and between it and culture generally marks Christian ethics as a field of study.

EVALUATIVE COMMENTS ON NIEBUHR'S THOUGHT

The vigor and persuasive power with which Niebuhr participated in the contemporary theological scene have attracted both negative criticism and enthusiastic respect, often from the same person. The direction taken by this criticism can be indicated by certain types of questions which his position evoked. However, no attempt will be made to reach a final assessment of either Niebuhr or his critics.

Some of the principal questions cluster about two centers in his position: his theological presentation with its emphasis on revelation and radical monotheism and his treatment of ethics as it focuses upon relativism.

Niebuhr speaks of the impossibility of understanding Christian revelation except from the faith posture which revelation itself creates. Does this mean only that one cannot appreciate an experience until one has passed through it for himself? And if so, then is not the participant in the experience cut off from any significant discourse about the experience with those to whom the revelatory event has not occurred? Can he speak to or hope for understanding from only those within the community where revelation has been doing its work? One can talk around revelation, it seems; can speak and act from the ground it affords, but one can never state directly what the content of revelation is without seriously misleading others as to its true nature. Yet if one is to carry on a dialogue with a culture which denies or is unaware of revelation, what possible grounds remain for intelligible discourse? To argue that every person speaks from a faith stance which is ultimately inaccessible to others may be correct as an observation, but since it appears that more people are able to understand each other on these grounds than the proponent of revelation can muster for his position, the argument remains indecisive. There is no universal court of appeals in which the reality of faith postures can be adjudicated. The answer lies in conversion or decision. As Niebuhr saw it, the full intelligibility of human existence swings into view only when man is encountered by the Ultimate One. It is God, not man, that at last is the supreme actor in providing the grounds for communication between the "outsider" and the "insider." Short of that resolution, a gulf stands between Niebuhr and his critic.

In a similar vein the agnostic question is raised as to how one judges among competing "revelations." What criteria can be offered by which to test the validity of revelation? Of course the manner in which this type of question is posed shows that the critic has not grasped Niebuhr's interpretation. That is revelation which itself provides the criteria by which all other options are tested; therefore whatever tests are offered as ultimately decisive are themselves outside the arena of the testable. They provide the grounds for evaluation, but are not themselves being evaluated. But even these, as they are held by finite, fallible humans amid the relativities of historical existence, provide no test for universal and absolute validity. After all, man is not himself a universal spectator of existence; he cannot pretend to possess, as over against the Ultimate Being, a standpoint of evaluation which escapes his finitude and sin. Interpretive presuppositions are inevitable, but they are to be held confessionally, and their validity can be assessed not simply by their initial convincement but by the degree to which, in the presence of an enormously varied human experience, they do justice to the full flavor of existence and bring intelligibility into its confusion.

In respect to Niebuhr's ethic, questions have often centered on his insistence on "relativity." His extreme concern for social relevance and his understanding of the way in which radical monotheism relativizes all finite beings and functions seem to have led him to an extravagant estimate of the role of "relativism." Some critics see this emphasis as derogating from the importance of ethical principle for the sake of expedience, or even threatening to undermine the integrity of the moral agent.

As a way of avoiding the wooden rigidity of much ethical speculation and the inherent difficulty of gearing ethical values into the dynamics of society, Niebuhr's "contextualist" or "situational" ethics acts both as a corrective and as a way of meeting unpredictable moral demands. If Niebuhr had employed the term "relationalism" to describe the ethical situation, possibly the taint of the term "relativism" could be removed and his position would be more adequately represented. It is in relations that values come to be; it is in faithfulness to relations that moral action takes place; it is in relation to God, the self, and one's companions that virtues are to be defined. In any case, what is distinctly inappropriate to Niebuhr's thought is any notion of "relativism" which would conceive good or bad as merely expressions of psychological approval or disapproval.

The questions raised above touch only the more obvious directions which criticism may take. The fertility and subtlety of Niebuhr's thought inevitably provoke questioning, but also prompt reassessment of one's own position. His views on the relation of value and being, his Christology, his dialectical manner of thinking, or any one of a number of issues he treated may at first puzzle, then interest, and finally persuade his listener or reader that he too must bend his mind to a more profound and complex formulation of these issues. So questioning begun in criticism or for information has a way of turning into appreciation, or more importantly, into a renewal of one's own quest for theological understanding.

NIEBUHR THE TEACHER

Niebuhr's influence has been felt as much as a teacher as by the books and articles he has written. In the classroom he lectured as one who vigorously reconsidered at the time what he is saying, and he thereby exhibited an amazing capacity for involving his students in the development of his thought. He moved about and through a subject from many angles, and seldom did one leave without feeling that he had not only watched a first-class supple mind at grips with a major issue, but that in some strange way he had participated in an intellectual exploration of territories scarcely known before.

Even as he demanded much of himself, so his students were held to the mark of careful preparation and hard thinking. Yet he did not seek a meek acceptance of his views. It was characteristic of him that he welcomed the challenge and thoughtful criticism of his students rather than a slavish discipleship. His was not a system of theology or theological ethics to be learned by rote or repetition; it was a way in which to walk, a method which, by opening new viewpoints, might even be turned against Niebuhr himself.

As a counselor of students of high degree and low, he was considerate and sensitive. Many a student in personal or vocational perplexity found in him a tactful and intelligent guide, one whose openness of manner preserved the dignity of the inquirer, yet in a quite unsentimental way accepted him into the orbit of his concern. It is no wonder that the high respect in which he was held usually merged into affection.

Niebuhr's influence continues to be felt in the academic world through these students, many of whom teach in theological seminaries, colleges, and universities. His past writings continue to challenge the attention of both the church and the world, as their various reprintings show. His writings charted new directions of theological inquiry as his restless, probing mind continued to pioneer on the frontier of human existence where the spirit of man is searched, wounded, and healed by the Eternal.

Bibliography

H. Richard Niebuhr, *Christ and Culture*, N.Y., Harper, 1956. (Harper Torchbooks).

Faith and Ethics, Paul Ramsey, ed., N.Y., Harper, 1957.

KARL BARTH

Daniel Jenkins

Karl Barth is considered by many students of theology to be the outstanding Protestant theologian of the twentieth century. As far back as 1937 H. R. Mackintosh, the shrewdest and most balanced of Scottish scholars, declared that in Barth "we have incontestably the greatest figure in Christian theology that has appeared for decades." Others have mentioned him in the same breath with Luther and Calvin. He is credited with having had the decisive influence in the remarkable change which has overtaken theology in the past generation.

To those who know him, Karl Barth is also one of the outstanding persons of our time. He was born in 1886, the son of a Swiss professor, and since his dismissal from his post at the University of Bonn by the Hitler regime he has spent the larger part of his working life as Professor of Theology in his native city of Basel. He is a brisk and vigorous man of bursting eloquence and lively humor, with a face of the greatest authority and distinction. The size and range of his theological output strikes awe into the hearts even of those trained in the remorseless schools of German scholarship, but he is also a lover of Mozart and likes nothing so much, after a day's hard work on his *Church Dogmatics,* as a drink and a smoke and a visit to the cinema. When he visited England in 1956 to receive a *Festschrift* on his seventieth birthday, he completely captivated the journalists of the secular press who interviewed him.

Yet as a theologian he is also much spoken against and the impression given of his teaching in short summaries is often hard to reconcile with the impression he makes as a man. His influence may be widely diffused, but the number of his professed followers, especially in the Anglo-Saxon countries, appears to be quite small. His voluminous works are more often referred to than actually quoted, and his distinctive position in theology is frequently described in singularly unattractive terms.

He is said to have brought original sin back into theology, to have emphasized the greatness of the gulf between God and man, and to have poured scorn on reason and philosophy. In all, he is made to appear like an old-fashioned Evangelical preacher of the type popularly known as "strict Calvinist."

Barth is certainly not that, and the peculiar impact which he has made upon the theological thought of our time is best understood when he is seen against his historical background. Like most of the Protestant students of his generation, he was brought up under the influence of theological liberalism. He spent some time at the feet of Harnack in Berlin and, like Tillich, was influenced by the movement of religious socialism. Then came the catastrophic event of the First World War and, although Barth was a citizen of a neutral country, he found himself questioning radically the assumptions upon which thought and life had been based in church and society. As a young pastor in Safenwil in Switzerland, he discovered that he had nothing to preach when he stood up before his people in the pulpit. In his perplexity he turned to that unfailing source of renewal to the men of the Reformation, the Epistle to the Romans. He did so, as he has said, like a man clutching at a rope when he was falling. When he wrote his commentary on Romans to describe what he had found, he discovered that the rope had rung a bell which could be heard all over Europe. This brilliantly sophisticated young liberal had learned again what the Epistle to the Romans was all about—that God, the living God, had come to deliver perplexed, self-contradictory men like himself from their sins through the power of Jesus Christ.

This was much more startling news in the theological world of 1918 than it would be today. Up to that time there had been two main lines of interest in Protestant theology. One was that of historical criticism of the Bible. This was of great value on its own level, but it often led men to disparage the significance of the testimony of the apostolic community to Jesus as being based not on history but on faith. The picture of the "historical Jesus" which, despite the critical work of Albert Schweitzer and others, still fascinated men, seemed often to owe as much to current notions of ideal manhood as they did to the New Testament. The other interest of many theologians was that of trying to find a justification for religious experience in a universe dominated by ideas, derived from scientific philosophy and other sources, which seemed to leave little room for such experience.

Such theology seemed always to be on the defensive and more anxious to accommodate the Christian faith to other influences in the world around it than to heed what the Bible really says. The result was that when preachers spoke about God they sounded as though they were doing little more than speaking about man in a loud voice. What Barth discovered from the Epistle to the Romans was that this was not the way to speak about God. He had received entry into what he called "the strange new world within the Bible," where God and not man was in the center. The effect of his commentary on Romans, which was a huge, breathless, exciting sermon rather than a commentary in the accepted sense, was to make men aware with new freshness and power that God had really come into the midst of human self-contradiction and despair and that what He thought about men was more important than what they thought about Him. What Kierkegaard had been trying brokenly to express in a largely negative way in Denmark nearly a century earlier was now boldly trumpeted forth.

Perhaps no other book of Barth's has had the same impact as the *Römerbrief,* and even now, after all these years and despite many changes of emphasis in his position, it remains the best introduction to his work. No book expresses his spirit more vividly and dramatically. Since it appeared, however, a vast corpus of literature has poured out from his pen. He must be among the most prolific not merely of theologians but of all writers. Even Erle Stanley Gardner cannot have produced more words than Karl Barth. He has published two sets of expositions of the Apostles' Creed, a series of Gifford Lectures, an outstanding book on Anselm, many pamphlets and occasional papers, and, in a different vein, a large volume of studies of nineteenth-century thought, translated as *From Rousseau to Ritschl.* All these, which would add up to a substantial life's output for an ordinary scholar, are dwarfed, however, by his gigantic *Church Dogmatics.* This remarkable work has developed throughout the years into one of the vastest literary projects ever undertaken by a single individual. Twelve volumes have already appeared, all of them very large and some of them running to nearly a thousand pages, with many long sections in small print—and the end, after over thirty years of work, is still not in sight. It is this great range of Alpine peaks which makes Barth's major contribution to theology and by which he would have his work assessed.

What are the qualities of Barth's work, as exemplified chiefly in the *Dogmatics,* which make intelligible the extent of his reputation and influence? There are at least seven which stand out.

First, his is the most massive and sustained theological enterprise of our time, rivaling the greatest systematic efforts of history. We are so accustomed to hearing of the dethronement of theology from her place as the "Queen of the Sciences" as compared with the "ages of faith" that the very existence of Barth's work is a testimony to the reality of God. Confronted by the long shelf of the *Dogmatics,* one is compelled to say, "Here, at least, is a man who believes in God." This is not, of course, a matter of their bulk alone. It is, as we shall see, a cause for regret that Barth has not found it possible to produce his work in more concentrated form. But he has created a great treasure house of theological truth, where fresh insights into familiar matters and into others which have been long neglected are constantly to be found. Whether one agrees with his general approach or not, no one seriously concerned with theology can read Barth on, say, the Trinity, the nature of religion, the attributes or perfections of God, predestination, angels, the nihil, time, and relations between men and women, or upon the significance of the "deep sleep" into which Adam fell before the birth of Eve or the divine beauty or capital punishment, war and peace, and be the same again. Here indeed is God's plenty. Barth has a great chapter on "sin as sloth" in the *Dogmatics* IV:1. This is a sin from which he himself is peculiarly free and he fills his readers with new zest for the theological task.

Second, this is more than a tour through the wide realm of theology with a guide of genius. It is a tour conducted by a man who knows what he is doing and where he is going, and who chooses his own route. Barth's overriding concern throughout the whole *Dogmatics* is so to state theological truth as to make clear the sovereignty and initiative of God in His revelation.

That he largely succeeds in doing this is his decisive theological achievement. His watchword is the same as that of Luther, "Let God be God." If since Schleiermacher the tendency has been to place man at the center of theology, with God pushed to the periphery, Barth firmly places revelation again at the center. And this God is the God who was in Christ. Barth is the theologian of the sovereignty of God, but because he is that he is no less the most christocentric of theologians. The chief motive lying behind his violent polemics against natural theology and against approaching revelation with inadequately examined philosophical assumptions which are appropriate only in another frame of reference is that he wishes to expose these as threats to the divine initiative and therefore to God's real coming in saving love. To look for God, in the first place, elsewhere than in His revelation in Christ when we have that revelation already before us is to imply that we know better than God who He is. Theology is "the Church's concentrated anxiety and concern about her own most intimate responsibility." That responsibility is to ensure that when the church tries to proclaim the Word of God to man it is, in fact, the Word of God which is being proclaimed, and not a word of man masquerading as a Word of God. This means that the church's proclamation must always be inspired and controlled and checked by reference to God's revelation in Christ as declared in the Bible.

This leads us to consider Barth's third great quality as a theologian. He performs superbly the main function of a theologian concerned to state systematically the Church's fundamental beliefs, which is what a dogmatic theologian is supposed to be. He leads the church back to the Bible as a medium through which God speaks to His people here and now. This is in contrast to a theologian like Paul Tillich. Tillich tries to relate the questions posed by modern man to biblical revelation and in so doing helps many people to see more clearly what biblical revelation is about. But his strength does not lie in his making the ideas of the Bible more luminous; it consists in his conveying meaning through terms which he has invented himself. Barth speaks to modern man by trying to show him that God in His revelation poses more radical questions to all men than any which even the most discerning and critically minded modern man has been able to put to God. He would not make a distinction, as Tillich does, between kerygmatic and apologetic theology, because the kerygma, that which the Bible proclaims, cannot be properly stated or grasped without facing and overcoming its contradiction in the hearts and minds of sinful men.

Whether Barth is an altogether faithful biblical exegete is a matter of dispute. He is certainly not a fundamentalist. He insists that it is essential that the Bible should be open to critical examination from all sides. Otherwise, men try to hinder the freedom of God to vindicate Himself in the truth of His revelation. His whole understanding of the dynamic, existential character of revelation, in which God is never an Object, rules out the possibility that Barth could ever have much real sympathy with fundamentalism. Yet his conviction of the normative character of the Scripture for the Christian life is so strong that he is often tempted to read more into the Bible than most other people can find there, and to treat critical considerations with a certain arbitrariness. One of the most notorious examples of this is his discussion of the relationship between men and women in the form of an exposition of the Creation story in Genesis. There may be some justice in the complaint of those who say that, although Barth himself may not be a fundamentalist, students who follow this procedure without having grasped the vital principle of his theology may easily become indistinguishable from fundamentalists. It is not enough for Barth to deplore the existence of "Barthians"; he has some responsibility for ensuring that his followers do not misunderstand and misapply his teaching.

Yet when all qualifications have been made, it remains one of Barth's greatest contributions that he has made the Scriptures come alive in a new way for many people in many lands who have to preach the Word of God. He of all men has made us see that when the great words of Scripture seem stale and platitudinous, it is not because they are no longer "relevant" but because we ourselves are no longer in the right place for hearing what they have to say. His theology is best described as a theology of the Word of God, and Barth is indeed a true doctor of Holy Scripture.

Fourth, Barth has achieved a notable critical reinterpretation of classical theology. For many Protestants brought up in the liberal tradition he has been a theological mentor who has awakened their interest in great figures of the past to whom otherwise they would have paid little attention. He has introduced many non-Lutherans to Luther. He has revivified the Calvinist tradition, although his freedom in handling Calvin has earned him the displeasure of Calvinist traditionalists, who brand his theology as a "new modernism" (the title of a book attacking Barth by Cornelius Van Til). He breaks boldly with Calvin over predestination and reinterprets him on the Trinity, but it is not simple enthusiasm which makes many believe that if Calvin were alive today he might be more disposed to agree with Barth than with those who stick close to the Calvinist letter. Barth has also uncovered much buried treasure among the Protestant scholastics. He has always been deeply attached to Anselm, and has said that his book on Anselm is the one which gave him most satisfaction to write. In recent years he has shown a growing sympathy with Thomas Aquinas even though he still maintains, against Thomist sympathizers who dispute his interpretation of Thomas, that the Thomist doctrine of the *analogia entis* is the root of a great deal of theological evil. Barth was one of the first writers of any kind to draw inspiration from the works of Kierkegaard, and it is through Barth that many people have approached Kierkegaard. Characteristically, he quickly dissociated himself from Kierkegaard lest he be thought to depend too much on existentialism, and he did not include an essay on Kierkegaard in his series of studies on nineteenth century thought. He always speaks in an illuminating manner of Schleiermacher, whom he greatly admires while he deplores much of his influence. And despite his alleged lack of concern with philosophy, he has much that is original to say about the philosophers of the Enlightenment and about Marx and Feuerbach and Nietzsche and Sartre.

Fifth, Barth has presented a vigorous reinterpretation of the radical Reformed doctrine of the Church. He is a firmly committed member of the Swiss Reformed Church and asserts that dogmatics is a responsible activity of the Church community. But he insists that the Church can never be taken for granted as automatically the possessor of divine grace. The Church has constantly to find her life in the events of proclamation and sacrament; she never simply has it by being there. The theology of Barth and his colleagues in the early days was known as "crisis theology," not in the sense that it was produced in a period of tension in world affairs but in the sense that it laid great emphasis upon the fact that men could not hear the Word of God without being thrust into a situation where the whole basis of their existence was imperiled—where their lives were at a crisis and where they were judged by God—and where their only hope was in the leap of faith. The expression of the idea at the time obviously owed a great deal to existentialist philosophy, but the idea itself is central to the New Testament understanding of faith and to the Reformed approach to the doctrine of the Church. Faith and crisis are inseparable. This is why judgment always has to begin at the household of faith. This, in its turn, is why the way of renewal in the life of the Church is always the way of reformation. Reformation is not something which happens at particular periods in the Church's history, so that after such a period the Church can relax and celebrate its own purity. Reformation must be a persistent activity in the Church's life. There is a sense in which it is true that whenever the Church gathers together out of the world for worship every Sunday it is making an act of reformation.

Barth sees the Church as living between the times of reconciliation and final redemption—he edited a series of pamphlets at one time with the title *Zwischen den Zeiten*—and emphasizes that the Church holds her true life only as she moves toward her coming Lord. She is, in her nature, a pilgrim Church, and once she settles down as an earthly institution she is in danger of being conformed to this world which passes away.

It is this aspect of Barth's teaching which causes greatest resistance among Catholics. They claim that he denies a real coming of God to man and any continuity and dependability in the divine grace. His sacramental teaching, especially about baptism, is certainly "left wing" and in his thinking about the Church in general he has a good deal of affinity with British Congregationalism. His concern, however, here as always, is to assert the Lordship of Christ in His own house. The Church owes her life not to her inherent vitality nor to temporal succession but

to her Lord. She has constantly to die that she might live, to
know even in her earthly form the fellowship of Christ's sufferings if she is to manifest the power of the resurrection. He
emphatically believes in a real coming of God to man, but it is
a coming in "the form of a servant." There is continuity in the
action of the divine grace and there is dependability; these may
have their adumbrations in the life of human institutions, but
they are ultimately apprehensible only from the Godward side,
in faith. Where men imagine that things are otherwise and that
they can produce guarantees of the divine reliability, they are,
as he says in his exposition of the Scots Confession of 1560 in
his Gifford Lectures, in danger of turning the Church into a
"filthy synagogue of Satan."

Barth's attitude to the Church as a human institution is closely
connected with his attitude toward religion. No one is more
aware of the ambiguity of human religion. It is he who coined
the aphorism, "Religion is the enemy of faith." Religion in this
sense he defines, in the *Dogmatics* I:2, as man's attempt to enter
into communion with God on his own terms. Man must, therefore, transcend his religion if he is to arrive at the real self-giving
of faith in which he dies and Christ lives in him. True religion,
which issues out of genuine faith, is a real possibility, but a
possibility only because revelation has taken place and men can
realize that they are able to transcend themselves in faith.

We may reasonably question whether Barth has said all that
needs to be said about so complex and many-sided a phenomenon as human religion and yet can recognize that what he
is saying is of the profoundest importance for the inner life of
the Christian community itself. The lesson of the failure of the
old Israel is taken to heart by Barth as by no other theologian.
Religion is not good in itself. Like all human activities it needs
to be redeemed. It was religion which crucified Christ and, as
religion goes, it was good religion. The watchword of the modern
ecumenical movement is "Let the Church be the Church." Barth
would probably agree with it, but would want to make clear
what the conditions are which enable the churches to become
truly churches of Jesus Christ.

Sixth, Barth brings wide sympathy and broad humanity into
his theological work. This will surprise those who think of him

rather as an opinionated and aggressive theologian, and it has to be admitted that he himself must bear a large part of the responsibility for giving this misleading impression. His characteristic method, in the German rather than in the Swiss manner, is to lay down his thesis in thick black type and in its starkest and most uncompromising form at the head of each chapter, as though to challenge anyone to dare deny it. His way of dealing with his critics is to go after them with a hatchet and cut them to pieces, making sure that nothing of them is left after he has finished. His treatment of Emil Brunner over natural theology and of the early Paul Tillich in the very first half-volume of the *Dogmatics* are cases in point. Those brought up according to the gentler conventions of Anglo-Saxon scholarly discourse may reasonably feel that there are more courteous and more constructive ways of conducting theological arguments. At the same time it is fair to say that, as many of those who have studied with him insist, he proceeds upon the assumption that his opponents are as tough as he is, that he expects to be answered in kind and that he retains his good humor.

His method is doubly unfortunate, however, because it serves to conceal the extent to which, as his argument develops, Barth does in fact take account of objections to his thesis and different approaches from his own. It also serves to conceal the extent to which he is sensitively aware to the movements of thought and life around him. We have already referred to his love of Mozart and the cinema. These are only slight indications of his conviction that the theologian is a man among men who must clearly recognize his complete involvement in the human situation with his fellows. In his exposition of the doctrine of man in the *Dogmatics* III:2, he does not directly use Bonhoeffer's ideas of "holy worldliness" and mature manhood but, as Bonhoeffer acknowledged, their ideas are very close to each other. In his comparatively recent paper on "The Humanity of God" (1956) he says that it is this side of the Christian faith which needs particular emphasis today, just as when he started the Otherness of God needed emphasis. Barth the theologian may not always provide us with the best exemplification of what this might mean, although Barth the man would, but even the theologian can give us a great deal of help in trying to work it out.

Seventh, Barth may be claimed as one of the genuinely ecumenical theologians of our time. He himself has taken little
direct part in formal conversations sponsored by the World
Council of Churches, although he did attend the Amsterdam
Assembly and has contributed to various ecumenical symposia.
But he is the acknowledged theological mentor of the General
Secretary of the World Council and many others who are active
in its affairs look to him for leadership. He has disciples in most
of the larger churches of Christendom and he is increasingly
studied and admired in the more advanced Roman Catholic
circles. The reason is that, although he speaks so uncompromis-
ingly out of the Reformed tradition, his purpose is to recall men
to those central realities of the Christian faith which provide
the most enduring inspiration for the ecumenical movement.
The chief cause of the disunity and ineffectiveness of churches
is that they do not believe enough in God. We have seen that
Barth's greatest contribution to theology is to recall men to what
belief in God really means. This makes men critical of their
ecclesiastical traditions, in their religious ambiguity, and at the
same time reminds them of their solidarity in sin and their
participation in a common hope in Christ. This gives them
strength to persevere through the disappointments and frustrations of the ecumenical enterprise in the knowledge that the
Church belongs not to themselves but to God.

Barth contributes to the ecumenical movement also because
his work has an ecumenical sweep and scope. He tries to see
Christian truth as a unity and places it firmly in a cosmic setting.
He has his blind spots, but there is very little that is sectarian
or provincial about Barth's theology. If it is true that the more
truly ecumenical Church toward which we all aspire cannot come
into being without theology of an ecumenical quality and range,
Barth is one of its chief architects.

The seven qualities we have mentioned indicate the greatness
of Barth's work, and the impact of his genius is such upon
those who have learned to appreciate him that it is often hard
for them to become aware of any of his limitations. But if there
were none, this would contradict some of Barth's own most
characteristic insights. And Barth has given himself to his
readers with such prodigal generosity and has been at work for

such a long time that some of his weaknesses have become visible even to his admirers.

The first weakness that suggests itself is that Barth does not always escape the danger of placing the theologian on a pedestal, above criticism. This is related to the excessive biblicism which we have already noted, since, if you read more into the Bible than can really be found in it, you are in danger of claiming the authority of Scripture for what are no more than your own opinions. Nothing could be further from Barth's professed intention than this. In the prolegomena to the *Dogmatics,* in the book on Anselm, and in various occasional papers Barth constantly insists that the theologian can only perform his functions of criticism, proclamation, and witness if he himself is constantly brought into the situation of radical self-criticism which confrontation with God's Word produces. But he sometimes leaves his reader wondering whether he has always succeeded in being faithful to his own best principles. He echoes Kierkegaard's famous question, "Can a theologian be saved?" in his commentary on Romans and he would still insist that this is a serious question, but he sometimes gives the impression that it is only the theologian who can be saved. When a theologian is moved to maintain that Jesus Christ is the only source of true revelation and that his method of interpretation of Jesus Christ is the only right one, he must be particularly careful to be humble and generous in his accounts of the positions of theologians who think differently and in his attitude toward other religious and philosophical traditions than his own. Barth succeeds in showing this care more frequently than his critics allow, but he is far from being invariably successful.

The very size of the *Dogmatics* is a partial indication of this. An unsympathetic critic, E. L. Mascall, has said that it takes so much time to read this theologian of the Word that no time is left to read the Word itself. The choice is between Barth and the Bible. This is ungracious, but Barth would perhaps have made us even more grateful than he has if he had given more consideration to how he could have spoken more economically. The words of Scripture, "God is in heaven, thou art on earth; therefore let thy words be few," have a very Barthian ring. It would have been reassuring if more concrete evidence had been provided that this exhortation applied even to Barth. Speaking of the first volume of the *Dogmatics,* he said, "I know where I mean to come out, if the Lord will." At that time he apparently thought of five volumes of five hundred pages each. Perhaps his work would have been even more influential, and his tendency to theologism more firmly checked, if he had managed to keep his work close to those limits.

Barth's second limitation arises from a defect of one of his very greatest qualities. Barth is incomparable at uncovering for us again the peaks of theology in their full majesty. One thinks especially here of the chapters on the Knowledge and the Reality of God in the *Dogmatics* II:1. He is not so good at leading the gentler of his readers over all the confused and broken foothills in which they easily get lost in these days and which they must traverse before they reach the peaks. In general, it can be said that the more fundamental the question is, the surer Barth's touch becomes. For this we cannot be too grateful, but it does appear to be the case that only those who are trained in rigorous theological schools or those with his own kind of imagination can readily keep company with him.

This is partly a matter of his style, which some find vivid and exciting while to others it seems turgid and repetitive. It is also a matter of his method of thinking. He has an unerring instinct for the distinctively theological point in any discussion, but he rarely indicates to the reader how he reaches it and he concentrates most of his energies upon repudiating any argument which seems to threaten his position. In the process he deals with many of the familiar criticisms which are made of him and produces many incidental felicities, but only the patient reader can discover these things and they are not always dealt with in a frame of reference familiar to the reader. Barth operates with a theological bulldozer, moving a vast amount of earth and then proceeding to build, with excellent materials, a great rough tower to the glory of the Lord. But he leaves plenty of mess for others to tidy up and a great deal of work for the builders of approach roads.

A final limitation of Barth as a theologian is his lack of interest in a number of important questions which he might reasonably be expected to be concerned with. For example, he appears singularly uninterested in the relation between Christianity and other faiths. What hints he gives us suggest that his attitude toward them would not necessarily be as unconstructive as most people assume, but it has to be admitted that, in all the wide spaces of the *Dogmatics,* the references to other religions are pitifully few. When Barth has given us so much, it seems unreasonable to ask for more, but the other religions of the world do pose questions of great importance to anyone who is trying to produce a work of systematic theology. Barth needs to define his attitude toward them carefully even if, as he is entitled to, he does not regard it as his function to enter into dialogue with them.

Yet it is doubtful whether this catalogue of limitations does more than underline the fact that Barth is one theologian among others and that other voices need to be heard as well as his. He is such a magnificent solo instrumentalist that it is easy to imagine that he is the whole orchestra. He has called his theology a corrective, and would claim that in the end this is the best that all systems, however elaborate, can hope to be, needing their own correctives in due season. The present writer is a part-time professor of theology, but he also has to preach to a congregation Sunday by Sunday and to spend much of his time alongside busy people much engaged in the day-to-day life of one of the world's great cities. He would like to say that he has found no theologian to be of more practical help than Karl Barth, in leading him and others to the knowledge and service of God revealed in Christ.

Bibliography

Karl Barth, *Church Dogmatics: A Selection,* N.Y., Harper, 1962. (Harper Torchbooks).

Georges Casalis, *Portrait of Karl Barth,* N.Y., Doubleday, 1963.

EMIL BRUNNER

J. Robert Nelson

It is remarkable that the two men who have exercised the greatest influence upon Protestant theology in this century have come from the small land of Switzerland. Emil Brunner of Zurich and Karl Barth of Basel have been the undisputed champions of the theological revival variously known as "dialectical theology," the "theology of crisis," or more generally "neo-orthodoxy." Neither of the two Swiss professors gave these names to his pattern of thought. The content, not the name, is important. Their basic purpose, said Brunner in 1931, was simply "to declare the *Word* of the Bible to the *World*."[1] But herein lay a difference between the two men. Barth addressed himself primarily to the community of faith, Brunner to the dubious or the uninformed both within and outside it.

Despite the fact that their names are often spoken in the same breath, Brunner and Barth in more than forty years of writing and teaching have never been colleagues and, though residents of the same part of Switzerland, have encountered each other on very few occasions. But they are linked together because at about the same time both came to the same conclusion about prevailing Protestant theology, and they prescribed roughly the same kind of antidote for its illness. "The Protestant theology of our day," announced Brunner, "is in a state of rapid dissolution. . . . The substance of Christian theology, the content of Christian faith, is in a stage of complete decomposition. Christianity is either faith in the revelation of God in Jesus Christ, or it is nothing."[2] He was launching a vigorous attack upon the whole body of theological liberalism which derived from Friedrich Schleiermacher, Albrecht Ritschl, and Adolf von Harnack, and which until World War II remained

[1] *The Word and the World* (London, SCM Press, 1931), p. 6.
[2] *The Theology of Crisis* (N.Y., Scribner's, 1930), p. 2.

regnant in Great Britain and America. Its most grievous faults were a humanistic picture of Jesus Christ, an optimistic view of man's essential goodness, and a progressive idea of history as inevitably leading to the Kingdom of God.

Brunner has not regarded himself as either a traditionalist or an innovator. He has tried only to be true to the historic faith of the Church as grounded in the Bible, and to make this intelligible and compelling for people of his own time. His so-called neo-orthodoxy did not involve a return to the rigid dogmatic confessions of the Lutheran and Calvinistic orthodoxy of the seventeenth century. Instead he was disposed from the outset to study the Bible with a mind trained in historical criticism (he detested biblicism!) and there to find, and therefrom to expound, the self-revelation and saving work of God in Jesus Christ. The Gospel he found there was not one of general religious and ethical values, as the liberals taught, nor of propositional dogmas, as the Roman Catholics and certain Protestants believed it to be. The foundation of biblical faith is the coming of the infinite God to finite man in the person of Jesus Christ. This is itself a paradox which the human mind can never resolve because of the mind's inherent limitation. The Word of God is like a rod thrust in the water: its shape is broken in contact with the world. Nevertheless, this event is critical for every person; it is literally a "crisis" which demands decision on the part of each man to say Yes or No to God in either faith or revolt.

How did Brunner come to this interpretation of Christian faith, so different from what prevailed in contemporary sermons and theological books? He has himself often indicated those to whom he was most indebted. The first was the south German pastor Christoph Blumhardt (1842–1919), a man of deep spirituality, intense mind, and ethical passion. Still greater was the influence of Hermann Kutter (1863–1931), a disciple of Blumhardt, who perceived how Christian thought was straying and boldly declared to his generation how it should be recalled. Through another dynamic Swiss theologian, Leonhard Ragaz (1868–1945), who was his teacher at Zurich, the young Brunner learned to know the works of Søren Kierkegaard. In many places in his writings Brunner pays special tribute to the brilliant Dane as the most important Christian thinker since Luther. It is significant that none of these mentors of the young Brunner was a powerful exponent of Switzerland's Reformed tradition, either Zwinglian or Calvinistic. But they taught with great force the reality and present relevance of the coming of God in Jesus Christ, with implications for radical change in both individual and society.

From the time of his birth, in 1889, through his university years, Brunner remained in his native land and was nurtured in its rich though limited culture. In 1911 he spent a semester at Berlin, but was not impressed by either Harnack or the great city. He felt greater affinity for Anglo-Saxon culture after his visit to England in 1913–14. Here he began to learn English, which he soon spoke flawlessly. The outbreak of the war necessitated his return to his homeland, where he spent two years in military service, guarding its neutral borders. In 1916 he was appointed pastor of the church at Obstalden, a mountain village in Kanton Glarus. The following year he married Margret Lauterberg, a niece of Hermann Kutter. For more than forty years she has given him much assistance in his literary output. And she raised a family of four sons, for whom Brunner has had the deepest fatherly affection. Much to their parents' grief, two sons died in their maturity, one from an illness and one in an accident. Another is a pastor, and the fourth a businessman.

Through the ecumenical leader Adolf Keller, arrangements were made for Brunner to study in the United States during 1919–20 at Union Theological Seminary. His relationship to America, as to England, grew stronger during the ensuing years. In the twenties he lectured extensively in both lands. He was visiting professor at Princeton 1938–39. And still later he gave major lectureships in these countries, where most of his many books were known through English translation.

The University of Zurich recognized the talent of the scholarly pastor-theologian by calling him to be professor of systematic and practical theology in 1924. While his fame grew as a theologian, few of his readers and admirers outside Zurich realized that Brunner also taught homiletics and pastoral care. He never allowed academic theology to stifle his pastoral calling, and for many years he was a preacher to overflow congregations in the old Fraumünster church.

During the thirties he was drawn into a number of international spheres of activity. Both the Faith and Order and the Life and Work streams of the growing ecumenical movement claimed his participation. The Group Movement, under Frank Buchman's leadership, attracted his interest; it seemed to offer the new life he longed for in the rather moribund Swiss churches. But when the Group Movement was changed into Moral Re-Armament, with the tacit loss of its christological center, it also lost the services of this eminent Christian.

It is notable that Brunner's experience and influence in Germany were never extensive. Hitler is to blame. For even though he has been a most prolific writer in German, Brunner's books were banned by the Nazis and he was not permitted to lecture in the land. The fact that Karl Barth was teaching at Bonn and was expelled by the Nazis after inspiring the rebellious Confessing Church has given this other great Swiss a much stronger role in German theology than Brunner's.

As he approached the age of retirement, a new and exciting chapter of his life opened unexpectedly. On the invitation of John R. Mott, Brunner agreed to be theological advisor to the worldwide Y.M.C.A. In 1949 he traveled through Asia, lecturing, teaching, and learning. His vision of the Church's mission was thereby enlarged. And in 1953 he returned to Japan for a two-year sojourn as professor at International Christian University in Tokyo. Here he found particular satisfaction in discussions with Christian laymen of various occupations, as well as with Buddhists and Shintoists. The coming of so prominent a European theologian had strong effect upon Japanese Christianity; in turn, the experience left an indelible impress on his mind.

It was on the homeward journey from Japan in 1955 that Brunner suffered a stroke, which ever since has hindered his work. In his *Dogmatik* Vol. III (1960) he apologizes to the reader for not having provided all the usual scholarly footnotes and expresses gratification that his health permitted him to finish the book and thus complete the series, which crowns his illustrious career as a theologian.

BRUNNER'S THEOLOGY BRIEFLY SKETCHED

The Doctrine of Jesus Christ

In his criticism of prevailing Protestant thought during the first quarter of this century, the young Brunner discerned its most vulnerable point to be that of Christology. In place of the Lord of the New Testament faith and the Christ whom Christians for centuries had believed and adored as the Son of God made man, many theologians had been describing a Jesus of Nazareth who was no more than a religious genius. Sharp attacks upon this humanistic and essentially unitarian portrayal of Jesus are found in Brunner's books. And it is significant that his first major book on Christian doctrine was precisely on this central issue. In 1927 he published *Der Mittler (The Mediator)*, which quickly won recognition in many lands, and which is still one of the best books on Christology. Thanks to the skilled work of translation by Olive Wyon, who thereafter made many of his books available in English, *The Mediator* soon held a commanding place in British and American theology. The importance of this book lies not in its new teaching, for the author expressly disavowed any such novelty. He wanted only to make a fresh restatement of the ancient and indispensable belief of the Church. But the timeliness of the book, as well as its lucidity of style and cogency of assertion, account for its wide effect on the thought of Christians.

Brunner's starting point is the problem of revelation. How does God, the omnipotent Creator and infinite Father, make Himself known? Not through the ideas of general religious principles, which arise in men's minds, nor through occult revelations. For Brunner the avenues to knowledge of God which are followed by both philosophers and mystics are blind alleys. Only upon His own initiative and through Himself does God reveal to man who He is and what His will is. So God chose one person at a particular time in man's history and amongst a particular people to be His self-revelation. The appearance of Jesus Christ was unique and unrepeatable. Comparisons between Jesus and other ancient religious prophets and teachers are interesting but pointless. He is not to be regarded as the

first among equals, but as the one and only incarnation of the
Word of God. In Jesus Christ "we are confronted with an absolutely incomparable new fact, or rather a new category which
transcends history and is thus no longer history at all, the fulfillment of time in the midst of time."[3] Brunner does not simply
retreat from the processes of reason by taking refuge in a dogmatic and defiant declaration of God's self-disclosure in Jesus
Christ. He shows consistent respect for the uses of the intelligent mind in respect to man's knowledge. But he simply holds
that the Christian faith cannot recognize reason alone as the
ultimate arbiter of truth.

The Old Testament prophets, as well as other religious teachers, have been heeded as bearers or interpreters of the Word of
God. But Jesus Christ was not a mere bearer of the Word: he
was the Word. The revelation of God is Jesus Christ. Brunner
emphasizes strongly the teaching of the Gospel according to
John—that whoever has seen or known the Son has thereby
known the Father. Such knowledge is mediated to us in the
present time by the message of the apostles, the original eyewitnesses; and this message is found first in the New Testament. Therefore, while rejecting a literalistic reading of the
Bible as a whole, Brunner stresses the primacy of the biblical
witness to the Word of God, who is Jesus Christ.

During the first four centuries of the history of the Church,
theologians struggled to find definitive words to speak of the
relation between the Father, the Son and the Holy Spirit, and
also to indicate how Jesus Christ was at once divine and human. Brunner sees the need for examining the same problems
today. Espousing the classic position of Irenaeus and Athanasius, he considers and rejects several theories about the person
of Jesus Christ which keep appearing in history. He gives no
ground to the idea that Jesus Christ was a mere human being
who was "adopted" by God to be the Son, or conversely that he
was a nonhuman, phantasmal appearance of the divine, or that
he was an angelic being neither really divine nor really human.
None of these speculations, either in ancient form or in contemporary dress, can account for the identity of the one whom
Christians call Lord and Savior.

[3] *The Mediator* (Philadelphia, Westminster, 1947), p. 86.

Asserting the divinity of Jesus Christ does not, in Brunner's judgment, imply acceptance as literal fact of the traditional idea of the virgin birth of Jesus. Some find it difficult to reconcile Brunner's "high Christology" with his skepticism about the manner of Jesus' birth. But his intellectual sincerity is evident here. He finds the biblical evidence, apart from the romantic stories in the Gospels according to Matthew and Luke, to be too scanty to warrant acceptance. Moreover, he reasons, the great miracle of the incarnation is not enforced but rather minimized by the idea of a supernatural birth without human father. Human paternity and normal birth make the coming of the Word of God into history an even greater wonder, and more important, they leave no room for doubt about the authentic humanity of Jesus Christ.

Defense of Jesus' true humanity is of much import for Christian theology. It keeps the faith from floating above the material realities of history upon a cloud of religious speculation. Some critics of *The Mediator* have charged Brunner with denying to Jesus an authentic humanity, a real personality, in his zeal to teach the divinity of Jesus Christ. But Brunner has disavowed this criticism.[4] He is content to accept the definition of the Council of Chalcedon (451) that Jesus Christ is at once true God and true man. But even this formula has its dangers, he says, if it is unduly intellectualized. The truth about the Lord is discovered not through theorizing on His nature but through personal encounter with Him.

This personal encounter, which for Brunner is a primary category of faith and theology, is possible today because of the resurrection of Jesus Christ. He does not shrink from asserting the reality and indispensability of the resurrection. This is something different from the virgin birth. It is the *risen* Lord whom the apostles witnessed, and to whom they bore witness. It was the assurance of their continued communion with him that gave the apostles something to proclaim to the world. Here is the basis for Christian faith and preaching, and hence for the Church. It is as inexplicable in historical terms as the incarnation itself, but none the less real. Without the resurrection, all

[4] *The Christian Doctrine of Creation and Redemption (Dogmatics* II) (Philadelphia, Westminster, 1952), p. 360.

discussion of the mystery of the person and saving work of Jesus Christ—indeed, all claims of the Christian faith—would be without meaning. But they have meaning, because he is risen.

God Known in Personal Encounter

Christians are always prone to falsify the knowledge of God by holding one or the other of two extreme positions. One is a false objectivism. This is exemplified by unquestioning biblical literalism, by the dogmatism inherent in the teaching office of the Roman Catholic Church, and by the confessional orthodoxy of certain Protestant traditions. This objectivism is like a frozen waterfall, giving the appearance of life and movement but actually immobile and lifeless. The other extreme is subjectivism. It is seen in those movements of Christian enthusiasts and mystics, as well as in romantic liberalism, which seek knowledge in experience and feeling. As Brunner declared in a famous series of lectures delivered in Sweden in 1937, both extremes, widespread as they are, are a threat to the integrity of the Christian faith.

As his chosen title asserts, the truth of God is known only in personal encounter—*Wahrheit als Begegnung,* or in English, *The Divine-Human Encounter.* The biblical witness to God shows Him always to be God-approaching-man; man is always man-coming-from-God; and their meeting point is Jesus Christ.[5] Man by his striving and seeking cannot know God. Only God can take the initiative to make Himself and His will known to man. What is known as divine revelation is a two-sided relation in which "God is completely and wholly the Giver, the first, and man is completely and wholly the receiver, the second."[6] But God does not overwhelm His creature; He treats man as the free and responsible being whom He loves, and whose choice is to accept God's grace in faith or to reject it in sin. This is the choice which confronts man when he hears or reads the gospel of Jesus Christ.

If the knowledge of God's truth and saving love comes

[5] *The Divine-Human Encounter* (Philadelphia, Westminster, 1943), p. 46. (New translation, 1963.)
[6] *Ibid.,* p. 69.

through real personal encounter, where does that encounter take place in human experience? Brunner is disposed to recognize several areas of history and experience wherein revelatory encounter occurs. He does not mean to weaken the faith that God reveals Himself as Lord and Savior uniquely and decisively in Jesus Christ. But he willingly admits the reality of God's revelation in the created world in which man lives. He sees the biblical revelation as twofold: the promise given in the Old Covenant between Yahweh and Israel, and the fulfillment of the promise in Jesus Christ. Because Jesus Christ is both true God and true man and is genuinely personal, the revelation in him is final and complete. But the revelatory action does not end with the termination of Jesus' earthly life. It continues in the witness of the Holy Scriptures, in the faith of the Church, and in the personal testimony of the Holy Spirit in the hearts of men. Finally the hope of man lies in the expectation that God will make Himself known in communion with man at "the end," when the consummation of the reign of God shall take place. Since revelation is thus a series of divine actions, God gives meaning to human history. His revelation is neither timeless nor confined to a certain point of time. He keeps encountering man.[7]

These views of Brunner's on revelation brought him into a famous disputation with Karl Barth in 1934—the theological *cause célèbre* of the decade. Unfortunately in the heat of dispute the two Swiss giants not only broke apart their former theological alliance but also allowed their sharp differences to be felt personally. In subsequent books Brunner has made frequent reference to this debate; and more than twenty-five years later referred to Barth's rebuttal entitled *Nein!* as that "terrible book."[8]

Despite mutual misunderstandings in their essays, the main issues between Brunner and Barth emerge as follows: Does God reveal Himself solely and exclusively in Jesus Christ as known in the Scriptures, or does He also use creation and on-going his-

[7] From the long treatise *Revelation and Reason* (Philadelphia, Westminster, 1946), Part I.

[8] *Natural Theology*, comprising "Nature and Grace" by Emil Brunner and the reply *"No!"* by Karl Barth (London, Geoffrey Bles, 1946).

tory as media of revelation? Has the image of God in man been so utterly defaced that man no longer has any capacity to receive God's revelation? Is there to be found in man no "point of contact" for the saving action and revelation of God? Is it legitimate at all for Christian theologians to speak of "natural theology" and "natural law" without capitulating to Roman Catholic doctrine?

Barth accused Brunner of deserting faith in the singularity of Jesus Christ as the revelation of God's saving truth, and thus of reopening the way for the 19th-century Protestant liberalism against which they had both contended. Brunner accused Barth of a christological one-sidedness which made him virtually reject the goodness of creation and the humanity of man. And years later Brunner often maintained that Barth in his huge book on the doctrine of creation had tacitly changed his mind and agreed with him. Undecisive as the argument proved to be, it stimulated extensive discussion of these questions, so vital to theology, and prompted numerous Christian thinkers to reappraise their views of the nature of man and the revelation of God.

The Doctrine of Man: the Creature in Contradiction

In an interview for British television in 1961, Brunner said that he considered his chief contribution to theology the 1937 book *Der Mensch im Widerspruch (Man in Revolt)*. A brilliant statement of the Christian understanding of what it means to be human, its importance is enhanced by the fact that it was published at a time when the Western world was awakening to the terrors of dehumanizing totalitarianism. The deadly trends of fascism and communism in Europe were being abetted by certain schools of psychology, biology, and philosophy which in effect stripped man of his God-given humanity.

In this work Brunner acknowledged his debt to two thinkers only a bit older than himself: Ferdinand Ebner and Martin Buber. They refined and developed the theme of the I-Thou relationship which has been highly influential in much modern theology. In this deep insight into personal communion between individuals and between a man and God, as opposed to the growing impersonalism and collectivism of modern life, Brunner saw the clue to interpreting in the present time the Christian idea of man's nature. Man is made for community with his Creator and his fellows, but this community derives first from his relation to the Creator as *Thou*.

This relationship is determined by man's inherent responsibility to God. Such responsibility is the common property of every man. The believer in God is conscious of it, the unbeliever does not acknowledge it. Yet neither can escape it. Nor does the plenteous grace of God annul it. The human *I* responds to the divine *Thou*; and the nature of that response determines the quality of his life. For Brunner, a Christian, in contrast to Buber, a Jew, this claim of responsibility to the personal, divine Thou is discerned in Jesus Christ, the Word of God. Brunner claims to have been the first Protestant theologian to make use of this I-Thou scheme, having referred to it in an essay in 1912.

There would be no basis for responsibility if man were not created in the image of God. The idea of the divine image in man is fundamental not only for the Christian understanding of man but for the history of Western civilization itself. Confused thinking on the matter has led to three confusing and pernicious lines of thought: (1) a distinction between the *image* of God, as rationality and freedom, which has been retained in man, and the *similitude* of God, as a divine element in human nature, which has been lost; (2) the concept that in the fall of man only a *relic* or vestige of the image remained; and (3) the secularized notion, since the Enlightenment of the 18th century, that the image is a fiction. Against these widespread ideas, Brunner has contended that the *imago Dei* is simply man's personal relation of total responsibility to the holy, loving God. It is this which makes man human.

But man is in contradiction, in revolt against God. This is his predicament. He is irresponsible, and so allows himself to be robbed of true life. It is not enough to say that there is within man something contradictory; rather, the whole man, because of his revolt against God, is against himself. "Sin is defiance, arrogance, the desire to be equal with God, emancipation, a deliberate severance from the hand of God."[9] There is

[9] *Man in Revolt* (Philadelphia, Westminster, 1947), p. 129.

no need to take the story of Adam's fall literally nor to posit the existence of a golden age to which man longs to return. The fact that man has contradicted both God and his own nature is self-evident in history, in psychology, and in ethics. Thus every man is Adam. And, to use Pascal's words, each man is aware of his misery only because he knows something of his defaced grandeur.

Of course the whole struggle of man's life is to overcome this contradiction of his nature. And the significance of Jesus Christ is precisely his effective—not merely exemplary—work in enabling persons to find restitution in terms of personal communion with God, moral responsibility to Him, and community with one another.

The Ethics of God's Command and the Earthly Orders

Evident throughout the writings of Brunner is a sustained and intensifying ethical concern which at times is expressed with genuine passion. He has never been an ivory-tower theologian. In accord with the essential genius of the Christian faith, he ponders doctrinal questions in relation to their ethical consequences.

His first effort to set forth a system of ethics for Protestant thought was in *Das Gebot und die Ordnungen* (1932); it appeared in English two years later with the title *The Divine Imperative*. Though Brunner agreed to that title, he later expressed regret that it misses the import of his original subject, "The Command and the Orders," for the book is built on these two concepts.

As a Christian he sees the starting point of ethical judgment and behavior in the relation to God through faith in Jesus Christ. Philosophers brood over the problems of human relations and endeavor to generalize concerning the nature of the Good. But if they follow the Hebraic prophetic tradition and its culmination in Jesus Christ, they will recognize that the Good is not to be defined in abstract theories but rather in terms of the known activity of God. The highest manifestation of God's activity is in the self-giving and crucifixion of Jesus Christ. "Here alone is the meaning of the word 'love' disclosed."[10] In the cross-event is seen the distinct difference between love as self-seeking (eros) and love as self-giving (agape).

Brunner defines Christian ethics as "the science of human conduct as it is determined by Divine conduct."[11] Now the essential character of God's conduct is self-giving love. This is not only taught by but also supremely exemplified in Jesus Christ. The same quality of love is God's primary *command* to mankind. To live in faith, to be fully responsible to God and thus to be completely human means to live in love. It is equally perilous to think of love legalistically as a principle of conduct and to consider it sentimentally as a mere emotion. Brunner shuns both distortions. Love is of the nature of God, and so it is His command to human beings created in His image. From this command are derived the various commandments, which include the tempering influences of righteousness, equity, and mercy. Man's obedience to the command and the commandments should be with singleness of heart, but the manner of obeying is always determined by the particular circumstances which call for decision and action. The countless variations of circumstance require the formulation of ethical laws; but these are derived from and are in consonance with the primary command of love. Moreover, the Christian ethical imperative, in contrast to other types, involves the dimension of time. There is much urgency for every person that he obey God's command *now*, with no excuse for delay. The leisurely approach of the "good pagan" to better patterns of living is not tolerated by the insistent command of God addressed to all men, and heard and heeded by those who have faith in Him.

Even such ethical considerations as these must be seen in relation to the several spheres of man's individual and communal life in which decisions are made and actions taken. Here Brunner adopts the idea of the "orders of creation." These are the five dimensions of human community which are written into the historical existence of mankind. Three of them are clearly outlined in the given nature of life: the male-female community, or family; the community of work, or economics; and the com-

[10] *The Divine Imperative* (Philadelphia, Westminster, 1947), p. 55.
[11] *Ibid.*, p. 86.

munity of law and nation, or the state. The fourth order, still essential, derives from man's intellectual impulses, the community of culture. And the fifth, springing from and embracing the impulses of faith, is the religious community, or Church. Lack of space forbids even an outline of his views on the meaning of each of the five orders; a few words must suffice.

Despite the vigorous tone of his writing, Brunner reveals himself as neither a traditionalist nor a social revolutionary. He is prepared to say that economic capitalism and communism are twin brothers: the extremes of individualism and collectivism meet each other, since both destroy human values. The divine command of love can be better obeyed today in a moderately controlled economy.

The state is ordained by God both to restrain evil and to conserve justice. But it is also susceptible to grossest corruptions, as witnessed in contemporary totalitarianism. Certainly Brunner's own considered loyalty to Swiss democracy has been an ingredient in his view of the state. And throughout the era of German Nazism and Russian communism he has been increasingly polemical in his criticism. He sees in the phenomenon of the *Totalstaat* the very opposite of love and the end of freedom.

Since 1932 Brunner has not felt constrained to write more on ethical problems of marriage and family. But those who know him personally have seen him as a nearly ideal instance of the Christian husband and parent. His example is more significant than his articulated thought on the subject. Also a man of rich cultural appreciation—a devotee of Bach and Rembrandt—with considerable knowledge of the physical sciences, he shared his thoughts on the community of culture in his Gifford Lectures, published as *Christianity and Civilisation* (1948).

The community of faith, the Church—the nature of which he holds to be the "presupposition for Christian Ethics as a whole" —merits more extensive treatment.

The Church—Not Institution but Fellowship

The participation of Brunner in the life of the Church in Zurich as well as in the world at large has been notable. Nevertheless he has been consistently critical of prevailing understandings of the nature of the Church and of practices which he regards as injurious to its proper life. As early as 1932 in *The Divine Imperative* he was developing thoughts on the Church which came to fruition in the fifties with the publication of *The Misunderstanding of the Church* and Volume III of his *Dogmatics*. His oft-repeated thesis is this: the Church as ecclesiastical institution has nothing to do with the Church (Greek: *ekklēsia*) of the New Testament. They are two different and contrary entities.

Brunner sees the New Testament *ekklēsia* as a free fellowship of faithful Christians, united in common life and worship by their faith in Jesus Christ and led in their service and witness by the Holy Spirit. This simple fellowship was truly of both divine and human nature and could rightly be called the Body of Christ, though it was virtually without institutional structure or official ministry. But the process of institutionalization began even in New Testament times. It is seen in the Pastoral Epistles, where frequent reference is made to regular ministry and sound doctrine. Thereafter came the Catholicizing process, the development of new doctrines about the sacraments, and, worst of all, the patronizing adoption of the Church by the Empire under Constantine and Theodosius. The Reformation promised to restore the Church to its character as *ekklēsia*; but the great Reformers acquiesced to a partly Roman Catholic notion of the Church. So Protestant churches, especially those in Europe enjoying particular favor of the state, are criticized by Brunner no less harshly than the Catholic.

To a large extent Brunner has followed, though not uncritically, the thinking of an earlier German scholar, Rudolf Sohm. He regards as wholly inadequate the common conception of the Church as the congregation where the Gospel is preached and the sacraments administered. He is especially distressed by the undisciplined practice of infant baptism. He can see no justification for the prevailing separation between clergy and laity. Even though he has given much time to the ecumenical movement, he sees neither need nor hope for the visible unity of institutional churches. What is deplorable is the lack of spiritual brotherhood in the churches, not their divisions as institutions.

In his own experience Brunner has found the true character

of the *ekklēsia* more often in voluntary associations of Christians than in the churches as such. Thus he gave much attention to the Group Movement until 1938, when it changed into Moral Re-Armament and lost its distinctly Christian character. He has been an ardent supporter of the Y.M.C.A., as well as the movement for laymen's institutes. And most significantly, when he reached Japan he found an indigenous expression of Christianity, the *Mukyokai*, or Non-Church Movement, which embodied his own theories about the New Testament *ekklēsia*. In later years he has done much writing to make the *Mukyokai* known in the West.

One of his reasons for criticizing the institutional churches is their lack of missionary zeal. He believes that the mission of the gospel would be better served if the true *ekklēsia* were more evident. Time and again he has asserted that his theological work is entirely in the service of mission. For years he has stressed the need for what he calls "eristics": a combination of both the apologetic commending of the faith and the polemical defense of it. He has demonstrated "eristics" in his treatment of non-Christian religions and the secular rivals of Christian faith.

BRUNNER'S INFLUENCE ON CHRISTIAN THOUGHT

The widespread effect of Brunner's many books has been evident for years. Several generations of theological students have used them assiduously. Their titles have become meaningful labels for types of theological concern. His published sermons and semipopular books and lectures have helped many people understand the complex questions aroused by Christian faith. Nevertheless he has not been the head of a particular "school" of theology. The adjective "Brunnerian" is seldom seen or heard. This is in accord with his wishes. He has been content to be the protagonist of living, biblical faith and the relentless antagonist of all that is inimical to it.

For exposing the weaknesses of Protestant liberalism and setting theology on a new course in this century Brunner has received much credit. Yet his own mind is literally a liberal one, free and open. And strangely enough, recent critics have described him as only a somewhat reformed liberal in theology.

This is a matter of definition of terms and of critical judgment. Most people still think of him, however, as one of the so-called neo-orthodox theologians.

His great books of Christian doctrine have manifested an unusual staying power. And there are scarcely any important doctrinal issues which he has neglected: God and creation, Christology, anthropology (i.e., man's nature), ethics, the Church, and the end of history and the future life. In the three volumes of his *Dogmatics* he has restated and summed up his thoughts on all these questions.

Brunner's career has been oriented toward both scholarship and teaching on the one hand and interpreting the Christian faith to the modern mind (both Western and Oriental) on the other. A favorite project has been the laymen's academy at Boldern, near Zurich, where he and his friends have tried to make the faith known to persons of many vocations.

Finally, he has over the years been the lucid, cogent, friendly teacher of a great many students from many countries. They remember his opening a 7 A.M. class with a rousing hymn, his orderly lectures delivered at times with passion, his wise counsel in courses on pastoral care, the hospitality of his home and the countless evenings of discussion there. These personal influences—consistent with his fondness for the I-Thou relation and for personal encounter—are as important and lasting as his books.

Bibliography

Emil Brunner, *The Divine Imperative*, Philadelphia, Westminster, 1947.

The *Theology of Emil Brunner*, Charles W. Kegley, ed., N.Y., Macmillan, 1962.

FRIEDRICH GOGARTEN

Theodore Runyon, Jr.

History is one of those all-important—if somewhat mystifying—words in current theological discussion. And no contemporary theologian has devoted himself more persistently to clarifying what we mean when we say "Christian faith is historical" than has Friedrich Gogarten. Gogarten's concern has been twofold: to rethink the traditional doctrines of the church in historical rather than metaphysical categories, and to show the relevance of Christian faith—understood as a kind of history—to a mankind which has become conscious of the overwhelming responsibility it carries for present history.

Born in 1887 in the Ruhr industrial city of Dortmund, Gogarten received his university training in Berlin, Jena, and Heidelberg. After serving as an assistant pastor in Bremen, he took a small country parish in Thuringia, bought himself a complete edition of Luther's works, and began to steep himself in the thought of the Reformer. Up to this point Gogarten had been a rather conventional "liberal" in the tradition of German idealism. His first book was on the religious thought of Fichte. But his absorption in Luther resulted in an abrupt break with the past, a break which first found expression in his sermons. The peasants who dutifully listened to those sermons might not have been aware of an emerging theological position, but students from the university at nearby Jena soon began making pilgrimages to the village church to hear the young pastor and spend the day discussing theology.

"The Crisis of Culture,"[1] an address delivered in 1920, first brought Gogarten to public attention. Spengler's *Decline of the West* was a best seller, and no one in postwar Germany needed to be reminded that civilization was in crisis. Gogarten's task

[1]Reprinted as "The Crisis of Our Culture," in *The Beginnings of Dialectic Theology,* ed. James M. Robinson (Richmond, John Knox, 1968), pp. 283-300.

was rather to clarify the relation of religion to the crisis. And here he differed sharply with many of his fellow theologians. The question they faced was this: Can Christianity as a Western religion survive the downfall of Western civilization? Many concluded that while Christianity as a historically conditioned form of religion may not survive, that matters little if the essential religious truths expressed in Christianity are preserved. And this is assured, they reasoned, for Christianity like all religions is an expression of the deep, inner religious consciousness of man. And this consciousness will persist even if Christianity passes away with Western civilization.

Gogarten's response is not so much a defense of Christianity's present forms as an attack on a liberalism which sees the crisis as limited to these forms. Liberalism is not radical enough. It continues to think of the religious consciousness of man as a kind of storm cellar from which he can emerge after the crisis has blown over. But this is hardly the Biblical understanding, which never conceives of crises as simply external, nor as excluding any part of man—least of all his religious consciousness. The real crisis, asserts Gogarten, is not defined by the instability of Western civilization but by that which shakes all foundations: the judgment of God. And the religious consciousness is no place to hide from this judgment, for it begins precisely with man and his religion—with the man who has named the depths of his own spirit "God," and thus completed the circle of reality within himself. For this man, his culture, *and* his religion there is no road to renewal which bypasses death. There are no "good" elements which might be salvaged. For this culture's highest good—the human spirit—is just that which has usurped the place of God. Therefore the death sentence must be pronounced; the *No* must be said. And at the present moment it may have to be said so loudly there seems little room left for a *Yes*. But the *No* of God's judgment is not the *No* of cynicism; it is not ultimately negative. "The death sentence is the entrance into life."[2] It is said in order that the *Yes* might be said, the *Yes* of God's new creation.

This new creation does not signal the end of crisis, however.

[2] *Ibid.*, p. 291.

If the life of faith means continually receiving oneself from the hand of the Creator, it is a life lived always at the end of human possibilities, never self-sufficient, always dependent for continued existence on help from beyond. Thus the fundamental crisis is permanent, written into the very nature of faith itself.

This awareness of the radical character of the crisis, along with the dialectic of judgment and grace under a sovereign God, made it natural for the young German pastor to join forces with a young Swiss pastor, Karl Barth, who was also disengaging himself from earlier theological idealism and striking out on a new course. In 1922, together with Eduard Thurneysen and Georg Merz (later joined by Rudolf Bultmann and Emil Brunner), they founded a journal which was to provide a forum for this new direction in theology known in Europe as "crisis theology" or "dialectical theology" and in America as "neoorthodoxy." The journal took its name from the title of one of Gogarten's articles, "Zwischen den Zeiten" (Between the Times).

FAITH AND HISTORICAL RELATIVITY

The book which was to secure Gogarten a permanent place in the theological world, *I Believe in the Triune God,* was published in 1926. Subtitled "An Examination of the Relation between Faith and History," it is a vigorous attack on the historicism tempered with idealism of Troeltsch, Harnack, and Seeberg. Their historical research had forced them to face the *relativity* of Christian ethical and doctrinal positions traditionally considered absolute. They finally had to ask, Is there anything in Christianity which is absolute? Troeltsch's answer is characteristic of the general view: Christianity is "the historical concretion of a universal truth."[3] The historical form, marked as it is by the peculiarities of a particular time and place, is not absolute. It is only the shell within which dwells an essential idea that is timeless. The absoluteness of Christianity is to be found in the universal value of its history-transcending essence.

But this solution does not satisfy Gogarten. Can an approach which grants validity to historical events only as they can be

[3] *Ich glaube an den dreieinigen Gott* (Jena, Diederichs, 1926), p. 96.

reduced to a universal essence unconditioned by time and place do justice to Christian faith? If Christian faith is the product of God's creative activity, and if this activity not only takes place in history but *makes* history, then the "essence" of faith most certainly cannot be nonhistorical. Quite the opposite. *Faith is history.*[4]

This claim is basic to Gogarten's whole approach. But it needs explanation, for certainly he does not mean by *faith* much of what passes under that name. Indeed, he protests those views which have gradually diluted the distinctively Hebrew-Christian understanding of the relation between man and God, substituting for it aesthetic experience, participation in a world spirit, or religious intuition. Nor is Gogarten any more friendly toward a sterile dogmatism which mistakes assent to theological propositions, however important, for faith. All these views are deficient because they fail to see that faith cannot be defined exclusively in terms of man's feelings, intuition, convictions, or ability to assent. Faith is faith only as God himself is actively involved, only as it is happening between God and man. "The final, most profound, yet simplest fact is that you cannot have God without God."[5] Faith in God must be called forth by God himself, the God who communicates to man his trustworthiness and elicits faith and obedience. Faith is therefore an event, a relationship in which the Creator is active with the creature.

It follows that "faith is history" does not mean that faith is simply *past* history. For just as "faith" must be carefully defined, so "history" cannot be understood in the ordinary schoolroom sense. It designates instead the process of interaction in which being and meaning are created ever anew. Therefore faith is present history, history now taking place. And if it is not present history it is nothing.

Gogarten recognized in the I-Thou approach being developed by Grisebach, Buber, Ebner, and Heim an interpretation of history akin to his own. And Bultmann's *Jesus and the Word,* the first edition of which appeared in 1926, applies a similar methodology to New Testament studies. The reality of history is neither the reality of ideas in the mind of the interpreter, who

[4]*Ibid.*, pp. 17 f.
[5]*The Beginnings of Dialectic Theology,* p. 298.

by virtue of these ideas makes the facts fit together in a meaningful pattern (subjectivism and idealism), nor the reality of the "facts" in themselves in their detached isolated state (objectivism and positivism). The truth cannot be known by coming down on one side or the other of a fence between subject and object. It is found instead in the interaction between subject and object—or better, in the case of God and man, between Subject and subject. Reality is an event which happens in the "between," in history.

Thus the problem of relativity as it concerns Christian faith is solved not by escaping from history into a realm of absolute ideals and universals but by living in history the *responsible* life of faith. And faith is itself a kind of relativity, man's relativity to God in every new moment.

In his next major work, *Political Ethics,* Gogarten examines the implications of this view of history for the relationships between men. Here again relativity is the problem. Historical research had mercilessly exposed the relativity of supposedly absolute ethical norms and standards. Seeking to rebuild on the wreckage, Christian ethical theorists were tempted to search for universal principles within Christianity which would be valid beyond the relativities of Christianity as a historical religion, on the assumption that if such universals could be found a system of Christian ethics could be formulated which would have all-embracing validity and lasting authority. From Gogarten's standpoint, however, historical contingency—while undermining an absolutist ethic—is not inimical to ethics as such. Indeed, the fact that history is composed of contingent relationships is what makes it unavoidably ethical. One has his being in creative encounter—being is always being-from-the-other (*Von-dem-Andern-sein*)—and his continuing existence in being-with-another (*Mit-dem-Andern-sein*). These are not secondary modes of existence preceded by a primary mode of being-in-and-for-oneself (*An-und-für-sich-sein*); rather, individuality is secondary and the interpersonal is primary.[6]

Accordingly, ethical decisions and actions are the result not of adhering to abstract, nonhistorical standards of what one does

[6] *Politische Ethik* (Jena, Diederichs, 1932), pp. 26 ff., 173. Thus "thou-I" would be a more appropriate characterization of Gogarten's approach.

or does not do, but of responding to each situation out of the being which one is in the relation to God and neighbor. The Christian life is a life of openness and obedience. The two go together. Obedience is understood not as strict compliance with laws and ideals but as that kind of openness which marks the genuine listener (*obedience* means literally "to hear toward") whose action is a creative response to what he hears. In ethics as elsewhere, therefore, the problem of relativity is overcome not by substituting nonhistorical absolutes for the relativities of history but by facing each situation as a call to responsible action in history out of the being one has in faith. Thus Gogarten provides us with one of the earliest formulations of a "contextual ethic," which has become a hallmark of most contemporary, theologically based ethical thought.

Not content to rest on the level of individual relations, Gogarten pursues the implications of his position for an ethic of the state. Contemporary Western theories of society and the state have their roots in the individualism of rationalism. They are I-oriented. The fundamental mode of existence is understood as "being-in-and-for-oneself." Society and the state are thus secondary, artificial realities created by man for the furtherance of his welfare, goals, and ideals. Over against this Gogarten sets an understanding of the state as a fabric of interresponsibility in which each has his being in his function of being-for-another.[7] The state is given power over the individual member to ensure that the needs of the body politic will be met by forced obedience, if necessary, where the individual is irresponsible regarding his duties. Such obedience is not true obedience in the intended sense, of course, but is necessary to maintain order in at least an external sense even if fallen man does not will it.

Discernible here is the influence of Luther's doctrine of civil authority, which grounds the magistrate's authority and power in the Fall. His Lutheran unwillingness to risk anarchy was to make Gogarten less prone to criticize the state in the first years

[7] Thus Gogarten's preference for the title "political ethics" rather than the usual "*social* ethics." The *polis* is an organic whole, in which each member has his function and duty for the maintenance of the body politic, rather than merely an *association* of individuals. Cf. pp. 115 f., 147 ff.

of the National Socialist regime in Germany than were many of his friends in the circle of dialectical theology. During the same period there was a gradual parting of the ways theologically between Gogarten and Barth, the latter accusing Gogarten, Bultmann, and Brunner of leaving the common ground of the earlier dialectical theology and making theology too dependent upon philosophical presuppositions.[8] This led to the discontinuation of the journal *Zwischen den Zeiten*, as well as the partnership which had created it.

Though continuing to teach (at the University of Breslau, from 1931 to 1935, and at the University of Göttingen, from 1935 until his retirement in 1955), Gogarten published no further major work until after World War II.

FAITH AND SECULARISM

In most of his major postwar works Gogarten continues his interest in history, but whereas his concern earlier had been to overcome idealism and answer the problem of historical relativism, he now turns to what he considers *the* problem confronting a technological age: the relation of Christian faith to secularism. And he does this by developing the implications of a theology of history for the traditional theological questions of Christology and soteriology (in *The Proclamation of Jesus Christ*), law and gospel (in his magnum opus, *Man between God and the World*), faith and works (in *The Fate and Hope of the Modern Era*), and subjectivism versus objectivism (in *The Reality of Faith*).

While the popular attitude toward secularism regards it as the archenemy of the faith, Gogarten asks whether a certain kind of secularization is not implicit in the Christian gospel itself. For example, the secular view sees the world as depopulated of those spirits once thought to have the world's well-being under their control. The task of maintaining the order of the world passes out of the hands of the demons, angels, "principalities and powers" and into the hands of man, who takes over the responsibility of ordering and caring for the world in accordance with his own needs and desires. Such a secularization is, however,

[8] *Zwischen den Zeiten*, Vol. XI (1933), p. 311.

by no means foreign to the Christian faith, in which man is understood as receiving his being from the God whose creative Word calls man not just into existence but into an existence-in-responsibility. The world is directly involved in this responsibility, for the being into which man is called is, in Pauline terminology, the being of a *son* (Galatians 4). A son is distinguished from a child in that, whereas the child is completely dependent upon the parent for his continued existence, the son—who has come of age and received an inheritance which is his to manage—has the ability to stand on his own, to be independent (*selbstständig*), no longer bound to the father by the necessities of his physical survival. The inheritance bestowed upon man is the *world*; he is given dominion over it and charged with the responsibility to "till it and keep it." His position with regard to the world thus frees him for a mature and noncompulsive relationship with the Father, while his filial relation to the Father frees him for a mature and noncompulsive attitude toward the world.[9]

Now we are in a position to understand the context of Gogarten's recurrent insistence that the examination and ordering of the world be delivered to man's reason with no strings attached.[10] His regular conversations with his physicist colleague at Göttingen, C. F. von Weizsäcker, convinced him of the very real necessity of clarifying the relation of formal and technological reason to faith, especially as it bears on the responsibility of the scientist. Again he finds the answer in Luther's understanding of faith and works and the doctrine of the two realms. Faith has no business anxiously hovering over reason lest reason discover something about the world that would undermine faith. A faith which could be so undermined would actually be pre-Christian, i.e., it would in effect assume that the world has a power over one's salvation which the early Christian message specifically denied that the world possesses. In genuine faith man receives the world and his existence as steward of the world

---

[9] Note the similarity between Gogarten's development regarding the nature and place of the world in Christian faith and Dietrich Bonhoeffer's seminal idea of "the world come of age."

[10] E.g., *The Reality of Faith* (Philadelphia, Westminster, 1959), pp. 90 ff.

—but not information about the world. The latter is *his* responsibility and is to be gained through his efforts. Nor need he justify himself before God by piously limiting his reason in the pursuit of this task. He is justified by faith alone, i.e., by the sustaining relationship with the Father, which frees him to explore his world with true "objectivity," unhampered by the subjective necessity of justifying his existence by his works.

However, contends Gogarten, if faith is not present, if man does not continue to receive his existence from the Father, then the crucial balance—reason operating within faith—cannot be maintained. Freedom and openness are destroyed, anxiety sets in, and a now heteronomous "faith" seeks to extend its authority and control over an autonomous "reason," and vice versa, in the anxious effort to re-establish the wholeness and unity of life lost with the death of genuine faith. It matters little which side in this struggle is victorious, for neither is what it was and is meant to be within faith. Both have been fundamentally perverted. Man without faith remains a son, to be sure, but a son who has betrayed the Father. Man without faith retains his mastery over the world, but as a master who is in the ironic position of having to squeeze his meaning and being out of that over which he is lord. Thus the change is not so much the loss of what man previously was as the turning of what he was into its negating opposite.[11] Just as honor betrayed becomes *dis*honor—which is worse than the mere absence of honor—so sonship betrayed becomes worse than the mere absence of relationship; it becomes a corrupted relationship, one of alienation and estrangement.

When this shift comes about and man looks to the world for his being and meaning, the world begins to take on a religious nature. That which was secular now becomes the source of life in a religious sense remarkably parallel to the ancient world, though without benefit of the ancient mythological picture. The reality is the same, however. Man is subject to the powers of the world; they control his meaning or lack of it. Nor are "materialists" the only ones who fall under this subjugation. Indeed, the two classic examples of bondage to the world are religious:

---

[11] Cf. Romans 1:22-25.

the Greeks' bondage to the cosmos and the Jews' bondage to the law. In both instances one's being was assured only if he adhered rigidly to what was understood as a religious order of things. Absolute conformity brought salvation. Is the picture so different today? Meaning, place, and position are guaranteed if one will conform to a group, class, or national self-image which grants the participant being—but only as long as he continues to conform. Nonconformity results in rejection and threatened loss of being. World views are propounded which promise to reduce the world to a meaningful and manageable whole—but only if one adheres to the assumptions and laws by which their originators seek to introduce order into experience. Stray from the path and chaos reigns again. In this misuse of reason, meaning can be had only at the price of conformity to the law of the world of man's mind. Gogarten's early rejection of idealism was based on the conviction that it was really a form of worldliness; it imposed a subjective scheme of things upon reality and insisted that reality conform to that scheme. A full-scale example of the same phenomenon was National Socialism. Operating on the basis of a quasi-mythological world view, National Socialism methodically destroyed all opposition to its ordering of the world in conformity with its own self-image. All such religio-secularistic attempts are inherently totalitarian. Any opposition calls forth a neurotic response simply because as long as opposition persists the system is in principle undermined, for it has failed to accomplish what it promises: to reduce all of reality to conformity with itself.

Thus the problem of secularism is not its irreligion but its continual tendency to become religious. *It is not secular enough.* Secularism in its various modern forms does not preserve the truly secular nature of the world but tends to give to the world—whether this be the material world, the world of religion, or the world of its own mind—the honor due God alone. Christian faith proposes to keep the world truly secular and thus safeguard man's freedom toward the world through a certain kind of existence, existence as a mature and responsible son under the Creator-Father. Where this existence-in-faith is not present, however, the freedom for which man was created cannot be present. He still remains man, to be sure, and as man he is that being who has his being *in relation*, that creature who must be fulfilled from beyond himself. But this is precisely his difficulty. If not fulfilled through a free relation to his Creator, he will—he *must*—turn to another source of fulfillment; he must enter into a compulsive relation to the world.

In the fateful situation of corrupted sonship God himself acts to restore to man the possibility of authentic sonship. And he does so in and through his own Son.

CHRISTOLOGY AND SOTERIOLOGY

In developing his doctrine of Christ, Gogarten insists that Jesus' divinity must be understood in and through his humanity. Jesus' revelation of God is to be found in his history rather than in a metaphysical nature in which he is consubstantial with the Father. Or, expressed in another way, his history *is* his metaphysical nature through which he reveals the Father to us and brings about reconciliation. In his history the Incarnational event —God assuming our flesh—takes place. What is the nature of this event?

Jesus of Nazareth is fully man, but since he is a man who is completely obedient to the Father, his being is being-from-the-Father. Lived out of the will of the Father, his life is the concrete expression of that will. In the history of Jesus of Nazareth the eternal will of God is enacted. He is that Son who *is* the second person of the Trinity, for in his life the eternal relation between the Father and the Son in the being of God becomes historical.[12] The basic difference, therefore, between ourselves and Jesus is not the difference between natural man and a supernatural being but the difference between sinful history and faithful history, between sonship betrayed and sonship maintained.

But to this must be added that Jesus' relationship is with the Father who wills to restore his estranged sons to fellowship with himself. Consequently, the Son who received his being from the Father reflects in his sonship the concern of the Father for the brothers. He enters into relationship with them and thus also receives his being from their sinful being. Having his being

[12] Cf. "Gottheit und Menschheit Jesu Christi," *Zwischen den Zeiten*, Vol. X (1932), pp. 3 ff.

entirely from God, Jesus turns toward man and, in fulfillment of the second half of the Great Commandment, receives his being *entirely* from man. (This illustrates how "being" as used by Gogarten cannot be understood substantially or quantitatively but as the quality of historical existence.) Thus his full divinity and full humanity are the result of the same divine will and are a description of the same history. He is "made to be sin" (II Cor. 5:21), while at the same time remaining "without sin" (Heb. 4:15) in perfect obedience to the Father. Passages such as these, which for a substantialist approach must remain inexplicable, take on new meaning and relevance when seen as history. The doctrine of the two natures of Christ is meant to be not an unintelligible mystery but an account of Jesus' life with God and man. At the same time, it is an account of the way in which man is restored to that life with God for which he was created, true sonship. Since true sonship is not available apart from faith, the question becomes: How does the action of God in Jesus Christ make faith—and true sonship—possible?

Acting in accordance with the will of the Father, Jesus turns toward the brothers, participating in their being-in-sin through his relationship to them. In so doing, he experiences more radically than can any man the intensity of the alienation between man and God, for he experiences it within his own history. On him the full weight of the curse of this alienation falls, coming to expression in the cry of dereliction. Is it surprising that the cross was interpreted by the early church as judgment, as the place where Christ as the representative of man takes upon himself the judgment which should rightly fall on all men? This is how it looks from man's side. On the cross the man who has received his being from a mankind-against-God is reduced to nothingness. But the cross is not only "the disclosure of the guilt-laden fate of perverted being that lies upon man and his world"; it is also the turning of this fate. It is not only the sign of divine judgment but also "the sign of the salvation brought to man by the crucified One." It is not only the condemnation of man's sin and his reduction to *Nichtigkeit*; also "on the cross the forfeited sonship is bestowed anew."[13] The man-against-God is reduced to nothingness—but in order that he might be raised

[13] *The Reality of Faith,* pp. 123, 125.

a new man by the Creator who re-creates, the God who forgives and restores, the God who quickens the dead (Rom. 4:17).

Man participates in this history which takes place in Jesus Christ as he encounters the Word directed toward him from the Father, communicated to him through the Son. For the Man who hangs on the cross as the representative of man is also the Son who is the representative of God. In the encounter with the Son, man meets that which both reduces him to nothing and raises him to new life and new sonship. For in the relation with Christ man receives himself and his being from the One who receives his being from the Father and whose being is therefore "historically identical" with that of the Father. In this way man participates in the salvation made available to him in Jesus Christ. But this participation is not metaphysical, nor mystical, nor is it a matter of the moral influence or spiritual interpretation of a story, nor any approach which views atonement as taking place exclusively, or even primarily, either in the supernatural world apart from man or within man's mind. It is fundamentally the reconciliation of persons. It is the event which takes place as man is confronted by the One who in his life, death, and resurrection is God's judgment upon man's life apart from him and is at the same time God's turning toward man in forgiveness and restoration to true sonship.[14]

In this historical event of atonement man is released from his bondage to the world and restored to his intended place over it through the re-establishment of the faith-relation to God. Once again he receives his fundamental meaning and being from the Father and is thus enabled to live in creative freedom toward a world which has been "secularized," stripped of its idolatrous pretentions. (This transformation can be expressed mythologically as the vanquishing of the demonic cosmic powers through the cross of Christ, a victory in which man benefits by virtue of his relation to the Victor. Cf. Rom. 8:38f.; Eph. 1 and 2; Col. 1 and 2.) Thus salvation is at the same time the secularization of the world, that secularization which, according to Gogarten, is at the heart of Christian faith.

Modern secular*ism,* on the other hand, developing out of the

[14] Cf. *Demythologizing and History* (London, SCM Press, 1955), pp. 68–79.

reorientation which took place in the Renaissance and Enlightenment, has purged the world of gods and devils by splitting all reality into "subject" and "object," the subject—the human mind—taking charge over the world as its object in a way it previously had never dared to do. The world is to be examined in and for itself, disregarding all supernatural associations, in order to define and isolate the intramundane law. The result of this methodology has been a technological advance without parallel. Unfortunately, however, technological control, though it does guarantee the burden of responsibility, does not guarantee meaning. The result is a situation in which man *alone* is responsible for the world—there are no more gods with whom to share the burden—while at the same time the ultimate meaning of this responsibility eludes him. Man feels increasingly victimized by the world about which he is accumulating ever greater amounts of objective information. Yet every attempt to derive meaning from within the world proves finally unsatisfactory. At the end of the subject-object era the *object* has become the real, the vis-à-vis (*Gegenüber*) from which the subject has to receive its being because it is the only reality apart from the subject. As a result, the subject is relativized by that over which it is supposed to exercise dominion. And the values of the subject are now "only relative," "only subjective."

The bankruptcy of the subject-object orientation as an exclusive approach to reality is clear. It has ended in a situation in which man is the victim and captive of that toward which he should—and indeed *must*—be free if he is to carry out his responsibility for the ordering and maintaining of the world under the Creator.

FAITH AND DEMYTHOLOGIZING

It should now be apparent why Gogarten felt called upon to enter the "demythologizing controversy" on the side of Bultmann. The real issue at stake, says Gogarten in *Demythologizing and History,* is the nature of faith and its relation to history.

A charge commonly lodged against Bultmann and his followers is that they have, by the application of rigorously critical methods to the New Testament, reduced the amount of objective, factual material in the gospel records to the point where the bridge between the historical Jesus and the preaching about him has collapsed. If the first Christians were not concerned with reporting the facts objectively in their preaching, but instead made generous use of the language of the then-current world views (*Weltanschauungen*) and of the ancient conception of the physical universe (*Weltbild*) in interpreting and proclaiming what they experienced, we are left with little or no solid ground in reliable fact to which we can point as reinforcing the claim of faith that God has acted decisively in objective history through the life, death, and resurrection of Jesus Christ. And if this be the case, how can we continue to speak of Christianity as a "historical" religion in any more than a strained and indeed mythological sense?

Two assumptions are implicit in this protest which need to be examined. One is that God's action in history is objective; the other, that faith is subjective. The two are, of course, correlated because they are both grounded in the subject-object world view and exemplify the way in which this view must of necessity see faith and history. History is viewed as an independent object which is available to be appropriated by a free and independent subject in an act which is called "faith." The objectivity of that which is espoused keeps faith from being completely subjective. Faith is thus understood in the traditional pattern of *notitia* plus *assensus,* taking notice of an objective fact and also assenting to its validity.[15] Now if there is no independent object toward which Christian faith is directed, but only the subjective faith of the early church, it follows that the believer is set adrift in a sea of subjectivism and relativism. There is no solid historical object in his faith, and the fear that such a faith is "docetic" seems justified.

But Gogarten must question both assumptions: the objectivism of history and the subjectivism of faith. The demythologizers no less than their opponents affirm that "the great acts of God are set before all human existence indestructibly, indissolubly and irremovably."[16] But the reality and permanence of these events, as they are understood in the Bible itself, lie not

15 *Ibid.,* p. 51.
16 *Ibid.,* p. 67.

in their independent objectivity but in their being used by God in communicating his intention toward man. This is made especially clear, as we have seen, in the revelation in Jesus Christ. The genuine history of Jesus *includes* his relation with the Father. His very being is being-from-the-Father. Moreover, the being he receives as the Son is God's being-for-man. So that *the history of Jesus is God's turning himself toward man to save!* But obviously neither the relation of Jesus to the Father nor the intention of God toward man enacted through the Son is available through an "objective" approach, not because they are irrecoverable but because both are recoverable only in and through a method appropriate to transmitting the kind of history with which we are here concerned. For this history has a verbal (*worthaft*) character; it intends to communicate. And its reality cannot be grasped apart from a reception of this communication. This is why preaching, far from breaking the connection with the historical Jesus, is actually the conserver and effectuator of the genuine history of Jesus. For he who would understand this history must be involved in it as it becomes the living Word of God to him. This history can be grasped and understood only as its reality becomes present, as it happens here and now. To attempt to reduce this to "objective" history is to engage in a "miserable rationalization of the New Testament history . . . [by which] the New Testament message loses its own historical character."[17]

Likewise, faith for Gogarten cannot be labeled "subjective," for faith is not a subject's affirmation of an object but rather its being confronted by the Word from beyond itself and incorporated into a relationship—into a new history—fundamentally conditioned by the history of Jesus Christ (as that history has just been described). Faith therefore transcends subjectivism by virtue of the fact that it is a historical mode of being, a being-from-the-other and with-the-other. Apart from this "other" and the historical interaction there is no genuine faith.

What happens in revelation and faith thus bursts the bonds of the subject-object approach and simply cannot be comprehended by it. To attempt to do so can lead only to a distortion of the genuine reality involved. The demythologizers recognize

[17] *Ibid.*, p. 76.

this and explicitly operate in a different context in their theological formulations. However, they do continue to use the objective approach where it is appropriate, namely, in historical critical research. The resultant alternation between methods is the source of much confusion to many of their opponents who themselves operate for the most part unconsciously in a subject-object context which is neither so strictly employed in criticism nor so clearly superseded in theological formulation. Thus much of what is said and written in the controversy is unfortunately beside the point. Rather than the destruction of historical truth, the demythologizers see their task as making possible a proper confrontation with a history understood not as a supernatural object but as the divine Word. Their negative contribution is in making it impossible to confuse faith with assent to certain thought forms of the first century. Consequently they have to be critical of the *form* of expression of the first century, but only in order to open up the genuinely historical *content* which was and is being communicated: God's Word to man.

Because of his defense of the existentialist stance in theology, Gogarten's name is today often linked with that of Bultmann, as it once was with Barth. In some respects the present classification is more justified than the earlier one, for Gogarten's Lutheran bias and philosophical interests made him something of an anomaly in dialectical theology. However, it would be a mistake simply to equate Gogarten with Bultmann. For one thing, several of the so-called "post-Bultmannians" are dependent upon Gogarten for their theological orientation, especially Gerhard Ebeling, Brunner's successor at Zurich,[18] and Ernst Fuchs, upon whom the mantle of Bultmann has fallen at Marburg. And Gogarten is credited with anticipating systematically in *The Proclamation of Jesus Christ*[19] many of the conclusions to which these younger critics of Bultmann have since come, on the basis of textual evidence. But perhaps it is his

[18] Cf. Ebeling's *The Nature of Faith* (Philadelphia, Muhlenberg, 1961).

[19] *Die Verkündigung Jesu Christi* (Heidelberg, L. Schneider, 1948). For an account of the "post-Bultmannian" development, see James M. Robinson, *A New Quest of the Historical Jesus* (London, SCM Press, 1961).

foremost American admirer, Carl Michalson, who in *The Rationality of Faith*,[20] a programmatic study of faith's relation to history, has given most explicit expression to Gogarten's central concern. For underneath Gogarten's earlier attacks on idealism, as well as his more recent conversations with secularism, lies but one aim: to examine systematically the implications for theology of the fact that reality, in general, and the reality of the Christian faith, in particular, must once again be viewed as it was in the Biblical period—as history.

[20] (N.Y., Scribner's, 1963.)

Bibliography

Frederick William Dillistone, *C. H. Dodd: Interpreter of the New Testament*, London, Hodder & Stoughton, 1977.

Garland Wayne Glick, *The Reality of Christianity: A Study of Adolf von Harnack as Historian and Theologian*, N.Y., Harper & Row, 1967.

Friedrich Gogarten, *The Reality of Faith*, Philadelphia, Westminster, 1959.

Ingmar Haolmstrand, *Karl Heim on Philosophy, Science, and the Transcendence of God*, Stockholm, Almquist & Wiksell International, 1980.

Larry Shiner, *The Secularization of History*, Nashville, Abingdon, 1966.

RUDOLF BULTMANN

John Macquarrie

Born at Wiefelstede, Oldenburg, on August 20, 1884, Rudolf Karl Bultmann has spent his entire life in biblical and theological studies. He was a student at the University of Marburg in the years when that center of learning boasted world-famous schools both in philosophy and in theology, and he continued his studies at Tübingen and Berlin. By 1912 he had become a private lecturer at Marburg, and later held academic posts at Breslau and Giessen. In 1921 he returned to Marburg as Professor of New Testament, and remained there until his retirement in 1951. In the meantime he had gained an international reputation as a scholar, and this was recognized by invitations to give the Shaffer Lectures in Yale University in 1951 and the Gifford Lectures in Edinburgh University in 1955.

It was as a radical critic of the New Testament that Bultmann first attracted attention. In an extensive study of the Synoptic Gospels,[1] Bultmann takes up the method of form-criticism which had been adumbrated by Johannes Weiss. On this view, the gospel narrative may be analyzed into units which can then be classified according to their forms, as apothegms, miracle stories, and so on. These units were formulated in the early Christian community to meet its devotional and apologetic needs, and later they were strung together like beads on a thread to make up the Synoptic Gospels. If this point of view is correct, it follows that the Synoptic Gospels give us information about the early Christian community and its beliefs rather than about Jesus himself, and that their value as biographies of Jesus is negligible. Even St. Mark's Gospel, on this view, is a theological document rather than a historical one.

The Fourth Gospel has likewise come under Bultmann's meticulous scrutiny, and he has produced a major commentary

[1] *Geschichte der synoptischen Tradition* (Göttingen, Vandenhoeck & Ruprecht, 1921).

445

on it.[2] In his view, Gnostic influences have entered very deeply into the thought of the Fourth Gospel, in which the sacrifice of history to theology has been carried to an extreme length.

These theories about the Gospels lead to a profound skepticism with regard to any historical facts they may be supposed to record. This skeptical attitude may be summed up in Bultmann's own statement that "we can now know almost nothing concerning the life and personality of Jesus."[3] We can indeed know something of his teaching, which Bultmann represents as primarily eschatological in character, and as an appeal for decision before the approaching end. But the historical Jesus himself remains in impenetrable shadow, and it is even denied that he ever claimed to be the Messiah. "The historical person of Jesus was very soon turned into a myth in primitive Christianity."[4] It is now impossible to get behind this myth to the historical facts of the matter.

Yet this skepticism about matters of fact has not made Bultmann skeptical about the Christian religion. On the contrary, he combines his negative historical findings not only with Christian faith but with a genuine evangelical concern to win acceptance for the Christian message in the modern secularized world, and he tells us himself that he experiences no discomfort in this combination. For him faith is not dependent on the findings of historical research. Like Karl Barth, Bultmann has reacted strongly against the older liberal school of thought which looked for the "real" historical Jesus, freed from theological interpretations of his person and work. Bultmann agrees with Barth in finding the essence of Christianity in the kerygmatic proclamation of the New Testament—a word of God addressed to man and demanding the response of faith. Some of Bultmann's critics say that he has been driven into this theological orientation because the negative results of his researches have left him with so little in the way of a factual historical foundation for his theology; but other critics allege that he has deliberately stressed the negative findings of historical research in order to make it

[2] *Das Evangelium des Johannes* (1941).

[3] *Jesus and the Word* (N.Y., Scribner's, 1934), p. 8.

[4] *Primitive Christianity in Its Contemporary Setting* (N.Y., Meridian, 1956), p. 200.

clear that faith is not at all dependent upon such research. Whatever the truth of the matter, the main theological interest in Bultmann lies in his attempt to interpret Christianity in such a way that one can be radically skeptical about the factual content of the gospel narrative and yet continue to believe in the essential message of the New Testament. Indeed, Bultmann would go further, maintaining that if the essential Christian message is to gain a hearing in the contemporary world, it must be disengaged from the form in which it is presented in the New Testament.

As we have already noted, Bultmann holds that the history of Jesus was speedily transformed into a myth. It is this myth which now confronts us in the pages of the New Testament, and it is futile to try—as Harnack and others did—to get behind it to the facts of the historical Jesus. These facts, whatever they may have been, have undergone an irreversible metamorphosis into the story of a divine pre-existent being who became incarnate and atoned by his blood for the sins of men, who rose from the dead and ascended into heaven, and who, it was believed, would shortly come again on the clouds to bring the present age to a close, to hold judgment upon men, and to establish the new age. This central story is, moreover, embellished and illustrated by all kinds of peripheral legends which tell of miracles and wonders, voices from heaven, victories over demons, and the like. Such a story is called a myth. It belongs to the undifferentiated thinking of a prescientific age, when occult forces, divine or demonic, were supposed to be everywhere active both in human affairs and in nature, and when any unexplained event was assigned to the direct agency of such forces.

Such a mythical way of thinking is impossible for men who live in the twentieth century. They have grown up in a scientific climate of thought, and their understanding of the world is inescapably influenced by it. "It is impossible to use electric light and the wireless and to avail ourselves of modern medical and surgical discoveries," says Bultmann, "and at the same time to believe in the New Testament world of demons and spirits."[5]

[5] "New Testament and Mythology," in *Kerygma and Myth*, H. W. Bartsch, ed., (N.Y., Harper, 1961), p. 5.

It is indeed impossible, unless we are to have split minds, with one set of beliefs about the world for religion and another set for our everyday living. If Christianity is inextricably bound up with the outworn mythology and cosmology of the first century of our era, then it would seem that unless we are prepared to make a sacrifice of the intellect, we must reluctantly say good-by to the Christian faith, as so many moderns have felt themselves compelled to do when confronted by the bewildering and unintelligible ideas of the New Testament.

Bultmann himself, however, when confronted with this situation, does not say good-by to Christianity. He believes that hidden in the mythical language of the New Testament lies a supreme truth—nothing less than God's word addressed to man. He is concerned that we in the modern world should hear this word and respond to it. We cannot, it is true, accept the mythical ideas of the New Testament, but these ideas, Bultmann thinks, are not part of the essential message but are simply historical accidents which inevitably attached themselves to the message in the age in which it was formulated. The message itself can be disengaged from its mythical setting. We have already seen that this is not to be done by trying to penetrate behind the myth to some supposed historical substratum. We have to take the myth as it stands and attempt to restate it in a form free from mythical ideas. The task of constructing such a restatement is what Bultmann calls "demythologizing."

Bultmann is therefore engaged in a task of translation. The message of the New Testament is to be translated out of the mythical language in which it has been handed down to us into a language which is intelligible in our times. "Demythologizing," says Bultmann, "is an hermeneutic method, that is to say, a method of interpretation and exegesis."[6] Hermeneutics is the scientific study of the principles of interpretation, and it is a study to which Bultmann has devoted considerable attention.[7] He points out that an interpreter can elucidate the meaning of a document only if he already has some preliminary understanding of the subject matter of the document. For instance, one cannot begin to understand what St. Paul has to say about

[6] *Jesus Christ and Mythology* (N.Y., Scribner's, 1958), p. 45.

[7] See his essay "The Problem of Hermeneutics," in *Essays, Philosophical and Theological* (N.Y., Macmillan, 1955), pp. 234–61.

sin unless one already has from experience some understanding of what sin is. Again, Bultmann claims that the interpreter will be most successful in his task if he approaches the document with the right questions in mind, that is to say, if the interest which guides his questions is sufficiently close to the interest which motivated the author of the document. People go wrong when they ask of the Bible questions which are remote from the interests of the biblical writers—for instance, when they seek information about scientific cosmology from Genesis or when they try to forecast contemporary political happenings from Ezekiel, to mention extreme cases.

Now the key to this hermeneutical problem is found by Bultmann in the concept of human existence. It is as existing, and therefore as already having some understanding of existence, that we are able to have that preliminary understanding which is necessary to us before the biblical writings can mean anything to us at all. And further, it is the question of existence which provides the required community of interest with the biblical writers, and which is therefore the right question to ask of the Bible. This question of existence is one to which each of us is driven by having to decide about his own existence, and the truth concealed under the mythical formulations of the Bible is a true understanding of human existence for which men can decide in the twentieth century just as they did in the first—a new self-understanding, as Bultmann often expresses it. To demythologize is therefore to translate from mythical language into existential language.

The first step in this new orientation is to address to the New Testament existential questions. What does this mean for my existence? What possibilities of existence are disclosed here? Into what understanding of myself does this bring me? But in order that such questions may be asked with the fullest awareness of their implications, we should first of all clarify and analyze that preliminary understanding of existence which we already bring to the task of interpretation. The peculiarity of man, as distinct from any mere inanimate thing, is that he not only exists but always has some understanding of his existence. And while this understanding of existence which is given with human existence may be—and usually is—vague and naïve, it is nevertheless capable of being brought to clarity through philosophical reflection and analysis. The type of philosophy which explicitly applies itself to the task of clarifying the structures of human existence is existentialism, so now we see the reason for the close connection of demythologizing with existentialist philosophy. In particular, Bultmann has found the philosophy of Martin Heidegger very enlightening for his purposes. It would be a mistake to suppose, as some do, that Bultmann has first accepted the philosophical teaching of Heidegger and has then interpreted the New Testament in such a way that it will conform to this secular philosophy. Rather, Bultmann has seen in the categories which Heidegger has forged the very tools which he needs for his own hermeneutical approach to the New Testament. In Heidegger we find an analysis of human existence which enables us to go about the task of existential interpretation with some hope of attaining clarity and precision. As another New Testament scholar, Erich Dinkler, has remarked, "Heidegger's analysis of human existence more than any other modern philosophy offers structures and defines terms fit for theologically clear speaking."[8]

Heidegger thinks that human existence gets misunderstood when we apply to it categories such as substance and accident or cause and effect. These categories are appropriate to objects in the world, but our existence is never such an object. He proposes to find a new set of categories, or "existentials," as he calls them, which will be appropriate for describing human existence, and these existentials will describe not fixed properties but possible ways of being for which man, as an existent, can decide. Heidegger's whole scheme cannot be indicated here, but it will be helpful to consider a few of his more important ideas and show how they provide a framework for Bultmann's exposition of the thought of St. Paul, which ranks among his best exegetical work.[9]

In Heidegger the fundamental possibilities are an authentic existence or an inauthentic existence. In an authentic existence, man lays hold on his potentiality for being and attains the full stature of his selfhood. In an inauthentic existence, his self is

---

[8] "Martin Heidegger," in *Christianity and the Existentialists*, Carl Michalson, ed., (N.Y., Scribner's 1956), p. 120.

[9] See *Theology of the New Testament*, 2 Vols. (N.Y., Scribner's, 1951–55).

scattered in its concern with the world of things, and its decisions are made for it by the collective mass of mankind. In St. Paul we find the corresponding distinction between the spiritual man who has found his true self in a new life and the natural man whose view does not rise above the horizons of the earthly. Heidegger's idea of the collective depersonalized mass of mankind as one of the basic existentials or possible ways of being provides a place in the scheme of existence for the Pauline concept of the "world" which, as Bultmann points out, is an existential rather than a physical concept, and usually designates the whole body of fallen mankind from which the individual can be liberated only by a radical decision of faith. Another of Heidegger's basic existentials is fallenness—the possibility of losing responsible selfhood through submitting to the tyranny of things and of the collective mass. This is alienation from man's true being. Bultmann gives a corresponding interpretation to the Pauline concepts of the "flesh" and "sin." These represent concern with the realm of the earthly, and alienation not only from man's true being but also from God. For Heidegger the way to authentic existence lies through resolvedness. The individual takes on himself responsibility for his existence and projects himself on his own potentiality for being. The Pauline counterpart is "faith," and in his interpretation of this concept we find Bultmann laying stress on the aspects of radical decision and commitment.

From these illustrations we can see how Bultmann uses the conceptual framework provided by Heidegger's existential analytic for an existential interpretation of New Testament ideas. And it can hardly be denied that by taking the idea of existence as his hermeneutical key, Bultmann is able to show the interrelationships subsisting among the various Pauline concepts and is also able to inject fresh meaning into such worn-out terms as "flesh," "world," "sin," "faith."

So far we have considered the application of the method of existential interpretation only to single concepts, but in demythologizing proper a similar approach can be made to whole areas of myth. Let us take as an example the eschatological myth which Bultmann, following Weiss and Schweitzer, regards as a fundamental and pervasive element in New Testament thought. As is well known, the mythology of the last things was taken over by the first Christians from Jewish apocalyptic. According to this myth, the world is viewed as the scene of a cosmic drama. The present age is shortly coming to an end through a supernatural intervention. There will be a final judgment, and men will be assigned to destinies either of bliss or torment. The first disciples' expectation of an imminent end proved to be wrong, and to people nowadays the whole belief, if taken at all literally, must look like an absurd superstition. As Bultmann has expressed it: "History did not come to an end, and, as every schoolboy knows, it will continue to run its course."[10] At least, if history ever did come to an end, it would presumably be halted through some purely physical cause, such as a change in the sun's radiation or a nuclear war on the earth. This is the kind of mythology which makes the New Testament appear so remote and unintelligible to minds that are accustomed to postmythical ways of thought.

But let us now apply the canons of existential interpretation to the eschatological myth, and we discover that we can begin to make sense even of this unpromising material. The ideas of the myth must be related to the here and now of actual individual existence. Every individual stands before the imminent end—his own death. As Heidegger puts it, our human existence is always a "being towards death." Again, in his everyday decisions about the existence for which he is responsible, every individual works out his own judgment. He makes his essence, and here and now either lays hold on his authentic being or loses it. When we understand it in this way, the eschatological teaching of the New Testament ceases to be merely a curious survival from the remote past. When they are transferred to the actual individual existence, the eschatological ideas recover something of their urgency, of the sense of responsibility and of the need for decision before the end. "In every moment," says Bultmann, "slumbers the possibility of being the eschatological moment. You must awaken to it."[11]

---

[10] *Kerygma and Myth*, p. 5.

[11] *The Presence of Eternity*, p. 155. This is the title given to the American edition of Bultmann's Gifford Lectures (N.Y., Harper, 1957). The original title is *History and Eschatology* (Edinburgh, Univ. Press, 1957).

It must have been the existential significance of the myth—though this had not yet been sorted out from the mythical formulation—that made eschatology so important for the first Christians. If we look at the Fourth Gospel, composed, as is generally believed, around the end of the first century when the hopes of an immediate end were beginning to fade, we do find that the cruder eschatology is beginning to give way to the existential interpretation of it. The writer of the Fourth Gospel no longer thinks of judgment and eternal life as purely future, but brings them into the here and now of Christian existence. Thus Bultmann is able to claim that demythologizing begins in the pages of the New Testament itself.

The kind of approach which has been exemplified in the case of eschatology may be applied to other areas of myth. Myths of creation, for instance, are interpreted not as fanciful accounts of how the world began but as expressions of the finite, creaturely, and dependent status of man's being. Myths of demonic powers which hold the world in subjection are interpreted not as expressions of a dualistic world view—which would in any case be abhorrent to the biblical belief that God is the author of all things—but as representing man's awareness of the tyranny of the world over his life. This tyranny appears to him like that of an alien power, yet it arises from his own decision for the world and against God. In each case the myth is understood as a primitive way of bringing to words some aspect of man's awareness of his own existence. In the myth, this existential awareness has been projected outward upon objects in the world, and the aim of demythologizing is to recapture the existential significance and restate it in a nonmythical form. And if someone asks why we should trouble to do this, Bultmann would reply that these ancient myths often contain important insights which have been lost to more sophisticated and perhaps more shallow generations to whom the myths have become meaningless. In particular, as we have already noted, he thinks that the Christian myth conceals in itself a supreme truth of existence, which is just as relevant to our existence as it was to the existence of men in ancient times.

We have still to consider how Bultmann handles the core of the Christian story—the cross of Christ and his resurrection from the dead. Here we must notice a distinction. The cross can be regarded as a fairly well attested event of history, and is recognized as such by Bultmann. He points out that there is a difference between the story of Christ and a pure myth—such as, let us say, the story of Osiris—in that Christ was a real figure and his death can be dated in world history; he was, as the creed says, "crucified under Pontius Pilate." On the other hand, Bultmann regards the resurrection as a myth and dismisses the stories of the empty tomb as legends. The resurrection simply expresses the significance of the cross. Yet the cross itself has been transposed from the plane of world history onto the level of the mythical cosmic drama. The cross becomes the act of atonement and reconciliation at the very heart of the drama.

"What a primitive mythology it is," says Bultmann, "that a divine being should become incarnate and atone for the sins of men through his own blood!"[12] Yet even this "primitive myth" finds its justification through demythologizing and existential interpretation. Here we must notice briefly the existentialist view of history, which Bultmann has learned from Heidegger and also from the English philosopher, R. G. Collingwood, though the latter could scarcely be called an "existentialist." On this view, the business of the historian is much more than just to discover what happened at a particular time in the past, or to show how particular events were related to other events. His business is conceived to be rather that of exploring the possibilities of human existence which are disclosed in history. This he can do because his own existence is historical and he can, so to speak, re-enact in himself the actions of historical persons. It is when the Christian believer re-enacts the cross in his own existence that he discovers its power as an atonement. To believe in the cross, according to Bultmann, is not to hold some theory of atonement but to make the cross one's own, and so to be reconciled both to one's true being and to God. Acceptance of the cross is the radical decision or commitment of faith. It is the decision to turn from the world to God, to give up self-sufficiency and to live by the grace of the unseen, and so to be at one with one's true self and with God. But this is also experienced as resurrection, the beginning of a new life. By losing his life

[12] *Kerygma and Myth*, p. 7.

the believer has found it. He has risen from the death of sin, when his being was scattered and lost in worldly concerns, to an authentic existence.

All this makes sense and enables us to understand the cross as an atonement and the way to wholeness, but so far nothing has been said of the incarnation. For the cross to have its atoning power, is it necessary first to believe that it was the Son of God who died? Bultmann would reply to this question with a counterquestion: "Does he help me because he is God's Son, or is he the Son of God because he helps me?"[13] In other words, we can say that in Bultmann's theology, Christology is subsequent to soteriology. It is because we experience the cross as atonement that we recognize that God was in Christ. Christology also is interpreted existentially. To say that Christ is God is not to make a metaphysical pronouncement about Christ's person, but to declare one's own attitude toward him. Bultmann's Christology is indeed not far removed from that of Albrecht Ritschl, who taught that a christological pronouncement has the status of a value judgment. This way of thinking has a long history in Lutheranism, going back to Melanchthon and Luther himself.

It is then God himself who addresses us through the crucified and risen Christ. It is God's kerygmatic word that lies concealed under the mythological formulations of the New Testament, and this word, Bultmann believes, is still of vital concern and presses us to the point of radical decision. It may seem that in the course of his thinking Bultmann has put aside many things that have been traditionally believed in the Christian Church and many ideas that have been cherished in Christian piety. Yet his motive in doing this has been to set free the essential message of the New Testament from what he regards as the embarrassment of its mythological formulation, and he has done this so that the same message may be heard and awaken the response of faith in our scientific age. The real stumbling block in the way of faith, as Bultmann recognizes, is acceptance of the cross and the surrender of self-sufficiency. Why then, he asks, make things more difficult for the modern man by putting in his way

[13] *Essays*, p. 280.

an additional stumbling block and asking him to swallow a mythology in which he cannot believe any more without destroying his intellectual integrity?

Desperate diseases, we are told, require desperate remedies. No one doubts that our Western civilization today is in the grip of a malaise, as a shallow secularism keeps advancing while religion and spiritual values decline. The Christian message seems to have lost its biting edge. It is not so much rejected as disregarded and dismissed as remote, irrelevant, and unintelligible. Bultmann's demythologizing may turn out to be none too desperate a remedy if Christianity is to count again; and surely Western civilization is unthinkable without a vital Christianity, for it would have ceased to be the Western civilization that we cherish. If demythologizing is not the remedy for Christianity, then something equally drastic is called for. But whether or not we think that demythologizing offers the way forward, we cannot but admire the fearless honesty and integrity with which Bultmann has faced the task—the greatest task now confronting those who still adhere to the Christian religion—of seeking to make Christianity once more a living issue for which men of our time can decide.

The impact made by Bultmann's ideas upon the theological world has been a major one, comparable in its magnitude to the impact made by Barth's theology of crisis a quarter of a century earlier. Since the controversy over Bultmann's views still goes on and shows no sign of abatement, it is impossible to predict what influence he may eventually have on the future course of theology. It can, however, be asserted that he is probably the most discussed theologian at the present time. Since he put forward his program for demythologizing the New Testament, a steady and voluminous stream of books and articles devoted to the subject has been flowing. Contributions have come from theologians of many nations and of many branches of Christendom. Philosophers too have joined in the debate, and this is a particularly interesting and welcome fact, for throughout much of the present century there has been a divorce between philosophy and theology, each regarding the other with indifference or even suspicion. While Bultmann's views have aroused plenty of opposition, something like a Bultmannian school has arisen among some of the younger theologians in Germany, and there are pockets of disciples to be found elsewhere. Although the debate still goes on, the main lines of criticism and of further development have already emerged. For Bultmann's theories, as expounded in the earlier part of this essay, conceal a number of unresolved problems and difficulties, and while his critics have seized upon these, his defenders and he himself have sought to meet the objections. In what follows we shall consider three major problems raised by Bultmann's theology.

The first problem is one which, in various forms, has long vexed the Christian Church—the problem of the relation of philosophy to theology. Bultmann's demythologizing, as we have seen, is closely tied up with existentialist philosophy. Has he had any success in reaching a new *rapprochement* between theology and philosophy? Has he worked out a proper relation between the two disciplines? It must be reported that his attempts to do so seem to have displeased both the theologians and the philosophers, and he has been severely criticized from both sides.

Theologians like Karl Barth are naturally suspicious of the place which Bultmann gives to existentialist philosophy in his exposition of Christianity. Barth himself fought hard to win autonomy for Christian theology and to deliver it from subservience to whatever brand of philosophy might be in fashion at a particular time. In his little book on Bultmann, Barth remarks that for a generation theology had been escaping from what he calls "an Egyptian bondage in which a philosophy lays down what the Holy Spirit is permitted to say."[14] It seems to Barth that Bultmann, by his deference to Heidegger, has initiated a move back to Egypt. For Bultmann has brought Heidegger's existential analytic into his scriptural exegesis, and in Barth's view the truth of Christianity can only be perverted and distorted when an attempt is made to wed it to a secular philosophy. It is not clear, however, that Bultmann does in fact make his exegesis dependent on the demands of a philosophy, and certainly it is not his intention to do so. As has been pointed

[14] *Rudolf Bultmann—ein Versuch ihn zu verstehen* (Zurich, Evangelischer Verlag, 1952), p. 52.

out above, he appropriates Heidegger's existential scheme as a useful tool for his exegetical studies, but he would argue that this tool by no means determines the meaning which he elicits from the biblical text. Its function is only a heuristic one. It opens our eyes to the meaning of the text and helps toward the elucidation of that meaning.

On the other hand, Bultmann finds himself under attack from the philosopher Karl Jaspers.[15] According to Jaspers, Bultmann's apparent interest in philosophy is quite spurious. The essence of philosophy is said to lie in its openness. Bultmann, on the contrary, has shown himself to be exclusive. He has taken one single philosopher—Heidegger—and concentrated on a single work by that philosopher, *Sein und Zeit*. In Jasper's view such a selective procedure is so far from qualifying Bultmann to be heard in philosophical circles that it rather shows him to be entirely lacking in the true philosophical spirit. Moreover Bultmann has used those ideas which he has taken from Heidegger to bolster up a sagging orthodoxy. He is willing to keep company with the philosophers so long as it suits his purpose, but then he appeals to a special divine revelation which, he says, is inaccessible to philosophy. Jaspers may have in mind a passage in which Bultmann himself asks whether a demythologized version of Christianity must not become another philosophy of existence—whether, in fact, Christian theology is not merely the precursor of existentialism and is now to be discarded. But Bultmann goes on to deny that this is the case. Philosophy, he claims, may conceive of an authentic existence, but theology knows of a gracious act which empowers such existence—God's gracious act in Christ, as proclaimed in the kerygmatic word. It is this appeal to a special act of God which annoys Jaspers and leads him to declare that Bultmann's professed interest in philosophy is not genuine. So Bultmann's ventures into philosophical territory are censured as severely by Jaspers as they are by Barth, though for different reasons.

The debates over the relation of theology to philosophy in Bultmann's thought have led to the first major independent development of Bultmann's ideas by one of his disciples—the Swiss theologian Fritz Buri. This younger thinker frankly ac-

[15] See his debate with Bultmann in *Die Frage der Entmythologisierung* (Munich, 1954).

cepts demythologizing and existential interpretation as the most promising way forward for theology in our time, though he looks to Jaspers rather than to Heidegger for his philosophical background. Buri thinks, however, that Bultmann's demythologizing needs to be carried much further. Quite arbitrarily, it seems to Buri, Bultmann has called a halt to demythologizing when he has come to the kerygmatic word which he unwraps from its mythological coverings. But this kerygmatic word, the appeal to which so annoys the philosophers, is itself, says Buri, just a last remnant of mythology. So he asks that we should go beyond Bultmann's demythologizing to what he calls "dekerygmatizing."[16] This would involve the frank recognition that there is in the New Testament no special or unique word of God that is inaccessible to human reflection in general. There is in principle no distinction between Christian theology and philosophies of existence, though there is the difference that theology possesses a wealth of symbolic material for exploration, and its concrete symbols, as Buri recognizes, can be a powerful aid in the quest for an authentic existence.

Buri's radicalizing of Bultmann's theology certainly meets the kind of objections that are put forward by Jaspers, but it may be asked whether it is not Bultmann who does more justice to the experience of Christianity as a religion of grace. The problem of the relation of theology to philosophy in Bultmann's thought turns into the question of whether there is a limit to demythologizing, and if so, why should there be a limit and where does it come? This is one of the major unresolved issues which Bultmann's theology raises, and no doubt it will be the subject of further debate.

A second major problem in Bultmann's thought is the relation of theology to history. Christianity is usually described as a historical religion, because its center is not a code of laws or a world view but an event or series of events focused in Jesus Christ—the "mighty acts" or the "salvation history," to use the terms generally employed by theologians. Now Bultmann, as we have seen, leaves very little in the way of factual objective history to the gospel narrative. What history there was, he tells us, has been transformed into myth, so that we can no longer

---

[16] See his essay "Entmythologisierung oder Entkerygmatisierung?," in *Kerygma und Mythos*, Band II (Hamburg, 1952), pp. 85–101.

get at the history. He himself transforms the myth into its existential significance and brings the "salvation history" into the present, that is to say, into the historical existence of the believer who here and now dies and rises with Christ. It is true that he can speak of the difference between the story of Christ as a real figure of history and the myths of the Hellenistic cults. It is true also that he can speak of the paradox of the Christ-event, which happened once in the past and which nevertheless happens again and again in every Christian in whose soul Christ is born, suffers, dies, and is raised up. But it seems clear that Bultmann attaches much more importance to what happens now than to anything that may be supposed to have happened long ago—and of course it is obvious that much can be said for this point of view.

Protestant theologians who stress the "once-for-all" character of the Christ-event have been particularly critical of Bultmann's skepticism with regard to the historical events in the gospel narrative. While some of their criticisms are wildly exaggerated, it is a fair question whether Christianity does not need some minimum of factual history to support its message. In one of his early works, R. G. Collingwood remarks that if Jesus was not a real historical person, it might be as futile to exhort men to follow him as it would be to urge an athlete to emulate the feats of Heracles.[17] Such a remark will appeal especially to the empirical temper of the English-speaking peoples. Does the Christian message summon us to a pure speculative possibility of existence, or to a possibility which has been actualized under the real conditions of historical existence? We could have no confidence about embarking on the first of these alternatives. So we come back to the question whether Christianity needs some minimum of factual history, and, if so, how much?

Bultmann's own position on this matter is ambiguous, but again we find that the problem has been taken up by his disciples.[18] Aware of the dangers of being committed to the wor-

[17] *Religion and Philosophy* (London, Macmillan, 1916), p. 53.

[18] For an instructive review of recent researches on these lines, see James M. Robinson, *A New Quest of the Historical Jesus* (London, SCM Press, 1961).

ship of a purely mythological Lord, some of the younger German followers of Bultmann are exploring the relation of the Christ of faith to the historical Jesus of Nazareth. One of them, Günther Bornkamm, says that the records which we have do not entitle us to be resigned or skeptical about the historical Jesus, and that "we must look for the history in the kerygma."[19] He and others have proceeded to do this, and so the whole question of history and theology in relation to demythologizing is still an open one.

A third major problem raised by Bultmann's theology is the question of how one is going to talk about God in the context of demythologizing. The Belgian Jesuit scholar Father Malevez criticizes the anthropological bias of Bultmann's approach to the New Testament, which, he says, is primarily concerned to teach us about God. Bultmann's theology, he finds, "is absolutely silent about the God whom it urges us to worship; there is nothing about his nature or attributes."[20] This objection is strongly worded, but there seem to be some grounds for it. Demythologizing, as we have seen, aims at translating mythical language into existential language, that is to say, into statements about possibilities of human existence. If this is carried through consistently, where is there room left to talk about God, or how is he to be brought into the picture?

Yet we do find Bultmann talking about God, and in particular he has much to say about the "acts" of God. Such talk, however, would fall under his own definition of mythology as "the use of imagery to express the otherworldly in terms of this world and the divine in terms of human life,"[21] since, when we speak of an act of God, we are applying the human conception of an "act" to God. But Bultmann's definition of mythology was a bad one, for as many critics have pointed out, it would cover not only myth but all kinds of symbolic and analogical language. Bultmann himself has had second thoughts about his definition, for he now tells us that when he talks of an "act of God," he is using not mythological but analogical language. This is certainly

[19] *Jesus von Nazareth* (Stuttgart, Kohlhammer, 1956), p. 20.

[20] Léopold Malevez, *The Christian Message and Myth* (London, SCM Press, 1958), p. 156.

[21] *Kerygma and Myth*, p. 10, n. 2.

a clarification, but it is at the same time a tacit admission that demythologizing does not succeed in performing the task which it sets out to accomplish. For obviously there is all the difference in the world between an existential statement which refers to human existence, and a statement which, though expressed in terms drawn from human existence, refers analogically to God. We must in fact conclude that when demythologizing has completed its work of translation, we shall have on our hands not only the existential statements which we were promised but also a set of analogical statements of quite another order. It follows that the work of restating the Christian message in a form free of myth is a good deal more complicated than Bultmann originally led us to believe, and up till now he has not carried out a systematic logical analysis of the different kinds of discourse that are involved, nor has he shown how they are related to each other. Of course there is always a drastic alternative to such complications, that is to say, to give up talking about an act of God and to follow Buri along the way of radical dekerygmatizing.

An examination of some of the questions that arise out of Bultmann's theology and of some of the criticisms to which he has been subjected show us that the subject is much more complex than might have been supposed at the end of the straightforward exposition of his ideas which formed the first part of this essay. It is clear that Bultmann leaves us with many unresolved problems and difficulties on our hands. Yet this need not surprise us, for no theology that has ever been constructed is free from difficulties. The test of the worth of a theology is whether it helps to solve some problems, whether it makes a worthwhile contribution to the religious thought of its own day, and whether it offers ground for further advance. Judged by this test, Bultmann's thought must rank high among the theologies of the twentieth century—indeed, the present writer would say that it offers the most promising way forward for Christian theology at the present time. No doubt in the light of further discussion some of Bultmann's positions will call for modification, just as some of his difficulties will be resolved. He has said himself that the task of working out a program of demythologizing would be arduous enough to occupy scholars for a generation.

But leaving aside speculation about the future, we can be grateful for his initiative and for his profound and honest contribution which does so much to keep the Christian faith a living issue in the contemporary world.

Bibliography

Rudolf Bultmann and others, *Kerygma and Myth*, Hans W. Bartsch, ed., N.Y., Harper, 1961. (Harper Torchbooks).

John Macquarrie, *The Scope of Demythologizing: Bultmann and His Critics*, N.Y., Harper, 1961.

DIETRICH BONHOEFFER

Franklin Sherman

Although he met death in a concentration camp before he had attained the age of forty, Dietrich Bonhoeffer during his lifetime had already become well known in Germany for his personal and theological contributions to the church's struggle against Nazism. Since his death in 1945, and largely due to the impact of his posthumously published prison letters and fragmentary *Ethics,* his influence has spread throughout the Christian world.

Born in Breslau on February 4, 1906, Dietrich Bonhoeffer enjoyed the advantages of a highly cultured home. His father was a noted physician who from 1912 onward served as professor of psychiatry at the University of Berlin. Having decided to study theology, Dietrich attended lectures at Tübingen in 1923–24, but then returned to complete his education at Berlin. Here he encountered the liberal heritage of Troeltsch, and himself had the opportunity to study under the aged Harnack; but the young Bonhoeffer felt himself drawn increasingly toward the new "theology of crisis" being set forth elsewhere by Karl Barth.

After a year's internship in a German-speaking congregation in Barcelona, he was appointed a lecturer (*Privatdozent*) in theology at Berlin (1930). Before assuming his duties, however, he undertook a year's further study at Union Theological Seminary in New York. Here he first made the acquaintance of Reinhold Niebuhr and was able to become familiar with American religious life. In Berlin once again, in the fall of 1931, he served both as lecturer at the university and as pastor to students at the School of Technology. During the same period, Bonhoeffer began to take an active part in ecumenical affairs, at first primarily in the World Alliance for Promoting International Friendship through the Churches, which he served as a youth secretary for some years.

An early and outspoken antagonist of the Nazi regime, Bonhoeffer, on February 1, 1933, just two days after Hitler had become chancellor, gave a radio address on "Changes in the Concept of 'Leader' in the Younger Generation" which was cut off the air before completion. Shortly afterwards, in an essay on "The Church and the Jewish Question," Bonhoeffer called on the church vigorously to resist anti-Semitism both in civil society and in its own ranks. By the fall of 1933, however, he was sufficiently discouraged by the victory of the "German Christians" in the church elections to be willing to leave Germany for England, where he became pastor of two small German-speaking congregations in London. During this time there began his lasting friendship with the ecumenical leader G. K. A. Bell, Bishop of Chichester.

In 1935 Bonhoeffer returned to Germany to become leader of a seminary established to train pastors for the Confessing Church, which since the Barmen Synod of 1934 had come to embody the most uncompromising opposition to Nazi efforts to "coordinate" church and state. Although outlawed by the Gestapo two years later, the seminary was continued in a disguised form until 1940. Meanwhile, however, Bonhoeffer had experienced his second "American interlude." In view of the threat of his being drafted into the German army or imprisoned as a conscientious objector, arrangements had been made by Reinhold Niebuhr to secure him a position in the United States. But no sooner had he arrived in New York (June, 1939) than he was conscience-stricken at having forsaken his Christian brethren in Germany, and within a few weeks decided that he must return to share their fate.

Bonhoeffer soon became an especial target of suspicion of the authorities, and was required to report regularly to the police,- and was forbidden to speak publicly or to have anything published. Yet at the same time his contacts with leaders of the resistance movement against Hitler (including high officials of the Military Intelligence Service) enabled him to secure credentials for travel on behalf of the resistance. At a fateful meeting with the Bishop of Chichester at Sigtuna, Sweden, in May, 1942, Bonhoeffer presented to the bishop for conveyance to the British government detailed information on the plans for overthrowing the Nazi regime, together with proposals for the subsequent establishment of peace. The proposals reached British foreign secretary Anthony Eden but were summarily rejected; "unconditional surrender" was to be the Allied policy.

The further suspicion that now fell on Bonhoeffer led eventually to his arrest on April 5, 1943. During the eighteen months that he was confined in Tegel Military Prison near Berlin, he was able to keep in touch with family and friends through correspondence (the letters published posthumously). The discovery of his connections with the group responsible for the July 20, 1944, attempt on Hitler's life led to his removal to maximum-security confinement, and finally to his execution at the concentration camp in Flossenberg on April 9, 1945, just a few days before the camp was liberated by the Allied forces.

The dramatic circumstances of Dietrich Bonhoeffer's death undoubtedly contributed to the impact made in English-speaking countries by the first of his books to be translated, *The Cost of Discipleship* (1948). Already when published in Germany in 1937, however, it had won considerable notice, both as a tract for the times and as a work of biblical interpretation. It is in the first chapter of this book that Bonhoeffer makes his famous attack on the "cheap grace" being marketed by the evangelical churches. Under cover of Luther's principle of justification by faith alone, he charges, believers have been relieved of the obligations of discipleship.

> Cheap grace means grace as a doctrine, a principle, a system. It means forgiveness of sins proclaimed as a general truth, the love of God taught as the Christian "conception" of God. . . . The Church which holds the correct doctrine of grace has, it is supposed, *ipso facto* a part in that grace. In such a Church the world finds a cheap covering for its sins; no contrition is required, still less any real desire to be delivered from sin.[1]

Distinguished from this is the "costly grace" that accompanies a life of discipleship. "Such grace is *costly*," writes Bonhoeffer, "because it calls us to follow, and it is *grace* because it calls us to follow Jesus Christ. It is costly because it costs a man his life, and it is grace because it gives a man the only true life."

[1] *The Cost of Discipleship*, 2d ed. (N.Y., Macmillan, 1959), p. 35.

This, he insists, is the grace of which Luther was speaking. For Luther, grace was the answer to an excruciating problem, whereas for his followers it has become an all too readily accepted presupposition. "When he spoke of grace, Luther always implied as a corollary that it cost him his own life."

On the difficult question of the relation between faith and works, Bonhoeffer points out that the standard Protestant formula has been something like this: "Only he who believes is obedient" (i.e., only works done in faith are truly good). Over against this Bonhoeffer places the converse: "Only he who is obedient believes" (only a faith expressed in works is truly faith). He then proceeds to expound, on the basis of relevant passages in the Synoptic Gospels, the notion of "discipleship," which, as he shows, uniquely combines these elements. Discipleship implies *faith* in the Lord one follows, and it implies *obedience* to the will of that same Lord. The Sermon on the Mount, to which Bonhoeffer devotes a good portion of the book, he interprets as a description of the life of discipleship. Jesus is here depicting the new righteousness that is to characterize the new community which he is gathering about himself. But conformity to these new criteria is possible only insofar as the disciples cling to Christ, who alone in his person has "fulfilled" all righteousness.

Bonhoeffer thus offers a christological interpretation of the Sermon: its demands have meaning only as utterances of the One whom the church worships as its Incarnate, Crucified, and Risen Lord. At the same time, he resists all efforts to interpret these demands in anything but their plain, literal sense. The words of Jesus call for "single-minded obedience." Discipleship necessitates a radical "breach with the immediacies of the world."

The concluding chapters of the book are devoted to placing the picture of the life of discipleship as we have it from the Synoptic Gospels into the context of Pauline theology. Bonhoeffer will hear nothing of a supposed conflict between these two parts of the New Testament: "The Jesus of the Synoptists is neither nearer nor further from us than the Christ of St. Paul." The great Pauline equivalent for "discipleship" is "baptism," which like the former involves the death of an old pattern of existence and the initiation of a new one. But baptism means entry into the church, which thus becomes the locus of the contemporary call to discipleship. "If you would hear the call of Jesus you need no personal revelation: all you have to do is to hear the sermon and receive the sacrament."

This emphasis on the communal context of the faith had already been evident in Dietrich Bonhoeffer's first published work, his doctoral dissertation entitled *Sanctorum Communio* ("The Communion of Saints"). The subtitle reveals the character of the project: "A Dogmatical Inquiry into the Sociology of the Church." The contribution of Ernst Troeltsch and his generation had been to focus attention on the sociological forms of the religious life. The Barthians, in contrast, were insisting on a purely theological conception of the church. The young Bonhoeffer now attempts to synthesize these two perspectives. The sociologist, he warns, must be wary of reducing the church to an example of some already established social type, without heeding the testimony of its own self-consciousness; this would be the "historicizing" misunderstanding of the church. But the theologian, for his part, must not overlook the sociological dimension; this would be the "religious" misunderstanding, which would have failed to take seriously "God's will that everything he reveals be revealed hiddenly, clothed in the garments of historical life—as in Christ, so in the church."

Human nature itself, Bonhoeffer reminds us, is inescapably social. It was the merit of the Hegelian philosophy to have made this clear. But Hegelianism tended to lose the concreteness of the individual by stressing the "structural openness" at the expense of the "structural closedness" of personal being. Crucial for the emergence of self-conscious personal life, Bonhoeffer emphasizes, is the encounter with the "limit," whether experienced as the claim of the other person or as the claim of the divine. As a matter of fact, these two claims coincide; for the divine Thou meets us precisely in the human thou. This is what Bonhoeffer calls an "ethical" as opposed to an "epistemological" interpretation of transcendence.

If man's very nature as a created being thus is social, the "fall" is equally communal. The doctrine of original sin implies the solidarity in guilt of the whole human race. Hence man's redemption must be equally corporate in character; and so it is, since it consists precisely in the creation of a community of the redeemed. In Jesus Christ as a "collective person," as "deputy" or "representative" for all mankind, the humanity of Adam is transformed into the humanity of Christ. Through his life, death, and resurrection, the communion of saints is realized.

There is thus the closest possible identification between Christ and the church. "The Church," writes Bonhoeffer, "is the presence of Christ, as Christ is the presence of God." Or as he puts it in an adaptation of a phrase from Hegel, the church is "Christ existing as community."[2] Therefore the principle of the church's life can be none other than the same deputyship or vicarious love that was shown forth in Christ's own life. The Christian is dependent on his brother for the word of grace and for the word of counsel. It is in order to make concrete this mutual dependence of the brethren that Bonhoeffer here advocates, as he was to do repeatedly, the restoration of private confession, as well as a greater willingness to heed the ethical consensus of the church.

In his second dissertation (the *Habilitationsschrift* which qualified him to lecture in theology), Bonhoeffer again devotes himself to the doctrine of the church, this time employing it as the resolution of a basic problem in theology that he epitomizes in the title of the dissertation: *Act and Being*. How shall revelation be conceived? Only in terms of a series of discrete "acts" of God, a sequence of revelatory "moments" in which God "touches" man's existence? Or does revelation have a continuity, an historical embodiment of such a character that man's "being in" revelation is conceivable? The former is the viewpoint of Karl Barth—a man with whose theology the young Bonhoeffer, as we have noted, had much sympathy. But with respect to its denial of all "being" categories (i.e., its rejection of ontology), Barth's theology, Bonhoeffer charges, is determined more by Kantian philosophy than by the Bible. For the Bible does know of a continuity of man's being both "in Adam" and "in Christ."

"Being" theologies are those which stress the embodiment of

[2] *Christus als Gemeinde existierend.* The word *Gemeinde* has a wide range of meanings, but here it clearly refers to the specifically religious community; the phrase could therefore equally well be rendered "Christ existing as the church."

revelation in some form whereby it is more readily available, whether in the ecclesiastical institution (Roman Catholicism), in "pure doctrine" (Protestant orthodoxy), or in "religious experience" (Protestant liberalism). As against all these, the merit of the Barthian theology, according to Bonhoeffer, is that it has restored the realization that God is not, after all, at man's disposal; the initiative in revelation remains his. But this "act" theology fails to reckon with the fact that God in his mercy has, in another sense, chosen precisely to place himself at man's disposal, in that he has entered into history in Christ and in the church. As Bonhoeffer states in *Act and Being,* in words that were later to be echoed by Karl Barth himself:

> The question after all is not so much the freedom of God beyond his revelation, God's eternal remaining with-himself, his aseity, but rather God's coming forth, his coming out of himself in the revelation, his *given* word, his covenant. . . . God is not free from man, but for man. Christ is the word of the freedom of God. God *is* here, not in eternal non-objectivity, but—let us say it with all due caution—"havable," graspable in his word in his church.[3]

This is what Bonhoeffer calls a "material" as contrasted to a "formalistic" understanding of God's freedom: it is a freedom-in-Christ.

In a further criticism of act-theology as it affects our understanding of the life of faith, Bonhoeffer notes that Rudolf Bultmann, with his interpretation of faith as consisting in repeated acts of "decision," is unable to explain the continuity of the deciding self. Again, for Bonhoeffer, the continuity is to be found in the believer's life within the church. Yet the church itself, as he must emphasize once more against the theologies of being, remains constantly dependent on the "event" of preaching. Thus in the church—which is to say, in Christ-existing-as-community—Bonhoeffer finds the unity of contingency and continuity, of transcendentalism and ontology, of *Akt* and *Sein.*

It was the advent of Hitler's National Socialist regime that gave occasion for Bonhoeffer's doctrine of the church to be put

[3] (N.Y., Harper, 1961), pp. 67 ff.

to an acutely practical test. The Nazi efforts to infiltrate the church with their hypernationalistic ideology had been met with the ringing testimony of the Barmen Declaration (May, 1934) to the sole sovereignty of Jesus Christ, with its concomitant repudiation of the "false teaching that the church can and must recognize yet other happenings and powers, images and truths, as divine revelation alongside this one Word of God." Barmen further had warned against permitting the structure of church government to fall under the state's totalitarian control. It soon became evident, however, that the majority of the church leadership were more disposed to compromise with the proposals of the regime, even including the application of anti-Semitic legislation to converted Jews within the church. Further inroads by the Nazi ideology together with the assumption of arbitrary power by the new Hitler-sponsored "national bishop" Ludwig Mueller caused the Confessing Church group at its second synod (held in Martin Niemöller's church at Dahlem in October, 1934) to declare that the existing church government had in fact divorced itself from the Christian church. In its stead, Dahlem set up a "Provisional Church Government" with a "Council of Brethren" at its head.

Bonhoeffer's assuming the pastorate in London had removed him from the German scene just prior to these fateful meetings, but their decisions clearly represented his own position, and he quickly became one of the staunchest defenders of both the Barmen and the Dahlem declarations. He startled many of the Confessing Church leaders themselves with his readiness to identify these synodical pronouncements with the will of God. The Barmen Declaration he regarded as a genuine "confession" to be considered just as determinative for purity of doctrine as the classic Reformation documents. He prized, too, the unity between Lutheran and Reformed elements that had become visible in the confessing situation, and strongly opposed the later tendency to separate these elements again. Through his contacts in the ecumenical movement, Bonhoeffer agitated continually through the mid-thirties for the recognition of the Confessing Church as the sole body that could legitimately speak for German Protestantism, and to his own countrymen he stated, in an article published in 1936 that gave to the ancient principle *extra ecclesiam nulla salus* a disturbingly specific application: "Who-ever knowingly separates himself from the Confessing Church in Germany separates himself from salvation."

This effort to define the limits of the church represented the negative side of Bonhoeffer's concern for the integrity of the community in Christ. The positive side came most fully to expression in his work as director of the seminary of the Confessing Church. Bonhoeffer had long since come to doubt the wisdom of entrusting theological education to the universities. Needed today, he had said, are "monastic-like schools" in which three things are taken seriously: pure doctrine, worship, and the Christian life. Alongside the seminary proper, he now established at Finkenwalde a "Brethren House" in which his long-standing emphasis on the concreteness of the communion of saints could find expression. Each resident pledged himself to share in a common regimen of daily prayer, oral confession of sin, shared livelihood, and readiness to answer any emergency call by the Confessing Church. When the seminary was forced underground in 1937, the Brethren House had to be discontinued. To preserve the fruits of the experiment, Bonhoeffer wrote the little book *Life Together* (published 1939), which had the largest sale of any of his writings during his lifetime, and which has been widely read in connection with the many similar ventures in communal living that have appeared in Protestantism since the end of World War II.

The book demonstrates that Bonhoeffer was well aware of the spiritual dangers attendant on such an enterprise. Its disciplines, he insisted, must be understood solely as means of preparation for effective service in the world, and its benefits received in trust for the whole church. He counseled the avoidance of all wish-dreams about what such life together would be like, and drew a clear distinction between the mutual deputyship of Christians and the merely human psychological phenomena of domination and dependency. "Let him who cannot be alone beware of community," he wrote. But he added, "Let him who is not in community beware of being alone."

Although he laid great emphasis upon the role of prayer in the life of both the individual and the community, Bonhoeffer apparently had little interest in the liturgical movement in a formal sense, and even had some suspicion of it. "Only he who cries out for the Jews dare also sing Gregorian," he once remarked. More important than the restoration of historic forms was learning to pray in one's own words. Similarly with respect to the interpretation of the Scriptures, he felt that the greatest need was not further training in "objective" scholarly research, but a recovery of the capacity to read the Bible as the Word of God, addressed to the community of faith.

We have a number of brief Bible studies from Bonhoeffer's hand, as well as one longer work based on his Berlin lectures and published in 1933 (English translation 1959) under the title *Creation and Fall: A Theological Interpretation of Genesis 1-3*. His interpretation here proves to be not only theological but christological. Genesis 1-3 deals with what is "in the beginning"; but, says Bonhoeffer, we are not "in the beginning" but "in the middle," and we know of the beginning only because the "end" has come upon us. The doctrine of the primeval state is "hope projected backwards." Thus Bonhoeffer's interpretation of the "image of God" in which man is created is christological. It consists in freedom; but this does not mean merely man's freedom from the limitations of the brute creation. Rather, just as God in Christ has shown his freedom to be a freedom not from but for man, so man's true freedom is a freedom for God and for his fellow man. This is the explanation of the *Imago dei* as an "analogy of relationship" that Barth later adopted from Bonhoeffer as a substitute for the Thomistic doctrine of analogy of being.

Creation and Fall is noteworthy for its anticipation of a number of themes that come to light again only in Bonhoeffer's last years. Among these is the insistence that God's presence is to be found not at the periphery of man's existence but at its center. This is the significance that Bonhoeffer sees in the placement of the Tree of Life "in the midst of the garden." Striking also is his interpretation of the creation of the woman to be man's "helper." Her deepest role is to help him not merely with his sundry tasks, but with his fundamental problem of learning to live within the limits of his finitude. "In his unfathomable mercy the Creator knew that this creaturely, free life can only be borne in limitation if it is loved, and out of his mercy he created a companion for man who is to be at once the embodiment of Adam's limit and the object of his love." When the primal pair do nevertheless transgress the limit, God still does not withdraw his mercy. He resolves to preserve even his fallen creatures: this is the significance that Bonhoeffer finds in the report at the close of Genesis 3 that "the Lord God made for Adam and his wife garments of skins, and clothed them." The orders of creation have become "orders of preservation on their way to Christ."

In the semester following his course on "creation and fall" Bonhoeffer devoted his Berlin lectures directly to the topic of Christology. Unfortunately these lectures never saw publication, nor has Bonhoeffer's manuscript for them been found; but his friend and posthumous editor Eberhard Bethge has made available a conflation of students' lecture notes that he believes to be a reasonably close equivalent to the original. This is included in the third volume of Bonhoeffer's *Gesammelte Schriften* (collected shorter writings), published in 1960.

Bonhoeffer divides the topic of Christology into three parts —the contemporary Christ, the historical Christ, the eternal Christ—although he was able to cover only two by the end of the semester. That he begins with the contemporary is significant; again, his stress is on "Christ existing as the church." As he puts it here in analogy to the Lutheran view of the Lord's Supper, the church *is* (not merely signifies) the Body of Christ. But even the historical Christ, he insists, did not exist in and for himself, but as a Christ "for me." This is the "deputyship" that he assumed not only for me but for the whole of nature and of history.

Bonhoeffer lays great stress on the "humiliation" of Christ and the "incognito" that makes him recognizable, whether historically or contemporaneously, only to faith. At the same time, he draws a sharp distinction between this humiliation and the incarnation as such. The humiliation is not God's becoming man (for this in itself is glorious), but the subjection of the Incarnate One to the conditions of existence under sin. Humiliation is concealment, while incarnation as such is revelation. The humiliation pertains to the fallen creation, the incarnation to the primal creation. The humiliation, therefore, is temporary, whereas the incarnation is permanent: with the return of Christ to the Father, humanity has been assumed into the eternal life of God himself.

With Luther, Bonhoeffer objects to any effort even to conceive of Christ's humanity and his divinity as separable entities. If Christ is the Logos (God's creative and communicative Word) made flesh, then, Bonhoeffer insists, everything that is asserted of the Logos can be asserted of the man Christ Jesus. The finite, as he maintains in conscious opposition to the Calvinist tradition, *can* contain the infinite.

The lectures on Christology remained incomplete, but in one of the concluding chapters of *The Cost of Discipleship,* Bonhoeffer further clarified his own position as well as its antecedents when he wrote:

> As they contemplated the miracle of the Incarnation, the early Fathers passionately contended that while it was true to say that God took human nature upon him, it was wrong to say that he chose a perfect individual man and united himself to him. God was made man. This means that he took upon him our entire human nature with all of its infirmity, sinfulness, and corruption, the whole of apostate humanity.[4]

Here Bonhoeffer reveals his dependence on the tradition, particularly strong in Greek theology, whereby the notion of humanity as an entity (rather than merely a plurality of individual men) makes it possible to conceive of the redemption as universal in its scope. As to the character of that redemption, Bonhoeffer describes it here as the restoration of the proper "form" of man as he was originally created in God's image. In Jesus Christ as the Incarnate, Crucified, and Risen One, this true image once again takes form in human history.

It was against such a background of ideas that Bonhoeffer undertook the project that was to occupy him during his final years: the writing of an ethic that should be both firmly grounded in Christology and oriented to man's concrete situation in the present hour. He was unable to complete the project, or even to pursue it very far into specific problems; what we

[4] P. 213.

have in the *Ethics* as published by Bethge in 1949 (English translation 1955) is more nearly a set of alternative beginnings for the book. Yet it has proved extremely influential, not only at the level of theological method but also as the testimony of a sensitive Christian conscience facing the collapse of the whole Western moral heritage in Nazi Germany.

The question of ethics, says Bonhoeffer, is the question of the "formation" of man. For Christians this can mean nothing other than "conformation" with Jesus Christ. To be conformed with the Incarnate One: this means to have the freedom to be the man one really is. While we are engaged in vain attempts to transcend our manhood, God affirms it by becoming man, real man. To be conformed with the Crucified: this means to submit oneself wholly to God's judgment, and thereby to be released from the world's criteria of success. To be conformed with the Risen One: this means to participate, though hiddenly, in the renewed humanity that the Risen Christ bears within himself. In all this, Bonhoeffer emphasizes, it is no alien form into which man is transformed, but rather his own proper form. "Man becomes man because God became man."

A life that is truly ethical, Bonhoeffer suggests, would combine simplicity with wisdom, in accordance with Jesus' counsel to be "wise as serpents and innocent as doves." But simplicity derives from single-hearted concentration upon God, while wisdom requires intimate acquaintance with the world. How are the two combinable? Only by virtue of the reconciliation between God and the world that has occurred in Christ.

> In Christ we are offered the possibility of partaking in the reality of God and in the reality of the world, but not in the one without the other. The reality of God discloses itself only by setting me entirely in the reality of the world, and when I encounter the reality of the world it is always already sustained, accepted and reconciled in the reality of God.[5]

Most ethical systems, Bonhoeffer notes, focus attention on those conflict situations in which life is threatened by some disvalue or by a clash of values. In the New Testament, however,

[5] *Ethics* (London, SCM Press, 1955), p. 61.

precisely because it springs from the reality of reconciliation, "the life and activity of men is not at all problematic or tormented or dark: it is self-evident, joyful, sure and clear." The Christian lives not by lists of prohibitions and requirements, but by God's commandment, which is distinguished from all human laws in that what it commands is freedom. The commandment of God is in fact nothing other than "the permission to live as man before God."

If Christian ethics thus is by nature wholly positive, it is also wholly concrete. The wise man, says Bonhoeffer, will be aware of the limited receptiveness of reality for "principles." The will of God is not a set of rules established in advance, but is "something new and different in each different situation in life." Bonhoeffer thus allies himself with what since has come to be known as "situation ethics" or "contextualism." But he carefully guards against the implication that God's will is therefore to be grasped solely by intuition; quite the contrary, "the whole apparatus of human powers," including the heart, the understanding, observation, and experience, is to be set in motion for the task of "proving" what is the will of God (Romans 12:2). It is in this connection that Bonhoeffer again calls for the restoration of private confession. Roman Catholicism, he says, with its strong emphasis in the training of its clergy on dealing with moral problems as encountered in the confessional, has tended to fall prey to legalistic casuistry. But Protestantism, with its almost exclusive emphasis on public preaching, has rested content with the enunciation of general moral principles that remain purely formal. Only by "rediscovering the divine office of confession," Bonhoeffer asserts, can the Protestant church "find its way back to a concrete ethic such as it possessed at the time of the Reformation."

In further explication of the way in which God's commandment confronts us, Bonhoeffer now introduces the concept of the "divine mandates"—marriage, labor, culture (sometimes listed by him under labor), state, and church. This he intended as a substitute for the traditional notion of the "orders of creation," to which he had long objected on account of its use to provide an unambiguous religious sanction for a given social order, whether the old order or the "new order" of National

Socialism. Already in 1932 he had proposed the substitution of the more functional concept of "orders of preservation," which were to be understood as retaining their legitimacy only so long as they actually served God's purpose to preserve the world for Christ. It was this latter category that Bonhoeffer had used in explanation of the pacifist position that he took during the 1930's. International peace, he had said, is the great "order of preservation" willed by God for our time. But he added the significant proviso that like all such orders it is relative, not absolute, and so can and must be broken when the higher criteria of truth and justice are endangered. Here was a little-noticed clue to Bonhoeffer's later willingness to cast his lot with military men in the resistance movement against Hitler.

By the time of his work on the *Ethics,* however, Bonhoeffer had become disillusioned by the uses to which even the concept of orders of preservation could be put in the defense of Nazism, and so had devised the new term "mandates." These are to be understood not as arising from below (i.e., from history itself) but as imposed from above; they are not earthly powers but divine commissions. True, the mandates do involve relationships of superiority and inferiority (father and child, teacher and learner, ruler and ruled, etc.), but the "superior" is distinctly limited. He is limited from above by the God who has conferred this deputyship upon him; from below by the just rights of the inferior; and laterally by the coexistence of the other mandates. The state thus has no warrant to invade and tyrannize the realm of culture or the family. Nor is the church called to dominate the other mandates; quite the contrary, it is the place where the commandment of Jesus Christ is to be made known as the "word of freedom" that emancipates each of the other mandates for the realization of its own essential character.

Bonhoeffer strenuously opposes what he calls the habit of "thinking in terms of two spheres," which assumes that life is divided into Christian and non-Christian sectors, the problem being somehow to relate the two. Whether it be the scholastic differentiation between nature and grace, the "pseudo-Lutheran" doctrine of two kingdoms, or the sectarian view of the struggle of the elect against a hostile world, the fault, he says, is the same: the assumption that there are realities outside the reality of

Christ. In truth, "there are not two realities, but only one reality, and that is the reality of God, which has become manifest in Christ in the reality of the world." He therefore proposes in place of the spatial concept of two spheres, the qualitative (or more precisely, eschatological) categories of "the ultimate and the penultimate." The ultimate reality of God's grace in Christ does not annihilate the penultimate reality of man's ongoing life in history, but rather validates it, while at the same time limiting it. The penultimate is preserved in order that it may become "the outer covering of the ultimate."

Within this realm of the penultimate, Bonhoeffer felt it crucially important that Christian ethics recover the ability to make distinctions between the relatively better and the relatively worse. In a widely noted section of the *Ethics* calling for a recovery of "the concept of the natural" in Protestant thought, Bonhoeffer points out that the Reformers' emphasis on the all-sufficiency of grace had unintended consequences:

> Before the light of grace everything human and natural sank into the night of sin, and now no one dared to consider the relative differences within the human and the natural, for fear that by their so doing grace as grace might be diminished. . . . The sole antithesis to the natural was the Word of God; the natural was no longer contrasted to the unnatural.[6]

The result was that the Christian conscience was left unassisted in vitally important decisions, while the realm of nature and of civil society was allowed to fall prey to forces of disorder. In a similar vein, Bonhoeffer objects to the church's glossing over of the difference between relatively good and relatively evil people, which has amounted sometimes to an actual preference for the latter (presumably on the grounds that they are more fit subjects for conversion). "Whatever humanity and goodness is found in this fallen world must be on the side of Jesus Christ," he writes. "It is nothing less than a curtailment of the gospel if the nearness of Jesus Christ is proclaimed only to what is broken and evil and if the father's love for the prodigal son is so emphasized as to appear to diminish his love for the son who remained at home."

6 P. 101

The idea of "the natural" seems to have functioned for Bonhoeffer as still another equivalent for the concept of orders of preservation: it is the tendency toward health that God has implanted in the very structure of existence. "Life is its own physician," he notes, and "so long as life continues, the natural will always reassert itself." Included in the notion are natural rights and duties as well as natural relationships between man and man. In a chapter which was to provide a detailed exposition of these matters, Bonhoeffer begins with "the natural rights of bodily life," defending the legitimacy of bodily pleasures such as those of sex, food, and recreation, and discussing the problems of corporal punishment, torture, euthanasia, murder, suicide, and birth control. He intended to continue with sections on "the natural rights of the life of the mind" and "the natural right to work and property," but the chapter remained unfinished.

In thus setting out to articulate what apparently would have amounted to a full-fledged theory of natural law, Bonhoeffer did not feel that he had swerved from his original aim of founding an ethic wholly on Christology. For it is from Christ as Mediator of creation (i.e., as Logos) that the character of all created things derives. The incarnation only reinforces this relationship. "Just as in Christ the reality of God entered into the reality of the world, so, too, is that which is Christian to be found only in that which is of the world, the 'supernatural' only in the natural, the holy in the profane, and the revelational only in the rational." In fact it is only the Christian believer, Bonhoeffer asserts, who is able to live a truly natural and "worldly" life, since only he is free from the need to deify the world. For the Christian knows that precisely in its secularity, the world has already been accepted by a gracious God.

Bonhoeffer seems to have had a premonition that this work on ethics would be the last book to which he would set his hand. "I often feel as though the best part of my life was already past," he wrote from prison in December, 1943, "and that all I have to do now is to finish my *Ethics*." What he could not foresee was that the letters he was writing to parents and friends during these very months would when published later (in German, 1951; English translation 1953), have an impact equal to or greater than that of any of his other works. In part this is due to the intimate portrait of the man Dietrich Bonhoeffer that they offer, especially of the remarkable intellectual life that he was able to sustain even in prison. He read avidly in everything from Plutarch to the church fathers to nineteenth-century romantic literature. The letters are most notable, however, for the theological discussions with his friend Eberhard Bethge in which he pursues the idea of "Christian worldliness."

The urgency of the theme derives from Bonhoeffer's conviction that we have arrived at the end of the "religious" era in our culture. From the thirteenth century onward, man has been learning how to get along without any hypothesis of "God"; indeed, he has lost practically all awareness of what "God" might mean. This development, which Christian apologists almost universally deplore as "secularization," Bonhoeffer describes simply as the world's arrival at "adulthood" (*Mundigkeit*), its having "come of age." This he regards as an irreversible development. What are its consequences for the Christian faith?

> The thing that keeps coming back to me [he writes in April, 1944] is, what *is* Christianity, and indeed what *is* Christ, for us today? The time when men could be told everything by means of words, whether theological or simply pious, is over, and so is the time of inwardness and conscience, which is to say the time of religion as such. We are proceeding towards a time of no religion at all: men as they are now simply cannot be religious any more. . . . Our whole nineteen-hundred-year-old Christian preaching and theology rests upon the "religious premise" of man. What we call Christianity has always been a pattern—perhaps a true pattern—of religion. But if one day it becomes apparent that this *a priori* "premise" simply does not exist, but was an historical and temporary form of human self-expression . . . what does that mean for Christianity?[7]

In the letters that we have available (others were destroyed when Bethge was arrested), Bonhoeffer is hardly able to begin an answer to his own question, but several things are clear.

[7] *Prisoner for God* (N.Y., Macmillan, 1954), p. 122. (British ed. is entitled *Letters and Papers from Prison*, as is 1962 U.S. ed.)

First, a Christianity appropriate to a world come of age would speak of God "not on the borders of life but at its center." Bonhoeffer has no patience with the effort to spy out human weaknesses and drive men to despair before the Gospel can be preached, or with the use of God as a stop-gap for the incompleteness of our scientific knowledge. "We should find God in what we do know, not in what we don't," he writes. "We must not wait until we are at the end of our tether: he must be found at the center of life: in life, and not only in death; in health and vigor, and not only in suffering; in activity, and not only in sin."

Secondly, the church in the new age will have to learn what it means to live in deputyship for man. Bonhoeffer was critical even of the Confessing Church in this respect:

> During these years the church has fought for self-preservation as though it were an end in itself, and has thereby lost its chance to speak a word of reconciliation to mankind and the world at large. So our traditional language must perforce become powerless and remain silent, and our Christianity today will be confined to praying for and doing right by our fellowmen. Christian thinking, speaking, and organization must be reborn out of this praying and this action.[8]

Thirdly, when the church does speak again, a new language will be required. It is in this connection that Bonhoeffer introduces his famous proposal for a "non-religious interpretation of Biblical terminology" (and of theological concepts generally). His remarks on the subject are so tantalizingly brief that in subsequent discussion there has been a natural tendency to identify them with the more fully articulated "demythologizing" program of Bultmann, although Bonhoeffer himself, on the basis of Bultmann's key essay of 1941, explicitly rejected such an identification. "I am of the view," he wrote, "that the full content, including the mythological concepts, must be maintained. The New Testament is not a mythological garbing of the universal truth—this mythology (resurrection and so on) is the thing itself—but the concepts must be interpreted in such a way as not to make religion a pre-condition of faith (cf. circum-

[8] P. 140.

cision in St. Paul)." In the latter respect, Bonhoeffer stated,
Bultmann had not gone far enough. Neither had Karl Barth,
who although he had begun the criticism of religion had lapsed
into a mere "positivism of revelation," a "take it or leave it"
attitude.

In undertaking a nonreligious interpretation of biblical concepts such as he proposes, the church would only be permitting
the Bible to assume its own true character again, Bonhoeffer
is convinced, for the Bible knows nothing of "religion" in the
ordinary sense. "Religion" is concerned with inwardness, the
Bible with the whole man. "Religion" is individualistic, while
the Bible is concerned with corporate existence. "Religion" is
metaphysical, i.e., interested in a world beyond; the Bible is
concerned with the renewal of this world. This nonreligiousness
is clearest in the case of the Old Testament, but it is equally
true of the New Testament, Bonhoeffer asserts, when it is interpreted as it should be, in the light of the Old. "Jesus does not
call men to a new religion, but to life."

In the subsequent discussion of Bonhoeffer's thought, it has
been much debated whether the theme of the "worldliness" of
Christianity as we have it in the letters represents a departure
from Bonhoeffer's earlier theology or is in continuity with it.
Undoubtedly there are grounds for both positions. The letters
do present a contrast with the tendency in *The Cost of Discipleship* to draw a sharp line of demarcation between church and
world; Bonhoeffer himself was quite aware of this contrast (see
his letter of July 21, 1944). But the motif of worldliness can
also be seen as in direct continuity not only with his *Ethics* but
also with his earlier work, especially *Creation and Fall* and the
lectures on Christology. It is in his doctrine of Christ, both as
the Mediator of creation and as the crucified Redeemer, appearing in humiliation to reconcile God and the world, that
Bonhoeffer's theme of "Christian worldliness" is rooted.

> Man is challenged to participate in the sufferings of God at
> the hands of a godless world. This is the decisive difference be-
> tween Christianity and all religions. Man's religiosity makes him
> look in his distress to the power of God in the world; he uses
> God as a *Deus ex machina*. The Bible however directs him to
> the powerlessness and suffering of God; only a suffering God

can help. To this extent we may say that the process we have described by which the world came of age was an abandonment of a false conception of God, and a clearing of the decks for the God of the Bible, who conquers power and space in the world by his weakness.[9]

[9] P. 164.

Bibliography

Dietrich Bonhoeffer, *Letters and Papers from Prison*, N.Y., Macmillan, 1962.

John D. Godsey, *The Theology of Dietrich Bonhoeffer*, Philadelphia, Westminster, 1960.

PAUL TILLICH

Walter Leibrecht

Paul Tillich has spoken to modern man with great penetration. It is the honesty with which he approaches reality and the freshness with which he discusses the perplexities and joys of our individual and collective lives that make his writings fascinating.

Tillich is a thinker working on the frontiers of thought. One might call him a philosopher's philosopher, as Einstein was a scientist's scientist. He has influenced many men in the field of philosophy and theology, and mainly through such men made an impact on contemporary thought. He is not one of those who counsels the skeptical modern man to abandon his autonomy as the root of his lostness and to subject himself without questioning to the doctrines and authority of the church. For Tillich, modern man has no possible way back to medieval heteronomy, to a faith understood as intellectual sacrifice. Where faith is possible only by the suppression of doubt, Tillich asserts, it will likely result in fanaticism or cynicism; indeed, it is modern man's doubt that testifies to the intensity of his quest for absolute truth. In his presentation of the Christian faith Tillich does not ignore modern man's intense desire for truth and, sharing this desire himself, he is constantly seeking the meaning of the Christian doctrines.

As there is no truth without doubt, so there is no being without nonbeing. And as truth is present in the moment of doubt, there is for Tillich no realm of life, even life in estrangement, which exists without relation to the ultimate. This, to him, is the very center of Christian faith. Man experiences the presence of the ultimate in the moment of utter estrangement and despair—which signifies that in the moment of separation he may be close to God as the origin of his being. As with Luther, Pascal, and others, it has been Tillich's experience that the way to God—to truth, to ultimate reality—leads through the desert. In the moment of despair, in the moment life is threatened by meaninglessness, man reaches out for meaning—for being. The word "being," which is of central importance in Tillich's vocabulary, is not a static but a dynamic word. Thus he speaks of the "power of being"—that to which I reach out and that by which my whole being can be grasped. Tillich refuses to speculate as a detached observer about being as such. Being itself is the very ground of my being, that by which I live. It is not a physical reality up in the clouds. It can be given expression only through the ultimate character of my faith.

Paul Tillich and Karl Barth offer two great theological alternatives in our generation. Barth's theology tends to be swallowed up in Christology; it rejects the possibility of any natural theology, describes the God-man relationship primarily in terms of sin and forgiveness and sees the human life as being determined by the historical acts of God's salvation. Barth concentrates on the acts of God and is highly dialectical in regard to the question of how these acts actually determine and shape human life.

Tillich starts from the central Christian conviction that the word became flesh—that the Logos entered reality and that reality, individual as well as cultural, is transformed through crisis and renewal by the power of divine grace. Man, by the very fact that he is and not merely by his being baptized, is related to the divine and dependent on it. For Tillich Christianity is the revelation not of new beliefs or doctrine but of a new reality which is at work renewing the old. Tillich deplores the attempts of many of the despisers of religion in our time to cut religion off from life and thus make it meaningless. This is the basic goal of secularism—to claim the world in its material reality for itself and to restrict religion to the realm of fancy and dreams.

Tillich feels that Barthian dialectical theology offers only a wooden sword in the struggle against secularism, since such theology tends to agree with secularism's basic assumption that in its creatureliness the world as such does not reveal its divine origin. Condemning natural theology, the followers of Barth seem not to recognize that life as such is related to its divine originator and is therefore sacred. Tillich is convinced that it is the task of the theologian to witness to the holiness of all being and to proclaim that everything that is, is only through the power and grace of God, and that therefore the profane and the sacred cannot be artificially separated.

Like Barth, Tillich rejects the nineteenth-century culture-Protestantism which tended to adapt religion to the demands of modern civilization to such an extent that civilization itself determined the content of faith. But while Barth repudiates the mediating role of theology, Tillich accepts it as an essential part of theology. In this sense Tillich continues the great nineteenth-century theological tradition of mediation, with its effort to overcome the schizophrenic split between the religious and the scientific consciousness of modern man. However, Tillich approaches the problem from an entirely new angle and does so within the intellectual and cultural situation of the twentieth century. Mediation is for him never an easy or uncritical adaption of religion to modern man's cultural or scientific maxims. He does not seek the absorption of the religious into the secular as present-day secularism demands. Nor does he share the romantic dreams of those who think it possible to return to a medieval order in which the secular is subservient to the ecclesiastical. Opposed both to a secularized culture separated from religious concern and to any sort of ecclesiastical imperialism, Tillich seeks a true reconciliation between the religious and the secular.

Tillich takes seriously the Johannine statement that "God so loved the *world* that he sent his only begotten son." Therefore a purely spiritual or ecclesiastical salvation would not for him be Christian salvation. Salvation—the reality of the "new being" as revealed in Jesus Christ—is always concerned with man and his world; divine grace reuniting and healing man's broken life encompasses the totality of man's world. From this centrally Christian concern for salvation Tillich as theologian and philosopher sets out on his task of mediation. Here is where he breaks with neo-orthodox colleagues who concentrate on theology yet often leave the fallen world to its own devices.

Religion is defined by Tillich as the dimension of depth in all of man's life functions, rather than as a special function of his spiritual life. But, contrary to the charge of some of his critics, he does not thereby reduce religion to a merely human act, for by "dimension of depth" Tillich refers to that which is ultimate, infinite, and unconditional in man's spiritual life. Hence he defines religion or faith as "ultimate concern," as concern directed toward the ultimate. And as ultimate concern religion is at the origin of all cultural expression, giving substance, meaning, judgment, and creative courage to all the functions of the human spirit. Both religion in its forms of expression and culture are grounded in the experience of ultimate concern and therefore belong together. Their separation in contemporary life, Tillich asserts, is artificial and must be overcome if religion is to remain pertinent and our culture creative. Both religion and culture can issue in demonic perversion and destruction wherever a finite entity or ideal rather than the ultimate is the focus of their unconditional concern.

In his basic approach Tillich is a philosopher of religion. The true theologian, he contends, cannot avoid being a philosopher; instead of using philosophical forms in an underhanded or uncritical way the theologian ought to be fully conscious of the philosophical framework within which he operates. Tillich rejects the kind of religious philosophy inherent in the approach of much neo-orthodox theology, according to which the meeting of God and man is merely accidental since God and man do not essentially belong together. Over against this approach Tillich opts for the ontological approach, according to which man discovers himself when he discovers God—discovers something that is identical with himself although it transcends him infinitely, something from which he is estranged but from which he has never been nor can be separated. Tillich is convinced that the ontological method—used, among many others, by Augustine—not only represents the true emphasis of Christian faith but is basic for every genuine philosophy of religion. He is also convinced that only on such a basis can the destructive cleavage between philosophy and theology be overcome and a reconciliation between religion and secular culture achieved. However, having discovered this ontological principle implicit in classic Augustinianism, Tillich sometimes carries his effort to overcome the gap between religion and culture to a point where the offered reconciliation is one of "mere thought." Although Tillich rejects the Hegelian reconciliation by thought and the Barthian reconciliation by faith and demands reconciliation in reality, he is tempted to fall back on a philosophy of consciousness whenever he moves from basic Christian existential experience into ontological analysis, applying the Hegelian maxim that everything that is real is also rational—a maxim which hardly seems commensurate with the words of the Creator in Genesis: ". . . and God saw that it was good."

Nonetheless Tillich the Christian existentialist keeps Tillich the ontologist from giving way to the notion of a philosophical salvation. Like Kierkegaard, he believes that the ultimate discloses itself only to the "passionate" man, the man who allows himself to be "grasped by the ultimate." As an adherent of the passionate approach Tillich holds that faith can be expressed not in terms of objective experience but only through symbols and myth—a problem he discusses in his many writings on the nature of symbol, myth, and religious language. But whereas Kierkegaard was satisfied with direct existential expressions of an existential religious attitude, Tillich attempts to translate this attitude into philosophic expressions and concepts.

Clearly recognizing the inner limitations of existentialism and existentialist psychoanalysis, Tillich nevertheless feels that these two movements have bestowed a "tremendous gift" on modern theology in terms of understanding the human situation. He interprets both existentialism and depth psychology as modern expressions of the age-old protest against philosophies of consciousness. In his view existentialism's emphasis on the unconscious and the irrational will and its analysis of human predicament and estrangement were transformed by Freud into a methodological scientific language. Existentialism and depth psychology are thus for him inseparable. Though their great significance lies in their detailed descriptions of man's existential predicament and estrangement, they are also significant insofar as they point at least indirectly to man's teleological nature. Existentialism and depth psychology are, however, both unable and unwilling to define this true nature of man; though they raise the ultimate questions of life in a profound way, they cannot answer the questions they ask. Neither do they in themselves have the capacity to heal the disruption they have discovered. In Tillich's opinion the psychologist may be able to treat a person's pathological symptoms, but he cannot deal with the basic existential estrangement that made escape into neurosis or psychosis desirable or necessary in the first place. States Tillich: "Neither existentialist analysis nor psychological methods can overcome the existential negativity, meaninglessness and guilt which not only the sick person, but man universally carries." This existential estrangement which cannot be healed by the most refined therapeutic techniques is, as Tillich puts it, "the object of salvation." In this regard Tillich has been instrumental in suggesting ways in which the psychologist and theologian can work together. He indicates how the theologian can benefit from the psychologist, but he also shows how the psychologist needs grace—the power to heal—in order really to address himself meaningfully to man's root problem and thus do more than merely relieve the patient's symptoms of his deeper suffering.

Parallel to his relating of religion and depth psychology, Tillich deals in ever new and fresh approaches with the basic relatedness of the center of our faith to the various secular spheres. The special merit of Tillich's many writings on theology vis-à-vis culture, science, and politics consists in their combination of profound thought penetrating into the very structure of reality and seeking the basic relatedness of religion to the field in question, and practical down-to-earth advice directed not only to ministers but to doctors, artists, educators, and others concerning the achievement of the kind of cooperation in creative tension through which reconciliation can be realized.

The key term in Tillich's understanding of religion and culture and their mutual relatedness is "ultimate concern." Faith as ultimate concern signifies first of all that it is an act of one's whole being and not only his mind. It also signifies that only that concern which is directed to the ultimate as such deserves to be called faith. Tillich has noted man's inclination to be idolatrous, to make something in the finite world his ultimate concern, and that wherever man focuses his ultimate loyalty on something which is not ultimate he brings destruction upon himself. The most ideal-sounding goal will corrupt us if we confuse the finite with the infinite. Whether it be the ideal of national honor as in fascism or the socialist state of communism, as soon as it is declared absolute all else is sacrificed to its achievement, and incalculable suffering follows for those who do not adhere to it. Likewise, if modern man makes success, ambition, happiness or honor his ultimate concern, it brings suffering upon himself and others and he becomes impervious to all the other concerns of life. Only the ultimate itself deserves ultimate concern. This does not mean, in Tillich's view, that we should withdraw from the world into some vague mysticism, shunning all involvement and practical action. On the contrary, if we are ultimately concerned, our inner being will not be dominated by one concern; rather, it will express itself in new integration and wholeness. If we are ultimately concerned, all our finite concerns will be informed by ultimate concern, becoming the media and expression of ultimacy itself.

The great painter, Tillich writes, is not a man who falls in love with the aesthetic effects of his painting, but one who creates a great work because he is ultimately concerned. The mark of the true genius is that he is dissatisfied with himself and ceaselessly tries to express something ultimate. A culture without ultimate concern, Tillich is convinced, will lose its creative power. He points to the loss of ultimate concern—of any sense for transcendent reality—in the civilization of the second half of the nineteenth century. He is merciless in his attack on the spirit of placid finitude which he sees expressed in the artistic, political, cultural, and even ecclesiastical world of the late nineteenth and early twentieth centuries. In his eyes Western bourgeois society and its civilization are doomed to destruction not from without but from within. Accordingly, his method has become radical analysis, attacking the "self-complacency and self-sufficiency" inherent in our culture.

The total world view of nineteenth-century man was shaped by his utter confidence in inevitable progress—progress defined by ever-increasing material wealth and opportunities. But World War I broke his world to pieces. He discovered that science, his precious instrument for mastering the world, had turned against him by becoming a means of mass destruction. When Tillich returned from that war, a social revolution was afoot in his native Germany. The question in his mind was, What is the task of the postwar generation? Was it the demand of the hour to mend the broken house of the nineteenth century—to join the ranks of the conservatives and nationalists, as most of Germany's educated people thought, particularly those active in the churches? Or was the world of the past beyond repair, making a new structure necessary? Tillich felt that after the revolution a new kind of civilization should be introduced. The immediate task for the intellectual, as he understood it, was to identify himself with the rebelling proletariat. The fact that the proletariat fought for the socialist cause and that socialism seemed to reject religion did not disturb him fundamentally. He felt that there was promise in the irreligious character of the rising proletariat, since it challenged hypocritical and smug middle-class religiosity. Tillich believed that among the frustrated unemployed and those of the working class who had been deprived of all opportunity creatively to express their true humanity he would find a deep desire for true self-realization. These men, he thought, could become the bearers of a new culture in which man could freely realize his own potential.

Together with some friends, Tillich founded a movement for religious socialism in Germany. They hoped to lead the proletariat to a new and deeper understanding of their goal, to interpret its deeper meaning to its followers. The principle out of which this new society was to grow was "theonomy." Theonomy as a divine demand Tillich set in opposition to modern man's oscillation between empty individualistic autonomy and imposed totalitarian heteronomy. Theonomy, he said, is not a divine law over and against man that demands his total subjection, nor is it a disguised form of heteronomy; it is a form of culture in which all concerns of life are informed by ultimate concern. Theonomy does not impose on man's reason beliefs which are strange to man's rational nature; rather, it is "autonomous reason united with its own depth."

Religion is here understood by Tillich as the root of culture—culture as the efflorescence of religion. Accordingly he is concerned to show what he feels is the essential relatedness of each cultural expression to its religious ground. Theonomy also, Tillich believes, creates a basis for a truly ecumenical encounter between Protestantism and Catholicism. Theonomy includes the

Protestant principle of protest against any form of idolatry, but unites Protestant prophetism with priestly sacramentalism by the awareness of the holiness of all being and the awareness that the presence of being, of God, always is dynamic, overcoming and renewing all that is old. The prophet speaking the word of crisis becomes the priest healing that which is broken.

But Tillich's hope for the realization of religious socialism informed by theonomy never came true. The dehumanized and dishonored proletariat felt its needs more directly expressed by a man like Hitler, who promised them bread and work, an automobile and security. Both politically and theologically, it was heteronomy and its accompanying totalitarianism which became the dominant trend in the Germany of the late 1920s.

A few weeks before the Nazis' rise to power, Tillich published a book in which he warned his countrymen against Nazism and its demand for ultimate loyalty to something which was not ultimate. The rise of the Führer was, for Tillich, a truly demonic development which could lead only to destruction. Along with Thomas Mann, Albert Einstein, and others, he had to leave his country in 1933, emigrating to the United States at the age of forty-seven though he had no knowledge of the English language. The fact that he has since become one of America's leading spirits is a compliment both to the man and his rare intellectual power and to the country ready to receive him as one of her own and to listen to him. Whereas in Germany Tillich was chiefly a philosopher, he has primarily been a theologian during his years in the United States.

Although religious socialism did not find its actualization in history, it did contribute importantly to modern thought. In particular it articulated new truth and insight about man's nature and the meaning of history. Tillich had spoken of the *kairos* of religious socialism. *Kairos* means the fulfilled time—the right moment to act in a given situation. Every kairos situation expresses its own inner demand. Kairos is the moment when time is invaded by eternity. In the kairos situation the restoring power of being is present—the power which transforms man and society and which fulfills what is potential in history and nature.

The concept of kairos informs Tillich's whole approach to

ethics. He is concerned not so much with the eternal law written down once and for all as with the ethical demand of a given situation. While he finds the material for his ethics in an ontological analysis of love, power, and justice, he rejects any casuistics and emphasizes the need for a new decision or act which will do justice to a situation's inner demand. Thus careful analysis is the precondition for ethical decision.

Kairos, eternity in time, becomes also the key for a new interpretation of history. Contrary to what some of the late romantics thought, history knows no static, timeless togetherness of the infinite and the finite; for Tillich history is a process of moving from one transition to the next—a process of eternal crisis and renewal. This is the way in which the power of being is present in history—not as a superhistorical reality but as the ultimate ground and power of every historical situation. Hence historical interpretation cannot rest content with the compilation of historical data but must grasp the depths of reality in which its divine foundation and meaning become visible. "Historical realism" reaches the ultimate ground of meaning of a historical situation and, through it, of being itself. Tillich shows that the historian must write as a man who participates in history—a man involved in the contemporary struggle. The historian has a kind of prophetic responsibility: he must be able to understand the structural necessities of the present and derive from such analysis a direction for action. Freedom to act is possible only by means of a thorough analysis of the given situation; man has the power to transform history only if he knows what is involved. Thus an understanding of kairos in history has profound ethical consequences. In every crisis situation man is confronted with a new creative possibility. Every historical situation has an aspect of destiny, but man can make a decision and, if it is based on a thorough understanding of what is given, he can act freely. This freedom is never infinite, however. Tillich's awareness that human freedom is always limited and finite leads him to emphasize the tragic element in human existence. With Kierkegaard and Heidegger he can say that "man is finite freedom," which means that while man cannot be man without actualizing his freedom, through the act of self-actualization he estranges himself from his original union with being, from his state of "dreaming innocence." Here we see the strong influence of Schelling in Tillich's thought.

Even ethical action cannot lead to reunion with God. It is not the awareness of the radical character of depravity which leads Tillich to the assumption that a mere ethical reconciliation is impossible, but his idealist notion that man, originally in paradisic unity with being and thus in a state of dreaming innocence, separates himself from the divine by exercising his freedom—i.e., by any act in which he realizes his freedom in a finite world. Once separation has taken place, once dreaming innocence is lost, it is impossible for man to achieve by his own efforts a reunion with God, with the ground of being. Thus we are estranged, and action leads only to further estrangement. Reunion with being—the overcoming of estrangement—is possible only when man's heart lets itself be grasped by the divine spirit, only when being itself, entering man, overcomes and conquers the resistance of estrangement and despair.

In his emphasis on the power of reconciliation which is necessary to reunite the separated one with the ground of being Tillich often seems closer to the Greek tradition than to biblical thought. In the Old Testament it is man's disobedience, his use of his freedom against the will of God, which estranges him from God, rather than his use of freedom as such. The Greek concept of freedom evokes a tragic connotation insofar as freedom is viewed both as the means by which man realizes his true being and as the means by which he separates himself from the grace of the gods. For the biblical writers man is constantly abusing his freedom by making himself the end of all things. But they do not look upon freedom as such as a destructive element; for the most part they praise it highly. Even Paul, in his interpretation of Adam's fall as having become the destiny of mankind, does not necessarily identify estrangement with man's self-actualization as such. Tillich tends to combine Greek and Christian insights concerning estrangement in his statement of the fundamental predicament of human existence. But in his thought the feeling of tragic inevitability is united with an overpowering feeling of guilt, revealing his deep kinship to Kierkegaard.

As a philosopher Tillich has asked unceasingly the question

of man's being, has relentlessly sought the meaning of man's life. The analysis of man's estranged situation is the center of Tillich's philosophical effort. It is the philosopher's task to analyze the human situation and to invite man to a radical act of self-knowledge. But knowledge cannot effect reconciliation. Only a new reality can do this, and it is the theologian's task to proclaim and open up this new reality. Thus it became a necessity for Tillich to be not only a philosopher but also a theologian. Tillich has a place in the great tradition of Christian mysticism; in his writing traditional theology is not simply recapitulated in orthodox fashion but becomes instrumental in the expression of his own encounter with the divine. He is a theologian as one who is "ultimately concerned."

At the same time, like many of the great mystics, Tillich has no intention of abandoning classic Christian doctrines. What he does is to show their true and deeper meaning by interpreting them symbolically. Symbol and myth are two of the most important categories in Tillich's thought. He rejects all literalistic interpretation of the biblical witness. The ultimate cannot be expressed directly, Tillich emphasizes, because the infinite is beyond the finite, and every finite picture we use to point to the infinite can be employed only analogically and symbolically. But he also rejects any reference to a particular Christian doctrine as "only a symbol." Symbol and myth are the highest forms of religious speech, and a true symbol participates in the reality which it symbolizes. As such, a symbol becomes a bearer of revelation, a self-manifestation of the ultimate.

It is not, Tillich insists, the task of the theologian to create new symbols; in fact symbols cannot be created: they grow and die. If we are fully conscious of the intellectual and spiritual atmosphere of our time we will know which symbols have the power to manifest the ultimate for our time. There are certain symbols, Tillich feels, which in the Middle Ages or the Reformation period were extremely powerful but which do not convey reality to the man of the twentieth century. He maintains, for instance, that just as the powerful symbol of the Virgin Birth lost significance in the piety of the Reformers, the symbol of God as the father often evokes the wrong connotations in modern man. No doubt Tillich has done great service to modern theology in showing that many biblical expressions are used symbolically rather than literally; he thereby has made many Christian teachings newly acceptable to modern men. However, his preoccupation with symbol, and particularly with the central symbol of the Christian faith, Jesus as the Christ, has often led him to lose interest in the historical aspect of the event symbolically interpreted.

Led by his awareness of the kairos situation in history—in which something new appears, creating a crisis for the old—Tillich finds a new interest in Christology, which for him becomes central to any serious effort of Christian thought. Since the presence of the new in our lives and in history is not static but is a "breaking into existence," the New Being which appears in Jesus as the Christ is to be understood as the breaking into existence of the power of the New Being. When Tillich's terms such as "kairos situation" and "the demand of the hour" were misused by adherents of Nazism and applied to their movement and leader, he had to make unmistakably clear what the ultimate criterion of every kairos situation is.

This criterion is the "logos," the New Being which appeared in Jesus, the Christ. Christ as Jesus, as the bearer of the New Being, surrenders his finitude and thus becomes completely transparent to the ultimate he reveals. Tillich says that Jesus is the Christ through his sacrificing that which is Jesus to that which is Christ. Since Jesus is able to do this without losing himself, he must first completely possess himself. This means that Jesus as the Christ is truly united with the ground of being and thus can be called the "true man." In him essential manhood is revealed. This and not any of his personal finite characteristics is what makes him the Christ. His personality, teachings, and acts are not the cause but the expression of his being the Christ. In Tillich's view any attempt to make the finite self of Jesus the object of religious devotion is to be rejected as idolatry. Neither Jesus himself nor the church but only that to which he witnesses is final. This does not mean that Tillich takes the biblical picture of Jesus lightly. In fact he continually uses the episodes, parables, and teachings of Jesus as the basis of his sermons. But through the presentation of these the ultimate itself becomes manifest. The New Being which is in Christ is for Tillich the creative power which is active in all history.

For Tillich the Christ-event is the key to the very structure of the universe; it is the revelation of the ultimate relationship of the divine and the human. It leads Tillich to the ontological statement that the holy and the profane cannot be separated, and to the insight that ultimate reality or the power of being is the power of history itself and cannot be understood in a supernaturalistic sense. It is the power of history constantly overcoming that which is old and reconciling that which is separated. This is the power of the New Being.

Tillich's emphasis on the universal meaning of that which was revealed in the Christ-event was a needed balance in contemporary theology. Nonetheless the question remains whether the revelation of God through Christ gives way for Tillich to some form of higher gnosis—to an ontology which perhaps makes faith unnecessary. Tillich deals with this problem himself in his book *Dynamics of Faith*. While faith always leads to gnosis, gnosis cannot, he says, substitute for faith. Faith is always conquering doubt and as long as we remain human, faith involves risk. Tillich's theology of the New Being finds powerful expression also in his volume of sermons titled *The New Being,* and more thorough expression in his *Systematic Theology*.

Tillich's emphasis on the healing function of the New Being has led him to a rediscovery of the original meaning of the word "salvation"—namely, healing, making whole that which is broken. It is this latter emphasis which has drawn him into vital discussions with men in the healing professions. Only the reality of the New Being of grace can heal that basic estrangement of man from his true self—from the ground of his being.

The power of the New Being, says Tillich, is expressed in love which overcomes all separations. If I am driven by love, I participate in the power of love and therefore in the power of being. Tillich's analysis of the nature of love is one of the deepest reflections of his philosophical mind. In his volume *Love, Power and Justice* he discusses libido, eros, philia, and agape not as different types of love but as aspects of the one true love, as forms of man's self-realization. Tillich confronts the self-realization through freedom which leads to estrangement with the self-realization through love, finding in the actualization of ourselves in and through love a way of fulfillment in which separation is overcome. Love does not always lead to freedom, but freedom can be truly experienced only through love. He further points out that there is no such thing as true love in which one does not do justice to and respect the freedom of the other person; both justice and freedom need love to remain just and free. Love makes us whole again, makes us real by making each of us a self-related being able to resist dissolving into something else.

If one embraces this reality of love, having recognized its truly healing function, must one, in Tillich's view, go back to the Christian faith to find its original source? In making self-realization the ultimate criterion of religion and love and by defining love as the power toward self-realization, does not Tillich elevate the eros concept of love over others? Is not his view tempered by Plato's concept of eros seeking fulfillment through self-realization of the individual and by the romantic ideal of the individual personality? Tillich united the basic insights of Greek thought and classic Christian theology in a form in which both become newly relevant to modern man. There are, however, tremendous inner tensions in his thought which cannot easily be overcome by the rationality of his system. His work does not present us with ready answers, but it does offer us new questions—questions which will stimulate the discussion of a whole generation of theologians.

Theologians in all ages have felt the urge to bless or accept the cultural status quo of their time. Even Karl Barth, after all the judgment he has pronounced over this fallen world, has, like Bonhoeffer, discovered great "promise" in the secularity of secularism. Both Barth and Bonhoeffer have created a theological vogue of talking about *Weltlichkeit* (secularity), which among their disciples often amounts to mere world acceptance with no attempt to inform the secular world and its culture with truly Christian meaning. Reinhold Niebuhr, after writing much on "crisis and renewal," has in recent years reached the conclusion that the kind of sober pragmatism according to which the best among the children of this world handle their affairs is, after all, the best way in which to act; Christian faith simply adds a sobriety, through its awareness of human sinfulness, and a dash of mercy. Although none of the neo-orthodox thinkers mentioned here can be accused of disinterestedness in the affairs of this world, their recent positions do not suggest themselves as a basis for a deeper renewal of our cultural life by the reality of Christ.

Tillich alone among the great Protestant thinkers of our time still strongly believes that the Gospel is of such nature and power that it transforms the whole of life. He believes that this Gospel is the power of reconciliation and renewal in this world and for this world in its totality. He alone really dares to spell out the forms and structures not only of crisis but of renewal and the ways in which reconcilation in reality is achieved. He dares to have a vision of what man essentially is, and of what culture essentially is in its God-given structure and purpose. Even if one cannot follow Tillich in some of his detailed conclusions and ontological analyses, one must admire him for the tremendous power of his faith and intellect in resolutely linking the center of our faith to all the realms of God's and man's world. He does so as a theologian who takes seriously the profound consequences of the Christian doctrine of creation and redemption for both our individual and our cultural life.

Bibliography

Paul Tillich, *The Courage to Be*, New Haven, Yale, 1959.

The Theology of Paul Tillich, Charles W. Kegley and Robert W. Bretall, eds., N.Y., Macmillan, 1952.

IV

Recent Theological Work

PIERRE TEILHARD DE CHARDIN

Christopher F. Mooney, S.J.

Pierre Teilhard de Chardin was almost unknown as a theologian before his death in 1955 at the age of seventy-four. But with the posthumous publication of his philosophical and theological works he immediately gained a notoriety and a renown which would have altogether amazed him during his life. He succeeded in disturbing scientists as well as philosophers and theologians and has found today both strong support and violent opposition among Christian and non-Christian alike. He has been called a genius, a harbinger of a new and strong Christianity, and also a dangerous innovator saved from ecclesiastical condemnation by his good faith alone. For some he is a daring thinker of great depth and originality, for others simply a scientist who has wandered from his exacting professional disciplines of geology and paleontology to speak in the poetic language of a personal religious experience.

All these paradoxical reactions to the thought of Pierre Teilhard de Chardin are in some measure justified. They spring from the paradox in the man himself. Teilhard was a Jesuit and a priest, a scientist, a philosopher, a theologian, a spiritual prophet, and a seer. He was a man of enormous personal charm. He suffered deeply during his life; yet that life was one of high adventure. His scientific writings fill ten large volumes, and his anthropological, philosophical, theological, and spiritual writings fill another fifteen. Then there are volumes of letters and spiritual journals. In the past twenty-five years he has had three biographers and has been the subject of thousands of critical articles and over a hundred books.

Born near Clermont-Ferrand, France, in 1881, Pierre was fourth of eleven children of a wealthy gentleman farmer, whose own father had married into French nobility, and whose wife, Pierre's mother, was the great grandniece of Voltaire. Pierre entered the Society of Jesus in 1899 and taught at the Jesuit secondary school in Cairo between 1905 and 1908, where in the heat of the Egyptian desert he began his lifelong study of minerals and fossils. Following his ordination to the priesthood in 1911, he pursued doctoral studies in geology and paleontology at the Sorbonne. These were interrupted in 1914 by his induction into the French army as a stretcher-bearer during World War I and were not completed until 1922, when he was appointed to the chair of geology at the Institut Catholique in Paris. In 1925 the Jesuit Superior General removed him from this position because of a paper he wrote on the relation of evolution to the doctrine of original sin. Considered henceforth by the Vatican to be a dangerous innovator, he was forbidden to publish anything of a philosophical or religious nature, and he was exiled to China.

He remained in China for twenty years, exploring with fellow Jesuit scientists the vast geological resources around Tientsin and Peking. His voluminous scientific writings brought him into contact with the leading paleontologists of the day and involved him in numerous expeditions, including the one that discovered the skull of the 400,000-year-old "Peking Man" at Choukoutien. After World War II he returned to Paris, where he became director of research at the National Center for Scientific Research. In 1948 he was asked to be a candidate for the chair of paleontology at the Collège de France, but his Superior General, fearing adverse publicity for his ideas on evolution and further difficulties with the Vatican, refused permission. Teilhard eventually had to leave Paris permanently. He settled in New York in 1951, at the invitation of the Wenner-Grenn Foundation for Anthropological Research, subsequently making two trips to fossil sites in South Africa. During all these years he wrote three books and a great number of essays on the philosophical and religious meaning of evolution and on Christian spirituality, all of which were finally published following his death in New York on Easter Sunday, 1955.

What did Teilhard want to do as a thinker, and why? This fundamental question must be answered before any summary can be made of his complex intellectual enterprise. Only then can we look more closely at the three different levels of his thought to see how he carried out his overall project.

Without fear of contradiction, I think we can say that Teilhard de Chardin was primarily a visionary, a seer. He once wrote:

"Nothing is profane to those who know how to see."[1] Teilhard *saw* something and wanted to show others what he saw. He wanted to be a guide for others; yet he suffered deeply for wanting to be a guide. He was severely disciplined by the Vatican authorities of his time; he spent most of his life in exile from his native Paris; and he was forbidden to publish anything of a philosophical, theological, or spiritual nature. Why then did he want to be a guide? Because he saw with crystal clarity the disjointedness between the sphere of the sacred, to which he was totally committed, and that sphere which is the product of modern science. This secular sphere was not at all interested in talk about God or Christ, but it was a sphere to which Teilhard, as a scientist, was also totally committed. Teilhard saw that those committed to the first sphere left out everything that appeared in the second and were largely unconcerned with the phenomenon of change in human life. On the other hand, he knew the second sphere to be authentic, because as a geologist and paleontologist he had come to understand evolution from the inside. But this second sphere left out the whole history of inwardness; it left out the study of what was most peculiar to the human species—namely, thought, spirit, growth in personal interrelatedness. Teilhard's overall project, therefore, was to unite these two spheres, the one redemptive and the other cosmic, and to expand the second so that science would deal with the phenomenon of thought and reflection. For his experience as a Christian convinced him that God was ultimately responsible for what was taking place in both spheres, and he wanted others to see what he saw. The following passages, selected from his writings between 1917 and 1940, will illustrate the intensity of his desire to make people see.

There are in reality two types of minds and two only: those who never get past the perception of multiplicity nor feel any need to do so, and those for whom the same perception of multiplicity must necessarily resolve itself into some unity. The pluralists and the monists, those who do not see and those who do. . . . I know it looks ridiculous and vain to play the part of being misunderstood. And yet, I honestly believe that I see something and I wish that something to be

[1] Pierre Teilhard de Chardin, *The Divine Milieu* (N.Y., Harper & Row, 1960), p. 38.

seen. . . . I want to teach people how to see God everywhere, to see Him in all that is most hidden, most solid and most ultimate in the world. These pages put forward no more than a practical attitude, or, more exactly, perhaps, a way of teaching how to see. . . . Seeing. We might say the whole of life lies in that verb. That is why the history of the living world can be summarized as the elaboration of ever more perfect eyes within a cosmos in which there is always something more to be seen. . . . To try to see more and better is not a matter of whim or curiosity or self indulgence. To see or to perish is the very condition laid upon everything that makes up the universe by reason of the mysterious gift of existence. I repeat that my only aim in these pages, my whole driving power, is to try to see.[2]

Why did this disjointedness in two sets of data, the religious and the secular, bother Teilhard so much? And why was he so intent that his readers see the unity he saw? The reason is that his whole life experience, and therefore his whole system of thought, was a response to what he felt to be the most pressing need of humanity today: the assurance of some successful outcome for the human enterprise, some hope for the future. He said many decades ago that the focus of all human anxiety and fear today is the future, the sense of being responsible for the future and for human life on our planet. Long before it was fashionable, Teilhard proclaimed that the whole of modern culture was oriented toward the future. What reasons are there for us to hope in this future? What guarantees are there that we have a future? Teilhard believed that there were enough people focusing upon reasons for despair in the human future; he wanted to focus unilaterally upon reasons for hope. A passage from *The Phenomenon of Man,* completed in 1940, gives a sense of his concern for our contemporary fear of the future.

The whole psychology of modern disquiet is linked with the sudden confrontation of space-time. Conscious or not, anguish, a fundamental anguish of being, despite our smiles, strikes in the depths of our hearts and is the undertone of all our conversations. In the first and most widespread degree, the "malady of space-time" manifests itself as a rule by a feeling of futility, of being crushed by the

[2] *Christianity and Evolution* (N.Y., Harcourt Brace Jovanovich, 1971), p. 101; *The Making of a Mind* (N.Y., Harper & Row, 1965), p. 269; *Divine Milieu*, p. 15; *The Phenomenon of Man* (N.Y., Harper & Row, 1959), pp. 31, 35.

enormities of the cosmos. Sickness of the dead end—the anguish of feeling shut in. . . . Fear of being lost in a world so vast that man seems to have lost all significance. Fear of being reduced to immobility. Fear of being unable to find a way out. . . . In the great game being played, we are the players as well as being the cards and the stakes. Nothing can go on if we leave the table. Neither can any power force us to remain. Is the game worth the candle, or are we simply its dupes? We will never take a step in a direction which we know to be blocked. There lies precisely the ill that causes our disquiet.[3]

Let us imagine, Teilhard wrote toward the end of his life, that a group of miners are trapped after an accident deep down in the earth. For these miners to summon up the courage needed for the difficult struggle to climb back up the shaft, they have to presuppose two things: some opening exists at the other end, and when that opening is reached, there will be air to breathe again and light to see. Now this is the case with our own generation. We are confronted with the realization that we are responsible for the march of humankind, an enterprise of staggering proportions, demanding long and painful labor, the end of which seems infinitely far away. It is useless to urge modern men and women to throw their energy behind such an effort if there is the least possible suspicion that the world is either hermetically closed or that the opening at the other end leads to what is inhuman or subhuman. A death which is total, into which our whole earthly achievement disappears forever, or, what comes to the same thing, a survival which is humanly deformed and on a level lower than the noblest aspirations of humanity: either one of these dismal prospects would be enough of itself to inject into the marrow of human action the incurable poison of weariness, discouragement, and fear. The taste for life would be stifled, and the magnificent élan of humanity would eventually come to an end.

Teilhard's overall project, then, was to elaborate a guarantee for the human future that would bring together the two spheres of his experience. This guarantee is in reality three guarantees, elaborated on three different levels of his thought: the scientific,

[3] *Phenomenon of Man*, pp. 227–29; *The Appearance of Man* (N.Y., Harper & Row, 1965), pp. 208–09; *Phenomenon of Man*, p. 231.

the philosophical, and the religious. Once he has these guarantees, he draws from them some very important consequences for human living, especially for Christian spirituality. Let us see now how he elaborates these guarantees and draws these consequences.

On each level of his thought Teilhard asked a question regarding human life and then provided a master idea that is the key to answering that question. The question on the first level of his thought, the scientific level, is this: What has been happening over the centuries to the phenomenon of life? For this biological phenomenon seems to be the antithesis to the physical phenomenon of entropy: entropy is a disintegration of energy in the universe, but life seems to represent energy on the increase. Teilhard's answer to his question about the phenomenon of life focused upon the pattern of the past which has been uncovered by modern science, and his master idea is what he called the law of complexity-consciousness. He started with a fact: in all known life the more developed consciousness will always correspond experimentally with the more complex organic structure. This is seen most clearly, of course, in the human person, where the most complex organic structure, the human brain, corresponds with the most sophisticated consciousness we know: the capacity for reflection. For Teilhard this scientific fact did not simply show that there has been change over millions of years but that there has been what he called "genesis"—from the French word *genèse,* which means "change in successive stages," "change oriented toward some goal," or more simply, "directional change." This scientific fact also accounted for his coining the term *cosmogenesis,* meaning "directional change in the universe." More important, however, he believed that this scientific fact showed that the goal of the evolutionary process is the human species, which at the present time has both the highest organic complexity and the highest degree of consciousness. This human consciousness, this power of reflection, was for Teilhard the key to the evolutionary process. In a world where change is directional, where it is a genesis, it is clear that the movement of evolution has been in the direction of the human person and therefore in the direction of human consciousness, in the direction of spirit, mind, thought, and love.

Teilhard's thought now moves to a second level where the question concerns not what has been happening to the phenomenon of life but what is happening to the phenomenon of *human* life. Having pointed to the pattern of the past revealed by the law of complexity-consciousness, Teilhard asked: Where is this pattern leading, where is the evolutionary process going, and what does it all mean? The master idea on this second level is Teilhard's analysis of the role of love energy in human development. For there is no reason at all to suppose, said Teilhard, that evolutionary development, by which growth in complexity brings growth in consciousness, should cease with the arrival of the human person. For this arrival of human beings in the cosmos is only the crossing of the first threshold of reflection. Whatever significant human change exists must now take place on the other side of this threshold, not in the biosphere but in that sphere which corresponds to the sphere of human mind and human thought, a sphere which Teilhard called a "noosphere." Evolution today, on the other side of this first threshold of reflection, should be called not cosmogenesis but "noogenesis," to indicate that what is going on in the human realm is a development of consciousness and interiority.

But what kind of development? Where is this development going? We see here the importance of Teilhard's master idea on this second level—namely, the role of "love energy." This is the energy that unifies, the same energy that unifies molecules but on the human level operates in the realm of interpersonal consciousness. Teilhard used the phenomenon of electromagnetic waves to illustrate how his master idea on the first level, the law of complexity-consciousness, operates also on the second level and meshes with his new master idea of unifying love energy. Through technology, humans have made an enormously complex use of electromagnetic waves to enable them to share thoughts over vast distances. Someone with an idea in the remote mountains of Tibet can communicate that idea immediately to someone else in New York provided there is the requisite technological complexity in the use of electromagnetic waves. Another image used by Teilhard to illustrate the operation of this unifying human energy is the image of the coil. Evolution, he said, is a coiling; the movement is not in a direct line but in the form of a coil. Unifying energy pushes up the coil by tightening it, thereby moving humanity closer and closer together around the surface of the earth. What is humanity moving toward? To understand Teilhard's answer, we have to think on the scale on which he thought, a scale of millions of years. What he envisioned at the end of the coiling process was a point, which he named Point Omega and which represented for him an experience of community for the human species we can at present only dimly perceive, a kind of common sharing of consciousness, what he called an experience of "more being." Human progress for Teilhard is thus synonymous with growth in consciousness for the human species—that is to say, growth in the capacity for union or in the capacity for love. This growth in the capacity for union and love began when the first threshold of reflection was crossed with the coming of thought and continues now and will continue in the future, again over a period of millions of years, up to the second threshold of reflection which is the Omega Point.

Teilhard was very conscious, of course, that many objections can be made to this vision of the human species moving toward greater and greater unity. The most telling objection is obviously our experience of disunity. All around us we see disruptions, revolutions, transitions of all types. We also have experienced in this century manifestations of unity that have been radically disruptive, such as totalitarianism in all its forms, unities that have been bad for humanity. Finally, we have the existence of evil in the world, the presence of hatred, the very antithesis of love. Teilhard was very sensitive to these types of objections, and he elaborated three answers. First, we cannot deny that there has been a steady growth in the unity of consciousness of the species. All we have to do is to contrast how humans related to each other a thousand years ago, or five hundred or even one hundred years ago, to see how differently we now relate to each other on a global scale. Tensions and turmoil continue in the political order today precisely because of this growing sense of interdependence of everyone upon everyone, as well as upon the growing sense of the dignity of all human beings. We are a very different species today from the times when humans allowed other humans to be enslaved. Second, the totalitarianisms which have pressured the species in so many ways in the twentieth century are examples of good energy gone awry. For these totalitarianisms have used force, not love and freedom, to unify peoples. Third, Teilhard admitted that his understanding of progress as growth in consciousness engendered a serious misunderstanding. For him growth in consciousness meant growth in the *capacity* for love and union among humans, not growth in love itself. Insofar as human progress means the growth in our *capacity* for love, it also means that we are growing in our capacity to refuse love.

Thus, despite his strong emphasis upon the movement toward higher consciousness, Teilhard admitted to a profound ambiguity in all human progress. Greater power to love seems to mean greater temptation to refuse love. Again, human progress for Teilhard takes place not in a straight line but in a coiling movement. The same cycle is repeated, and each time there is a little advance. Each new crisis is the product and the result of a previous achievement. Each new advance thus increases the temptation to stop or to regress. The future success of evolution in Teilhard's analysis thus appears to be jeopardized from the inside by the frailty of human love. This is why he was searching for some guarantee that humanity would ultimately use its freedom well, by finally choosing to love rather than to hate, to unite rather than to disperse. Within evolution, however, he could find no such ultimate guarantee. Hence at the end of this second level, his thought begins to search for some guarantee outside the evolutionary process. This Teilhard found by postulating, not proving, the existence of an Omega that is not a point at the end of the process but a personal and divine source of love. This postulate is something like Pascal's wager. The last part of Teilhard's great work, *The Phenomenon of Man*, develops this idea of a divine, personal Omega. Only such a transcendent absolute, he argued, "loving and lovable at this very moment," can activate the love energy of the world and bring the evolutionary process to a successful completion.

Many commentators have pointed out that what Teilhard was really trying to do, in postulating a divine, personal Omega who alone can activate the love energy of the world, was to develop a proof for the existence of God, an ultimate pledge of hope for the species. In truth, all that Teilhard came up with at the end of *The Phenomenon of Man* was a conjecture, a philosophical hypothesis, a necessary assumption, perhaps, but not a proof. He himself was the first to acknowledge this fact, which is why Teilhard, the scientist, was forced to move to a third level of his thought, the level of Christian theology, in order to find some ultimate source of hope for the human species. He had to appeal to Christian revelation to move from the level of philosophical hypothesis to the level of historical fact. At the very end of *The Phenomenon of Man* Teilhard wrote an epilogue titled "The Christian Phenomenon." Here he identified the Christ of revelation with the Omega of evolution, and by so doing he gave to evolution the well-defined reality of the historical Jesus. The historical Jesus is the ultimate guarantee that the human species will survive, for Christianity tells us there is a very precise goal for this creation which God has brought into existence. This goal is the second coming of Jesus, the Parousia. Christianity also tells us that, in the person of Jesus, God has actually entered into the evolutionary process. The second coming at the end of time has been preceded by the first coming at the time of the Incarnation, which Teilhard referred to as a prodigious biological operation. Since we know from Christian faith that Jesus has entered into the biological process, as this has been discovered by science, and that he will bring this process to a successful completion at the end of time, Teilhard was able to speak of the process, on this third level of his thought, no longer as a biogenesis or a noogenesis but as a "Christogenesis." This third level also has its own master idea: Christ as the physical center for the evolutionary process and the source of love energy in that process.

We should note that Teilhard's Christology was very different from traditional Christology. Unlike theologians before his time, Teilhard used two sources of knowledge. The first was the data of Christian revelation, especially the cosmic texts of Paul in the eighth chapter of Romans, the first chapter of Colossians, and the first chapter of Ephesians. All these texts are concerned with the lordship of Christ over the whole of creation, the spiritual as well as the material. It is clear also in Paul that there is a strong physical relationship between Christ and the cosmos. This physical relationship, of course, is emphasized by Paul's theological reflection upon the mysteries of the Incarnation and the Holy Eucharist. It is not surprising that Teilhard focused his theological attention not only upon the Parousia and the Incarnation but also upon the Eucharist, as the symbol of physical and organic unity between Christ and the cosmos, and on the phenomenon of the church, looked upon as the microcosm of the unity of the whole human species. These data of Christian revelation are then compared, on this third level of Teilhard's thought, with a second source of knowledge, the data that science has discovered about the evolutionary process, data that give an inductive vision of the world and human beings. Teilhard was not trying to cast these two sources of knowledge, these two sets of data, into a single mold but rather to confront them with each other and to compare them. He was always convinced, however, that a pole of truth exists and that these two sources of knowledge somehow meet in common vision in the future, since God is the source of both sets of data.

On this third level of his thought, then, what Teilhard saw was not just intellectual coherence but also some extraordinary consequences for human living. There are, therefore, some very distinctive Teilhardian emphases in Christian spirituality. On this level of Christian faith he wanted to be a guide to survival in the area of knowledge, and he also wanted to be a guide to action.

Teilhard's spirituality may be described as a spirituality of creation and creativity: he summons us to a human task. Why? Because he saw the human task as a collaboration with God's creative action, which in and through the historical evolutionary process builds up the body of Christ. It is fairly easy to see how the third level's master idea of "Christ as a physical center" becomes, when extended into a spirituality, another way of speaking of the more traditional doctrine of the divine omnipresence. Teilhard's great work on the spiritual life is *The Divine Milieu*, completed in 1927. Unlike the English word *milieu*, the French word *milieu* means both "center" and "environment," and so it is clear that Teilhard used the phrase *Divine Milieu* as a proper name for the person of Jesus. Jesus is the divine atmosphere, the divine omnipresence ceaselessly at work in creation. In another essay Teilhard spoke of the world as a crystal lamp, illumined from within by the light of Christ. Hence Teilhard's call to the Christian was to collaborate with God as God is experienced in the secular world. The effort of the Christian must be not so much to *bring* God to the secular world but to *find* God there. This emphasis, of course, is very different from the one we have been used to in much Christian writing. This collaboration is very important to Teilhard's spirituality, because in his system of thought the end of the evolutionary process will not come until certain necessary preliminary stages are accomplished in and through this collaboration between God and human beings. The final building up of the body of Christ, in preparation for the second coming at the Parousia, is in fact conditioned by the very nature of the creative process, which is a collaboration among free human beings. This collaboration, Teilhard said, is a necessary, though insufficient, condition for the coming of the Parousia.

Teilhard used a vivid image to illustrate this human collaboration with the creative action of God leading to the Parousia, that of the master artist and the apprentice. In the shop of the master artist the apprentice does all the preliminary work. In the case of a painting, the apprentice sketches the outlines of all figures in the painting, chooses perspectives as well as colors, and begins to sketch in the details of the painting. As time proceeds, the master artist inspects the painting, makes adjustments and suggestions, and highlights the consequences of emphasizing certain details in the painting. Finally, the apprentice can progress no further with the preliminary sketch and must call in the master artist to complete it. The work of the apprentice is thus the necessary condition for the completion of the painting, since the preliminary sketch and ideas constitute the contours and the content of the painting. But this work is also insufficient, since only the master artist has the requisite skill and knowledge to bring the painting to its successful conclusion.

This creative spirituality of Teilhard, this collaborative effort between the human and the divine, can be a very costly form of Christian discipleship. In *The Phenomenon of Man* Teilhard noted that "the human epic represents nothing so much as a way of the cross."[4] In *The Divine Milieu* Teilhard developed his great theme of the passivities of life, those of growth and those of

---

[4] *Phenomenon of Man,* p. 313.

diminishment; those events in our lives over which we have no control, and which inevitably bring with them fear, anxiety, and pain. The ultimate passivity, of course, is death. This phenomenon of death has an enormous importance in Teilhard's spirituality. Death is not a friend, but neither is it an enemy. The reason is that death is central to the whole creative process, not just a single part of the redemptive process. Here again there is that characteristic change of emphasis: death can be life-giving, whether it is one of our intermediate deaths or our final death, and detachment is essential to creative growth. Consider the following quotations from *The Divine Milieu:*

> The great victory of the Creator and Redeemer, in the Christian vision, is to have transformed what is itself a universal power of diminishment and extinction into an essentially lifegiving factor. God must in some way or other make room for himself, hollowing us out and emptying us, if he is finally to penetrate into us. And in order to assimilate us into him, he must break the molecules of our being so as to recast and remodel us. The function of death is to bring about this opening up of our innermost selves which God desires. It will force us to undergo the disunion he is waiting for. It will put us into the state organically needed if the divine fire is to descend upon us. And in that way its fatal power to decompose and dissolve will be harnessed to the most sublime operations of life. . . . Jesus on the Cross is both symbol and reality of the immense labor of the centuries, which little by little raises up created spirit to restore it to the depths of the divine *milieu.* He represents and, in a true sense, he is creation, as it re-ascends the slopes of being, supported by the hand of God, sometimes clinging to things for support, sometimes tearing itself from them in order to transcend them, and always compensating by physical suffering for setbacks caused by its moral failures. . . . The Cross is not something inhuman but superhuman. It has been placed on the crest of the road that leads to the highest peaks of creation. The Christian's task is not to swoon in its shadow but to climb in its light.[5]

This emphasis in Teilhard's spirituality upon creation and creativity has been responsible for what is perhaps the most serious objection to his Christian writings—namely, that he has a sense neither of sin nor of the mystery of evil. In *The Divine Milieu,* for example, there is no development of any purgative

[5] *Divine Milieu,* pp. 68–69, 87–88.

way. Teilhard deliberately avoided talking of sin and the reformation of one's life, because he was concerned in his total system of thought with generating optimism and hope. His experience, although probably not ours to the same extent, was of a theological tradition that drew very pessimistic conclusions from the human experience of sin, especially original sin. In one of his theological essays Teilhard said that this theological tradition "cuts the wings of our hope for humanity."[6] He blamed an overemphasis on sin for the unconcern on the part of many Christians to build the earth and to contribute to the human enterprise. Teilhard would not have denied, of course, that there is risk in choosing optimism regarding life rather than pessimism. But he would have said that there is just as much risk in choosing pessimism. A good example of such pessimism is *The Imitation of Christ,* a classic of Christian spirituality, but a very negative one, emphasizing mistrust of the world, advising separation as much as possible from its activities, and offering no invitation at all to life and creativity. Just because Teilhard did not talk about sin explicitly does not mean it is not there; it is just not emphasized. We have already noted his emphasis upon the frailty of human love, the refusal of community with others and with Omega, the failure of the whole evolutionary process. This can only be attributed to a failure of love or the presence of sin. Also, Teilhard's emphasis on human progress was an emphasis upon growth in the *capacity* to love. Human progress is therefore not the same as moral progress. Human progress in the Teilhardian sense necessarily involves the possibility of moral regress in individual lives. Indeed, no more terrifying pages on hell have ever been written by any master of the spiritual life than those found in *The Divine Milieu.*

In summary we can say that Teilhard de Chardin's overarching objective was to find some unity and coherence between the two spheres of sacred and secular, the one resting upon faith in the divine, the other upon faith in the human. If he could make others see what he saw, Teilhard felt, then he could assuage modern anxiety by offering persons hope for the final success of human evolution, for the ultimate survival of all that earth has

[6] *Christianity and Evolution,* p. 79.

developed in complexity and consciousness, all that is *best* in the world. This hope he rooted in the person of Jesus in whom the love of God Omega is revealed. Only what God has done in Christ can bring assurance that human creativity is indeed a participation in divine creativity and that the outcome of the whole enterprise will be on the side of life, not on the side of death.

One final question: Can Teilhard's thought be true? His writings have been criticized as one-sided and unbalanced; he has been accused of leaving out or de-emphasizing whatever did not fit into an optimistic outlook on world developments, human history, theology, and spirituality. How then can such thought be true? The most obvious answer to this objection is that visionaries are not "balanced" people. They are people with a message. Being "balanced" is an extremely difficult thing for any visionary intent upon delivering a message. What kind of truth does Teilhard's evolutionary system have, then? Biological truth? Philosophical truth? Theological truth? Is Teilhard's message false because it is unbalanced? What are his criteria for truth? He himself told us that he had two criteria for truth. The first was coherence. Does his message make sense out of the world around us? Does it unify the experiences we have in life? "If a system of thought," said Teilhard, "enables us to grasp a little more of the world and helps us to harmonize its elements, we can be sure we are closer to the truth. Truth is nothing but the total coherence of the universe in regard to each of its elements."[7] Teilhard's second criterion for truth was fruitfulness—personal, social, and cultural. Does his message lead to a creative human life? Teilhard would say that we must first do what he suggests we do, and then we shall discover whether or not what he says is true.

As a final judgment, then, on the evolutionary system of Pierre Teilhard de Chardin, I think we can say that whether one is favorable or hostile to his efforts to elaborate a guarantee for success of the evolutionary process will depend in large measure upon one's theological, spiritual, and intellectual temperament. Such temperament will determine whether one can resonate with the style of Christian living that Teilhard urges upon us, with the

[7] *Human Energy* (N. Y., Harcourt Brace Jovanovich, 1962), pp. 54–55.

fundamental harmony of the universe that he tries to transcribe for us. He once wrote to a close friend that people made a big mistake in comparing his writings to those of Darwin. What they should do, he said, is to compare his writings with the music of Richard Wagner. Teilhard wanted to be not only the apologist for hope and survival but also their musician. Like any great musician Teilhard wanted to create a mood and an attitude toward life which would unify all things secular and sacred in a single movement toward the future. Let us end with his own words:

All over the earth at this moment, at the heart of the new spiritual atmosphere created by the appearance of the idea of evolution, there flow the currents of love of God and faith in the world, the one current highly sensitive to the other. In me, by pure chance, the ratio of each has been favorable and their fusion has taken place spontaneously, too weak yet to be propagated with explosive force, but still sufficient to make it clear that fusion itself is possible and that some day or other the chain reaction will come.[8]

[8] *The Heart of the Matter* (N.Y., Harcourt Brace Jovanovich, 1978), p. 102.

Bibliography

Pierre Teilhard de Chardin, *The Phenomenon of Man,* N. Y., Harper & Row, 1959.

Christopher F. Mooney, *Teilhard de Chardin and the Mystery of Christ,* N. Y., Harper & Row, 1966.

KARL RAHNER

Anne E. Carr

Karl Rahner was born on March 5, 1904, in Freiburg in southern Germany. He entered the Society of Jesus in 1922, shortly after his older brother Hugo (a noted patristics scholar), and began his philosophical and theological studies in Jesuit schools at Feldkirch, Austria; Pullach, near Munich; and Valkenburg in Holland. In preparation for teaching philosophy, he attended the University of Freiburg where, in addition to traditional Thomist studies in the Catholic faculty, he participated in Martin Heidegger's seminars. There he wrote his first philosophical-theological work, *Spirit in the World,* a study of Aquinas' metaphysics of knowledge formulated in the context of German philosophical currents from Kant to Heidegger. This study was rejected as a philosophical thesis by his Thomist adviser, and Rahner went on to complete a degree in theology at the University of Innsbruck, where he began teaching in the Catholic faculty in 1937. He taught there until the faculty was closed by the Nazis in 1939. During World War II he did pastoral work in Vienna, and after the war he resumed teaching at Pullach for several years. In 1948 he returned to Innsbruck where his theological lectures and writings drew increasing attention in the following decade. He was influential in the preparatory work for the Second Vatican Council and was chosen as a *peritus* for the council by Cardinal Franz König of Vienna. In 1964 Rahner succeeded Romano Guardini in the chair of Christian Worldview and Philosophy of Religion at the University of Munich. He moved to the University of Munster in 1967, where he was professor of dogmatic theology until he retired in 1971 and returned to Munich. In 1981 he went back to Innsbruck. Rahner continued to lecture and to write in his retirement, bringing the number of his publications, in many languages, to more than four thousand. He died in Innsbruck on March 30, 1984, at the age of eighty, completing a life which he once described in an interview as "monotonous" in its regularity but which, in its theological creativity, was extraordinary.

Rahner wrote many important books, but his characteristic form is found in his numerous occasional essays, centered upon particular questions in the practical and intellectual faith life of Christians and of the church. His essays have been collected over the years in the series *Theological Investigations,* which in English includes twenty volumes (the German *Schriften zur Theologie* numbers sixteen). Although this occasional form indicates that his theological work did not develop according to a tightly conceived methodological plan, Rahner is a profoundly systematic thinker, casting each question within the framework of an overarching theological vision. This vision captured the minds and hearts of theologians and lay people alike, making Rahner something of a twentieth-century Aquinas in the universities, seminaries, and parish meeting rooms of the Catholic world as well as a spokesman for contemporary Catholic thought in the ecumenical community. This theological vision is adumbrated in his early philosophical-theological work *Hearers of the Word* (1941) and synthesized in his recent *Foundations of Christian Faith: An Introduction to the Idea of Christianity* (1976). It is apparent in his powerful spiritual writings, such as the early *Encounters with Silence* (1938) or *Spiritual Exercises* (1965), and readily accessible in brief form in his many encyclopedia articles. This view, despite Rahner's disclaimers of any special concern with questions of method, has issued in his distinctive approach to theology.[1]

What is Rahner's theological vision? Perhaps it can best be described as an apprehension of the whole that maintains the distinction of its parts, unity in diversity: the sacred and the secular, essence and existence, the divine and the human, theology and philosophy, grace and nature, or in Rahner's characteristic language, transcendence and history. He advocates an approach to theology that takes account of both the a priori framework of interpretation, the "transcendental," by which he means the conditions of possibility for Christian revelation and dogma, and the a posteriori, the "categorical,"

[1] "Reflections on Methodology in Theology," in *Theological Investigations,* XI (N.Y., Seabury, 1974), pp. 68-114, hereafter cited as TI.

the historical data. The unifying core of Christianity, for Rahner, is the message and the reality of the personal self-communication of God in the Incarnation and in grace, what the tradition calls "uncreated grace." All his theology can be understood as an explication of this strictly mysterious unity in which God is personally related to humankind and to the world, beyond the demands of nature, in such fashion that the world and humankind are both united to God in intimate relationship and set free in their own autonomy and distinction precisely by this relationship. This religious vision of dynamic unity-in-difference sets the pattern for Rahner's approach to theological questions and for the systematic coherence of his thought. Its center is found in ordinary human existence or experience, which may be reflected upon from both philosophical and theological, both transcendental and historical, points of view. Each perspective ineluctably leads to the other because they are united in the oneness of the person—what Rahner describes as the unity of existence and reflection, or as being and knowing.

There are several starting points from which Rahner develops his fundamental insight about God's presence and self-communication to human persons and to the world of their experience. One starting point may be found in the *philosophical foundation* which he proposes in his early work for the possibility of theology after Kant's critique of metaphysical knowledge of knowledge of God. Rahner begins with the (Heideggerian) phenomenon of human questioning. That persons ask the metaphysical question of being as such indicates both knowing and unknowing. There cannot be inquiry about that which is totally unknown; yet inquiry asks after that which is not known. Following both Aquinas and Kant, Rahner insists that all human knowledge is grounded in the sensible, finite world of experience. His reflection on the actual "performance" of the human questioner in the world demonstrates the experience of transcendence precisely in the knowledge and freedom of ordinary human life. This experience of transcendence or subjectivity is a prereflective or original knowledge which human persons are, rather than have, in the very process of existence and experience.

Rahner's reflection on ordinary human knowledge of the world shows a concomitant experience of the self in which human self-awareness is also made reflexive. Thus he describes human persons as subjects or as spirit, beings who are always in the world but at the same time transcendent of the world of experience in knowledge. Similarly, analysis of the human experience of freedom, responsibility, and love shows that freedom is not merely the ability to choose this or that in the world of experience but is the spiritual or subjective freedom to create an identity to order one's loves and so to choose the self one becomes in a world-transcendent or spiritual fashion. This unthematic experience of transcendence is not a special or privileged moment but an element of all human experience in the world. This is Rahner's approach to the fundamental human question, the metaphysical question, which human beings not only ask but *are* in their ordinary everyday experience as "spirit in the world."

What is the reach of this human experience of transcendence in subjectivity, knowledge, freedom, and love? In his first major philosophical work, *Spirit in the World* (1939), Rahner joins the "turn to the subject" of modern philosophy with his own Thomistic tradition, mediated especially by the work of the Louvain Jesuit philosopher Joseph Maréchal. He argues that the scope of human transcendence in ordinary knowledge is unlimited, unbounded, infinite. He uses the metaphor of "horizon" to show that in human self-performance, or questioning and knowing, being as such is already revealed in a dim, unreflexive knowledge *(Vorgriff)* of God. At the same time, God is never the direct object of knowledge but remains concealed and unknown, the mysterious, infinite horizon which is only glimpsed in the knowledge of the concrete things and persons of experience. In *Hearers of the Word* (1941), his other major philosophical work, Rahner characterizes the human person not only as spirit-in-world and thus open to a possible revelation of God but also as fundamentally free and historical. His analysis shows that insofar as human persons are free, they transcend the finite world of experience in freedom and love within the infinite horizon of freedom. The specific form of finite freedom in the world of space and time is historicity. Human transcendence of the world is realized only in historical experience; one is spirit only in the earthly context of historical temporality. Consequently, human persons can and must look for a possible revelation on the basis of transcendence as historicity. The *Vorgriff* is only "known" as the horizon of concrete, temporal experience. If God is to be further revealed, to communicate with persons who are transcendent precisely in their knowledge, freedom, and historicity, then it must be through a word, a human symbol, a spatiotemporal event, commensurate with the specifically human structures of knowledge and freedom in history. If God were not to speak at all, the message of human history would be God's silence, the silence of the infinite horizon of human spirit. This, in brief summary, is Rahner's philosophical foundation for a contemporary theology.

Yet, even in these early "philosophical" works, Rahner is not merely a philosopher but a philosopher-theologian whose philosophy always serves an intrinsically theological purpose, whose philosophy is done within a theological framework. His early works have as their purpose an analysis of the transcendental conditions for the possibility of a historical revelation. Thus Rahner is frequently identified as a transcendental Thomist, one who unites the transcendental questioning of Kant with the theology of Aquinas or, using "transcendental" in a slightly different way, who shows the intrinsic character of human transcendence in and of the world toward the infinite horizon who is God. Rahner's approach to theology is often called a transcendental method, one which asks the question of the conditions for the possibility of any aspect of Christian faith. Indeed, this characterization is accurate, and Rahner himself has written of the importance and necessity of transcendental theology today, suggesting an intrinsic analogy between the structures of Christianity as understood in the tradition and the structures of human subjectivity as they have been uncovered in recent transcendental and existential thought. He has devoted a major part of his theological work to a transcendental theology in his "turn to the subject," his focus on the person who receives Christian revelation. He characteristically asks, with regard to any "object" of Christian belief, what are the subjective conditions of possibility in the human recipient of revelation implied by the particular data of revelation he questions. His transcendental method is, in fact, a theological anthropology, centered on the human subject of revelation.

At the same time, it is important to note that transcendence, for Rahner, is always transcendence in history, or history as transcendent. This dual structure implies a dual method: an examination of *both* the essential human structures implied in Christian revelation *and* examination of the historical, concrete data of Christian revelation itself. Essence *and* existence, transcendence *and* history are simultaneous, concomitant realities; one is not had without the other. Just as "knowledge" of the infinite horizon of being is co-known only in human judgment of the being of the concrete object of knowledge, the transcendental structures of the human subject of revelation are co-known only in knowledge of the concrete data of the history of revelation. Rahner's program, from the very beginning, calls for a twofold method of theological reflection, a theological anthropology which, at every stage, requires careful analysis of the historical data of Christian faith, what has happened and is happening in historical existence, and inquiry about the human subject, the essential structures of human subjectivity that are implied in this particular history. His own bibliography includes a number of historical studies—a lengthy work on the history of penance, for example.

In addition to the more philosophical approach, a second starting point from which Rahner develops his fundamental insight about the presence and self-communication of God is the *theological foundation* he proposes in his early work on grace and Christology. In his writings on nature and grace, for example, Rahner develops his doctrine of the "supernatural existential"—that is, humankind's existential ordination toward grace.[2] In contrast to the previous "extrinsicist" Catholic theory of nature and grace as disparate realities, he describes grace not as a static thing but as the dynamic and personal self-communication of God for which human beings are created, another dimension

[2] "The Scholastic Concept of Uncreated Grace" and "The Relationship between Nature and Grace," in TI, I (Baltimore, Helicon, 1961), pp. 319-46, 297-318; "Nature and Grace," in TI, IV (Baltimore, Helicon, 1966), pp. 165-88; "Grace," in *Sacramentum Mundi* 2, ed. Karl Rahner et al. (N. Y., Herder & Herder, 1968), pp. 415–27.

of God's self-gift in the Incarnation. Such self-communication, he argues, presupposes an open readiness ("obediential potency") for this unexacted gift. There is really no pure nature—only graced nature or nature which is already and always supernaturally oriented toward grace. Such a supernatural existential pervades conscious human existence, knowledge, and experience, even if only in an implicit and unthematic way. Grace, the self-communication of God, is thus a conscious element of human experience. The idea of a pure nature is an analytic or "remainder concept," what would have been had God not intended Christ and grace as the ultimate purpose of the personal world. Just as grace already envelops the nature that it both presupposes and alters, so theology supersedes philosophy even while presupposing it in its own autonomy.[3] For grace, or the supernatural existential, involves a concomitant new human knowledge, not as a new object of knowledge but as an expansion of the a priori horizon of which persons are already conscious in being conscious of themselves. Hence, every philosophy may contain elements that are anonymously theological. From the perspective of theology, pure philosophy is also a remainder concept, what would have been had revelation not occurred.

A similar pattern of unity-in-difference is apparent in Rahner's early Christological reflections where his work is essentially a retrieval of past formulations of dogma, particularly the dogma of Chalcedon, through questions suggested by contemporary exegesis, philosophy, history, and science. He describes his effort as an "anxious seeking for the question" which inspired the dogmatic formula, a simultaneous preserving and overcoming of the past. While he does not develop a systematic synthesis, certain fundamental themes structure his distinctive Christological vision.[4]

A major theme is the unity and diversity of the doctrines of creation and Christ which Rahner derives from a philosophical rethinking of the formula of the two natures. He describes the union between the divine and human natures in Christ (their

---

[3] "Philosophy and Theology," in TI, VI (Baltimore, Helicon, 1969), pp. 71–81; "Philosophy and Theology," in *Sacramentum Mundi* 5, pp. 20–24.

[4] "Current Problems in Christology," in TI, I, pp. 149–54; "Theology of the Incarnation," in TI, IV, pp. 105–20.

"unconfused" distinction and the "inseparable" unity in the language of Chalcedon) as a dialectical or "unifying" unity. This dynamic unity-in-diversity is the basis for the unity and diversity which Rahner maintains between philosophy and theology, the orders of creation and redemption, secular and salvation history, nature and grace, symbol and reality. This Christological view is the center from which Rahner develops a method that consists in a dual movement from ontology or anthropology to the doctrine of Christ, then from Christology to ontological or anthropological presuppositions. It is apparent, for example, in his discussion of the relationship between the theory of human evolution and the meaning of the Incarnation. Creation can be understood as an evolutionary movement intended by God to reach its finality in Christ. The presupposition or preparation required for God's self-communication is given historically in the Incarnation and grace. Because the self-communication of God is always first in the divine intention, creation and incarnation are not "two disparate, adjacent acts of God . . . but are two moments or phases" in the single process of God's self-gift to humankind. Thus hominization, the emergence of spirit from matter, occurs under the action of God as the necessary preparation for the Incarnation. The human person is what comes to be when God's self-gift occurs *ad extra*.[5]

Rahner's Christology culminates in a theology of symbol in which Christ is understood both as the self-expression or *Realsymbol* of God and as the unique expression of the meaning of the human person. His discussion of symbol represents a powerful example of his method, which involves both retrieval of past tradition and new formulation, and shows how content and method are intimately related in his thought.[6] Substantively, the single mystery of divine self-communication is given in the doctrine of Christ. That doctrine points backward to the dialectical ontology of the doctrine of God (the immanent

[5] "Christology within an Evolutionary View of the World," in TI, V (Baltimore, Helicon, 1966), pp. 157–92; "History of the World and Salvation History," *ibid.*, pp. 97–114; "The Order of Redemption within the Order of Creation," in *The Christian Commitment* (N. Y., Sheed & Ward, 1966), pp. 38–74.

[6] "The Theology of the Symbol," in TI, IV, pp. 221–52.

Trinity) and forward to the doctrine of the human person (creation, grace, the beatific vision—the economic Trinity) as a single unity in its diverse moments. It indicates a theological ontology of symbolic reality within the very being of God, an ontology already grasped by the early Logos tradition. It indicates a theological anthropology in which the human person is the extension and continuation of this primordial ontology of symbol: the person is understood, when reflected upon in the light of the mystery of Christ, as the symbol that emerges when God is expressed in the world. The human person, as material spirit, is thus understood not only as the evolutionary achievement of consciousness, and so of history and freedom in matter, but also and more radically as the one prepared to be the embodiment of God in the world of matter and history, the possibility of incarnation.

Rahner's Christology shows methodological continuity with his early philosophical studies of human knowledge, freedom, and historicity. He writes, "Christology is at once the beginning and end of anthropology, and . . . such an anthropology is really theology."[7] The more one thinks of Christ's humanity as the presence and *ek*-sistence of God into the world, Rahner says, the more Christ is understood as the central mystery and expression of human existence. Christology cannot form the absolute point of departure for ontology and anthropology, since statements about Christ are originally made with the help of a general doctrine of creation and the ontology and anthropology implicit in it. But Christology can be used retrospectively in assertions about the human person and the human world: it indicates dimensions of ontology and anthropology that might have remained hidden had not the Incarnation revealed them as the conditions for its possibility. The mystery of the human person cannot be described adequately without reference to the mystery of Christ; because humankind is the "articulate mystery of God," all theology is anthropology. Thus the radical Christocentrism of Rahner's theological enterprise becomes apparent. In contrast with Barth, for example, this Christocentrism must be held in tension with an equally firm philosophical point of departure in which the very nature of human subjectivity is

[7] "Current Problems in Christology," p. 185.

understood to entail the implicit knowledge of God as the horizon and goal of human transcendence. Philosophical theology is therefore transcendental anthropology. Natural theology, which explores the unlimited horizon of the human spirit that alone makes the idea of God possible, is an inner moment in revelation theology. Thus Rahner maintains that anthropocentrism and theocentrism are not opposing positions but the same reality understood from two perspectives which mutually illuminate each other.[8]

Rahner elaborates this dual approach in his discussion of revelation. He holds that the universal salvific will of God (I Tim. 2:5), the order of grace or salvation, constitutes the one goal of human history; salvation history coincides with, although it is not identical with, world history. Following his fundamental principle of the unity of being and knowledge in the one human person, Rahner argues that the new order of grace implies an elevation of the human spirit to a new "formal object" of knowledge, a new (although not in a temporal sense), perhaps unthematized, horizon of knowledge correlative to the new being of grace. Rahner calls this a priori, unthematic knowledge which is constituted by God's personal self-communication a "transcendental revelation" between God and persons. It is the supernatural existential considered from the point of view of the knowledge integral to it.

> The history of revelation and what is usually called revelation as such is the historical self-unfolding in predicamental terms, or, even more simply and correctly, the history of that transcendental relation between God and man which is constituted by God's communication of a supernatural kind, made to every mind by grace, but inescapably and always, and which in itself can rightly be termed revelation.[9]

Hence, revelation has two sides—the transcendental reality, always and everywhere given, and the objective, official Christian revelation, its full and constitutive manifestation, as

---

[8] "Current Problems in Christology," p. 185.
[9] Karl Rahner and Joseph Ratzinger, *Revelation and Tradition* (N.Y., Herder & Herder, 1966), p. 13.

explicitly accepted or rejected. The transcendental reality in its immediacy is made reflexively conscious only through its mediation in history, in socially structured language, thought, and action. Transcendental revelation means not a new content apprehended by the human mind but a change in the horizonal constitution of the mind in its new supernatural ordination, whether or not grace is explicitly accepted. It means that, whether or not one objectively knows it, one lives under a new but universally present horizon, that of grace. Although mediated through the Christ-event, that grace is prior to it because of God's original Christological, salvific intention.[10]

Rahner's theory of the supernatural existential and its concomitant transcendental revelation enables him to argue that conscious life and action in grace are not only characteristic of the justified. Grace is universal, extended prior to justification and outside the historical church; God's self-gift is neither intermittent nor rare.

> Theology has been too long and too often bedevilled by the unavowed supposition that grace would be no longer grace if it were too generously distributed by the love of God! Our whole spiritual life is lived in the realm of the salvific will of God, of his prevenient grace, of his call as it becomes efficacious: all of which is an element within the region of our consciousness, though one which remains anonymous as long as it is not interpreted from without by the message of faith. Even when he does not "know" it and does not believe it, . . . man always lives consciously in the presence of the God of eternal life.[11]

This is not to say that every individual is necessarily justified, but insofar as one has the capacity for moral action, for example, one is open to the God who is offered, whether this offer is accepted or refused in concrete human decision. In each moral choice, one takes a positive or negative stance not only toward a particular object or person but also toward the totality of one's own existence and ultimately toward God. Rahner concludes that, since human existence is saturated by grace, every authentic decision and action is salvific (or sinful) in relation to that order of grace. Even when it is unreflected or "anonymous," this supernatural ordination toward grace manifests itself in the

[10] *Ibid.*, p. 22; "Philosophy and Theology," in TI, VI, p. 78.
[11] "Nature and Grace," in TI, IV, pp. 180–81.

dynamics of individual and social life in the history of religions, for the religious aspirations of humankind necessarily symbolize nature as enveloped by grace. Hence the preaching of the church does not bring totally unheard of news; rather, it awakens and makes explicit what the human person really is, an anonymous Christian or one who is called to be a Christian and who, even as a sinner, is enfolded in an inescapable sphere of grace.[12]

Rahner insists theology must recognize that its conceptual content symbolizes a transcendental event, an experience of mystery that it can never totally grasp. Transcendental experience can be consciously operative even where it is not explicitly recognized. Anonymous theism exists wherever one is open to the infinite mystery which is the ground of human existence. Because human nature is touched and changed by God's self-gift in Christ, wherever in the depths of experience one accepts one's own ultimate mystery there is anonymous Christianity, even if one denies its conceptual expression in official Christianity. Does such a theology imply that the church, its sacraments, and missionary activity are unnecessary? No, the church remains the visible sacrament of salvation, "the historical manifestation" of the grace of God's self-communication "as absolutely present, close and forgiving, . . . the grace which is at work everywhere. . . ." This grace has a dynamic tendency toward tangible expression in the life of the church, but it does not always find that expression. It is clear that the church today is a "little flock" in a diaspora situation in which official Christianity is less and less an effective historical power. Theology can reconcile the two principles of the universal salvific will of God and the necessity of Christian faith only if it recognizes that wherever the grace of Christ, an ecclesial grace, is at work, individuals are anonymously but actually related to the Christian church.[13]

This position seems to minimize the possibility and meaning of sin. But Rahner holds that sin is included in this view of the Incarnation as the summit of God's creative intention; the

---

[12] Ibid., "Christianity and the Non-Christian Religions," in TI, V, pp. 115–34.
[13] "Anonymous Christians," in TI, VI, pp. 390–98; "The Problem of the 'Anonymous Christian,' " in TI, XIV (N. Y., Seabury, 1976), pp. 280–94.

redemptive aspect of the Incarnation and grace is derived from this systematic starting point. The cosmos evolves toward spirit, toward freedom and grace. Wherever there is freedom in relation to the world and in transcendence toward God, "there can also be guilt and freedom which closes itself against God." It is on the basis of a view of history which has the self-communication of God as its goal that the redeeming power over sin is found in the grace of the Incarnation: "sin is from the outset embraced by the will to forgive" because the history of the world is the very history of God. Freedom, guilt, and sin are integral to this view and must not be misunderstood as merely "unavoidable difficulty which is all part of the development."[14] Far from reducing sin to insignificance, Rahner says that human persons were never so convinced of their own evil, conscious of their fallibility, as today. Contemporary experience is one of terrible doubt and insecurity; human goodness is utterly open to question.

Rahner discusses this experience under the rubric *simul justus et peccator*. Freed from the polemics of the sixteenth century, he writes, Catholic theology may understand the Reformation recognition of the self as sinner even when one knows divine forgiveness. This paradox can be integrated with the Roman position on the reality of the "new creation" that grace effects, for it remains true that there is no certitude of salvation in this life. Even in grace, one continues to sin in such a way that one's orientation ("fundamental option") toward God is threatened. One never completely grasps the depths of one's own being during this pilgrim existence and must constantly live in hope. The unity of nature and grace destroys neither the ambiguity of human freedom nor the ambiguity of human history.[15] The reality of sin and evil remains, even in a Christocentrically evolving world.

At the same time, Rahner asserts that within the ambiguities of freedom and history, authentic Christianity, whether explicit or anonymous, will manifest itself in human experience. Christians will see its expression not only in the life of the church but also in the lives of those who will never explicitly accept Christian faith.

[14] "Christology within Evolutionary View," pp. 185–86.
[15] "Justified and Sinner at the Same Time," in TI, VI, pp. 218–30.

Hence theology must look to the world in its effort to discern the hidden relationships of grace to the world, the "connections by correspondence" between Christianity and human experience. Thus, systematic or dogmatic theology is apologetic or kerygmatic; it presupposes a common ground between the kerygma and the human subject. It attempts so to formulate theological statements that they have intrinsic connection with human experience. Such connections are present because personal, transcendent "nature" is an inner moment of the dynamism of grace. If grace is the transformation of experience, then its presence and significance can be discovered in human experience itself. This is not to deduce theology from experience, Rahner believes, but to discover inherent relationships between the two. Theology would then stress what Rahner calls the fundamental and formal structures of the human spirit in its worldly context which are the implicit conditions for the possibility of every dimension of Christian revelation.[16]

Such theology is needed in the present, Rahner contends, for a number of philosophical and theological reasons. Chief among these is the structure of Christian revelation itself, which is essentially a revelation for human persons, for salvation. Because God's self-gift is given to persons both transcendentally in personal self-communication and categorically in Jesus Christ and an explicit word revelation, this self-gift is necessarily a conscious experience, historical and concrete. The experience may be an unthematized one, but its full realization demands conceptual articulation.[17]

In Rahner's early theology, prior to the Second Vatican Council, his stress on human historical experience is concerned chiefly with the subjective dimensions of the meaning of Christian faith and with the human person conceived primarily as knower. The emphasis is on the clarification of the central dogmas of Christianity within the "hierarchy of truths" of faith and their implications for human understanding. He is convinced that the "turn to the subject" which is characteristic of modern and contemporary philosophy must be integrated within Catholic theology. His works on the supernatural existential, on

[16] "Theology and Anthropology," pp. 41–42.
[17] Ibid., p. 35.

the experience of grace, and on Christology and evolution are examples of this attempt to work out the relationship between transcendence and historicity in terms of human knowledge, particularly as the thematization of the implicit dimensions of prereflective knowledge.

Rahner argues, for example, that because the reality of grace (and its concomitant revelation) penetrates the totality of conscious human life, this experience can be thematized in various ways. He suggests that one experiences grace as the very mystery of God's presence in conscientious decisions, in generous love for another, in silent sacrifice, and in facing death in faith.[18] Or, he reasons, if contemporary exegesis points to Jesus' developing consciousness of his identity and mission, such an evolutionary understanding is analogous to the experience of all persons as they come to know themselves in relation to the dimly known source and horizon of their own existence. In Jesus' case, this developing awareness need not contradict his unobjectified awareness of his identity and task (his divinity and salvific role).[19] Or when the scientific theory of evolution is understood in relation to the Christian doctrines of creation and Christ, it indicates the way in which God's creative action occurs dynamically through natural and historical causes and reaches its goal in Christ. Hence, Rahner's effort is to bring the ancient dogmas into fruitful contact with the questions posed by contemporary philosophy, science, exegesis, and history in order to demonstrate new implications for the human subject.

Since Vatican II, however, this emphasis has altered somewhat. Rahner's attention now focuses more on the changing secular context of Christian faith. The radical cultural and spiritual transformations of recent times have created a new situation for theology. What is the meaning of human existence in a pluralistic, secularized, technological culture, and how does this new situation relate to traditional Christianity? Signs of this broadened focus in Rahner's thought are found in his theological dialogues with various Marxist themes—hope, the future,

[18] "Reflections on the Experience of Grace," in TI, III (Baltimore, Helicon, 1967), pp. 86–90.
[19] "Dogmatic Reflections on the Knowledge and Self-Consciousness of Christ," in TI, V, pp. 193–215.

ideology, political theology. He has suggested that theology may find its most significant dialogical partner not in philosophy but in the natural and social sciences which shape human self-understanding in the present.[20] Further, the difficulties of the present theological context have led him to consider the kinds of religious experience possible in a culture in which the silence and the distance of God seem more apparent than ever before. Rahner calls for a new "mystagogy" in which the sources of religious experience within a secular culture might be explored.[21]

Thus, he suggests, the power of human freedom as it is experienced today, in which humankind participates in planning the human future to the point of "self-creation," reveals as well the dimension of the unknown and uncontrollable. In the unprecedented human ability to master and manipulate, persons also experience themselves, paradoxically, as "disposed into freedom" and so can come to the mystery of their own being—who is God—through the experience of human freedom in its ultimate limitations as well as its apparently infinite capacities. In the new responsibility that persons experience in relation to freedom, Rahner points to the anonymous or reticent experience of God: God is described as the source of the highest human qualities of honesty, objectivity, humility, and integrity. Christian mystagogy would thus concentrate on finding new openings into the incomprehensible mystery of human existence, an access which, under different sociological conditions in the past, could be taken for granted. In the experience of the mystery of the self, the mystery and the meaning of God can be experienced and newly understood.[22]

Rahner's broadened focus on the cultural context of the human subject of faith includes new understanding of the church's teaching function. He writes that the church finds itself in a new position, especially in relation to theology, as listener and discerner and should seldom exercise its power of final

[20] "Ideology and Christianity" and "Marxist Utopia and the Christian Future of Man," in TI, VI, pp. 43–58, 59–68; "Christianity and the 'New Man,' " in TI, V, pp. 135 53; "Philosophy and Philosophizing in Theology," in TI, IX, pp. 46–63.
[21] "Atheism and Implicit Christianity," in TI, IX, pp. 145–64.
[22] "The Experiment with Man," *ibid.*, pp. 205–24.

judgment. Pluralism within theology, philosophy, and the other disciplines indicates the impossibility of a common theology and of new dogmatic formulations. Over and over again, Rahner points to the historical conditioning that affects any theological statement, hence any dogmatic statement, and to the constant possibility of error in theology. Moreover, in the present pluralism, no one person can adequately understand the various theological languages and specializations and their inherent problematics in such a way as to mediate them in a common synthetic view or to pronounce judgment on their truth or adequacy. Nevertheless, Rahner insists on the reality and universality of transcendental grace and revelation: the fundamental mystery of human existence is the Christian mystery, and it is anonymously or explicitly present wherever human life is lived authentically, no matter what words are used to define and describe it.[23]

The church exists to serve and to proclaim precisely this mystery of the self-communication of God to the human world in the humanity of Jesus of Nazareth. Rahner's early reflections on ecclesiology focus on the church as the fundamental sacrament, the visible sign of God's offer and gift of grace in Christ. Just as Jesus Christ is the *Realsymbol* of God's self-communication, so the church, in which Christ and the Spirit continue to dwell on earth, is the fundamental symbol or sacrament of Christ's grace. As sacrament, the church is both sign and cause of grace, signifying and rendering effective God's irrevocable gift to humankind in Christ. Rahner's essays on the important role of the faith of the recipient of the sacraments (in addition to their *ex opere operato* character), on the significance of the charismatic or dynamic element in the church, on questions of freedom in the church, and on the church of sinners and the sinful church are examples of his contributions to Roman Catholic ecclesiology. He argues as well that the church of the future will be a "diaspora church" in an unbelieving culture to which members will belong by choice, not simply because of birth. He urges the importance of individual, personal conviction and the nourishment of faith in

[23] "The Historicity of Theology," *ibid.*, pp. 64–82; "Pluralism in Theology and the Unity of the Creed in the Church," in TI, XI, pp. 3–23; "Intellectual Honesty and Christian Faith," in TI, VII (N. Y., Herder & Herder, 1971), pp. 47–71.

the small groups or "pockets" of Christians who will constitute the church of the future.[24]

These themes are carried further in Rahner's post–Vatican II reflections on the church in which he argues persuasively for a declericalized church concerned fundamentally with service, a church that preaches and teaches morality without moralizing, recognizes the equality of women, and offers a spirituality of genuine depth in relation to the incomprehensible mystery of God. He writes of a church of "open doors" which recognizes the indefiniteness of its borders and its own "marginal settlers" who are not fully members and yet not entirely outside. Rahner calls for a church "from below" or "from the roots" which is open, ecumenical, democratized; he calls for a church which has the courage to take stands on social and political issues and to operate in critical fashion toward social conditions and institutions marked by sin. This vision of "the shape of the church to come" corresponds with Rahner's theological interpretation of the Second Vatican Council as the church's discovery and realization of itself, for the first time, as a truly pluralistic, nondogmatic, non-Western, world-church. The full ramifications of this "theological caesura in church history" will become apparent in the future as the church continues its historical pilgrimage as the people of God.[25]

The question of the future is an abiding theme in Rahner's theology. In contrast to Bultmann's radical existentialism, Rahner maintains the importance of a real future, one that implies the really hidden, the mysterious, the unknown, and the uncontrollable as the horizon of Christian eschatology. At the same time, since human beings are spirit in history, present experience is intrinsically related to both past and future; the

---

[24] *Free Speech in the Church* (N. Y., Sheed & Ward, 1960); *The Dynamic Element in the Church* (N. Y., Herder & Herder, 1964); *The Church and the Sacraments* (N. Y., Herder & Herder, 1967); "Freedom in the Church," in TI, II (Baltimore, Helicon, 1964), pp. 89–107; "Considerations on the Active Role of the Person in the Sacramental Event," in TI, XIV, pp. 161–84; "The Church of Sinners," in TI, VI, pp. 253–69; "The Christian in His World," in TI, VII, pp. 88–99.
[25] *The Shape of the Church to Come* (N. Y., Seabury, 1974); "Basic Theological Interpretation of the Second Vatican Council," in *Concern for the Church* (TI, XX) (N. Y., Crossroad, 1981), pp. 77–89.

future is already implied in the present and grows out of it. Eschatological statements, for Rahner, represent an extrapolation from the present reality and experience of grace, God's self-communication, to its future mode of definitive fulfillment.[26] This fulfillment is both individual and collective, corporeal and spiritual—the resurrection of Christ as the beginning and symbol of the resurrection of Christians. The mystery of eternity is already dimly known to Christian experience in the radical character of unconditioned faith, love, and hope. Eternity is not the prolongation of time in its movement toward death but is the fulfillment of time. In an early essay, Rahner suggests that death, as the event "from the outside" which entails ultimate human diminishment and passivity, can also be an act of the highest human freedom, the definitive act of personal life. The Christian dies in Christ and so recapitulates Christ's redemptive acceptance of death. Rahner's later writings on collective hope continue this theme of active receptivity: the Christian's attitude toward the future combines both active work in the world to bring about the "utopian" future for which human beings plan and hope and awareness that God's absolute future is a gift which transcends any human plan. The radical openness of Christianity toward the future distinguishes it from "ideology," which, for Rahner, identifies the mystery of the future—God's future— with some particular human vision or scheme.[27]

Although Rahner is not a moral theologian in the specialized sense, his theology has singular significance for moral thought in suggesting a programmatic revision of traditional Catholic natural law perspectives. He shows that the conditions for the possibility of the ordinary human experience of freedom are rooted in the self-conscious and self-disposing capacity of the human subject to shape the self in a final way before God. This basic human freedom is expressed in the person's "fundamental option," that inner and most immediate self-direction which can never be completely objectified. The condition for the possibility of this basic freedom is, once again, the dynamic outreach of the self toward the horizon of mystery (the *Vorgriff*). This unifying

---

[26] "The Hermeneutics of Eschatological Statements," in TI, IV, pp. 323–46.
[27] *On the Theology of Death* (1961; reprint edition, N.Y., Seabury, 1973); "The Concept of the Future," in TI, X (N. Y., Herder & Herder, 1973), pp. 235–41.

core of knowledge and commitment is modified by the reality of grace as its intrinsic fulfillment and expansion and is expressed outwardly in the relations of the self toward others—in love of neighbor. Thus Rahner can affirm, on the one hand, that love of God is one with love of the neighbor and, on the other, that the deepest experience of the self is one with the experience of God.[28] Human love for another—or others—is only achieved within the dynamism of the self toward God. God is truly loved in the concrete love of the neighbor.

The fundamental option of the human person is always expressed in free decision, in outward "works" toward the neighbor, because of the original unity of spirit and matter: the categorical, bodily character of human spirit in the world. It is through human choice and activity that the fundamental option creatively shapes the self in a world of other selves and in the abiding ambiguity of human life in time. For Rahner, the moral significance of human action is finally measured by its freedom and according to freedom's loving or sinful orientation. He is critical of any moral theology that emphasizes mere conformity to external norms or coerced obedience to a moral law. A pretheoretical moral knowledge analogous to the unthematic knowledge of God, a "global moral instinct," guides decisions that must be made before the theory to justify them is available. All moral theology is the product of this kind of graced moral knowledge. Within certain "essential" boundaries or limits derived from the nature of the person (as self-conscious and free) freedom is open, "existential," creative. This is Rahner's important distinction between essential and existential ethics: while there can be many licit courses of action (discernible through an essential ethics), it may be that, in the immediacy of grace, there is *one* decision to which God calls the individual in a particular situation (discernible through an existential ethics).[29]

Earlier versions of natural law had viewed human nature as a

---

[28] "On the Question of a Formal Existential Ethics," in TI, II, p. 230; "Reflections on the Unity of Love of Neighbor and the Love of God," in TI, VI, pp. 231–49; "Experience of the Self and Experience of God," in TI, XIII (N. Y., Seabury, 1975), pp. 122–32.

[29] "Works," in *Encyclopedia of Theology: The Concise Sacramentum Mundi*, ed. Karl Rahner (N. Y., Seabury, 1975), pp. 1829–32; "Formal Existential Ethics," pp. 227–28.

static, objective entity within a cosmocentric perspective, according to Rahner. He points out that the traditional definition "rational animal" compared human beings downward, with animal natures, rather than emphasizing the decisive openness of human beings toward God in an anthropocentric or theocentric framework. When the conditions for the possibility of the thinking, deciding self and the creativity of the human subject are taken into account, it becomes clear that "person" as the subject who shapes the self in time and history must be seen in dialectical relationship with enduring human "nature." Human nature thus includes both immutable and mutable aspects, and these are known only through critical, empirical reflection. Rahner claims that what had frequently passed for "nature" in traditional scholasticism is really uncritical, external observation of factual continuities in human societies, elements that may not be nature at all but changeable human creations. The normative content of natural law can be discerned only through constantly renewed critical reflection; it is not an immutable code. To act rationally is to preserve and enhance human freedom. Thus, the task of moral theology is to translate the fundamental structures of the human as self-conscious and free—what "is"—into moral "oughts" in the present historical situation. This task is accomplished through disciplined reflection on experience and on the conditions for the possibility of human freedom and personhood. For Rahner, moral theory is rooted in practice, in the experience that particular modes of action conform or conflict with the limiting and empowering conditions of possibility for freedom itself.[30]

Rahner's theology has met with wide approval but also with a variety of criticisms. Hans Urs von Balthasar, for example, argues that Rahner's anthropocentric focus on the subject or hearer of revelation and his theory of anonymous or implicit Christianity reduce God's Word to a merely philosophical or human word which diminishes the objective and supernatural character of divine revelation and renders the missionary task of the church superfluous.[31] Rahner's persistent response to this

[30] "The Experiment with Man" and "The Problem of Genetic Manipulation," in TI, IX, pp. 205–24, 225–52.

[31] Hans Urs von Balthasar, *Cordula oder der Ernstfall* (Einsiedeln, Johannes, 1966).

sort of criticism "from the right" is that the transcendental and the categorical, or the theocentric and the anthropocentric, are indissolubly united in the Incarnation and in grace. It is only because God's strictly mysterious self-gift has already and always been given universally to humankind that transcendental reflection on graced human subjectivity is possible at all. Another criticism, which Rahner says is the only one he takes very seriously, comes from his former student Johann Baptist Metz, a proponent of political theology. This critique "from the left" finds Rahner's theological anthropology too privatized and individualistic; it fails to take into account the societal situation of persons and the crucial importance of historical praxis in its emphasis on the "already and always" fulfillment of a world of grace. Rahner responds by agreeing with Metz that the social and political context of human freedom must be concretely developed in theology. However, he points out that he has always insisted that

> transcendental experience (of God and of grace) is always mediated through a categorical experience in history, in interpersonal relationships and in society. If one not only sees and takes seriously these necessary mediations of transcendental experience but also fills it out in a concrete way, then one already practices in an authentic way political theology or . . . a practical fundamental theology. On the other hand, such a political theology, if it truly wishes to concern itself with God, is not possible without reflection on those essential characteristics of man which transcendental theology discloses.[32]

Thus Rahner concludes that transcendental and political theology are complementary, not contradictory; a concrete mystagogy is at the same time, in Metz's language, mystical and political.

Rahner's responses to these different criticisms indicate two fundamental characteristics of his through: (1) his unshakable

[32] Karl Rahner, "Introduction," in James J. Bacik's *Apologetics and the Eclipse of Mystery: Mystagogy according to Karl Rahner* (Notre Dame, University of Notre Dame Press, 1980), pp. ix–x; Johann Baptist Metz, *A Theology of the World* (N. Y., Herder & Herder, 1969), pp. 98–100; *Faith in History and Society: Toward a Practical Fundamental Theology* (N. Y., Seabury, 1980), pp. 154–66.

conviction that the core of Christian faith is the irrevocable self-gift of God in Jesus Christ, the absolute bringer of salvation to the whole of human history and experience; and (2) his openness to the mystery of the future and to the new questions that emerge in the course of human history as the history of salvation. Nowhere is this openness to new questions more apparent than in the continuing discussions of Christology that are found in the later volumes of *Theological Investigations*. In a series of essays and in a book he coauthored with New Testament scholar Wilhelm Thüsing, Rahner has taken seriously the new findings of biblical exegesis with regard to the historical Jesus and the Resurrection as the center of New Testament faith. He has shown how his own incarnational, "descending Christology" needs to be supplemented by "Christology from below" or an "ascending Christology." He maintains that the two methods require and are dependent upon one another and that recent approaches to the history and humanness of Jesus are not only more helpful for preaching but also are, in fact, expressions of the traditional faith of Chalcedon in contemporary language.[33]

Rahner's confidence in graced human experience, despite and within the enduring ambiguity of time and history, is echoed in the whole of his theology and in his many spiritual writings, both of which reflect the influence of the tradition of the mystics in his thought. The Ignatian spirituality of "finding God in all things" is translated into his own mystagogy as the "mysticism of everyday life," as is the Thomistic theme of the hidden God who is adored in and through the symbols of earthly and sacramental life.[34] Theology, for Rahner, springs from and is directed toward worship and adoration. There is an intrinsic relation between this theology and his spiritual writings: both center on the self-communication of God and the graced freedom of human response in the struggle of prayer, intelligent thought, and loving commitment to the neighbor and the earthly task. This close relationship between theology and spirituality may account for the wide influence of Rahner's theology on both Christian lay persons and theologians.

[33] TI, XIV, Part 3.
[34] See, e.g., TI, III, especially "The Ignatian Mysticism of Joy in the World," pp. 277–93 and TI, VII.

From the beginning of his career, Rahner was persuaded that the integration of Catholic theology with the modern focus on the subject would enable theology to be responsive both to the faith life of individual Christians and to the intellectual life and pastoral needs of the church in relation to modern culture. His theological anthropology has realized both goals. Rahner's influence on Catholic thought has been enormous. He has written with insight and power on a wide range of theological questions, inserting each issue into a genuinely theological framework to probe its relation to the Holy Mystery, the triune God who has been given to human beings in unfathomable closeness in Jesus Christ and in the Spirit of grace, and the free response of persons to that gift as the single mystery of human life in time.

Bibliography

Karl Rahner, *Foundations of Christian Faith: An Introduction to the Idea of Christianity,* N. Y. Crossroad, 1978.

Leo J. O'Donovan, ed., *A World of Grace: An Introduction to the Themes and Foundations of Karl Rahner's Theology,* N.Y., Crossroad, 1980.

HELMUT THIELICKE

Geoffrey Bromiley

LIFE

Helmut Thielicke has few peers in twentieth-century Germany, either as a constructive church leader or as a productive theologian. Born in December 1908 at Barmen, he studied philosophy and theology at Greifswald, Marburg, Erlangen, and Bonn. He graduated Doctor of Philosophy in 1931 and Doctor of Theology in 1934. Upon ordination, he spent the first years of his ministry as a pastor and theological teacher in Württemberg. An early work, *History and Existence,* however, brought him to the unfavorable notice of the National Socialist authorities. In this work he criticized the idealizing of the so-called orders of creation, including race and people, which offered to the "German Christians" their main support for acquiescence in the Hitler regime. Indirectly, but plainly enough, he suggested that the Third Reich was simply a titanic self-projection of Promethean humanity.

Once the implications of this particular work became apparent, he was expelled from a teaching post at Heidelberg. Indeed, during the war years he came under a ban on all writing, speaking, and traveling. Fortunately, this ban was soon relaxed to allow him to preach in his place of residence and the immediate environs, thus making possible the great preaching of the later period of the war. Thielicke also succeeded in smuggling out the first version of his work titled *Death.* It was published in Switzerland and found its way into courses for German prisoners of war in various places.

The collapse of National Socialism and the end of the war allowed Thielicke to resume his interrupted academic career. In 1945 he took up a theological professorship at Tübingen, where he served with distinction for nine years, acting also as rector of the university and president of the rectors' conference in 1951. Translation to a similar post at Hamburg came in 1954, and there, too, Thielicke held office as university rector in 1961. During the Tübingen and Hamburg years he began to assemble and publish his two most important series, *Theological Ethics* and *The Evangelical Faith*.

Although teaching and writing claimed Thielicke's main attention during the postwar years, he still found opportunities for preaching on radio and television and also in the pulpit of St. Michael's, Hamburg, where he ministered to large congregations drawn from many races and classes. His growing reputation both as preacher and theologian opened up a wider ministry that led him to Asia, Africa, America, and Australia on extensive lecturing and preaching tours. As he considered the decline in church life and Christian knowledge in his own country, he attempted a countermovement, not merely in the form of more popular works like his *Hidden Question of God* and *Being Human . . . Becoming Human* but also through the founding of an information project in Hamburg. By means of adult instruction, group discussion, short popular writings, and presentations on radio and television, this project was designed partly to help Christians relate their faith to modern developments and problems and partly to teach those who had only a minimal acquaintance with Christianity—such as two students who told Thielicke that they had never even heard of the Lord's Prayer.

Despite indifferent health in his later years, Thielicke continued a tremendous program of teaching and writing. Covering a vast range of subjects, he has published more than two hundred larger and smaller works, culminating in a revision of his early work on death, *Living with Death,* in 1980 and a full-scale history of modern thought, *Glauben und Denken in der Neuzeit,* in 1983. The extent to which Thielicke's spoken and written efforts will have a decisive influence on Christian life and theology, only time can tell. Of the immediate impact of his work, whether as preacher, ethicist, or theologian, there can be little question.

PREACHING

Although Thielicke's career has been primarily that of a theologian, he has never been in any sense a remote professor making only occasional and amateurish forays into the sphere of proclamation. In fact, he first came into wider prominence for his preaching rather than his theology, with his pulpit ministry during the war and the postwar period and with the publication of sermons delivered (and letters written) in this time of almost apocalyptic trial, when there were incessant air raids, staggering losses on the Russian front, increasing shortages, and finally the traumatic problems of the occupation. Thielicke provided prophetic messages and tracts for the times which admirably combine situational relevance, theological depth, and vital proclamation of judgment and grace. Perhaps no one matched so well the desperate needs of that time of supreme storm and stress.

Thielicke himself believed that in the last resort life may be reduced to a few elementary questions and a few fundamental truths. These emerge when we are plunged into the deep crises of existence and peripheral concerns and comforts lose their point. They are the result not of study or reflection but of contact with exhaustion, terror, hunger, sickness, and death. They do not take the form of academic problems or facile assurances and promises; they involve an encounter with the harsh realities that strip away every sham, demand an ultimate answer, and leave room only for a faith that believes, not because of obvious demonstration but because of a defiance despite all appearances to the contrary. The very titles of Thielicke's presentations, "The Silence of God," "The Question of Christ," "Death," "The Final Dereliction," "The God of Ends," and "In the Depths," give evidence of the utter realism with which he issued the divine call to a needy people.

A list of the elementary questions and fundamental truths is hardly possible in the present context, but one or two examples may be given. A typical question is: Why does not God intervene in days of human agony? What is the reason for God's terrible silence when the world is full of the tumult of war and the cries of the wounded and dying? In face of this question, the truth emerges that God works through silence as well as speech. God's silence is finally the awful silence of Gethsemane and Golgotha when God is with us in the fellowship of death and the depths, and behind Gethsemane and Golgotha stand the higher thoughts of God that come to glorious fulfillment on Easter Day. Another question arises at once when individual disaster strikes. Why did God cause this or let it happen? Why indeed is all life, both individual and social, so scarred by what seems to be meaningless tragedy, futility, and cruelty? The truth in this instance is that to ask why is to ask the wrong question, for the question itself in this form presupposes meaninglessness. The real question that one should ask is: To what end? Jesus himself puts the question in this form when asked to explain the blindness of the man in John 9. Or rather, Jesus answers the question as though it were put in this form. When confronted with tragic human events, we are not to attempt an explanation but to consider how these events may still serve the divine purpose. When we do this, difficult though it may often be immediately to discern such a purpose, we shall be proof against the mortal injuries that are inflicted by the little word *why*. Thus Thielicke believed that he saw a divine visitation rather than blind fate in the ruins and rubble of shattered Nazi Germany—a visitation of grace as well as judgment. Additionally, he perceived in the very correction of the question a liberation for alignment with the deepest purpose of God as this was manifested in the cross of Christ.

Behind the penetrating analyses contained in these and similar examples lay some profound reflections on the role of proclamation which Thielicke had occasion to express in the no less trying period of postwar prosperity, materialism, and religious indifference. As he stated many times, Thielicke firmly believed that proclamation must precede theology. The Gospel as declaration, whether in sermon or sacrament, has radical priority over theological thinking. The latter arises out of encounter with the Word. It may take different forms in relation to what is finally a common theme. The theme itself, not its doctrinal formulation, stands at the heart of Christian ministry. Its proclamation constitutes the church's primary task.

The Word, of course, has for Thielicke a fixed form in the various aspects of liturgy. This given element safeguards the integrity of the Gospel. In times of feeble or irrelevant preaching, it may be "almost choked by pulpit twaddle," but it preserves the essential message for an age when new life will breathe into the dead bones. Nevertheless, Thielicke never believed that mere recitation fulfills the task, even when ancient texts are not left in antiquated forms but updated and expounded. Proclamation relates to living hearers. It is a venture in presentation. It must correspond to the requirements of the hour. If it can only quote or paraphrase biblical or liturgical idioms, it may achieve timeless orthodoxy but will fail to accomplish the needed incarnation of the Word.

At this point Thielicke saw that preachers must walk a knife-edge between tedious irrelevance and accommodating betrayal. This problem arises whether an expository or a thematic course is taken. Exposition undoubtedly inclines to irrelevance, and the thematic sermon is always in danger of accommodation. On the one side, hearers no longer recognize their own concerns or self-understanding in the passages expounded, receiving answers to questions they are no longer asking. On the other side, up-to-date deliberations that aim directly at contemporaries change, distort, or completely absorb the evangelical content. Thielicke often combined in his sermons an indirect expository element with a thematic core, but his chief concern was to address listeners in such a way as to work through their immediate problems to the basic questions which he thought to be the real human questions in every age and for which he was confident the Gospel alone has the real answers. Preachers may or may not announce a text. But like Jesus himself, they will always begin, at least in an evangelistic or missionary address, with the situation of the hearers. In authentic proclamation this will lead on to a biblical saying or truth in which, unexpectedly, the hearers will see their situation in a totally new light.

Apart from his pulpit ministry, Thielicke has attempted this form of proclamation in his more popular writings. In *The Hidden Question of God* he examines various modern problems, phenomena, and theses. Probing more deeply into them, e.g., into the medical problem of abortion or the legal problem of punishment, he tries to show that these are ciphers for what are ultimately religious problems. The aim in proclamation is to press through to basic issues by counterquestioning. Behind all other questions lie the question of humanity itself and, deeply concealed behind that, the question of God. For most people in

Thielicke's world, the concept of God might seem to be of little relevance or necessity. If they ask about God at all, it is no longer in the search for a gracious God, but with the query, anxious or cynical, whether there is a God at all, whether there is even any need for a God, whether the concepts of God are not outmoded and dispensable. By working through the immediate problems of individual and social life, raising probing counterquestions, Thielicke hopes to show that all these problems lead by different routes to the question of something unconditional that constitutes the ground of human life. Thielicke then identifies this element as the God whom we may know in Jesus Christ and the knowledge of whom is the underlying answer to every other question.

Thielicke's anthropology, *Being Human . . . Becoming Human,* follows the same pattern on a larger scale. Adopting themes from various other works, Thielicke here traverses the fields of human insecurity, norms, technology, and time, covers the issues raised in medicine, law, and sociology, investigates theories in the spheres of philosophy, biology, and psychology, and insists that behind or below everything that has to do with humanity the real question always confronting us is that of human identity. What does it mean to be human? How does one achieve authentic humanity? For Thielicke, of course, this question cannot be divorced from the question of God. It is in relation to God that one perceives and achieves true human identity. As Thielicke constantly reiterates, the image of a person is the image that God has of that person. Knowledge of the self comes with the knowledge of God.

Because, by counterquestioning, the concerns of the age open the door to the evangelical message, Thielicke argues that preachers do best to begin by putting themselves in the situation of their hearers. In commending this principle he is in no sense thinking of psychological strategy. Indeed, he strongly resists such practices as raising the issue of nuclear war merely to catch attention or to induce fear. The technological problem of perfected means and confused ends is a legitimate theme, but only if by means of it access is gained to the deeper issues of humanity and God. Along similar lines Thielicke objects to the adoption of new forms of worship, e.g., rock music, if the purpose is merely to draw in people of a particular group. Experimentation with new liturgical expression has a valid place, but what Thielicke calls psycho-strategy will fail, partly because it is so easy to see through, but chiefly because it is the worst enemy of the Word itself.

This leads to what is perhaps Thielicke's most important conviction as a preacher. He certainly believes that one should adopt a right procedure in proclamation, but his final confidence lies in the self-evident truth of the message as the Holy Spirit speaks and applies it to the hearers. If proclamation leads people to the ultimate questions, at the level of ultimacy Thielicke presents the content of the Gospel in all simplicity, believing that it will cast its own new and authentic light on all matters of human concern. Nor does it carry its truth merely as an idea or construct, for God speaks the message as the Spirit of presentation and disclosure. God's Spirit is the Spirit of neither repetition nor assimilation. God is the Spirit of the addressed word who "makes present the past event of salvation, and makes it present as also the future one." God is the Spirit who by shedding the light of the Gospel effects a new relationship to God, brings about a radical reorientation in self-understanding, and creates a new and true identity.

ETHICS

The situation Thielicke faced in National Socialist Germany posed many critical problems for Christians. Should they engage in resistance in spite of loyalty oaths? Should they deceive so that they would shelter the persecuted? Should Christian partisans torture captured enemies in order to protect their colleagues? Did the country's plight justify plotting to remove Hitler? Apart from these extreme instances of borderline decision, Thielicke after the war found himself increasingly plunged into the practical perplexities of the postwar age, the sexual revolution, the growing crime rate, medical dilemmas, and political and economic pressures. It is hardly surprising, then, that Thielicke's first full-scale work as a scholar should take the form of a multivolumed ethics, begun under the wartime ban, in which he attempted to cover such important areas of human life as politics, medicine, law, aesthetics, and sex.

Thielicke's first ethical task was to explore the theological foundations of Christian ethics. In this regard he followed a path which Karl Barth and Emil Brunner had already pioneered a decade or so before. Yet the initial theological exploration is fully in accord with what he was attempting in his missionary proclamation. This time, however, he reversed the procedure. Instead of beginning with human questions and pressing back through them to the real question (and answer) as lit up by the Gospel, he now began with the light of the Gospel, with the Christian understanding of human and historical reality, with the primary relationship with God to which the problems of life ultimately lead under the pressure of counterquestioning. He brought not only individual life but also the social, political, and economic structures of the world into this primary relationship, seeking the implications of justification, sanctification, and Christian freedom for human existence in all its dimensions. In a striking comparison, he referred in this respect to theological cardiology. Justification is the theological heart, but this heart does not exist for itself alone. It must pump blood into all the members. Only too often the heart may have been beating strongly, but the blood has not found its way to various areas of the body, i.e., to one or another aspect of Christian conduct. His task was to clear the vessels for a fuller flow. Thielicke also pointed out that for him ethics forms the link between theology proper and proclamation. Like proclamation, if from a different angle, it deals with humanity in its secularity. It is thus doubly instructive. On the one hand, it shows how the way can be traversed from the secular situation to the Gospel. On the other hand, it shows how the way can be traversed from the Gospel to the secular situation.

At the basis of Thielicke's understanding lie two connected convictions. The first is that Christians, in virtue of their new life in Christ, are citizens of two eons. The second is that the imperative of their new life is contained in its indicative, so that commands are not imposed as duties but arise spontaneously as the complement of the invitation, or as the task corresponding to the gift. The tension of existing in both the old and the new eons is preserved by the law, which, when properly distinguished in good Lutheran fashion from the Gospel, dispels the false security of personal attainment, yet without making legalistic demands. The imperative contained in the indicative is in effect a command that we countersign the pledge God has signed, that we continually advance by continually returning to the beginning (Luther), and that we increasingly be what we already are. In this regard the law still serves a positive teaching function as a reminder, guide, and source of comfort.

Belonging to the old eon as well as the new, believers are in a world God created, one in which humans bear a lasting divine likeness in virtue of the image God has of them, but they also suffer under the burden of the human fall. For Thielicke the Fall has decisive ethical implications that the experience of history amply confirms. It means that natural law can no longer offer satisfactory norms because it comes under the unavoidable sway of relativity. It means that even God's law takes a predominantly negative form in order to make plain that we humans are not what we ought to be. It means that emergency orders—e.g., those of law or the state—have come into play to arrest the headlong plunge of the human race into a chaos of violence and wickedness. It means that Christians have to recognize two kingdoms or dominions, the spiritual kingdom to which they belong by faith and the secular kingdom, that of the emergency orders, to which they still belong as they must live out the new life in the old eon. It means that the "laws" of the Sermon on the Mount have a relevance that is eschatological; they apply to everyday life only to a limited degree and mainly in the individual sphere, their primary reference being to the innocence of life before the Fall and to life at the end when God's work of new creation in Christ comes to its consummation. It means that utopian dreams of establishing here and now either a perfect Christian society or a society that is ideal by any model have no hope of successful realization and can lead only to frustration and disillusionment, if not to actual disaster.

Thielicke's pessimistic or, as he would say, realistic analysis is tempered by more hopeful qualifications. Natural law still has a limited value in the conduct of secular affairs. Emergency orders may be necessary, but they do not excuse regimes of reaction and repression. Although rulers are ministers of God in the execution of justice, they too, like the orders they represent, participate in human fallenness and come under divine judgment if they become totalitarian tyrants. The secular kingdom has a charge not merely to control human vice but also to promote human virtue. It certainly offers no basis for a double morality, for secularized autonomy, for total separation from the spiritual kingdom. The "laws" of the Kingdom of God impinge on the conduct of Christians in secular affairs, restraining the impulses toward secularization and demanding a place for some actualization of love in structures, however modest this might necessarily be. Although dreams of ultimate perfection are mistaken, they have the positive role of keeping alive the hope of penultimate progress in both the individual and the social sectors.

Thielicke undoubtedly believes that being a Christian in a fallen world is a little easier in direct personal dealings than in those that have greater structural dimensions. Yet even here problems arise for which there are no ready solutions or recommendations. This explains the many efforts to deradicalize the Sermon on the Mount by giving it only a historical application, by distinguishing between intention and action, or by establishing the two levels of precept and counsel. Most people, of course, are usually involved in actions that have more than a purely individual reference; thus the problems in applying an unconditional rule of love multiply rapidly. Thielicke offers the example of the Christian businessman who knows well enough what it means to love his neighbors at the personal level but fails to see how he is to act toward an unsuccessful competitor whom he is driving toward bankruptcy. He also engages in the fancy that the good Samaritan might have been the mayor of his city and felt a responsibility to stop the violence that left the traveler half-dead by the roadside. Should he just track down and punish the robbers? Or should he inquire why those responsible have taken to a life of crime and propose steps to remedy the situation? But might not such courses, even if successful, entail some measure of conflict between the justice that demands the punishment of crime and the love that demands the rehabilitation of criminals, or the removal of the conditions that produce them?

In fact, Thielicke firmly believes that love must find social expression. He also clearly realizes, however, that the tangled situations resulting from the Fall pose insoluble problems when sincere people differ as to the right decisions, not because two courses are both right but because they are both to some extent wrong. Human conditions in this eon seldom leave room for absolutes. Even in the apparently simple matter of telling the truth, hosts of complications arise that force the most honest persons—and not just diplomats or politicians—into compromises. Truth itself, for Thielicke, is relative to people and circumstances. White lies may be relatively justifiable in unjust situations. Conventional untruths serve a purpose as polite formulas that ease social dealings. Physicians conceal what they think to be the truth in order to avoid shattering the morale of critically ill patients. Situational problems of this kind abound in every sphere of life when ethical norms collide, and whatever course is adopted will unavoidably involve a certain measure of wrong.

Thielicke does not raise these problems in an effort to establish casuistical rules for every conceivable contingency. He emphasizes that he deals with particular difficulties only by way of illustration. No detailed guidance can or should be given. The most that can be attempted is laying bare the situation and suggesting, with the help of models, various constructive lines of action according to the basic theological principles. At the same time, Thielicke does arrive at some significant ethical conclusions.

First, he acknowledges the primacy of the person in the relation between person and structure. We cannot wait, of course, for the conversion of people before tackling structural evils. Structures take on a life of their own and unquestionably affect persons. Nevertheless, the person is the ultimate problem, not the structure. Great Babylon, as Thielicke likes to quote from Francis Thompson, is simply a macrocosm of our Babylonian heart. Acts do not make the person, but the person does the acts (Luther). Reforming the world's structures will not of itself solve the world's problems.

Second, and in consequence, we cannot escape responsibility for the hard choices we have to make by throwing all the blame on the situation. The need to compromise may be a necessity, but we cannot make a virtue of this necessity. It is a necessity of our own making, not a compulsion of external fate. Hence Thielicke dislikes the concept of *tragic* moral choices, for tragedy in the stricter Greek sense implies subjection to destiny. Compromise is indeed unavoidable in a fallen world, but the world that makes it unavoidable is our own world. It is an institutionalization of our own rebellion. If we are victims, we are victims of our own nature and action.

Third, although the compromises people make in ambiguous situations may be the right courses of action, they still contain an element of wrong. People can evade neither the guilt incurred nor the possibility that one guilty action may set them on a slippery slope leading to successively more guilty actions. Christians may not plead ambiguous situations as an excuse for watering down the divine imperatives. In facing these imperatives they have to confess, "I ought but I cannot," not "I can because I ought." With the fallen world that demands compromises, they stand under the judgment of God. Even in doing what they think best in difficult circumstances, Christians have to admit that these actions are wrong as well as right. Their actions may follow the most loving course they can perceive, but this fact alters nothing. Few actions can claim to be loving in a pure sense, and other factors are involved as well as love. The devastating truth Christians have to face, and have to try to present to others, is that realistically, in the given human situation, no actions are free of guilt. There can be no convincing excuse, rationalization, or vindication for even relatively good decisions face to face with the divine absolute.

Finally, and for this reason, the Christian life must be lived in terms of the gracious justification of sinners through the "compromise" that God wrung out in the work of Christ. In their lives as citizens of two eons believers have an alien righteousness. This is the indicative to which they must constantly return as they fulfill the implied imperative. Here is the true being that they are to express in the twisted life and structures of fallen humanity. As Thielicke puts it, "Both compromise and the radicalness that attempts anticipation of the future are wrong if they lead to self-justification. " "But they are good" if those who adopt them "realize that their action is of no avail before the last judgment, if they live in expectation of the coming kingdom and see that what they do in this aeon is set under the forgiveness and also the patience of God." Then "God causes them to be good, for those who live in justification are right before God."

THEOLOGY

In proclamation Thielicke tries to push through from human problems to ultimate questions and answers as these problems are set in the new light of the Gospel. In ethics he begins with the new light and tries to show its implications for the living of the life of faith in the eon of the Fall. A task that still remains is that of examining and exposing the new light itself. Acceptance of this task leads Thielicke to the sphere of dogmatic theology in his *Evangelical Faith* (three volumes).

Even in dogmatics Thielicke never loses his primary interest in proclamation. He takes it as axiomatic that the Gospel has two sides. It is a divine message, but it also has a human address. This means that theologians may adopt either a theological or an anthropological approach. They may begin with the message or begin with the recipients. Either course is legitimate, but in Thielicke's view an initial focus on the recipients has proved historically to run the almost unavoidable risk of an accommodation of what is said to those to whom it is said. Along these lines he offers an illuminating criticism of anthropocentric theology, with Rudolf Bultmann as a prize exhibit. The existential and hermeneutical concentration of this Cartesian theology, as he calls it, either leaves no room for genuine theological content or so gravely distorts it as to rob it of its true meaning and force.

Thielicke realizes that theocentric or non-Cartesian theology faces the opposite danger of being a mere repetition of biblical and historical material. As in his preaching, he allows that attention must be paid to changes in vocabulary, situation, and thought-forms. His real alternative to Cartesian theology is not orthodoxy but a theology of the Holy Spirit. As he sees it, the God who gives (or is) the message also makes the transition from the divine message to the human recipient. Presenting the message, God constitutes the hearers true recipients, not just in intellectual apprehension but in personal appropriation *to* its truth. As God's Word is spoken, it has in God's Spirit a creative force that brings about the death of the self-encircling self and the creation of the self in Christ that is theonomously instead of autonomously oriented. This created work is possible because the truth of the Word is uniquely truth in person into which its hearers are called and which establishes faith as a new category of knowledge and understanding.

From the introductory volume it might seem that Thielicke would simply develop a theology of the Holy Spirit. To do this, however, would be to overlook the fact that what the Spirit presents is the Word, which is supremely Christ himself as the divine Word-event in and with which God "enters into his own unique compromise" with fallen humanity. What is first demanded, then, is a discussion of revelation under the two headings of God the Father as its source and God the Son as its form. This discussion enables Thielicke to take up many subjects that have occupied modern theology—e.g., natural revelation, the use of the word *God,* the personal nature of God, the Trinity, the relation between faith and history, the problem of Christ's person and work, the virgin birth, and the resurrection of Christ. Important features of this comprehensive treatment include the constant reference to God's actual work, the recognition that terms such as *person* can be applied to God only as they receive their content from God, and the insistence that ordinary historical epistemology is not wholly appropriate to the historical phenomenon of Christ. Above all is the insight that in Christ, by his incarnation, death, and resurrection, God has reconstituted humanity in the relationship to God disrupted by the Fall and that this central truth gives unity and totality to all other truths unfolded by human investigation.

Although the Word-event of the self-revealing God forms the indispensable core of dogmatics, as it is also the core of the Gospel, the application of this creative content to hearers is of special interest to Thielicke the preacher, especially in view of the suggestion of the later Barth that theology in the Schleiermacher tradition has validly, if inadequately, tried to fill the gap left by the absence of a proper theology of the third article of the Creed. In his

Evangelical Faith, therefore, Thielicke devotes a whole volume to the presentation of the Gospel in the ministry of the Holy Spirit. He does this under the headings of the power, the means, the form, the exclusiveness, and the transcending of presentation. Sanctification, Scripture, preaching, sacraments, church, the religions, and the last things all call for investigation under these headings. In the course of his deliberations Thielicke also takes the opportunity to enter into sympathetic but forthright dialogue with liberals, fundamentalists, and especially Roman Catholics. Significant points are his understanding of the relationship between the Old and the New Testaments as one of promise and fulfillment, his effort to get beyond the older eucharistic debates, his combination of the exclusiveness of the Gospel with an appreciative approach to world religions, the realistic facing of death and the failure of attempts to repress its factuality through various forms of pseudo-immortality, and his commitment to resurrection on the basis of the true, ongoing identity of the believer in God.

Beyond the individual discussions, however, the most valuable feature of his third volume is the insistence that God is the supreme and indispensable factor in the appropriation of the Gospel as well as in the Word-event it narrates. At the level of human response, no human element compels acceptance even though this element is itself a product of the Spirit. Neither individual believers nor the church can boast of a perfect sanctification that forms a separate basis for justification or faith. Holy Scripture, for all its inspiration and canonicity, has no demonstrable infallibility that forces readers to accept its truth. In none of its aspects does the ministry have a psychologically irresistible force that brings growth to the church by the mere use of human abilities and techniques. By human criteria Christianity has no religious uniqueness that enables it to make a tenable claim to superiority over all other religions. The message of the Resurrection does not have the scientifically historical demonstrability that grants empirical certainty to the hope of the eschaton.

Thielicke has no wish to contest the reality of sanctification, scriptural authority, ministry, Christian uniqueness, or the Resurrection. On the other hand, he has no desire to secure for them a false inviolability by protecting them from the involvement in a fallen world that is a mark of God's own action.

Rather, his purpose is to see here the instruments of the divine involvement by giving them a place in the operation of God the Holy Spirit. He views them as a part of the divine Word-event in accordance with the incarnational pattern of the supreme act of revelation and reconciliation in Christ. In bridging the gap between God's work and the human response to this work, the decisive thing is that the Word of this work creates its own hearers in self-disclosure by the Spirit. Those who proclaim it have no need, therefore, to resort to existential, hermeneutical, or intellectual constructions to make the connection. The Holy Spirit uses the events and their proclamation to evoke the response of faith and to complete the saving circle.

CONTRIBUTION

The main outlines of Thielicke's theological contribution should now be plain. His works present some difficulties to nontechnical readers. He assumes a wide acquaintance with modern thought, he ranges over many topics, he is verbose, he tends to be repetitive so that one often gets the impression of learning by recollection, and he comes out with so many forthright judgments that constant protest or even violent objection may arise at points of detail. Nevertheless, his fundamental theses, or concerns, are simple and emerge with reasonable clarity.

First, Thielicke passionately believes that God's incarnational work is the solution to the separation between God and the world which is a problem in the modern epoch. Early in his career he had to ask himself how God and humanity can still be perceived as belonging together. He could not accept the prospect of a Godless world or a worldless God. But he also could not accept the apparent alternatives of a sacralization that preserves a little niche for God in a predominantly secular structure or of a secularization that subsumes God under purely secular concepts. He found an answer to his dilemma in the divine involvement with humanity in the saving work of Christ and the ensuing ministry of the Spirit. What the Gospel proclaims is divine action within the world, which is a model for the church's own action as it plunges into the world's concerns. The church does so not to make the world's agenda its own agenda but to work through the world's agenda to God's agenda, which is finally the world's real agenda as well.

Second, Thielicke recognizes that when we press back to the true agenda, the primary item is the alienation of humanity resulting from alienation from God. This world is a fallen world, and while its institutions may offer some protection against the worst excesses of alienation, they themselves participate in the Fall and are therefore alienating factors. Even Christians who have received the Gospel message and who experience God's gracious work of renewal have to live their lives in the complex situation of individual and structural alienation. They cannot fulfill the absolute demands of God; yet they are not just victims of supraindividual forces. Each individual is a microcosm of humanity at large. With individual renewal, then, only small if not insignificant steps can be taken as the divine requirements are brought to bear on human problems. We can entertain no extravagant dreams of utopian solutions. We are justified in hope *(spe)* and not in fact *(re)*. We have to make compromises, but we must admit that even if these are the best possible courses, they are partly wrong and need the divine forgiveness. We can draw up no blueprints for right actions in all conceivable circumstances. Nevertheless, the position is not hopeless. The new eon has dawned, the work of restoration has begun, the final consummation is assured, and even now, for all the entanglement in an alienated eon, advances in good can be made.

Third, Thielicke can have this confidence only because he believes that since the ultimate human problem is alienation from God, the ultimate solution is the restoration of the broken fellowship by God. This is the point of the Word-act recounted in the Gospel. This is the point of the ministry of the Spirit. True to his initial insight, Thielicke does not see this being accomplished apart from humanity. The Incarnation means solidarity with humanity and involvement in a particular period of its history. The ministry of the Spirit means the use of human instruments and encounter with the problems, actions, discoveries, and insights of changing centuries and civilizations. Through it all God has been and is at work. Humanity alone cannot reforge the broken link. On its own, humanity cannot achieve its true identity or dignity. It depends on God's faithfulness for its ongoing identity as God's creature, on God's grace for an alien dignity, and on God's love for its restoration to fellowship which brings the full realization of both dignity and identity. It does not depend on God's faithfulness, grace, or love in vain. For all the perplexing and multiplying problems that face the human race, and the people of God within it, God has given it once again, by God's saving action and the mediation of God's Word and Spirit, the opportunity to be and become human. The efforts of believers are first and faltering steps in this direction.

A final point—and Thielicke ends where he begins—is that the primary task of the church, confident in the power of the Spirit, is to proclaim and actualize the Gospel of God's reconciling work in the world. The truth of God is truth for humanity. It is liberating truth that gives direction in all areas of life. It is *the* truth that the world desperately needs, not as mere intellectual insight but as "truth in person" in which the world may "be" by the Holy Spirit. To present this truth, believers have to be in tune with their age but not so absorbed into it that they have nothing of their own to offer. Ethics and theology, when they are true to their calling, serve this task of proclamation of the truth and of its outworking in individual and structural renewal. They carry this out by so focusing on the Gospel and its implications for action that the delicate balance is preserved between irrelevance on the one side and false relevance on the other. But ethics and theology must not forget their servant role. They must never degenerate into talk for talk's sake. Indeed, the church as a whole must not lose sight of this primary task. As an institution it must not become a dead crater that no longer spills out glowing lava. As Thielicke the preacher finally observes (in *The Hidden Question of God*), "whether a church is living or dead depends exclusively on its proclamation."

Bibliography

Helmut Thielicke, *Being Human . . . Becoming Human*, N.Y., Doubleday, 1984.

Jan Flipsen, *Spannung zwischen Glaube und Welt. Kritische Analyse der Theologischen Ethik Helmut Thielickes*, Rome, 1970.

JACQUES ELLUL

Douglas Sturm

The world is in perpetual contradiction with the will of God.[1]

To Jacques Ellul, a French Protestant theologian, the central theme of Christian theology is God's incessant contention with the world. The world is in a condition of alienation, but it is not, ultimately, to be abandoned. The intention of the struggle, however impossible it may seem at times, is to restore the world to its rightful character. Indeed this central theme of Christian theology characterizes Ellul's own life as citizen, churchman, and Christian intellectual.

Ellul was born of mixed ancestry in Bordeaux in 1912. His father's intense sense of honor, which on one dramatic occasion preceding the Great Depression led to loss of employment, instructed him in the ways of courage. His mother's artistic proclivities taught him the ways of elegance. Despite conditions of poverty, the close-knit family was deeply imbued with traditional values of integrity and industry. There was, however, nothing explicitly Christian about the family, although Ellul's mother was Protestant. His father, of Greek Orthodox background, was a devotee of Voltaire and an open-minded liberal on the subject of religion. The economic circumstance of Ellul's family and his intimate acquaintance with life around the quays of Bordeaux engendered sensitivity to the miseries of the lower classes in the social order.

At the age of sixteen, Ellul entered college where, introduced to the thought of Karl Marx, he found in *Das Kapital* a thoroughly convincing explanation of the conditions in the modern world. Ellul never assumed Marxism as an article of faith, and he found revisions in content necessary given changes in the course of history since Marx's death. But from that time forward, he has insisted that

---

[1] *In Season Out of Season* (French edition, 1981; San Francisco, Harper & Row, 1982), p. 204. Most of the section on Ellul's life is derived from this text, based on interviews conducted by Madeleine Garrigou-Lagrange.

Marx's mode of understanding the modern social world is the most powerful and persuasive available.

Ellul reports that, during the same period, he was embroiled in a protracted, deeply individual struggle with God eventuating in a conversion to Christianity. Although Christianity was responsive to the sufferings and sensibilities of his inner life and personal relations with others, it was devoid of explanatory power in interpreting the structure and dynamics of societal existence. Thus Ellul held together, as he has continued to do, a profound faith informed by biblical revelation and a social understanding instructed by Karl Marx, without confusing the two, but without synthesizing them into a single system of thought.

During his twenties, Ellul assumed an active role in French politics. Through *Esprit,* a movement of Catholic personalists, and *Ordre nouveau,* a group of anarchist-socialists, Ellul organized small groups throughout southwest France committed to social change. His aim was to stimulate a fundamental cultural revolution opposed to the powers of nationalism and political centralism and especially to the overreaching structures of modern technology.

In 1938, Ellul was named professor of law at the University of Strasbourg, but two years later he was removed by the Vichy government on trumped-up charges. Until the end of World War II, Ellul, sustaining his family through farming, was part of the resistance movement, assisting Jews to escape from the Nazis. He became a deputy mayor of Bordeaux following the liberation of Europe, intending to press for radical reconstruction of the social order. But his intent was constantly frustrated by the intricacies and inertial quality of political administration, resulting in his increasing disillusionment about prospects for social change.

Given the frustrations of acting through direct political administration, Ellul was led by the compulsions of a "revolutionary Christianity" to promote social transformation through the Reformed Church. For several years, he cultivated the creation of Protestant professional associations to bring biblical imperatives to bear on professional practice as a means of infusing the social order with the qualities of Christian life. Some time after that project floundered, Ellul, as a member of the national council of the Reformed Church of France, assisted in the creation of a committee on strategy with the intention of restructuring the entire organizational pattern of the church to make its constituents more aware of and responsive to global problems of social existence. Despite meticulous preparation over the course of years, the plans were resisted and eventually scuttled.

Ellul cooperated for a time with committees of the World Council of Churches, but he was led eventually to an open dissent at the Conference on Church and Society in 1966. He disagreed with them partially because of the council's increasing bureaucratization but primarily because of the theological superficiality and social naiveté of its support of liberation movements in the Third World.

Yet Ellul continued to work in the church, sharing for many years in the leadership of a small parish outside Bordeaux and participating for a decade on a committee for the reform of theological studies.

Outside the church, while Ellul has remained disillusioned with prospects for effective social change through official political channels, he has devoted significant energies to various causes. He is widely known for his work on local and regional levels with street gangs where his aim has been not the adjustment of youth to social expectations, for society is corrupt, but their empowerment to transcend their circumstances and to assume responsibility for their own lives. Moreover, he has been active in an environmentalist movement opposing organized forces seeking the massive economic development of the coast of Aquitaine (southwest France).

For all that, Ellul, ever an activist in church and society despite repeated failures, has been primarily a lay Christian intellectual, given to interpretations of the character of modern civilization and the countervailing character of Christian faith. From 1944 until his recent retirement, he taught at the University of Bordeaux in legal studies and in the history and sociology of institutions. He is internationally acknowledged for his writings; these include more than thirty-five books, most of which have been translated into English.

The books, by design, fall into two categories—sociological and theological. The sociological works, inspired in orientation by Marx, penetrate into the principles governing the forms of modern social life. The theological texts, manifesting the influence initially of John Calvin and subsequently of Karl Barth and Søren Kierkegaard, present the challenge of biblical revelation to the modern world. Ellul is not, however, a systematic theologian. He has not attended to traditional doctrinal questions. Rather, his focus has been the ethical import of the faith.

In some cases, Ellul's books are intended as parallels. Thus *The Technological Society,* the most famed of his sociological books, and *The Technological System* are paired with *The Meaning of the City,* an interpretation of the significance of cities throughout the Old and New Testaments. Similarly *The Political Illusion* is paired with *The Politics of God and the Politics of Man.*[2] The pairing does not mean that the two sides are connected in any simple or systemic way; in accordance with this method, they are related dialectically.

METHOD OF INTERPRETATION: DIALECTIC

> It is true that there is a dialectic within my work, and it is entirely central in that I have discovered progressively that in the world we live in there are no means of thinking and acquiring knowledge that are not of a dialectical nature.[3]

Ellul has characterized his work as a "composition in counterpoint," informed by a "principle of confrontation." Since, in his judgment, the entire course of human history is governed by conflicts among contradictory forces, the only ultimately adequate mode of thought is dialectic.

From Marx, Ellul derives the insight that historical change

[2] *The Technological Society* (French edition, 1954; Knopf, 1964); *The Technological System* (French edition, 1977; N.Y., Continuum, 1980); *The Meaning of the City* (French edition, 1975; Grand Rapids, Mich., Eerdmans, 1970); *The Political Illusion* (French edition, 1965; N.Y., Knopf, 1967); *The Politics of God and the Politics of Man* (French edition, 1966; Grand Rapids, Mich., Eerdmans, 1972).

[3] *In Season Out of Season,* p. 201. Much of the section on Ellul's method is derived from his essay "On Dialectic," *Jacques Ellul: Interpretive Essays,* ed. Clifford G. Christians and Jay M. Van Hook (Urbana, University of Illinois Press, 1981), pp. 291–308.

results from a clash of opposing social forces. There is no history without opposition. From Barth, Ellul transmutes this insight into a broader comprehension of the relation between God and the world. There will be no fundamental transformation of the world without the intervention of God, for otherwise the world will persist in its given condition.

But dialectical thought, which focuses on the conflicts and contradictions in reality, is not a modern invention. Nor does it originate in ancient Greece, as some interpreters have argued. According to Ellul, dialectical thought is evident in Hebrew Scriptures beginning in the eighth century B. C. The interactive relationships depicted in the Bible between God's command and the people's response, between promise and fulfillment, between history and the Kingdom of God are all cases of a dialectical form of thinking in which antithetical forces are nonetheless discerned as belonging to each other and being driven, in their opposition, to an eventual stage of reconciliation.

Thus the two sides of Ellul's work, sociological and theological, are in one sense independent of each other. The sociological studies can be understood, as they have been, to make claims about central features of human life in the modern period without any attention being paid to Ellul's theological concerns. Similarly, his theological arguments and interpretations of biblical revelation can be appropriated, though less easily, in the absence of knowledge about his sociological interpretations.

Yet, in Ellul's mind, the two sides belong together. For a full comprehension of their import, they must be considered, each relative to the other. The link between them is dialectical. The sociological studies are efforts, from the perspective of faith, to state as fully and accurately as possible the character of this world, the specific context and condition of human life in this historical epoch. The theological studies, in turn, are formulated as messages of hope and the possibility of new life addressed precisely to persons in this world. In Ellul's affirmation, both are accomplished in light of eschatological expectations—in the prospects, that is, of what God purposes in the contention with the world.

The form of Ellul's dialectical method, as applied to the

structure of his overall work, presses him to adopt a controversial but cogent method of approaching his sociological and theological studies. In each case, the method is holistic.

Hence, in sociology Ellul expresses severe doubts about the adequacy of statistical and experimental methods, for, even if highly sophisticated, they are inherently limited. They deal only with sharply demarcated segments and aspects of the social order. What they neglect is, however, what is most critical —namely, the basic milieu of the common life, the social totality, the structural features of the historical epoch. A discursive method, while lacking in the seeming precision of a statistical formula, may be in fact more precise in delineating the determining features of social existence.

In theology, Ellul announces that the biblical revelation is the criterion, content, and beginning point of his work. Here, too, he voices grave reservations about prevailing modes of interpretation. Diverse schools of hermeneutics, form criticism, and textual analysis may shed some light on the biblical books, but they tend to overlook what is of paramount significance; that is, the theological meaning of the text in its entirety. The church canonized the text as a whole, for it is through the text as a whole that the Word of God is conveyed.

Ellul employs the same holistic method in his approach to particular books of the Bible—Jonah, II Kings, Revelation. What is critical to Ellul is the message conveyed through the structure of the entire book, but he is no literalist. He is unconcerned with the historical factuality of every story in the Bible—for instance, of Cain's construction of the first city or of Jonah's reluctance to call Nineveh to repentance. The theological issue central in the interpretation of Scripture is not whether its narratives are historically true, but what kind of word God is conveying in and through them as opposed to the historical realities of human life.

Given Ellul's dialectical method, three interconnected questions constitute the core of his intellectual work. The sociological question is: What is the character of the modern world? The theological query is: What is the axis of the biblical revelation, and what is its import for human history? Granting the contradiction between the modern world and biblical revelation, the ethical concern is: What are the qualities of a Christian style of life?

CHARACTER OF THE MODERN WORLD: TECHNIQUE

No social, human, or spiritual fact is so important as the fact of technique in the modern world.[4]

Five decades ago, Ellul had arrived at the central thesis of all his subsequent sociological studies: the primacy of technique in modern Western civilization.[5] *Technique,* in the special meaning Ellul assigns to that term, is the decisive factor in the formation of the West's economic, political, and cultural systems. Its influence is more than institutional. It has become a way of life. It is the ethos informing the inner sensibilities of persons and determining what they consider sacred and supreme. Technique has created a civilization of means.

All civilizations employ technical operations of one kind or another; that is, procedures and tools to reach a desired end. But in traditional settings, such operations are applied in limited domains, are subordinated to human interests, are of only local significance, and are used or not at the discretion of the user. In modern times, however, technical operations are a matter of rational intent and commitment. Deliberate efforts are made to discover alternative means to a given purpose and to ascertain which among them is most efficient. Systematic ways are constructed to apply results throughout all domains of human activity. The quest for the "one best means" in every sphere of life has become a primary social obsession.

Thus technique, to Ellul, is not merely a particular tool or procedure. It is a total complex of methods designed rationally to introduce maximal efficiency throughout all life. It is an ensemble of means. It is the effort to gain control over the world, to master the resources of nature, to organize the energies of humankind, and to subject all things to the principle of efficient ordering.

[4] *The Technological Society,* p. 3.
[5] See *The Technological Society, The Technological System,* and *In Season Out of Season.*

In the modern world, technical development has assumed an impetus of its own. All major social institutions are given to its furtherance. Technical advance is the sign and criterion of progress. The technical expert has become indispensable in all sectors in the formation and administration of policy. Technical solutions are considered the only appropriate response to technical problems. Technologies are linked together in complicated and extensive systems in many areas—economic production and distribution, urban planning, military operations. Moreover, technique has become a global phenomenon. In its wake, it destroys all that stands contrary to its principles. Since technique, for instance, depends on the plasticity of nature and adaptability of persons to its concern with efficient ordering, it is wholly at odds with those cultures and subcultures oriented toward the rhythms of elemental nature or toward the authority of traditional ways.

Ellul devotes particular attention to propaganda in the modern world because propaganda, itself a technology, is more importantly a condition for technological civilization.[6] Propaganda is a set of methods employed by an organization to elicit the participation of a mass of individuals in its activity. Propaganda manipulates the sentiments and dispositions of a people, and its purpose is to draw them into unified and active support of the organization. The ultimate concern of propaganda is not just attitudinal, but practical. It is to incorporate individuals into the organization's own designs.

In the modern Western world, propaganda is carefully calculated to address each person individually but to do so en masse. It is a total phenomenon in two senses. Taken as a whole, it presents a myth about the world, a story about who we are and what is important in life. It is an all-pervasive presence, forming through multiple media a virtually inescapable environment of human living. Furthermore, propaganda is highly organized for maximal effect. Its intent is to mobilize the masses to enact the myth it presents.

Propaganda has become a functional necessity for both the

---

[6] *Propaganda: The Formation of Men's Attitudes* (French edition, 1962; N.Y., Knopf, 1965).

modern state and the individual. The state, acknowledging the need of popular support (public opinion) for its programs, even as it lays heavy claim on the financial resources and lives of its citizens to complete them, is driven to propaganda to shape the people's desires to conform to government policy. The individual, on the other hand, in the context of a technological society whose complexities defy comprehension and whose direction and character are beyond one's control, is in dire need of propaganda for several purposes: as a key, however simplified, for understanding events; as a ground to devote one's life to its persistence; as a reason for adjusting to the traumas and demands of industrial and urban living; and as an explanation, if not justification, for the absurdities and catastrophes of modern existence. Propaganda, Ellul concludes, is a remedy for ignorance, incoherence, and isolation.

But, Ellul argues, however functionally necessary propaganda may be, it has deleterious effects, psychologically and socially. Propaganda is given to stereotypes. It closes the mind to new ideas and blunts critical judgment. It stimulates action without thought and mechanizes work. Moreover, propaganda enhances the role of technicians in the social and political order. It destroys genuinely interpersonal communication. It therefore creates a dilemma for democracy; although propaganda is in direct conflict with principles of democratic politics, democracy cannot avoid its use in a technological society. Again, it forces the Christian community into an impossible circumstance. Without propaganda the voice of Christianity is not heard, but propaganda constitutes a total system, a civilization of means, a whole style of life whose inner character is utterly anti-Christian.

The political consequences of technique in the modern world have been twofold: the "politization" of the common life and the creation of political illusions.[7] By politization, Ellul means the gigantic growth of the centralized state and the bureaucratization of its administration of rules and programs made necessary by the extension of technique throughout the social order. This process lies behind Ellul's judgment that the nation-state today is the

[7] *The Political Illusion.* For Ellul's argument that "politization" has radically altered the status of law, see *The Theological Foundation of Law* (French edition, 1946; London, SCM Press, 1960).

most significant institutional reality. It is virtually impossible, Ellul argues, to distinguish between social and political, private and public spheres of life. One result of politization is the increasing dependency of peoples on the state and their subsequent assumption that the fundamental criterion of human dignity and true liberty must be effective political participation; that is, gaining some control over the institutions that affect the conditions of their life.

That assumption, which underlies liberation movements (some theologically inspired) in many countries, is an exemplary case of the illusions of modern politics. First, it is an illusion, carefully nurtured by politicians and citizens, to think that bureaucracies can be controlled by either individuals or parliaments. Bureaucracies endure by the inner laws of their being: continuity, specialization and rationalized efficiency, anonymity and secrecy. They are virtually impenetrable. Second, it is an illusion to think that citizens, were they given the opportunity, possess the maturity and competence needed for participation in political processes. They lack the inclination, time, and knowledge requisite for considered judgments in contemporary political issues. Efforts of Christian churches to engage in political action are notorious, in Ellul's judgment, for their incompetence. Third, it is an illusion to think that political solutions are possible anyway, especially in regard to the most central problems of existence: justice, truth, peace, and human fulfillment. At best, political systems accomplish minor accommodations in the balance of power and distribution of material resources.

In the transition from medieval Christendom to the modern world, technique has also been a powerful instrument of desacralization.[8] It has destroyed traditional gods and obliterated sacred places in the name of efficient ordering. But according to Ellul, in a paradoxical twist typical of such transitional periods, it has given rise to a new form of the sacred since, from a sociological perspective, the idea of the sacred fulfills a necessary function in social life. That is considered sacred which, because of its inescapable and all-encompassing presence, threatens one but which, if one will only conform to its commands, will protect. The sacred is thus both awesome and

---

[8] *The New Demons* (French edition, 1973; N.Y., Seabury 1975).

comforting. In its functions, the sacred is that which establishes an order in the universe, is a guide for conduct, and integrates the individual into the solidarity of a group.

In Ellul's interpretation, the form of the sacred in contemporary civilization consists of four factors: two ordering principles (technique and nation-state) and, since the sacred exists in polar tension with its opposite, two principles of transgression (sexuality and revolution). The irrationality of sexuality and the destructiveness of revolution are the seeming negations, respectively, of technical ordering and state control. But, given the character of the sacred, the negations are appropriated into the full dynamics of the predominating principles. Thus sexuality, partly as a form of release and partly as a symbol of aggressive power, serves the perpetuation of the technological order that it seems to oppose. Similarly, revolution, a threat to existing state structure, is but a means for re-creating the form of the nation-state itself.

In a penetrating analysis, Ellul depicts the prevalent myths and rituals derived from the modern form of the sacred. Although there are many such myths (e.g., class struggle, happiness, progress, productivity), the most fundamental are two: belief in history as the locus for the meaning of life, and acceptance of science as the power for unraveling the mysteries necessary for salvation. Moreover, although there are many signs of religious ritual in the modern age, ranging from rediscovery of the occult to ecstatic celebrations of consumer society, the supreme form is political religion epitomized most extremely in Stalinism, Hitlerism, and Maoism but evident in all modern states. In the secular religion of a technological age, the *homo politicus* has become the perfect equivalent of the traditional *homo religiosus*.

Within this context, the Christian church, in contrast to its original faith, is guilty of a "terrible conformity" to the world.[9] It is a "false presence" in the modern age by assuming that Jesus Christ's lordship over history means that history is progressing toward the Kingdom of God, that technological civilization is a stage in the process, that happiness (as a comfortable standard of living) is the proper goal of life, and that the church should, in

[9] *The False Presence of the Kingdom* (French edition, 1963; N.Y., Seabury, 1972).

moments of social conflict, side with progressive political movements. The church, whether of rightist or leftist persuasion, whether acting out of the legacy of Bonhoeffer's or Teilhard's acceptance of modernity or the revolutionary impulse of the ecumenical movement or liberation theology, is in its approach to politics usually incompetent, always selective (moved by a "passon for the latest thing"), and in any case, guilty of apostasy, of "a betrayal, either of revealed truth or of the incarnate love."

More generally, the emergence of technological civilization is a betrayal of the genius of Western tradition.[10] Against those who condemn the West in its entirety for its perversities, Ellul insists that out of the West given the influence of Christianity, there was formed the prospect of a civilization of and for the individual, a civilization in which freedom qualified only by reasoned discourse would constitute the foundation of social order. But that prospect, with the onset of the modern age, suffered an agonizing reversal. Reason was reduced to technical rationality. The individual was dissolved into the mass. Freedom was transmuted into concern for security and comfort. The political left, initially adopting the role of Christianity in resisting the change, finally capitulated to the myths and prejudices of the technological world.

The conclusion of Ellul's sociological work is grim but intended as a note of stark realism. Ours is an age of abandonment. The West, as evidenced in the reactions of the theater of the absurd and the art of nihilism to the destructiveness of the world of technique, has gone mad.

CENTRAL AXIS OF BIBLICAL REVELATION: JESUS CHRIST

If Christians have a special mission here, it is due to the fact that they are witnesses to an event on which all other events are based, an event which took place in history, . . . an event which sums up and guarantees all other events, personal and historical, and renders history and life absolutely irreversible. This event is the intervention of God in the course of human history, it is Jesus Christ.[11]

[10] *The Betrayal of the West* (French edition, 1975; N.Y., Seabury, 1978).
[11] *The Presence of the Kingdom* (French edition, 1948; London, SCM Press, 1951).

Jacques Ellul is not a systematic theologian. He never presents a philosophically argued accounting of the faith. Nowhere does he develop a sophisticated theological method. Nor does he engage in apologetics, the effort to persuade the cultured despisers of faith of the truth of the Gospel.

Ellul's theological investigations are, by his own affirmation, grounded in biblical revelation. Most of his theological studies are direct expositions of biblical texts which, as noted, he understands to constitute a whole. The axis around which the texts are organized and which draws them together as an organic totality is the manifestation of God, the Wholly Other, in Jesus Christ. Moreover, Ellul's appropriation of the Bible, both Old and New Testaments, as a thoroughly Christian document and as the only source through which an understanding of faith is possible, bears the mark of the classic Protestant principle *sola Scriptura*. Ellul's theology is thus simultaneously Christocentric and bibliocentric.

Out of this beginning, Ellul's theology focuses on traditional themes of Reformed Christianity: the sovereignty of God over history; the strength and solidity of sin in history; and the presence of hope for a new creation, a New Jerusalem, beyond history but inclusive of history. In each instance, however, the theme is intended for and is a judgment on the modern world.

In a commentary on II Kings, "the most political of all the books of the Bible," Ellul finds in narrative form an affirmation of the sovereignty of God and how that sovereignty is possible without detracting from the autonomy of human action.[12] Ellul admits that the problem, stated theoretically, is rationally insoluble. Either God is truly sovereign and human freedom is a sham, or humans are autonomous and God's power is limited.

Yet Ellul claims that, in the stories, the problem vanishes with the affirmation that God's action is only suggestive, never coercive. God, through the prophets, announces and predicts, but individuals must act. The manner in which the individuals act is their responsibility. Thus Elisha announces that Jehu will be king of Israel, but Jehu of his own volition assassinates the incumbent, kills Jezebel, and massacres the members of the house of Ahab and disciples of Baal. Therefore Jehu ambig-

---

[12] *The Politics of God and the Politics of Man.*

uously fulfills the prophecy of God and acts out of his own self-regarding interest.

Ahaz, on the other hand, without benefit of prophecy but as a pure political realist, acts single-mindedly to save the state. He commits the "sin of Jeroboam" in exploiting religion as a tool of political power, even as in the modern world sacred realities, including the "golden calves" of communism and capitalism, science and history, are used to the same effect. Thus Ahaz appears politically efficacious, but, Ellul insists, there are two kinds of efficacy: efficacy as success according to the measure of this world and efficacy as faithfulness to the Wholly Other. Only the latter conforms to the sovereign measure of God.

Ellul points to Hezekiah as a third case, a king who, confronting impossible political odds, simply acknowledges the limits to political action and discerns the ultimate question transcending the politics of history: Who, after all, is the Lord? The politics of the sovereign God transcend the politics of history, engage the authentically free action of the faithful, and break open the prospect of a miraculous intervention into the ordinary routines of historical logic.

Jehu, Ahaz, and Hezekiah are therefore free agents, but nonetheless all are cast in a drama in which God is sovereign Lord.

In a powerfully illuminating study of Scripture from Genesis to Revelation, Ellul argues that, until the New Jerusalem, the city (which in the modern world is synonymous with technique) is presented as a symbol and reality of the rebellion of humankind against God.[13] Cain, the first murderer, established the first city. It is, for him, a countercreation, an effort to find a place of security independent of God.

The true character of the city is typified throughout the Bible by the name of Babylon, a place where understanding and communication are lacking. God's curse on the city, however, is not on its inhabitants; it is on the city as a whole, its inner spirit, for the spirit of a city, of all cities throughout history, claims autonomy for itself. It sets itself apart from others. Cities, like nations and civilizations, take on a life of their own. A city is a closed world. Moreover, given its dealings with commerce and coercion, it is destructive of human relationships.

[13] *The Meaning of the City.*

Cities are not wholly without hope, however. Though Sodom is destroyed, Nineveh repents and is saved. But its salvation depends on toppling the spiritual power that holds the city in its grip. Again, Jerusalem is a special case. Like other cities, it is a countercreation, but God determined to dwell in its midst. The symbol of Jerusalem indicates that given the human circumstance, there is no avoiding life in the city, and although God curses the city, God accepts the suffering of the curse and will not leave the city dweller without hope. The climax of the biblical account of the city lies in the event of Jesus Christ in whom the spirit of God's Word conquers the spiritual powers of the city, revealing the possibility of a final city, a New Jerusalem.

Until that time, however, the city is a place of alienation.[14] As a totality, it enslaves those who depend upon it and live within it. It is of the order of necessity, forcing its members to serve its interests. Yet, for the sheer continuance of human existence, it belongs as well to the order of preservation. Without it, life would be impossible. In sum, from a biblical perspective, the city is of a dialectical character. Though it destroys, it also sustains.

According to Ellul, the modern world, where the city is the civilization of technique, is a unique moment in the development of human life. It is an age of abandonment.[15] God is silent. We live in the dead of night. The crisis of our time is hopelessness. Even the church, in its mediocrity and conformity to the trends and interests of this world, is a sign of abandonment. It has forgotten its origins and purpose. We must live in the world of technique, but it is a place of futility. The sovereign God is absent.

In this circumstance, hope assumes a special significance. It is a challenge to the silence of God, a passion for the impossible. It is a claim against God's absence, an expression of a theology of promise. Hope, in effect, is the act of inciting God to intervene. As such it is, in itself, an apocalyptic act, for the very presence of hope in an age of hopelessness is a counterreality betokening the possibility of a new age.

[14] *The Ethics of Freedom* (Grand Rapids, Mich., Eerdmans, 1976), pp. 23–50. (French editions of various portions of this text, 1973 and 1975.)

[15] *Hope in the Time of Abandonment* (French edition, 1972; N.Y., Seabury, 1973).

Christian hope as a counterreality within the order of this world is, in Ellul's interpretation, the central theme of John's Book of Revelation, which in its entirety Ellul takes as presenting the basic structure of Christian theology.[16] In the first part of the book, the church is depicted as not simply a social phenomenon but a mediation of the lordship of Jesus Christ over history. In the second part, the four horsemen of the apocalypse represent the fundamental agencies of historical struggles: political power, economic interest, forces of death, and the Word of God.

The third part is the keystone of the whole, for it announces the incarnation of God in Jesus Christ as a new creation, a new beginning. In contrast, the two beasts portray the primacy of the political (the city), the totalitarian drive of social authority with its universal propagandistic intent. The spiritual power of the political is the inversion of the Incarnation because, measured against God's love, it is the power of chaos; it divides and separates. In Ellul's assessment, evil is not the violation of higher commands but the rupturing of relationships between person and person, and between humanity and God.

The fourth part of the Book of Revelation describes the character of God's judgment. Here Ellul draws a critical distinction: God judges all humanity but destroys none; God destroys human works (the city) as countercreations but does not condemn them as expressions of human action; God's damnation is reserved for the spiritual powers that alienate humanity from God and are thus forces of death. Ellul, in short, proposes a principle of universal salvation. Given the unconditional love of the sovereign God, it is theologically impossible that any person be damned.

Hence, in the final part of the book, the new creation is symbolized as a New Jerusalem, marking a radical change from original creation. Original creation was a garden, but Cain constructed something quite different—a city. Although God curses the city as an autonomous power, God will not annul history altogether. God has been present in the struggles of history, even when silent. In the new creation, God will take up the city but reverse its character and orientation. What was a

[16]*Apocalypse: The Book of Revelation* (French edition, 1975; N.Y., Seabury, 1977).

work of revolt will become a work of reconciliation. The judgment of God is both destructive and reconstructive. In the new city, however, neither church nor political authority will be needed because God's love will be perfectly and ceaselessly realized.

These five moments in the Book of Revelation, Ellul insists, are not to be understood as a temporal sequence. Rather, taken altogether, they manifest a "permanent depth" in every present time. The "last things" of the apocalypse signify the ultimate and conclusive purpose of the sovereign God, faith in whom supplies a perspective from which the full dialectical reality of existence can be discerned. On this basis, Ellul, following his mentor Karl Barth, makes a radical distinction between revelation and religion, reserving the latter term to refer to those beliefs and myths that are continuous with the social forces of this world.[17] Faith, apprehending the truth of revelation in Jesus Christ, reaches beyond those forces toward the Wholly Other and is thereby enabled to perceive the character of this world in its stark actuality. Theology, the articulation of the meaning of faith, is therefore distinct from sociology but provides for the possibility of a sociology that is honest and frank. Faith also, Ellul argues, promotes a certain style of life, a way of acting in this world.

CHRISTIAN STYLE OF LIFE: FREEDOM

Freedom is not one element in the Christian life. . . . It *is* the Christian life.[18]

Jacques Ellul once outlined a tripartite agenda for Christian ethics constructed on the theological virtues of Paul: hope (an ethics of freedom), faith (an ethics of holiness), and love (an ethics of relationship). The first of the three is foundational, for it constitutes the beginning and basic quality of Christian life. The other two, on which Ellul has yet to complete major studies, are related dialectically as separation from and renewed discovery of the world.

[17] *Living Faith: Belief and Doubt in a Perilous World* (French edition, 1980; San Francisco, Harper & Row, 1983).
[18] *The Ethics of Freedom*, p. 104.

Christians, living at the intersection between this world and the New Jerusalem, are called "to create a new style of life," a style at odds with the expectations of the earthly city.[19] They do not possess a set of higher laws for the governance of society since, as Ellul repeatedly contends, there are no specifically Christian principles for politics or economics. Nor should Christians pretend to direct the nations toward the Kingdom of God as the true purpose of their development because these two realities are incommensurable. Rather, they are to embody a new way of life. Thus Christian ethics to Ellul, although he does not use this language, is an ethics of character, not of duty (as conformity to a higher law) or of purpose (as movement toward a future goal).

As such, Christian ethics is indicative, not imperative; it is a description of the character of Christian life. Moreover, its point of departure is the individual, not the social structure; the possibility of creative renewal resides only in the individual. In addition, it is addressed to and is intended only for Christians; non-Christians cannot be expected to represent the hope revealed in Jesus Christ. Furthermore, the Christian style of life, located at the point of struggle between the powers of this world and the possibility of new creation, is "agonistic"; it includes responsibility for the needs of the present order but intends to represent the antithetical order of the Kingdom of God. Thus the position of Christians is at the same time dualistic and revolutionary. Though they belong to two cities, their ultimate fidelity is to the lordship of Jesus Christ.

As the foundational quality of the Christian style of life, freedom, according to Ellul, means possibility.[20] Freedom, which Ellul insists is open only to those who deliberately and explicitly confess the lordship of Jesus Christ, is two-sided. On its negative side, freedom is emancipation from the order of necessity, from enslavement to the powers of this world. Ellul distinguishes between institutional structures—political, economic, technological—that constitute the milieu of the common life and the power that holds persons enthralled to them as systematic totalities. Through the lordship of Jesus Christ,

[19] *The Presence of the Kingdom.*
[20] *The Ethics of Freedom,* pp. 133–219.

liberation from such power is made possible. One may continue to live in such institutions, but they no longer determine the character of one's life or dictate the necessities of one's conduct.

On its positive side, freedom subordinates all other considerations to the glory of God and the love of neighbor. Love, as the restoration of a lost communion between an I and a Thou, is addressed to the singularity of specific persons. It is, in its orientation to the needs of the neighbor, individualistic and particularistic since each person is unique and each occasion exhibits its own exigency.

Ellul, however, declares that, belonging to two cities, Christians are bound by a double morality.[21] On the one hand, for Christians, the good is nothing but the will of God. The good is not a cultural inheritance or a human creation. It is not a purpose that inheres in the evolution of history. It is not a set of imperatives deducible from the structure of reason or human nature. The good, which is what God wills, is apprehended only in a personal relationship with God. Since the will of the living God is new at each moment, the moral work of the Christian must be assumed afresh at each moment, expressed in what the Christian is and does. Ellul's doctrine of God's sovereignty drives him toward a radical ethical situationalism and leads him to reject all efforts to identify Christianity with any political and moral causes, either conservative or socialist.

On the other hand, human life is lived always in historical context, in the matrix of moralities that are artificially constructed and temporal, even if immemorial. Such moralities are not expendable. Whatever their character, they articulate the perceptions and beliefs, expectations and hopes, judgments and felt needs of ordinary life. Without a moral universe of some kind, human life is impossible. To repudiate such moralities is to reject not only the conditions of historical existence but also human life itself. Moralities belong to the order of preservation and are useful in sustaining life even if that life is captured by the powers of this world. Although living ultimately in accordance with a higher good, Christians must, out of love of neighbor, live

[21] *To Will and To Do: An Ethical Research for Christians* (French edition, 1964; Philadelphia, Pilgrim Press, 1969), pp. 73–110.

in and cooperate with the moralities of social life while at the same time remaining in constant tension with them. That is their agony.

Ellul specifies, in very broad terms, several dimensions of Christian presence in the world.[22] First, Christians, through deep study of basic structural features of social life (e.g., technology) and the inner psychic life of a culture (e.g., a sense of hopelessness), should exercise a prophetic ministry after the manner of a Jonah in forewarning a people of its probable future. Second, Christians, engaged in sundry social movements and organizations, should fulfill a ministry of reconciliation through defusing the explosiveness of issues and mediating among conflicting parties. ("One of the great functions of Christians in the political world is to calm down debate.") Third, Christians inherit a ministry of desacralization. They have a "stern duty" to profane the sacralities of ordinary social existence (e.g., state and money) and explode the myths that justify them (e.g., liberalism and socialism). Fourth, against the totalities of technology, nation-state, and economy, Christians have a ministry of "opening up the world," of demonstrating through disposition and deposition that there are alternatives to the presumed necessities of social order and that there is more to life than food and raiment, than technical advance and national security.

Moreover, Christians, out of their faith in the Wholly Other, should introduce into the political world two principles of a democratic character (which is not to be confused with existing democratic regimes): a principle of open communication and a principle of social resistance.[23] The former principle requires a critique of political mythologies, the promotion of reason (as distinct from technical rationality) in political discourse, and an attitude of respect for political adversaries and minority judgments. The latter principle requires the re-creation of a substantial private sphere into which the state may not intervene and the formation of multiple "centers of conflict and poles of tension" throughout the social order. Thus Ellul applauds the emergence of protest movements outside routine political channels as a means of forming zones of free life and of increasing

[22] *False Presence of the Kingdom*, pp. 176–211.
[23] *The Political Illusion*, pp. 199–240.

tension within an otherwise highly technologized social system.[24] Christians, he concludes, should be "troublemakers, creators of uncertainty, agents of a dimension incompatible with society."

On the issue of violence, in particular, historical moralities and Christian morality are irreconcilable.[25] This is a point of "Christian radicalism," a point where Christianity must be adopted in pristine form without accommodation. Unfortunately, Ellul nowhere defines exactly what violence means or how it is differentiable from other kinds of power. He is clear in his criticism of two forms of violence: the overt use of violent methods for revolutionary purposes and the covert presence of violence in established institutions.

In the former case, Ellul, directing his criticism against Christian movements encouraging revolutionary violence in the Third World, asserts that "the singling out of the poor" is an authentic Christian theme, that a revolutionary transformation of the social order is an appropriate cause, and that socialism will likely prove to be a more adequate economic system than capitalism. But identifying socialism as specifically Christian is erroneous. It is in strict contravention of Christian morality to employ violence in any cause. While the use of violence may be understandable as an expression of frustration or despair, Christians may never themselves employ violence as a means of action. Moreover, no distinction between just and unjust kinds of violence or between violence that liberates and violence that enslaves is sensible, for all violence is the same.

In the latter case, Ellul argues that violence, though often masked, is intrinsic to the order of necessity. All states are founded on and subsist by violence; it is impossible, Ellul observes, to be a Christian and an effective politician. Economic relations, even those of so-called free enterprise, are violent. Racism and class domination are forms of violence. Violence is, in effect, the general rule of social institutions.

The alternative is the "violence of love," the sacrificial employment of one's energies in constructing and conducting

[24] *In Season Out of Season*, pp. 129–38, though compare *The Ethics of Freedom*, pp. 398–435.

[25] *Violence: Reflections from a Christian Perspective* (French edition, 1972; N.Y., Seabury, 1969).

nonviolent methods of social change on behalf of the truly poor, particularly the forgotten poor of the world. Not only may Christians never condone or cooperate with forces of violence, but they are, Ellul contends, to blame whenever violence occurs, for that signifies a failure of their prophetic vocation.

The Christian style of life is therefore representative of the dialectical relationship of God to the world. Living in and suffering with the world, Christians are meant to embody the possibility of a new creation that transcends the world. The substance of freedom is the presentation of hope in the context of an age of hopelessness.

Jacques Ellul's works, taken as a whole, constitute an impressive vision of the meaning of life, its conditions and possibilities. Serious questions may be raised about the theoretical ambiguities of his dialectical method, the technocentric totalism of his sociology, the Christocentric exclusivism of his theology, and the theocentric situationalism of his ethics. But he must be honored for the single-minded devotion of his life and thought to the two-sided cause of Christian realism and Christian revolution. While Ellul is not a systematic theologian, he is a prophet to the modern age.

Bibliography

Jacques Ellul, *The Ethics of Freedom*, Grand Rapids, Mich., Eerdmans, 1976.

Darrell J. Fasching, *The Thought of Jacques Ellul: A Systematic Exposition*, N.Y. and Toronto, Edwin Mellen Press, 1981.

CARL F. H. HENRY

Gabriel Fackre

If the twentieth century "evangelical renaissance"[1] in North America has produced a Michelangelo, that exemplar is surely Carl Henry. Premier theologian, key figure in its formative institutions, chief public interpreter of its ways and critic of its wanderings, this renaissance man has left his mark on an epoch. Yet there is no Sistine Chapel or public piazza on the American scene where all can view these works of genius. Religious pluralism and parochialism are such that a Henry can write an encyclopedic six-volume work on epistemology that will go unreviewed in major journals of academia, or he can lecture across the continent and around the world but be known only on the circuit of evangelical para-institutions. However, durability and impact count, especially in a pragmatic culture. As evangelical presence is now widely felt through American society and its churches, its intellectual leaders are getting a hearing. In this company Henry has no peer.

Carl Ferdinand Howard Henry was born of immigrant parents, Karl F. and Johanna (Vaethroeder), in New York City, January 22, 1913, and raised on Long Island in Central Islip, New York. After baptism and confirmation in an Episcopal congregation to which religiously indifferent parents sent their children, Henry became a teenage church dropout. Equipped with some sports writing skills learned in high school, he took a job upon graduation as a reporter for the *Islip Press,* moving later to an editorship at the *Smithtown Star* and from there to the *Port Jefferson Town Echo,* as well as serving as a regional reporter for the *New York Tribune.*

On June 10, 1933, a three-hour conversation with a friend eventuated in a personal experience of conversion and evangelical commitment and in his subsequent immersion and

---

[1] As identified by Donald Bloesch in his book *The Evangelical Renaissance* (Grand Rapids, Mich., Eerdmans, 1973).

membership in a Baptist congregation on Long Island. This new stance of faith had vocational implications. As Henry considered how best he could serve his Lord, he entered Wheaton College in Illinois, the "evangelical Harvard," in 1935, receiving both his A.B. and M.A. from that institution. Declining an offer to take an influential post at the Moody Bible Institute in public relations, he chose instead to go on to Northern Baptist Seminary in Chicago. He was ordained in 1941 and served as student pastor in the Humboldt Park Baptist Church, and for a short time as interim pastor at First Baptist Church of Elmhurst, but his academic gifts were taking him toward another form of ministry. Completing doctoral work at Northern Baptist Seminary (Th.D.), he was invited to teach philosophy and religion at his alma mater, where he eventually became a full professor. His agile and disciplined mind set high standards for the students, who esteemed him as a person of warmth and brillance, and indeed a "terror" in his examination expectations.[2] During this period Henry was active as one of the organizers of the National Association of Evangelicals in 1943, writing for its organ, *United Evangelical Action,* and was instrumental in creating its Commission on Social Ethics. In 1940, while in Chicago, Henry married Helga Bender, whom he had met at Wheaton; from their lifelong felicitous union came two children, Paul Brentwood and Carol Jennifer.

In these early years of academic preparation and teaching, Henry found time to write *A Doorway to Heaven* (1941) and *Successful Church Publicity* (1942). A major work was forthcoming in 1947, *The Uneasy Conscience of Modern Fundamentalism.* In this seventy-five-page tract—"the manifesto of neo-evangelicalism," according to Dirk Jellema—Henry criticizes the separatist tendencies of rigid orthodoxies, on the one hand, and their lack of social ethics, on the other.

In 1947 Henry was invited to serve on the first faculty of the newly founded Fuller Theological Seminary in Pasadena, California, created to provide evangelical congregations with a learned ministry. Having previously declined a seminary

[2] When teacher evaluation forms were introduced at Eastern Baptist Theological Seminary, Henry received the highest rating as "the best prepared and most stimulating teacher." Letter from Thorwald W. Bender, February 2, 1984.

presidency and deanship, he was drawn to Fuller because of its special academic goals and promise. He began his work there not only as a professor of philosophy and theology but also served, for the first year of the institution's existence, as acting dean. The intellectual stimulation of colleagues and students at Fuller, and the opportunities for research and writing, made these years happy ones. During that time a prolific writing career developed, giving voice to the burgeoning evangelical movement. In rapid succession a series of doctrinal works came from his pen, including *Remaking the Modern Mind* (1948), *Giving a Reason for Our Hope* (1949), *The Protestant Dilemma* (1949), *Notes on the Doctrine of God* (1949), *Fifty Years of Protestant Theology* (1950), *The Drift of Western Thought* (1951), and *Glimpses of a Sacred Land* (1953). His published dissertation (Ph.D., Boston University, 1949), entitled *Personal Idealism and Strong's Theology* (1951), marked him as a constructive critic of Augustus Hopkins Strong, the most influential theologian in the American Baptist Convention. In 1957 a major book in a field in which he began to specialize—ethics—was published, *Christian Personal Ethics,* as well as his *Evangelical Responsibility in Contemporary Theology.* In these varied works in theology, philosophy, and ethics, Henry's concern for the rational articulation and defense of faith became increasingly manifest.

Henry had captured the attention of key evangelical figures, and in 1955 and 1956, when a new journal was in process of formation by Billy Graham and H. Nelson Bell, he was asked as an architect of evangelical theology to give *Christianity Today* editorial leadership. Accepting the invitation, he took a leave from Fuller (one extended by faculty and administration for three succeeding years), making a permanent commitment to the enterprise in 1959. During his twelve-year tenure as editor-in-chief, Henry—and the staff he gathered around him—established *Christianity Today* as the most influential organ of American evangelicalism, with a paid circulation of 170,000. In fact, through the writers Henry assembled and the magazine's new coverage and commentary, a "new evangelicalism" emerged, one that expressed unswerving commitment to evangelical distinctives yet sought to show their relevance to contemporary social issues and to demonstrate the intellectual viability of evangelical faith. In his editorial leadership Henry aimed to reduce the partisanships that historically divided evangelicals; he encouraged movement on a common front. For example, his recommendation for an evangelism effort in the United States subsequently issued in the national endeavor called "Key 73." This ecumenical evangelicalism took form in the World Congress on Evangelism in 1966 in Berlin; it was sponsored by *Christianity Today* and chaired by Henry, with Billy Graham as honorary chairman. Another expression of the concern for evangelical collegiality was a series of symposia gathered and edited by Henry, including *Contemporary Evangelical Thought* (1957), *Revelation and the Bible* (1959), *The Biblical Expositor* (three volumes; 1960), *Basic Christian Doctrines* (1962), *Christian Faith and Modern Theology* (1964), *Jesus of Nazareth: Saviour and Lord* (1966), and *Fundamentals of the Faith* (1969).

In 1968 Henry acceded to the wishes of a group in the executive committee of *Christianity Today*'s board of directors to step down as editor, that group seeking tighter control of the contents and stance of the magazine. Henry departed for a period to Cambridge, England, to begin his massive work on the doctrine of God. He returned to become professor-at-large at Eastern Baptist Theological Seminary in Philadelphia until 1974, when he began devoting most of his time to writing and lecturing. In 1968 he also helped organize the Institute for Advanced Christian Studies, a mobile think tank of evangelical scholars seeking to relate Christian faith to the intellectual disciplines. The group launched in 1982 a major venture with the William B. Eerdmans Publishing Company: a series of volumes by distinguished philosophers, historians, scientists, and others on the relation of rational faith to modernity.

In 1974 Henry became a lecturer for World Vision, Inc., an evangelical social service agency, and thus an itinerant who, as he expressed it himself,

> flew some 2 million miles by air, lecturing, preaching and teaching, wearing a suit bought in Majorca, a beret from Spain, shoes resoled in Korea, carrying a Bible rebound in the Philippines, and meeting people everywhere who scarcely suspect what God can do for the

individual whose mind and heart have been stretched by the good news of the Gospel.

Henry has become a kind of world evangelist—"the thinking man's Billy Graham," as he is sometimes called.

Although at home most of all in the world of words and books, Henry has had a rich history of human relationships—family, friends, colleagues and, yes, enemies, too. Helga, his "good and godly" spouse, has been at his side in all his ventures, a companion of mind and heart, as have been his two children, who continue the family's evangelical commitments.[3] Gordon Clark, philosopher and theologian, is Henry's chief intellectual mentor both in the thirst for ideas and in the specifics of the history of philosophy. Yet Edgar Brightman, a personalist philosopher of a very different theological perspective with whom he did doctoral studies at Boston University, has left an impression on him because of his intellectual rigor and fairness of spirit. Cornelius Van Til and Edward Carnell, the latter a colleague at Fuller, were reinforcing influences in their evangelical orthodoxy, "presuppositionalist" on the one hand and apologeticist on the other. W. Harry Jellema, former Indiana University teacher, also shaped his thinking. Billy Graham, who visited him at Pasadena to urge him to become editor of *Christianity Today*, has been a close friend and co-worker. So too has been Everett Harrison, former professor of New Testament at Fuller. Laity in the evangelical movement have meant much to Henry, including lifelong friendships with A. Lewis Shingler of Pasadena; Cleo Shook, formerly of the U.S. AID program; and Richard Ostling, religion editor of *Time*, who served as *Christianity Today*'s news editor during a portion of Henry's tenure. Leadership in the American Theological Society, including its presidency in 1981, and movement among "the establishment" have also brought friends in those circles.

Theological combat as well as parochialism within both the liberal and evangelical communities have left their mark on Henry's life. Often treated as an outsider in denominational and ecumenical circles, Henry was given token time on assembly

[3] His son, Paul Henry, has written *Politics for Evangelicals* (Philadelphia, Judson, 1974).

agendas or accorded a marginal relationship at best to the working life of the institutions of "mainline Christianity." His awkward departure from the editorship of *Christianity Today,* including the removal of his column, "Footnotes," and the dropping of his name from the masthead during a succeeding editorship, has left wounds. While Henry is a polemicist for his point of view, he is also a gentle man and does not respond in kind to personal affront. More and more his generosity of spirit and ecumenical evangelicalism are ready to honor "each soldier where he fights well."[4] Thus the ardor and range of his thought, as well as his human decency, have over time won the respect of friend and foe, securing for him a front-rank place in world evangelicalism and American Christianity; he is a "maker of the modern theological mind."[5]

REVELATION AND
AUTHORITY

In his various roles as teacher, writer, editor, initiator, and organizer, Henry manifests an arrowlike purpose: the rational articulation and defense of Christian faith.[6] As dogmatic theologian, he seeks to render intelligible the fundamentals of the Gospel in the face of intellectual confusions within Christian theology, and as apologetic theologian, he aims to demonstrate its intellectual superiority over competing world views.[7] Henry is a communicator who sees his task as clarifying the identity of the Christian religion while at the same time manifesting its profundity in the contest with current alternatives. As such, his theological work is marked by frequent juxtapositions between core belief and what he holds to be distortions of it, or challenges to it. We will pay attention, therefore, to these competing views,

---

[4] Letter to the writer, February 8, 1984.

[5] See Bob E. Patterson's excellent study, *Carl F. H. Henry,* in the series *Makers of the Modern Theological Mind* (Waco, Tex., Word, 1983).

[6] Longtime friend Everett Harrison remarks that one of Henry's favorite phrases is "to strike a blow for the faith." Letter to the writer, February 19, 1984.

[7] The line between dogmatics and apologetics is never sharp for Henry since clarifying confusions within has to do with the invasion of alien themes from without.

most of which are to the left of Henry, but some are on the right.[8]
In these exchanges, the contours of his own position are
sharpened.

As a newspaperman, Henry knew that information gathering
required reliable sources, and in his subsequent work of
theological communication, soundness at the source of disclosure became of decisive importance. Very early he made the
point that the questions of authority and revelation are the
commanding theological issues of the time.[9] His six-volume *God,
Revelation and Authority* shows an investment of energy
commensurate with this lifelong conviction; indeed, "in every
church epoch it is the fate of the Bible that decides the fate of
Christianity."[10] Thus the reliability of where we go to find out
what is ultimately so is basic for interpreting faith. To this subject
of the *authority* of Scripture, and its underlying premise of divine
revelation, we now turn, giving attention to its critical themes:
inspiration, inerrancy, illumination, and their relation to *reason.*

The Authority of Scripture

For the believer, God is the "fontal authority" (P. T. Forsyth),
but the flow from that fountain is the authority issue in theology,
the question of palpable "mediate" authority (I; IV). That access
point for Henry is the Scripture of the Old and New Testaments.
Therein God has disclosed the divine purpose; in this Word the
rational Logos has unveiled the divine being and doing. What
information God wants us to have is given in the original (inerrant)

[8] As modernity's challenge is the historical context in which Henry does his
work, the left gets much of the criticism. But his influential early volume, *The
Uneasy Conscience of Fundamentalism* (Grand Rapids, Mich., Eerdmans, 1947),
is evangelical self-criticism regarding the lack of social relevance. Evangelicalism
and fundamentalism were synonymous for him at this stage—he pled for a
"progressive fundamentalism"—but the latter term is used in a more critical
sense in *Evangelical Responsibility in Contemporary Theology* (Grand Rapids,
Mich., Eerdmans, 1957) where it is associated with a narrow-spirited polemicism.

[9] At mid-century he asserted that "the pivot . . . is the question of revelation
. . . and with it an adequate objective authority." *The Protestant Dilemma*
(Grand Rapids, Mich., Eerdmans, 1949), pp. 39,56.

[10] Carl Henry, *God, Revelation and Authority,* IV (Waco, Tex., Word, 1979),
p. 380, hereafter cited as GRA. In some instances, only the volume number(s)
will be included in the text and enclosed in parentheses. Vol. I and II were
published in 1976, Vol. III in 1979, Vol. V in 1982, and Vol. VI in 1983.

writings as those are conveyed to us in the doctrinally sound (infallible) copies and reliable translations to which we have access (IV). Thus the Bible's authority rests on God's revelatory action, deeds done and meanings conveyed in the trustworthy propositions of the prophetic-apostolic testimony (IV).

Why do we need this "special revelation"? The answer is that reason in revolt obscures the communication between God and human beings that marks the origins of history in paradise, and even continues in the sullied but surviving image of God in us (II; IV; V). This latter "general revelation" of God in nature and history, perceived by the real but dimmed light of reason and conscience, does render us accountable for our disobedience and makes us open to something more but does not give us saving knowledge. Moreover, it does not make a "natural theology" possible (I; II; III; IV; VI). The light that comes to dispel the darkness shines in the incarnate Word and is transmitted to us in the "epistemic Word," the Scripture (IV). As the deposit of God's revealed truths, the Bible has unrivaled authority.

The authority of Scripture is put in question by naturalisms, ancient and modern, which turn to human experience and its wisdom to legitimate their world views. In the modern setting the heirs of the Renaissance and Enlightenment dominate Western culture with their antisupernaturalist ontology and humanist value systems.[11] That regency is also challenged by forms of Christian theology that allow the world's agenda to compromise biblical authority with philosophical, moral, social, economic, aesthetic, affective, and spiritual experiences, or constructs, dictating the meaning of theological assertions (IV).

The Inspiration of Scripture

The authority of Scripture is secured by the "plenary verbal inspiration" of the originals (or "autographs"). This "God-breathed" quality is testified to in its own words: "All scripture is

---

[11] From early, middle, through later writings, Henry challenges "naturalism." See comments in *The Uneasy Conscience of Fundamentalism*, p. 70 and *passim; The Remaking of the Modern Mind* (Grand Rapids, Mich., Eerdmans, 1946), pp. 264ff.; *The Protestant Dilemma*, pp. 23ff.; through editorials in *Christianity Today* to the essay in *This World*, no. 7 (Winter, 1984), pp. 95–105. See also GRA, I, pp. 17–30, 135–51; IV, pp. 10ff.

inspired by God . . ." (II Tim. 3:16).[12] The Holy Spirit has worked in and through the biblical authors in such a manner that their words are guided ("breathed-out") to their proper end (IV). That does not mean the "dictation" of a heavenly text to earthly amanuenses, a view associated more with the Koran or Book of Mormon (IV). Biblical inspiration honors the particularity of human agency, which is evident from the different vocabulary ranges, styles, and cultural idioms of the authors, as well as their manifest struggle and personal journey (IV; VI). Inspiration means the ever-present concursive operation of the Holy Spirit in the writing process and the superintendence of the same, so that what is produced is always what God intends and as such is errorless. To the latter point we shall return, but first one very important feature of the "how" of revelation must be identified. Carl Henry is a determined defender of propositional revelation—"revealed shareable propositional truths" (I; III).

Propositions are sentences to which the responses yes or no are appropriate. *Webster's New Collegiate Dictionary* describes them as "expression(s) in language or signs of something that can be believed, doubted, or denied, or is either true or false"(2a). A theological proposition makes claims about certain subjects: who God is; what God has done, is doing, and will do; who we are; what we are to do; and what we shall be. In Henry's view, these assertions cannot be construed as reliable unless they are "univocal," in contrast with "equivocal" (contradictory) or "analogical" (saying what they are like rather than what they are), statements.[13] A long-standing tradition in philosophy and theology, influenced by Kant, has been formative of current nonevangelical faith and thought, one which Henry believes casts epistemological doubt on all statements made in Scripture and derivative doctrinal reflection. Of particular concern to him are those commendable efforts at biblical retrieval that undercut their possible contribution by ambiguity about their cognitive weight. Here Karl Barth and neo-orthodoxy in general come under heavy criticism. The interpretation of Scripture as

[12] GRA, IV, pp. 129–61 for exposition and related texts.
[13] On the unremitting attack on analogy and the defense of univocal propositions, see GRA, II, pp. 53–54; III, pp. 362–66; IV, pp. 117–21; V, pp. 86–88, 261–62, 355–356.

"witness" to revelation rather than revelation itself, or revelation as an "event" rather than the communication of revealed truths, he believes, loses God's self-disclosure in the mists of human subjectivity. Henry seeks to preserve the rationality of the Bible, which in this case means the revelatory deliverance of knowledge about God in intelligible sentences.[14]

The propositional status of revelation must also be asserted against the widespread contemporary assumption of cultural relativity, which claims that biblical statements are so wed to their historical context that abiding transcultural truth is not possible. On the one hand, it declares that the reader is so rooted in the culture of another day that what is said in Scripture cannot even be understood today, much less be relevant to another time with its own contextual issues and sensibilities. Henry writes, "No flashpoint of contemporary religious dialogue bears more critically than this upon the significance of the Christian faith."[15] While acknowledging the "culture-relatedness" of biblical writers in the sense that they borrow the idiom of their time to make their point, Henry believes that the revelatory assertions made in Scripture have a fixed transcultural meaning extractable by grammatical-historical analysis. The biblical author was not so bound by the premises of that day, nor is the believer by those of this one, that truth-bearing propositions cannot be carried over time and space from source to receiver, giving trustworthy, unchanging, intelligible information, "abiding instruction" (I; III; IV; V).

Plenary verbal inspiration is an understanding of the divine self-disclosure as the very speaking of God, the revelation of truth in "conceptual-verbal" form (III). The Bible is the epistemic Word even as Jesus Christ is the incarnate Word, and Christianity is a book religion (III; IV). Yet its incarnational

[14] Henry's engagement with the thought of Barth is intensive and extensive. Acknowledging that Barth does speak of the cognitive weight of biblical assertions, Henry believes that the location of that truth claim by him in the moment of revelatory encounter and the distinction of Barth's theology between the Word and the biblical words undercut their propositional status and thus the truth claim of Christian faith. See the following places where his struggle with Barth on this issue goes on: GRA, I, pp. 203–12; II, pp. 40–41, 143–47, 158–62; III, pp. 224–29; IV, pp. 148–61, 174–92, 196–200, 257–71, 298–303; V, pp. 39, 53, 97, 299, 366–70.

[15] GRA, V, p. 398.

center and historical character cannot be forgotten, since God "shows" as well as "speaks." While the divine speech interprets the divine deeds, the heart of the inscripturated truth is a record of God's activity, a narrative that runs from creation to consummation with its turning point in the life, death, resurrection, and ascension of Jesus Christ.[16] In particular, Henry returns time and again to the words and work of Christ and thus places a strong Christological norm at the center of his authority structure (II; III). However, this structure is not one in which an incarnate Word is juxtaposed to the written Word, but one in which the latter comes to plenitude and clarity of meaning in the former (III; IV).

While Henry shares with twentieth-century salvation history theologians this attention to the deeds of God and to the Christological center, he takes pains to distinguish his view from those who would (1) reduce the Bible to the recounting of divine deeds, (2) polarize Jesus Christ with scriptural teaching considered less worthy, (3) understand the prophetic and apostolic interpretation of the deeds of God as only human formulations secondary in significance to the deeds, (4) isolate some deeds and interpretation as a trustworthy core within an errant context, or (5) argue for a "canon within the canon" (II; III; IV). Revelation is the whole cloth of the Bible, not a red thread within it, albeit set forth progressively in the historical flow of the Bible (II; III).

The Inerrancy of Scripture

Implicit in claims to biblical authority, and a logical inference from verbal inspiration, is the teaching of biblical inerrancy. Can God lie or the Spirit inspire error? Can the Bible be authoritative as an inspired literary deposit if it appears to be a broken and erroneous testimony? In addition to these considerations, the text itself witnesses, Henry declares, to Christ's own assurance of the reliability of the Hebrew Bible, as he quotes it with confidence (II; IV; V). Further, the spirit and form of the "thus saith the Lord" declarations that pervade Scripture argue for its errorlessness. Alternative views of "limited," or "partial,"

[16] From time to time Henry sets out simply and forcefully the highlights of the Christian narrative. See especially GRA, IV, pp. 468–69; also I, p. 34; V, pp. 15–16, 54.

inerrancy are either contradictory or an invitation to a slippery slope the end of which is the rejection of biblical authority (IV). Thus by biblical warrant and rational argument, inerrancy is seen to be integral to the meaning of authority.

What is inerrancy? This teaching asserts that the autographs are safeguarded from error in whatever they teach as doctrine—not only in theological and moral matters but also in scientific, historical, and geographical ones. As noted earlier, this does not mean the dictation of a text but the superintendence of it with allowances for authorial individuality and historical context. With the latter is included a respect for literary genre, and thus the refusal to impose standards of modern historiography on poetic license or oriental hyperbole, latitude in the traditions of citation (as is shown in the quotations of the Old Testament in the New), the employment of metaphor (the "sun rising" was not a scientific statement then nor is one now), the ways of ancient numerology (divergent estimates reflecting the practice of generalization), and so on (IV). When logical or factual contradictions appear to persist, what then? Some can be attributed to transmission frailties, as noted regularly by ancient exegetes who presupposed errorless text. Other challenges at this level which assume the finality of empirical data that seem to contradict the biblical chronicle are methodologically ambiguous, since all empirical tests must be tentative (I; III; IV). Still other problems require patience, with the assumption that the biblical record will be validated at some future time, as newer archaeological discoveries are tending to corroborate (IV).

In these matters, the infallibility of received copies must be distinguished from the inerrancy of inaccessible autographs. In the former case, the errorless potency of the original persists even in semantic details and the power of Providence continues to secure them. Approved copies, therefore, are not error-prone, nor is their doctrinal and moral teaching in doubt. Since truth is carried not by isolated words but by propositions or sentences, the doctrinal reliability of the copies can be asserted even with the linguistic and factual inaccuracies that are discernible along the edges of the documents (IV).

Whenever inerrancy is questioned, the Bible's authority is either undercut or in serious jeopardy, as is the case with such views as the following: (1) Neo-Protestant views assert the authority of the Bible, but either (a) deny its cognitive status by holding Scripture to be the occasion for encounter or existential decision, or to be only functionally authoritative through its "performative" language; (b) construe Scripture as a witness to events rather than a deposit of trustworthy propositions; (c) treat the Bible as a compendium of ideas or images; (d) consider the Bible to be vast scriptural authority in a "canon within a canon"—Jesus Christ, or Jesus recovered by historical scholarship, or a motif such as justification, covenant, liberation, etc.; or (e) read a sociological theory, philosophical system, or political program into the Scriptures (I; IV; V). (2) Traditional Roman Catholic views declare for inerrancy but assert the magisterium to be the key to its meaning (IV). (3) Neo-Catholic views seek to relate the magisterium to contemporary experience and in that fusion look for a canon within a canon (IV). (4) Evangelical views (a) claim limited inerrancy for doctrines and morals or "soteric knowledge" but withhold confidence in matters of science and history; (b) construe the Bible essentially as a vehicle of conversion; or (c) allow claims to the present work of the Spirit in charismatic sensibility to exercise authority over the inspired text (III; IV).

In the case of evangelicals whose limited inerrancy views are "unstable" and invite deterioration of the Bible's authority, Henry believes that efforts at rational persuasion are more in order than recrimination, crusades, and accusations of apostasy (IV). Further, "unbalanced preoccupation with inerrancy" is a costly evangelical diversion. To Henry, "the mark of New Testament authenticity is first and foremost proclamation of the crucified and risen Jesus as the indispensable and irreplaceable heart of the Christian message."[17]

Related to the issue of inerrancy is the function of biblical scholarship. Henry's exegetical emphasis is on historical-grammatical work with texts, seeking the intended common-sense meaning, with obscure texts illumined by clear ones (the "analogy of faith"), and assuming the unity of Scripture, providing the horizon that renders the Bible its own best

[17] GRA, IV, p. 365.

interpreter (II; IV). In contrast to those who indict the historical-critical method as such, Henry affirms its limited usefulness (Jonah could be a theological tale, not an empirical narrative, although arguments for either are not conclusive), as long as the antisupernaturalist premises that have often controlled such inquiry are detached from it. Henry is firmly committed to textual criticism since proximity to the autographs, and thus the distinction of superior from inferior texts, is a desideratum (IV).

The Illumination of Scripture

Although Scripture can be understood by individuals who use the rational faculty available to them by virtue of the *imago Dei*, only in persons moved by the fiducial work of the Holy Spirit does the Word reach its proper end of changing heart and mind. The Spirit's gift of "illumination" is a regeneration that sets the soul on fire at the beginning of the journey of faith. The Spirit brings a new birth that takes the believer into a framework of faith which affects how the Bible is read by those who espouse inerrancy. This new disposition carries with it the assumption, the "epistemic axiom," that Scripture will tell the truth and that the use of reason will confirm it (II). The Holy Spirit guides the believer in the reading of Scripture to its truth and enlivens its truth, as well as convicts and converts (II; IV). However, faith so illumined must be rational. Epistemologically this is a "moderate presuppositionalism," one that returns us full circle to the authority of Scripture, established as it is for Henry in a believer by the work of the Spirit, not by reason. Yet reason plays a very important role in Henry's theology. To that point we now turn.

Reason

For Carl Henry reason is grounded in the very being of God, the eternal Logos. Therefore, he is deeply concerned about the anti-intellectual currents of the times (III; V). His view of human nature holds that the Fall has not so impaired the image of God in us that reason is disqualified in the discernment of ultimate truth.[18] Thus we must "be prepared to make a defense . . . for the hope" that is in us (I Pet. 3:15). While the believer comes to faith by regeneration (the new birth by the work of the Spirit), those converted are called to give reasons for faith and to assess and challenge the rationality of alternative views. Reason, as the mind's grapple with evidence, the use of ordered thought and obedience to the laws of logic, expresses itself in Christian apologetics. Apologetics seeks to show, on the one hand, that attacks on Christian faith are unpersuasive and alternatives to Christian belief are contradictory or inadequate, and on the other, that Christian faith is a coherent and consistent view (I). Indeed, reason is a test of truth, since the claims of Christian faith must be subject themselves to the laws of logic (I; IV). Human beings in the ordinary course of living, as well as in the practice of intellectual disciplines, cannot function without rational norms and attention to evidence (I; III; IV). Henry's dialogue with alternative views comes down time and again to these tests: Is this position intellectually self-consistent? Does it at any point contradict itself?

An example of his employment of logic in disputation is his critique of theological relativism. How can an ideological relativist claim with a straight face the absolute truth of an assertion that all propositions are culture-relative? The premise of the argument denies its own exposition, or it exempts itself from its thesis and thus undercuts it (IV). A similar charge is made by Henry against logical positivists who grant validity only to sentences with empirical warrants and thereby render nonsensical their own nonempirical premise (I; V). Thus, Henry seeks to reduce to logical absurdity various opposing world views. Correspondingly, he challenges his critics to find inconsistency in his own understanding of Christian faith. Hence "logical consistency is a negative test and coherence a subordinate test" for religious truths.[19]

The concern for reason is reflected also in Henry's philosophical interest and competence. He believes faith has its own ontology, one that must be in conversation with and critical of nonrevelational world views. The influence of Gordon Clark

[18] Indeed, "the Fall conditions man's will more pervasively than his reason." GRA, I, p. 226.
[19] GRA, I, p. 232.

and Edgar Brightman is apparent here, as is a philosophical commitment that continues through his membership in the American Philosophical Association (I).

In all these matters, a discursive interpretation of Christian faith is to the fore, but it would be wrong to identify Henry simply as a "rationalist." He contests evangelical positions that seek to validate Christian faith in toto by reason, and he also argues with others who think we can come to faith by reason. These limitations do not, of course, deny that the Holy Spirit uses reason as an instrument of persuasion. Henry believes that theology is developed out of a fundamental framework of faith, a "revelational axiom" into which one is brought by an act of faith through the power of the Holy Spirit (I; II). Reason functions as partner to that in clearing the ground of presumedly rational objections to faith and after that in showing the logical warrants for faith.

GOD AND CHRISTIAN FAITH

Henry's massive volumes on revelation and authority are so designed that the content of, as well as the method of, discerning truth is set forth. Under the word *God* in the title is to be found the outline of a full-scale dogmatics. Drawing on Henry's earlier writing as well as the subject material in his magnum opus, we identify briefly some of those doctrinal propositions.

The doctrine of God is to the foreground as the logical companion of the doctrine of revelation—the God who "stands" is the One who "speaks" and "shows." And the deeds of that same God—as the One who "stoops" and "stays"—constitute the material for the traditional doctrines of creation, humanity, Christ, church, salvation, Providence, and the last things.

In a wide-ranging debate with philosophical and theological alternatives, classical and contemporary (such as Platonism, Aristotelianism, Scholasticism, positivism, personalism, existentialism, process thought), Henry argues the case for "evangelical theism" (V; VI). Unabashedly defending supernaturalism, Henry declares God to be the living personal Spirit of the Bible, infinite, eternal, immutable, omniscient, omnipresent, omnipotent, foreordaining (election/divine decrees) as well as foreknowing, yet not in violation of human freedom (V; VI). Critical of liberal and neo-orthodox theologians who focus too exclusively on the divine love, Henry stresses the parity of divine righteousness and benevolence, with a concern that the accountability of the sinner before the holiness of God not be lost from view (VI). The One with these attributes and perfections is the triune God, whose three persons, economic and immanent, express tripersonality in unipersonality. The fact that only God knows the depths of the divine being, and our own formulations do not "exhaustively" define that ultimate reality, does not preclude the knowability of God and the reliability of biblical teaching about the One Who Is (V).

Following the acts in the biblical drama, Henry turns to the doctrine of creation, developing it against the background of the revived creationist-evolutionist controversy of the 1980's. He expounds the well-known orthodox themes on the goodness but not the divinity of finite being (creation out of nothing), human nature as uniquely made in the image of God, with special attention to our rational and spiritual capacities and the creation of angels as "messengers of God." Henry examines evolutionist and young-earth scenarios of the world's origin and argues that the Genesis account does deal with the "how" as well as the "what" and "why," interpreting the order of the days and the acts of God at each level to be theologically significant—although not so the length of the days, therefore leaving room for the results of careful geological research. In the same vein, he asserts the reality of a paradise before the Fall and the historicity of the Fall—that of Adam and Eve and Satan and the demonic legions—although he recognizes that the literary genre is to be honored for what it is in the details, rather than those details being forced into the doctrine (VI).

Henry follows classical theology in the doctrine of the person of Christ, holding to Christ's deity, humanity, and unity. Continuing the current stress of Protestant orthodoxy on the virgin birth, the miracles of Christ, and the bodily resurrection, he argues against a view of natural law as a closed system. On the work of Christ, he continues the evangelical accent on Calvary and finds a central place for the penal substitutionary view of the Atonement, yet not to the exclusion of the Galilean Christ whose teaching figures prominently in his epistemology and ethics (II;

III; VI). Here too is a strong emphasis on the uniqueness of Christ in the face of modern pluralism and its tendencies to relativize particularist truth claims (III; VI). In subjective soteriology, Henry continues the Protestant emphasis on salvation by grace through faith, stressing the personal experience of regeneration and the fruit it bears in a sanctified life and evangelistic commitment (VI). The church is understood in a fashion commensurate with these soteriological themes as a regenerate community marked by baptismal profession at the age of accountability and showing signs of its faithfulness through witness in word and deed. Proclamation and defense of the Gospel are its principal mission but one that includes as well personal and social ethical concern carried out primarily by the Christian believer at work in the world.

Carl Henry points to "the God who stays" as One whose providence watches over the world both in its microcosmic and macrocosmic circumstances, and who by the gift of faith and the ministry of prayer enables us to face with trust and hope the enigma of evil. God leads the world to its completion and fulfillment when Christ personally returns to judge the living and the dead at the general resurrection, with the elect going to eternal bliss and the damned to their eternal destiny with Satan and his minions, as the Kingdom comes and God unveils the divine glory (VI). He shuns making further eschatological details, a test of Christian fellowship, although his own view is broadly premillennial.

ETHICS

Quoting Alvah Hovey approvingly, Henry says that "in the order of logic Christian ethics must follow Christian theology."[20] We honor that sequence here, although Henry's ethical concern is manifest wherever his theology is expounded. In fact, ethics was the emphasis of his influential early book *The Uneasy Conscience of Fundamentalism* and characterized his major intellectual effort, *Christian Personal Ethics*, until the launching of his 1978–83 project in a wider systematics. Also, his editorship of *Baker's Dictionary of Christian Ethics* reflects the importance of this subject for him. The moral decay in culture and the

[20] *Christian Personal Ethics* (Grand Rapids, Mich., Eerdmans, 1956), p. 197.

inadequacy of secular moral theory, on the one hand, and the concern about unclarity in personal and social ethics in the churches, on the other, constitute the reference points for the development of his views.

In his textbook work on ethics (identified in the title as "personal ethics" but far more wide-ranging), Henry criticizes a variety of ancient and contemporary theories—naturalisms, idealisms, existentialisms—and finds that these "speculative ethics" divorced from revelation are too much prey to the human revolt against God and thus mired in relativity and sterility. Respecting the potential of moral sensitivity in all humans through the continued but distorted image of God, he believes that these impulses must be enriched and redirected by an understanding of "the good as the will of the Lord" given in Scripture.[21] At its center is to be found the disclosure of *agape* in the person of Jesus Christ where its embodiment and teaching provide our definitive moral norm. Yet a Christocentric perspective cannot be juxtaposed to the concern of law and justice in the Old Testament and elsewhere in the Bible. Neither can it be reduced to the liberals' Jesus of history; it must be united with obedience to the crucified and risen Lord of apostolic testimony.[22] Thus "comprehensive moral principles," absolute in character, together with specific rules in some areas of application, and Christ as perfect exemplification, give guidance to the regenerate believer and also provide a rationally compelling model for the world at large.[23]

Social ethics for Henry means the relating of these biblical standards to human life in communities and institutions in which one must confront questions of justice, peace, order, law, and freedom without succumbing to such current ideologies as Marxism and liberation theology (IV). Faulting fundamentalists past and present for their interiorizing of piety, he calls evangelicals to be the "vanguard" rather than the "rearguard" of efforts in society to make and keep life human. The impact of the Christian community on society, however, is not to be mounted through the kind of social action too often attempted by liberal

[21] *Ibid.*, pp. 209–18.
[22] *Ibid.*, pp. 219–35, 327–418.
[23] See also his critique of John Yoder's pacifism in GRA, IV, pp. 531–37.

and mainstream church bodies. Henry writes, "The use of political compulsion to regenerate society is alien to both American politics and to the Protestant religious heritage."[24] The chief tasks of the church are preaching the Gospel and carrying out evangelism. Through this mission, lives are changed and, in turn, make their social witness—one carried out through the ministry of the laity in their vocations and in terms of responsible Christian citizenship. It also can be exercised in the preaching and teaching of the church as it holds the state and other institutions accountable to transcendent reality. Para-church ministries of social service are natural avenues of Christian discipleship (World Vision, the largest evangelical social agency, and one with which Carl Henry has long been affiliated, is a good example). The church in general and theology in particular seek to provide sound general principles from Scripture for the guidance of Christians living out their social commitment in the world, yet without prescribing or endorsing specific programs. The church endeavors to establish in its own household the practice of righteousness, serving thereby as a model for the larger community.

THE THEOLOGICAL
ACHIEVEMENT OF CARL HENRY

The conventional wisdom about the demise of theological giants in the latter half of the twentieth century invites some second thoughts. Indeed, the writing of Carl Henry has not received the attention in the wider culture of a Barth, Niebuhr, or Tillich, nor has it influenced the broad sweep of Christian thought as have some of these earlier figures. However, the extensive and formidable nature of Henry's systematic work has begun to evoke comparison with some of the century's notables. Like others of eminent stature, he speaks for a considerable constituency, an evangelical presence he has helped to shape and bring to self-awareness and one which universally acknowledges him as its pre-eminent voice. As the evangelical community itself comes more and more to constitute the mainstream of North

[24] *Aspects of Christian Social Ethics* (Grand Rapids, Mich., Eerdmans, 1964), p. 144.

American church life and thought, an awareness is developing that there may be other giants in the land.[25]

On the specifics of theological content, Henry's influence has been felt both in and beyond evangelicalism in his argument for the cognitive weight of biblical and theological assertions. His stress on propositional revelation and his criticism of views that reduce faith to the experience of personal encounter or historical event, or reduce theological language to evocative or expressive functions, have earned considerable attention. His insistence that Christian faith makes universal truth claims as well as personal ones has become a force to be reckoned with in contemporary theological debate. Closely associated with this is his defense of the metaphysical status of theological claims and his related espousal of the role of reason in theological discourse. The revived interest in apologetics among evangelicals is in no small measure due to Henry's practice of that art.[26]

The written Word makes its own way in the world but not without its chief expositors and protagonists. Henry has been one of those, both giving expression to the recovery of concern for the Bible in the late twentieth century and contributing to it. While his argument for inerrancy has had little influence beyond segments of evangelical thought and piety, his unflagging defense of biblical authority, including its inspiration and cognitive claims, has had significant impact. His magnum opus as it goes into translation in languages from German to Mandarin promises to become the chief evangelical voice for biblical authority around the world for many years to come.

While occupying the center of his early intellectual endeavors, Henry's work in ethics has given a lasting bequest to the evangelical heritage. His effort to make an important place for social concern in evangelical thought and mission, including

[25] See Leslie R. Keylock, "Evangelical Protestants Take Over Center Field," *Publishers Weekly* (March 9, 1984), pp. 32–33. For the writer's definition of *evangelical*, see Gabriel Fackre, "Evangelical, Evangelicalism," in *Westminster Dictionary of Christian Theology*, ed. Alan Richardson and John Bowden (Philadelphia, Westminster, 1983), pp. 191–92. The name of Carl Henry appears more and more in the typologies of modern theology as representing a point of view and significant constituency. For example, see Avery Dulles, *Models of Revelation* (Garden City, N.Y., Doubleday, 1983), pp. 37–41, 250–52.

[26] Bob E. Patterson, *Carl F. H. Henry*, (Waco, Tex., Word Books, 1983), p. 9.

involvement with contemporary issues of justice, helped to change the direction of a movement. Further, Henry's early and continuing attention to personal ethics, so easily lost from view by the church at large in its concentration on macro-questions, and so eroded by modern relativisms, anticipated and helped to inform the current concern with Christian norms for personal behavior.

In these and other areas the achievement of Henry is marked by firmness of conviction; yet it is one held together in a remarkable way with openness to dialogue and collegiality with others in the faith community who see things differently.

HENRY'S CRITICS

As Henry has taken religious epistemology as the framework for his major systematic work, his critics can be ranged along a continuum of its options. To Henry's far left are those who assume that human experience, in one or another sense, is the source and norm of truth and as such tells us nothing of the God to whom Henry testifies. Naturalism in its various expressions accuses Henry of supernaturalist myth-making that cannot stand up under the scrutiny of empirical and rational verification procedures, or represents the ideology of the ruling classes and the escapist projection of a premodern subculture. Closer to the middle are critics who believe that universal human experience must be related to the lore of faith in a critical fashion, and they fault Henry for too exuberant claims for special revelation. Thus earlier liberals and neo-naturalists and later process, secular, existentialist, and liberation theologians declare that evangelical orthodoxy fails the tests put to it by the modern mind, the deepest human sensibilities, or the most rigorous moral imperatives. Still closer in are those who share his commitment to special revelation but hold that Henry has succumbed to an Enlightenment rationalism by construing it too exclusively in propositional terms. Still others, even persons of similar evangelical persuasion, believe that the Enlightenment contributions to critical scholarship have not been honored by Henry in his determined defense of biblical inerrancy. To the right of Henry are fellow inerrantists who believe him to be too moderate in spirit and theology about matters of both orthodoxy and rationality. Still further to the right are fundamentalists and the hyper-orthodox who hold that he has accommodated to modernity, has combined faith with social ethics or with the wrong social ethics, or has given insufficient attention to apocalyptic or too much latitude to biblical criticism.

Among Henry's friendly critics in the ranks of a developing evangelical-ecumenical partnership, the following kinds of questions are posed.

1. Cannot cognitive truth claims and propositional revelation be defended with the recognition, at the same time, of (a) the analogical character of faith language with its overlap of identity but acknowledgment of divine mystery, (b) the enrichment and corrigibility of theological assertions as the Spirit lets "ever new light and truth break forth from God's Holy Word" and thus the development of doctrine, and (c) the inseparability of personal trust from the truth claims of faith (*fiducia* bonded to *assensus*) and thus the status of theological assertions as "affirmations" rather than "propositions"?

2. Can there be an "epistemic Word" that is granted parity with the incarnate Word in such a way that the perfections of Christ's humanity appropriate to the latter are paralleled by claims for the perfections of human authorship in the former? Is the lordship of Christ over the Bible given due honor by a theory of inerrancy which links historical and scientific matters with the revelation of the eternal Word? Indeed, given the dispute among evangelicals about the meaning of the word *inerrancy*, can it function as a modern battle cry? And does the "domino theory," which sees the inevitability of doctrinal erosion in the wake of deviance on inerrancy, have the empirical and rational warrants befitting Henry's esteem of reason?

3. Should not the church have a higher profile in Henry's authority structure since (a) it functions covertly at various points as an instrument of Providence in the canonization and transmission process, as a resource in the identification of classical doctrine in Scripture, and as a principle of selection among doctrines in the case of teachings accented by evangelicals, and (b) Scripture testifies to the presence of the Spirit in the church, giving therein knowledge as well as power? As such, do

the church and its traditions not serve as a guardian against the "pick and choose" temptations of biblical interpretation by functioning as ministerial while Scripture remains magisterial?

4. Is "reason" given too prominent a place as an authority, in one sense, and too inadequate a place in another sense? The process of deductive reasoning is always in the hands of a finite and sinful reasoner and as such is subject to the limitations and agenda of the one doing the reasoning, making inordinate confidence in it suspect. Reason, as thought rising from a given time and place, while vulnerable to the same conditions of creation and the Fall, may also propose contextual questions to and give fresh perspective on faith, serving thereby as a catalytic agent to a deeper understanding of the Bible and the Gospel, although always under the norm of the latter.

5. If the experience of today's human context—with special respect to the perils of nuclear war, economic justice, and political tyranny—is accorded a catalytic role in the interpreting of Scripture, should not the biblical judgments on war and peace, solidarity with the poor, and liberation of the oppressed play a larger role in social ethics and the mission of the church in our time?

CONCLUSION

Critical attention and the impressive proportions of the work we have examined, gives force to Henry biographer Bob E. Patterson's description of him as "the prime interpreter of evangelical theology, one of its leading theoreticians, and now in his seventies the unofficial spokesman for the entire tradition."[27] The test of time contributes as well to this judgment. In an era of transient theologies and the accommodation of faith to ideologies of both the right and left, Carl Henry has embodied his own ideal of consistency and has demonstrated an uncommon theological durability. As such he has played a decisive role in making evangelical thought an articulate conversation partner in the theological dialogue of the twentieth century, as well as "striking a blow for the faith."

[27] See Patterson, p. 131.

Bibliography

Carl F. H. Henry, *God, Revelation and Authority,* Vol. I–VI, Waco, Tex., Word, 1976–83.

Bob E. Patterson, *Carl F. H. Henry*, in the series *Makers of the Modern Theological Mind*, Waco, Tex., Word, 1983.

PAUL RICOEUR

Mary Gerhart

In his introduction to *The Phenomenological Movement* (1969), Herbert Spiegelberg noticed that among the younger philosophers, "the outstanding contribution to phenomenology, both in size and originality," had been made by Paul Ricoeur.[1] While there may be no good reason to quarrel with Spiegelberg's assessment, there is a sense, as Ricoeur himself states in his theory of narrative, that only the conclusion of a story provides the justification for the particular way in which the preceding events have been emplotted. At the end of a story, that is, we see for the first time how such and such is the case—after all. Because of this privilege inherent in endpoints, we should perhaps begin with Paul Ricoeur's latest work on hermeneutic phenomenology and present all his earlier work in its light. To do so, however, would deprive the reader of both the story and the discovery of its conclusion.

During an interview for *The New Chicago* in 1979, Paul Ricoeur was asked to give a brief account of his role in the creation of a "university" for fellow captives in a German POW internment camp where he spent five years between 1940 and the end of World War II. Before the war, Ricoeur had read classics as part of his secondary education, studied metaphysics at the Sorbonne, and taught classics and philosophy in lycées. Only after the war did he become professor of the history of philosophy at the University of Strasbourg and professor of metaphysics at the Sorbonne in Paris. During the war, Ricoeur taught the POW "university's" history of philosophy—and taught it entirely without books! Ricoeur reminisced:

> Sometimes there were moments of great doubt, wondering whether we were studying the 14th or 15th century. With Plato and Aristotle

[1] Herbert Spiegelberg, *The Phenomenological Movement: A Historical Introduction*, Vol. I (The Hague, Martinus Nijhoff, 1969), p. 563.

things worked well: we had good memories. But the 5th and 7th centuries with Boethius and all—we weren't sure when they lived or what they said. . . . luckily nobody could check on what we were teaching!

Nevertheless, the course was given and taken with enthusiasm, and after the war, the degrees of the prisoners were recognized by the French government.[2]

Ricoeur's role in this "university without walls" within walls suggests one of the key characteristics of his life and thought: In whatever else he has done, Ricoeur has demonstrated an ability to draw upon, to build upon, and to modify the entire Western philosophical tradition. This ability has made him a bridge builder par excellence: between American and Continental philosophy; among phenomenology, structuralism, deconstructionism, hermeneutics, and critical theory; between traditional and contemporary understanding of religious texts. Furthermore, just as his teaching during the war perforce resembled the early Greek academy, his teaching and writing have retained the flavor if not always the literal elements of those early dialogues. His fidelity to questions of what it means to be human and of the relationship between thought and action has been the leading thread to each of the new directions—he called them detours—his thought has taken.

Paul Ricoeur was born in Valence, the capital of Drôme in southeastern France, on February 27, 1913, six months before Germany invaded France at the beginning of World War I. Orphaned at an early age, he was raised in Brittany by his grandparents in the Calvinist Huguenot tradition. From his teacher of classics at the Faculté des Lettres de Rennes, he developed a strong interest in philosophy and went to study metaphysics at the Sorbonne in 1934–35, receiving his Agregation de Philosophie in 1935.

While Ricoeur was a student at the Sorbonne, his thought was influenced by the evening seminars he attended in Gabriel Marcel's home. Marcel's famous distinction between a "problem" (a dilemma that admits of solution) and a "mystery" (a

---

[2] David Skelding, "Paul Ricoeur: A Civil Philosopher," *The New Chicago*, Vol. I (Winter, 1979), pp. 2–8.

conundrum for which no resolution is possible) introduced Ricoeur to the paradoxes of existentialist thought. As he said later in a book of essays on Husserl (he had translated Husserl's *Ideen* during the war after the German guards began to allow prisoners to read German-authored books provided by the Red Cross), existentialism both reintroduces a "sense of the negative" into philosophy and holds forth the possibility of a "liberating presence."[3] In Marcel's seminar he gained an appreciation for the grandeur and the tragedy of the human project, a grandeur most manifest in freedom. In his conversations with Marcel, which were published in 1968, Ricoeur recalled the issues Marcel discussed with his students in the seminars. Marcel was preoccupied at that time with constructing a phenomenology of the "owned body," that is, "my body precisely as mine."[4]

Ricoeur departed from existentialist thought after the war, however. He "relocated" Marcel's preoccupation with the body-subject in the reflexive philosophical tradition of Descartes, Kant, and Nabert. For Ricoeur,

> a reflexive philosophy considers the most radical philosophical problems to be those which concern the possibility of *self-understanding* as the subject of the operations of knowing, willing, evaluating, etc. Reflexion is that act of turning back upon itself by which a subject grasps, in a moment of intellectual clarity and moral responsibility, the unifying principle of the operations among which it is dispersed and forgets itself as subject.[5]

Ricoeur also became committed, in ways that existentialism was not, to reflect on both the uses and the limits of philosophical method.

From 1935 until he enlisted in the military as a commissioned officer in 1939, Ricoeur taught classics and philosophy as a

---

[3] *Husserl: An Analysis of His Phenomenology* (Evanston, Northwestern Univesity Press, 1967), pp. 210–11.

[4] Gabriel Marcel, *Tragic Wisdom and Beyond, Including Conversations Between Paul Ricoeur and Gabriel Marcel* (Evanston, Northwestern University Press, 1973), p. 222.

[5] "On Interpretation," in *Philosophy in France Today,* ed. Alan Montefiore (Cambridge, Cambridge University Press, 1983), p. 188.

professor de lycée,[6] as his father had taught English in a lycée before him. In 1935, the same year he married Simone Lejas, Ricoeur became a cofounder of *Terre Nouvelle*, a monthly review. He and his colleagues, described as "fiery young Christians," were impatient with the anti-Marxist polemics of *Esprit*, a journal founded in 1932 by Emmanuel Mounier.[7] During this time he published five articles—the first of which, entitled "Responsabilité de la Pensée," indicated the theme of all that was to follow.[8]

After the war, Ricoeur returned to Paris and from 1945 to 1948 served as an Attaché de Recherches at the Centre National de la Recherche Scientifique. A book on Jaspers written with Michel Dufrenne was followed by Ricoeur's first attempt at a "sympathetic dialectic" between two positions, *Gabriel Marcel et Karl Jaspers: Philosophie du mystère et philosophie du paradoxe* (1947). This dialectic made explicit both the contrasting "rhythms" of two philosophies of existence and the difficulties of their search for a "personalist epistemology." For different reasons, Ricoeur found neither existentialism nor phenomenology tuned finely enough for an adequate understanding of reality.

Ricoeur became Docteur ès Lettres from the University of Paris in 1949. His dissertation, Volume One of his "Philosophy of Will," *Freedom and Nature: The Voluntary and the Involuntary (Philosophie de la volonté: Le volontaire et l'involontaire*, 1950), provided the radical starting point of his hermeneutic phenomenology. From that time on, specifically while he was teaching at Strasbourg (1948–56) and publishing his work on Husserl, a position emerged that is distinctively his own.

Ricoeur's attempt to be as disclosive as possible about his own method distinguishes his early work from his work after 1950. Method, for Ricoeur, is not a prescribed form into which

---

[6] In Colmar, 1934–35, and in Lorient, 1936–39.

[7] John Hellman, *Emmanuel Mounier & the New Catholic Left, 1930 to 1950*, (Toronto, University of Toronto Press, 1981), p. 104. After the war, the only new review to survive was *Esprit*. Ricoeur became one of its most important contributors and a close associate of Mounier. After the war the Ricoeurs moved to Châtenay-Malabry to live in the "personalist community" that Mounier founded. The Ricoeurs were the only Protestants in the group of usually six or seven families.

[8] "Responsabilité de la Pensée," *Être*, 1 (Nov. 10, 1936–37), pp. 4–5.

reflection is pressed; method is developed in terms of the object to be analyzed. In discovering what limits a method, there is the possibility that "one also discovers what justifies and founds" it.[9] A special problem of method occurs when the object of analysis is the essential structure of human being, when the centrality of human consciousness in the subject is studied by the subject who is conducting the inquiry. In this case there is no possibility of doing an analysis directly and completely.

Ricoeur's strategy in his first major work was to recognize the reciprocal interaction of the voluntary and the involuntary when a subject says, "I will" (that is, "I decide," "I move my body," "I consent"). On the side of the voluntary, the intentional objects of these expressions could be specified in terms of noematic analysis (the decision or project, the action or motion, the acquiescence or consent). On the side of the involuntary, the respective realms of these three intentional objects could also be designated (needs, motives, values; skills, emotions, habits; character, the unconscious, life). The point of this analysis was to disclose the possibility of freedom through the mediations which actually occur between the voluntary and the involuntary. However fragile the actual freedom experienced, it surely resides in the decision-making subject.[10]

Volume Two of the "Philosophy of Will" was published under the title *Finitude et Culpabilité* in two parts, both in 1960: *Fallible Man (L'homme faillible)* (Ricoeur considered giving the subtitle "Grandeur and Limitation of an Ethical Vision of the World" to the English edition of Part One, but he decided that would delineate the problem too exclusively in terms of ethics) and *The Symbolism of Evil (Symbolique du Mal)*. In Part One, Ricoeur studied the precarious interaction between the voluntary and the involuntary in order to discover the ways in which the essential operations in decisive action are likely to be interrupted or distorted. Whereas existentialism tended to conflate the

[9] "Sympathie et respect: Phénoménologie et éthique de la second personne," *Revue de métaphysique et de morale,* LIX (1954), p. 380.

[10] Although he regards the act of decision as disclosing the height of human freedom, Ricoeur avoids a "decision-emphasis" in his work by making explicit the limits of direct reflection and the necessity of interpretation before existential decision. See, for example, the collection of his essays, *History and Truth (Histoire et Vérité,* 1955; Evanston, Northwestern University Press, 1965).

experiences of finitude and guilt, Ricoeur distinguished between them so that he could address the problem of human evil and weakness. Fallibility could not be contained within a direct analysis of essential human structure. Neither is fallibility a transient, random phenomenon. Ricoeur approached fallibility in an empirics of the will—that is, as an experience actually but not essentially common to all human beings.

With *The Symbolism of Evil,* the genius of Ricoeur's schema became clear. In this book, three problems were discussed. First, the turn to symbol is necessary because philosophy has said all it can legitimately say about the problem of evil when it construes the conditions for its possibility and empirically accounts for it as a state of affairs. For philosophy to say more it must change its method: from direct phenomenological description of the essential structure of being human to indirect phenomenological *interpretation* of experiences of being human. What cannot be said is that human beings *must* experience a rupture from their best intentions. What must be acknowledged is that human beings do in fact experience a disparity between what they set out to do or not do and what they achieve by their actions.

Second, interpretation is necessary because symbolic meaning is given only indirectly: "the first, literal, patent meaning analogically intends a second meaning which is not given otherwise than in the first."[11] In *The Symbolism of Evil,* interpretation was confined to indirect discourse. The data are classical avowals of the experience of the disparity between human intention and its consequences: evil experienced as deviation; evil experienced as transgressing a boundary; evil internalized as guilt. Four classical Western myths of creation are first interpreted in the light of a phenomenological analysis of the avowals and then compared. Several of the exegeses are daring and creative. For example, the word *fall* does not occur in the Genesis story, Ricoeur points out, and responsibility for evil is spread out "in time and scattered among many roles" (243). Here, too, we find an unexpectedly early challenge to sexist interpretations of the story: "Eve, then, does not stand for woman in the sense of 'second sex.' Every woman and every man

[11] "The Hermeneutics of Symbols: I," in *The Conflict of Interpretations: Essays on Hermeneutics* (Evanston, Northwestern University Press, 1974), p. 290.

are Adam; every man and every woman are Eve" (255). But the most original part of the book, anticipating his later work in books on Freud and on metaphor, is his preliminary exploration of the act of interpretation. Understanding is always done from somewhere, claims Ricoeur: "Wherever a person dreams or raves, another person arises to give an interpretation" (author's translation, 350). Human beings are interpreters through and through.

Third, the act of appropriation completes the acts of interpretation and understanding. By means of the notion of the "cycle of myths," Ricoeur provides a model for both the interpretation and the appropriation of the myths which are shown to be potentially meaning-filled. In his view, appropriation of the meanings of a particular religious text is an inclusive act—i.e., informed by, rather than exclusive of, texts of traditions other than one's own. But the pluralism of the data interpreted does not preclude investment in a particular text or tradition. The turn to the Hebrew creation myth for what appears to him to be the most appropriate understanding of evil is a good wager for the philosopher to make.

Although not all symbols are religious for Ricoeur, his symbolism of evil is an explicitly religious concept for which no argument is needed to establish its religious relevance. After *The Symbolism of Evil,* Ricoeur would continue to address the issue of religious language and understanding in articles and lectures.[12] One may speak, nevertheless, of his "detour" into psychoanalysis—a detour not only from his projected third volume, a poetics of the will, but also from a direct consideration of religious language. In a sense this detour reflects an acknowledgment that his contemporaries, like himself, are heirs of the Enlightenment who are not only disenchanted but also dispossessed by being born into an "Age of Suspicion": "Something has been lost, irremediably lost: immediacy of belief. But if we can no longer live the great symbolisms of the sacred in accordance with the original belief in them, we can . . . aim at a second naïveté in and through criticism" (351). Since there could be no criticism

---

[12] For Ricoeur's contribution to religious understanding, see David Pellauer, "Paul Ricoeur and the Specificity of Religious Language," *JR,* 61 (July, 1981), pp. 264–84; and David Klemm, *The Hermeneutical Theory of Paul Ricoeur* (Lewisburg, Penn., Bucknell University Press, 1983), pp. 109–63.

without interpretation, hermeneutics had a permanent place in his work. Since there could be no interpretation without contest, he moved to a consideration of Freudian psychoanalysis as his next project.

Ricoeur gave the Terry Lectures at Yale University in 1963, published as *Freud and Philosophy: An Essay on Interpretation (De l'interprétation: essai sur Freud,* 1965). This major work, in which Ricoeur understood Freud's work as pre-eminently a theory of interpretation, was both controversial and well received. Today many religious thinkers realize the value of Freud's work. In the early sixties, its helpfulness was not so clear and, for many, is still not apparent. For Ricoeur, Freud was someone to be thought with as well as to argue against: "Freud has already reinforced the belief of unbelievers; he has scarcely begun to purify the faith of believers."[13] Freud was representative of a "hermeneutics of suspicion": a rejection of the object of faith, a suspicion that what appears to be given in immediate consciousness, in reality, masks hidden desire. Whereas Wittgenstein berated Freud for "cheating" the patient of the immediacy of what is intended in spoken language,[14] Ricoeur agreed with Freud that the force and meaning of language can conceal a false consciousness, the intentionality of which is disguised even from the self. However, unlike Freud, Ricoeur did not leave psychoanalytic theory in the grip of suspicion; instead he completed the archaeology of desire in Freudian hermeneutics with a teleology of desire from Hegel's phenomenology. The regressive analysis of figures of memory was linked with a progressive analysis of figures of possibility. Meaning, then, for the one who undergoes psychoanalysis is not to be found in the lost memory; ideally, meaning is constructed in terms of the present and future in view of a new understanding of the past.

Ricoeur's book on Freud can today be seen as the beginning of a major insight regarding the famous nineteenth-century critiques of religion. Before Freud, Feuerbach is remembered

[13] "The Atheism of Freudian Psychoanalysis," *Concilium,* 6 (June, 1966), p. 36.

[14] As quoted in John B. Thompson, *Critical Hermeneutics: A Study in the Thought of Paul Ricoeur and Jurgen Habermas* (Cambridge, Cambridge University Press, 1981), p. 33.

for his treatment of religion as a mere projection of desire, his hypothesis being that human beings project onto an inaccessible God their best desires for themselves. Because God is the projection of human desire, Feuerbach argued, God is not real. Marx, Freud, and Nietzsche offered no new critique of religion, but in distinctively different ways they extended the Feuerbachian assertion into new areas: Marx into economic theory, Freud into theories of culture and sexuality, and Nietzsche into value formation and radical pluralism. Most philosophical critiques of all three practitioners of suspicion fault Feuerbach's logic; the fact that an object is projected by human imagination says nothing about its status in reality. An object which is imagined can be either real or not real, existent or nonexistent. Just to refute Feuerbach's logic, however, is not enough. Ricoeur perceived that the real problem was the lack of a theory of imagination that would provide for our time a status in reality for the objects of imagination, a theory he developed later on several fronts. Whereas Feuerbach (and Marx and Freud after him) had a totally negative view of imagination, Ricoeur patiently recovered the positive role of the imagination in human understanding and action. The third part of *Freud and Philosophy* can be read, then, as a preliminary solution to the problem. By taking Freud's regressive analysis (i.e., an analysis which depends solely on constructing an explanation of origins) seriously but not literally, Ricoeur was able to present a credible projective analysis—specifically, one constructed from Hegel's phenomenology of spirit. By allowing the Freudian critique to inform consciousness before surpassing the critique, Ricoeur made good his wager that "by interpreting, we can hear again."[15]

Soon after he finished his book on Freud in 1965, Ricoeur's life underwent several changes. As early as 1958 he had spent one term as visiting professor of philosophy of religion at Union Theological Seminary in New York City. In 1966, with Alasdair MacIntyre, he gave the Bampton Lectures at Columbia University (published as *The Religious Significance of Atheism*, 1966). During the same year the decentralization of the French university system took place, and Ricoeur volunteered to leave the Sorbonne, where he had been professor of metaphysics since

[15] *The Symbolism of Evil* (Boston, Beacon, 1960), p. 351.

1956, to take a position at what was soon to become the University of Paris at Nanterre. There the faculty elected him dean, and during the two years of protests and demonstrations, it fell to him to mediate between the reformist students and the more conservative forces in the university. In 1967 he lectured at DePaul University, was awarded an honorary doctorate at the seventy-fifth anniversary of the founding of the University of Chicago, and was offered the John Nuveen Chair of Theology at Chicago, a post which had been vacated by the death, in 1965, of Paul Tillich, its first occupant. Ricoeur accepted a one-term appointment to the chair and taught two courses in 1968. He also left Nanterre to teach for two years at the University of Louvain. Having given extraordinary service to his own university—particularly in a time of crisis—he was prepared, in 1970, to regularize his appointment at the University of Chicago and became the John Nuveen Professor in the Divinity School, with appointments in the Department of Philosophy and in the Committee on Social Thought. From 1970 on, he divided his time between the University of Chicago and the University of Paris at Nanterre. He continues to serve as professor emeritus and to teach at both institutions.[16] The announcement of Ricoeur's acceptance of the appointment at Chicago described him as "a scholar of broad and towering intellect," one who would bridge European and American thought.

Ricoeur's bridge building can be seen most clearly in his interpretation theory which he began to develop in the early seventies. From 1969 to the mid-seventies, Ricoeur worked simultaneously on a theory of metaphor, on imagination, and on hermeneutics—work published in *The Rule of Metaphor: Multi-disciplinary Studies of the Creation of Meaning in Language (La métaphore vive, 1975)* and in *Interpretation Theory: Discourse and the Surplus of Meaning* (1976). The turn to metaphor occurred shortly after his book on Freud, and the theory developed when Ricoeur began to answer questions not adequately answered in the context of his theory of symbol: In what sense is symbol linguistic? To what do symbolic objects refer? His interest in metaphor was concurrent with his new focus on language, and the books showed his familiarity with such

---

[16] Ricoeur is also an active member of Amnesty International.

theorists as Beneviste, Richards, Derrida, and Austin. In *The Rule of Metaphor,* Ricoeur challenged the correspondence theory of truth by showing that on the level of sense, the metaphoric process creates new meanings which cannot be translated without remainder into another linguistic expression: their "place" in the system of language is nowhere. But it is on the level of reference that the metaphoric process can be said to possess the potential for "remaking" reality. A prelinguistic "ontological vehemence" erupts as new meaning inside the system of language, in spite of and on the ruins of literal meanings. Correlatively, there is no literal object to act as the referent of the metaphor. Metaphor refers to a change in the logical distance between lexical meanings and to a reality inaccessible to direct description.

The hermeneutical tradition of Schleiermacher, Dilthey, and, more recently, Gadamer acquired new rigor and a larger scope by means of Ricoeur's work on metaphor and interpretation. Ricoeur distinguished between regional hermeneutics (the art and rules of exegesis) and general hermeneutics (reflection on the structures of the event of interpretation). The problem addressed in the nineteenth century by Schleiermacher was to show how and in what sense distance is overcome in the interpretation of foreign subjects. Dilthey, his contemporary, asked for norms operative in the life sciences which would be sufficiently rigorous and explicit to provide a model capable of rivaling the Enlightenment positivistic model dominant in the natural sciences. Gadamer, Ricoeur's contemporary, described central experiences which call into question the Enlightenment ideal of what it means to know. Ricoeur's specific contribution to the history of the tradition was to provide a number of corrections which, taken together, rescued the tradition from its romanticist biases—biases which have tended to isolate its past achievements from some humanists as well as scientists.

The first correction Ricoeur made was to develop a concept of text capable of overcoming the subjectivist bias within the hermeneutical tradition. For the nineteenth-century theorists, the goal of interpretation was to adopt the subjective stance of the author—to feel as the author had felt. For Ricoeur, this goal was not only incapable of being achieved but also mystifying.

Instead of groping for the—for all practical purposes, inaccessible—author, he concentrated on the text as a mediator of meaning. The key term operative in his formulation of the problem is *distanciation*.[17] For Gadamer, distanciation is to be overcome. For Ricoeur, however, distanciation is constitutive to discourse: in the way the meaning of the speech-event surpasses the event; in the way the written text surpasses the transitory spoken word; in the way the intention of the author is surpassed by the text; in the way the original audience is surpassed by other audiences. Although distanciation must eventually be overcome in interpretation, it is first a condition of its success.

Ricoeur brought about a second correction of the hermeneutical tradition with his theory of productive imagination. The nineteenth-century theoreticians were primarily interested in the literal (historical) and spiritual (psychological) aspects of objects for interpretation. Imagination was understood by Schleiermacher and Dilthey as perceptual, and while neither was satisfied with the Humean notion of imagination as the product of association, they did not question Hume's assumption that to imagine was to reproduce some object which was absent. Ricoeur put imagination on a new basis by conceiving of it as linguistic rather than perceptual. This new basis is available since contemporary linguistics is no longer positivistic, as in Dilthey's time, and is drawn from the semiological rather than the natural sciences. By taking a "linguistic turn" within hermeneutics Ricoeur was able, as his predecessors were not, to account for both the transmission of lexical meaning and the imaginative display of new meaning. The turn to language is best understood as a new starting point; it does not preclude either an affective or a praxis-orientation to interpretation.

The third correction Ricoeur made was to overcome the nineteenth-century dichotomy between understanding and explanation. Instead of relegating explanation to the natural sciences, Ricoeur conceived of understanding and explanation in a dialectical relationship. Moreover, explanation (like distanciation) is not a product of method but an essential element of the first moment of discourse: the speaker explains in order that the

---

[17] See his "Hermeneutical Function of Distanciation" in the special issue of his essays, *Philosophy Today*, 17 (Summer, 1973), pp. 129–41.

listener comes to understand. Here, the process of explanation originates in the "exteriorization of the event in the meaning."[18] The process of explanation is extended by the written text and assisted by the codes of literary genres. Interpretation, then, is a special kind of understanding which makes explicit the dialectic between explanation and understanding, and it creates a logical space for diverse kinds of explanation, including those of the social and natural sciences. Whereas Heidegger, for example, short-circuited many questions about interpretation by making the question of knowing into the question of being, Ricoeur chose to take the "long route" to ontology—a route which enabled him to raise the question of being at the end instead of at the beginning of an interpretation. On the one hand, he denied the claims that "well-formed" languages are alone capable of making and evaluating the meaning and truth of nonlogical statements, like metaphors. On the other hand, he challenged those emotive theories of language which deny all but the subjective referents of metaphoric language. His notion of the "conflict of interpretations" calls into question linguistic reductionism and clarifies the need to arbitrate among opposing interpretations.

As Ricoeur moved from symbol to the conflict of interpretations, to metaphor, to interpretation theory, he expanded upon the notion of action. In a paper, "The Model of the Text: Meaningful Action Considered as a Text" (1971),[19] he investigaged the sense in which the human sciences may be said to be hermeneutical, since their object has some characteristics in common with those of a text and since they use procedures similar to those of text interpretation. His theory of action has a critical edge in that it addresses the issues of power, oppression, and ideology. His analysis is based on an understanding of language as a primary and privileged way in which human beings participate in and shape their world. This participation is multidimensional and disclosive of being not only in an immediate sense but also as language and action point beyond

[18] See his "Explanation and Understanding," in *Interpretation Theory: Discourse and the Surplus of Meaning* (Fort Worth, TCU Press, 1976), p. 74.
[19] See his *Hermeneutics and the Human Sciences* (Cambridge, Cambridge University Press, 1981), pp. 197–221.

themselves: to the way in which the speaker and the hearer, the writer and the reader, the actor and the one acted upon are situated in the world—and to the kind of world in which they are situated.

Ricoeur's hermeneutical theory and his analysis of action came together in *Time and Narrative (Temps et récit,* 1983). Here he addressed three aspects of the relationship between narrative and action. He reiterated the continued need to preserve the "fullness, the diversity and the irreducibility of the various *uses* of language." He brought together various forms of storytelling and narrative by showing their temporal unity. Finally, he examined the relationship between time and narrative, particularly the capacity of a text to "mark, organize and clarify temporal experience."[20] This capacity is to be found in history as well as fiction, even though the historian today is likely to regard history less as a narration of individual action than as a social, economic, and cultural event understood on the model of the sciences which explain initial causes. Ricoeur, on the other hand, saw the explanatory function of the sciences as being grafted onto the narrative function; "directly or indirectly, history is always the history of [human beings] who are the bearers, the agents and the victims of the currents, institutions, functions and structures in which they find themselves placed."[21] In his view the referent of history is not, strictly speaking, the past, since the past is unavailable for verification. The discourse of history, like that of fiction, attempts to grasp the past "only *indirectly*" through interpretation of documents, records, data, and narrations. Both historical and fictional texts are constituted by two functions. Their narrative function refers to "the field of action" and its values which are under the constraint of temporality. Their metaphoric function refers to "the field of sensory, affective, aesthetic and axiological values which make the world one that can be *inhabited.*"[22] In interpretation, the worlds of historical and fictional texts "intervene" in the world of action in order to configure it differently, ultimately to transfigure it.

[20] "On Interpretation," pp. 175–77.
[21] *Ibid.,* p. 180.
[22] *Ibid.,* p. 186.

More a philosopher than a theologian, Ricoeur nevertheless created new possibilities for religious understanding in the contemporary situation. Particularly in his biblical hermeneutics, Ricoeur's originality developed out of and against the opposed positions of Bultmann and Barth. In Bultmann, Ricoeur took seriously the need to mediate the understanding of sacred texts by means of a "second naïveté." After Barth, Ricoeur preserved an emphasis on the initiative taken by God ("the Word from beyond") toward the human being.

The earliest collection of his biblical hermeneutics (*Semeia* 4, 1975) contains the pivotal essays on the specificity of religious language and on parable. A dialectic between philosophical and religious understanding manifestly informs these essays. His turn to language, his hermeneutical theory, and his theory of metaphor guided his approach to religious texts, which in this sense become a region of the more general notion of text. At the same time, however, the texts as specifically religious invited and directed his philosophical reflection. In this sense, philosophical hermeneutics functions as an organon for biblical hermeneutics.

Ricoeur worked with several different genres of the Christian and Hebrew testaments: parable, proverb, prophecy, law, and hymn. He regarded genre as a principle of production and as a mode of praxis. Genre, in his view, both encodes and decodes the written text. The religious text is first a poetic text and, as such, refers to a new mode of being in a possible world. The form of the text as religious, however, "bursts" under the pressure of such limit-expressions as are central to the genres of the Scriptures, limit-expressions such as "Kingdom of God," "covenant," and "second coming." As religious, the text also refers to the conditions for the possibility of a new mode of being. In a later collection of his essays on religion, *Essays on Biblical Interpretation* (1980), Ricoeur developed a "hermeneutic of the idea of revelation" in which religious texts point in different ways, according to how they are structured as genres, to a hidden God.

Ricoeur's philosophical style has been congruent with his hermeneutical theory. His criteria for judging a good interpretation—whether or not it accounts for all or most of the significant details and whether or not its accounting is done at a high level of persuasion—are also basic to his conception of philosophy. Just as interpretation is always an interpretation of a text, so too philosophy is always reflection on reality or on articulated experience. Insofar as those "data" are articulated experiences—in ordinary language, in poetic narrative language, in theoretical language—the philosopher recognizes the limits as well as the extent of language, for the articulation of experiences always takes place in a dialectical relationship with reality. Philosophy is self-contained as a realm of discourse, but at the same time it is parasitic on the things outside itself—things nonphilosophical. Philosophy is dependent in its independence.

A characteristic expression to be found in Ricoeur's work is that such and such a position "is both less than and more than . . ." Religious language, for example, is less than poetic language in that it is one kind of poetic language. At the same time religious language is more than poetic language in that it modifies the latter by intensifying it, transgressing it, and taking it to its limit.[23] Or, faith is both less than and more than philosophical reflection. Several assumptions are disclosed by this expression. Ricoeur uses the expression to call attention to the overlapping of positions and fields: to show that the other position is not adequate but that neither is it useless in the discussion. The expression also exemplifies his attempt to take another position in order to see where it might lead. Rather than being preoccupied with the presuppositions of another position, Ricoeur is interested in where it goes and where it breaks down, how it carries through and illuminates the issues under investigation. Ricoeur's willingness to consider opposing positions is a daring insouciance of sorts. Moreover, it is in accord with his political belief that in a socialist democracy every position has the right to be heard. Indeed, he wagers that the ability to hear and to learn from another's position is the necessary precondition of the possibility of reconciling radically opposed beliefs.

Ricoeur identified his own philosophical tradition as that of hermeneutical phenomenology—in brief, philosophy that is reflexive and interpretative.[24] It is helpful to consider two general

[23] The Specificity of Religious Language," *Semeia*, 4 (1975), p. 170.

[24] "On Interpretation," p. 186. For a typology of four contemporary models of philosophy, see Paul Ricoeur, *Main Trends in Philosophy* (N. Y., Holmes & Meier, 1979), pp. v–viii.

aspects of Ricoeur's work in this light. First, his work may be seen largely as a synthesis of major relevant positions of the problem. His critical and constructive use of the philosophical tradition frequently calls for close attention to the departures and differences between his own position and the positions of others which he appropriates.

A second characteristic of his work can be seen in the detours taken as he worked toward the third volume of his major project, a poetics of will. In these detours, Ricoeur addressed a number of issues at a high level of specificity, and a casual survey of these issues does not yield an apparent unity. The threads of continuity are there, nevertheless, and the search for them is rewarding. At the same time it should be noticed that each of Ricoeur's writings is self-contained and therefore accessible even without a grand sense of "l'oeuvre."

Philosophy and theology have undergone many changes since 1950, when Ricoeur published his first major book. This change can be seen in the tempering of philosophical ideals through both the use and critique of phenomenology and linguistic analysis, in the cleansing of religious motives through the constructive employment of the hermeneutics of suspicion, and in the broadening of the spectrum of languages to be taken seriously in philosophy by means of new theories of symbol, metaphor, and narrative. Ricoeur has participated in all these shifts in direction, and his contributions to the history of thought will remain.

Bibliography

Paul Ricoeur, *The Symbolism of Evil,* Boston, Beacon, 1960.

Charles E. Reagan, ed., *Studies in the Philosophy of Paul Ricoeur,* Athens, Ohio, Ohio University Press, 1979.

EDWARD SCHILLEBEECKX

Robert J. Schreiter, C.Pp.S.

The name of the Dutch theologian Edward Schillebeeckx is closely associated with the renewal of Roman Catholic theology during and since the Second Vatican Council. His works on marriage, ministry, sacraments, and other topics helped Roman Catholics think about these aspects of church life in a new way. His work in hermeneutics has aided theologians in developing more adequate ways of bringing together current experience with the Christian tradition. And his two large volumes on Jesus, published in the 1970's, have helped Catholics and Protestants, believers and nonbelievers, come closer to understanding what God's saving activity in Jesus Christ can mean for the contemporary situation.

The work of Schillebeeckx, then, has appealed to a wide variety of audiences, which has been his intent. He has seen his task as a theologian to speak not only to other theologians or Christians but also to all contemporary men and women. That he has been to some extent successful in doing this is evidenced in his being awarded the prestigious Erasmus prize for promoting European civilization in 1982, the only theologian ever so honored.

Schillebeeckx's oeuvre spans forty years and some four hundred publications, including eighteen books. Within his writings he has explored most of the great themes of the Christian tradition, although he has not produced what might be called a systematic theology. His respect for the complexity of human experience and his depth of erudition often make his texts difficult to read; yet theologians and lay people alike continue to struggle with his work. This is no doubt due to his serious consideration of contemporary experience and to his keen focus upon understanding what it means to be a Christian in a technological and secularized society.

That concern for the contemporary experience of the Christian has marked the progress of Schillebeeckx's work in two important ways. First of all, in an effort to maintain a dialogue with contemporary human experience, he has tried to keep as close as possible to those edges of human life where experience is struggling for articulation. This means that some of his writings seem to become dated more quickly because of the language he uses. Second, in order to express contemporary experience adequately, he has utilized a variety of interpretive frameworks—Thomism, existential phenomenology, analytic philosophies of language, neo-Heideggerian hermeneutics, the social critical theory of the Frankfurt school, French structuralism, and semiotics—and he has retained bits and pieces of each of these as he has progressed in his thought. For those not familiar with the intellectual currents of both North America and Europe in the past forty years, this range of frameworks can lead to some perplexity. For these reasons, Schillebeeckx's intellectual biography is especially important in understanding the development of his theology.

Edward Schillebeeckx was born into a middle-class Flemish family in Antwerp, Belgium, in 1914. He entered the Dominican order at Ghent in 1934 and was ordained a priest in 1941. The most important intellectual influence on him during this period was his teacher, the philosopher D. De Petter. De Petter was developing a new Thomist theory of knowledge, which drew upon insights from phenomenology and the social sciences, emphasizing the role of intuition as the key to bringing together empirical reality and the human mind. De Petter's Thomism, with its respect for concrete human experience and optimism about the knowability of God through human experience, provided the principal intellectual framework for Schillebeeckx's theology down to the mid-1960's.[1]

Schillebeeckx taught theology in the Dominican house of studies during the Second World War, and in 1945 he went to the Dominican faculty in Paris, Le Saulchoir, to pursue doctoral work. Paris provided two important influences on his thought. Le Saulchoir was one of the major centers of the *nouvelle théologie*,

---

[1] None of De Petter's work has been translated into English. His contributions to philosophy can be found in a series of articles published in *Tijdschrift voor Philosophie* 1 (1939), pp. 84–105; 2 (1940), pp. 515–50; 9 (1949), pp. 3–26; 17 (1955), pp. 199–254; 21 (1959), pp. 737–44.

which advocated a *ressourcement,* or regrounding of theology in historical study of the patristic and medieval periods. Yves Congar and M.-D. Chenu (who served as Schillebeeckx's thesis adviser) were the leading minds of the faculty. Their commitment to historical research and involvement in the contemporary life of the church have been mirrored in Schillebeeckx's own life and work.

The second major influence in Paris Schillebeeckx found in the currents of existentialism and phenomenology which made up the mainstream of French intellectual life in the immediate postwar period. Schillebeeckx attended lectures in the Sorbonne, Ecole des hautes études, and the Collège de France. He met and had several conversations with Albert Camus and Maurice Merleau-Ponty. He had been somewhat prepared for this by De Petter, but in the Parisian environment his affinity for an existentialist phenomenology developed markedly.

He completed his doctorate in 1951, with a thesis on the sacraments, published in revised version the following year as *De Sacramentele Heilseconomie* (The Sacramental Economy of Salvation). The work is an historical study in patristic and medieval sacramental theology, intended to serve as a basis for a renewed understanding of the sacraments. That renewed understanding was to appear in a second volume, never published as such, but presented in abbreviated form in 1958 and published in 1963 in English as *Christ the Sacrament of the Encounter with God.* In this work, Schillebeeckx sees Christ as the primordial sacrament, from whom flows the sacraments of the church. The sacraments are seen as more than instruments of divine grace; they are the means for personal encounter with Christ, the primordial sacrament. Thus, by recovering earlier understandings of sacrament (especially the patristic notion of sacrament as *mysterion*) and combining this with an existentialist view of the human person, Schillebeeckx brought the theology of the sacraments more into line with contemporary human experience. It was for his work in sacraments that he first achieved his reputation as a theologian intimately acquainted with the tradition and with the currents of contemporary thought.

Schillebeeckx had returned to teach at the Dominican house in Louvain upon completing his doctoral studies. In 1957 he was called to the Chair of Dogmatics and History of Theology at Nijmegen in the Netherlands, where he was to remain until his retirement in 1983.

The Dutch situation provided another major influence on the direction of his thought. The Dutch Catholic Church was undergoing an emancipation in that society which was evoking a great deal of energy in the church. Attempts were being made to create a Christianity more consonant with the demands of the modern world. The Dutch bishops' Christmas letter of 1960 (in which Schillebeeckx had a hand) outlined a liberal agenda for the upcoming Vatican Council. The letter brought to the attention of the world what was happening in the country and that church.

Schillebeeckx accompanied the Dutch bishops to the council. He served as their theological adviser and came into international prominence for his lectures to groups of bishops on the schemas then on the council floor. Curial conservatives blocked his being named a *peritus* to the council itself—an augury of the troubles that would recur in the future.

Contact with other theologians and the international church broadened Schillebeeckx's horizons, a process which continued with the first of many visits to the United States shortly after the council. The free exchange of ideas and the challenges of living in a secular society he found invigorating. His lectures from that visit, published as *God the Future of Man* (1969), show the major shifts that were then going on in his thought.

During the 1960's, Schillebeeckx had published studies on marriage, Eucharist, and clerical celibacy—all topics under debate among Catholics at that time. By 1966 it was clear that he was moving out of the Thomism in which he had framed his theology. Elements of it were to remain, but he had abandoned it as an explicit framework in search of models that more adequately addressed contemporary problems and situations. He embarked on a study of different interpretive approaches— the "new" hermeneutics of some of the followers of Martin Heidegger, the analytic philosophies of language of the English-speaking world, and the social critical theories of the Frankfurt school (Adorno, Horkheimer, Habermas). The neo-Heideggerians helped him come to terms with the radically historical character of human existence; the analytic philosophers, with a secular, empirical world view; and the Frankfurt school, with suffering and struggle in society. He published his studies on these in *The Understanding of Faith* (English edition, 1974).

All these factors—ferment in the Dutch Church, international experience, confrontation with secularization, exposure to new interpretive frameworks—contributed to a significant shift in both the style and the substance of Schillebeeckx's work, evident especially in three ways. First of all, his awareness of the complexity and texture of the contemporary situation had an effect on his writing style. His sentences become longer and more convoluted, as though trying to be both as inclusive and as specific as possible—all at once. Second, he shifts away from intra-church themes to issues of church and world. It is in the writing from this point (in the late 1960's) onward that his work becomes of greater ecumenical interest. Although he will return to issues of interest only to church people (notably in his little book *Ministry* in 1980), his audience has increasingly become Christians in general and contemporary men and women as a whole. Third, he centers more on understanding the human experience which is the channel through which God's revelation comes to us. This latter point is especially characteristic of the method he chose to develop his Christology.

His two volumes of Christology, *Jesus* (1974; English edition, 1978) and *Christ* (1977; English edition, 1979), brought his thought to a much wider audience. These two volumes begin not with dogmatic statements as their point of departure but with a mapping out of the experience of the early disciples of Jesus as a way for contemporary people to come to a confession of Jesus as the Christ. To that extent, they are not a Christology in the traditional sense; that is, they do not deal with the full confession of the Christian church about the divinity of Christ. A third, as-yet-unpublished volume is expected to address that matter. What has appeared thus far has been so attractive because of the experiential approach to a growth in understanding of Jesus, commensurate with the ways of contemporary human experience.

Schillebeeckx's focus on the edges of present-day human experience and his utilization of new ways to express traditional

Christian teaching have brought him into conflict with Vatican authorities on three occasions—in 1968, 1976, and 1982. He was exonerated in the first two instances; the third has not been resolved as of this writing.

Given his long career to this point, with promises of a third volume on Christology and a major work in hermeneutics yet to be written, how would one characterize Schillebeeckx's theology? It has certainly been central to the renewal of the Roman Catholic Church since the Second Vatican Council, both in Schillebeeckx's own works and in his editorial leadership of the international journal *Concilium*. Within the English-speaking world, he has been arguably the most influential Catholic Continental theologian on the church as a whole (although Hans Küng might be a rival for this claim). Karl Rahner may have had more influence on theologians and clergy, but Schillebeeckx's influence seems to have been wider.

Yet the theology of Edward Schillebeeckx is harder to encapsulate in a few statements than that of a Karl Rahner might be. The diversity of interpretive frameworks and development of ideas on the same theme no doubt account for some of that. Perhaps the best way to approach the content of his theology is by looking at why he has been so widely read by both theologians and nontheologians.

It has been said that great theologians struggle with a single problem throughout their theology, and the impact of that struggle on other theological themes creates new insights into the Christian message. If one were to single out that problem in Schillebeeckx's theology, it would be the church's relation to the world. His first published writings had to deal with the response of Christians to humanism in France.[2] He had wanted to write his doctoral thesis on a church-world question, but the practicalities of needing to lecture on sacraments led him to that topic. The theme has never been far from his thoughts and has been increasingly present in his work since the mid-1960's. *Church* is understood here in a broad sense. Up to the mid-1960's the concern was expressed most often in terms of sacraments, ministry, and spirituality which the church provided for

[2] "De Christelijke situatie," *Kultuurleven* 12 (1945), pp. 82–95, 229–42, 585–611.

Christians to carry out their lives in the world. Since that time, the focus has been more on the individual believing Christian in a secular world and in oppressive societies. One can see something of a progression in his understanding of the relation of church to the world. In his earliest writings, the relation centers upon what message Christians have for the world. By the late 1950's, there is talk of the dialogue of the church with the world. The late 1960's witness another shift, in which questions are raised about how one can be simultaneously faithful to the church and to secular reality. The late 1970's and early 1980's present even further movement, where it is asked what difference there is between being fully Christian and being fully human in the world.

That attention to the nexus between Christianity and the world in which it finds itself has its repercussions on the entirety of Schillebeeckx's theology. It seems most helpful to look at his theology in that light.

Schillebeeckx has not developed a systematic doctrine of God, but three themes recur in his treatment of that topic. The first theme is God as *mystery*—a term he has associated with God throughout his writings. God dwells beyond where our concepts can grasp, yet we are called into the reality of God's presence. In Schillebeeckx's early writings, this idea is developed within the context of sacraments as the *mysteria* which lead us to God, or through Christ, the primordial sacrament. His writings of the 1970's and the 1980's consider God as mystery which holds together contemplation and politics in what he has called a "political holiness." God is beyond our reach, dwelling in mystery, although God reaches out to us for the sake of the fulfillment of our humanity and our world.

The second theme is related to the first: God is ahead of us, in eschatological promise. Like many European theologians, Schillebeeckx rethought Christian eschatology in the latter part of the 1960's, and many features of the reflection have remained with his thought. God goes before us as promise, bringing the world out of its suffering and contradictions with God's eschatological proviso (that is, God's ultimate completion of human action for the betterment of the world). The image projected is not one of God far ahead, waiting for a stumbling humanity to catch up with its destiny. The image is more one of God's being immediately ahead, leading us, even coaxing us onward to the building up of the Kingdom of God.

The third theme holds the first two from spinning off their center around the human reality. It is, to use a favored phrase of Schillebeeckx's, a "God mindful of humanity"—kind, abounding in love, always close to the human condition, especially in its suffering. The graciousness of God, already stressed by De Petter, is seen in Schillebeeckx's work on the sacraments and on revelation. God deeply wants to relate to humanity and human history, so much so that revelation can be understood only in the complexities and ambiguities of human history. God does not choose some alternate route through which to be revealed. Schillebeeckx sees this also at the heart of the message of Jesus, supported by his experience of God as *Abba*. That conviction of the utter closeness of God prevents indifference to a God beyond us and discouragement at a God ahead of us.

Correlative to Schillebeeckx's understanding of God is his understanding of humanity, which has been a much more systematically developed theme in his work. In his book *Christ* he sets out what he calls a system of coordinates for developing an anthropology; i.e., six factors which have to be considered in any anthropology: being related to corporality, nature, and ecological environment; being in community; being related to social and institutional structures; being conditioned by time, culture, and space; dealing with both theory and practice; and having both religious and "para-religious" consciousness.[3] These elements reflect Schillebeeckx's directions in developing an anthropology; it is always thoroughly situated in concrete historical circumstances, seen as much socially as individually, preoccupied with the relation between thought and action, and concerned with the nature of religious consciousness.

Two other factors have to be added to fill out the shape of Schillebeeckx's anthropology. The first factor is his focus on human experience. His early contact with existentialism had already helped him articulate a sense of the irreducible worth and integrity of the human individual. That he talked of sacramental

---

[3] *Christ: The Experience of Jesus as Lord* (N.Y., Crossroad, 1979), pp. 734–43.

activity as "encounter" suggested the importance of taking human experience seriously. By the 1970's experience was to become a theme in itself, through which theological themes of revelation and grace would be rethought. Experience is not taken uncritically, however, or in the sense of nineteenth-century liberal theology. Much of what Schillebeeckx has to say about experience has to do with critical consciousness, the experience of the brokenness of the world, and the ultimate inadequacy of human concepts.

That leads to the second factor, the theme of suffering. Suffering is one of the most profound and threatening human experiences. Under the influence of Theodor Adorno, Schillebeeckx examined the negative side of human experience in suffering. He spoke particularly of the "contrast experience"— that is, the difference between what is and what ought to be. He perceived a contrast experience to be a means by which people could abandon preconceived ideas of humanity and quest for an experience beyond suffering—a new vision of the *humanum*, what it will mean to be human. Reflection on suffering led Schillebeeckx to the work of Jürgen Habermas, which has dealt with the manifold ways in which a society creates suffering for some of its members through oppression and blocked communication. This stream of thought has informed Schillebeeckx's approach to social questions. Habermas has had an influence on liberation theology via the work of German theologian Johannes Metz (to whom Schillebeeckx has felt an affinity). It explains, too, why the language of emancipation, emancipatory freedom, and orthopraxis (as an expanded sense of orthodoxy) in Schillebeeckx's theology is so reminiscent of what one sees in Latin American liberation theology.

Schillebeeckx's anthropology has to be situated within his understanding of the world. Schillebeeckx has a positive evaluation of the world as God's creation. Following out a Thomist concept of proportionate analogy of being, Schillebeeckx sees the world as a fit vehicle for God's revelatory activity, since the being of the world is analogously related to the being of God. The grace of God works in and through the world, not alongside it. Human history becomes the means by which God's Kingdom will be realized, although it takes the activity of

God to bring that to completion. Schillebeeckx does not want to posit a sacred history apart from or opposed to human history. God works in and through the human. This position has had two important implications for his thought.

First of all, Schillebeeckx takes human history seriously. Thus he has tried to introduce categories of action into his theology, and the most important one has been the category of *praxis*. The term is used primarily as it has been understood in critical social theory as a combination of theory and practice, with somewhat more emphasis on the practice. It is crucial to have more than good theory; how that theory is carried out and informed by the experience of action is of equal significance. Schillebeeckx's concern not only for properly understanding a situation but also for action which leads to emancipation or liberation from oppressive circumstances can be found throughout his work from the late 1960's onward. Politics is not something separate from religion; to think that is a possibility only masks a politics which wishes to maintain the status quo.

His serious consideration of human history has been one of the attractive aspects of his theology to many people. If God is said to be acting through human history, then God must be sought there.

The second implication has to do with Schillebeeckx's use of historical material. Starting with his contact with the *nouvelle théologie*, Schillebeeckx has immersed himself again and again in the history of the Christian tradition. This has been particularly evident in his work on the sacraments, marriage, ministry, and Christology. The results of that immersion are always bracing and frequently liberating. As a result of his work on the sacraments, he freed Christians to approach the separated sacraments via the primordial sacrament, Christ. In his study on marriage, he showed that it was not only a saving mystery but also a human reality in its own right and should not be sacralized unduly. His study of the historical Jesus has given new hope to many people by making the reality of Jesus accessible to them. His work on the history of Christian ministry in the West has been perhaps his most controversial, since it challenges the necessity of maintaining current forms in the Catholic Church. His earnest study of that history has enabled him to state the results of his research, even when it could cause him personal difficulties.

Connected with this quest for history has been sensitivity to ideology, or the false consciousness perpetrated by those who wish to maintain the status quo in society at the expense of one or more groups in society. Ideology critique he sees to be central to the theological task, both for the world and within the church. For this reason, he has from time to time lent his support to the "critical communities," grass-roots church groups in the Netherlands, that engage in ideology critique in the name of greater justice in church and society. Ideology is the creation of a false history which does not accurately mirror the relationships within society. The prophetic word of judgment has to be spoken against the creation, and the maintaining, of ideology.

The prominence which Schillebeeckx accords human experience and history is a salient factor in how he understands theology. The other dimensions of his understanding follow directions set forth in the documents of the Second Vatican Council. The Word of God stands as the final norm of theology. The magisterium, or ecclesiastical teaching office of the bishops, is subjected to the Word of God and works continually to interpret that Word faithfully. Schillebeeckx sees the magisterium in that dialogical fashion, as a servant of the Word and the church to maintain the integrity of the apostolic witness.

A correlational model similar to Paul Tillich's shapes Schillebeeckx's theological method. It is not a correlation of a divine answer to a human question as much as it is a dialogue between God and human experience. Schillebeeckx's study in hermeneutics has made him acutely sensitive to the power and limitations of language and to the fact that meaning is usually communicated adequately only within limited language models or *language games,* to borrow the term of Ludwig Wittgenstein. In the 1980's he has become increasingly aware of the cultural boundaries of language and meaning, and of the need to create an intercultural hermeneutics more sensitive to those cultural boundaries.

Schillebeeckx's work in Christology is an example of how this method is set to work. The starting point is the human difficulty in discerning the experience of God's salvation in contemporary society. After setting out those difficulties in the first part of the book *Jesus*, Schillebeeckx turns to the first century and explores how the disciples came to experience Jesus and his message as revelatory of God's saving activity. Schillebeeckx concludes that the image of Jesus as prophet was central to their developing understanding. It was the prophetic call of Jesus, forgiving their sins and calling them back together to preach the message of the Kingdom, that helped the disciples recognize and affirm that God had raised Jesus from the dead. Schillebeeckx goes on in *Jesus* to show how the disciples used models in their environment to articulate their experience of Jesus. In the process no model was left unchanged, but available models were always the starting point for shaping experience. This emphasizes once again how much the revealing activity of God is embedded in history. In the last part of the book, Schillebeeckx returns to contemporary questions, particularly about the universality of God's salvation in Jesus Christ. Something of the same pattern is seen in the book *Christ,* where Schillebeeckx begins with the development of the New Testament theologies of grace but then turns to contemporary questions of evil and suffering, anthropology, politics, and social ethics. That lively bringing together of the history of Christian tradition with contemporary experience is what makes his work so rich. While the Christology has yet to be completed, some lines are already evident: a greater balance in understanding the humanity and divinity of Jesus; a stronger emphasis on soteriology, or understanding of salvation, than has usually been the case in Christology; a greater role for the Spirit; and a clearer view of the coming Kingdom of God as the work of a God mindful of humanity.

Schillebeeckx has not written a systematic theology of the church, even though this theme pervades his work. The image of the church as a sacrament of God's grace for the world is a common one in his work in the 1950's and the early 1960's. Later he speaks of church as the community of grace, emphasizing more its role in the world than its internal functions. Mediation and dialogue are categories expressive of the church's relation to God and the world in the early phase; discipleship and orthopraxis become more important terms in the later work. In that latter stage, more attention is given to the church's liberating activity in the world, countering the oppressive forces which block the saving activity of God. Ministry in the church is seen as serving that capacity, both building up and giving leadership for the sake of the liberating activity in which the church is to be engaged. Liturgy is to be perceived as a worldly activity, bringing together in thanksgiving and praise the saving grace of God and the realities and sufferings of the world. As is the case in his Christology, Schillebeeckx seems to be viewing the church in a more pneumatological (Spirit-centered)—or as he would say, pneumatological-Christological—light, emphasizing the Spirit side of the presence of Christ in the church.

A theme which has shown up again and again in Schillebeeckx's work since the early 1970's has been that of a social ethics, or what J. B. Metz has called a political theology. Schillebeeckx's concern for human experience is not entirely centered upon the individual. It is also quite communal. On that basis, he has been willing to speak out on issues of war and peace, on economic oppression, and on the problems of society. He sees this not as a by-product of theology but as central to the theological enterprise. God's saving activity means the emancipation from oppression of all kinds, and the theologian needs to name both where that has been happening and where salvation still needs to happen. His speech upon receiving the Erasmus prize in 1982 is a vivid example of this view.[4]

How would one assess Schillebeeckx's place among theologians today? That is a hazardous task with a living and still very productive theologian. An encyclopedic knowledge of the Christian tradition, a polymath of contemporary currents of thought, a commitment to the analysis of today's society— Edward Schillebeeckx represents the change through which Roman Catholic theology has gone since the Second World War. His first publications appeared in the year that war ended, and they dealt with the changed situation the church would have to face. The experience of the Vatican Council came at the time his own theology was changing. He continues to define future directions for Christians in the mid-1980's. His theology has

[4] The speech may be found in *God Among Us: The Gospel Proclaimed* (N.Y., Crossroad, 1983), pp. 249–53.

become more truly catholic, or ecumenical, through the years. By the 1980's it was raising questions about a multicultural church in dialogue with other great religious traditions. His principal theological works were once written primarily for the specialist; now his intended audience has come to include an increasingly theologically literate laity. Human need, rather than need for system, has marked the shaping of his theology. A willingness to rethink a problem, to change his mind, and to enter new avenues has been a constant and continuing factor in his thought.

Edward Schillebeeckx's work not only exemplifies the best of what has happened to theology in the Roman Catholic Church in the past forty years but also presents some themes in which to frame contemporary human experience in a more enduring way: the utter graciousness of God's leading humanity forward to completion; God's commitment to humanity, especially in suffering; and the enduring significance of God's revelation in Jesus Christ. In the midst of much suffering, oppression, and even despair about the future of the planet, the studied optimism of the Dutch theologian Edward Schillebeeckx can help Christians face more squarely the challenges lying ahead to create a more human environment and a community of grace.

Bibliography

Robert J. Schreiter, *A Schillebeeckx Reader,* N.Y., Crossroad, 1984.

John Bowden, *Edward Schillebeeckx: Portrait of a Theologian,* N.Y., Crossroad, 1983.

WOLFHART PANNENBERG

Carl E. Braaten

Wolfhart Pannenberg was born in 1928 in Stettin, Germany, now a part of Poland. Though baptized as a child, he was not raised in a devout Christian family. As a teenager he participated in the defense of his country during the last days of World War II. After the war he began university studies in Berlin; then he went to Göttingen (1948) for instruction in philosophy under Nicolai Hartmann. His conversion to Christianity followed an intellectual path. In 1950 Pannenberg went to Basel to study philosophy with Karl Jaspers and theology with Karl Barth. He continued his studies at the University of Heidelberg in 1951, at that time a faculty enjoying a renaissance of Lutheran dogmatic theology under the leadership of Peter Brunner and Edmund Schlink. He received his doctorate in 1953 with a dissertation on the doctrine of predestination in Duns Scotus.[1] He became an instructor in theology *(Dozent)* in 1954 after receiving his license to teach *(Habilitation)* with a book on the idea of analogy from early Greek philosophy to Thomas Aquinas.[2] In 1958 Pannenberg became professor of systematic theology at a church seminary *(Kirchliche Hochschule)* at Wuppertal. Three years later he assumed the same position at the University of Mainz. Since 1968 Pannenberg has been professor of systematic theology at the University of Munich.

In the early 1960's Wolfhart Pannenberg's name first broke upon the world scene as the inaugurator of a new program of theology going beyond that of Barth or Bultmann. The situation in theology and the church, at least in Europe, was dominated by the split between Bultmann's hermeneutics and Barth's dogmatics. This fact was amusingly brought out in a letter Barth wrote to Bultmann shortly before Barth's death. Barth compared the two

[1] *Die Prädestinationslehre des Duns Skotus* (Vandenhoek & Ruprecht, 1954).
[2] *Analogie und Offenbarung: Eine kritische Untersuchung der Geschichte des Analogiebegriffs in der Gotteserkenntnis,* unpublished *Habilitationsschrift* (University of Heidelberg, 1955).

of them to a whale and an elephant eyeing each other by the shores of the Pacific. While the whale is squirting a mighty stream of water into the air, the elephant is making loud trumpeting sounds from his trunk. They can see and even hear each other, but neither understands a word the other is saying. They speak in different tongues. Barth became favored by the conservatives, Bultmann by the liberals. The younger generation of scholars confronted an impasse, and that triggered a search for a breakthrough.

REVELATION AND HISTORY

In the early 1950's four students at the University of Heidelberg[3] began to meet weekly in search of a unified comprehensive vision of theology that would overcome the unhealthy polarization between the schools and the fruitless divisions between the field specializations. The exegetical, historical, systematic, and practical disciplines were locked in by their own special methods. Students of theology preparing for the Christian ministry lacked a way to integrate the results of their studies into a whole view. Pannenberg, who had just returned from studies with Barth and Jaspers at Basel, joined the Heidelberg team of four as the systematic theologian. Later Martin Elze, a church historian, and Trutz Rendtorff, another systematic theologian interested in social ethics, became members of the team. Some of the most prominent figures in theology at that time were teaching at the University of Heidelberg—Gerhard von Rad, Günther Bornkamm, and Hans von Campenhausen, among others.

As a doctoral student of Paul Tillich at Harvard University, I went to Heidelberg in 1957 to write a doctoral thesis on "Revelation, History, and Faith in the Theology of Martin Kähler." Tillich had introduced me to the thought of his systematics professor at the University of Halle, Martin Kähler, who had made the greatest impression on him. Kähler had struggled to overcome the same hiatus between revelation, history, and faith that had bedeviled German theology since Immanuel Kant's distinction between the noumenal and the phenomenal realms, something which G. E. Lessing once called

[3] Ulrich Wilckens, Dietrich Roessler, Klaus Koch, and Rolf Rendtorff.

"the ugly ditch." While I was working on Kähler's distinction between kerygma and history, and also between the two different German words for history, *Historie* and *Geschichte*,[4] I began to hear rumors about this young team of German scholars conspiring weekly to solve *the* greatest puzzle in the history of modern theology. How can facts of history mediate the reality of revelation and the truth of salvation? This issue was sharply focused in the nineteenth century as the relation between the Jesus of history and the Christ of faith, and in the twentieth century as the relation between the historical Jesus and the kerygmatic Christ.

In 1961 the first results of the Heidelberg team were published in a volume of essays edited by Pannenberg, and titled *Offenbarung als Geschichte*.[5] What was needed was a new concept of revelation which could bridge the gulf between the historical-exegetical and the existential-systematic methods and results. Revelation is not something suprahistorical that occurs above and beyond history to which faith alone enjoys some mysterious private access. Nor is revelation in the biblical sense the communication of supernatural truths about God that one can find in so many words in the Bible. Rather, revelation is an indirect self-disclosure of God in the course of historical events. Revelation does not happen *in* history or *above* history but *as* history. The Word of God declares what God has been doing in the actual sequence of events open to historical investigation. This concern for the real historical character of revelation was expressed in direct antithesis to existentialist and salvation-history theology which placed revelation in an "invulnerable area" exempt from any objectively rational critical methods of examination.

Pannenberg proposed seven dogmatic theses to explain his new concept of revelation as history.

1. The self-revelation of God, according to the biblical witnesses, did not take place directly, after the fashion of a theophany, but indirectly through God's historical acts.

[4] Martin Kähler, *The So-Called Historical Jesus and the Historic Biblical Christ*, translated, edited, and with an introduction by Carl E. Braaten (Philadelphia, Fortress, 1964).

[5] *Revelation as History*, ed. Wolfhart Pannenberg, trans. David Granskou (N.Y., Macmillan, 1968).

2. Revelation happens at the end of revelatory history, not at the beginning.

3. In contrast to special manifestations of deity, the historical revelation is open to anyone who has eyes to see. It has universal character.

4. The universal revelation of the deity of God is not yet realized in Israel's history but was realized first in the destiny of Jesus of Nazareth, insofar as the end of all events took place beforehand in what happened to him.

5. The deity of Israel's God is revealed by the Christ-event, not as an isolated occurrence but only insofar as it is an integral part of God's history with Israel.

6. The universality of the eschatological self-demonstration of God in the destiny of Jesus comes to expression in the development of non-Jewish concepts of revelation in the Gentile Christian churches.

7. The Word is related to revelation as prediction, instruction, and report.

These seven theses encapsulate Pannenberg's bold departure from the current options of the day, whether Barth's revelation positivism, Bultmann's existentialist demythologizing, or Cullmann's history-of-salvation. What is new in Pannenberg's proposal is that only the totality of God's historical activity can be taken as the self-revelation of God. Pannenberg dusted off an old leaf from German idealism, particularly that of Hegel, who advanced the idea that only the totality of reality as history comprises the self-communication of the divine. Here we find the origin of Pannenberg's notion of universal history as the indirect self-revelation of God. To make use of this idea Pannenberg had to solve some problems. First, if history as a whole is the revelation of God, how can one particular event of history—the Christ-event—possess absolute revelatory significance? The left-wing Hegelians of the nineteenth century, David F. Strauss for one, had said it cannot be. Second, if history as a whole is revelation, it would seem that the revelation of God in Jesus Christ can be superseded in the future. The exponents of the Hegelian line were unable to show how history in its totality can be the self-revelation of God without relativizing the Christ-event, without making Jesus Christ only one among many significant stages in a progressive development.

Pannenberg saw that a renewal of Hegel's attempt to combine the idea of universal history with a Christocentric theology of revelation must take care lest it repeat Hegel's failure to take seriously the finitude of human experience, the real openness to a still incalculable future, and the uniqueness of the individual, which Søren Kierkegaard underscored in his attack against "the system," meaning Hegel's philosophy. If the totality of history is really the self-revelation of God, the end of history alone can provide the ultimate perspective from which to understand the total course of world history as revelation. But is not this precisely the meaning of Jesus Christ in an age of universal history? Does not the New Testament present Jesus Christ as the proleptic presence of the eschatological future of all history? Hegel's philosophy of history did not incorporate our knowledge of the eschatological dimension of history, provided by more recent biblical inquiries into the Old Testament, late Jewish apocalypticism, and early Christian tradition. This idea that we have in Jesus the end of history preoccurring, that he is the real anticipation of the final end of the universal history, constitutes Pannenberg's most significant modification of Hegel's view of universal history as the indirect self-revelation of God.

The decisive assertion that the end of history is already anticipated in the person of Jesus can be made only within the framework of the apocalyptic concept of history. Apocalyptic eschatology cannot be dehistoricized or demythologized as Bultmann did in interpreting the Christ-event and the New Testament kerygma. Rather, in Jewish apocalypticism Pannenberg finds the indispensable presupposition for understanding the eschatological character of the Christ-event. In this milieu we encounter an understanding of history from creation to the eschaton as reality in its totality. The fulfillment of history was expected at the end of the whole world history. Of course, the end has not yet occurred; history is still running its course; the future is still open. Nevertheless, Christianity came upon the scene of world history with the apostles' announcement that an end-of-history kind of event has already taken place in Jesus' resurrection from the dead. The resurrection of Jesus can be understood only against the background of the apocalyptic view of history and its expectation of a final resurrection of the dead. Did Jesus really rise from the dead?[6] Pannenberg says yes, and it is an historical as well as an eschatological event, happening in the midst of history ahead of time, so to speak. Moreover, it can be shown by the methods of historical criticism to be an historical event, with a high degree of probability.

When revelation happens as history, it does not require a special insight of faith or illumination by the Holy Spirit in order to be known. Pannenberg affirms the logical priority of knowledge to faith. Revelatory history is objectively knowable by reason alone. Reason is the only faculty humans possess to observe, remember, or reconstruct an account of historical events. Revelation is not a supernatural or spiritual kind of knowledge mediated any differently from other historical knowledge. Revelation speaks in the "language of facts." These facts have inherent power to convince of their truth and reality. No additional boost from the outside is needed to make them revelatory. If they are revelatory, then one's subjective enthusiasm does not make them more so.

At this point we are entering upon that part of Pannenberg's concept of revelation that has aroused the most controversy. What has caused offense is the assertion that acts of God and facts of history can be integrated within the same field of interpretation. There are not two kinds of history, secular history and holy history.[7] God does not act in some *heilsgeschichtlichen* ghetto where only a few souls with a peculiar *blik* are able to see what is going on. That would place their statements beyond the range of historical verification. The old supernaturalism of orthodoxy has crept into modern theology under the guise of a suprahistorical idea of revelation. For Pannenberg every last vestige of supernaturalism must be effaced. By this he means that the modern equivalents of the medieval dichotomy between nature and grace have placed the Christian idea of revelation

[6] Pannenberg makes his case for the resurrection of Jesus of Nazareth in *Jesus—God and Man*, trans. Lewis L. Wilkins and Duane Priebe (Philadelphia, Westminster, 1968), pp. 53–114.

[7] Pannenberg develops his theology of universal history in the form of essays in *Basic Questions in Theology: Collected Essays*, trans. George Kehm (Philadelphia, Fortress, Vol. I, 1970; Vol. II, 1971).

outside the range of reason and therefore irrelevant to the rational quest for meaning and truth. Then theological statements become a function of personal experience or existential encounter, bringing faith and the Spirit along in this retreat into the sphere of subjectivity. Pannenberg is suspicious of every theory of theological knowledge which introduces an element of subjective uncertainty into the objective ground and content of faith. All revelation lies in historical events, and it is not an arbitrary interpretation superimposed from the outside, arising from a person's conversion experience. In no sense does faith or the Holy Spirit enhance the revelatory content of the historical facts. Revelation is objectively there, subject to operations of historical reason.

THE HISTORICAL JESUS AND CHRISTOLOGY

Every new theological movement needs to establish its Christian identity via Christology. At least since Schleiermacher, Christology has become the testing ground of all theological theories and statements that aim to be acceptable as specifically Christian. Pannenberg's next major publication after announcing his new view of revelation was his Christology, *Jesus—God and Man*. He began this work with the assertion: "Its teaching about Jesus Christ lies at the heart of every Christian theology."[8] Thus Pannenberg continues the Christocentric line in Protestant theology that runs from Schleiermacher through Ritschl to Barth and Tillich.

Pannenberg's Christology begins with a methodological concern for the right starting point. The traditional way of doing Christology was to start "from above," with the incarnational dogma of the ancient church as defined in the creeds of Nicaea and Chalcedon. Ever since the quest of the historical Jesus began in the eighteenth century, it has become increasingly clear that church dogma can no longer be the point of departure in Christology but must itself be legitimated with reference to our knowledge of the historical Jesus and the early Christian trajectories of interpretation. Christology today must start "from below," to show that the apostolic kerygma or ecclesiastical

[8] *Jesus—God and Man*, p. 19.

dogma is grounded in the Jesus of history. In starting Christology "from below" Pannenberg does not end with a "low" Christology. A "low" Christology is one which follows the ancient Ebionitic tendency to treat Jesus as a "mere man," in contrast to a "high" Christology which finds in Jesus' unity with the Father the revelation of the identity of God. Pannenberg's proposal is to do a Christology "from below" which is a true Christology "from above."

What is Christology, then? The note of history is struck again. Christology is the interpretation of the history of Jesus. There is nothing that can be called Christian that is not based on that. Jesus of Nazareth was a proclaimer of the oncoming Kingdom of God within the horizon of late-Jewish apocalyptic expectations. Jesus was not one of the apocalyptic visionaries, but the distinctiveness of Jesus' message and ministry can be understood only within the framework of apocalyptic eschatology. That was the context within which Jesus preached his message of the Kingdom of God and in whose terms that message was heard and believed. However, neither the *fact* that Jesus preached nor *what* he preached would be an adequate basis of Christology. Without the historical event of the Resurrection, Jesus would have been one more zealous eschatological preacher soon forgotten. The Resurrection acted like a magnet to draw Christological titles from numerous sources into the service of announcing the identity and meaning of Jesus as the Messiah awaited by Israel. Thus, in one sense Christology began with the first witnesses to the risen Lord Jesus Christ. Faith in Jesus as the Christ was an Easter event. Yet in another sense Christology began in the person of Jesus himself, for the risen Lord is an empty symbol without connection with the historical life and ministry of Jesus.

In addition to his strong emphasis on the resurrection of Jesus as the pivot of Christology, Pannenberg offers a number of equally significant, constructive proposals for Christological thought. First, he resists the modern tendency to write Christology strictly out of soteriological interests. Melanchthon's statement, "To know Christ is to know his benefits," has had a reductionistic effect on modern thought. It has fallen prey to the danger of each age's projecting onto Jesus Christ its own feelings and desires for salvation. Tillich's famous statement that

Christology is a function of soteriology is unacceptable. Second, Jesus' unity with God can be established only retrospectively from the Easter event. His pre-Easter life has proleptic significance. The idea of prolepsis is the key to understanding the relation between the present and the future. Third, the mode of God's presence in Jesus is affirmed in terms of God's revelational unity with Jesus. From this revelational approach Pannenberg seeks to do justice to the concern of classical Christology to stress the essential unity of Jesus with the Father. Fourth, through Christology Pannenberg opens a way to rethink the doctrine of the Trinity, thus helping to reinforce the revival of trinitarian thinking in the twentieth century, starting with the creative initiatives of Barth and including other contemporary theologians such as Karl Rahner, Jürgen Moltmann, and Eberhard Jüngel. Fifth, the most starkly original idea in Pannenberg's overall scheme is that of the retroactive power of the future to create all things from the beginning. This idea lies at the heart of his incorporation of eschatology into all dimensions of theology, including in particular his idea of God as the "power of the future."

THE ESSENCE OF ESCHATOLOGY

Pannenberg took up the theme of the future in eschatology because he became convinced that Jesus shared the apocalyptic hope of Judaism for the *future* of God's approaching Kingdom. Jesus modified that hope by his career and message, but his own person and meaning can be grasped only within the horizon of the apocalyptic world of thought. In apocalypticism the whole of reality is historicized, and the meaning of all history will be disclosed in the end—eschatologically. The neo-orthodox theology of Barth, Brunner, and others made no positive use of the idea of the Kingdom of God. That had been spoiled by the social-ethical interpretation of the Kingdom of God in Protestant liberalism and the Social Gospel movement (Ritschl and Rauschenbusch). Pannenberg links up with the consistently eschatological concept of the Kingdom of God advanced by Albert Schweitzer and Johannes Weiss. Instead of being a liability to modern theology, Jesus' eschatological view of the

Kingdom of God proves to be an asset. Pannenberg asserts: "This resounding motif of Jesus' message—the imminent kingdom of God—must be recovered as a key to the whole of Christian theology. . . . Our starting point then is the kingdom of God understood as the eschatological future brought about by God himself."[9] The Kingdom of God is the power of God's own future determining the destiny of everything that exists in the present and in every past age. Although Jesus proved to be mistaken about the *imminence* of the inbreaking Kingdom, it was precisely the force of his eschatological expectation that gave an end-time orientation to his whole life and qualified his message throughout.

We can summarize Pannenberg's view of Jesus' message of the Kingdom in a few theses. (1) The eschatological rule of God which Jesus preached was the power determining his whole life. (2) Through Jesus' complete surrender of himself to the rule of God, he is the decisive revelatory medium of God's eschatological Kingdom. (3) The resurrection of Jesus from the dead was the divine vindication of Jesus' ministry as the present medium of God's eschatological revelation and salvation. (4) The future of the eschatological Kingdom does not cease to be future in relation to its real presence in Jesus' own ministry. (5) The presence of the future Kingdom is explained as a proleptic presence, as an anticipation of God's eschatological rule. Thus, Jesus becomes a down payment on the fulfillment of all things projected by Jewish hope. (6) The general resurrection is still awaited by believers from the fulfilling end of time and reality. The glory of God and final salvation remain still a matter of the future, although fore-glimmerings of it have appeared already in history by the grace of God.

Pannenberg attempts to breathe new life into the traditional eschatological ideas. Many theologians have stopped trying to make sense of the symbols of Kingdom of God, new creation, resurrection of the dead, final judgment, and the end of the world. They seem at first sight alien to modern consciousness. In Pannenberg's interpretation the basic meaning of such eschatological ideas has to do with the meaning and destiny of humanity.

[9] *Theology and the Kingdom of God* (Philadelphia, Westminster, 1969), p. 53.

In Jewish eschatological hope the coming rule of the Messiah will inaugurate a new world of peace and righteousness. These are conditions humans long for but cannot establish within the kingdoms of this world based on human rule. Only the direct rule of God can establish a truly human society. If such a society of peace and justice is to prevail in the end for all peoples, and not just for the last surviving generation, there will need to be a transcendent solution, mediated through what is called the resurrection of the dead and the transformation of the natural conditions of human existence—in short, a new heaven and a new earth.

Eschatological ideas such as these deal with the future worthy of human hope; but are they predictive in character? There is no denying that they have the logical form of predictions; they seem to predict particular events that will happen in the future course of things. However, Pannenberg does not take them as literal predictions about forthcoming political developments or as intuitive foreknowledge about contingent events sometime in the future. Instead, statements that refer to the eschatological future formulate the conditions of an ultimate realization of the essential humanity of human beings as the consequence of the establishment of God's righteous rule. The realization of the essential humanity of human beings requires a society in which every individual finds a fitting place, a society in which the antagonisms between the interests of individual persons and the interests of society as a whole are overcome. If the unity of individual and social destiny is an indispensable condition of a true realization of humanity, it is not enough to have that happen in a future social order, as Marxist humanists envision. For there would remain the question of the share of past generations in human destiny in such a future society. Rather, the condition of the possibility of having all individuals—past, present, and future—participate in a future society in which the essence of humanity is realized is simply inconceivable apart from the future resurrection of all the dead. That alone makes it possible to have the totality of individuals participate in the realization of the social destiny of humanity. Simply stated, apart from hope for the general resurrection, there can be no hope for final salvation and fulfillment for the totality of humankind.

Eschatological symbols and ideas do not tell us by what course of events the essential future of humanity will be realized. Pannenberg is willing to leave a lot of questions open, particularly the question about the nature of the transition from the sequence of ordinary historical events to the order of eschatological events. There is a limit to what human speculation can manage on this point. Suffice it to say that Pannenberg is working to develop an ontology penetrated by eschatology—an eschatologized ontology. The classical Christian tradition never succeeded in fully transforming Greek ontology into the key of biblical eschatology. In an eschatological ontology, the essence of things lies in their future, not in a timeless realm above and beyond history. The Kingdom is still future insofar as the essence of things has not yet been realized. Yet it is just this future Kingdom that is the essence of things past and present. The essence of things depends on the temporal process and will be decided only by way of its outcome. Eternity is not conceived of as nontemporal; it also is constituted by the historical process, especially by its outcome.

In this scheme, the final future of the temporal process will definitively decide about the essence of things. The future of the divine Kingdom and judgment will decide about the nature and destiny of humanity. Meanwhile, the essential future is not only future but also really present through symbols of anticipation; thus it can provide identity to our personal life—although the process of our lives is still open, and no one knows what concrete events the future will bring. Eschatological symbols remind us that humans yearn for progress in time as well as for a lasting fulfillment in eternity. A future without eternity amounts to meaningless change, and this in turn threatens our personal destiny. This personal identity lives from its essence, its essential future, which participates in the mystery of eternity. About this mystery Pannenberg, like other classical theologians, cannot tell us very much; otherwise it would no longer remain mystery.

So much stress on the renewal of the eschatological thematic in theology calls for further explanation and justification. For all its biblical weight, what is its relevance for human existence and Christian faith today? Pannenberg makes a strong case for eschatology in terms of the human quest for meaning, especially as this comes to its most complete expression in religion. All of Pannenberg's thinking begins with a fundamental analysis of the human experience of meaning and proceeds to establish the essential conditions of its possibility in time and history. He draws heavily on the thought of Wilhelm Dilthey, even more than he does on that of Hegel. Dilthey showed that meaning in all experience is a matter of the relation between the parts and the whole. Words have meaning, but the concrete meaning of a word can be established only by discovering its use in a specific linguistic context. As words in a sentence, so also individual events derive their meaning from their relation to the larger context of life. Human beings experience meaningful events by relating them to the whole context of life mediated through the faculties of memory and anticipation. However, human life is still running forward in an unfinished historical process. Life in the present stretches forward through anticipating the end of life which makes it whole and finished. Dilthey asserted that the final significance of the events of our life can be measured only at the end of life, in the hour of death. Because of the historicality of meaning, the future acquires a decisive function, and only the final future can render a judgment on the ultimate meaning of existence.

The problem is that the most certain future of human existence is death. Death destroys life and does not bring a promising fulfillment. Death can hardly constitute the meaning of life, actualizing the true essence of what it means to be human. To be sure, death brings about the finish of life, but it is not the essential future humans anticipate when they are ultimately serious. The power of death is deadly, and if that commands the place of final meaning, it will work retroactively upon life in the present, spreading the virus of anomie, nihilism, hedonism, or cynicism. In other words, if death is the eschaton of life, it is destructive of the very meaning humans seek through symbols of hope, grounded in memories of promise. At this point, Pannenberg correlates his theology of the Resurrection with his fundamental analysis of the problematique of meaning in history. In light of resurrection hope, death becomes demoted to the rank of a penultimate eschaton of earthly existence.

The future of hope is not limited to individuals, for the

meaning of individual existence is conditioned by the larger social context. The social conditionedness of an individual contributes to personal identity. The essential future of an individual person cannot be separated from the essential future of society and humanity as a whole. This connection between the essence of individual and society was originally expressed in the eschatological symbols of the Bible, which hold that the decision concerning each individual person is connected with the general resurrection of the dead, the final judgment, the end of world history, and the consummation of all things in a new creation, a new heaven and earth.

HERMENEUTICS AND THE IDEA OF GOD

Pannenberg defines theology as the "science of God."[10] He connects the question of God with his phenomenological-ontological analysis of meaning in history and existence, working out his views in connection with the heritage of hermeneutic that includes such thinkers as Schleiermacher, Hegel, Dilthey, Heidegger, Gadamer, and Habermas. The idea of God is linked with a contextual theory of meaning, and the claim of theology to "scientific" (wissenschaftlich) validity stands or falls with the success of the hermeneutic method for understanding meaning. The history of hermeneutics in modern times began with Schleiermacher. Hermeneutics is not merely a collection of rules for interpreting texts; more broadly it is a theory of understanding in general. The context of the interpreter is related to the text to be interpreted. Schleiermacher used psychology to penetrate the author's mind originally at work in the production of the text. Dilthey built on Schleiermacher's ideas but expanded the scope of hermeneutics. He went beyond psychology as a basis for hermeneutics and developed a theory of historical consciousness. If history runs through all life and language, then they are necessarily incomplete until history has come to an end. Weaving together ideas drawn from a critical analysis of the theories of Heidegger, Gadamer, and Habermas, Pannenberg reaches the conclusion that the category of totality is a fundamental

[10] *Theology and the Philosophy of Science*, trans. Francis McDonagh (Philadelphia, Westminster, 1976), Chap. V.

prerequisite of perceiving anything meaningful at all. The special subject matter of theology as a science of God is *reality as a whole*—the totality of reality. This whole implied in the experience of meaning and in hermeneutical reflection provides anthropological grounding for the idea of God. Discourse about God as the "all-determining reality" corresponds to the theme of the whole. The old enterprise of natural theology is thus given new foundations in contemporary hermeneutical theory. The progression of thought seems to be from language about the whole implied in hermeneutical experience to the idea of the totality of history to the eschatological future, thus bringing the whole theme into the radius of reality revealed by the biblical God of history. In this way the language of faith about revelation does not rest on a mere postulate of faith about revelation but is connected with hermeneutical questions implied in the struggles of human existence.

Pannenberg is breaking with the neo-orthodox position which places theology on the basis of either the positivity of the church's discourse or the positivity of biblical language. A wider frame of reference than the positivity of Christianity is needed to make theology viable as an academic discipline within the universe of sciences. Pannenberg's major concern is for the truth, not only the meaning, of Christian faith. But the truth of Christianity cannot be decided within the context of an inquiry that deals merely with the Christian religion. It must deal with the reality of God as such on which Christian faith rests. What is the appropriate context for dealing with the question of God? Frequently, he complains, the question of God has been trapped in some kind of dogmatic positivism or religious subjectivism. As the object of theology, the idea of God functions as a hypothesis which can be tested indirectly with respect to traces of the divine mystery in the things of the world and in human experiences. If God is to be understood as the all-determining reality, everything must be shown to be determined by this reality and to be ultimately unintelligible without it.

Talk about God in this scheme is intended to meet the intellectual challenges of modern atheism. Language about God no longer becomes privy to faith or imprisoned in the church and its confessional theology. For this reason Pannenberg argues that theology belongs as one of the academic disciplines of a university. Wherever there goes on a study of the totality of reality from the point of view of what ultimately determines its meaning and destiny, both as a whole and in all its parts, there is theology. It may be called philosophical theology or ontological metaphysics, but it is theology because it investigates God as the all-determining power involving all reality. Much of modern philosophy is not theological because it chooses to postpone the question of God, or deliberately to avoid it by refusing to formulate the question of reality as a whole. The problem of atheism in modern culture is acute, but atheism cannot survive in the long run, because the question of God will arise whenever things are studied in relation to reality as a whole.

In seeking to overcome the isolation of Christian theology from its dogmatic ghetto, Pannenberg proposes that Christian theology must be legitimated within a more comprehensive theology of the history of world religions. Not many theologians have taken this route, preferring to examine the Christian texts and traditions in an exclusive manner. Pannenberg here takes the side of Ernst Troeltsch, the great systematic theologian of the "history-of-religions" school early in the twentieth century, whose thought was eclipsed by Barth's definition of revelation as antithetical to religion. For Pannenberg, revelation without religion is an empty word. The nature of religion is to give expression to the experience of reality as a whole, namely, God. An historic religion is the locus of explicit perception and articulation of the self-revelation of God in the complex of human experience. If Christianity is restricted to a sphere of revelation, it pays the high price of losing every way of making claim to universal validity in relation to the religious dimensions of human experience. In departing from the Barthian way, Pannenberg is joining Tillich's call, made shortly before his death, for the renewal of systematic theology by situating it within the context of research and dialogue with the great religious traditions of the world. For Pannenberg such a theology of the history of the religions would provide the context in which a theology of Christian faith would function, allowing it to pursue its special task as a hermeneutic of the Christian tradition. Other religions could be dealt with side by side in the same scholarly fashion.

The clear difficulty in our time is that the great Western universities by becoming secularized have banished the study of religion from a theological perspective. Religious studies go on at best from the more limited perspectives of the history and phenomenology of religion, or the psychology and sociology of religion and the like. What Pannenberg is calling for does not find hospitality in most universities. The fact of religious pluralism poses the most severe test. There can be no such thing as a *neutral* theology of the history of religions. If Christian theology is treated as a branch of the history of religions, its understanding of the experience of God and the world in the Jewish-Christian context will definitely influence every decisive account of the non-Christian religions. No scholar can approach the study of the religions with a *tabula rasa*. The perspectives and interests of faith are bound to a truth-claim implied in the revelation on which any given religion depends, and these will affect the descriptive and evaluative accounts one makes about all other religions. Pannenberg attempts to neutralize this problem by drawing a distinction between the heuristic and the probative factor in scholarly endeavor. A theologian's personal faith belongs to the heuristic context, but one's personal faith cannot be used as the basis for an argument which claims to be true. Theology has to do with truth, and the claim to truth requires proof; otherwise it stands as a naked assertion, a mere function of one's piety. Assertions about the Word of God in the Bible and in Jesus Christ must be tested if they are intended as real assertions with cognitive character, not simply as expressive linguistic gestures. For this reason theology belongs in the university, where assertions have to be advanced and defended on their merit, not by appeal to the authority of a church or a given religious tradition.

Practical Consequences

One must be impressed by the strength of Pannenberg's drive to inquire into the whole truth and to see things from the most comprehensive viewpoint. He will not allow theology to withdraw into a ghetto to carry on a monologue, as though it could survive in the modern world by restricting itself to the claim of a particular community unchallenged by others. His call to enter the open forum of intellectual discussion is proving to be productive of a new synthesis that is both deeply anchored in the traditions of Christian faith and unrestrictedly open to new frontiers of experience and knowledge. He has been called a "conservative radical," a characteristic of his approach clearly typified by his ecumenical and political involvement. Pannenberg is an ecumenical activist in a strictly theological sense of the word. He has been an imaginative participant in the ecumenical dialogues with Catholics and Jews and a theological leader in the Faith and Order Commission of the World Council of Churches. He has frequently offered bold proposals to advance trends leading to the unity of the church, drawing upon the constructive potential of his leading ecclesiological concept—the Kingdom of God announced by Jesus and embodied in the apostolic communities that witnessed the risen Lord and that experienced his presence in the power of the Spirit in the context of the Eucharist.[11]

Early in his career Pannenberg developed an ethic of the Kingdom of God that promoted social change.[12] During the student revolutions of the 1960's, Pannenberg's response was somewhat sympathetic, but in the meantime his thinking has taken a decided turn against revolutionary movements whose appeal to the future reacts with disdain toward the cultural values embodied in classical traditions. He looks upon liberation theology as an illegitimate appropriation of the symbols of the Christian tradition, especially the eschatological symbol of the Kingdom of God. Pannenberg is critical of liberation theology's flirtation with the Marxist theory of praxis and its romance with socialist ideology and utopian rhetoric. In a heated exchange with Helmut Gollwitzer, Pannenberg has explained his opposition to any alliance of Christian theology with Marxist socialism.[13] Socialists speak of the ideals of freedom, justice, and

[11] See *The Church,* trans. Keith Crim (Philadelphia, Westminster, 1983).

[12] See Pannenberg's most recent statement in the field of ethics, *Ethics,* trans. Keith Crim (Philadelphia, Westminster, 1981).

[13] See Pannenberg's essay "Der Sozialismus—das wahre Gottesreich?" in *Müssen Christen Sozialisten sein?* 1976.

peace, and so do Christians and classical liberals. The issue is the *way* in which these goals are reached and such values implemented. He does not accept the socialist way nor the assumption of the Christian left that Christianity can bind the integrity of biblical faith to one particular way.

The socialist way, not its ideal, is the direct target of Pannenberg's opposition to the Christian left. He understands the socialist way to call for the end of the private ownership of the means of production so that true freedom of every individual may be accomplished. That is nonsense; its underlying premise requires an optimistic view of human nature, contradicting the biblical estimate that sin and evil lie deep in the infrastructure of every person. Individuals by nature are more interested in seeking their own freedom at the expense of others than in pursuing the rational insight that the well-being of each is somehow dependent on the realization of the common good. This deep tendency of each person to secure his or her own freedom at the cost of others is not exclusively manifest in a system of private ownership; it expresses itself with equal vigor in the individual's striving for power, influence, or fame.

The tragedy of modern socialism is that the socialist revolution and the socialization of the means of production have not generated a consensus of individuals free of coerciveness. Many excuses are made for this delay in the realization of true freedom, while the interim period in which coercion is required becomes indefinitely prolonged. In every case some particular group assumes the competence to decide the true interest of all and what sacrifices individuals must make to bring about the socialist aims. It is no accident, Pannenberg claims, that wherever the socialist revolution has been successful, this has led to some of the most enslaving political conditions known to humanity. This is, moreover, not due to any unfortunate set of circumstances which could in principle be rectified next time. We are faced here with a basically false doctrine of human nature embedded in the foundations of socialist theory. Nor can the socialist of today be pardoned on the grounds of naïveté, certainly not after so many socialist revolutions have invariably produced totalitarian systems of domination. Virtually no grounds support the promises of socialism. On the contrary, the facts of historical experience contradict them.

Christian faith lives in the expectation of the Kingdom of God as a coming rule of peace and righteousness, which will definitively put an end to our human systems of domination and oppression. But there is no causal connection between the socialist plan to get rid of the private ownership of the means of production and the coming of God's Kingdom. Christians do not have the duty to be socialists for the Kingdom's sake.

The Christian's hope for the Kingdom of God is deeply suspicious of every political scheme to inaugurate a world of peace and justice. Only God in time will bring about such a world, which does not mean that God's rule of peace and righteousness is thoroughly otherworldly, something for the next life. The real presence of this eschatological Kingdom has been embodied in the Christ-event and is signaled by those who receive his rule through faith and hope. This is, of course, precisely what Marxists and socialists (including some liberation theologians) recognize as a kind of religious opiate. Pannenberg has taken the offensive against the socialist superstition that the realization of the true humanity of human beings will be established as a direct consequence of the elimination of private ownership of the means of production, as though this is the sole or even the chief obstacle to the flowering of the goodness of human nature. This superstition is no harmless illusion, for in our century it has been combined with the kind of political fanaticism that has offered up the lives of millions of people on the altar of socialism, without having succeeded in minimizing in the least the power of domination. Slavery and oppression continue under socialism in new and different forms. Instead of pushing Christians toward the socialist option, Pannenberg believes that theologians would do better to remember the realistic anthropology of the Bible and dispel the superstition that something like the Kingdom of God, with its promised peace and freedom, justice and righteousness, can be brought about by the socialist revolution.

Pannenberg is now in mid-career as a theologian, and his plans for future theological work seem boundless. In 1983 he published a massive work on Christian anthropology, transcending anything of its kind in the twentieth century.[14] Currently he is working on a multivolume work of Christian systematics, dealing with the basic questions of fundamental theology, the doctrine of God, anthropology, Christology, ecclesiology, and eschatology. These are likely to build on the foundations he has already laid, but he will undoubtedly explore new paths of knowledge and integrate wider fields of data into a comprehensive vision of the meaning and truth of a theological vision of reality as a whole.

[14] *Anthropologie*: *Anthropologie in theologischer Perspective* (Vandenhoek & Ruprecht, 1983).

Bibliography

Wolfhart Pannenberg, *Jesus—God and Man,* trans. Lewis L. Wilkins and Duane A. Priebe, Philadelphia, Westminster, 1968.

E. Frank Tupper, *The Theology of Wolfhart Pannenberg,* Philadelphia, Westminster, 1973.

JÜRGEN MOLTMANN

Christopher Morse

Jürgen Moltmann first came to prominence internationally following the publication of his *Theology of Hope: On the Ground and the Implications of a Christian Eschatology* in 1964 (1967).[1] For at least a decade no contemporary theological work was more widely read and discussed. In Germany alone the book went through six printings in the first two years. Shortly thereafter, translated editions were published in several European countries and in England, the United States, and Japan. Responses came from Roman Catholics as well as Protestants, from Christians of Latin America, Africa, and Asia, and from Marxist humanists in Eastern Europe. A new period of ecumenical dialogue had been initiated.

Through the ensuing years and cultural changes since the sixties Moltmann has remained a prolific author, lecturer, and leading theological contributor. Rather than simply reaffirm and defend earlier positions, he has moved on to venture new constructive proposals in what are to date his three other major works, *The Crucified God: The Cross of Christ as the Foundation and Criticism of Christian Theology*, 1972 (1974); *The Church in the Power of the Spirit: A Contribution to Messianic Ecclesiology*, 1975 (1977); and *The Trinity and the Kingdom: The Doctrine of God*, 1980 (1981), a title which announces the beginning of a systematic doctrinal series. In addition, his list of published writings in English includes several volumes of essays and addresses, primarily on themes developed in the major works: *Religion, Revolution and the Future*, 1969, dedicated to the memory of Martin Luther King, Jr.; *Hope and Planning*, 1971; *The Passion for Life: A Messianic Lifestyle*, 1978; and *The Future of Creation*, 1979, the collection which perhaps best introduces the range of his thought up to this point. From a number of other shorter books two further ones, *The Experiment Hope*, 1975,

---

[1] Dates in parentheses are of the editions in English.

which deals with topics in social ethics, and *Man: Christian Anthropology in the Conflicts of the Present,* 1974, should be mentioned to round out the picture. A current project is the doctrine of creation. Whatever proves to be the future direction and impact of his thought, Moltmann's is clearly one of the most influential theological voices of the past twenty years.

Who is the man? In a brief autobiographical reflection he has spoken of himself.[2] Born in 1926 in Hamburg, Moltmann was only seventeen when he was sent to war in 1944. The beginning of the second half of this century, as far as theology is concerned, can be dated from Dietrich Bonhoeffer. Considered from this reference point, at the time of Bonhoeffer's execution by the Nazis at Flossenbürg in April 1945, Moltmann was himself a prisoner of the Allies. His capture by the British forces had occurred two months earlier in Belgium. Later he was interned in camps in Scotland and then near Nottingham in England, but his release did not come until three years had passed. As Bonhoeffer was meeting his death in hope—"This is the end; for me the beginning of life"—the young Moltmann was just beginning to face a life of seeming hopelessness.

> We lost our names and became numbers. We lost our home and our country; we lost our hope and our self consciousness; and we lost our community. What we experienced in those years was *ochlos,* an unorganized, uneducated, imprisoned, and suffering mass of people without a face, without freedom, without history.[3]

No one could have predicted that beyond the barbed wire he would later emerge as one who would take up the cause of theology in postwar Germany. He least of all could have imagined that in the next quarter-century his name was to become identified around the world with the theology of hope.

The Christian faith, so he has written, was not a vital force in Moltmann's home in Hamburg as he was growing up. Nor by the time of his induction into the military had he ever contemplated

[2] "Why Am I a Christian?", in *Experiences of God* (Philadelphia, Fortress, 1980), pp. 1–18.
[3] *The Passion for Life: A Messianic Lifestyle* (Philadelphia, Fortress, 1978), p. 97.

theological study. His earlier interests were in mathematics and physics. The nourishment for the soul that he took with him as he went to war consisted of writings by Goethe and Nietzsche. As the misery of the war years intensified, the sustenance on which he had relied proved insufficient. The unrelenting despair of the prison camp reflected not only the hunger and defeat of armies but also the utter devastation of a world, both social and individual, as he had known it. Looking back, Moltmann would later recall that a prison chaplain's rather unwelcome gift of a New Testament with appended Psalter came to provide the only means for articulating the sense of loss he experienced. There followed no dramatic conversion to faith as some instant happening, but out of the darkness of those years the reality of a God in the midst of suffering impressed itself upon him increasingly.

Repatriation in the spring of 1948 brought Moltmann into contact firsthand with efforts in Germany to reorganize the nation and the church. In both areas he sensed a rigid opposition to new initiatives and a determination to reclaim as far as possible the stability of the pre-Nazi period. The appeal in rebuilding was to the past rather than the future. The Protestant church bodies appeared intent upon reverting to their earlier forms of leadership instead of reshaping themselves according to the new lessons taught by years of shared resistance to established power in the name of the Gospel. With the collapse of the Third Reich and the growing disclosure of its record of atrocities, persons who had sanctioned the assimilative tendencies toward a Nazi-oriented national religion had been discredited. But even the respected Confessing Church movement that had maintained the opposing struggle proved less resistant in peace than in war. This same year Moltmann began his study of theology at Göttingen.

The pervasive theological influence he encountered was that of Karl Barth, who was then at Basel. Moltmann was introduced to Barth's theology through such teachers as Otto Weber, Hans Iwand, and Ernst Wolfe, each of whom had been active in the Confessing movement. For awhile he felt what every student who first becomes aware of the depth and comprehensive content of Barth's dogmatics tends to feel. There was nothing more left to be said. His teachers were not uncritical Barthians, however, and through their own breadth of scholarship and inspiration, as well as, later, that of the Dutch theologian of mission Arnold A. van Ruler and others, Moltmann's own theological agenda began to emerge.[4]

In 1952 he received his degree and was installed as the pastor of a rural parish in Wasserhorst near Bremen where he served for five years. His doctoral thesis, a study of Christoph Pezel, a sixteenth-century Reformed theologian and leading disciple of Melanchthon, was completed in 1957.[5] Moltmann then moved from the pastorate to a teaching position at Wuppertal, an academy of the Confessing Church. His *Habilitationsschrift* dealt with the implications of the Calvinist doctrine of the perseverance of the saints and, like his doctoral thesis earlier, was submitted under Weber at Göttingen.[6] University professorships in systematic theology followed, first at Bonn and then at Tübingen, where most of his teaching career has been spent. Moltmann's guest lectureships have been numerous and global. His chief introduction in this country came when he was visiting professor at Duke in 1967–68.[7]

The focal point of Moltmann's agenda, and the link which most clearly connects the theology of hope with his subsequent work, is the theme of the eschatological significance of the cross. Readers of the four major texts published to date will not find a straight line of systematic development unfolded from one volume to the next. Moltmann himself has characterized the first three of these books as programmatic in style and content with overlapping emphases, and in introducing a new doctrinal series with *The Trinity and the Kingdom* he disclaims any desire to formulate a dogmatic system. The *eschatologia crucis*, nevertheless, marks the distinctive concentration of his theology and provides a consistency of intent which informs all the variations. Main attention thus far has been devoted to those dimensions of

[4] For a discussion of this background, see M. Douglas Meeks, *Origins of the Theology of Hope* (Philadelphia, Fortress, 1974).

[5] *Christoph Pezel und der Calvinismus in Bremen* (Bremen, Einkehr, 1958).

[6] *Prädestination und Perseveranz, Geschichte und Bedeutung der reformierten Lehre "de perseverantia sanctorum"* (Neukirchen, Neukirchener Verlag, 1961).

[7] Critical responses to Moltmann's thought by American theologians given at a symposium at Duke during this time appear in *The Future of Hope: Theology as Eschatology*, ed. Frederick Herzog (N.Y., Herder & Herder, 1970).

this theme which may be grouped under three rubrics: revelation, the doctrine of God, and mission—or what he has called the "practice of hope."

ESCHATOLOGY AND REVELATION

In an Advent sermon on the text of Luke 21:25–36 Martin Luther remarked that scarcely any other words of God are so neglected as those wherein God's coming is foretold. Moltmann challenges this neglect in *Theology of Hope* and argues that the words of God's coming are in fact the scriptural key to a renewed understanding of the doctrine of revelation and its radical consequences for contemporary culture. What is at stake, in Moltmann's judgment, is the accommodation of Christianity to established power and the Gospel's exposure of the idolatry of all attempts to deify the status quo. Do we have here simply a manifesto reflective of the sixties, a theology in effect conforming despite itself to the status quo of a decade of revolutionary rhetoric and protest? To decide this question one must first ask another. Why this turn to the subject of eschatology, or the ultimate future, and to the neglected words which foretell of God's coming?

To be sure, the climate of the late fifties and the sixties was conducive to such a project. Moltmann has observed that the theme of hope was "in the air." One need think only of such names as John XXIII, Martin Luther King, Jr., John F. Kennedy, and Alexander Dubcek to recall the ferment for change that arose during those years. The civil rights struggle with its terrible pain notwithstanding was based upon the defiant confidence, at once so impressively sober and passionate, of God's promise of freedom now at last. Campus unrest, whatever its excesses, represented the channeled energies of thousands of students and faculty against irrational policies of war in Vietnam and the social lethargy of the universities. Under the inspiration of socialist humanists like Dubcek in Czechoslovakia, serious conversations began for the first time between Christian and Marxist intellectuals. Overcoming their former stereotypes of each other, participants in these dialogues discovered the issue of hope to be their common concern and the necessity of rethinking their assumptions concerning the future a common task.

The spirit of the times alone cannot account for the theology of hope. Had that been so the tragic deaths, defeats, and periods of reaction which followed the initial expectations would have shown it to have been an exercise in illusion. The primary reasons for the undertaking were theological. Behind Moltmann's effort was a heightened interest in eschatology on the part of both Old and New Testament scholars and in the questions which their work posed for contemporary theology. This interest extended to a variety of traditions within the canon, including the promise of Yahweh narrated in the Hexateuch as that which kept Israel on the move in expectation of being met in coming events with covenant faithfulness, the prophetic references to the impending Day of Yahweh, the apocalyptic visions of a new heaven and a new earth, the passages in the Synoptic Gospels about Jesus' preaching the Kingdom of God at hand and the imminent coming of the Son of Man, the Pauline emphasis upon the revelation (apocalypse) of God's righteousness in the cross and the promise of its vindication in all things despite what can be seen at present, and the Apocalypse of John, which begins with the Lord God who not only is and was but is "to come" (Rev. 1:8) and ends, " 'Surely I am coming soon.' Amen. Come, Lord Jesus!" (Rev. 22:20). Gerhard von Rad, Walther Zimmerli, and Rolf Rendtorff were among the most influential from the Old Testament side, and Ernst Käsemann and Ulrich Wilkens from the New. What their research suggested to systematic theologians was not that the diverse and intricate traditions of Scripture were all reducible to a single fixed pattern of eschatological interpretation, but that a sense of imminent expectation and future directedness is central, not peripheral, to the shape of the canon. Why then had this sense of imminence and the understanding of God's Word as promise not been as central in dogmatic theology?

Neither Barth nor Bultmann had been oblivious of the eschatological question, and in an earlier generation each had indeed raised it in his own reaction to nineteenth-century Protestant liberalism. In their separate ways both had sought to take account of the critical insight of Johannes Weiss at the end of the last century that the Kingdom of God in the proclamation of Jesus is an impending state of affairs which cannot be equated simply with some relation of the soul, moral ideal, or presently existing spiritual community. It is *at* hand, not *in* hand. Yet, in Moltmann's view, the sense of history that Von Rad and Zimmerli saw initiated by God's promise to Israel and the societal reality of God's righteous vindication of Christ in the cross that Käsemann saw posited by the promise in the Pauline understanding were insufficiently spelled out in either Barth's or Bultmann's positions. In each case the eschatological event of revelation was located in a subjectivity—God's for Barth, ours for Bultmann—which was transcendental, and thus in danger of becoming incidental, to the time, space, and affairs of this world. For Barth the eschatological revelation has its locus in what can only be acknowledged as God's own history as a free Subject. For Bultmann the eschatological event of salvation, while not a state of consciousness, is an existential moment occurring within the historicity of the believing subject. Such, in essence, is Moltmann's reading in *Theology of Hope* of the dominant patterns of eschatological interpretation then current in theology. One may question if his accusation of an otherworldly transcendentalism is justified, especially in the case of Barth with his insistence that there is no Word of God without a worldly event and that God's free history is only revealed as distinguishable from our own because it remains eternally a history of love taking time for our own. At any rate, what Moltmann seeks in *Theology of Hope* is not to dispense with Barth and Bultmann and return to precritical cosmological arguments to interpret God's relation to the world but to develop a yet more biblically accordant interpretative option in which eschatology is less dependent upon cosmological, ontological, or anthropological modes of thought. In this effort to find new concepts his chief source of stimulation was the philosophy of Ernst Bloch.

Bloch's masterwork on the principle of hope, *Das Prinzip Hoffnung*, had been published in 1959, and its impact soon became apparent among theologians intent upon rethinking the significance of eschatology. Wolfhart Pannenberg, Gerhard Sauter, Johannes Metz, and others, including Moltmann, found themselves provoked to fresh approaches by it. In light of Bloch's identity as a theoretical atheist and left-wing Hegelian in the tradition of the young Marx, this influence might seem surprising. What one discovers in this philosophy of hope, however, is that Bloch draws upon apocalyptic aspects of biblical tradition, and eschatological perspectives often relegated to the radical fringe groups within Christian history, as root metaphors for reconceiving both human nature and the nature of reality at large.

What is primary about all historical reality, Bloch argues, is the pre-eminence of the future over the past. Human consciousness is essentially anticipatory, or it ceases to be. Without hope, as without hungering, one cannot long exist. Neither Freud's retrospective portrayal of the unconscious as that which is no-longer-conscious *(Nicht-Mehr-Bewussten)* nor Heidegger's introspective phenomenology of the self achieving authenticity through recognition of the threat of nothingness does justice to the decisive importance for human existence of that which is not-yet-conscious *(Noch-Nicht-Bewussten)*. Bloch's prospective interpretation is not limited to an account of human consciousness. It offers a critical revision of ontological as well as anthropological claims. Being itself involves the ongoing dynamic created by that which is not-yet *(Noch-Nicht-Seins)*. Such a reconception allows us to speak of transcendence without recourse to an otherwordly eternity either above us or within us. We can remain with the materiality of this actual world in all its sufferings and still acknowledge transcendence in terms of the future. This requires that we give up thinking vertically in the categories of an ahistorical idealism and begin to think horizontally. It is this horizontal and world-historical understanding of transcendence, Bloch contends, that we see exemplified in the biblical prophets.

With the discovery of Bloch, Moltmann suddenly found his biblical, theological, and political concerns coming into focus. While not totally adopting Bloch's concepts, he adapted several of the most important ones to express what he saw to be the significance of biblical eschatology for an understanding of the way God is known. A major difference for any Christian theology of hope is that the future in prospect is not futurity in general but the future of Jesus Christ. Eschatology cannot be a theory of the world process as such. It is an *eschatologia crucis*.

The central thesis Moltmann develops in *Theology of Hope* is that it is more consonant with the biblical testimonies to understand God as revealed in an "apocalypse of the promised future" than in an "epiphany of eternal presence." The distinction he draws, briefly put, is as follows.

In the form of classical Greek thought that we find first in Parmenides of Elea in the fifth century B.C. and then in Plato and his heirs, ultimate reality tends to be conceived as fully and simultaneously complete. Being, therefore, has no future; being simply *is* despite all changes in temporal appearance. This kind of thinking is carried over into Christian theology in some of its most formative dogmatic traditions regarding revelation. God is said to be self-disclosed in a presence of ultimacy which is always permanent and, so to speak, forever simultaneously in place. The temporal appearances through which God becomes known to us are truly revelatory only insofar as they may happen to mirror or correspond to this eternal presence. In the case of language and the scriptural stress upon God revealed through words, the correspondence is like that of a symbol or name referring to that which is already there and posited in completion. Barth, unlike many others since Kant, does not claim that this eternal presence is posited as an experiential datum, whether immediate or inferential, prior to the language which is its revelatory medium. But even with Barth, Moltmann argues, the presupposition of truth as referential correspondence to that which already is remains. The truth of a medium of revelation lies not so much in its efficacy in relation to a subject revealed as in its transparence to an already established subject. Hence even Barth's more biblically oriented account of revelation betrays a Parmenidean bias in its insistence that the Word of God is. "It is never 'not yet'" (*noch nicht*)."[8]

The pervasive eschatological expectations of Scripture, as

---

[8] Karl Barth, *Church Dogmatics: The Doctrine of the Word of God*, Vol. 1, Part 2, (Edinburgh, T. & T. Clark, 1956), p. 52. In a later volume, however, Barth himself stresses the "not-yet" of the presence of Christ's eternal Parousia, *Church Dogmatics: The Doctrine of Reconciliation*, Vol. 4, Part 3, the second half (Edinburgh, T. & T. Clark, 1961), pp. 903–904.

Moltmann assesses them, diverge sharply from this epiphanic line of thinking. The contrast becomes striking in four respects. First, the reality of God in biblical faith always involves a future. The coming of God's will and way over all that presently opposes it in creation *is* the revelation of God. Future as *adventus,* as God's coming vindication, is the mode in which God is present to faith. Advent is not a denial of presence here and now; it is the kind of presence that a Parmenidean ontology fails to recognize. Both the immanence of God and the transcendence of God are present in God's imminence. Second, God is disclosed not as in place but as taking place. This is the meaning of apocalypse, the opening up of all reality to the coming of God. The Resurrection is an *eschatologia crucis* because it is the future as the vindication of the crucified Christ taking place. The cross and the Resurrection are God's way of being God, God's apocalypse which is not yet established but present as impending reality. Third, the creaturely forms of signification through which the self-disclosure of God is mediated do not function as descriptive references corresponding to some completed state of being but as statements of hope and anticipations of a further coming of God. Revelatory language is promissory. It names God only through expressing God's promise of self-commitment in covenant for a future. Fourth, the identity, or selfhood, of God is perceived as God's faithfulness in keeping the word of promise to come as Lord in all the events of history. This view differs markedly from a Parmenidean conception of being or from modern notions of selfhood influenced by Kantian concepts of a transcendental and ahistorical Ego. God's being as person is inseparable from God's coming glory as Lord of all creation. Ousia is revealed only as Parousia. As promise the Word of God is not transparent but initiatory in the sense that it initiates the experience of encountering God's faithfulness ever anew in all the events of this earth.

The Cross and God's Triunity

If revelation is to be understood eschatologically not as an "epiphany of eternal presence" but as an "apocalypse of the promised future," how does this change in perspective affect the conception of God? What are the implications of saying that God takes place as the coming Lord in the cross? In *The Crucified God* and later in *The Trinity and the Kingdom* Moltmann addresses the question of the doctrine of God.

To stress such terms as *imminence, anticipation, promise, future,* and the *not-yet* is to risk suggesting a disregard for the incarnation of God in the events concerning Jesus of Nazareth. It is, therefore, to the Incarnation that Moltmann next directs his attention. If God's way of being is the reality that takes place in the cross, then it takes place in earthly suffering and rejection. That which is not established at present but impending is nevertheless concretely present as enfleshed in the particular sufferings of the Rejected One, Jesus. The coming glory of God, as seen from the standpoint of what happens regarding Jesus, is neither an ethereal ideal nor a vacuous wish. It occurs, as Luther interpreting Paul emphasized, not in what appears according to the human wisdom to be glorious or the highest good but *sub contrario,* beneath its very opposition, in the sufferings of the cross. In this context God is incarnate.

According to Moltmann, when the Incarnation is thus understood in terms of the eschatology of the cross, the theological basis for affirming that God's being is triune can be recognized. Such a linkage of the concepts of incarnation and trinity within an eschatological framework has its theoretical antecedent in Hegel. Moltmann's own case for this claim to God's triunity is argued, in sum, through the following steps.

If it is truly the case that the import of the canonical witness for faith is that the passion of Jesus Christ is to be identified as the pathos of God, then the ontic reality of God must be said to involve crucifixion and resurrection. This is precisely what the classical Parmenidean conception of being, with its derivative presuppositions in Christian thought regarding God as supreme substance or as absolute subject, cannot say. This ontology could not take account of the apocalyptic reality of the Resurrection in the interpretation of God's revelation, and it fails equally to take account of the incarnate reality of the Crucifixion in the interpretation of God's being.

In contrast the Scriptures attest to an incarnate reality of the cross, and they do so by speaking of the self-giving on the part of God from two vantage points, at once distinguishable and inseparable. One of these, which is the more commonly acknowledged in Christian doctrine, is the suffering surrender of the Son. The other is the suffering surrender of the Father. This second perspective is conveyed through such New Testament references as God's so loving the world that God "gave his only Son" (John 3:16), or as Paul radicalizes this self-giving, "did not spare his own Son but gave him up for us all" (Rom. 8:32), for our sake even "made him to be sin who knew no sin" (II Cor. 5:21), "a curse for us" (Gal. 3:13). This reciprocal depiction of the suffering intrinsic to the cross, in Moltmann's view, reaches its most profound expression in Jesus' cry of dereliction in the words of Psalm 22:1, "My God, my God, why hast thou forsaken me?" (see also Matt. 27:46; Mark 15:34). To acknowledge this cry of the Son to the Father as incarnate reality is to acknowledge God's calling out to God in suffering for the vindication of the will and way of God. Speaking ontically, the passion narratives suggest a confrontation within the reality of God, an over-againstness and otherness even to the point of self-forsakenness within God's own being.

No suggestion of two gods or of an ultimate dualism, however, appears in the Gospel traditions. The depths of god-forsakenness are not proclaimed as other than God; on the contrary, they are seen as the very depths of otherness within God. God's being is a being-one-with-another in a unity of Spirit, a being united solely in the reciprocity of willing surrender and of distinguishable though mutual self-abandonment. As scripturally rendered, God the Son suffers being lost through surrender to the Father even to the point of god-for-sakenness. God the Father suffers loss of being through surrendering the Son, not a loss of identity as the ancient concept of Patripassianism wrongly implied but a loss of being God in any way other than by not sparing the Son. The Son in distinction from the Father suffers dying. The Father in distinction from the Son suffers the death of the Son. The oneness that takes place in this incarnate inseparability of suffering in the cross is, therefore, to be thought of not as a single mathematical unit but as a dialectical unity of Spirit. It is this unity of mutual self-surrender proceeding from the relation of the Father and the Son that faith confesses as God the Holy Spirit who eschatologically transforms the sufferings of the present time and of all history from being a surrender to death into being a surrender to life.

This latter point regarding the Holy Spirit Moltmann emphasizes as the crucial reason for the contemporary importance of understanding the trinitarian significance of Christ's passion. What is ultimately at issue in the doctrine of God's triunity is the perennial question of theodicy, the vindication of the just. When the theodicy question is raised as the cry of dereliction in the cross, it takes on a different meaning from the one generally assumed. No longer is it a matter of a theoretical vindication of the way of God to human sufferers. Now it becomes God's own vindication of human sufferers in reality as God's way of being. The Holy Spirit as the reciprocal relation both to dying in rejection and to the death of one's beloved is confessed in faith to be the "Giver of life." Ultimate reality is shown in the cross to be enfleshed in all dying with its rejection and in all the suffering of the death of one's beloved. This is not a masochistic deification of suffering or of the status quo of oppression as itself an eternal presence. The enfleshment is the material incarnation of God's apocalyptic overcoming of all suffering and oppression, an overcoming presently taking place and initiated by God's self-committing promise but not yet established as complete. By attending to both the historical and eschatological significance of the cross, Moltmann concludes, we are enabled to recognize God's triunity not as some idealist abstraction of threefold self-enclosed being divorced from the pain of this earth, but as in truth the ultimate reality of this earth's pain and its overcoming in which we all participate.

The Practice of Hope and Mission

From this discussion of the Trinity, just as in the case with revelation, it is clear that Moltmann attaches considerable importance to the social and political consequences of doctrine. Following the completion of *Theology of Hope,* he declared his intention to develop yet further the implications of a Christian eschatology for the "practice of hope" as a political theology, an interest shared with Roman Catholic theologian Johannes Metz. Each of his four major texts deals with certain aspects of this practice and of mission. Throughout all his work this remains a primary concern.

By concentrating upon the eschatology of the cross, Moltmann from the beginning moves beyond the superficial alternatives of pessimism and optimism in his examination of hope. Hope is based upon the Resurrection of the Crucified One as this is revealed in the form of promise. In pursuing this perspective Moltmann finds God's promise to be related directly to historical practice. A *missio* arises out of the *promissio*. We can see this connection throughout the Bible in that the promise of God initiates the movement of faith. The Abrahamic paradigm comes immediately to mind: "Go from your country and your kindred and your father's house to the land that I will show you. And I will make of you a great nation, and I will bless you, and make your name great, so that you will be a blessing" (Gen. 12:1–2). Likewise in the New Testament the proclamation that Christ is risen with the promise of his resurrected presence initiates the apostolic witness. To paraphrase Anselm of Canterbury's classic rationale for theology, "faith seeking understanding" (*fides quaerens intellectum*), one can say that for Moltmann the most comprehensive posture of faith in the biblical traditions may be summed up as "promise seeking mission" (*promissio quaerens missionem*).

No human agency can produce or control the promise that initiates liberation in history. On this point, which has prompted criticism from some people who otherwise are sympathetic with his political aims, Moltmann continues to stand unambiguously within the Reformed tradition. Nor is promise merely another name for possibilities which may be inherent in present social conditions and which can be extrapolated from them. By promise, most simply put, Moltmann means the kind of significance Scripture has for faith when it is heard as a witness to God. Human beings do signify the Scripture through their words and actions, but only God can make these words and actions significant to faith as God's own promise. Only God determines when our words and acts come to be God's Word.

Yet Moltmann's equally emphatic opposition to supernaturalistic conceptions which tend to remove God from the affairs of this world is expressed in his claim that God's Word as promise creates the experience of history. This experience of history involves the practice of hope. By this claim Moltmann seeks to integrate three lines of thinking. The first is the biblical perspective of living between promise and fulfillment. There is a peculiarly Hebraic perception of reality narrated in the Hexateuch as Israel moves through the contradictions of the wilderness on the way to a promised land. This consciousness may be seen as well in the prophetic messianism of the Old Testament and in the New Testament's witness to the Parousia of Christ. The promised coming in each instance calls the present into question and opposes all that presently obstructs this coming. Thus hope in God's promise creates a practice of resistance rather than acquiescence to all authorities that seek to foreclose or forestall the future. A second source is the post-Enlightenment European tradition of philosophical reflection regarding historical consciousness. The contribution of Judeo-Christian eschatology to the secular sense of history in the West has often been a subject of study. With the outbreak of the French Revolution a new form of critical consciousness emerges which puts all institutions in a crisis of judgment and undermines all self-legitimating appeals to divine right. Historical consciousness is experienced as critical consciousness. The third line of thinking Moltmann draws upon is that of the more recent Frankfurt school of critical social theory represented by T. W. Adorno and M. Horkheimer. History is best understood as an adjudication process in which lawful rights are contested, and truth prevails not as a transcendental ideal but out of conflict as the negation of all that serves to negate these rights.

From these three sources Moltmann elaborates the thesis of God's own trinitarian reality as a history of the trial of Jesus Christ, a trial in which the contested rights of those considered the godforsaken and the least of the earth are adjudicated in the verdict of the Resurrection. The practice of hope is the actual participation in the sufferings of Christ's trial though concrete involvements on location in current struggles for liberation against the negations of freedom imposed by the vicious circles of economic, political, and cultural alienation. This is the mission that God's promise seeks.

In *The Church in the Power of the Spirit* Moltmann relates this thesis to a comprehensive treatment of ecclesiology. Mission does not derive from the church, nor does the church produce the Kingdom. Mission is the trinitarian life of God from which the church derives, a life which involves the universal coming of the Kingdom as its own way of being. The church, therefore, has its reality not in self-legitimating efforts at self-perpetuation but in embracing all activities, whether considered religious or secular, which lead to the liberation of human life from every form of oppression threatening it. Such an embrace is not to be confused with a mindless conformity to any social or political ideology, a giddy seduction merely by whatever the current rhetoric about freedom. Rather, it determines both the identity and relevance of the true practice of liberation with the critical rationality of faith in God's promise at the cross, a locus of discernment both eschatological and historical from within the sufferings of the present time. In seeking to signify the promise of the cross through Word and sacrament and partisanship with the least of earth whom Jesus called the brothers and sisters of the coming Son of Man, the church comes to its own life as a manifestation of the Spirit.

Viewed in its overall scope, Moltmann's theology in its most substantive expressions provides a texture of discourse remarkable for its interdisciplinary character. This quality no doubt accounts in large part for the widespread interest such texts as *Theology of Hope* and *The Crucified God* have aroused. Reflections from biblical theology, church history, the history of philosophy, and dogmatic tradition are woven together with contemporary modes of social and political thought. Inevitably some loose ends appear in the fabric of the argument. The exegetical claims made from Scripture and the philosophical conceptions, mainly from Bloch and Hegel, which are used to interpret their significance for today are not always harmoniously wedded. Quarrels may be raised as well with points in Moltmann's descriptions of positions that he is attacking. From some of the newer liberation theologians, for whom his work has been so influential, has come the objection that what is said regarding the practice of hope lacks a sufficient grounding and concrete engagement in social struggle. On the other hand, some of the initial criticisms of one-sidedness, of proposing a futurist eschatology which overlooks God's presence and of ignoring the role of present experience in the knowledge of God, now appear in retrospect to reflect misunderstanding.

Many others have addressed issues similar to the ones that have continued to occupy Moltmann. No one has been more instrumental in showing how and why reflection on the eschatology of the cross matters for our life today.

Bibliography

Jürgen Moltmann, *The Crucified God*, N.Y., Harper & Row, 1974.

Christopher Morse, *The Logic of Promise in Moltmann's Theology*, Philadelphia, Fortress, 1979.

DAVID TRACY

Matthew L. Lamb

If conversation means allowing the participants to seek a fuller understanding of what is being discussed, then the art of conversation is the art of questioning by which the solidity of opinion is opened up to new possibilities of meaning. A person who possesses the art of questioning is a person who is able to prevent the suppression of questions by the dominant opinion. A person who possesses this art will himself seek for everything in favor of an opinion. Dialectic consists, not in trying to discover the weakness of what is said, but in bringing out its real strength. Conversation requires not the art of arguing but the art of thinking whereby what is said is strengthened by reference to the subject matter being discussed.[1]

The theological enterprise bids each new generation of theologians to enter into conversations stretching back millennia as well as to engage in the pluralist discourses of their own times. What is being discussed in any and all theology is not only the diverse human conversations in so many different languages and cultures but also the transformations of those dialogues disclosed by the ground and source of human dialogue, Divine Mystery—for Christians, the Word of God.

Among contemporary theological writings, few express as fully as David Tracy's the character of a wide-ranging conversation. To read his works is to enter into very demanding conversations in which are disclosed very creative turns or transformations. Indeed, David Tracy's life and work are dedicated to an exploration of those arts of questioning and of thinking which, if practiced responsibly, make theological discourse genuinely public and intellectually serious. Genuine conversation is the hallmark of his catholicity, the universality of which calls for an "ecumenical self-exposure" wherein the past and present conflicts of interpretation "may yet become a genuine conversation."[2]

[1] Hans-Georg Gadamer, *Wahrheit und Methode* (Tübingen, J. C. B. Mohr, 1965), p. 349.
[2] David Tracy, *The Analogical Imagination: Christian Theology and the Culture of Pluralism* (N.Y., Crossroad, 1981), p. 437, herafter cited as AI.

Tracy was born in Yonkers, New York, on January 6, 1939. His early education at Cathedral College and St. Joseph's Seminary in Yonkers (1958–60) underwent the profound transformations of studying Catholic theology at the Gregorian University in Rome (1960–64) during the pontificate of Pope John XXIII and the Second Vatican Council. He returned to Rome in 1965, spending the next two years there working on a doctoral dissertation dealing with the theological method of Bernard Lonergan, S.J., whose lectures and writings had introduced Tracy into the art and potential scope of human questioning. With Lonergan as a guide, Tracy was able to recover classical and medieval conversations in philosophy and theology, with their significant breakthroughs in theory and interiority, and also to engage in the very different modern conversations arising from the Reformation and the Enlightenment, with their emphases upon religious subjectivity, modern science, and historical consciousness.

His first book, *The Achievement of Bernard Lonergan,* traces Lonergan's achievements in disclosing transformed methodological contexts. The significance of these contexts for Tracy is their ability to enable serious, nonauthoritarian conversations. So many intellectual discourses of the past and the present have been broken off into exclusive monologues and marked by polemical misunderstandings within Christianity and modernity. These can, however, be critically and rigorously recovered and transposed into humanly and ecumenically inclusive dialogues. Manifold conflicts, such as those between the past (*via antiqua*) and the present (*via moderna*), between Catholicism and Protestantism, between faith and science, between theism and atheism, are indicative of how the worlds of intelligence and of faith could become a "chaotic pluralism." The achievement of Lonergan, in Tracy's view, consists in the critically transformed methodical contexts fostering genuine conversations already in process and making others concretely possible. This is especially important for Catholic theologies. Recent developments make painfully clear how easily the genuine conversations found in the works of Bernard Lonergan, Karl Rahner, Edward Schillebeeckx, Johann Baptist Metz, Hans Küng, and many others can be misunderstood and jeopardized within certain sectors of Catholicism.[3]

After two years at the Catholic University of America in Washington, D.C., David Tracy joined the Divinity School of the University of Chicago in 1969. With the congenial collaboration of his many colleagues at the University of Chicago, Tracy embarked upon an ambitious project of thematically reconstructing the theological discourses operative within the subject specializations, or disciplines, of fundamental, systematic, and practical theologies. Within the limits of this introductory essay it is impossible to convey the rich texture and multiplicity of conversations which imbue his writings. Rather, I shall concentrate upon the arts of questioning and of thinking which those writings exhibit, the underlying related and recurrent ways in which Tracy patterns his reconstructions of theological discourse. Moreover, since Tracy himself has recently provided a succinct overview of his project of reconstruction, I shall approach it somewhat differently.[4]

A HERMENEUTICS OF THEOLOGICAL CONVERSATION

The motif of conversation, as a hallmark of Tracy's theological enterprise, allows for what might be called a "backward reading"

[3] See Tracy's *Achievement of Bernard Lonergan* (N.Y., Herder & Herder, 1970), esp. pp. 232–69, hereafter cited as ABL, where Tracy indicates the inclusive character of Lonergan's approach to method and how this character radically transforms method from its modern derailment into technical, or logical, rules. A recent book, coauthored with Stephen Happel, draws upon work that Tracy did in 1967–68 while at the Catholic University of America, *A Catholic Vision* (Philadelphia, Fortress, 1984). Since 1976 Tracy has been on the editorial board of the international theological journal *Concilium*, and very much involved in the efforts to promote the many dimensions of theological discourse it represents. Cf. David Tracy, Hans Küng, and Johann B. Metz, eds., *Toward Vatican III: The Work That Needs to be Done* (N.Y., Seabury, 1978). Also, Tracy's "Particular Questions within General Consensus," in *Consensus in Theology? A Dialogue with Hans Küng and Edward Schillebeeckx*, ed. L. Swidler (Philadelphia, Westminster, 1980), pp. 33–39; and his essay in *Twenty Years of Concilium—Retrospect and Prospect*, ed. Paul Brand, Edward Schillebeeckx, and Anton Weiler (N.Y., Seabury, 1983), pp. 30–36.

[4] See "The Foundations of Practical Theology," in *Practical Theology*, ed. Don S. Browning (N.Y., Harper & Row, 1983), pp. 61–82, hereinafter cited as FPT.

of his writings. Later positions cast new light upon previous ones. This is by no means unusual in ongoing conversations. There is the fundamental significance of the hermeneutical circle, in which the developing whole gives new meaning to its parts. As applied to conversations, Hans-Georg Gadamer points out how

> we say that we "conduct" a conversation, but the more fundamental a conversation is, the less its conduct lies within the will of the participants. Thus a fundamental conversation is never one that we want to conduct. Rather, it is generally more correct to say that we fall into conversation, or even that we become involved in it. The way in which one word follows another, with the conversation taking its own turnings and reaching its own conclusion, may well be conducted in some way, but the people conversing are far less the leaders than the led. No one knows what will "come out" in a conversation. Understanding or its failure is like a process which happens to us.[5]

Walter Benjamin expresses an analogous insight with his metaphor of the angel of history moving backward into the future, with its face turned resolutely toward the past as a storm from paradise drives it ever forward.[6] What is going forward in theological, or any, conversations can often only be discerned clearly through a hermeneutical backward glance.

Such a reading of Tracy, I suggest, would indicate how his writings to date are efforts to bring the subdisciplines of fundamental, systematic, and practical theologies into conversation with the analogical tasks of developing what he had earlier, in reference to Lonergan, analyzed as the dialectical and foundational specializations of theology in general.[7] Both *Blessed Rage for Order* and *The Analogical Imagination*, as well as subsequent articles, are creative and critical contributions toward transforming theological conflicts of interpretation from what he terms "a chaotic pluralism" to "a responsible and

---

[5] Gadamer, *Wahrheit und Methode*, p. 361.

[6] Walter Benjamin, *Illuminations*, ed. Hannah Arendt (N.Y., Shocken Books, 1969), pp. 257ff. Another expression is found in T. S. Eliot's *Four Quartets* which begins, "Time present and time past/ Are both perhaps present in time future,/And time future contained in time past."

[7] ABL, pp. 247–55. In my *Solidarity with Victims* (N.Y., Crossroad, 1982), pp. 94–95, hereafter cited as SV, I put forward this suggestion.

collaborative pluralism." Tracy's writings rank pre-eminently among those dedicated to transforming theology into genuinely "public forms of discourse."[8]

Now pluralism has foundational import for theology, according to Lonergan. Both the problems and the enriching possibilities of pluralism led Lonergan to develop what he referred to as general and special foundational theological categories.[9] Tracy combines this concern for general and special categories with a revised notion of Tillich's theological method of mutually critical correlations. Tracy revises the latter by insisting how the interplay of questions and answers leads to revisions in both our Christian traditions and our contemporary situations.[10] Instead of general and special categories, we now have mutually critical correlations between "the meaning and truth of an interpretation of the contemporary situation" (general) and "the meaning and truth of an interpretation of the Christian fact" (special).[11] Just as the categories render the ongoing questions-answers more determinate for Lonergan, so the three subdisciplines of fundamental, systematic, and practical theologies "concretize," or provide "specificity" to, Tracy's notion of theology as mutually critical correlations.[12]

In such a reading, the subdisciplines are distinguished but by no means separated, and the same holds true for the publics in which their distinct but interrelated conversations occur. Fundamental theologies are "expressed but not exhausted" in

[8] FPT, p. 81; see his contributions to David Tracy and John Cobb, *Talking About God: Doing Theology in the Context of Modern Pluralism* (N.Y., Seabury, 1983), pp. 1–7, hereafter cited as TAG; also AI, pp. xi–xii, 28ff., 79ff., 446ff.; his *Blessed Rage for Order: The New Pluralism in Theology* (N.Y., Crossroad, 1975), pp. 3–14, ABL pp. 89ff., hereafter cited as BRO.

[9] Bernard Lonergan, *Method in Theology* (N.Y., Crossroad, 1972), pp. 271–81, hereafter cited as MIT; note how Lonergan's discussion of "Pluralism and the Unity of Faith" on pp. 326–30 refers to the issues raised in foundations. On general and special categories, see p. 282: "While the transcendental notions make questions and answers possible, categories make them determinate. Theological categories are either general or special. General categories regard objects that come within the purview of other disciplines as well as theology. Special categories regard the objects proper to theology."

[10] ABL, pp. 264–65; BRO, pp. 32–63.

[11] FPT, p. 62; TAG, pp. 5–7; AI, pp. 47–62.

[12] FPT, p. 65.

the public of the academy. Systematic theologies are similarly expressed relative to the publics of the churches, while practical theologies are related primarily "to some particular social, political, cultural, or pastoral movement or problematic."[13] Often overlooked by even very attentive readers of Tracy are what I would term two sets of mutually critical correlations in his complex reconstructions of ongoing theological conversations. One set consists of the "general rubric of mutually critical correlation of the meaning and truth of an interpretation of the Christian fact and the meaning and truth of an interpretation of the contemporary situation."[14] These are operative in theology generally, according to Tracy, and *a fortiori* in each of the three subdisciplines.

The other set of mutually critical correlations, however, flows from the first set and further determines the arts of questioning and of understanding in the three subdisciplines. If one reads back from his more recent works, it seems Tracy is also attempting to establish mutually critical correlations between the subdisciplines of fundamental, systematic, and practical theologies. In *The Analogical Imagination* he acknowledges that each of the three subdisciplines involves "differences" or "distinctions" relative to a common set of five "rubrics": (1) primary reference groups; (2) modes of argument; (3) ethical stances; (4) self-understandings of the theologian's personal faith or beliefs; and (5) formulations of what primarily counts as meaning and truth in theology.[15] To date, it is true, Tracy tends to emphasize the *differences* in these five common rubrics operative in fundamental, systematic, and practical theologies. This emphasis on difference relates to what he calls an abstract-concrete schema:

> But if one keeps the abstract-concrete schema in mind, one can note that fundamental theology is concerned with the *most abstract possibilities and necessities* that *are* fundamental for understanding some of the necessary presuppositions of systematic and practical theologies. Abstractions are necessary to correct confusions in the

[13] TAG, p. 3; AI, pp. 3–46, 56.
[14] FPT, pp. 62–65; TAG, pp. 5–8; AI, pp. 58–62; BRO, pp. 32–63.
[15] AI, p. 56; also TAG, pp. 2–5.

concrete. Abstractions never replace the concrete. For fundamental theology, thus considered, to replace systematic and practical theologies would prove not merely imperialistic but a prime instance of the "fallacy of misplaced concreteness."[16]

Although this might read as if the role of abstract theory is to correct confusions in concrete praxis, both Tracy's appreciation of the dialectics of theory-praxis and his choice of analogy as claiming similarities-in-differences tend against such a reading. For what about the need, in our postmodern situation, to correct confusions in so many competing, often contradictory, theories?

Abstract possibilities and necessities are not conceptualist or essentialist criteria à la neo-scholasticism or Hegelianism. Rather, they are the enriching possibilities and the contingently conditioned necessities disclosed in the transformative praxis of intellectualist theorizing.[17] Thus Tracy acknowledges both the presence of praxis and the need to articulate ethical stances in all three subdisciplines.[18] Moreover, this second set of mutually critical correlations among the three subdisciplines seems to enlighten the turns in Tracy's own theological conversations. *Blessed Rage for Order* is primarily dedicated to questions in fundamental theologies; yet systematic and practical theological correctives are present throughout the work.[19] Similarly, *The Analogical Imagination* is primarily dedicated to questions in systematic theologies, although fundamental and practical theological correctives are even more in evidence.[20]

As Tracy is now working on a volume dedicated to practical theology, one wonders how his articulations of a more comprehensive notion of critical reason determined by analogical transpositions of praxis and phronesis will not only "affect ractical theology" but will also provide critical correctives to fundamental and systematic theologies.[21] This is especially

[16] AI, p. 89.

[17] ABL, pp. 76ff., 140.

[18] FPT, pp. 67, 70–81; AI, pp. 63, 122, 246 n. 26, 301 n. 99, 369–79, 390–95, 429; BRO, pp. 13, 33, 44, 81, 210ff., 237–57.

[19] BRO, pp. 24, 26, 33, 238–50.

[20] AI, pp. 22, 56–59, 62–64, 69–79, 85, 93, 95, 97, 160, 183ff., 241, 377ff., 390–98.

[21] FPT, pp. 67, 70–72.

intriguing since *The Analogical Imagination* already admits that some fundamental theologians, namely, Lonergan along with political and liberation theologians, employ philosophical models of praxis and transformation relative to truth and value questions.[22] In a similar vein, Tracy holds that "praxis is theory's own originating and self-correcting foundation" so that "praxis sublates theory, not vice-versa."[23] Will this lead Tracy—as it has Alasdair MacIntyre, Richard Bernstein, Johann B. Metz, and liberation theologians in their different ways—to a realization of how the recovery of practical rationality beyond objectivism and relativism is not only an intellectual but also a political—and for the theologian an ecclesial—task?[24] To what extent would truly practical theologies analogously sublate, with their similarities-in-differences, systematic and fundamental subdisciplines? We must await the ongoing turns in the conversations for Tracy's answers and further questions.

A Dialectics of Theological Conversation

Because there are so many conversation partners in *Blessed Rage for Order* and *The Analogical Imagination*, readers and reviewers sometimes miss the direct discourse of Tracy's own positions. A hermeneutical reading of these books, with such a reading's attention to how later developments throw light upon previous positions, might prove helpful in distinguishing these modes of discourse. For one thing, such a reading highlights the dialectics operative throughout Tracy's own direct discourse.

For example, some reviewers thought Tracy was adopting

[22] AI, pp. 63, 70–73, 390–98.

[23] Ibid., p. 69.

[24] Cf. A. MacIntyre, *After Virtue* (Notre Dame, University of Notre Dame Press, 1981), pp. 238–45; R. Bernstein, *Beyond Objectivism and Relativism: Science, Hermeneutics, and Praxis* (Philadelphia, University of Pennsylvania Press, 1983), pp. 223–31; J. B. Metz, *Glaube in Geschichte und Gesellschaft* (Mainz, Grünewald, 1977), pp. 29–76, 120–35, 204–11; also his *Emergent Church*, trans. P. Mann (N.Y., Crossroad, 1981); S. Torres and J. Eagleson, eds., *The Challenge of Basic Christian Communities* (N.Y., Orbis, 1981). These studies indicate how the publics of academy, church, and society are in need of profound transformations in order to realize more genuine conversation in dialogical communities.

basically liberal theological positions in *Blessed Rage for Order*.[25] In *The Analogical Imagination* Tracy revises both his previous distinctions between theological subdisciplines and his characterization of political and liberation theologians of praxis as neo-orthodox.[26] In *Talking About God* he further clarifies what he understands by mutually critical correlations between Thomist and process understandings of God and world order.[27] Yet even within *Blessed Rage for Order* his criticism of liberal theologies for their "nearly complete commitment to the modern Enlightenment view of humanity's rational possibilities" should have signaled how his revisionist model was anything but a liberal agenda under a new name.[28] Tracy's analysis of the models of orthodox, liberal, neo-orthodox, radical, and his own revisionist model of theologizing, is, I believe, best understood as an analogical ordering wherein the revisionist model sublates and transforms, with its similarities-in-differences, some of the basic concerns of the other models.[29] It is clear that Tracy in *Blessed Rage for Order* is *not* dealing with typically *modern* forms of secularity, whether expressed in modern science, moral discourse, or the life-worlds of the everyday. He explicitly develops a critique of "the modern secular mind" and situates his revisionist theologizing as seeking mutually critical correlations "between the principal values, cognitive claims, and existential faiths of both a reinterpreted *post-modern consciousness* and a reinterpreted Christianity."[30] A decade later, readers are perhaps in a better position to appreciate how Tracy's discussions of limit-questions in science, morality, and the everyday life-world, as well as his analyses of limit language and metaphysics, in *Blessed Rage for Order* were aimed at disclosing

[25] See Avery Dulles, "Method in Fundamental Theology," *Theological Studies*, Vol. 37, no. 2 (June, 1976), pp. 304–16; Van A. Harvey, "The Pathos of Liberal Theology," *The Journal of Religion*, Vol. 56, no. 4 (October, 1976), pp. 382–91.

[26] BRO, pp. 239–46; AI, pp. 84 n. 28, 390–98.

[27] TAG, pp. 17–38; also AI, pp. 439–40 n. 7.

[28] BRO, p. 241.

[29] *Ibid.*, pp. 22–42. Note also how pluralism led Lonergan to introduce the foundational significance of models, MIT, pp. 284ff., to which Tracy refers in BRO, pp. 23, 35 n. 9. Also Lamb, SV, pp. 75–99.

[30] BRO, p. 32 (emphasis mine); also pp. 10–14.

the profound transformations occurring in the contemporary shifts from modern to postmodern cultures.[31]

Similarly, some readers and reviewers of *The Analogical Imagination* perceived in it a lack of concrete and reflective dialectics.[32] Yet I believe a hermeneutical reading itself indicates how Tracy's notion of analogy maintains mutually critical correlations between hermeneutics and dialectics. His analogical understanding of hermeneutics and his own theological recovery of the notion of a classic are open to dialectical transformations. The authority of "classic texts, symbols, persons, and images can operate as the authority of persuasive disclosure, not authoritarian coercion." The entire thrust of his recovery of the notion of the classic is to transform, or revision, classics so that they "need not be handed over to the classicists," any more than we should allow tradition to "become the personal property of traditionalists."[33] Such a program can be carried out only if analogy incorporates dialectics into its hermeneutical agenda.

The analogical imagination, therefore, is dialectically open to "the actuality of the not-yet concealed in our present inhumanity in all its darkness." There is need for a "liberating" scholarship in order that "authentic conversation" recover "that dialectical sense within analogy itself."[34] Tracy himself engages in such a liberating scholarship by carefully analyzing how theologies centered on manifestations of God's presence, as well as those centered on proclamation of God's saving action in our sinful world, can be critically related with theologies centered on the imperatives of prophetic action redemptively transforming

[31] *Ibid.*, pp. 91–203. On the significance of postmodernity for shifts in hermeneutics and the dialectics of theory-praxis, cf. David Tracy's and Matthew Lamb's essays in *Ein Neues Paradigma von Theologie?*, ed. Hans Küng and David Tracy (Zürich, Benziger, forthcoming). For a very readable introduction to some of the issues involved in the shift to postmodernity, see Harvey Cox, *Religion in the Secular City: Toward a Postmodern Theology* (N.Y., Simon & Schuster, 1984).

[32] See the reviews of John B. Cobb, Jr., and Gregory Baum in *Religious Studies Review*, Vol. 7, no. 4 (October, 1981), pp. 281–90; Gordon D. Kaufman, "Conceptualizing Diversity Theologically," *The Journal of Religion*, Vol. 62, no. 4 (October, 1982), pp. 392–401.

[33] FPT, p. 71.

[34] AI, p. 455; pp. 414ff.

human history.[35] So the "tensive power of the negative" is transformatively disclosed in the classic events grounding liberation theologies as "a liberating praxis wherein the actions of whole peoples whose disclosive, ignored, forgotten, despised story is at last being narrated and heard in ways which may yet transform us all." For our contemporary situation is marked with "satanic explosions of anti-Spirit. These events challenge *all* interpretations by paradigmatically expressing a repressed truth in our situation: the Holocaust, the Gulag, Hiroshima." Hence Tracy can be quite explicit about "the dialectic of the classics" within our contemporary postmodern situation.[36]

Such a reading of *The Analogical Imagination* enables us to understand how Tracy's analyses of Christian classics, religious classics, and classics in general are not meant to impose some conceptualist univocal meanings upon these very different forms of classics. Rather, Tracy's intention is to contribute to, and theologically explicate, ongoing conversations among diverse Christian traditions, among the world religions, and within our very divided and nuclear-armed world. He carefully analyzes the analogical similarities-in-differences which provide some of the main intellectual, religious, and Christian warrants—indeed imperatives—for moving from sometimes bitter conflicts of interpretation toward more just and ecumenical conversations. Public discourse in its many dimensions (academic, ecclesial, social) is dependent upon the meanings conveyed in its various classics and their continually new interpretations. Tracy's efforts to elaborate analogical understandings of their similarities and very real differences do evidence that "art of questioning able to prevent the suppression of questions by the dominant opinion" of which Gadamer has written.[37] An attention to both dialectics and praxis is intrinsic to these hermeneutical efforts.

Christian classics find their focal meanings and truths in the

---

[35] *Ibid.*, pp. 371–445. In these chapters Tracy distinguishes the trajectories or routes theologies adopt as those of manifestation and proclamation. This parallels his earlier treatment of religious classics, pp. 202–18. But on pp. 390–98 he indicates how political and liberation theologians interpret the theological classics of manifestation or proclamation in the context of prophetic and transformative praxis in history.

[36] *Ibid.*, pp. 398, 410; p. 361 (emphasis mine); pp. 345–52.

[37] Gadamer, *Wahreit und Methode*, p. 349.

event and person of Jesus Christ witnessed to in the New Testament. Christian faith, as a knowledge born of Christ's Spirit of love, is both challenged and often purified by scholarly efforts at ever more accurately understanding the genre and narrative forms which "free the theologians to employ the world disclosed by the narrative as a new and critical corrective of all present practice and thought in the tradition." For "the intrinsic dialectical relationship of situation-event-response" operative in the New Testament witnesses themselves is a "dialectic of freedom and response" normative for all subsequent Christian traditions. Thus only "when the *orthopraxis* of discipleship is authentic" will "the *orthodoxy* of the confessions ring true."[38]

> Every great religious tradition (as the prophetic-reformatory core of Judaism and Christianity should also remind us) has produced radically ambiguous effects. Consider, for example, the central symbol of Christianity, the Christ symbol. That symbol has produced in its history of effects not only the healing, disclosive, and transformative realities of genuine religious redemption for millions but sometimes has produced, unintentionally to be sure but no less fatally, anti-Semitism, sexism, class prejudice, racism, and an arrogant exclusivism.[39]

This later explication of the radical ambiguity of concealment as well as disclosure in all classics, whether Christian, religious, or secular—"Every great work of civilization, as Walter Benjamin reminds us, is also a work of barbarism"[40]—indicates how Tracy by no means reifies classics but is attentive to the "intrinsically dialectical experience" grounding all classic expressions.[41] Insofar as "from the beginning to the end of the entire hermeneutical process . . . authentic praxis" should be "operative," it is important to realize with political and liberation theologians that in history there is a very "breakable connection" between the way humans "ought to live and the way things really are."[42]

[38] AI, pp. 325ff.; pp. 255–87, 305; p. 270.
[39] FPT, p. 70; also AI, pp. 202–18.
[40] FPT, p. 70.
[41] AI, pp. 115, 121, 175, 218.
[42] FPP, p. 71; AI, p. 1630.

As Tracy continues to converse with past and present scholars, social theorists, philosophers, and theologians regarding a reconstruction of practical theologies in our pluralistic situation, perhaps the mutually critical correlations between fundamental, systematic, and practical theologies will become more pronounced. Already this seems to me to be emerging in his most recent works. Tracy recently began designating fundamental, systematic, and practical theologies as "subdisciplines" rather than "disciplines."[43] He has also concisely articulated the foundational importance of praxis within these subdisciplines:

> In a manner analogous to the necessity for the praxis of the value of critical theory for the fundamental theologian, the systematic theologian, precisely as interpreter of the tradition, must ethically honor the complex and demanding praxis of authentic interpretation and its attendant criteria. . . . The very praxis of interpretation will also open one to the further test of transformative praxis. . . . As disclosive, the Christian vision, like any classic vision, is also in some sense transformative for the interpreter. As applicable, this vision is both grounded in praxis and open to a final test of truth—the test of transformative praxis and critical theological ethical reflection. . . . The task of practical theology . . . is to test this vision and, in that testing, transform it.[44]

Perhaps we already have a clue in the ways in which *The Analogical Imagination* intensified the significance of history and of hermeneutics relative to *Blessed Rage for Order*. Not only did this lead Tracy to reformulate his understandings of the subdisciplines within the theological enterprise, it also led him to reflect, at the very beginning of *The Analogical Imagination*, on the diverse social contexts in which theology is practiced.[45] Whether or not analogous intensifications in regard to dialectics and praxis occur in his next major work, the present introduction to his past reconstructions of ongoing theological conversations is no more than an invitation to engage oneself in the new and transformative possibilities of meaning his writings disclose.

Contemporary theology and culture have already been

[43] FPT, p. 65; AI, pp. 61ff.
[44] FPT, pp. 71–72.
[45] BRO, pp. 237–40; AI, pp. 3–31, 84–85 n. 28.

enriched by David Tracy's very creative participation in the ongoing efforts to render genuine and empowering conversations both more possible and more inclusive. He is indeed a person whose arts of questioning and of thinking strengthen those inclusive possibilities of conversation by allowing the subject matter itself to lead the way.

> Conversation occurs *only* where the conversation partners allow the subject matter to take over. Conversation occurs only when we free ourselves for the common subject matter and free ourselves from the prisons of our vaunted individualism. . . . Only the realities of genuine self-respect and self-exposure to the other in conversation with the classic expressions of the human spirit is likely to free us all to the fuller reality of a liberating analogical imagination in this pluralist situation.[46]

Whatever turns the conversations in David Tracy's further works will take, his dedication to the subject matter of theology assures that they will be both insightful and challenging.

[46] AI, p. 452.

Bibliography

David Tracy, *The Analogical Imagination: Christian Theology and the Culture of Pluralism,* N.Y., Crossroad, 1981.

William M. Shea, et al., "David Tracy's *The Analogical Imagination,*" Horizon: *The Journal of the College Theology Society,* Vol. 8, no. 2 (Fall, 1981), pp. 313–39.

JOHN B. COBB, JR.

David Ray Griffin

"Creative transformation" has become the central notion in the thought of John Cobb. His own spiritual-intellectual journey can itself be described as a series of transformations.

GEORGIA PIETISM

John Cobb's parents, John and Theodora, both grew up in Georgia. They met in the Student Volunteer Movement before World War I, then went to Japan as missionaries in 1919, where they served, except during World War II, until 1965. John, Jr., the youngest of three children, was born February 9, 1925. Except for returning to Georgia at ages six and fourteen when his parents had furloughs, he lived in Japan, mainly in Hiroshima and Kobe, until 1940, when all unessential Americans were encouraged to leave. (He was attending a Canadian school, and Canada was already at war with Germany, Japan's ally.) Young John, then fifteen, returned to Georgia to live with his grandmother, finished high school, and attended a junior college, Emory at Oxford.

Throughout this period, Cobb lived in terms of the Georgia Protestant pietism he had imbibed with his mother's milk. Feeling like an outsider in both Japan and Georgia, he experienced his main sense of community, beyond his family, with God, with whom it seemed natural to converse. In junior college days, his pietism involved an extremely ascetic dimension; for example, money that might have been spent on candy or bus fare was sent to a mission for lepers in the Sudan. His pietism also contributed to strong moral convictions; he brought blacks to his Georgia church and publicly countered the lies in the anti-Japanese propaganda after Pearl Harbor. The negative effect that his pietistic moralism had on others is suggested in a cartoon in the college annual picturing John with a halo around his head and several more dangling from his arm. It was titled

691

"Spares." He muses: "That my sanctity was only skin deep was illustrated by the rage I felt and expressed at this cartoon—which I must admit was one of the funniest in the annual."

Transition to Modernity

A transitional period began with Cobb's decision, before he had finished junior college and after he had pondered pacifism, to join the United States Army in 1944. Because of his background, he was chosen for the Japanese language program, which was filled mainly with academic-minded Jews and Irish Catholics. For the first time he was in the company of intellectuals, and he became aware of the relativity of his own world view, learning that others regarded Georgia Protestantism as a phenomenon of interest sociologically but not intellectually. Cobb began an avid reading program which exposed him to the intellectual world of the twentieth century, but this exposure did not undermine his faith, which had rested upon personal experience, not upon fundamentalist convictions.

The one clearly extraordinary experience Cobb has had occurred during this period: "One night I knelt beside my bed for prayer in the most perfunctory way, when suddenly the room seemed filled with a presence of the most blessed sort. For a few brief moments I experienced what I can only describe as joy. It passed, I said thank you, and went to bed." He contrasts this experience with another, when he came to the realization that he preferred to go not into government foreign service but into some kind of Christian ministry. Although there were a suddenness and a clarity to this "calling" experience, he can accept a thoroughly psychological explanation of it. That experience of blessed presence during prayer "simply gave itself to be understood as the presence of God and as a gift totally disconnected from expectation, merit, or anything else in my own life." This experience is germane to his ongoing ambivalence about the desirability, as well as the reality, of personal immortality: "If it were not for that event, I could only regard literally everlasting life as a curse, but if such life partook of that quality, it would be unmitigated blessing." Coming as it did shortly before Cobb's Chicago years, this experience could perhaps be interpreted as a proleptic confirmation that there was *something* to his pietistic faith—which was about to be demolished.

The Destruction of Faith

The intellectual stimulation and advice he had received from his army friends led Cobb to enroll in the University of Chicago. He chose an interdepartmental program in which he could study all the objections to Christianity produced by the modern world. He describes the motivation and the effect: "I was determined to expose my faith to the worst the world could offer. Within six months of such exposure my faith was shattered." This shattering was not due to particular *arguments*. Rather, "the vision, perspective, or frame of reference of the modern sensibility simply altered my own vision of reality." This interpretation, from about 1965, reflects two motifs of Cobb's first period of reconstruction: (1) Christian faith has to do centrally with a preconceptual perspective, or "vision of reality," and (2) the distinctively "modern" vision of reality is incompatible with Christian faith.

A central effect of this shattering of faith was upon his prayer life, previously his mainstay: "God, who had been my constant companion and Lord up to that point, simply evaporated, and my prayers bounced back from the ceiling unheard." Even after Cobb's faith had returned intellectually, the previous naturalness of prayer did not. Because of his honesty about his struggle with prayer, many people have found his later writing on the subject refreshingly authentic.[1]

Since Cobb's sense of community and self-identity had primarily involved his relationship to God, the loss of belief was far from a merely intellectual matter. He has always felt kinship with those persons, such as Friedrich Nietzsche and Thomas J. J. Altizer, who portray the "death of God" as a catastrophic event.

A Context for Reconstruction

After a year, deciding that he needed to turn to some affirmative religious study at the same level of sophistication as the negative

[1] "To Pray or Not to Pray: A Confession," in *Prayer in My Life*, ed. Maxie Dunnam (Nashville, The Upper Room, 1974), pp. 83–112.

study he had been undertaking, Cobb entered the University of Chicago Divinity School:

> My occasional prior contacts with members of its faculty, chiefly Joachim Wach and James Luther Adams, had assured me that they had taken account somehow of the problems that had destroyed my faith, and though I was quite unable to see how, it seemed that I should expose myself to what they had to say.

Again, openness led to transformation, this time a constructive one.

A major influence on him during his divinity school days was Richard McKeon of the philosophy department, who led him to philosophical relativism. He was persuaded by McKeon that numerous systems are each capable of handling the range of philosophical problems quite well from their particular perspectives and that "almost all serious criticisms of major thought-systems are primarily a function of approaching those thought-systems with alien presuppositions."

The other major intellectual influence upon Cobb was Charles Hartshorne. Cobb says, "It was through his teaching that I was once again able to take the idea of God seriously." Hartshorne introduced him to the thought of Whitehead, and a Hartshornean Whiteheadianism has cohabited with philosophic relativism in Cobb's mind.

Cobb was able to begin reconstructing his faith in the context of the divinity school community, which was the first to which he really felt he belonged. In retrospect he sees many weaknesses in his education there. For example, there was little exposure to the new ideas from the Continent (this was 1947–50). But it was a "serious community of inquiry in which," Cobb says, "I felt all possible encouragement to think honestly and clearly and independently. I would not trade that for the finest scholarship, although I greatly admire and envy in others a scholarship I do not share." In this period, "Questions of professional preparation receded far into the background, for I was preoccupied with questions of belief for myself," he states.

During this time of intellectual turmoil, Cobb had become engaged to a friend from high school days, Jean Loftin, despite two obstacles: the difficulties his pietistic attitudes had created in his accepting both his own sexuality and that of "nice girls,"[2] and a passage he read a few weeks before the wedding stating that the inability to whistle—one of *his* inabilities—was a sign of physiological homosexuality! The ensuing weeks were for him as close to hell as the earlier mystical experience was to heaven. Fortunately, he was, he says, too cowardly to call off the wedding, and the Cobbs have had a happy and fruitful marriage, raising four sons.

Cobb's intellectual reconstruction of faith can be described in terms of several stages. Of course, these stages do not signify abrupt beginnings and endings. Each period of dominant interest usually overlapped the previous one by several years. Also, in most respects, each new understanding of what Christian faith and theology should be in our time did not mean a rejection of the previous phase so much as a relativizing of it.

CHRISTIAN NATURAL THEOLOGY

The first person to bring Whitehead's thought to Chicago was Henry Nelson Wieman. Wieman increasingly favored a strictly "empirical theology" free from all dependence upon dubious speculation, and he tended to stress only that side of Whitehead's thought, whereas Hartshorne stressed the metaphysical side. Confronted with these opposing emphases, Cobb read Whitehead for himself and saw that Hartshorne's stance was closer to Whitehead's own.

The systematic issue still remained: Can faith, and hence theology, do without philosophical speculation? Cobb's doctoral dissertation, titled "The Independence of Christian Faith from Speculative Belief," dealt with Wieman, Schleiermacher, and Tillich, who in various ways argued for such independence. Cobb contended, by means of internal criticism, that such independence is an impossible ideal and that it would accordingly be best to make one's speculations explicit, so that they could be criticized. This relationship between faith and speculative philosophy remained his central concern until the late sixties.

Cobb had to rush through his work at Chicago in order to

[2] Some of Cobb's later reflections on sexuality can be found in "Spirit and Flesh: Dipolarity Versus Dialectic," *Philosophy of Religion and Theology: 1972*, ed. David Ray Griffin (American Academy of Religion, 1972).

return to Georgia to take care of his older brother. By returning to Georgia he enabled his mother to return to Japan. Having to take whatever position he could find close to Atlanta, Cobb served seven mountain churches and taught in a junior college. Following his dissertation examination in 1952 (after which Hartshorne said, "He's one smart cookie"), he took a job that Ernest Colwell, former president of the University of Chicago and then vice-president at Emory, had arranged with the outgoing dean of the School of Theology there. Since the faculty in systematic theology had not been consulted and was additionally outraged because of Cobb's Chicago background, he was compelled to sign a statement that he would never teach a course in that field at Emory. Had he remained there, he would have become a full-time member of the philosophy department. As it was, after five years Colwell was invited to become president of the School of Theology at Claremont, and he in turn invited Cobb and James M. Robinson to be the core of the new faculty there. Cobb finally had the opportunity to teach systematic theology. For those of us who have been deeply influenced by Cobb's thought and person, this call has to be viewed providentially.

In this context he published his first book, *Varieties of Protestantism* (1960), in which he argued that the central concerns of each denomination do not necessarily conflict with each other. Many years later he would reach a similar conclusion about Christianity and Buddhism.

Cobb next wrote the book which is still his best piece of scholarship, *Living Options in Protestant Theology: A Survey of Methods* (1962). While continuing the argument of his dissertation that speculative beliefs are unavoidable (and this time he included a critique of Barth's "revelational positivism"), he also argued (against neo-Thomism and Boston Personalism) the impossibility of a strictly "natural" theology, in the sense of one based upon data equally open to all persons regardless of their historical background. For example, the "arguments for the existence of God," as developed by philosophers within the Christian tradition, already presuppose the vision of the world as created—e.g., in the perception of it as "contingent." Combining his two conclusions—that Christian theology presupposes a speculative philosophy serving as a natural thelogy and that there can be no *neutral* natural theology—Cobb points to the need for a *Christian* philosophy or natural theology. With the qualifier *Christian* we indicate our awareness that even the most abstract speculation is carried out from the standpoint of a *particular* perspective, or vision of reality, which is derived from a historically conditioned "community of faith." There is no such thing as philosophy per se, but only Hellenic philosophy, Christian philosophy, Buddhist philosophy, Humean philosophy, and so on. Cobb continued this argument in *A Christian Natural Theology: Based on the Thought of Alfred North Whitehead* (1965).

His insistence upon the relativizing adjective *Christian* showed the continuing influence of McKeon's relativism and put Cobb at odds with Schubert Ogden and David Tracy, who believe that the only criterion for choosing a philosophical support for the theological task should be its intrinsic excellence, judged on purely philosophical grounds. Cobb maintained that that criterion needed to be supplemented by the philosophy's appropriateness to the Christian vision of reality (since other philosophies might be equally excellent from the viewpoint of people with other visions of reality). He suggested that Whitehead's philosophy was appropriate in this sense, as it embodied the Christian vision of the world as creation. Hence, he could agree with those liberal and neo-orthodox theologians who believed that classical theology's use of Greek philosophy, especially Aristotle, had distorted Christian faith, while arguing that the use of Whitehead's philosophy would not.

Cobb's chief concern was God, and he was primarily interested in Whitehead's philosophy because it provided an intellectually cogent way to affirm the reality of God, including God's efficacy in our lives and in the world in general. But Whitehead's doctrine of God is inextricably bound up with his whole metaphysical system. What he meant by God, and the reasons he had for speaking of God, make no sense apart from his quite novel ideas about what the world is made of and about the nature of human perception. So Cobb's "Christian natural theology" includes the discussion of God's reality and efficacy within a discussion of how the world looks through eyes informed by Whitehead's vision.

Given his empirical bent, it was important to Cobb to stress the experiential rootage of talk about God. Most empiricism, equating perception with *sense* perception, has concluded that there can be no direct experience of God. However Whitehead portrays sense perception as derivative of a more basic kind of relatedness, called "prehension," in which one directly grasps previous events, which themselves have prehended previous ones. This non-sensory preconscious prehension is at the root of our response to reality and is a kind of response which we share with all other events—from animals, cells, and atoms below to God above.

By portraying all levels of reality as having a basic type of relatedness in common, Whitehead could explain how every level of reality could influence every other level. Hence, he could explain how mind and body could influence each other—always a big mystery to dualists. He could thereby explain how God could influence us (i.e., because we can prehend God) and in fact how God can affect all things in the world (i.e., because all individuals have some ability to prehend the actualities in their environment and because God is present in everything's environment). Cobb points out that this makes a Whiteheadian-based theology strikingly different from the tendency of most modern thought, which has denied the meaningfulness of talk about God or at most has limited God to some sphere of distinctively human experience, such as conscience or language. Whitehead had reopened the possibility for speaking of the world as God's creation and for seeing God, as Holy Spirit, directly and intimately related to every detail of the world process.

God's effect upon the world is not, however, total determination of its events. God's power is persuasive, not coercive. This means that the idea of a good creator and provider is not undermined by the problem of evil—another one of those "objections to Christian faith" Cobb had studied. God acts in the world by providing novel possibilities for its creatures. God's "primordial nature," as Whitehead calls this aspect of God, is God's appetitive envisagement of primordial potentialities. It is only because this reservoir of previously unactualized possibilities is energizing in the world that we can understand how novelty is possible (as in the increasing complexity of the evolutionary process). God acts thus not as another coercive force but as a persuasive lure. By stressing this side of Whitehead's thought, Cobb carries on the main thrust of Wieman, who, without employing the speculative Whiteheadian ideas, looked upon the process of "creative transformation" as God in the world.

Whitehead also portrays God, in turn, as prehending the world and thus having a "consequent nature." With this doctrine, Whitehead rejects the long-standing idea, inherited by the early Christian theologians from Greek thought, that to be divine is to be beyond change and passion in all respects. Whitehead's doctrine that God is affected by the world, as the "fellow sufferer who understands," provides a philosophical way of recovering the biblical notion that what we do "unto the least of these" we do unto God, and for making more sense out of prayer than traditional theism ever did.

This "consequent nature" of God was the side Hartshorne had most stressed. It provided a basis for affirming the meaningfulness of life. Hartshorne has long considered personal or "subjective" immortality highly improbable. Our lives have permanent meaning, even in the light of the eventual death of our planet, because we have "objective immortality," being remembered and cherished everlastingly by God.

This is central to Cobb's own eschatology. He also stressed that Whitehead's view of the person, according to which the soul is distinct from the brain, does make life after death possible. Perhaps through prehensions of God and other souls the series of experiences could find support beyond the body. Cobb has continued to be open to this possibility and to think about forms of continued existence that would be more a blessing than a curse.[3] But he has never made this an essential part of this theology.

During this period, Cobb understood the essence of Christian faith to be a particular preconceptual "vision of reality." As preconceptual, this vision is tied to no particular set of conceptual beliefs. But it is not merely a noncognitive *blik* which can be neither true nor false; it does say something about the nature of reality and hence can in principle be true. One can argue for its truth by formulating a convincing conceptual system which expresses this vision. Further, since the Christian vision of reality sees the world *as creation*, Cobb disagreed with

[3] "What is the Future?", in *Hope and the Future of Man*, ed. Ewert H. Cousins (Philadelphia, Fortress, 1972).

Bultmann's view that faith could be characterized as a self-understanding and explicated by means of a philosophy, such as that of Heidegger's *Being and Time,* which provided concepts for understanding human existence from within but none for understanding God and other creatures in themselves. Partly because he understood the nature of faith differently, Cobb took issue with the use of linguistic, existentialist, and phenomenological analysis as adequate for explicating Christian faith; thus he disagreed with the dominant schools of philosophy of religion and theology in the fifties and sixties. Only a full-fledged metaphysics can explicate the essence of Christian faith, since it is a vision of reality as a whole, not just of the self.

THE STRUCTURE OF CHRISTIAN EXISTENCE

However, Cobb's engagement with the Heideggerian tradition, partly through the influence of his fellow "transplant" from Emory, James M. Robinson,[4] did have an important effect upon his understanding of Christian faith. He came increasingly to see the essence of faith as a particular "structure of existence," which involves a way of relating to others and a way of structuring the various dimensions of the psyche (body, emotions, reason, will, spirit).[5] The Christian vision of reality, requiring a Christian natural theology for its explication, was still seen as necessary, but more as the necessary support for a particular mode of existing than as the essence of faith itself.[6] This shift could be seen in part as a return, in sophisticated form, to his Methodist pietism, in which being a Christian was more a matter of experience and of living than of believing certain ideas. While expressing his agreement with the Bultmannians that faith is fundamentally a mode of existence, Cobb relativizes their position. He finds their equation of Christian faith and unfaith with authentic and inauthentic existence, understood as two

[4] Cobb and Robinson edited three books in a series called "New Frontiers in Theology." The first two involved the influence of Heidegger: *The Later Heidegger and Theology* (1963) and *The New Hermeneutic* (1964).

[5] See "The Intra-Psychic Structure of Christian Existence," *Journal of the American Academy of Religion,* 36 (December, 1968), pp. 327-39.

[6] See "Christian Natural Theology and Christian Existence," *The Christian Century,* 82 (March 3, 1965), pp. 265-67; reprinted in *Frontline Theology,* ed. Dean G. Peerman (Atlanta, John Knox, 1967).

permanent possibilities for human existence, radically unhistorical. He finds it incredible to suppose that the complex structure of modern Westerners, as illuminated in *Being and Time,* emerged full-blown with the first appearance of beings worthy of the name human. In his view, there have been many stages of development between us and our apelike ancestors. Also, he finds it unilluminating to lump together modes of being as diverse as those of an Eastern mystic and a Western "other-directed" individual. Finally, seeing the essence of Christian faith as a *permanent* possibility of human existence implies that it is independent of all changing theological-cosmological ideas. One bad effect of this false belief is that it encourages theologians to think they can ignore the difficult task of relating the Christian vision of reality to the cosmological ideas expressed in the natural sciences.

Cobb employs Whitehead's ideas, in conversation with Erich Neumann, Karl Jaspers, and Lewis Mumford, to develop an evolutionary understanding of the rise of animal, primitive, and then axial existence, which has a plurality of structures. Although there can be successive stages within one tradition, e.g., Hindu and Buddhist, Homeric and Socratic, prophetic and Christian, the various traditions cannot be put into some kind of hierarchy. Buddhist existence is basically different from Christian, not a "preparation" for it or an "inauthentic" actualization of the general axial structure. The authentic-inauthentic language makes sense only *within* a particular structure. For example, "spiritual existence," in which one is radically responsible for one's own structure, has an inauthentic mode (self-preoccupation) and an authentic mode (freedom for genuine concern for the other).

Cobb tried out these ideas while lecturing as a Fulbright professor in Mainz, Germany, in 1965-66, and published them as *The Structure of Christian Existence* (1967).

TRANSITION FROM SCHOLASTICISM TO THE CALL FORWARD

For Cobb, the major figure at Mainz was Wolfhart Pannenberg.[7] His influence increased Cobb's sense of the importance of eschatological hope for Christian faith.

[7] The third of the Cobb-Robinson series, *Theology as History* (N.Y., Harper & Row, 1967), was devoted to Pannenberg's thought.

Another influence in that period was the "death of God" movement, with Cobb's best friend from Chicago days, Thomas Altizer, at the center of attention.

One irony of this movement, from Cobb's perspective, was that it appeared just as he was beginning to be able to talk about God and the effects of God in the world without extreme discomfort. In one sense it had no effect upon him, for it was a rejection of the wholly transcendent God, who had already died for him at Chicago, and of a corresponding theological approach (most of whose leaders had been Barthians) which he had rejected.

But it did have an effect. As Altizer saw, Cobb's response to it in *God and the World* (1969) was a transitional work. In retrospect, Cobb regards his work up through 1965 as "Whiteheadian scholasticism," in which he sought to show how Whitehead's thought could be employed to make sense of most of the concerns of neo-orthodoxy. Partly through the influence of the "death of God" movement, and especially of Altizer, he came to reject this maximalist approach, which relied partly on Whitehead's authority, and to favor speaking about God only from his own authentic convictions, which were coming to center on God as the source of novelty.

The central part of *God and the World* is chapter 2, which focuses on the image of God as "The One Who Calls" us forward. It reflects Cobb's greater appreciation for Wieman—although Cobb rejects Wieman's identification of God and creative transformation, seeing God instead as the *source* of such transformation. This chapter also reflects Cobb's change of focus from God's eternal nature to God's concrete effects at particular times—a change already begun in *The Structure of Christian Existence,* which portrayed God's effects in terms of changing structures of human existence. This chapter also shows Cobb's growing conviction that the theological task is not exhausted by developing an intelligible conceptuality for one's time. People live more by images than concepts; the theologian must participate in the process of shaping helpful images.

Chapter 2 has been the most influential part of this book. However, in chapter 3 Cobb applied the results of his metaphysical and epistemological labors of the previous decades to the questions of God's reality, location, and efficacy. Chapter

2 could not have been written without chapter 3. As Cobb later said: "Images are powerful only when those who hold them believe, consciously or unconsciously, that the images are appropriate to reality."[8]

In the remainder of this essay, I will discuss Cobb's position during the decade and a half from 1969 to 1984 as a single movement, dealing with the issues thematically instead of sequentially. It is true that some of the themes developed later than others, but all of them can be seen as elements in a single emerging stance.

FROM ECOLOGICAL CRISIS TO ECOLOGICAL-POLITICAL THEOLOGY

The most abrupt and datable transformation in Cobb's thinking came in 1969, as the implications of the ecological crisis hit him. Reinhold Niebuhr had been one of his heroes; he had been reading the liberation and political theologians with much concurrence. But he had continued to separate his political interests from his theological work, reflecting the departmental distinction between systematic theology and ethics. He says that only the realization in 1969 "that the whole human race was on a collision course with disaster shook me out of this dualism."[9]

Between 1970 and 1981 Cobb published two books[10] and fifteen papers on ecological concerns. The incorporation of an ecological stance was in one sense relatively natural. As he came to see, all the needed elements were already there in Whitehead's thought and even more explicitly in Hartshorne's. The doctrine that all actualities have experience and hence intrinsic value means that a purely anthropocentric ethic, in which other creatures are viewed merely as means for our ends, is inappropriate. A reverence for all being, especially for all life, is called for. In distinction from Schweitzer's unlivable ethic of *equal* reverence for all life, process thought allows for gradations of intrinsic value, corresponding to our sense that

[8] *Process Theology as Political Theology* (Philadelphia, Westminster, 1982), pp. 72–73.

[9] *Ibid.*, pp. x–xi.

[10] *Is It Too Late? A Theology of Ecology* (N.Y., Bruce Books, 1971); *The Liberation of Life: From the Cell to the Community,* with Charles Birch (Cambridge, Cambridge University Press, 1981).

some forms of life are intrinsically more important than others. Further, Whitehead offers an ecological view stating that an individual is not a "substance" which is what it is prior to its relations. Rather, reality is composed of events, each of which is a creative synthesis of the elements in its environment. (Cobb has recently come to refer to process thought as providing an "ecological model" of reality, which has, among other things, led him to criticize the departmental approach to education.) Finally, the idea that the ultimate locus of value is God's experience means that our ethic should consider instrumental as well as intrinsic value and should endeavor to sustain the entire biosphere.

Since he now saw inherited Christian faith itself as significantly responsible for our plight—as a consequence of its view that the earth's only value was as the stage for the divine-human drama of salvation—Cobb began to think not only of making the Christian vision of reality intelligible but also of transforming it.

The ecological issue involved political issues to a degree, but it was not until 1982 that he published a programmatic book arguing that process theology can and must become a political theology, in which both sociological theory and ecological theory are combined.[11] Process theology must overcome its abstractness and deal with the concrete issues of the day. Process theologians must come to relate their work to the sociopolitical matrix in which they are embedded, not just to the history of ideas. He stresses that Whitehead's thought points to the degree to which our perspective and interests are conditioned, even if not totally determined, by the immediate world out of which we arise.

This move represents a reappropriation of the concerns of what Cobb calls the earlier tradition of "process theology," the sociohistorical school of Shirley Jackson Case and Shailer Mathews, which had dominated Chicago Divinity School prior to the arrival of Wieman and then Hartshorne. Case and Mathews had stressed that theological reflection in the early church had been in the service of the church's social mission and that this should be the case today. Most critics point to this school's optimistic assumptions, but Cobb points out that it also had no adequate way to speak of God. With the former weakness

[11] *Process Theology as Political Theology.*

remedied by Reinhold Niebuhr, and the latter by Whitehead and Hartshorne, Cobb believes process theology should return to its earlier understanding of the theological task as that of speaking out of our tradition to the most urgent needs of the day.[12]

This move also represents an agreement—an all-too-belated one, Cobb believes—with the main formal point of liberation and political theologians: the rejection of the theory-application model in favor of a theory-praxis model. The point is that one's theory, or systematic theology, cannot be developed in one context, such as the history of Western ideas, and then "applied" to another context. The theory must be developed out of reflection upon the context one is concerned to transform, or it will probably be irrelevant or even counterproductive.

FROM ESSENCE TO CHRIST AS CREATIVE TRANSFORMATION

Closely related to the rejection of the dualism between theology and ethics is Cobb's rejection of his earlier search for an essence of Christian faith. There is no self-identical core to be found in the various embodiments. Christianity is more like an onion than an apple. Cobb has come to agree with Case and Mathews that the essence of a movement is its history. He clarifies this notion in terms of Whitehead's idea of a "living person," which is not a self-identical substance but a serially ordered sequence of occasions of experience with a particular kind of order. The self-identity of a person is based not upon an unchanging essence, shared by all the experiences—what does the ninety-year-old man have in common with the one-year-old baby he was?—but upon a particular mode of relatedness from moment to moment. This is a relatedness (called "hybrid physical feelings" by Whitehead) in which one does not keep repeating inherited forms but transforms one's character by incorporating new forms which arise from time to time in response to new situations. For the church to be Christian today is not for it to preserve any particular past form, but to live responsibly and creatively out of its tradition, especially its memory of Jesus.

[12] "Process Theology and the Doctrine of God," *Bijdragen*, 41 (December, 1980), pp. 350–67; *Process Theology as Political Theology*, p. 65.

This change in Cobb's thinking has been accompanied by a change in his Christology. Earlier he sought to provide a plausible and conceptually clear account of Jesus' distinctive structure of existence, including his relation to God. He had avoided the term *Christ* as being a source of confusion. Now he has come to speak of Christ as the divine Logos—the primordial nature of God—incarnate in the world.[13] This Logos is the source of all creative transformation in the world. So Christ *is* creative transformation. Due to the unique role creative transformation played in the structure of Jesus' existence, it is appropriate to identify him as *the* Christ. Christ as creative transformation is at work in all things.

Since Christianity is the movement which has made Christ central to it, it is natural that creative transformation has particularly characterized its history. To be faithful to Christ today is to continue this process. We are called to appropriate our Christian history responsibly in relation to the major challenges of the day, such as natural science, the ecological crisis, racism, global economic injustice, the encounter with other religions, the feminist critique of patriarchal religion, the anti-Judaism of historic Christianity, and the threat of nuclear war.

This rejection of essentialist thinking, and of the theology-ethics (theory-application) distinction, has led Cobb to abandon the idea of writing a "systematic theology." He earlier had seen the central theological task as hermeneutical: making the unchanging essence of Christian faith intelligible for contemporaries. Now he sees theology as seeking to transform reality, including Christian faith itself, not as simply interpreting it and then leaving the "relevance" to ethicists and other "practical theologians." Writing a systematic theology would imply that Christianity had an unchanging essence which could be stated in abstraction from the concrete issues of the day.

FEMINISM AND BUDDHISM

Cobb's new view does not mean that truth is not important for its own sake, nor that theology should not deal with perennial issues, such as the problem of evil. Nor does it mean that the

[13] *Christ in a Pluralistic Age* (Philadelphia, Westminster, 1975); *Process Theology: An Introductory Exposition*, with David Ray Griffin (Philadelphia, Westminster, 1976), Chap. 6.

concrete issues of the day are to be limited to sociopolitical problems. The feminist critique of patriarchal Christianity and the encounter with other religious traditions are two contemporary challenges which, he believes, require a self-transformation on the part of Christianity.

In relation to feminism he has stressed, as Mary Daly had already seen, that the Whiteheadian view of God does not share the stereotypically masculine qualities: God's consequent nature is responsive, and God's activity in the world is persuasion, not unilateral imposition. A Whiteheadian view does not oppose "man" to "nature" but sees humanity as part of the organic web of life. It rejects the self-enclosed, autonomous ego in favor of a relational view of the self which is constituted by its relationships to others. Further reflection has led Cobb to dissatisfaction with his earlier suggestions about Christ and the Trinity.[14] He has recently suggested that *Christ* should be identified with the incarnation not only of the second "person" of the Trinity (the principle of creative transformation) but also of the whole triune God, so that Christ is responsive as well as creative love. He no longer holds that Christ must be called "he," since the second person of the Trinity can be called "Sophia," not only Logos.[15]

Given Cobb's childhood, it is not surprising that he has been concerned about the appropriate missionary stance of Christianity in relation to other religions. He has become active in interreligious dialogue, primarily with Buddhism. He had been dissatisfied with his conclusion in *The Structure of Christian Existence* that Christianity and Buddhism simply confront each other as equal but diametrically opposed structures of existence. Through collaboration with a Buddhist, Cobb came to a new way of seeing the relation: Whitehead and Nagarjuna differ not ontologically but only by differing valuations of the ultimate reality of codependent arising, or the many becoming one, which Buddhists call "emptiness" and Whitehead calls "creativity."[16]

[14] In *Christ in a Pluralistic Age,* "Postscript," and *Process Theology: An Introductory Exposition,* Chap. 8.

[15] "Christ Beyond Creative Transformation" (scheduled for publication in a book to be edited by John Roth). He also sees this move to a triune incarnation as enabling him to speak of Christ's identity with the poor, their suffering, and the truth which they can see but the rich cannot.

[16] "Mosha-Dharma and Prehensions: A Comparison of Nagarjuna and Whitehead" (with Ryusei Takeda), *Process Studies,* 4 (Spring, 1974), pp. 26–36.

The negative evaluation by Nagarjuna and the positive one by Whitehead are related to their attention to the different ultimates of Buddhism and Christianity. The Buddhist focuses on emptiness, which is beyond all forms; the Christian on God, who is the source of forms.[17] On this basis, Cobb has come to see Buddhist atheism and Christian theism as both true. They are complementary approaches to the one inconceivably complex reality. Each side can be enriched by creative transformation of itself by appropriating what the other has seen.[18]

By stressing complementarity Cobb rejects the hitherto dominant approaches. He obviously rejects dismissing other religions as false or as mere preparations for Christianity. He also rejects the notion that all traditions are at bottom identical. That notion can result in subtle Christian imperialism, if other religions are understood in terms of Christian categories of "faith" and "God," or Vedantist imperialism, if it is assumed that the Christian God is finally to be understood as the impersonal infinite.

Cobb's rejection of essence thinking is related to his interest in moving beyond understanding to mutual transformation, since the latter is unlikely to occur when each party assumes it is entrusted with a nonnegotiable essence to protect.

Cobb's interest in the helpfulness of a Whiteheadian approach to the whole gamut of human concerns has found institutional expression. In 1971 he and Lewis Ford launched a journal, *Process Studies;* in 1973 he and I established the Center for Process Studies, with the support of the School of Theology at Claremont and Claremont Graduate School.

About 1975, when Thomas Altizer and I had to decide on a title for a book we were editing on Cobb's theology, the most appropriate one seemed to be *John Cobb's Theology in Process;*[19] in the intervening years, this theological process has continued. A personal biography could equally well be titled "John Cobb in Process." Anyone looking for a self-identical essence would find little in common with the pietistic prig

---

[17] "Buddhist Emptiness and the Christian God," *Journal of the American Academy of Religion* (March, 1977), pp. 11–26.

[18] *Beyond Dialogue: Toward a Mutual Transformation of Christianity and Buddhism* (Philadelphia, Fortress, 1982).

[19] Cobb had previously edited *The Theology of Altizer: Critique and Response* (Philadelphia, Westminster, 1971).

lampooned as "Spares" by his college classmates. Cobb has developed a warm, forgiving, encouraging, concerned, generous spirit which reflects well upon his new God. These characteristics, his originality and clarity of thought, his self-deprecating sense of humor, and his continued sense of responsibility to his institutions, his fellow creatures, and his God make him beloved by his colleagues and students alike.

Bibliography

John B. Cobb, Jr., *Christ in a Pluralistic Age,* Philadelphia, Westminster, 1975.

David Ray Griffin and Thomas J. J. Altizer, *John Cobb's Theology in Process,* Philadelphia, Westminster, 1977.

HANS KÜNG

Leonard Swidler

In 1957, the year he received his doctorate in theology from the Institut Catholique in Paris, Hans Küng's dossier was, as he later remarked in a letter to the Vatican, "to judge by the number, already started by the Index" Department of the Holy Office in Rome. He was then twenty-eight years old, and from that time forward he frequently, at times constantly, had to defend himself vis-à-vis the Vatican and/or the German bishops.

EARLY YEARS

It was not always that way. As a young lad Küng was convinced he had a vocation to the priesthood. He was born March 19, 1928, into a devout Catholic family at Sursee near Lucerne, Switzerland, and although he attended a coeducational gymnasium in Lucerne and absorbed the culture and freedom-loving heritage of the Swiss, he eagerly went off to seven years of strict seminary discipline and study in Rome in 1948. It was, as Küng later related,

> an education in the strict Tridentine spirit—during seven whole years in which I would be allowed to travel home once, at most twice. . . . I wanted above all an intense scholarly schooling, which the papal Gregorian University with six semesters of philosophy and eight semesters of theology appeared to guarantee. I wanted the strict inner and outer discipline of the papal Collegium Germanicum, which like the Gregorian was run by Jesuits.[1]

The years 1948–55 were

> great years in Rome . . . Pius XII at that time stood at the height of his power and prestige . . . the triumphalistic definition of the

[1] Excerpts from *Hans Küng: His Work and His Way* by Herman Häring and Karl-Josef Kuschel. Copyright © 1979 by William Collins Sons & Co., Ltd. Reprinted by permission of Doubleday & Company, Inc., and Fontana Paperbacks, Collins.

Assumption of Mary into heaven and so forth. . . . Yes, in the beginning I accepted all of that unreservedly. . . . And in conversation with students from German universities I criticized at that time the "pride" and "hypercriticism" of the screaming rationalistic German theology professors who had their doubts about this matter.[2]

MATURATION

However, this uncritical enthusiasm for the church authority position began to change to a more mature, differentiating attitude and led to what Küng calls a "critical loyalty." Küng attended lectures by the outstanding Bible exegete Stanislas Lyonnet (who was silenced and banned by the Holy Office in 1961). He also came to know in a small study circle Yves Congar, the great Catholic "reform" theologian, who had been silenced and exiled—he came to Rome! Küng chaired a study circle on dialectical materialism for the rector of the Papal Collegium Russicum, Gustav A. Wetter, and another study circle on sociology for the papal adviser Gustav Gundlach. At the same time a crisis in church leadership was occurring, with the suppression of ecumenism, especially in Germany ("Monitum," 1948; "Instructio," 1949), the devastation of the "New Theology" in France ("Humani generis," 1950), and the suppression of the French worker priests (1953). According to Küng, there was a "constant inflation of magisterial declarations by addresses and encyclicals of a pope who memorized, and ultimately only read, what others—who I knew only too well—had written. The daily—if you will—look behind the scenery of this pontificate had led to a 'demythologisation' of this pope whom we had all before idealized."[3]

"JUSTIFICATION"

In 1951, Küng wrote a thesis for his Licentiate in Philosophy on the atheistic humanism of Jean-Paul Sartre and in 1955 a thesis for his Licentiate in Theology on the doctrine of justification in Karl Barth, a fellow Swiss and the most influential Protestant

[2] *Ibid.*, p. 132.
[3] *Ibid.*, p. 133.

theologian then alive. In this latter work he was supported by his professors at Rome and by another Swiss, a well-known Catholic theologian, Hans Urs von Balthasar (also an expert on Barth's theology), who urged Küng to expand his work on Barth into a doctoral dissertation. This Küng did during his year and a half at the Sorbonne and Institut Catholique in Paris (1955–57) with the title "Justification, La doctrine de Karl Barth et une réflexion catholique" under Louis Bouyer. The dissertation appeared simultaneously as a German book, published by Von Balthasar in Switzerland (1957). The book, which argued that Barth's doctrine of justification and the Council of Trent's were fundamentally the same, caused a sensation in Protestant and Catholic theological worlds.

DOSSIER

It was precisely this bridging of the presumably unbridgeable that brought immediate and manifold delations (technical term for tattling) to Rome. At the time Küng judged the chances of the book's being placed on the Index of Forbidden Books about fifty-fifty. However, the support of his teachers, especially Sebastian Tromp, Franz Hürth, Louis Bouyer, and Guy de Broglie, fended off that effort. But that move started his dossier—and it has been active ever since.

Küng at that point spent a year and a half in pastoral work in Switzerland, and then following the urging of Heinrich Fries (whose successor he became in 1960 at the University of Tübingen), Hermann Volk (whose assistant he became in 1959 at the University of Münster and who later became the Cardinal Archbishop of Mainz), and Karl Rahner, the most renowned contemporary Catholic theologian, he opted for the academic life in Germany. In 1960, he was called to the Catholic Theology Faculty of Tübingen and in the same year published another "sensational" book, *The Council, Reform and Reunion* (over the strong doubts of Professor Volk and Cardinal Julius Döpfner of Munich, but with an introduction by Cardinal König of Vienna), which urged a whole battery of reforms in the spirit of Pope John XXIII's *aggiornamento*.

Under the influence of the newly announced council (in

January 1959, by John XXIII) and the encouragement of his church history colleague Karl August Fink, Küng began an intensive study of the whole conciliar tradition, which resulted in the publication in 1962, the year Vatican II began, of *Structures of the Church*. All of the seemingly settled problems of authority, decision-making, etc., were all laid open again in the simple presenting of the historical evidence. This apparently made the Vatican so uneasy that they called Küng to a proceedings against the book. It took place in 1963, during the second session of the council (Küng was an "expert" appointed to the council by the pope) at the temporary Roman residence of Bishop Leiprecht of Rottenburg (in which diocese Tübingen lay). Fortunately for Küng the great ecumenist Cardinal Augustin Bea (who came from Swabia—Tübingen's province) was put in charge of the proceedings. Küng later recalled:

> Well, it was the period of the Council, and so I was forgiven a certain amount. At all events a solemn session took place in Rome with Cardinal Bea in the chair along with the Bishop of Basel [Küng's home diocese] as well as professors from the Gregorian. I had to answer various questions that had been drawn up by the Holy Office. Later I had to repeat my answers in writing in Latin. Without a doubt it was thanks to Cardinal Bea, whom I had got to know during my first years in Rome when he was Visitator at the German College in the days when he was a simple Jesuit priest and Pius XII's confessor, that the proceedings came to a happy conclusion and were terminated without any obligation of any kind being laid upon me.[4]

FREEDOM AND UNFREEDOM IN AMERICA

Earlier that same year (1963) Küng made the first of what might be described as his "triumphal tours" through the United States. Again restrictions by church authorities—this time episcopal rather than papal—played a significant role. It all started with the so-called Catholic University affair. Küng's name was struck from a list of proposed speakers for the Lenten series at Catholic University, Washington, D.C. Usually such an action would have remained a secret, but in those heady days it was reported to the national press and loud protests spread across the nation. In the midst of the outcry Küng arrived in the States for a previously

[4] *Ibid.*, p. 160.

scheduled lecture tour. He was forbidden to speak by the archbishops of Philadelphia, St. Paul, Los Angeles, San Diego, and others, but wherever he did speak, the crowds ranged up to six thousand! He spoke on freedom and unfreedom in the church. Hans Küng had suddenly become the symbol of the new freedom of the Catholic Church.

VATICAN II

Küng was very active at Vatican II, noting that he

> had possibilities, directly or indirectly, of bringing about important changes, for example in the Constitution on the Church insofar as I drew up various important Council speeches of bishops: for example on the charismatic dimension of the Church, on the significance of the local Church, on the sinful Church and the necessity of continual reform, on the three-fold offices of ordination and other similar matters. It was likewise possible to exercise influence through public statements in the world press: my timely orientation of the large newspapers in reference to the curial maneuvers to set aside the Declaration on the Jews as well as the Declaration on Religious Freedom put the brakes on these maneuvers.[5]

THE CHURCH

He further recalled that

> at the beginning of the second session—after a careful study of the revised schema of the Constitution on the Church—I decided after days of reflection to begin my book *The Church*. I had intended in later decades to dedicate myself to the writing of something like a *Spirit of Catholicism* (the German title is the "Essence" [*Wesen*] of Catholicism) according to the model of my great predecessor in dogmatics at Tübingen, Karl Adam. But now seemed to be the time to write a book on the essence of the Church—in a very different manner of course. . . . A year after the close of the Council the manuscript was after endless effort finished and in 1967 it was published.[6]

THE INQUISITION

The Holy Office, which had its name changed to the Congregation for the Doctrine of the Faith (it was earlier called

[5] *Ibid.*, p. 170.
[6] *Ibid.*, pp. 170–72.

the Congregation of the Index, and before that, the Congregation of the Holy Inquisition), was displeased enough with the book to reprimand the diocese of Rottenburg for having given the book an Imprimatur and to order that further distribution and translation of the book be halted until after the author had had a discussion with representatives to be named by the Doctrinal Congregation. Küng received the Vatican notification two days after Christmas.

On May 4, 1968, Küng received a letter from the Doctrinal Congregation telling him to appear at 9:30 A.M. at the Palace of the Holy Office for a "discussion" four days hence! Küng wired that it was impossible to keep the appointment, but that he was "in principle . . . prepared to participate in a discussion," that he looked upon "the invitation to a discussion as significant progress compared to the procedure customary in the past. . . . You can be assured of my cooperation."[7] He added five conditions he felt were essential if a fair discussion were to be held: (1) access to the documents in his Vatican dossier; (2) a written statement of the problem areas ahead of time from the Congregation; (3) because of the scholarly nature of his book, the Congregation's discussants should be competent experts in exegesis, history, and dogmatics, and Küng should be informed who they would be; (4) the discussion would be in his native tongue, German; and (5) Küng would be financially reimbursed for the expenses involved. Eventually numbers two through five were more or less granted but never number one—secrecy was to be maintained. Küng also eventually had extended discussions both with Vatican officials and committees of the German bishops—quite contrary to the myth that Küng stubbornly refused to go to Rome.[8]

The Church AND Infallible INVESTIGATIONS ENDED

Not only did the investigation of Küng's book *The Church* drag on for years, but it was added to after 1970 when on the centenary of the declaration of papal infallibility at Vatican Council I Küng published *Infallible? An Inquiry.* A year later, in the summer of 1971, Küng was notified by the Vatican that his new book was

---

[7] Leonard Swidler, *Küng in Conflict* (N.Y., Doubleday, 1981), p. 11.
[8] See, e.g., *ibid.*, pp. 129–32, 180, 226, 315.

under investigation and he was given a number of questions to answer. The documents of this dispute fill 135 pages in *Küng in Conflict*. It was an intense, at times acrimonious debate between Küng and the Vatican and a certain conservative portion of the German bishops. Through it all Cardinal Döpfner of Munich, the president of the German Bishops' Conference, effectually served as Küng's "protector" vis-à-vis Rome—though between him and Küng very frank, even vigorous, but always deeply friendly, exchanges took place. The case finally "ended" in a compromise Declaration by the Congregation for the Doctrine of the Faith (February 15, 1975) whereby Küng was admonished not to advocate his teachings on infallibility, but there was no question of his having to recant or suffer any censure: "With this declaration, the proceedings of the Congregation for the Doctrine of the Faith in this matter are ended for now"—the last two words proved to be ominous.[9]

ATTACK ON KÜNG's *On Being a Christian*

However, for Küng it was out of the fire into another frying pan, for the German Bishops' Conference also issued, two days later, a Declaration in which it not only greeted the termination of the proceedings against Küng's two books *(The Church* and *Infallible? An Inquiry),* but also delivered to him a set of instructions on how to proceed theologically and issued their first statement against his new book, *On Being a Christian* (German edition, 1974; N.Y., Doubleday, 1976). This book quickly turned into Küng's best best-seller, over 160,000 German copies alone being sold, besides the hundreds of thousands of copies in English, French, Spanish, Italian, Portuguese, Dutch, and Japanese. Because of the book's popularity, controversy over it spread quickly—not so much because of what it said but because of what it supposedly did *not* say. At the height of the controversy Cardinal Döpfner suddenly died and was replaced as Cardinal Archbishop of Munich by Joseph Ratzinger (after 1982 the head of the Vatican's Doctrinal Congregation), who had once been one of Küng's colleagues and collaborators but later turned in a **conservative direction and became his opponent. More ominous**

[9] *Ibid.,* p. 164.

was the replacement of Döpfner as president of the German Bishops' Conference by Cardinal Joseph Höffner of Cologne, who in single-minded fashion led a relentless attack on Küng.

The debate peaked when on January 22, 1977, Küng met with a number of German bishops and theologians for a day in what became known as the Stuttgart Colloquium. The theological issues of *On Being a Christian* were thoroughly discussed. However, every time an agreement was about to be reached, Cardinal Höffner broke it up with steely demands on Küng that he give simple yes answers to catechism-simple questions. The controversy simmered on through the time of the publication of Küng's next magnum opus, *Does God Exist?*, in 1978, and the election of two new popes, John Paul and John Paul II, the same year. However, all seemed on the surface basically resolved, for the German bishops had made a public declaration on Küng's *On Being a Christian*, and the requested Christological clarifications would seem to have been made in the latter part of *Does God Exist?* That calm, of course, turned out to be deceptive.

PUBLICATIONS

In 1978 Küng was fifty years old; he had an extraordinary publication record to his credit. By 1984 he had published more than thirty books, fifteen of which were major works, often ranging from five hundred to almost nine hundred pages, and over four hundred publications of all sorts; a full bibliography up to 1978 can be found in *Hans Küng, His Work and His Way*. His writings range not only over theology but also over modern art and music, psychology, philosophy, feminism, anti-Semitism, racism, economics, politics, etc., etc. Obviously not all of Küng's major books can be analyzed here. However, at least a brief evaluation of his two largest, most widely read, and perhaps most important books—namely, *On Being a Christian* and *Does God Exist?*—is in order.

On Being a Christian

I remember well how in the summer of 1971 while walking along the Rhine, Küng told me about his starting to work on a small, popular-level book about what it meant to be a contemporary Christian—perhaps about a hundred pages in length. Three years later it ended up the 720-page *On Being a Christian*. In a careful review, the Protestant theologian Werner H. Kelber of Rice University spoke of

> the stupendous achievement of Küng's latest work. It is cause for rejoicing without end. One appreciates his unflinching support of biblical, historical, and theological inquiries, of a critical questing in which he has proved himself a courageous and creative leader. . . . His relentless criticism of Roman authoritarianism and ecclesiastical paternalism is as much to the point as his rebuke of Luther's anti-Judaism, Reformation fanaticism, Protestants' indifference toward their churches, and "the dogmatic repression of the problem of religion by Karl Barth and 'dialectical theology.'" . . . A deep concern for social justice and a moving reflection on the conditions of South America are combined with a sober reservation toward political theologies and uncritical modernism.[10]

Kelber goes on to note that Küng exhibits a rare mastery over biblical criticism and New Testament theology (Kelber's specialty is New Testament), philosophical and historical theology, church history and ethics, and the history of religion and cultural history. He writes, "The result is a composition of systematic coherence and intrinsic plausibility" (Kelber's use of that last word has a special irony, as will be seen below in connection with the remark by Cardinal Volk of Mainz). Further, Küng's work was said by Kelber to be free of such habitual vices as cheap apologetics, unreflected skepticism toward the sciences, or theological sleight of hand; a profound sense of honesty and humanity permeates the book from start to finish. Kelber added that "reference must also be made to the artistic quality of this work. This reviewer has read the book in both the German and English versions. Küng's German is brisk, lucid, and of unpretentious clarity." He concluded: *"On Being a Christian* is not only one of Küng's masterpieces, but it will rank among the theological classics of the twentieth century."

[10] Leonard Swidler, ed., *Consensus in Theology? A Dialogue with Hans Küng and Edward Schillebeecxk* (Philadelphia, Westminster, 1980), p. 142.

Does God Exist?

As in *On Being a Christian*, so also in *Does God Exist?*, Küng takes extremely seriously the problems generated in modern times. The reader gets the distinct feeling that the conclusions were not foregone when Küng started wrestling with these issues—and the reader is right. Küng ends up agreeing with many of the central criticisms of modern thought on the God question. The reader also senses that here is a sure guide who has gone through the modern circle of flame surrounding God—one who, like all thinking men and women today, has also been struck at the very core of his being by the arguments of contemporary thought and science against the existence of God, but who, unlike most of us, by dint of a penetrating analysis and massive research has not only grappled with those problems but has solved them.

Like all good contemporary theology, *Does God Exist?* is presented within an historical matrix, focusing on the major thought patterns of modern Western history as exemplified in breakthrough thinkers, starting naturally with Descartes, and moving on through Pascal, Spinoza, Kant, Hegel, Feuerbach, Marx, Nietzsche, Freud, Adorno, Horkheimer, Heidegger, Wittgenstein, and others. Important personal, social, and intellectual historical information is painstakingly presented after obviously thoroughgoing research. Küng penetrated very sympathetically to the heart of the thought of these giant thinkers, carefully drawing out its significance for the God question. That is largely the first half of the book. The second half is basically Küng's—affirmative—response to the fundamental questions: Can we know reality? Does God exist?

In dealing with the first question, Küng faces squarely the option of the absurdity of life, of nihilism. He states starkly:

Nihilism is *possible*. The pervasive questionableness of reality itself makes nihilism possible. . . . *Nihilism is not disprovable*. There is no necessarily convincing argument against the possibility of nihilism. It is even at least possible that this human life is ultimately meaningless, that accident, a blind fate, chaos, absurdity and illusion rules the world, that everything ultimately is ambiguous, meaningless, worthless, nothing.

However, Küng also argues that *"nihilism is not provable. . . .* Here it is a *matter of trust or mistrust* in which without certainty and guarantee I put myself on the line. . . . Either I hold reality to be trustworthy—or not." Thus, although a no to reality is truly possible, Küng offers several reasons why humans ought to be inclined toward a yes, and he concludes that neither simple reason nor belief is the sole ultimate basis of our knowledge of reality. Rather

> if I in a consistent manner do not close myself to reality, but rather open myself to its working, if I do not withdraw myself from the light of being but rather dare to give myself over to it, I will thus perceive—*neither before, nor only afterwards,* but in the very act itself—that I am doing the right thing, indeed, "the most rational" thing. For what beforehand is not subject to proof or experience . . . I experience *in the act of trust itself.*

As with the fundamental question of the meaningfulness of reality, Küng finds the question of the existence of God one that not only can be neither proved nor disproved but also ultimately cannot be avoided, for, "the no to God means an ultimately ungrounded basic trust in reality. . . . Whoever denies God does not know why ultimately s/he trusts reality." As with the meaningfulness of reality, one affirms the existence of God by a free act of reasonable trust: "If I do not withdraw myself from the primal and final ground, sustainer, and goal of reality, but rather dare to give myself over to it, I will thus perceive—*neither before nor only afterwards,* but *in the very act itself*—that I am doing the right thing, indeed at bottom 'the most rational thing.'"

Bernard Häring, the world's most renowned Catholic moral theologian, wrote: "The most recent study on atheism is that of Hans Küng, *Existiert Gott?* . . . It is one of the most profound treatises from a philosophical, psychological, and theological point of view, and perhaps the best of Hans Küng.[11]

ATTACK ON KÜNG'S CATHOLICITY

On December 18, 1979, Küng was the object of a previously unheard-of Vatican document, a Declaration that he "can no

[11] *Free and Faithful in Christ,* vol. II: *The Truth Will Set You Free* (N.Y., Seabury, 1979), p. 378, n. 1.

longer be considered a Catholic theologian or function as such in a teaching role." In the past, Catholic theologians who fell into severe disfavor with Rome were either censured, silenced, made to recant, suspended from priestly office, excommunicated, burned at the stake—or all of the above. Küng suffered none of them. Why this novum? To those familiar with the relationship of German universities, the German state, and Rome the answer was obvious. If authoritative evidence could be presented that Küng was not a Catholic theologian and therefore could not function as one in teaching, then the local Catholic bishop of Tübingen, where Küng teaches, would have legal grounds to request the state to replace Küng as professor of Catholic theology at the university. This was to be done on the basis of the Concordat between the Vatican and Hitler's Germany in 1933. It was all carefully planned out and executed in a series of secret meetings by key Vatican and German hierarchs that reads like a plot of an international intrigue—which it was.[12]

Why this extraordinary effort on the part of so many to diminish the stature and influence of Hans Küng as a Catholic theologian? I would like to suggest four basic reasons: (1) his effectiveness in communication; (2) his absolute honesty; (3) his dynamic, historical, critical understanding of truth statements; (4) his placing of the historical person of Jesus at the center of Christian belief and practice. But of course the ultimate good (5) was to reduce significantly Küng's popularity and influence.

1. Clarity of Communication

Almost no matter what Küng wrote, if only a few thousand scholars and educated laity read his books, Rome and the German hierarchy would hardly have concerned themselves with him. However, as noted, his books have sold hundreds of thousands of copies in many languages all over the world. Moreover, people read and understood them because they made sense to them, spoke to them in their modern idiom, addressed their real problems, and made the idea of being a Christian come alive for them.

But there's the rub. In 1977, Cardinal Höffner complained to Küng that because his books were selling so many copies, they,

[12] See *Küng in Conflict*, pp. 383 ff., 401 ff., where the secret plot is described by Bishop Moser of Rottenburg.

the bishops, were compelled to call him to task. Why? Cardinal Volk of Mainz, at the same 1977 Stuttgart Colloquium, explained: "Your book [*On Being a Christian*] is for me too plausible!" *(Ihr Buch ist mir zu plausibel!)*

But this "plausibility," this clarity of style, does not come trippingly on the pen. It is the result of an immense amount of hard work. One of his close assistants, Dr. Karl-Josef Kuschel, has described in detail how *Does God Exist?*, almost nine hundred pages long, was written in three years.

He wrote that the mere physical strength which Küng invests in writing books demands respect. Küng's workday is eighteen or nineteen hours long, and when it is a matter of finishing a book, his last reserves are mobilized. In this Küng demands much of his co-workers (three academic associates and one secretary) in their daily contribution, but he demands most of himself.

In writing *Does God Exist?* the following plan was usually followed. Before a large chapter was begun, the entire concept was deliberated upon and the design, execution, and construction of the chapter analyzed and discussed by the circle of co-workers. Then Küng began to write. For many months—from spring 1975 until the end of August 1977—Küng constantly worked from nine in the morning until late at night. Even before the first typed draft, Küng had written out for himself two or three handwritten drafts in which he gave the first shape to the material, which was based on primary and secondary literature. Here lay the real creative process of writing. Küng then dictated this handwritten draft into a dictaphone so that the secretary could produce the first typed draft.

For Küng, dictation is not only a technical expedient in the production of a manuscript but also has an important function in relation to language and content. The flowing style of Küng's books (and the ease with which they can be understood) is due not least to the "oral testing" of the text by reading it aloud. Again and again Küng and Kuschel read the manuscript aloud to one another and, through that very process of "listening," were able immediately to pick out complications of both a stylistic and a substantive nature.

This first typed copy was then thoroughly revised and discussed by Küng and Kuschel for content and language, with

Küng deciding which corrections he would adopt. Then the secretary made the second typed copy. This copy as a rule went to the other two academic co-workers, who were also in constant personal contact with Küng. After this, if necessary, a third typed copy was produced.

Yet even after all this revision procedure, Küng was still not satisfied. In certain chapters where the systematic theologian ventured into a specialized area foreign to him, the counsel of specialists was sought. After this, and after several rereadings by Küng himself, the manuscript was sometimes typed for the fourth time.[13]

After such herculean efforts to attain clarity, it must have been a bit stunning to hear the accusation: Ihr Buch ist mir *zu plausibel!*

2. "Honesty Is the Best Policy"

Another reason for Küng's difficulties is his total honesty. For him it is a virtue that cannot be displaced by other considerations—he says as much in the book titled *Truthfulness: The Future of the Church* (1968). A number of other Catholic theologians are aware of the results of historical and other critical studies, but at certain crucial points they "fudge" their application to Christian doctrine. In many cases it is a matter of having a fundamentally different ecclesiology; they start out with what the church has traditionally taught on some matter through some authoritative expression, e.g., a conciliar or papal document, and assume that it cannot be faulted, not "essentially," although they will nowadays allow for "development." The difficulties come when the "development" moves from, for example, Gregory XVI's and Pius IX's solemn condemnations of religious freedom to Vatican II's solemn approbation of religious freedom. Küng, and others, would say that in such instances one cannot meaningfully, honestly, speak about "development" but would have to admit the possibility of error in at least one of the two contradictory positions (the latter position is obviously his choice in this case). Such probity precipitates papal problems.

3. Historical and Dialogical Understanding of Truth-Statements

Probably the most important reason why Küng has difficulties

[13] See *Consensus in Theology?*, pp. 152–58.

with church authorities is that his understanding of truth-statements is formed within the horizon of the historical and dialogical methods. He is of course far from being the only Catholic theologian to hold such an understanding, but he does so with a consistency that is not matched by all. Fundamentally, Küng's method of doing theology is historical and hence dynamic, unafraid of the idea of change. This world view is completely at odds with the traditional static one. As Thomas Kuhn has shown in the history of science, the shift from one "paradigm" by which reality is understood to a new one is always fraught with resistance and turbulence before the new paradigm is accepted—one thinks pre-eminently of the agonies of Copernicus, Kepler, and Galileo in moving from the geocentric to the heliocentric paradigm. Given the acceleration of change in the contemporary world, one hopes that Küng will be functioning as Copernicus, Kepler, and Galileo and beyond, all rolled into one.

The second creative—and trouble-causing—characteristic of Küng's method of doing theology is dialogue. Dialogue, specifically interreligious dialogue, has been officially and unofficially mandated and practiced by Catholics for two decades now. There have been wide experience, reflection, and writing on the subject. Anyone at all conversant with these knows that what makes such dialogue possible now is the "relativizing" of the human perception of statements about truth. In the past hundred years the wide acceptance of the findings of historicism, sociology of knowledge, and language analysis has made critical thinkers see all statements about reality as "relational," related to the time and culture, the sociological class and circumstances, and the language of the speaker. This perception of the relational character of all statements is a *sine qua non* of authentic dialogue, for it assumes that no one person or group can, by the very nature of finite knowledge and the statements of it, know everything about a topic. Rather than being certain about having the full "truth" about a matter, such critical persons claim that one is certain it is impossible ever to have the full "truth" about something expressed by one person or group. We come to dialogue not primarily to teach but primarily to learn. As a result dialogue always entails a risk: we might be persuaded by our partner's position on an issue, and thus if we would act with integrity, we would have to change. That can be painful; it challenges the static notion of truth. Küng is ready to "bite the bullet"; his opponents are only too ready to fire it.

4. The Historical Jesus at the Center

Küng speaks of two "poles" of Christian theology—the living Jesus of history and our own human experience—and of how there needs to be a critical correlation between the two so that Jesus in fact can affect the lives of Christans; it is this end that tradition and the church are to serve. As Küng states it:

> *The source, standard and criterion of Christian faith is the living Jesus of history.* Through historical-critical research into the life of Jesus the Christian faith is historically responsible in the light of the contemporary consciousness of problems and is protected from faulty interpretations arising from within or outside the Church. Schillebeeckx is correct in affirming that, "It is not the historical image of Jesus but rather the living Jesus of history who stands at the beginning and is the source, standard and criterion of that which the first Christians interpretively encountered in him." . . . Christianity is not founded on myths, legends or tales, nor solely on a doctrine (for it is not a religion of a book). Rather, it is based primarily on the historical personality of Jesus of Nazareth who was seen as the Christ of God. . . . No contradiction can be permitted between the Jesus of history and the Christ of faith. We must be able to identify the Christ of faith as the Jesus of history. . . . we can make it clear that the center of Scripture, the Christian message, the Gospel, is the living Jesus.[14]

5. Attack Backfires

If the ultimate goal of the Vatican's and the German Bishops' Conference's attack was to reduce significantly the popularity and influence of Küng, it backfired spectacularly. Before the December 1979 attack, Küng normally had about 150 students in his lecture classes. As a result of the attack, Küng is no longer a member of the Catholic Theology Faculty of the University of Tübingen, but he remains professor of ecumenical theology and director of the Ecumenical Institute of the University and can sit on doctoral committees in the Catholic Theology Faculty. (He of course also remains a priest in good standing.) In the three

[14] *Consensus in Theology?*, pp. 6, 7, 17.

succeeding years, his lecture courses regularly drew first one thousand, then thirteen hundred, and then fifteen hundred students! Further, he has also arranged to teach every fourth semester in the United States.

INCREASING DIALOGUE AND INVOLVEMENT

From the beginning of his public life, Küng has been committed to ecumenical dialogue, and there has been a steady progress in the process of his opening ever more fully to the dialogue. This can be seen most clearly in his attitude toward non-Christian religions. He evidences an increasing openness to them, moving from his book *The Church* (1968), to *On Being a Christian* (1974), to *Does God Exist?*, to after 1980. For Küng, the non-Christian religions have now become, along with the modern critical world, fully equal dialogue partners with his Christianity. At the same time his involvement with feminism and other liberation theology issues has become even deeper, as illustrated by his establishing a special section of his Ecumenical Institute devoted to "Woman and Christianity." Hans Küng is like a sensitive antenna of the contemporary Christian movement.

Notes on Contributors

NOTES ON CONTRIBUTORS

SYDNEY E. AHLSTROM was, at the time of his death in July 1984, Samuel Knight Professor of American History and Modern Religious History Emeritus at Yale University where he had been a faculty member since 1954. His *Religious History of the American People,* a winner of the National Book Award, is regarded as the classic work in its field. A specialist in matters having to do with the history of theology in the United States, he helped prepare a generation of notable scholars in this field while maintaining a productive scholarly life of his own.

CARL E. BRAATEN is Professor of Systematic Theology at the Lutheran School of Theology at Chicago. His books include *History and Hermeneutics, The Future of God: The Revolutionary Dynamics of Hope, Eschatology and Ethics: Essays on the Theology and Ethics of the Kingdom of God, The Flaming Center: A Theology of the Christian Mission,* and *Spirit, Faith and Church.* He is also the editor of *dialog,* a journal of theology.

GEOFFREY W. BROMILEY, Senior Professor of Church History and Historical Theology at Fuller Theological Seminary, is also a presbyter in the Church of England, licensed in the Diocese of Los Angeles. The author of *Thomas Cranmer, Theologian* and *The Anglican Reformers and Baptism,* he is noted for having translated and edited such works as Karl Barth's *Church Dogmatics,* Jacques Ellul's *The Ethics of Freedom,* Helmut Thielicke's *The Evangelical Faith* and *Becoming Human . . . Being Human: An Essay in Christian Anthropology,* and the *Theological Dictionary of the New Testament.*

ROBERT McAFEE BROWN is Professor of Theology and Ethics at Pacific School of Religion in Berkeley, California. Among his writings are books about Protestant, Catholic, and Jewish thinkers, respectively *P. T. Forsyth: Prophet for Today, Gustavo Gutiérrez,* and *Elie Wiesel: Messenger to All Humanity.* His most recent book is *Unexpected News: Reading the Bible with Third World Eyes.*

FRITZ BURI is Professor Emeritus of Dogmatics at the University of Basel. Four of his books that have been translated into English are *Christian Faith in Our Time, Theology of Existence, Steps on the Way*

729

to a Philosophical Theology, and *How Can We Still Speak Responsibly of God?*

GEORGE B. CAIRD, New Testament scholar and Dean Ireland Professor of the Exegesis of Holy Scripture at the University of Oxford since 1977, died in April of 1984. From 1970 to 1977 he was Principal of Mansfield College, Oxford. His published works include *The Truth of the Gospel, The Apostolic Age, Principalities and Powers,* and *The Language and Imagery of the Bible,* as well as exegetical studies and commentaries. He also achieved recognition as a writer of modern hymns.

ANNE E. CARR is Associate Professor of Theology at the Divinity School of the University of Chicago. She is the author of *The Theological Method of Karl Rahner* and numerous articles on contemporary theology and women's studies in religion.

GABRIEL FACKRE, Abbot Professor of Christian Theology at Andover Newton Theological School, is the author of *The Christian Story: A Narrative Interpretation of Basic Christian Doctrine, The Religious Right and Christian Faith,* and *The Rainbow Sign: Christian Futurity.*

JOSEPH FLETCHER, Robert Treat Paine Professor Emeritus at the Episcopal Theological School, Cambridge, Massachusetts, is now Visiting Professor of Medical Ethics at the University of Virginia's School of Medicine. He is the author of *Christianity and Property, Morals and Medicine, William Temple: Twentieth Century Christian, The Ethics of Genetic Control, Humanhood: Essays in Biomedical Ethics,* and other works.

A. DURWOOD FOSTER is Professor of Christian Theology at the Pacific School of Religion and the Graduate Theological Union, Berkeley, California. He is the author of *The God Who Loves.*

MARY GERHART is Professor of Religious Studies at Hobart and William Smith Colleges. She is the author of *The Question of Belief in Literary Criticism: An Introduction to the Hermeneutical Theory of Paul Ricoeur* and coauthor of *Metaphoric Process: The Creation of Scientific and Religious Understanding. She has served as editorial chair of Religious Studies Review* and on the editorial boards of other journals in the field of religion.

DAVID RAY GRIFFIN, Professor of Philosophy of Religion at the School of Theology at Claremont and Executive Director of the Center for Process Studies, is the author of *A Process Christology* and *God, Power, and Evil: A Process Theodicy* and the coauthor of *Process Theology: An Introductory Exposition*. He is also the coeditor of *John Cobb's Theology in Process, Mind in Nature: Essays on the Interface of Science and Philosophy*, and the corrected edition of Alfred North Whitehead's *Process and Reality*.

S. C. GUTHRIE, JR., Professor of Theology at Columbia Theological Seminary in Decatur, Georgia, helped translate Oscar Cullmann's *Christology of the New Testament*.

ROBERT T. HANDY, Henry Sloane Coffin Professor of Church History at Union Theological Seminary in New York City, recently published a second edition of *A Christian America: Protestant Hopes and Historical Realities*. Among his other books are *A History of the Churches in the United States and Canada, We Witness Together, Members One of Another*, and *The Protestant Quest for a Christian America, 1830–1930*.

MARTIN J. HEINECKEN, Professor Emeritus of Systematic Theology at Lutheran Theological Seminary at Philadelphia, is the author of such works as *The Meaning of the Cross, God and the Space Age, The Moment Before God: An Interpretation of Kierkegaard*, and *Christian Teachings: Affirmations of Faith for Lay People*.

HANS HOFMANN, formerly a Professor of Theology, Philosophy, and Psychology of Religion at Harvard Divinity School, was Executive Director of the Institute for Human Development in Cambridge, Massachusetts, from 1964 to 1970. He later served as Director of Mental Health at the Health Services of the University of Massachusetts in Boston, and he is now living in retirement in Sedona, Arizona. His writings include *The Theology of Reinhold Niebuhr, Breakthrough to Life*, and *Discovering Freedom*.

CLYDE A. HOLBROOK, Danforth Professor of Religion Emeritus at Oberlin College, has written *Faith and Community, Religion: A Humanistic Field, The Ethics of Jonathan Edwards*, and *The Iconoclastic Deity: Biblical Images of God*. He also edited Jonathan Edwards' *Original Sin* (Yale edition).

DANIEL JENKINS is Weyerhaeuser Professor Emeritus of Systematic Theology at Princeton Theological Seminary. His two most recent books are *The British—Their Identity and Religion* and *Christian Maturity and Christian Success;* others of his works are *Beyond Religion, The Strangeness of the Church,* and *Equality and Excellence.*

MATTHEW L. LAMB is Associate Professor of Systematic Theology in the Theology Department of Marquette University in Milwaukee, Wisconsin. He has written *History, Method and Theology* and *Solidarity with Victims* and has edited *Creativity and Method: Essays in Honor of Bernard Lonergan.* He has also published numerous articles in philosophical and theological journals.

WALTER LEIBRECHT, who has taught at Harvard Divinity School, Garrett-Evangelical Theological Seminary, and the University of Chicago Divinity School and has headed Chicago's Ecumenical Institute, is now President of Schiller International University, with headquarters in London. The university also has campuses in Madrid, Paris, Heidelberg, and Strasbourg. The author of *Being a Christian in Today's World* and the editor of *Religion and Culture: Essays in Honor of Paul Tillich,* Dr. Leibrecht is also President of the Paul Tillich Society in Germany.

JOHN MACQUARRIE taught Systematic Theology at the University of Glasgow (1953–62) and was Professor of the same subject at Union Theological Seminary, New York City (1962–70). He is currently Lady Margaret Professor of Divinity at Oxford University and Canon of Christ Church, Oxford. He is cotranslator of Martin Heidegger's *Being and Time* and author of such works as *An Existentialist Theology, The Scope of Demythologizing, Twentieth-Century Religious Thought, Principles of Christian Theology, God-Talk, In Search of Humanity,* and *In Search of Deity.*

BERNARD E. MELAND, Professor of Systematic Theology at the University of Chicago from 1945 to 1964 and now retired, has written such books as *Seeds of Redemption, The Reawakening of Christian Faith, Higher Education and the Human Spirit, Faith and Culture, The Realities of Faith, The Secularization of Modern Cultures,* and *Fallible Forms and Symbols: Discourses on Method in a Theology of Culture.*

CARL MICHALSON was Professor of Systematic Theology at Drew University at the time of his death in 1965. His books include *The Hinge of History: An Existential Approach to the Christian Faith, Faith for Personal Crises, Japanese Contributions to Christian Theology,* and

The Rationality of Faith. A posthumous work, *Worldly Theology,* was published under the direction of John D. Godsey.

CHRISTOPHER F. MOONEY, S.J., a member of the Pennsylvania Bar, is Academic Vice-President of Fairfield University. He has previously served as Chair of the Theology Department at Fordham University, President of Woodstock College, and Assistant Dean at the University of Pennsylvania Law School. He holds doctorates in both theology and law, and in recent years his major interest has been the interface between religious and legal values. He has written five books: *Teilhard de Chardin and the Mystery of Christ* (which won the National Catholic Book Award), *The Making of Man, Man Without Tears, Religion and the American Dream,* and *Inequality and the American Conscience.*

CHRISTOPHER MORSE, Associate Professor of Systematic Theology at Union Theological Seminary, New York City, is the author of *The Logic of Promise in Moltmann's Theology.*

J. ROBERT NELSON is Professor of Systematic Theology and former Dean at the Boston University School of Theology. Among his books are *The Realm of Redemption, Overcoming Christian Divisions, Criterion for the Church, Crisis in Unity and Witness, Church Union in Focus* and, most recently, *Human Life: A Biblical Perspective for Bioethics.*

RICHARD R. NIEBUHR, Hollis Professor of Divinity at Harvard Divinity School, is the author of *Resurrection and Historical Reason: A Study of Theological Method, Schleiermacher on Christ and Religion, Experiential Religion,* and *Streams of Grace: Studies of Jonathan Edwards, Samuel Taylor Coleridge and William James.*

WILHELM PAUCK died in 1981 in Palo Alto, California. Charles A. Briggs Graduate Professor of Church History Emeritus at New York's Union Theological Seminary, he had taught at Union from 1953 until his retirement in 1967. From 1967 to 1972 he was Distinguished Professor of Church History at Vanderbilt University Divinity School. His publications include *Karl Barth: Prophet of a New Christianity?, The Church Against the World, The Heritage of the Reformation, Harnack and Troeltsch: Two Historical Theologians, Paul Tillich: His Life and Thought* (with Marion Pauck), and *The Reformers and Their Heirs* (a posthumous collection of essays edited by Marion Pauck). He also translated, edited, and introduced *Luther's Lectures on Romans* and *Melanchthon and Bucer.*

WARREN A. QUANBECK at the time of his death in 1979 was Professor of Systematic Theology at Luther Theological Seminary in St. Paul, Minnesota. In addition to writing such books as *Search for Understanding, A Study Document on Justification, Luther Today,* and *Introduction to the New Testament,* he contributed essays to some twenty other works. He also served as a representative of the American Lutheran Church to numerous pan-Lutheran and ecumenical organizations and gatherings.

HERBERT R. REINELT is Professor of Philosophy at the University of the Pacific in Stockton, California.

THEODORE RUNYON, JR., is Professor of Systematic Theology at Emory University's Candler School of Theology, Atlanta, Georgia. A former student of Friedrich Gogarten at the University of Göttingen, he assisted in the translation of Gogarten's *Reality of Faith.* He is the editor of *Hope for the Church* and *Sanctification and Liberation.*

ROBERT J. SCHREITER, C.Pp.S., is Associate Professor of Theology and Dean of the Catholic Theological Union in Chicago. His books include *Constructing Local Theologies* and *A Schillebeeckx Reader.*

FRANKLIN SHERMAN, Dean and Professor of Christian Ethics, Lutheran School of Theology at Chicago, is the author of *The Courage to Care: A Study in Christian Social Responsibility* and *The Promise of Heschel,* the translator of Paul Tillich's *Socialist Decision, and an editor of Luther's Works* (American edition).

MATTHEW SPINKA died in 1972; he was Waldo Professor Emeritus of Church History at the Hartford Seminary Foundation. Among his books: *The Quest for Church Unity, John Amos Comenius: That Incomparable Moravian, The Church in Soviet Russia, Christian Thought from Erasmus to Berdyaev, Nicholas Berdyaev: Captive of Freedom,* and four volumes about the Czech religious reformer John Hus: *John Hus and the Czech Reform, John Hus: A Biography, John Hus at the Council of Constance,* and *John Hus' Concept of the Church.*

DOUGLAS STURM, Professor of Religion and Political Science at Bucknell University, composed this volume's essay on Jacques Ellul while a Research Fellow with the Project on Religion and Public Life in America sponsored by the Institute for the Advanced Study of Religion at the University of Chicago. He is a past President of the Society of Christian Ethics and is Chairman of the editorial board of the *Journal of Law and Religion.*

LEONARD SWIDLER is Professor of Catholic Thought and Interreligious Dialogue at Temple University, cofounder and editor of the *Journal of Ecumenical Studies,* and a consultor of the Catholic-Jewish Relations Committee of the National Conference of Catholic Bishops (U.S.). He has written such books as *Women in Judaism: The Status of Women in Formative Judaism, Biblical Affirmations of Women,* and *Jewish-Christian-Muslim Dialogue,* and he has edited such books as *Küng in Conflict, Consensus in Theology? A Dialogue with Hans Küng and Edward Schillebeeckx,* and (with Gerard Sloyan) *The Oberammergau Passionsspiel 1984.*

GUSTAF WINGREN, Professor Emeritus of Systematic Theology at the University of Lund in Sweden, is the author of *Creation and Law, Man and the Incarnation, The Living Word, Luther on Vocation, Theology in Conflict, Gospel and Church, The Flight from Creation, An Exodus Theology,* and *Credo.*

WILLIAM JOHN WOLF is Howard Chandler Robbins Professor of Theology Emeritus at the Episcopal Divinity School, Cambridge, Massachusetts. His publications include *Man's Knowledge of God, The Religion of Abraham Lincoln, No Cross, No Crown: A Study of the Atonement, Thoreau: Mystic, Prophet, Ecologist,* and *An Abridgment of Maurice's Kingdom of Christ.*